2ND EDITION

Fundamentals of Management

Core Concepts and Applications

Ricky W. Griffin
Texas A & M University

Houghton Mifflin Company
Boston   New York

I would like to dedicate this work to Sherry and Paul Hamm, Connie and Wayne Maxwell, and Luke and Arlene May—brothers and sisters all, in the truest sense of the words.

Sponsoring Editor: Kathleen L. Hunter
Associate Sponsoring Editor: Joanne Dauksewicz
Editorial Associate: Damaris R. Curran
Project Editor: Elizabeth Gale Napolitano
Editorial Assistant: Joy Park
Senior Production/Design Coordinator: Jennifer Waddell
Manufacturing Manager: Florence Cadran
Marketing Manager: Melissa Russell

Cover Design: MINKO T. DIMOV, MINKOIMAGES

PART OPENER PHOTO CREDITS: *Part One:* Woody Woodworth/Superstock; *Part One inset photo:* Jon Riley/Tony Stone Images, Inc.; *Part Two:* Rick Stiller/Gamma Liaison; *Part Two inset photo:* Tim Brown/Tony Stone Images, Inc.; *Part Three:* D.C. Lowe/Tony Stone Images, Inc.; *Part Three inset photo:* Alfred Wolf/Tony Stone Images, Inc.; *Part Four:* Ron Sherman/Tony Stone Images, Inc.; *Part Four inset photo:* Francisco Cruz/Superstock; *Part Five:* Rosenfeld Images LTD/Science Photo Library/Photo Researchers, Inc.; *Part Five inset photo:* Malcolm Fielding, Johnson Matthey/Science Photo Library/Photo Researchers, Inc.

PHOTO AND CARTOON CREDITS: *Chapter 1:* page 6: Mark Richards/Contact Press Images; page 10: © Susan Van Etten; page 12: © The New Yorker Collection 1996 Ed Fischer from cartoonbank.com. All Rights Reserved; *Chapter 2:* page 38: © 1999 Frank Cotham from cartoonbank.com. All Rights Reserved; page 39: Jennifer Binder; page 40: Reprinted with the permission of Lockheed Martin Corporation; page 44: Christopher Liu/ChinaStock. (*Photo and cartoon credits continue on page 467.*)

Printed in the U.S.A.

Library of Congress Catalog Card Number: 99-72014

ISBN: 0-395-96231-5

3456789-VH-03 02 01 00

Brief Contents

Contents

4 Managing Decision Making 94

5 Entrepreneurship and New Venture Management 120

Preface

Over the last four decades, literally hundreds of books have been written for basic management courses. As the body of material comprising the theory, research, and practice of management has grown and expanded, textbook authors have continued to mirror this expansion of material in their books. Writers have understood the importance of adding new material pertinent to traditional topics, like planning and organizing, while simultaneously adding coverage of emerging topics, such as diversity and total quality management. As a by-product of this trend, our textbooks have grown longer and longer, making it difficult to cover all the material in one course.

Another emerging trend in management education is a new focus on teaching in a broader context. That is, more often the principles of management course is now being taught with less emphasis on theory alone and more emphasis on application of concepts. Teaching how to successfully apply management concepts often involves focusing more on skills development and the human side of the organization. This trend requires that textbooks cover theoretical concepts within a flexible framework that allows instructors to make use of interactive tools such as case studies, exercises, and projects.

This text represents a synthesis of these trends toward a more manageable and practical approach. By combining concise text discussion, standard pedagogical tools, lively and current content, an emphasis on organizational behavior, and exciting skills-development materials, *Fundamentals of Management* answers the call for a new approach to management education. This book provides almost infinite flexibility, a solid foundation of knowledge-based material, and an action-oriented learning dimension that is unique in the field. Indeed, when its first edition was published in 1997, it quickly became a market leader in the fundamentals area. This second edition builds solidly on the successes of the earlier edition.

■ Organization of the Book

Most management instructors today organize their course around the traditional management functions of planning, organizing, leading, and controlling. *Fundamentals of Management* uses these functions as its organizing framework. The book consists of five parts, with fifteen chapters and one appendix.

Part One introduces management through two chapters. Chapter 1 provides a basic overview of the management process in organizations, while Chapter 2 introduces students to the environment of management.

Part Two covers the first basic management function, planning. Chapter 3 introduces the fundamental concepts of planning and discusses strategic management. Managerial decision making is the topic of Chapter 4. Finally, Chapter 5 covers entrepreneurship and the management of new ventures.

The second basic management function, organizing, is the subject of Part Three. In Chapter 6 the fundamental concepts of organization structure and design are introduced and discussed. Chapter 7 discusses organization change and innovation. Chapter 8 is devoted to human resource management.

Many instructors and managers believe that the third basic management function, leading, is especially important in contemporary organizations. Thus, Part Four devotes five chapters to this management function. Basic concepts and processes associated with individual behavior are introduced and discussed in Chapter 9. Employee motivation is the subject of Chapter 10. Chapter 11 discusses leadership and influence processes in organizations. Communication in organizations is the topic of Chapter 12. The management of groups and teams is covered in Chapter 13.

The fourth management function, controlling, is the subject of Part Five. Chapter 14 introduces the fundamental concepts and issues associated with the management of the control process. A special area of control today, managing for total quality, is discussed in Chapter 15.

Finally, the Appendix provides coverage of important tools for planning and management.

■ Skills-Focused Pedagogical Features

With this text I have been able to address new dimensions of management education without creating a text that is unwieldy in length. Specifically, each chapter in this book is followed by an exciting set of skills-based exercises. These resources were created to bring an active and behavioral orientation to management education by requiring students to solve problems, make decisions, respond to situations, and work in groups. In short, these materials simulate many of the day-to-day challenges and opportunities faced by real managers.

Among these skills-based exercises are three different *Building Management Skills* (one more than in the first edition) organized around the set of basic management skills introduced in Chapter 1 of the text. Another exercise is entitled *You Make the Call*. This feature follows a real company and its managers through a series of situations corresponding to chapter content (the names used in this feature have been altered to protect the identity of the actual business and managers that are described). The *Skills Self-Assessment Instrument* exercise helps readers learn something about their own approach to management. Finally, an *Experiential Exercise* provides additional action-oriented learning opportunities, usually in a group setting.

In addition to the end-of-chapter exercises, every chapter includes important standard pedagogy: learning objectives, chapter outline, opening incident, boldface key terms, summary of key points, questions for review, questions for analysis, and an end-of-chapter case with questions.

■ A Complete and Effective Teaching Package

In addition to the text itself, instructors have available to them an array of support materials that will facilitate instruction and education.

■ *Instructor's Resource Manual* (David W. Murphy, Madisonville Community College)   This resource includes suggested class schedules, detailed teaching notes for each chapter, and video guide teaching notes. The teaching notes for each chapter include: chapter summary; learning objectives; detailed chapter lecture outline (including opening incident summary); highlighted key terms; teaching tips; group exercise ideas; discussion starters; references to the transparencies; responses to review, analysis, and case questions; and information to help facilitate the skills-development exercises.

■ *Test Bank* (Tom Quirk, Webster University)   The *Test Bank* includes over 2000 questions, 130 questions per chapter and 60 in the appendix. Each question is identified with the corresponding learning objective and page number(s) for reference. In addition, the questions have an estimate of the level of difficulty and are identified by type of question—knowledge, understanding, or application.

■ *Computerized Test Bank*   This program is designed for use on IBM and IBM-compatible computers. With this program, the instructor can select questions from the *Test Bank* and produce test masters for easy duplication. This program gives instructors the option of selecting their own questions or having the program select them. It also allows instructors to customize tests by creating new questions, editing existing ones, and generating multiple versions of tests.

■ *Manager: A Simulation* (Jerald R. Smith and Peggy A. Golden of Florida Atlantic University)   *Manager* is a business game that provides students, who act as management teams, with simulated real-world experience in managerial decision making. An instructor's disk is provided with *Manager*; it explains how to play the game, provides suggestions for grading, and analyzes and evaluates student decisions.

■ *Power Presentation Manager*   This CD-ROM will provide instructors with a number of tools that can be used to create attractive, lively, and informative classroom presentations. Instructors will be able to easily build classroom lecture presentations by choosing appropriate line art, PowerPoint slides, pieces from the overhead transparency program, and selected video clips as part of a "script." In addition, instructors can create completely original presentation slides, and copy and edit text from lecture outline files provided.

■ *Internet*   With the Second Edition, we are pleased to offer our new student and instructor web sites, which provide additional information, guidance, and activities that enhance the concepts presented in this text. Among other things, the student site includes term paper help, interactive personal self-assessments, Internet links for each chapter, and real-world videos. The instructor site provides lecture outlines, PowerPoint slides, and instructor resources.

Color Transparencies   Approximately 80 full-color transparencies illustrate major topics in the text. Two types of transparencies are included: highlights of key figures from the text, and additional images that can be used to enhance lecture presentations.

PowerPoint Slides   These visually appealing and engaging slides, developed by the author, illustrate text content with outlines, charts, exhibits, and artwork, and they allow instructors to lecture directly from the slides. Where PowerPoint software is available, instructors can edit the slide program to include their own illustrations or notes, and they can print out the slides to use as class handouts.

Videotape Package   To illustrate important concepts from the text, real-world video examples from leading organizations are provided for each part. The video segments run from 12 to 23 minutes to allow time for classroom discussion. The Video Guide at the back of the *Instructor's Resource Manual* provides suggested uses, teaching objectives, an overview, issues for discussion, and a skills perspective section for each video segment.

Acknowledgments

I would like to acknowledge the many contributions that others have made to this book. My faculty colleagues at Texas A&M University and my assistant, Phyllis Washburn, have contributed enormously both to this book and to my thinking about management education. At Houghton Mifflin, an outstanding team of professionals including Kathy Hunter, Damaris Curran, Joanne Dauksewicz, and Liz Napolitano have made more contributions to this book than I could even begin to list. A special thanks is also due the many reviewers who helped shape the content and form of the material in this book. While any and all errors are of course my own responsibility, thanks to Sam Chapman (Diablo Valley College), Dr. Anne Cowden (California State University), Dr. Joseph S. Hooker, Jr. (North Greenville College), Joe Dobson (Western Illinois University), Sheryl A. Stanley (Newman University), Roberta B. Slater (Pennsylvania College of Technology), and George W. Jacobs (Middle Tennessee State University) for their help. My wife, Glenda, and our children, Dustin and Ashley, are, of course, due the greatest thanks. Their love, care, interest, and enthusiasm help sustain me in all that I do.

I would like to invite your feedback on this book. If you have any questions, suggestions, or issues to discuss, please feel free to contact me. The most efficient way to reach me is through e-mail. My address is rgriffin@tamu.edu.

R. W. G.

1

Understanding the Manager's Job

OBJECTIVES

After studying this chapter, you should be able to:

■ Define management, describe the kinds of managers found in organizations, and identify and briefly explain the four basic management functions.

■ Justify the importance of history and theory to management and explain the evolution of management thought.

■ Discuss contemporary management issues and challenges.

It once seemed as if there might one day be a McDonald's restaurant on every corner. But although there are certainly a large number of the venerable hamburger restaurants around today, Starbucks Corporation has, at least for the time being, replaced McDonald's as the highest profile and fastest growing food and beverage company in the United States. Starbucks was started in Seattle in 1971 by three coffee aficionados. Their primary business at the time was buying premium coffee beans, roasting them, and then selling the coffee by the pound. The business performed modestly well and soon grew to nine stores, all in the Seattle area. The three partners sold Starbucks to a former employee, Howard Schultz, in 1987. Schultz promptly reoriented the business away from bulk coffee mail-order sales and emphasized retail coffee sales through the firm's coffee bars. Today, Starbucks is not only the largest coffee importer and roaster of specialty beans in the United States but also the country's largest specialty coffee bean retailer.

What is the key to the extraordinary growth and success of the Starbucks chain? One important ingredient is its well-conceived and implemented strategy. Starbucks is on a phenomenal growth pace, opening a new coffee shop somewhere almost every day. But this growth is planned and coordinated at each step of the way through careful site selection. And through its astute promotional campaigns and commitment to quality, the firm has elevated the coffee-drinking taste of millions of Americans and fueled a significant increase in demand.

Starbucks has also created an organization that promotes growth and success. Managers at each store have considerable autonomy over how they run things, as long as the firm's basic principles are followed. Starbucks also uses a state-of-the-art communication network to keep in contact with its employees.

Another ingredient to Starbucks' success is its relationship with its employees. The firm hires relatively young people to work in its restaurants and starts them at hourly wages that are somewhat higher than most entry-level food-services jobs. The company also offers health insurance to all of its employees, including part-timers, and also has a lucrative stock-option plan for everyone in the firm.

Yet another key to the success of Starbucks is its near-fanatical emphasis on quality control. For example, milk must be heated to a narrow range of 150 to 170 degrees, and every espresso shot must be pulled within twenty-three seconds or else discarded. And no coffee is allowed to sit on a hot plate for more than twenty minutes. Schultz also refuses to franchise his Starbucks stores, fearing a loss of control and a potential deterioration of quality.

Its phenomenal growth rate notwithstanding, Starbucks is also continually on the alert for new business opportunities. One area of growth is into international markets. In 1996, for example, the firm opened its first two coffee shops in Japan and another in Singapore; by late 1998 there were fifty-four stores in Asia. Starbucks entered the European market in 1998 by purchasing the Seattle Coffee Co., a small chain in England. Using this operation as a base, Starbucks plans to open new stores throughout Europe, with a goal of having five hundred continental sites by the year 2003.

Another way that Starbucks can grow is through brand extension with other companies. For instance, the firm has collaborated with Dreyer's to distribute five flavors of Starbucks coffee ice cream to grocery freezers across the country. Starbucks has also collaborated with Capitol Records on two Starbucks jazz CDs that are sold in Starbucks stores. And Redhook Brewery uses Starbucks coffee extract in its double black stout beer. All things considered, then, Starbucks' future looks so bright that its employees may need to wear the sunshades the firm might soon begin to sell![1]

"One reason a lot of youths don't find corporate America so attractive is because of the IBM image: I'll become a blue suit. Starbucks makes you feel like a partner."

Karen Hunsaker, Starbucks employee

This book is about managers like Howard Schultz, Starbucks' regional managers who oversee dozens of coffee shops, and the manager of your neighborhood Starbucks shop, and the work they all do. In Chapter 1 we examine the nature of management, its dimensions, and its challenges. We explain the concepts of management and managers, discuss the management process, and summarize the origins of contemporary management thought. We conclude by introducing critical contemporary challenges and issues.

An Introduction to Management

management A set of functions directed at the efficient and effective utilization of resources in the pursuit of organizational goals
efficient Using resources wisely and in a cost-effective way
effective Making the right decisions and successfully implementing them

Management is a set of functions directed at the efficient and effective utilization of resources in the pursuit of organizational goals. By **efficient**, we mean using resources wisely and in a cost-effective way. By **effective**, we mean making the right decisions and successfully implementing them. In general, successful organizations are both efficient and effective.

Today's managers face a variety of interesting and challenging situations. The average executive works sixty hours a week; has enormous demands placed on his or her time; and faces increased complexities thanks to globalization, domestic competition, government regulation, and shareholder pressure. Rapid change, unexpected disruptions, and both minor and major crises further complicate the task. The manager's job is unpredictable and fraught with challenges, but it is also filled with opportunities to make a difference.[2]

■ Kinds of Managers

Many different kinds of managers are at work in organizations today. Figure 1.1 illustrates how managers within an organization can be differentiated by level and by area.

top managers The relatively small set of senior executives who manage the overall organization

Levels of Management One way to differentiate among managers is by their level in the organization. **Top managers** make up the relatively small group of executives who manage the overall organization. Titles found in this group include president, vice president, and chief executive officer (CEO). Top managers create the organization's goals, overall strategy, and operating policies. They also officially represent the organization to the external environment by meeting with government officials, executives of other organizations, and so forth.

Howard Schultz at Starbucks is a top manager, as is Deidra Wager, the firm's senior vice president for retail operations. Top managers make decisions about activities such as acquiring other companies, investing in research and development, entering or abandoning various markets, and building new plants and office facilities.

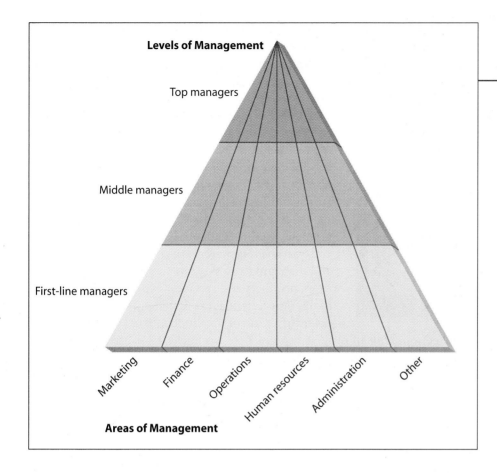

Levels of Management

Top managers

Middle managers

First-line managers

Marketing · Finance · Operations · Human resources · Administration · Other

Areas of Management

FIGURE 1.1
Kinds of Managers by Level and Area

Organizations generally have three levels of management, represented by top managers, middle managers, and first-line managers. Regardless of level, managers are also usually associated with a specific area within the organization, such as marketing, finance, operations, human resources, or administration.

Middle management is probably the largest group of managers in most organizations. Common middle-management titles include plant manager, operations manager, and division head. **Middle managers** are primarily responsible for implementing the policies and plans developed by top managers and for supervising and coordinating the activities of lower-level managers.[3] Plant managers, for example, handle inventory management, quality control, equipment failures, and minor union problems. They also coordinate the work of supervisors within the plant. Jason Hernandez, a regional manager at Starbucks responsible for the firm's operations in three eastern states, is a middle manager.

First-line managers supervise and coordinate the activities of operating employees. Common titles for first-line managers are supervisor, coordinator, and office manager. Positions such as these are often the first ones held by employees who enter management from the ranks of operating personnel. Wayne Maxwell and Jenny Wagner, managers of Starbucks coffee shops in Texas, are first-line managers. They oversee the day-to-day operations of their respective stores, hire operating employees to staff them, and handle other routine administrative duties required by the parent corporation. In contrast to top and middle managers, first-line managers typically spend a large proportion of their time supervising the work of subordinates.[4]

middle managers The relatively large set of managers responsible for implementing the policies and plans developed by top managers and for supervising and coordinating the activities of first-line managers

first-line managers Managers who supervise and coordinate the activities of operating employees

Organizations need many kinds of managers. Steven Jobs is the top manager at Apple Computer. He recently returned to the firm he founded back in 1976 in an effort to save it from bankruptcy. Jobs is very effective at inspiring other managers and motivating them to work harder. His charisma also helps inspire confidence in customers, investors, and other employees. Although Apple Computer may have a difficult time returning to its earlier prominence in the industry, with Jobs as the top manager many observers believe that the firm at least has a fighting chance.

planning Setting an organization's goals and deciding how best to achieve them

decision making Part of the planning process that involves selecting a course of action from a set of alternatives

organizing Grouping activities and resources in a logical fashion

Areas of Management Regardless of their level, managers may work in various areas within an organization. *Marketing managers* work in areas related to the marketing function—getting consumers and clients to buy the organization's products or services (be they Ford automobiles, *Newsweek* magazines, Associated Press news reports, flights on Southwest Airlines, or cups of latte at Starbucks). These areas include new-product development, promotion, and distribution. *Financial managers* deal primarily with an organization's financial resources. They are responsible for activities such as accounting, cash management, and investments.

Operations managers are concerned with creating and managing the systems that create an organization's products and services. Typical responsibilities of operations managers include production control, inventory control, quality control, plant layout, and site selection. *Human resource managers* are responsible for hiring and developing employees. They are typically involved in human resource planning, recruiting and selecting employees, training and development, designing compensation and benefit systems, formulating performance appraisal systems, and discharging low-performing and problem employees. *General managers* are not associated with any particular management specialty. Probably the best example of an administrative management position is that of a hospital or clinic administrator. Administrative managers tend to be generalists; they have some basic familiarity with all functional areas of management rather than specialized training in any one area.

■ Basic Management Functions

Regardless of level or area, management involves the four basic functions of planning and decision making, organizing, leading, and controlling. This book is organized around these basic functions, as shown in Figure 1.2.

Planning and Decision Making In its simplest form, **planning** means setting an organization's goals and deciding how best to achieve them. **Decision making**, a part of the planning process, involves selecting a course of action from a set of alternatives. Planning and decision making help maintain managerial effectiveness by serving as guides for future activities. Part II of this book is devoted to planning and decision making

Organizing Once a manager has set goals and developed a workable plan, the next management function is to organize people and the other resources necessary to carry out the plan. Specifically, **organizing** involves determining how activities and resources are to be grouped. Although some people equate this function with the creation of an organization chart, we will see in Part III of this book that it is actually much more.

Leading The third basic managerial function is leading. Some people consider leading to be both the most important and the most challenging of all managerial activities. **Leading** is the set of processes used to get people to work together to advance the interests of the organization. For example, Howard Schultz's leadership skills have clearly played an important role in the success of Starbucks. We cover the leading function in detail in Part IV.

Controlling The final phase of the management process is **controlling**, or monitoring the organization's progress toward its goals. As the organization moves toward its goals, managers must monitor progress to ensure that the organization is performing so as to arrive at its "destination" at the appointed time. Part V of this book is devoted to the controlling function.

■ Fundamental Managerial Skills

To carry out these management functions properly, managers rely on a number of specific skills. The most important management skills are technical, interpersonal, conceptual, diagnostic, communication, decision-making, and time-management skills.[5]

Technical Skills **Technical skills** are the skills necessary to accomplish or understand the specific kind of work being done in an organization. Technical skills are especially important for first-line managers. These managers spend much of their time training subordinates and answering questions about work-related problems. First-line managers must know how to perform the tasks assigned to those they supervise if they are to be effective managers.

Interpersonal Skills Managers spend considerable time interacting with people both inside and outside the organization. For obvious reasons, then, the manager also needs **interpersonal skills**—the ability to communicate with, understand, and motivate individuals and groups. As a manager climbs the organizational ladder, she must be able to get along with subordinates, peers, and those at higher levels of the organization. Because of the multitude of roles managers must fulfill, a manager must also be able to work with suppliers, customers, investors, and others outside of the organization.[6]

Conceptual Skills **Conceptual skills** depend on the manager's ability to think in the abstract. Managers need the mental capacity to understand the overall workings of the organization and its environment, to grasp how all the parts of the organization fit together, and to view the organization in a holistic manner. This skill enables them to think strategically, to see the big picture, and to make broad-based decisions that serve the overall organization.

FIGURE 1.2
The Management Process

Management involves four basic activities—planning and decision making, organizing, leading, and controlling. Although there is a basic logic for describing these activities in this sequence (as indicated by the solid arrows), most managers engage in more than one activity at a time and often move between the activities in unpredictable ways (as shown by the dotted arrows).

leading The set of processes used to get members of the organization to work together to advance the interests of the organization

controlling Monitoring organizational progress toward goal attainment

technical skills The skills necessary to accomplish or understand tasks relevant to the organization

interpersonal skills The ability to communicate with, understand, and motivate individuals and groups

conceptual skills The manager's ability to think in the abstract

diagnostic skills The manager's ability to visualize the most appropriate response to a situation

communication skills The manager's abilities to both effectively convey ideas and information to others and effectively receive ideas and information from others

decision-making skills The manager's ability to correctly recognize and define problems and opportunities and to then select an appropriate course of action to solve problems and capitalize on opportunities

time-management skills The manager's ability to prioritize work, to work efficiently, and to delegate appropriately

Diagnostic Skills Successful managers also possess **diagnostic skills**, or skills that enable them to visualize the most appropriate response to a situation. A physician diagnoses a patient's illness by analyzing symptoms and determining their probable cause. Similarly, a manager can diagnose and analyze a problem in the organization by studying its symptoms and then developing a solution.

Communication Skills **Communication skills** refer to the manager's abilities to both effectively convey ideas and information to others and effectively receive ideas and information from others. These skills enable a manager to transmit ideas to subordinates so that they know what is expected, to coordinate work with peers and colleagues so that they work well together properly, and to keep higher-level managers informed about what is going on. In addition, communication skills help the manager listen to what others say and to understand the real meaning behind e-mails, letters, reports, and other written communication.

Decision-Making Skills Effective managers also have good decision-making skills. **Decision-making skills** refer to the manager's ability to correctly recognize and define problems and opportunities and to then select an appropriate course of action to solve problems and capitalize on opportunities. No manager makes the right decision all the time. However, effective managers make good decisions most of the time. And when they do make a bad decision, they usually recognize their mistake quickly and then make good decisions to recover with as little cost or damage to their organization as possible.

Time-Management Skills Finally, effective managers usually have good time-management skills. **Time-management skills** refer to the manager's ability to prioritize work, to work efficiently, and to delegate appropriately. As already noted, managers face many different pressures and challenges. It is easy for a manager to get bogged down doing work that can easily be postponed or delegated to others. When this happens, unfortunately, more pressing and higher-priority work may get neglected.[7]

■ The Science and the Art of Management

Given the complexity inherent in the manager's job, a reasonable question relates to whether management is a science or an art. In fact, effective management is a blend of both science and art. And successful executives recognize the importance of combining both the science and the art of management as they practice their craft.[8]

The Science of Management Many management problems and issues can be approached in ways that are rational, logical, objective, and systematic. Managers can gather data, facts, and objective information. They can use quantitative models and decision-making techniques to arrive at "correct" decisions. And they need to take such a scientific approach to solving problems whenever possible, especially when they are dealing with relatively routine and straightforward issues. When Starbucks considers entering a new market, its managers look closely at a wide variety of objective details as they formulate their plans. Technical, diagnostic, and decision-making skills are especially important when practicing the science of management.

The Art of Management   Even though managers may try to be scientific as much as possible, they must often make decisions and solve problems on the basis of intuition, experience, instinct, and personal insights. Relying heavily on conceptual, communication, interpersonal, and time-management skills, for example, a manager may have to decide between multiple courses of action that look equally attractive. And even "objective facts" may prove to be wrong. When Starbucks was planning its first store in New York, market research clearly showed that New Yorkers preferred drip coffee to more exotic espresso-style coffees. After first installing more drip coffee makers and fewer espresso makers than in their other stores, managers had to backtrack when the New Yorkers lined up clamoring for espresso. Starbucks now introduces a standard menu and layout in all its stores, regardless of presumed market differences, and makes necessary adjustments later. Thus, managers must blend an element of intuition and personal insight with hard data and objective facts.[9]

The Evolution of Management

Most managers today recognize the importance of history. Knowing the origins of their organization and the kinds of practices that have led to success—or failure—can be an indispensable tool to managing the contemporary organization. Thus, in the next section we trace the history of management thought. Then we move forward to the present day by introducing contemporary management issues and challenges.

■ The Importance of Theory and History

Some people question the value of history and theory. Their arguments are usually based on the assumptions that history has no relevance to contemporary society and that theory is abstract and of no practical use. In reality, however, both theory and history are important to all managers today.

A theory is simply a conceptual framework for organizing knowledge and providing a blueprint for action. Although some theories seem abstract and irrelevant, others appear very simple and practical. Management theories, used to build organizations and guide them toward their goals, are grounded in reality.[10] In addition, most managers develop and refine their own theories of how they should run their organizations and manage the behavior of their employees.

An awareness and understanding of important historical developments are also important to contemporary managers.[11] Understanding the historical context of management provides a sense of heritage and can help managers avoid

No one knows the origins of Stonehenge, a mysterious circle of huge stones rising from Salisbury Plain in England. But one fact that is known is that whoever built the ancient monument must have relied heavily on a variety of management tools and techniques. For example, the stones were probably cut more than 300 miles away, in Wales, and transported to Salisbury Plain. This enormous feat alone would have required careful planning and co-ordination and the united efforts of hundreds of laborers.

the mistakes of others. Most courses in U.S. history devote time to business and economic developments in this country, including the Industrial Revolution, the early labor movement, and the Great Depression, and to such captains of U.S. industry as Cornelius Vanderbilt (railroads), John D. Rockefeller (oil), and Andrew Carnegie (steel). The contributions of these and other industrialists left a profound imprint on contemporary culture.[12] Shell Oil, Levi Strauss, Ford, Lloyd's of London, Disney, Honda, and Unilever all maintain significant archives about their past and frequently evoke images from that past in their orientation and training programs, advertising campaigns, and other public relations activities.

■ The Historical Context of Management

The practice of management can be traced back thousands of years. The Egyptians used the management functions of planning, organizing, and controlling when they constructed the great pyramids. Alexander the Great employed a staff organization to coordinate activities during his military campaigns. The Roman Empire developed a well-defined organizational structure that greatly facilitated communication and control.

In spite of this history, however, management per se was not given serious attention until the nineteenth century. Two of its first true pioneers were Robert Owen (1771–1858) and Charles Babbage (1792–1871). Owen, a British industrialist and reformer, was one of the first managers to recognize the importance of an organization's human resources and the welfare of workers. Charles Babbage, an English mathematician, focused his attention on efficiencies of production. He placed great faith in division of labor and advocated the application of mathematics to problems such as the efficient use of facilities and materials.

The Classical Management Perspective

At the dawn of the twentieth century, the preliminary ideas and writings of these and other managers and theorists converged with the emergence and evolution of large-scale businesses and management practices to create interest and focus attention on how businesses should be operated. The first important ideas to emerge are now called the **classical management perspective**. This perspective actually includes two different viewpoints: scientific management and administrative management.

classical management perspective Consists of two distinct branches—scientific management and administrative management

Scientific Management   Productivity emerged as a serious business problem during the first few years of this century. Business was expanding and capital was readily available, but labor was in short supply. Hence, managers began to search for ways to use existing labor more efficiently. In response to this need, experts began to focus on ways to improve the performance of individual workers. Their work led to the development of **scientific management**. Some of the earliest advocates of scientific management included Frederick W. Taylor (1856–1915), Frank Gilbreth (1868–1924), and Lillian Gilbreth (1878–1972).[13]

scientific management   Concerned with improving the performance of individual workers

One of Taylor's first jobs was as a foreman at the Midvale Steel Company in Philadelphia. It was there that he observed what he called **soldiering**—employees deliberately working at a pace slower than their capabilities. Taylor studied and timed each element of the steelworkers' jobs. He determined what each worker should be producing, and then he designed the most efficient way of doing each part of the overall task. Next, he implemented a piecework pay system. Rather than paying all employees the same wage, he began increasing the pay of each worker who met and exceeded the target level of output set for his or her job.

soldiering   Employees deliberately working at a slow pace

After Taylor left Midvale, he worked as a consultant for several companies, including Simonds Rolling Machine Company and Bethlehem Steel. At Simonds he studied and redesigned jobs, introduced rest periods to reduce fatigue, and implemented a piecework pay system. The results were higher quality and quantity of output and improved morale. At Bethlehem Steel, Taylor studied efficient ways of loading and unloading rail cars and applied his conclusions with equally impressive results. During these experiences, he formulated the basic ideas that he called scientific management. Figure 1.3 illustrates the basic steps Taylor suggested. He believed that managers who followed his guidelines would improve the efficiency of their workers.[14]

Taylor's work had a major impact on U.S. industry. By applying his principles, many organizations achieved major gains in efficiency. Taylor was not

FIGURE 1.3
Steps in Scientific Management

Frederick Taylor developed this system of scientific management, which he believed would lead to a more efficient and productive workforce. Bethlehem Steel was among the first organizations to profit from scientific management and still practices some parts of it today.

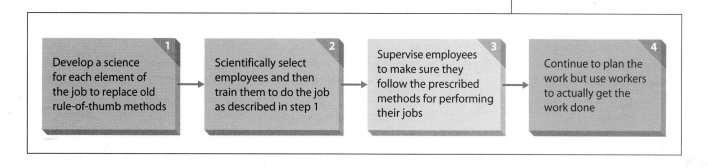

1	2	3	4
Develop a science for each element of the job to replace old rule-of-thumb methods	Scientifically select employees and then train them to do the job as described in step 1	Supervise employees to make sure they follow the prescribed methods for performing their jobs	Continue to plan the work but use workers to actually get the work done

"Well, being single and a robot, I'm able to put in a lot of overtime."

Early management pioneers working during the era of the classical management perspective placed little regard on the value and importance of human behavior to organizational effectiveness. Instead, they generally viewed workers from a "machine" perspective, much like robots who were supposed to do as they were told and who were interchangeable with other workers. It wasn't until the Hawthorne studies and the emergence of the behavioral management perspective that managers came to appreciate the importance of human behavior in the workplace. Unfortunately, however, some managers today still ignore the individual needs of their workers and assume that work always takes precedence over other things.

without his detractors, however. Labor argued that scientific management was just a device to get more work from each employee and to reduce the total number of workers needed by a firm. There was a congressional investigation into Taylor's ideas, and evidence suggests that he falsified some of his findings.[15] Nevertheless, Taylor's work left a lasting imprint on business.[16]

Frank and Lillian Gilbreth, contemporaries of Taylor, were a husband-and-wife team of industrial engineers. One of Frank Gilbreth's most interesting contributions was to the craft of bricklaying. After studying bricklayers at work, he developed several procedures for doing the job more efficiently. For example, he specified standard materials and techniques, including the positioning of the bricklayer, the bricks, and the mortar at different levels. The results of these changes were a reduction from eighteen separate physical movements to five and an increase in output of about 200 percent. Lillian Gilbreth made equally important contributions to several areas of work, helped shape the field of industrial psychology, and made substantive contributions to the field of personnel management. Working individually and together, the Gilbreths developed numerous techniques and strategies for eliminating inefficiency. They applied many of their ideas to their family; their experiences raising twelve children are documented in the book and movie *Cheaper by the Dozen*.

Administrative Management   Whereas scientific management deals with the jobs of individual employees, **administrative management** focuses on managing the total organization. The primary contributors to administrative management were Henri Fayol (1841–1925), Lyndall Urwick (1891–1983), and Max Weber (1864–1920).

Henri Fayol was administrative management's most articulate spokesperson. A French industrialist, Fayol was unknown to U.S. managers and scholars until his most important work, *General and Industrial Management*, was translated into English in 1930.[17] Drawing on his own managerial experience, he attempted to systematize the practice of management to provide guidance and direction to other managers. Fayol also was the first to identify the specific managerial functions of planning, organizing, leading, and controlling. He believed that these functions accurately reflect the core of the management process. Most contemporary management books (including this one) still use this framework, and practicing managers agree that these functions are a critical part of a manager's job.

After a career as a British army officer, Lyndall Urwick became a noted management theorist and consultant. He integrated scientific management with the work of Fayol and other administrative management theorists. He also advanced modern thinking about the functions of planning, organizing, and controlling. Like Fayol, Urwick developed a list of guidelines for improving managerial effectiveness. Urwick is noted not so much for his own contributions as for his synthesis and integration of the work of others.

Although Max Weber lived and worked at the same time as Fayol and Taylor, his contributions were not recognized until some years had passed. Weber was a German sociologist, and his most important work was not translated into English until 1947.[18] Weber's work on bureaucracy laid the foundation for contemporary organization theory, discussed in detail in Chapter 6. The concept of bureaucracy, as we discuss later, is based on a rational set of guidelines for structuring organizations in the most efficient manner.

administrative management
Focuses on managing the total organization

Assessment of the Classical Perspective   The classical perspective served to focus serious attention on the importance of effective management and helped pave the way for later theories and approaches. Many of the concepts developed during this era, such as job specialization, time and motion studies, and scientific methods are still in use. On the other hand, these early theorists often took an overly simplistic view of management and failed to understand the human element of organizations.

The Behavioral Management Perspective

Early advocates of the classical management perspective essentially viewed organizations and jobs from a mechanistic point of view—that is, they essentially sought to conceptualize organizations as machines and workers as cogs within those machines. Even though many early writers recognized the role of individuals, these management pioneers tended to focus on how managers could control and standardize the behavior of their employees. In contrast, the **behavioral management perspective** placed much more emphasis on individual attitudes and behaviors and on group processes and recognized the importance of behavioral processes in the workplace.

behavioral management perspective
Emphasizes individual attitudes and behaviors and group processes

The behavioral management perspective was stimulated by a number of writers and theoretical movements. One of those movements was industrial psychology, the practice of applying psychological concepts to industrial settings. Hugo Munsterberg (1863–1916), a noted German psychologist, is recognized as the father of industrial psychology. He suggested that psychologists could make valuable contributions to managers in the areas of employee selection and motivation. Industrial psychology is still a major course of study at many colleges and universities.

Another early advocate of the behavioral approach to management was Mary Parker Follett.[19] Follett worked during the scientific management era, but quickly came to recognize the human element in the workplace. Indeed, her work clearly anticipated the behavioral management perspective, and she appreciated the need to understand the role of human behavior in organizations. Her specific interests were in adult education and vocational guidance. Follett believed that organizations should become more democratic in accommodating employees and managers.

The Hawthorne Studies   Although Munsterberg and Follett made major contributions to the development of the behavioral approach to management, its primary catalyst was a series of studies conducted near Chicago at Western Electric's Hawthorne plant between 1927 and 1932. The research, originally sponsored by General Electric, was conducted by Elton Mayo and his associates.[20] The first study involved manipulating illumination for one group of workers and comparing their subsequent productivity with the productivity of another group whose illumination was not changed. Surprisingly, when illumination was increased for the experimental group, productivity went up in both groups. Productivity continued to increase in both groups, even when the lighting for the experimental group was decreased. Not until the lighting was reduced to the level of moonlight did productivity begin to decline (and General Electric withdrew its sponsorship).

Another experiment established a piecework incentive pay plan for a group of nine men assembling terminal banks for telephone exchanges. Scientific management would have predicted that each man would try to maximize his pay by producing as many units as possible. Mayo and his associates, however, found that the group itself informally established an acceptable level of output for its members. Workers who overproduced were branded "rate busters," and underproducers were labeled "chiselers." To be accepted by the group, workers produced at the accepted level. As they approached this acceptable level of output, workers slacked off to avoid overproducing.

Other studies, including an interview program involving several thousand workers, led Mayo and his associates to conclude that human behavior was much more important in the workplace than researchers had previously believed. In the lighting experiment, for example, the results were attributed to the fact that both groups received special attention and sympathetic supervision for perhaps the first time. The incentive pay plans did not work in determining output because wage incentives were less important to the individual workers than was social acceptance. In short, individual and social processes played a major role in shaping worker attitudes and behavior.

human relations movement
Argued that workers respond primarily to the social context of the workplace

Human Relations   The **human relations movement**, which grew from the Hawthorne studies and was a popular approach to management for many years, proposed that workers respond primarily to the social context of the workplace, including social conditioning, group norms, and interpersonal dynamics. A basic assumption of the human relations movement was that the manager's concern for workers would lead to their increased satisfaction, which would in turn result in improved performance. Two writers who helped advance the human relations movement were Abraham Maslow and Douglas McGregor.

In 1943, Maslow advanced a theory suggesting that people are motivated by a hierarchy of needs, including monetary incentives and social acceptance.[21] Maslow's hierarchy, perhaps the best-known human relations theory, is described in detail in Chapter 10. Meanwhile, Douglas McGregor's Theory X and Theory Y model best represents the essence of the human relations movement (see Table 1.1).[22] According to McGregor, Theory X and Theory Y reflect two extreme belief sets that managers have about their workers. **Theory X** is a relatively negative view of workers and is consistent with the views of scientific management. **Theory Y** is more positive and represents the assumptions that human relations advocates make. In McGregor's view, Theory Y was a more appropriate philosophy for managers to adhere to. Both Maslow and McGregor notably influenced the thinking of many practicing managers.

Theory X   A pessimistic and negative view of workers consistent with the views of scientific management
Theory Y   A positive view of workers; it represents the assumptions that human relations advocates make

Theory X Assumptions	1. People do not like work and try to avoid it.
	2. People do not like work, so managers have to control, direct, coerce, and threaten employees to get them to work toward organizational goals.
	3. People prefer to be directed, to avoid responsibility, and to want security; they have little ambition.
Theory Y Assumptions	1. People do not naturally dislike work; work is a natural part of their lives.
	2. People are internally motivated to reach objectives to which they are committed.
	3. People are committed to goals to the degree that they receive personal rewards when they reach their objectives.
	4. People will both seek and accept responsibility under favorable conditions.
	5. People have the capacity to be innovative in solving organizational problems.
	6. People are bright, but under most organizational conditions their potentials are under-utilized.

Contemporary Behavioral Science in Management Munsterberg, Mayo, Maslow, McGregor, and others have made valuable contributions to management. Contemporary theorists, however, have noted that many assertions of the human relationists were simplistic and inadequate descriptions of work behavior. Current behavioral perspectives on management, known as **organizational behavior**, acknowledge that human behavior in organizations is much more complex than the human relationists realized. The field of organizational behavior draws from a broad, interdisciplinary base of psychology, sociology, anthropology, economics, and medicine.

Organizational behavior takes a holistic view of behavior and addresses individual, group, and organization processes. These processes are major elements in contemporary management theory. Important topics in this field include job satisfaction, stress, motivation, leadership, group dynamics, organizational politics, interpersonal conflict, and the structure and design of organizations.[23] A contingency orientation also characterizes the field (discussed more fully later in this chapter). Our discussions of organizing (Chapters 6 through 8) and leading (Chapters 9 through 13) are heavily influenced by organizational behavior.

Assessment of the Behavioral Perspective The primary contributions of the behavioral perspective relate to ways in which this approach has changed managerial thinking. Managers are now more likely to recognize the importance of behavioral processes and to view employees as valuable resources instead of mere tools. On the other hand, organizational behavior is still imprecise in its ability to predict behavior and is not always accepted or understood by practicing managers. Hence, the contributions of the behavioral school have yet to be fully realized.

TABLE 1.1
Theory X and Theory Y

Douglas McGregor developed Theory X and Theory Y. He argued that Theory X best represented the views of scientific management and Theory Y represented the human relations approach. McGregor believed that Theory Y was the best philosophy for all managers.
Source: Douglas McGregor, *The Human Side of Enterprise*, pp. 33–34; 47–48, © 1960, reproduced with permission of The McGraw-Hill Companies.

organizational behavior Contemporary field focusing on behavioral perspectives on management

■ The Quantitative Management Perspective

The third major school of management thought began to emerge during World War II. During the war government officials and scientists in England and the United States worked to help the military deploy its resources more efficiently and effectively. These groups took some of the mathematical

quantitative management perspective Applies quantitative techniques to management

management science Focuses specifically on the development of mathematical models

operations management Concerned with helping the organization more efficiently produce its products or services

approaches to management that Taylor and Gantt had developed decades earlier and applied them to logistical problems during the war.[24] These officials and scientists learned that problems regarding troop, equipment, and submarine deployment, for example, could all be solved through mathematical analysis. After the war, companies such as Du Pont and General Electric began to use the same techniques for deploying employees, choosing plant locations, and planning warehouses. Basically, then, this perspective is concerned with applying quantitative techniques to management. More specifically, the **quantitative management perspective** focuses on decision making, economic effectiveness, mathematical models, and the use of computers. There are two branches of the quantitative approach: management science and operations management.

Management Science Unfortunately, the term *management science* appears to be related to scientific management, the approach developed by Taylor and others early in this century. But the two have little in common and should not be confused. **Management science** focuses specifically on the development of mathematical models. A mathematical model is a simplified representation of a system, process, or relationship.

At its most basic level, management science focuses on models, equations, and similar representations of reality. For example, managers at Detroit Edison use mathematical models to determine how best to route repair crews during blackouts. The Bank of New England uses models to figure out how many tellers need to be on duty at each location at various times throughout the day. In recent years, paralleling the advent of the personal computer, management science techniques have become increasingly sophisticated. For example, automobile manufacturers Daimler-Benz and Chrysler use realistic computer simulations to study collision damage to cars. These simulations give them precise information and avoid the costs of "crashing" so many test cars.

Operations Management Operations management is somewhat less mathematical and statistically sophisticated than management science and can be applied more directly to managerial situations. Indeed, we can think of **operations management** as a form of applied management science. Operations management techniques are generally concerned with helping the organization produce its products or services more efficiently and can be applied to a wide range of problems.

For example, Rubbermaid and The Home Depot use operations management techniques to manage their inventories. (Inventory management is concerned with specific inventory problems such as balancing carrying costs and ordering costs and determining the optimal order quantity.) Linear programming (which involves computing simultaneous solutions to a set of linear equations) helps United Air Lines plan its flight schedules, Consolidated Freightways develop its shipping routes, and General Instrument Corporation plan which instruments to produce at various times. Other operations management techniques include queuing theory, breakeven analysis, and simulation. All these techniques and procedures apply directly to operations, but they are also helpful in such areas as finance, marketing, and human resource management.

Assessment of the Quantitative Perspective   Like the other management perspectives, the quantitative management perspective has made important contributions and has certain limitations. It has provided managers with an abundance of decision-making tools and techniques and has increased their understanding of overall organizational processes. It has been particularly useful in the areas of planning and controlling. On the other hand, mathematical models cannot fully account for individual behaviors and attitudes. Some people believe that the time needed to develop competence in quantitative techniques retards the development of other managerial skills. Finally, mathematical models typically require a set of assumptions that may not be realistic.

Contemporary Management Theory

Recognizing that the classical, behavioral, and quantitative approaches to management are not necessarily contradictory or mutually exclusive is important. Even though each perspective makes specific assumptions and predictions, each can also complement the others. Indeed, a complete understanding of management requires an appreciation of all three perspectives. In addition, contemporary management theory based on systems and contingency perspectives builds from these earlier perspectives in a variety of ways.

■ The Systems Perspective

The systems perspective is one important contemporary management theory. A **system** is an interrelated set of elements functioning as a whole.[25] As shown in Figure 1.4, by viewing an organization as a system, we can identify four basic elements: inputs, transformation processes, outputs, and feedback. First, inputs are the material, human, financial, and information resources the organization gets from its environment. Next, through technological and managerial processes, inputs are transformed into outputs. Outputs include products, services, or both (tangible and intangible); profits, losses, or both (even not-for-profit organizations must operate within their budgets); employee behaviors; and information. Finally, the environment reacts to these outputs and provides feedback to the system.

Thinking of organizations as systems provides us with a variety of important viewpoints on organizations such as the concepts of open systems, subsystems, synergy, and entropy. **Open systems** are systems that interact with their environment,

FIGURE 1.4

The Systems Perspective of Organizations

By viewing organizations as systems, managers can better understand the importance of their environment and the level of interdependence among subsystems within the organization. Managers must also understand how their decisions affect and are affected by other subsystems within the organization.

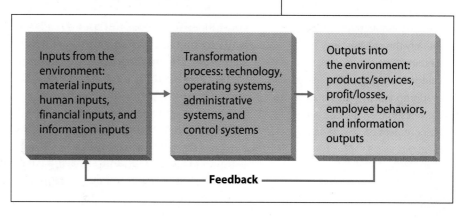

| Inputs from the environment: material inputs, human inputs, financial inputs, and information inputs | Transformation process: technology, operating systems, administrative systems, and control systems | Outputs into the environment: products/services, profit/losses, employee behaviors, and information outputs |

Feedback

system An interrelated set of elements functioning as a whole

open system An organizational system that interacts with its environment

closed system An organizational system that does not interact with its environment

subsystem A system within another system

synergy Two or more subsystems working together to produce more than the total of what they might produce working alone

entropy A normal process leading to system decline

universal perspective An attempt to identify the one best way to do something

contingency perspective Suggests that appropriate managerial behavior in a given situation depends on, or is contingent on, a wide variety of elements

whereas **closed systems** do not interact with their environment. Although organizations are open systems, some make the mistake of ignoring their environment and behaving as though their environment is not important.

The systems perspective also stresses the importance of **subsystems**—systems within a broader system. For example, the marketing, production, and finance functions within Mattel are systems in their own right but are also subsystems within the overall organization. Because they are interdependent, a change in one subsystem can affect other subsystems as well. If the production department at Mattel lowers the quality of the toys being made (by buying lower-quality materials, for example), the effects are felt in finance (improved cash flow in the short run owing to lower costs) and marketing (decreased sales in the long run because of customer dissatisfaction). Managers must therefore remember that although organizational subsystems can be managed with some degree of autonomy, their interdependence should not be overlooked.

Synergy suggests that organizational units (or subsystems) may often be more successful working together than working alone. The Walt Disney Company, for example, benefits greatly from synergy. The company's movies, theme parks, television programs, and merchandise licensing programs all benefit one another. Children who enjoy a Disney movie like *Mulan* want to go to Disney World and see the Mulan show or parade and to buy stuffed animals of the film's characters. Music from the film generates additional revenues for the firm, as do computer games and other licensing arrangements for lunch boxes, clothing, and so forth. Synergy is an important concept for managers because it emphasizes the importance of working together in a cooperative and coordinated fashion.

Finally, **entropy** is a normal process that leads to system decline. When an organization does not monitor feedback from its environment and make appropriate adjustments, it may fail. For example, Studebaker, W. T. Grant, and Penn Central Railroad went bankrupt because each company failed to revitalize itself and keep pace with changes in its environment. A primary objective of management, from a systems perspective, is to continually re-energize the organization to avoid entropy.

■ The Contingency Perspective

Another recent noteworthy addition to management thinking is the contingency perspective. The classical, behavioral, and quantitative approaches are considered **universal perspectives** because they tried to identify the "one best way" to manage organizations. The **contingency perspective**, in contrast, suggests that universal theories cannot be applied to organizations because each organization is unique. Instead, the contingency perspective suggests that appropriate managerial behavior in a given situation depends on, or is contingent on, unique elements in that situation.[26] Stated differently, effective managerial behavior in one situation cannot always be generalized to other situations. Recall, for example, that Frederick Taylor assumed that all workers would generate the highest possible level of output to maximize their own personal economic gain. We can imagine some people being motivated primarily by money—but we can just as easily imagine other people being motivated by the desire for leisure time, status, social acceptance, or any combination of these (as Mayo found at the Hawthorne plant).

■ Contemporary Management Issues and Challenges

Managers today face an imposing set of challenges as they guide and direct the fortunes of their companies. Coverage of each topic, introduced next, is thoroughly integrated throughout this book.

Downsizing   One major management challenge that is all too common today is *downsizing*, which occurs when an organization purposely becomes smaller by reducing the size of the workforce or by shedding entire divisions or businesses. From around the mid-1980s through today, it has become commonplace for firms to announce the elimination of thousands of jobs. For example, in recent years General Motors, IBM, and AT&T have undergone major downsizing efforts involving thousands of employees. Even some Japanese firms—long thought to be immune to this challenge—have had to downsize as a result of problems in the Japanese economy. Organizations going through such downsizing have to be concerned about managing the effects of these cutbacks, not only for those who are being let go, but also for those who are surviving—albeit surviving with a reduced level of job security.

Diversity and the New Work Force   A second important challenge today is the *management of diversity*. Diversity refers to differences among people. Although diversity may be reflected along numerous dimensions, most managers tend to focus on age, gender, ethnicity, and physical abilities/disabilities. The internationalization of businesses has also increased diversity in many organizations, carrying with it additional challenges as well as new opportunities. Motivating employees from different age categories, from senior citizens to Generation X-ers, is a related issue.

Information Technology   New technology, especially as it relates to information, also poses an increasingly important management challenge. The Internet and World Wide Web, local area networks and intranets, and the increased use of e-mail and voicemail systems are among the most recent technological changes in this area. Among the key issues associated with information technology are employee privacy, decision-making quality, and optimizing a firm's investments in new forms of technology as they continue to emerge. A related issue confronting managers has to do with the increased capabilities this technology provides for people to work at places other than their office.

New Ways of Managing   Another important management challenge today is the complex array of new ways of managing. As noted earlier, theorists once advocated "one best way" of managing. These approaches generally relied on rigidly structured hierarchies with power controlled at the top and rules, policies, and procedures governing most activities. Now, however, many managers are seeking greater flexibility and the ability to respond more quickly to the environment. Thus, organizations today are often characterized by few levels of management, broad, wide spans of management, and fewer rules and regulations. The increased use of work teams also goes hand-in-hand with this new approach to managing.

Globalization   Globalization is yet another significant contemporary challenge for managers. Managing in a global economy poses many different challenges and opportunities. For example, at a macro level, property ownership arrangements vary widely. So does the availability of natural resources and components of the infrastructure, as well as the role of government in business. Another important consideration is how behavioral processes vary widely across cultural and national boundaries. For example, values, symbols, and beliefs differ sharply among cultures. Different work norms and the role work plays in a person's life can influence patterns of both work-related behavior and attitudes toward work. They also affect the nature of supervisory relationships, decision-making styles and processes, and organizational configurations.

Ethics and Social Responsibility   Another management challenge that has taken on renewed importance is ethics and social responsibility. Scandals in organizations ranging from Drexel Burnham Lambert Inc. (stock market fraud) to Beech-Nut (advertising baby apple juice as being 100 percent pure when it was really chemically extended) to the Japanese firm Recruit (bribery of government officials) have made headlines around the world. From the social responsibility angle, increasing attention has been focused on pollution and business's obligation to help clean up our environment, business contributions to social causes, and so forth.

Managing for Quality   Quality also poses an important management challenge today. Quality is an important issue for several reasons. First, more and more organizations are using quality as a basis for competition. Second, enhancing quality lowers costs. Whistler Corporation recently found that it was using 100 of its 250 employees to repair defective radar detectors that were built incorrectly the first time. Quality is also important because of its relationship to productivity.

Service Economy   Finally, the shift toward a service economy also continues to be important. Traditionally, most businesses were manufacturers—they used tangible resources like raw materials and machinery to create tangible products like automobiles and steel. In recent years, however, the service sector of the economy has become much more important. Indeed, services now account for well over half of the gross domestic product in the United States and play a similarly important role in many other industrialized nations as well. Service technology involves the use of both tangible resources (such as machinery) and intangible resources (such as intellectual property) to create intangible services (such as a hair cut, insurance protection, or transportation between two cities). While there are obviously many similarities between managing in a manufacturing and a service organization, there are also many fundamental differences.

Summary of Key Points

Management is a set of functions directed at achieving organizational goals in an efficient and effective manner. A manager is someone whose primary responsibility is to carry out the management process within an organization. Managers can be differentiated by level and by area. By level, we can identify top, middle, and first-line managers. Kinds of managers by area include marketing, financial, operations, human resource, administrative, and specialized managers.

The basic activities that comprise the management process are planning and decision making, organizing, leading, and controlling. These activities are not performed on a systematic and predictable schedule. Effective managers also tend to have technical, interpersonal, conceptual, diagnostic, communication, decision-making, and time-management skills. The effective practice of management requires a synthesis of science and art, that is, a blend of rational objectivity and intuitive insight.

Theories are important as organizers of knowledge and as road maps for action. Understanding the historical context and precursors of management and organizations provides a sense of heritage and can also help managers avoid repeating the mistakes of others. Evidence suggests that interest in management dates back thousands of years, but a scientific approach to management has emerged only in the last hundred years.

The classical management perspective had two major branches: scientific management and administrative management. Scientific management was concerned with improving efficiency and work methods for individual workers. Administrative management was more concerned with how organizations themselves should be structured and arranged for efficient operations. Both branches paid little attention to the role of the worker.

The behavioral management perspective, characterized by a concern for individual and group behavior, emerged primarily as a result of the Hawthorne studies. The human relations movement recognized the importance and potential of behavioral processes in organizations but made many overly simplistic assumptions about those processes. Organizational behavior, a more realistic outgrowth of the behavioral perspective, is of interest to many contemporary managers.

The quantitative management perspective and its two components, management science and operations management, attempt to apply quantitative techniques to decision making and problem solving. These areas are also of considerable importance to contemporary managers. The contributions of quantitative management have been facilitated by the tremendous increase in the use of personal computers and integrated information networks.

Two relatively recent additions to management theory, the systems and contingency perspectives, appear to have great potential both as approaches to management and as frameworks for integrating the other perspectives. Challenges facing managers today include downsizing, diversity and the new workforce, information technology, new ways of managing, globalization, ethics and social responsibility, the importance of quality, and the continued shift toward a service economy.

Discussion Questions

Questions for Review

1. What are the four basic functions that comprise the management process? How are they related to one another?

2. Identify different kinds of managers by both level and area in the organization.

3. Identify the different important skills that help managers succeed. Give an example of each.

4. Briefly summarize the classical and behavioral management perspectives and identify the most important contributors to each.

5. Describe the contingency perspective and outline its usefulness to the study and practice of management.

Questions for Analysis

1. The text notes that management is both a science and an art. Is one of these aspects more important

than the other? Under what circumstances might one ingredient be more important than the other?

2. Recall a recent group project or task in which you have participated. Explain how the four basic management functions were performed.

3. Some people argue that CEOs in the United States are paid too much. Find out the pay for a CEO and discuss whether you think he or she is overpaid.

4. Explain how a manager can use tools and techniques from each major management perspective in a complementary fashion.

5. Which of the contemporary management challenges do you think will have the greatest impact on you and your career? Which will have the least?

Building Effective Technical Skills

EXERCISE OVERVIEW

Technical skills refer to the manager's abilities to accomplish or understand work done in an organization. More and more managers today are realizing that having the technical ability to use the Internet is an important part of communication, decision making, and other facets of their work. This exercise introduces you to the Internet and provides some practice in using it.

EXERCISE BACKGROUND

The so-called information highway, or the Internet, refers to an interconnected network of information and information-based resources using computers and computer systems. Whereas electronic mail was perhaps the first widespread application of the Internet, increasingly popular applications are based on home pages and search engines.

A *home page* is a file (or set of files) created by an individual, business, or other entity. It contains whatever information its creator chooses to include. For example, a company might create a home page for itself that includes its logo, its address and telephone number, information about its products and services, and so forth. An individual seeking employment might create a home page that includes a resume and a statement of career interests. Home pages are indexed by key words chosen by their creators.

A *search engine* is a system through which an Internet user can search for home pages according to their indexed key words. For example, suppose an individual is interested in knowing more about art collecting. Key words that might logically be linked to home pages related to this interest include art, artists, galleries, and framing. A search engine will take these key words and provide a listing of all home pages that are indexed to them. The user can then browse each page to see what information they contain. Popular search engines include Yahoo!, Lycos, and Webcrawler.

EXERCISE TASK

1. Visit your computer center and learn how to get access to the Internet.

2. Use a search engine to conduct a search for three or four terms related to general management (for example, management, organization, business).

3. Now select a more specific management topic and search for two or three topics (if you cannot think of any terms, scan the margin notes in this book).

4. Finally, select three or four companies and search for their home pages.

Building Effective
Diagnostic
Skills

EXERCISE OVERVIEW

Diagnostic skills enable a manager to visualize the most appropriate response to a situation. This exercise encourages you to apply your diagnostic skills to a real business problem and to assess the possible consequences of various courses of action.

EXERCISE BACKGROUND

For some time now college textbook publishers have been struggling with a significant problem. The subject matter that constitutes a particular field, such as management, chemistry, or history, continues to increase in size, scope, and complexity. Thus, authors feel compelled to add more and more information to new editions of their textbooks. Publishers have also sought to increase the visual sophistication of their texts by adding more color and photographs. At the same time, some instructors don't have time to cover the material in longer textbooks. Moreover, longer and more attractive textbooks cost more money to produce, resulting in higher selling prices to students.

Publishers have considered a variety of options to confront this situation. One option is to work with authors to produce briefer and more economical books (such as this one). Another option is to cut back on the complimentary supplements that publishers provide to instructors (such as videos and color transparencies) as a way of lowering the overall cost of producing a book. Another option is to eliminate traditional publishing altogether and provide educational resources via CD-ROM, the Internet, or other new media.

Confounding the situation, of course, is cost. Profit margins in the industry are such that managers feel the need to be cautious and conservative. That is, they cannot do everything, and must not risk alienating their users by taking too radical a step. Remember, too, that publishers must consider the concerns of three different sets of customers: the instructors who make adoption decisions, the bookstores that buy educational materials for resale (at a retail markup), and students who buy the books for classroom use and then often re-sell them back to the bookstore.

EXERCISE TASK

With this background in mind, respond to the following:

1. Discuss the pros and cons of each option currently being considered by textbook publishers.

2. Identify the likely consequences of each option.

3. Can you think of other alternatives that publishers in the industry should consider?

4. What specific recommendations would you make to an executive in a publishing company regarding this set of issues?

Building Effective Communication & Interpersonal Skills

EXERCISE OVERVIEW

Communication skills refer to the manager's abilities to both effectively convey ideas and information to others and to effectively receive ideas and information from others. Interpersonal skills refer to the ability to communicate with, understand, and motivate individuals and groups. This exercise applies these skills from a contingency perspective in selecting modes of communication to convey various kinds of news.

EXERCISE BACKGROUND

You are the regional branch manager for a large insurance company. For the last week you have been so tied up in meetings that you have had little opportunity to communicate with any of your subordinates. You have now caught up on things, however, and have a lot of information to convey. Specifically, here are the things that people need to know and/or that you need to do:

1. Three people need to be told that they are getting a pay raise of 10 percent.

2. One person needs to be told that she has been placed on probation and will lose her job if her excessive absenteeism problem isn't corrected.

3. One person needs to be congratulated for receiving his master's degree.

4. Everyone needs to be informed about the schedule for the next cycle of performance reviews.

5. Two people need to be informed that their requests for transfers have been approved, whereas a third was denied. In addition, one other person is being transferred even though she did not submit a transfer request. You know that she will be unhappy.

You can convey this information via telephone calls during regular office hours, a cell phone call as you're driving home this evening, a formal written letter, a handwritten memo, a face-to-face meeting, or e-mail.

EXERCISE TASK

With this background in mind, respond to the following:

1. Choose a communication mode for each message you need to convey.

2. What factors went into your decision about each situation?

3. What would be the least appropriate communication mode for each message?

4. What would be the likely consequences for each inappropriate choice?

Mark Spenser owns and manages Sunset Landscape Services (SLS), a nursery, landscape, and lawn care business located in Central City, Texas. Mark moved to Central City in 1970 to attend the state university there. After receiving his degree in horticulture, Mark decided to remain in Central City and start his own business. He spent three years as assistant manager at a small nursery located in a neighboring town and then launched Sunset Landscape Services in 1978.

Mark's timing could not have been better. Beginning in the late 1970s, Central City enjoyed a dramatic increase in population and economic growth, fueled primarily by unprecedented expansion and growth in the university. During the next ten years, Central City's population grew from less than 70,000 to more than 120,000. Surrounding communities grew as well, and several major new businesses moved into the area.

Mark anticipated the real-estate boom through an analysis of state demographics and population trends and conversations with local leaders who were for the first time actively courting new businesses. He realized that only two small local nurseries were in operation, and predicted that an increase in housing construction would fuel demand for both initial landscaping services by building contractors and follow-up nursery sales as homeowners began to establish their lawns and flower beds.

Like most new businesses, SLS struggled a bit at first. Mark did a good job of planning how his business would be run and setting up an efficient organization. He also did an excellent job of hiring employees and of getting them to work hard. He had a more difficult time, however, keeping his costs in line with his income and ordering new plants at the most efficient times. Finally, he took a couple of business courses at the university and learned how to manage various parts of his business better. Today, SLS is a thriving business that is well respected throughout the community.

DISCUSSION QUESTIONS

1. What kind of manager is Mark Spenser?

2. Can you identify examples of management functions and management skills in this case?

3. What emerging contemporary management challenges might be most relevant for Mark Spenser and SLS? Why?

SELF-AWARENESS

Introduction: Self-awareness is an important skill for effective management. This assessment is designed to help you evaluate your level of self-awareness.

Instructions: Please respond to the following statements by writing a number from the following rating scale in the column. Your answers should reflect your attitudes and behavior as they are *now*, not as you would *like* them to be. Be honest. This instrument is designed to help you discover how self-aware you are so that you can tailor your learning to your specific needs.

6	Strongly agree	**3**	Slightly disagree
5	Agree	**2**	Disagree
4	Slightly agree	**1**	Strongly disagree

_____ 1. I seek information about my strengths and weaknesses from others as a basis for self-improvement.

_____ 2. When I receive negative feedback about myself from others, I do not get angry or defensive.

_____ 3. In order to improve, I am willing to be self-disclosing to others (that is, to share my beliefs and feelings).

_____ 4. I am very much aware of my personal style of gathering information and making decisions about it.

_____ 5. I am very much aware of my own interpersonal needs when it comes to forming relationships with other people.

_____ 6. I have a good sense of how I cope with situations that are ambiguous and uncertain.

_____ 7. I have a well-developed set of personal standards and principles that guide my behavior.

_____ 8. I feel very much in charge of what happens to me, good and bad.

_____ 9. I seldom, if ever, feel angry, depressed, or anxious without knowing why.

_____ 10. I am conscious of the areas in which conflict and friction most frequently arise in my interactions with others.

_____ 11. I have a close relationship with at least one other person in which I can share personal information and personal feelings.

For interpretation, turn to page 457.

Source: D. Whetten/K. Cameron, _Developing Management Skills,_ 2nd ed., pages 38–39. © 1991 Addison-Wesley Educational Publishers, Inc. Reprinted by permission of Addison Wesley Longman.

Experiential Exercise

JOHARI WINDOW

Purpose: This exercise has two purposes: to encourage you to analyze yourself more accurately and to start you working on small group cohesiveness. This exercise encourages you to share data about yourself and then to assimilate and process feedback. Small groups are typically more trusting and work better together, as you will be able to see after this exercise has been completed. The Johari Window is a particularly good model for understanding the perceptual process in interpersonal relationships.

This skill builder focuses on the _human resources model_ and will help you develop your _mentor role._ One of the skills of a mentor is self-awareness.

Introduction: Each individual has four sets of personality characteristics. One set, which includes such characteristics as working hard, is well known to the individual and to others. A second set is unknown to the individual but obvious to others. For example, in a working situation a peer might observe that your jumping in to get the group moving off dead center is appropriate. At other times you jump in when the group is not really finished, and you seem to interrupt. A third set is known to the individual but not others. These are situations that you have elected not to share, perhaps because of a lack of trust.

Finally, there is a fourth set, which is not known to the individual or to others, such as why you are uncomfortable at office parties.

Instructions: Look at the Johari Window below. In quadrant 1 list three things that you know about yourself and that you think others know. List three things in quadrant 3 that others do not know about you. Finally, in quadrant 2 list three things that you did not know about yourself last semester that you learned from others.

Sources: Adapted from Joseph Luft, *Group Processes: An Introduction to Group Dynamics* (Palo Alto, Calif.: Mayfield Publishing Co., 1970), pp. 10–11 and William C. Morris and Marshall Sashkin, *Organizational Behavior in Action* (St. Paul, Minn.: West Publishing Co., 1976), p. 56.

My Own Perceptions

	Things I Know About Myself	Things I Do Not Know About Myself
Things Others Know About Me	**Quadrant 1** **"The Open Self"** Characteristics apparent to me and to others	**Quadrant 2** **"The Blind Self"** Characteristics not apparent to me
Things Others Do Not Know About Me	**Quadrant 3** **"The Concealed Self"** Characteristics known to me but kept hidden from others	**Quadrant 4** **"The Unknown Self"** The Blind Area

Other Persons' Perceptions

CASE STUDY

The Sky's the Limit

Back in 1975, two high school friends decided to start a business in the embryonic software market. The first commercial microcomputers were just coming to market, and the two friends had fallen in love with both the technology and what they saw as its long-term potential. Their first product was a version of the programming language BASIC. The fledgling business grew steadily as they modified and extended their BASIC programs for new computers just entering the market. In 1979, the two friends, William Gates and Paul Allen, moved the business—called Microsoft—to Seattle. And the rest, as they say, is history.

Microsoft's big break came in 1980 when IBM selected Gates and Allen to write the operating system software for its new line of PCs. Gates and Allen bought the rights to an existing program for $50,000, modified it a bit, and named it MS-DOS (for Microsoft Disk Operating System). Even though IBM was a relative latecomer to the PC market, its dominance in the computer industry brought it instant respect. And because other software developers wanted their products to run on IBM computers, MS-DOS quickly became the industry standard.

Paul Allen became seriously ill in 1983 and left the firm in Gates' capable hands. Microsoft developed relationships with other computer manufacturers and began introducing new application software like Word (for word processing), Excel (a spreadsheet), and PowerPoint (a presentation package). When the firm made its initial public stock offering, Gates became the PC industry's first billionaire. Popular new products like Windows 95, Windows 98, and Microsoft Office and deals with new industry giants like Compaq and Dell cemented Microsoft's place at the top of its industry. Today, Word controls 90 percent of the worldwide market for word processing, and Excel has 87 percent of the spreadsheet market. Windows 95 and Windows 98 together have 83 percent of the operating systems market. And the firm's total annual revenues are approaching $10 billion.

Because of the clout Microsoft has throughout the industry—and perhaps because of its continuing success—both the firm and Gates are widely feared and criticized in some quarters. Other software developers complain about the company's unfair business practices. Some computer manufacturers fear that they may become too dependent on Microsoft as the sole provider of software for their products. And even the government keeps a wary eye on Microsoft for possible antitrust practices, as evidenced by the lawsuit brought against the firm by the U.S. Department of Justice in 1998.

But Gates keeps his eye on the future and steers Microsoft unwaveringly toward it. For example, he personally oversaw the fifteen-year development of one of the firm's newest success stories, Windows NT, an operating system for computer networks. And he actively participates in every major decision made by the firm's top managers. He also fosters communication throughout the organization, however, and stresses the need to keep the firm lean and nimble, always wanting to avoid the bureaucratic procedures that saddle many big companies. And he keeps a close eye on the bottom line at all times, closely analyzing monthly and quarterly sales reports.

In many ways, however, Gates' biggest role at Microsoft is as its public persona. He appears at all major news conferences, makes all major announcements, and travels extensively to keep in touch with suppliers, computer manufacturers, customers, strategic allies, and government officials. He typically works sixteen hours a day and seldom takes any time off. Even when he is away from "work", he still keeps up with business via e-mail. Microsoft employees look at Gates with something bordering on awe. Some, for example, visibly copy his mannerisms. They also recognize that because of Gates' personal work habits and schedule, he expects no less from them.

The firm's dominance in its core software markets continues to grow, and its products are gaining ever-wider recognition and acceptance. But a few thunderclouds are looming on the horizon. For one thing, Microsoft faces formidable competition from America On-Line, especially since that firm acquired Netscape, in the emerging markets related to the Internet. And for another, computer giants like IBM and Compaq are seeking new alliances to avoid being too much at the mercy of Microsoft. But the chances of these thunderclouds raining on Gates' parade are quite slim.

Case Questions

1. Identify examples in this case of the four management functions and ten management roles.
2. Which management skills do you think have played the biggest role in Bill Gates' success?
3. What future events could derail Microsoft?

Case References: "Microsoft's Future," *Business Week,* January 19, 1998, pp. 58–68; David Kirkpatrick, "He Wants *All* Your Business—And He's Starting to Get It," *Fortune,* May 26, 1997, pp. 58–68; *Hoover's Handbook of American Business 1998* (Austin, Texas: The Hoover's Business Press, 1998), pp. 978–979; and David Kirkpatrick, "Microsoft: Is Your Company Its Next Meal?" *Fortune,* April 27, 1998, pp. 92–102.

CHAPTER NOTES

1. "Starbucks Cultivates Caffeine Rush," *USA Today*, April 30, 1998, pp. 1B, 2B; Jennifer Reese, "Starbucks—Inside the Coffee Cult," *Fortune*, December 9, 1996, pp. 190–200 (quote on page 196); "Grounds for Success," *Entrepreneur*, May 1998, pp. 120–126; and "Brewing a British Coup," *USA Today*, September 16, 1998, pp. 1D, 2D; "Reading the Tea Leaves, China Sees a Future in Coffee," *Wall Street Journal*, February 5, 1999, p. B1.

2. Stanley Bing, "Help! I Need Somebody," *Fortune*, March 4, 1996, pp. 41–43.

3. Rosemary Stewart, "Middle Managers: Their Jobs and Behaviors," in Jay W. Lorsch (ed.), *Handbook of Organizational Behavior* (Englewood Cliffs, N.J.: Prentice-Hall, 1987), pp. 385–391.

4. Steven Kerr, Kenneth D. Hill, and Laurie Broedling, "The First-Line Supervisor: Phasing Out or Here to Stay?" *Academy of Management Review*, January 1986, pp. 103–117; and Leonard A. Schlesinger and Janice A. Klein, "The First-Line Supervisor: Past, Present, and Future," in Lorsch (ed.), *Handbook of Organizational Behavior*, pp. 358–369.

5. See Robert L. Katz, "The Skills of an Effective Administrator," *Harvard Business Review*, September–October 1974, pp. 90–102 for a classic discussion of several of these skills.

6. See Thomas Teal, "The Human Side of Management," *Harvard Business Review*, November–December 1996, pp. 35–44.

7. For a recent discussion of the importance of time-management skills, see David Barry, Catherine Durnell Cramton, and Stephen J. Carroll, "Navigating the Garbage Can: How Agendas Help Managers Cope with Job Realities," *The Academy of Management Executive*, May 1997, pp. 26–42.

8. Gary Hamel and C. K. Prahalad, "Competing for the Future," *Harvard Business Review*, July–August 1994, pp. 122–128.

9. James Waldroop and Timothy Butler, "The Executive as Coach," *Harvard Business Review*, November–December 1996, pp. 111–117.

10. Peter F. Drucker, "The Theory of the Business," *Harvard Business Review*, September–October 1994, pp. 95–104.

11. "Why Business History?" *Audacity*, Fall 1992, pp. 7–15. See also Alan L. Wilkins and Nigel J. Bristow, "For Successful Organization Culture, Honor Your Past," *The Academy of Management Executive*, August 1987, pp. 221–227.

12. Daniel Wren, *The Evolution of Management Theory*, 4th ed. (New York: Wiley, 1994) and Page Smith, *The Rise of Industrial America* (New York: McGraw-Hill, 1984).

13. Wren, *The Evolution of Management Theory*.

14. Frederick W. Taylor, *Principles of Scientific Management* (New York: Harper and Brothers, 1911).

15. Charles D. Wrege and Amedeo G. Perroni, "Taylor's Pig-Tale: A Historical Analysis of Frederick W. Taylor's Pig-Iron Experiment," *Academy of Management Journal*, March 1974, pp. 6–27 and Charles D. Wrege and Ann Marie Stoka, "Cooke Creates a Classic: The Story Behind Taylor's Principles of Scientific Management," *Academy of Management Review*, October 1978, pp. 736–749.

16. Robert Kanigel, *The One Best Way* (New York: Viking, 1997); Oliver E. Allen, "'This Great Mental Revolution,'" *Audacity*, Summer 1996, pp. 52–61.

17. Henri Fayol, *General and Industrial Management*, trans. J. A. Coubrough (Geneva: International Management Institute, 1930).

18. Max Weber, *Theory of Social and Economic Organizations*, trans. by T. Parsons (New York: Free Press, 1947) and Richard M. Weis, "Weber on Bureaucracy: Management Consultant or Political Theorist?" *Academy of Management Review*, April 1983, pp. 242–248.

19. Wren, *The Evolution of Management Theory*, pp. 255–264.

20. Elton Mayo, *The Human Problems of an Industrial Civilization* (New York: Macmillan, 1933) and Fritz J. Roethlisberger and William J. Dickson, *Management and the Worker* (Cambridge, Mass.: Harvard University Press, 1939).

21. Abraham Maslow, "A Theory of Human Motivation," *Psychological Review*, July 1943, pp. 370–396.

22. Douglas McGregor, *The Human Side of Enterprise* (New York: McGraw-Hill, 1960).

23. See Gregory Moorhead and Ricky W. Griffin, *Organizational Behavior*, 5th ed. (Boston: Houghton Mifflin, 1998) for a recent review of current developments in the field of organizational behavior.

24. Wren, *The Evolution of Management Thought*, Chapter 21.

25. For more information on systems theory in general, see Ludwig von Bertalanffy, C. G. Hempel, R. E. Bass, and H. Jonas, "General Systems Theory: A New Approach to Unity of Science," I–VI *Human Biology*, Vol. 23, 1951, pp. 302–361. For systems theory as applied to organizations, see Fremont E. Kast and James E. Rosenzweig, "General Systems Theory: Applications for Organizations and Management," *Academy of Management Journal*, December 1972, pp. 447–465. For a recent update, see Donde P. Ashmos and George P. Huber, "The Systems Paradigm in Organization Theory: Correcting the Record and Suggesting the Future," *Academy of Management Review*, October 1987, pp. 607–621.

26. Fremont E. Kast and James E. Rosenzweig, *Contingency Views of Organization and Management* (Chicago: Science Research Associates, 1973).

2

The Environment of Organizations and Managers

OBJECTIVES

After studying this chapter, you should be able to:

- Discuss the nature of the organizational environment and identify the environments of interest to most organizations.
- Describe the components of the general and task environments and discuss their impact on organizations.
- Identify the components of the internal environment and discuss their impact on organizations.
- Identify and describe how the environment affects organizations and how organizations adapt to their environment.

Back in 1938, the U.S. Congress passed the Fair Labor Standards Act (FLSA). Among its other provisions, the FLSA mandated that hourly employees working in excess of 40 hours a week must be paid a premium wage of 1.5 times their normal hourly rate for those additional hours. The FLSA also specified that, because of the nature of their work, managerial and professional employees were exempt from this regulation. That is, because these individuals are paid salaries rather than hourly wages, they receive the same pay regardless of the number of hours they work during any given period. Although it is up to the organization itself to define which jobs are exempt and which are not, a number of legal standards have been used over the years for making these distinctions.

Recently, however, the distinctions between exempt and non-exempt jobs have become blurred in some organizations. For example, some people worry that an organization might reclassify some of its wage-based, lower-level jobs as managerial positions and then refuse to pay overtime to those individuals. Even more extreme are charges that some organizations today are pressuring hourly employees to work "off-the-clock"— to work when they are not being paid at all! Sometimes this behavior is legal, but other times it's not.

Because of the massive corporate downsizing programs in the recent years, some firms believe that the remaining employees need to carry a greater workload. This situation means working harder and being more productive. It may also mean working longer hours. In some cases it's a matter of work spilling over into what used to be free time. At AT&T, for example, workers are encouraged to participate in the firm's Ambassador Program by selling AT&T products to their friends, relatives, and neighbors during nonwork hours. Employees can win prizes for their efforts, but earn no additional income.

But other cases are more troubling. In the state of Washington, for example, a jury recently ruled that Taco Bell was guilty of pressuring its employees to do paperwork such as timesheets and schedules at home. And workers were sometimes asked to do some food preparation work after arriving at work—but before "clocking-in." Mervyn's, a chain of discount stores, has been sued by a group of its lower-level managers called team coordinators. These managers charge that they were routinely ordered to work through lunch and to take home paperwork. And Albertson's, the nation's fourth-largest grocery chain, has been charged with pushing employees to work past their assigned quitting time without receiving additional wages.

In some of these cases, of course, an individual employee might simply be misinterpreting events and suggestions from his or her boss. In other situations companies charge that unions are distorting the situation to make the business look bad. And even in cases where the law is being broken, the actions might be the isolated tactics of only one or a few managers working outside formal organizational policies to get a bit more productivity out of their employees. But regardless of the circumstances, it does seem as if some organizations are seeking ways to get more and more work out of fewer and fewer people. And although various legitimate ways to do so may be available, some managers may be crossing the line in how they are seeking to get more from their employees—without having to give anything in return.[1]

"They know ... the first to go will be the ones the boss thinks are not giving 150%. That atmosphere makes it very difficult for most people to say, 'No, I won't work the weekend.'"

Alice Freedman, consultant

All managers need a thorough understanding and appreciation of the environment in which they and their organizations function. Without this understanding they may not be aware of either the social or the legal costs of requiring or pressuring employees to work "off-the-clock" or to "volunteer" for the boss's pet project. This chapter is devoted to the environmental context of management. We first describe the general and then the task environments of business. Then we examine the ethical and social and the international environments of management. We conclude with a discussion of the internal environment of an organization, its culture.

The Organization's Environments

external environment Consists of the general environment and the task environment

general environment The set of broad dimensions and forces in an organization's surroundings that create its overall context

task environment Specific organizations or groups that affect the organization

The organization's **external environment** consists of two sets of forces. The **general environment** is the set of broad dimensions and forces in its surroundings that create its overall context. The **task environment** consists of specific external organizations or groups that influence an organization. In addition, organizations have an internal environment.

■ The General Environment

The general environment consists of several basic dimensions, including economic, technological, and political-legal dimensions. These dimensions have the potential to influence the organization in important ways. Two other parts of the general environment, social and international, are discussed separately later in this chapter.

economic dimension The overall health and vitality of the economic system in which the organization operates

The Economic Dimension The **economic dimension** of an organization's general environment is the overall health and vitality of the economic system in which the organization operates.[2] Particularly important economic factors for business are general economic growth, inflation, interest rates, and unemployment rates. For example, during the late 1980s, high interest rates made it difficult for a business to borrow money for expansion, high unemployment made it easier to hire people and to keep wages relatively low, and high inflation continued to increase costs and prices. But in the 1990s, economic conditions changed. Lower interest rates facilitated expansion, but low unemployment forced many employers to pay higher wages to attract workers.

technological dimension The methods available for converting resources into products or services

The Technological Dimension The **technological dimension** of the general environment refers to the methods available for converting resources into products or services. Although technology is applied within the organization, the forms and availability of that technology come from the general environment. Computer-assisted manufacturing and design techniques, for example, allow McDonnell Douglas to simulate the three miles of hydraulic tubing that run through a DC-10. The results include decreased warehouse needs, higher-quality tube fittings, fewer employees, and major time savings.

The Political-Legal Dimension   The **political-legal dimension** of the general environment refers to government regulation of business and the relationship between business and government. This dimension is important for three basic reasons. First, the legal system partially defines what an organization can and cannot do. Although the United States is basically a free-market economy, there is still major regulation of business activity. McDonald's, for example, is subject to multiple political and legal forces, including food-preparation standards and local zoning requirements. Second, probusiness or antibusiness sentiment in government influences business activity. For example, during periods of probusiness sentiment, firms find it easier to compete and have fewer concerns about antitrust issues. On the other hand, during a period of antibusiness sentiment firms may find their competitive strategies more restricted and have fewer opportunities for mergers and acquisitions because of antitrust concerns. Finally, political stability has ramifications for planning. No company wants to set up shop in another country unless trade relationships with that country are relatively well defined and stable. Hence, U.S. firms are more likely to do business with England, Mexico, and Canada than with Haiti and El Salvador. Similar issues are also relevant to assessments of local and state governments. A new mayor or governor can affect many organizations, especially small firms that do business in only one location and are susceptible to deed and zoning restrictions, property and school taxes, and the like.

political-legal dimension   The government regulation of business and the general relationship between business and government

■ The Task Environment

Because the impact of the general environment is often vague, imprecise, and long term, most organizations tend to focus their attention on their task environment. This environment includes competitors, customers, suppliers, regulators, and strategic allies. Although the task environment is also quite complex, it provides useful information more readily than does the general environment because the manager can identify environmental factors of specific interest to the organization rather than having to deal with the more abstract dimensions of the general environment. Figure 2.1 depicts the task environment of McDonald's.

Competitors   An organization's **competitors** are other organizations that compete with it for resources. The most obvious resources that competitors vie for are customer dollars. Reebok, Adidas, and Nike are competitors, as are A&P, Safeway, and Kroger. McDonald's competes with other fast-food operations like Burger King, Wendy's, Subway, and Dairy Queen. But competition also occurs between substitute products. Thus, Chrysler competes with Yamaha (motorcycles) and Schwinn (bicycles) for your transportation dollars, and Walt Disney World, Club Med, and Carnival Cruise Lines compete for your vacation dollars. Nor is competition limited to business firms. Universities compete with trade schools, the military, other universities, and the external labor market to attract good students, and art galleries compete with each other to attract the best exhibits.

competitor   An organization that competes with other organizations for resources

Customers   A second dimension of the task environment is **customers**, or whoever pays money to acquire an organization's products or services. Most of McDonald's customers are individuals who walk into a restaurant to buy food.

customer   Whoever pays money to acquire an organization's products or services

FIGURE 2.1
McDonald's Task Environment

An organization's task environment includes its competitors, customers, suppliers, strategic partners, and regulators. This figure clearly highlights how managers at McDonald's can use this framework to better identify and understand their key constituents.

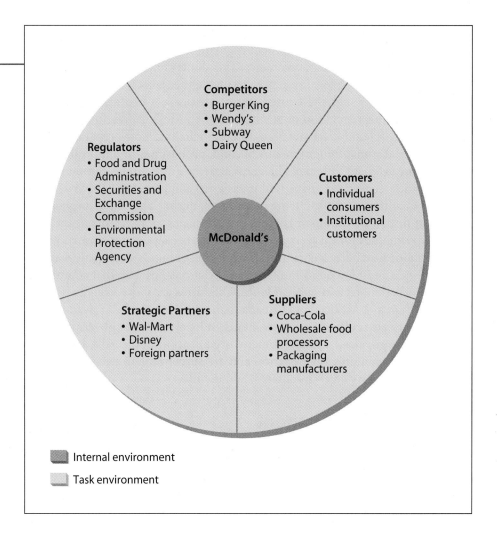

But customers need not be individuals. Schools, hospitals, government agencies, wholesalers, retailers, and manufacturers are just a few of the many kinds of organizations that may be major customers of other organizations. Some institutional customers like schools, prisons, and hospitals have recently started buying food in bulk from restaurants like McDonald's.

Dealing with customers has become increasingly complex in recent years. New products and services, new methods of marketing, more-discriminating customers, and a decrease in brand loyalty have added uncertainty to how businesses relate to their customers. McDonald's recently introduced a new sandwich called the Arch Deluxe, intended to appeal to adult customers. Unfortunately, the product failed because most adult customers preferred existing menu choices like the Quarter Pounder. Companies face especially critical differences among customers as they expand internationally. McDonald's sells beer in its German restaurants, for example, and wine in its French restaurants. Customers in those countries see those particular beverages as a normal part of their meal, much as customers in the United States routinely drink water, tea, or soft drinks with their meals. And the firm recently opened its first restaurant with no beef on the menu! That restaurant is in India, where beef is not a popular menu option. Instead, the local McDonald's uses lamb in its sandwiches.

Suppliers **Suppliers** are organizations that provide resources for other organizations. McDonald's buys soft drink products from Coca-Cola; individually packaged servings of catsup from Heinz; ingredients from wholesale food processors; and napkins, sacks, and wrappers from packaging manufacturers. Common wisdom in the United States used to be that a business should try to avoid depending exclusively on particular suppliers. A firm that buys all of a certain resource from one supplier may be crippled if the supplier goes out of business or is faced with a strike. This practice can also help maintain a competitive relationship among suppliers, keeping costs down.[3] But firms eager to emulate successful Japanese firms have recently tried to change their approach. Japanese firms have a history of building major ties with only one or two major suppliers. This relationship enables the companies to work together better for their mutual benefit and makes the supplier more responsive to the customer's needs.

supplier An organization that provides resources for other organizations

Regulators **Regulators** are elements of the task environment that have the potential to control, legislate, or influence an organization's policies and practices. There are two important kinds of regulators. The first, **regulatory agencies**, are created by the government to protect the public from certain business practices or to protect organizations from one another. Powerful federal regulatory agencies include the Environmental Protection Agency (EPA), the Securities and Exchange Commission (SEC), the Food and Drug Administration (FDA), and the Equal Employment Opportunity Commission (EEOC).

regulator A unit that has the potential to control, legislate, or otherwise influence the organization's policies and practices

regulatory agency An agency created by the government to regulate business activities

Many of these agencies play important roles in protecting the rights of individuals. The FDA, for example, helps ensure that the food we eat is free from contaminants and thus is an important regulator for McDonald's. At the same time, many managers complain about too much government regulation. Most large companies must devote thousands of labor hours and hundreds of thousands of dollars a year to comply with government regulations. To complicate the lives of managers even more, different regulatory agencies sometimes provide inconsistent—or even contradictory—mandates.

The other basic form of regulator is the interest group. An **interest group** is organized by its members to attempt to influence organizations. Prominent interest groups include the National Organization for Women (NOW), Mothers Against Drunk Driving (MADD), the National Rifle Association (NRA), the League of Women Voters, the Sierra Club, Ralph Nader's Center for the Study of Responsive Law, Consumers Union, and industry self-regulation groups like the Council of Better Business Bureaus. Although interest groups lack the official power of government agencies, they can exert considerable influence by using the media to call attention to their positions.

interest group A group formed by its own members to attempt to influence business

Strategic Allies A final dimension of the task environment is **strategic allies** (also called **strategic partners**)—two or more companies that work together in joint ventures or other partnerships.[4] As shown in Figure 2.1, McDonald's has several strategic partners. For example, one arrangement calls

strategic partner or ally An organization working with one or more other organizations in a joint venture or similar arrangement

for McDonald's to build small restaurants inside Wal-Mart stores. The fast-food company recently signed a long-term deal with Disney; McDonald's will promote Disney movies, and Disney will build McDonald's restaurants in its theme parks. And many of the firm's foreign stores are built in collaboration with local investors. Strategic partnerships help companies get from other companies the expertise they lack. They also help spread risk and open new market opportunities. Indeed, most strategic partnerships are actually among international firms. For example, Ford has strategic partnerships with Volkswagen (sharing a distribution and service center in South America) and Nissan (building minivans in the United States).

■ The Internal Environment

Organizations also have an internal environment that consists of their owners, board of directors, employees, and the physical work environment (another especially important part of the internal environment is the organization's culture, discussed separately later in this chapter).

owner Whoever can claim property rights on an organization

Owners The **owners** of a business are, of course, the people who have legal property rights to that business. Owners can be single individuals who establish and run a small business, partners who jointly own the business, individual investors who buy stock in a corporation, or other organizations. McDonald's has seven hundred million shares of stock, each of which represents one unit of ownership of the firm. The family of McDonald's founder Ray Kroc stills owns a large block of this stock, as do several large institutional investors. In addition, thousands of individuals own just a few shares each. McDonald's, in turn, also owns other businesses. For example, it owns several large regional bakeries that supply its restaurants with buns. The bakeries are incorporated as separate legal entities and managed as wholly owned subsidiaries by the parent company.

board of directors Governing body elected by a corporation's stockholders and charged with overseeing the general management of the firm to ensure that it is being run in a way that best serves the stockholders' interests

Board of Directors A corporate **board of directors** is elected by the stockholders and is charged with overseeing the general management of the firm to ensure that it is being run in a way that best serves the stockholders' interests. Some boards are relatively passive. They perform a general oversight function but seldom get actively involved in how the company is really being run. This trend, however, is changing, as more and more boards are more carefully scrutinizing the firms they oversee and exerting more influence over how they are being managed.

Employees An organization's employees are also a major element of its internal environment. Of particular interest to managers today is the changing nature of the workforce as it becomes increasingly more diverse in terms of gender, ethnicity, age, and other dimensions. Another trend in many firms is the increased reliance on temporary workers—individuals hired for short periods with no expectation of permanent employment. The usage of temporary workers has grown by more than 400 percent since 1982, and almost 2.5 million temporary workers are actively involved in the workforce today. Employers prefer to use "temps" because they provide greater flexibility, earn lower wages, and often do not participate in benefits programs. But managers have to deal with what often amounts to a two-class workforce and with a growing number of employees who have no loyalty to the organization where they work, because they may be working for someone else tomorrow.[5]

The permanent employees of many organizations are organized into labor unions, representing yet another layer of complexity for managers. The National Labor Relations Act of 1935 requires organizations to recognize and bargain with a union if that union has been legally established by the organization's employees. Presently, around 23 percent of the U.S. labor force is represented by unions. Some large firms such as Ford, Exxon, and General Motors have several unions. Even when an organization's labor force is not unionized, its managers do not ignore unions. For example, Kmart, J. P. Stevens, Honda of America, and Delta Air Lines all actively work to avoid unionization. And even though people think primarily of blue-collar workers as union members, many white-collar workers such as government employees and teachers are also represented by unions.

Physical Work Environment   A final part of the internal environment is the actual physical environment of the organization and the work that people do. Some firms have their facilities in downtown skyscrapers, usually spread across several floors. Others locate in suburban or rural settings that often resemble a college campus. Some facilities have long halls lined with traditional offices. Others have modular cubicles with partial walls and no doors. The top one hundred managers at Mars, makers of Snickers and Milky Way, all work in a single vast room. Two co-presidents sit in the very center of the room, while others are arrayed in concentric circles around them. Increasingly, newer facilities have an even more open arrangement where people work in large rooms, moving between different tables to interact with different people on different projects. Freestanding computer workstations are available for those who need them, and a few small rooms might be off to the side for private business.

The Ethical and Social Environment of Management

The ethical and social environment has become an especially important area for managers in the last few years. In this section we first explore the concept of individual ethics and then describe social responsibility.

■ Individual Ethics in Organizations

Ethics are an individual's personal beliefs about whether a behavior, action, or decision is right or wrong.[6] Note that what constitutes ethical behavior varies from one person to another. For example, one person who finds a

ethics An individual's personal beliefs regarding what is right and wrong or good and bad

ethical behavior   Behavior that conforms to generally accepted social norms

unethical behavior   Behavior that does not conform to generally accepted social norms

managerial ethics   Standards of behavior that guide individual managers in their work

twenty-dollar bill on the floor believes that it is okay to stick it in his pocket, whereas another feels compelled to turn it in to the lost-and-found department. Further, although **ethical behavior** is in the eye of the beholder, it usually refers to behavior that conforms to generally accepted social norms. **Unethical behavior**, then, is behavior that does not conform to generally accepted social norms.

Managerial Ethics   **Managerial ethics** are the standards of behavior that guide individual managers in their work.[7] One important area of managerial ethics is the treatment of employees by the organization. This area includes things such as hiring and firing, wages and working conditions, and employee privacy and respect. Unfortunately, there seems to be a growing concern that organizations may be intruding too much on employee privacy. For example, one recent survey of almost one thousand firms found that 15.7 percent of them videotaped employees performing their jobs, 14.9 percent stored and randomly reviewed e-mail by their employees, and 10.4 percent taped and reviewed telephone conversations.[8]

Numerous ethical issues also stem from how employees treat the organization, especially in regard to conflicts of interest, secrecy and confidentiality, and honesty. A conflict of interest occurs when a decision potentially benefits the individual to the possible detriment of the organization. For example, a buyer at J.C. Penney was charged with giving certain suppliers large orders in exchange for financial kickbacks to small companies he owned and with selling outright to some suppliers the bids that had been submitted to J.C. Penney by their competitors.[9]

Managerial ethics also come into play in the relationship between the firm and its employees with other economic agents. The primary agents of interest

Managerial ethics must be interpreted from the point of view of their organizational context. In some organizations, for example, norms are such that people feel empowered to bend rules and to pay little or no regard to ethical conduct. But in others, norms and organization culture reinforce strictly ethical behaviors. As shown in this cartoon, if a senior executive never questions his or her own ethics—and if no one dares to question the executive's actions—the potential for ethical problems increases significantly.

"I no longer worry about what's right and what's wrong. No one would dare tell me what was wrong."

include customers, competitors, stockholders, suppliers, dealers, and unions. The behaviors between the organization and these agents that may be subject to ethical ambiguity include advertising and promotions, financial disclosures, ordering and purchasing, shipping and solicitations, bargaining and negotiation, and other business relationships.

Managing Ethical Behavior Spurred partially by the recent spate of ethical scandals and partially from a sense of enhanced corporate consciousness about the importance of ethical and unethical behaviors, many organizations have reemphasized ethical behavior on the part of employees.[10] This emphasis takes many forms, but any effort to enhance ethical behavior must begin with top management. It is top managers, for example, who establish the organization's culture and define what will and will not be acceptable behavior. Some companies have also started offering employees training in how to cope with ethical dilemmas. At Boeing, for example, line managers lead training sessions for other employees, and the company also has an ethics committee that reports directly to the board of directors. The training sessions involve discussions of ethical dilemmas that employees might face and how managers might handle those dilemmas. Chemical Bank, Xerox, and McDonnell Douglas have also established ethics training programs for their managers.

Organizations are also going to greater lengths to formalize their ethical standards. Some, such as General Mills and Johnson & Johnson, have prepared guidelines that detail how employees are to treat suppliers, customers, competitors, and other constituents. Others, such as Whirlpool and Hewlett-Packard, have developed formal **codes of ethics**—written statements of the values and ethical standards that guide the firms' actions. Several years ago NYNEX won an award from the Center for Business Ethics at Bentley College for its code of ethics and its commitment of people and resources to ensure that all employees fully understand how the code affects them.[11] The Code of Ethics of Lockheed Martin is illustrated in Figure 2.2.

Individual ethics help people decide what is right and wrong. And it is individual ethics that cause some people to generously donate their time to help others. An increasingly popular choice that some people make is a so-called "volunteer vacation"—a trip paid out of their own pocket with the goal of contributing their time, talent, and effort to help others. The people shown here, for example, are spending their vacations building a home for a poverty-stricken family in Matamoros, Mexico. Their ethics have led them to conclude that this activity is the "right" use of their time.

code of ethics   A formal, written statement of the values and ethical standards that guide a firm's actions

■ Social Responsibility and Organizations

As we have seen, ethics relate to individuals and their decisions and behaviors. Organizations themselves do not have ethics, but do relate to their environment in ways that often involve ethical dilemmas and decisions. **Social responsibility** is the set of obligations an organization has to protect and

social responsibility   The set of obligations an organization has to protect and enhance the societal context in which it functions

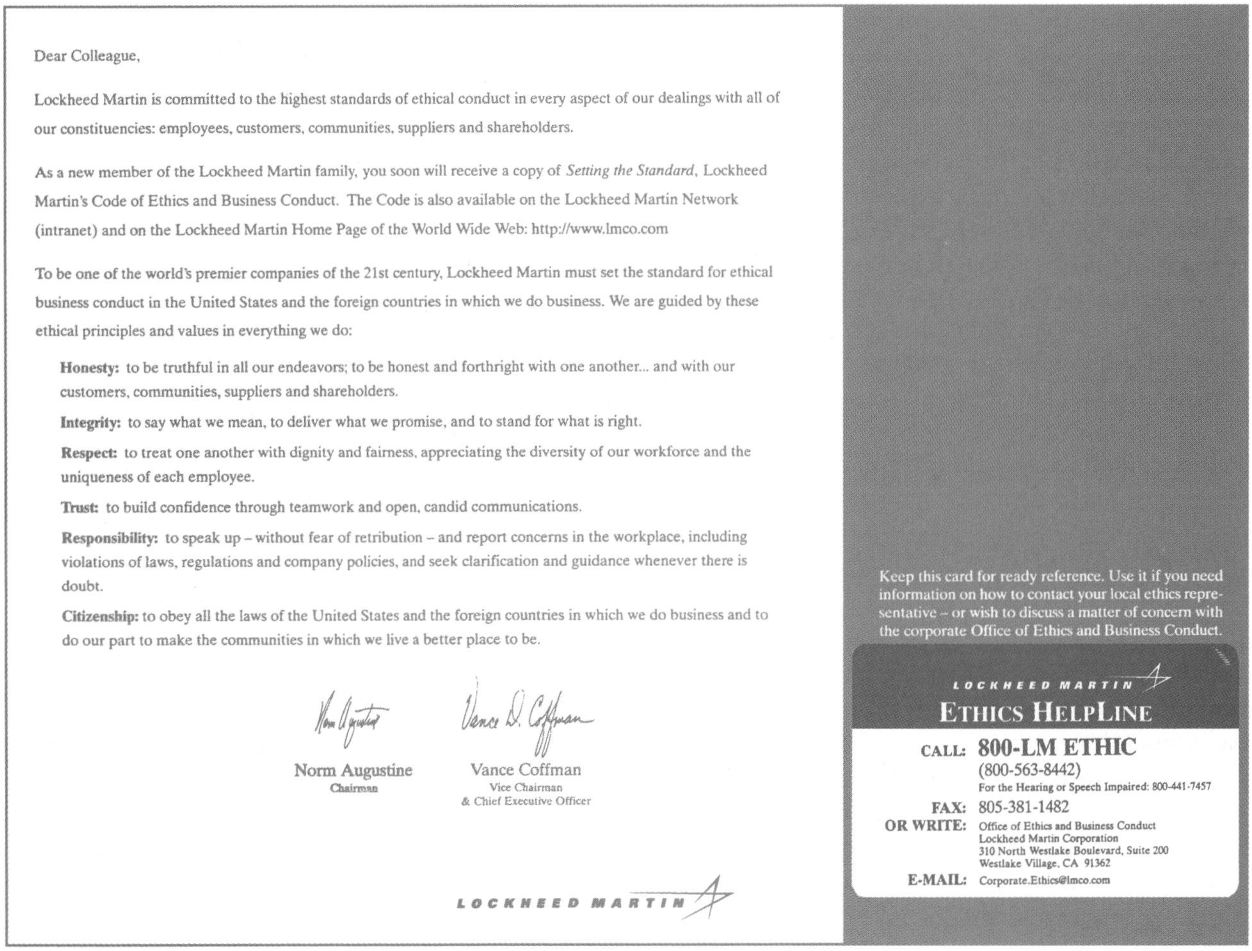

Dear Colleague,

Lockheed Martin is committed to the highest standards of ethical conduct in every aspect of our dealings with all of our constituencies: employees, customers, communities, suppliers and shareholders.

As a new member of the Lockheed Martin family, you soon will receive a copy of *Setting the Standard*, Lockheed Martin's Code of Ethics and Business Conduct. The Code is also available on the Lockheed Martin Network (intranet) and on the Lockheed Martin Home Page of the World Wide Web: http://www.lmco.com

To be one of the world's premier companies of the 21st century, Lockheed Martin must set the standard for ethical business conduct in the United States and the foreign countries in which we do business. We are guided by these ethical principles and values in everything we do:

Honesty: to be truthful in all our endeavors; to be honest and forthright with one another... and with our customers, communities, suppliers and shareholders.

Integrity: to say what we mean, to deliver what we promise, and to stand for what is right.

Respect: to treat one another with dignity and fairness, appreciating the diversity of our workforce and the uniqueness of each employee.

Trust: to build confidence through teamwork and open, candid communications.

Responsibility: to speak up – without fear of retribution – and report concerns in the workplace, including violations of laws, regulations and company policies, and seek clarification and guidance whenever there is doubt.

Citizenship: to obey all the laws of the United States and the foreign countries in which we do business and to do our part to make the communities in which we live a better place to be.

Norm Augustine
Chairman

Vance Coffman
Vice Chairman
& Chief Executive Officer

LOCKHEED MARTIN

Keep this card for ready reference. Use it if you need information on how to contact your local ethics representative – or wish to discuss a matter of concern with the corporate Office of Ethics and Business Conduct.

LOCKHEED MARTIN
ETHICS HELPLINE
CALL: **800-LM ETHIC**
(800-563-8442)
For the Hearing or Speech Impaired: 800-441-7457
FAX: 805-381-1482
OR WRITE: Office of Ethics and Business Conduct
Lockheed Martin Corporation
310 North Westlake Boulevard, Suite 200
Westlake Village, CA 91362
E-MAIL: Corporate.Ethics@lmco.com

FIGURE 2.2
Communicating Ethical Principles and Values

enhance the society in which it functions. On the surface, most people seem to agree that organizations should be socially responsible. In truth, though, those who oppose wide interpretations of social responsibility use several convincing arguments.[12] Figure 2.3 summarizes some of the more salient arguments on both sides of this contemporary debate.

Arguments For Social Responsibility People who argue in favor of social responsibility claim that because organizations create many of the problems that need to be addressed, such as air and water pollution and resource depletion, they should play a major role in solving them. The critics also argue that because corporations are legally defined entities with most of the same privileges as private citizens, businesses should not try to avoid their obligations as citizens. Advocates of social responsibility point out that while governmental organizations have stretched their budgets to the limit, many large businesses often have surplus revenues that could potentially be used to help solve social problems. For example, IBM routinely donates surplus computers to schools, and many restaurants give leftover food to homeless shelters.

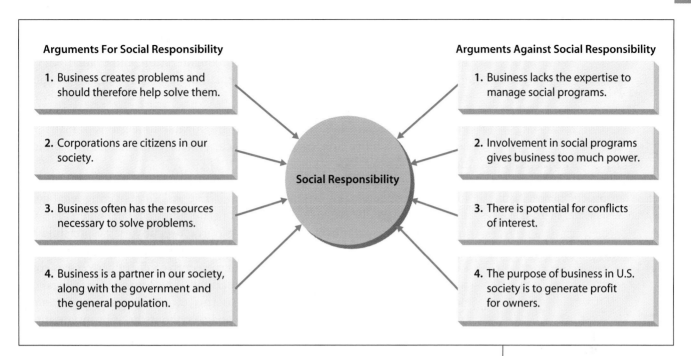

Arguments For Social Responsibility

1. Business creates problems and should therefore help solve them.

2. Corporations are citizens in our society.

3. Business often has the resources necessary to solve problems.

4. Business is a partner in our society, along with the government and the general population.

Social Responsibility

Arguments Against Social Responsibility

1. Business lacks the expertise to manage social programs.

2. Involvement in social programs gives business too much power.

3. There is potential for conflicts of interest.

4. The purpose of business in U.S. society is to generate profit for owners.

FIGURE 2.3
Arguments For and Against Social Responsibility

Arguments Against Social Responsibility   Some people, however, argue that widening the interpretation of social responsibility will undermine the U.S. economy by detracting from the basic mission of business: to earn profits for owners. For example, money that Chevron or General Electric contributes to social causes or charities is money that could otherwise be distributed to owners as a dividend. Ben & Jerry's Homemade Inc. has a very ambitious and widely touted social agenda. But some shareholders recently criticized the firm when it refused to accept a lucrative exporting deal to Japan simply because the Japanese distributor did not have a similar social agenda.[13]

Another objection to deepening the social responsibility of businesses points out that corporations already wield enormous power and that their activity in social programs gives them even more power. Another argument against social responsibility focuses on the potential for conflict of interest. Finally, critics argue that organizations lack the expertise to understand how to assess and make decisions about worthy social programs. How can a company truly know, they ask, which cause or program is most deserving of its support, or how money might best be spent?

■ Managing Social Responsibility

The demands for social responsibility placed on contemporary organizations by an increasingly sophisticated and educated public are probably stronger than ever. As we have seen, there are pitfalls for managers who fail to adhere to high ethical standards and for companies that try to circumvent their legal obligations. Organizations therefore need to fashion an approach to social responsibility the same way that they develop any other business strategy. That is, they should view social responsibility as a major challenge that requires careful planning, decision making, consideration, and evaluation. Organizations use both formal and informal dimensions to manage social responsibility.

Formal Organizational Dimensions   Some formal dimensions of managing social responsibility are legal compliance, ethical compliance, and philanthropic giving.

legal compliance   The extent to which an organization complies with local, state, federal, and international laws

Legal compliance is the extent to which the organization conforms to local, state, federal, and international laws. The task of managing legal compliance is generally assigned to the appropriate functional managers. For example, the organization's top human resource executive is responsible for ensuring compliance with regulations concerning hiring, pay, and workplace safety and health. Likewise, the top finance executive generally oversees compliance with securities and banking regulations. The organization's legal department is also likely to contribute to this effort by providing general oversight and answering queries from managers about the appropriate interpretation of laws and regulations.

ethical compliance   The extent to which an organization and its members follow basic ethical standards of behavior

Ethical compliance is the extent to which the members of the organization follow basic ethical (and legal) standards of behavior. We noted earlier that organizations have increased their efforts in this area—providing training in ethics and developing guidelines and codes of conduct, for example. These activities serve as vehicles for enhancing ethical compliance. Many organizations also establish formal ethics committees, which may be asked to review proposals for new projects, help evaluate new hiring strategies, or assess a new environmental protection plan. Such a committee might also serve as a peer review panel to evaluate alleged ethical misconduct by an employee.[14]

philanthropic giving   Awarding funds or gifts to charities or other worthy causes

Finally, **philanthropic giving** is the awarding of funds or gifts to charities or other social programs. Dayton-Hudson Corp. routinely gives 5 percent of its taxable income to charity and social programs. Giving across national boundaries is also becoming more common. For example, Alcoa gave $112,000 to a small town in Brazil to build a sewage treatment plant. And Japanese firms like Sony and Mitsubishi make contributions to a number of social programs in the United States. Unfortunately, in this age of budget cutbacks, many corporations have also had to limit their charitable gifts. And many firms that continue to make contributions are increasingly targeting them to programs or areas where the firm will get something in return. For example, compared to just a few years ago, firms today are more likely to give money to job-training programs than to the arts. The logic is that the companies get more direct payoff from the former type of contribution—in this instance, a better-trained workforce from which to hire employees.[15]

Informal Organizational Dimensions   In addition to these formal dimensions for managing social responsibility, there are informal ones. Leadership, organization culture, and how the organization responds to whistle blowers each help shape and define people's perceptions of the organization's stance on social responsibility.

Leadership practices and organization culture can go a long way toward defining the social responsibility stance an organization and its members adopt.[16] For example, Johnson & Johnson executives for years provided a consistent message to employees that customers, employees, communities where the company did business, and shareholders were all important—and primarily in that order. Thus, when packages of poisoned Tylenol showed up on store shelves in the 1980s, Johnson & Johnson employees didn't need to wait for orders from headquarters to know what to do: they immediately pulled all the packages from shelves before any other customers could buy them.[17]

Whistle-blowing is the disclosure by an employee of illegal or unethical conduct on the part of others within the organization.[18] How an organization responds to this practice often indicates its stance toward social responsibility. Whistle blowers may have to proceed through a number of channels to be heard, and they may even get fired for their efforts. Many organizations, however, welcome these contributions. A person who observes questionable behavior typically first reports the incident to his or her boss. If nothing is done, the whistle blower may then inform higher-level managers or an ethics committee if one exists. Eventually, the person may have to go to a regulatory agency or even the media to be heard. For example, Charles W. Robinson Jr. once worked as a director of a SmithKline lab in San Antonio. One day he noticed a suspicious billing pattern the firm was using to collect lab fees from Medicare; in this case, SmithKline was charging Medicare considerably more than the lab was charging its other customers for the same tests. Robinson pointed out the problem to higher-level managers, but his concerns were ignored. He subsequently took his findings to the U.S. government, which sued SmithKline and eventually reached a settlement of $325 million.[19]

whistle-blowing The disclosing by an employee of illegal or unethical conduct on the part of others within the organization

The International Environment of Management

Another important competitive issue for managers today is the international environment. After describing recent trends in international business, we examine levels of internationalization and the international context of business.

■ Trends in International Business

The stage for today's international business environment was set at the end of World War II. Businesses in war-torn countries like Germany and Japan had no choice but to rebuild from scratch. Because of this position, they essentially had to rethink every facet of their operations, including technology, production, finance, and marketing. Although it took many years for these countries to recover, they eventually did so, and their economic systems were

Most international business managers see the People's Republic of China as the most important emerging marketplace in the world. Its vast population and growing interest in consumerism combine to offer tremendous potential for a wide array of products and services. For example, even farmers in China's most remote regions hunger for new technology such as the satellite dish shown here. Products like televisions, cellular telephones, computers, and automobiles are also experiencing strong demand as the citizens of China take their place alongside consumers from Japan, Europe, the United States, and the rest of the world.

subsequently poised for growth. During the same era, U.S. companies grew complacent. Their customer base was growing rapidly. Increased population spurred by the baby boom and increased affluence resulting from the postwar economic boom greatly raised the average person's standard of living and expectations. The U.S. public continually wanted new and better products and services. Many U.S. companies profited greatly from this pattern, but most were also perhaps guilty of taking it for granted.

But U.S. firms are no longer isolated from global competition or the global market. A few simple numbers help tell the full story of international trade and industry. First of all, the volume of international trade increased more than 3,000 percent from 1960 to 1997. Further, while 162 of the world's largest corporations are headquartered in the United States, there are also 126 in Japan, 42 in France, 41 in Germany, and 34 in Britain.[20] Within certain industries, the preeminence of non-U.S. firms is even more striking. For example, only one each of the world's ten largest banks and ten largest electronics companies is based in the United States. Only two of the ten largest chemical companies are U.S. firms. On the other hand, U.S. firms account for six of the eight largest aerospace companies, four of the seven largest airlines, six of the nine largest computer companies, four of the five largest diversified financial companies, and six of the ten largest retailers.[21]

U.S. firms are also finding that international operations are an increasingly important element of their sales and profits. For example, in 1996 Exxon Corporation realized 80 percent of its revenues and 64 percent of its profits abroad. For Avon, these percentages were 64 percent and 68 percent, respectively.[22] From any perspective, then, it is clear that we live in a truly global economy. Virtually all businesses today must be concerned with the competitive situations they face in lands far from home and with how companies from distant lands are competing in their homeland.

Approaches to Internationalization	Advantages	Disadvantages
Importing or Exporting	1. Small cash outlay 2. Little risk 3. No adaptation necessary	1. Tariffs and taxes 2. High transportation costs 3. Government restrictions
Licensing	1. Increased profitability 2. Extended profitability	1. Inflexibility 2. Helps competitors
Strategic alliance/ Joint ventures	1. Quick market entry 2. Access to materials and technology	1. Shared ownership (limits control and profits)
Direct investment	1. Enhances control 2. Existing infrastructure	1. Complexity 2. Greater economic and political risk 3. Greater uncertainty

■ Levels of International Business Activity

Firms can choose various levels of international business activity as they seek to gain a competitive advantage in other countries. The general levels are exporting, licensing, strategic alliances, and direct investment. Table 2.1 summarizes the advantages and disadvantages of each activity.

Importing and Exporting **Exporting**, or making the product in the firm's domestic marketplace and selling it in another country, can involve both merchandise and services. **Importing** is bringing a good, service, or capital into the home country from abroad. For example, automobiles (Mazda, Ford, Volkswagen, Mercedes-Benz, Ferrari) and stereo equipment (Sony, Bang and Olufsen, Sanyo) are routinely exported by their manufacturers to other countries. Likewise, many wine distributors buy products from vineyards in France, Italy, and/or California and import them into their own countries for resale.

Licensing **Licensing** is an arrangement whereby a firm allows another company to use its brand name, trademark, technology, patent, copyright, or other assets. In return, the licensee pays a royalty, usually based on sales. For example, Kirin Brewery, Japan's largest producer of beer, wanted to expand its international operations but feared that the time involved in shipping the beer from Japan would cause the beverage to lose its freshness. Thus, Kirin has entered into a number of licensing arrangements with breweries in other markets. These brewers make beer according to strict guidelines provided by the Japa-nese firm, and then package and market the product as Kirin Beer. The foreign brewers pay a royalty to Kirin for each case sold. Molson produces Kirin in Canada under such an agreement; the Charles Wells brewery does the same in England.[23]

TABLE 2.1
Advantages and Disadvantages of Various Approaches to Internationalization

When organizations decide to increase their level of internationalization, they can adopt several strategies. Each strategy is a matter of degree, as opposed to being a discrete and mutually exclusive category. And each has unique advantages and disadvantages that must be considered.

exporting Making a product in the firm's domestic marketplace and selling it in another country

importing Bringing a good, service, or capital into the home country from abroad

licensing An arrangement whereby one company allows another company to use its brand name, trademark, technology, patent, copyright, or other assets in exchange for a royalty based on sales

strategic alliances   A cooperative arrangement between two or more firms for mutual benefit

joint ventures   A special type of strategic alliance when the partners share in the ownership of an operation on an equity basis

Strategic Alliances   In a **strategic alliance**, two or more firms jointly cooperate for mutual gain.[24] For example, Kodak and Fuji, along with three major Japanese camera manufacturers, recently collaborated on the development of a new film cartridge. This collaboration allowed Kodak and Fuji to share development costs, prevented an advertising war if the two firms had developed different cartridges, and made it easier for new cameras to be introduced at the same time as the new film cartridges. A **joint venture** is special type of strategic alliance in which the partners actually share ownership of a new enterprise. Strategic alliances have enjoyed a tremendous upsurge in the past few years.

direct investment   When a firm headquartered in one country builds or purchases operating facilities or subsidiaries in a foreign country

Direct Investment   **Direct investment** occurs when a firm headquartered in one country builds or purchases operating facilities or subsidiaries in a foreign country. The foreign operations then become wholly owned subsidiaries of the firm. Mercedes-Benz recently invested $1.1 billion to construct a new factory in Alabama to build its sport utility vehicle.[25] Similarly, Ford and General Motors have also recently built new plants in Brazil.[26] A major reason many firms make direct investments is to capitalize on lower labor costs. That is, the goal is often to transfer production to locations where labor is cheap. Japanese businesses have moved much of their production to Thailand because labor costs are much lower there than in Japan. Many U.S. firms are using *maquiladoras* for the same purpose. *Maquiladoras* are light-assembly plants built in northern Mexico close to the U.S. border. The Mexican government extends special tax breaks to the plants, and the area is populated with workers willing to work for very low wages.

maquiladoras   Light-assembly plants built in northern Mexico, close to the U.S. border, that receive special tax breaks from the Mexican government

■ The Context of International Business

Managers involved in international business must also be aware of three major areas of concern: controls on international business, the existence of economic communities, and cultural variations across national boundaries.

Controls on International Trade   In some instances, the government of a country may decide that foreign competition is hurting domestic trade. To protect domestic business, such governments may enact various barriers to international trade. A **tariff** is a tax collected on goods shipped across national boundaries. Tariffs can be collected by the exporting country, countries through which goods pass, and the importing country. Import tariffs, which are the most common, can be levied to protect domestic companies by increasing the cost of foreign goods. Japan charges U.S. tobacco producers a tariff on cigarettes imported into Japan as a way to keep their prices higher than the prices charged by domestic firms. Tariffs can also be levied, usually by less developed countries, to raise money for the government.

tariff   A tax collected on goods shipped across national boundaries

quota   A limit on the number or value of goods that can be traded

   Quotas are the most common form of trade restriction. A quota is a limit on the number or value of goods that can be traded. The quota amount is typically designed to ensure that domestic competitors will be able to maintain a certain market share. Honda is allowed to import 425,000 autos each year into the United States. This quota is one reason Honda opened manufacturing facilities here. The quota applies to cars imported into the United States, but the company can produce as many other cars within our borders as it wants, as they are not considered imports. **Export restraint agreements** are designed to convince other governments to voluntarily limit the volume or value of goods exported to a particular country. They are, in effect, export quotas. Japanese steel producers voluntarily limit the amount of steel they send to the United States each year.

"Buy national" legislation gives preference to domestic producers through content or price restrictions. Several countries have this type of legislation. Brazil requires that Brazilian companies purchase only Brazilian-made computers. The United States requires that the Department of Defense purchase only military uniforms manufactured in the United States, even though the price of foreign uniforms would be half as much. Mexico requires that 50 percent of the parts of cars sold in Mexico be manufactured in Mexico.

Economic Communities   Just as government policies can either increase or decrease the political risk facing international managers, trade relations between countries can either help or hinder international business. Relations dictated by quotas, tariffs, and so forth can hurt international trade. Currently, a strong global movement is underway to reduce many of these barriers. This movement takes its most obvious form in international economic communities.

An international **economic community** is a group of countries that agree to markedly reduce or eliminate trade barriers among themselves. The first—and in many ways still the most important—of these economic communities is the **European Union (EU)**. The map in Figure 2.4 identifies the member nations of the EU. Similarly, the passage of the **North American Free Trade Agreement (NAFTA)** represents the first step toward the formation of an economic community that comprises North American countries.

National Culture   Another environmental challenge for the international manager is the cultural environment and how it affects business. Cultural values and beliefs are often unspoken; they may even be taken for granted by those who live in a particular country. Cultural factors do not necessarily cause problems for managers when the cultures of two countries are similar. Difficulties can arise, however, when little overlap exists between the home culture of a manager and the culture of the country in which business is to be conducted. For example, most U.S. managers find the culture and traditions of England familiar. The people of both countries speak the same language and share strong historical roots, and there is a history of strong commerce between the two countries. When U.S. managers begin operations in Japan or the People's Republic of China, however, most of this familiarity disappears.

Cultural differences between countries can have a direct impact on business practice. For example, the religion of Islam teaches that people should not make a living by exploiting the misfortune of others and that making interest payments is immoral. Consequently, in Saudi Arabia few businesses provide

export restraint agreements
Accords reached by governments in which countries voluntarily limit the volume or value of goods they export and import from one another

economic community   A group of countries that agree to markedly reduce or eliminate trade barriers among themselves (a formalized market system)

European Union (EU)   The first and most important international market system

North American Free Trade Agreement (NAFTA)   An agreement between the United States, Canada, and Mexico to promote mutual trade

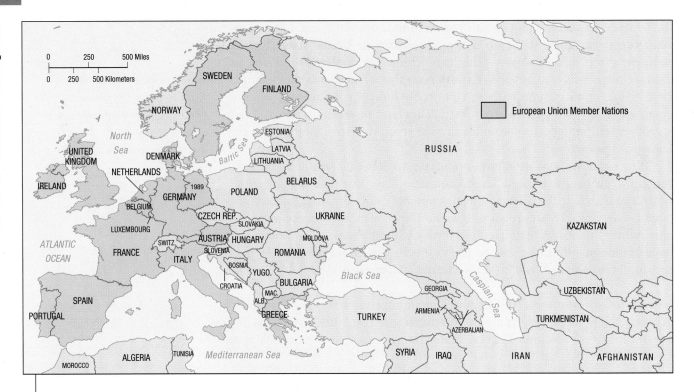

FIGURE 2.4
European Union Member Nations

auto-wrecking services to tow stalled cars to the garage because that would be capitalizing on misfortune), and in the Sudan banks cannot pay or charge interest. Given these cultural and religious constraints, automobile towing and banking don't seem to hold great promise for international managers in those particular countries!

Some cultural differences between countries can be even more subtle and yet have a major impact on business activities. For example, in the United States most managers clearly agree about the value of time. Most U.S. managers schedule their activities very tightly and then adhere to their schedules. Other cultures don't put such a premium on time. In the Middle East, for example, managers do not like to set appointments, and they rarely keep appointments set too far into the future. U.S. managers interacting with managers from the Middle East might misinterpret the late arrival of a potential business partner as a negotiation ploy or an insult, when it is rather a simple reflection of different views of time and its value.[27]

Language itself can be an important factor. Beyond the obvious and clear barriers posed by people who speak different languages, subtle differences in meaning can also play a major role. For example, Imperial Oil of Canada markets gasoline under the brand name Esso. When the firm tried to sell its gasoline in Japan, it learned that Esso means "stalled car" in Japanese. General Motors executives couldn't understand why the Chevrolet Nova was not selling well in Latin America until they learned that, in Spanish, *no va* means "it doesn't go." The color green is used extensively in Moslem countries, but it signifies death in some other countries. The color associated with femininity in the United States is pink, but in many other countries yellow is the most feminine color.

The Organization's Culture

The **culture** of an organization is the set of values that helps its members understand what the organization stands for, how it does things, and what it considers important. Culture is an amorphous concept that defies objective measurement or observation. Nevertheless, because it is the foundation of the organization's internal environment, culture plays a major role in shaping managerial behavior.[28]

organization culture The set of values, beliefs, behaviors, customs, and attitudes that helps an organization's members understand what it stands for, how it does things, and what it considers important

■ The Importance of Culture

Several years ago, executives at Levi Strauss believed that the company had outgrown its sixty-eight-year-old building. Even though everyone enjoyed its casual and relaxed atmosphere, the company needed more space. So Levi Strauss moved into a modern office building in downtown San Francisco, where its new headquarters spread over twelve floors in a skyscraper. It quickly became apparent that the change was affecting the corporate culture—and that people did not like it. Executives felt isolated, and other managers missed the informal chance meetings in the halls. Within just a few years, Strauss moved out of the skyscraper and back into a building that fosters informality. For example, the new site is adjacent to a park area where employees converge for lunchtime conversation. Clearly, Levi Strauss has a culture that is important to the people who work there.[29]

Culture determines the "feel" of the organization. The stereotypic image of Microsoft, for example, is a workplace where people dress very casually and work very long hours. In contrast, the image of Bank of America, for some observers, is a formal setting with rigid work rules and people dressed in conservative business attire. And Texas Instruments likes to talk about its "shirt sleeve" culture, in which ties are avoided and few managers ever wear jackets. Southwest Airlines maintains a culture that stresses fun and excitement. The firm's CEO, Herb Kelleher, explains the company's emphasis on fun in an orientation video set to rap music. Of course, the same culture is not necessarily found throughout an entire organization. For example, the sales and marketing department may have a culture quite different from that of the operations and manufacturing department. Regardless of its nature, however, culture is a powerful force in organizations, one that can shape the firm's overall effectiveness and long-term success. Companies that can develop and maintain a strong culture, such as Hewlett-Packard and Procter & Gamble, tend to be more effective than companies that have trouble developing and maintaining a strong culture, such as Kmart.[30]

■ Determinants of Culture

Where does an organization's culture come from? Typically it develops and blossoms over a long period of time. Its starting point is often the organization's founder. For example, James Cash Penney believed in treating employees and customers with respect and dignity. Employees at J.C. Penney are still called associates rather than employees (to reflect partnership), and customer satisfaction is of paramount importance. The impact of Sam Walton, Ross Perot, and Walt Disney is still felt in the organizations they founded. As an organization grows, its culture is modified, shaped, and refined by symbols, stories, heroes, slogans, and ceremonies. For example, an important value at Hewlett-Packard is the avoidance of bank debt. A popular story still told at the company involves a new project being considered for several years. All objective criteria indicated that HP should incur bank debt to finance the project, yet Bill Hewlett and David Packard rejected that approach simply because "HP avoids bank debt." This story, involving two corporate heroes and based on a slogan, dictates corporate culture today. And many decisions at Walt Disney Company today are still framed by asking, "What would Walt have done?"

Corporate success and shared experiences also shape culture. For example, Hallmark Cards has a strong culture derived from its years of success in the greeting cards industry. Employees speak of the Hallmark family and care deeply about the company; many of them have worked at the company for years. At Kmart, in contrast, the culture is quite weak, the management team changes rapidly, and few people sense any direction or purpose in the company. The differences in culture at Hallmark and Kmart are in part attributable to past successes and shared experiences.

■ Managing Organizational Culture

How can managers deal with culture, given its clear importance but intangible nature? Essentially, the manager must understand the current culture and then decide whether to maintain or change it. By understanding the organization's current culture, managers can take appropriate actions. At Hewlett-Packard, the values represented by "the HP way" still exist. Moreover, they guide and direct most of the firm's important activities. Culture can also be maintained by rewarding and promoting people whose behaviors are consistent with the existing culture and by articulating the culture through slogans, ceremonies, and so forth.

But managers must walk a fine line between maintaining a culture that still works effectively versus changing a culture that has become dysfunctional. For example, many of the firms already noted, as well as numerous others, take pride in perpetuating their cultures. Shell Oil Company, for example, has an elaborate display in the lobby of its Houston headquarters building that tells the story of the firm's past. But other companies may face situations in which their culture is no longer a strength. For example, some critics feel that Ford's culture places too much emphasis on product development and not enough on marketing. This atmosphere sometimes results in new products that fail to live up to expectations.[31]

Culture problems sometimes arise from mergers or the growth of rival factions within an organization. For example, Wells Fargo and Company, which relies heavily on snazzy technology and automated banking services, recently acquired another large bank, First Interstate, which had focused more attention on personal services and customers satisfaction. Blending the two disparate organization cultures has been difficult for the firm as managers have argued over how best to serve customers and operate the new enterprise.[32] Arthur Andersen, one of the Big Five accounting firms, faces a different type of cultural problem. Its relatively new Andersen Consulting Group has grown so much in size and importance that it threatens to usurp power from the original accounting group. Differences in culture between the two groups have hampered efforts to reconcile their goals and agendas.[33]

To change culture, managers must have a clear idea of what they want to create. Schwinn has tried to redefine itself to be more competitive and to break free of its old approaches to doing business. The firm's new motto—"Established 1895. Re-established 1994."—represents an effort to create a new culture that better reflects today's competitive environment in the bicycle market. Likewise, when Continental Airlines "reinvented" itself a few years ago, employees were taken outside the corporate headquarters building in Houston to watch the firm's old policies and procedures manuals set afire. The firm's new strategic direction is known throughout Continental as the "Go Forward" plan, intentionally named to avoid reminding people about the firm's troubled past and to, instead, focus on the future.

One major way to shape culture is to bring outsiders into important managerial positions. The choice of a new CEO from outside the organization is often a clear signal that things will be changing. Indeed, new CEOs were the catalyst for the changes at Schwinn and Continental noted above. Adopting new slogans, telling new stories, staging new ceremonies, and breaking with tradition can also alter culture. Culture can also be changed by methods discussed in Chapter 7.[34]

Summary of Key Points

Managers need to have a thorough understanding of the environment in which they operate and compete. The general environment consists of economic, technological, political-legal, sociocultural, and international dimensions. The task environment consists of competitors, customers, suppliers, regulators, and strategic partners.

The internal environment consists of the organization's owners, board of directors, employees, physical environment, and culture. Owners are those who have property rights claims on the organization. The board of directors, elected by stockholders, is responsible for overseeing a firm's top managers. Individual employees and the labor unions they sometimes join are other important parts of the internal environment. The physical environment, yet another part of the internal environment, varies greatly across organizations.

The ethical and social environment of management is also quite important. Understanding the differences between ethical and unethical behavior, as well as appreciating the special nature of managerial ethics, can guide effective decision making. Understanding the meaning of and arguments for and against social responsibility can help a manager effectively address both formal and informal dimensions of social responsibility.

The international environment of management is also very important. Current trends have resulted in the increasing globalization of markets, industries, and businesses. Organizations seeking to become more international can rely on exporting, licensing, strategic alliances, and direct investment to do so. Controls on international trade, economic communities, and national culture combine to determine the context of international management.

The organization's culture is the set of values that helps its members understand what the organization stands for, how it does things, and what it considers important. Culture is a very important ingredient in organizational success. It is generally determined by factors such as the firm's founder, as well as symbols, slogans, stories, heroes, ceremonies, successes, and shared experiences. Culture can be managed, although changing it may be difficult.

Discussion Questions

Questions for Review

1. Identify and discuss each major dimension of the general environment and of the task environment.

2. Do organizations have ethics? Why or why not?

3. What are the arguments for and against social responsibility?

4. Describe the four basic levels of international business activity. Do you think any organization will achieve the fourth level? Why or why not?

5. Describe various barriers to international trade.

Questions for Analysis

1. Can you think of dimensions of the task environment that are not discussed in the text? Indicate their linkage to those that are discussed.

2. What is the relationship between the law and ethical behavior? Can illegal behavior possibly be ethical?

3. How do you feel about whistle-blowing activity? If you were aware of a criminal activity taking place in your organization, and if reporting it might cost you your job, what would you do?

4. What industries do you think will have the greatest impact on international business? Are any industries unlikely to be affected by the trend toward international business? If so, which ones? If not, explain why not.

5. What is the culture of your college or university? How clear is it? What are its most positive and negative characteristics?

Building Effective Time-Management Skills

EXERCISE OVERVIEW

Time-management skills refer to the manager's ability to prioritize work, to work efficiently, and to delegate appropriately. This exercise provides you with an opportunity to relate time-management issues to environment pressures and opportunities.

EXERCISE BACKGROUND

As discussed in this chapter, managers and organizations must be sensitive to a variety of environment dimensions and forces reflected in the general, task, and internal environments. The problem faced by managers is that time is a finite resource. There are only so many hours in a day and only so many things that can be done in a given period of time. Thus, managers must constantly make choices about how they spend their time. Clearly, of course, they should try to use their time wisely and direct it at the more important challenges and opportunities they face. Spending time on a trivial issue while an important issue gets neglected is a mistake.

Time-management experts often suggest that managers begin each day by making a list of what they need to accomplish that day. After the list is compiled, the manager is then advised to sort these daily tasks into three groups: those that must be addressed that day, those that should be addressed that day but which could be postponed if necessary, and those that can easily be postponed. The manager is then advised to perform the tasks in order of priority.

EXERCISE TASK

With the background information above as context, do the following:

1. Across the top of a sheet of paper, write the three priority levels noted above.

2. Down the left side of the same sheet of paper, write the various elements and dimensions of the task and internal environments of business.

3. At the intersection of each row and column, think of an appropriate example that a manager might face. For example, think of a higher-priority, a moderate-priority, and a low-priority situation involving a customer.

4. Form a small group with two or three classmates and discuss each person's examples. Focus on whether or not there is agreement as to the prioritization of each example.

EXERCISE OVERVIEW

Decision-making skills refer to the manager's ability to correctly recognize and define problems and opportunities and to then select an appropriate course of action to solve problems and capitalize on opportunities. Many managerial decisions have an ethical component. This exercise demonstrates the potential role of ethics in making decisions.

Building Effective
Decision-Making Skills

EXERCISE BACKGROUND

Read and reflect on each of the following scenarios:

1. You are the top manager of a major international oil company. Because of a recent oil spill by another firm, all the companies in the industry have been subjected to scrutiny regarding the safety of various work practices. Your safety manager has completed a review and informed you that your

firm has one potential problem area. The manager estimates a 3 percent probability of a problem occurring within the next five years. The cost of preventing the problem would be about $1.5 million. However, if you do nothing and a problem develops, the cost will be $10 million, plus your firm will receive a lot of bad publicity.

2. You manage a small fast-food restaurant. The owner just told you to cut the payroll by twenty hours per week. You have two obvious choices. One candidate for layoff is a retired woman who works part-time for you. She lives on a fixed income, is raising three grandchildren, and really needs the money she earns from this job. The other is a college student who also works part-time. He is one year away from getting his degree, and must work to pay his tuition and fees.

3. You have decided to donate $1,000 to a worthy cause in your neighborhood on behalf of the small business you own. Based on your own research, you have learned that the groups and charities most in need of funds are a local homeless shelter, a youth soccer league, an abortion clinic, and a tutoring program for illiterate adults.

EXERCISE TASK

With the background information above as context:

1. Make a decision between the two courses of action for scenario one.

2. Decide which employee to lay off in scenario two.

3. Decide where to donate your money in scenario three.

4. What role did your personal ethics play in making each decision?

5. Compare your decisions with those of a classmate and discuss any differences.

Building Effective Communication Skills

EXERCISE OVERVIEW

Communication skills refer to the manager's ability to both effectively convey ideas and information to others and effectively receive ideas and information from others. International managers face additional communication challenges because of differences in language, time zones, and so forth. As a way to sharpen your communication skills, this exercise examines the impact of different time zones on business activities.

EXERCISE BACKGROUND

Assume that you are a manager in a large multinational firm. Your office is in San Francisco. You need to arrange a conference call with several other managers to discuss an upcoming strategic change by your firm. The other managers are located in New York, London, Rome, Moscow, Tokyo, Singapore, and Sydney.

EXERCISE TASK

Using the information above, do the following:

1. Determine the time differential in each city. For example, if it is 10 A.M. in San Francisco, what time is it in the other locations you need to call?

2. Assuming that people in each city have a "normal" workday of 8:00 A.M. to 5 P.M., determine the optimal time for your conference call. That is, what time can you place the call so as to minimize the number of people who are inconvenienced?

3. Now assume that you need to visit each office in person. You need to spend one full day in each city. Use the Internet to review airline schedules, take into account differences in time zones, and develop an itinerary.

You Make the Call

As Sunset Landscape Services grew and prospered, Mark Spenser led his firm to occupy a unique niche in the local business community. He also had to make a number of difficult choices, however, having recently entered a complex new business arena. He knew that the booming local and regional economy was a strong contributor to his success, but he was smart enough to know that he could not rely on economic growth alone to fuel his business.

Mark recognized immediately that it was necessary to establish and maintain good relationships with various constituents. Thus, he worked hard to develop close relationships with various suppliers and his local banker. He made sure that he demonstrated his loyalty to them, and this practice paid off in a variety of ways. For example, when SLS hit a tight spot in 1985, his suppliers extended extra credit and his banker provided a short-term loan for working capital.

Mark also paid close attention to his competitors. In addition to the two local nurseries already in business in Central City, he often checked the prices and product lines at the nursery at the nearby Wal-Mart store and the local grocery store, which also carried plants and plant supplies. Mark also had to deal with various inspectors from the U.S. Department of Agriculture and even had his taxes audited one year. He also put a premium on customer service in his business, treating every customer with respect and insisting that all employees do the same.

One of the more difficult issues Mark faced from the very beginning, however, has been a bit more personal in nature. Within the first few months of opening, he was called on to make contributions to the local United Way campaign and to support little league baseball, community soccer, Girl Scouts and Boy Scouts, and other similar programs. Although he believed that each program was worthwhile, he had to say no, simply because he could not afford so many donations. As his business grew, however, Mark increasingly found it possible to say yes, and today he supports a number of local social programs and activities.

One of Mark's most recent ventures grew out of the passage of the North American Free Trade Agreement. Because Central City has a mild climate, some local residents like to use cactus plants in their landscaping. Although some cactus plants can be obtained from domestic suppliers, Mark determined that he could obtain a wider variety of plants at a lower cost from suppliers based in northern Mexico. On the other hand, he also found that trying to import plants across the border was not as easy as he had anticipated.

DISCUSSION QUESTIONS

1. What elements of the general and task environments are reflected in this case?

2. How might a manager with limited resources decide which social programs to support?

3. What are the advantages and disadvantages to Sunset Landscape Services of exploring avenues for doing business in Mexico?

Skills Self-Assessment Instrument

GLOBAL AWARENESS

Introduction: As we have noted, the environment of business is becoming more global. The following assessment is designed to help you understand your readiness to respond to managing in a global context.

Instructions: You will agree with some of the following statements and disagree with others. In some cases you may find it difficult to make a decision, but you should force a choice. Record your answers next to each statement according to the following scale:

| **4** Strongly agree | **2** Somewhat disagree |
| **3** Somewhat agree | **1** Strongly disagree |

_____ 1. Some areas of Switzerland are very much like Italy.

_____ 2. Although aspects of behavior such as motivation and attitudes within organizational settings remain quite diverse across cultures, organizations themselves appear to be increasingly similar in terms of design and technology.

_____ 3. Spain, France, Japan, Singapore, Mexico, Brazil, and Indonesia have cultures with a strong orientation toward authority.

_____ 4. Japan and Austria define male-female roles more rigidly and value qualities like forcefulness and achievement more than Norway, Sweden, Denmark, and Finland.

_____ 5. Some areas of Switzerland are very much like France.

_____ 6. Australia, Great Britain, the Netherlands, Canada, and New Zealand have cultures that view people first as individuals and place a priority on their own interests and values, whereas Colombia, Pakistan, Taiwan, Peru, Singapore, Mexico, Greece, and Hong Kong have cultures in which the good of the group or society is considered the priority.

_____ 7. The United States, Israel, Austria, Denmark, Ireland, Norway, Germany, and New Zealand have cultures with a low orientation toward authority.

_____ 8. The same manager may behave differently in different cultural settings.

_____ 9. Denmark, Canada, Norway, Singapore, Hong Kong, and Australia have cultures in which employees tolerate a high degree of uncertainty, but such levels of uncertainty are not well tolerated in Israel, Austria, Japan, Italy, Argentina, Peru, France, and Belgium.

_____ 10. Some areas of Switzerland are very much like Germany.

For interpretation, turn to page 457.

ETHICS OF EMPLOYEE APPRAISAL

Purpose: Many management activities occur within an ethical context. The appraisal of employee performance is one of those activities that can raise ethical issues. This skill builder focuses on the *human resources model*. It will help you develop the *mentor role* of the human resources model. One of the skills of the mentor is the ability to develop subordinates.

Introduction: Much attention has been given in recent years to ethics in business, yet one area often overlooked is ethical issues when hiring or appraising employees. Marian Kellogg developed a list of principles to keep in mind when recruiting or appraising.

How to Keep Your Appraisals Ethical: A Manager's Checklist

1. Don't appraise without knowing why the appraisal is required.

2. Appraise on the basis of **representative** information.

3. Appraise on the basis of **sufficient** information.

4. Appraise on the basis of **relevant** information.

5. Be honest in your assessment of all the facts you obtain.

6. Don't write one thing and say another.

7. In offering an appraisal, make it plain that this is only your personal opinion of the facts as you see them.

8. Pass appraisal information along only to those who have good reason to know it.

9. Don't imply the existence of an appraisal that hasn't been made.

10. Don't accept another's appraisal without knowing the basis on which it was made.

Instructions: Read each incident individually and decide which rule or rules it violates, marking the appropriate number on the right. In some cases, more than one rule is violated. In your group go over each case and come to a consensus on which rules are violated.

Incidents:

1. Steve Wilson has applied for a transfer to Department O., headed by Marianne Kilbourn. As part of her fact finding, Marianne reads through the written evaluation, which is glowing, and then asks Steve's boss, Bill Hammond, for information on Steve's performance. Bill starts complaining about Steve because his last project was not up to par, but does not mention Steve's wife has been seriously ill for two months. Marianne then decides not to accept Steve's transfer.
   Rule violation # _____

2. Maury Nanner is a sales manager who is having lunch with several executives. One of them, Harvey Gant, asks Maury what he thinks of his subordinate George Williams, and Nanner gives a lengthy evaluation.
   Rule violation # _____

3. Phillip Randall is working on six-month evaluations of his subordinates. He decides to rate Elisa Donner less than average on initiative because he thinks she spends too much time, energy, and money making herself look attractive. He thinks it distracts the male employees.
   Rule violation # _____

4. Paul Trendant has received an application from an outstanding candidate, Jim Fischer. However, Paul decides not to hire Jim because he heard from someone that Jim only moved to town because his wife got a good job here. Trendant thinks Jim will quit whenever his wife gets transferred.
   Rule violation # _____

5. Susan Forman is on the fast track and tries to make herself look good to her boss, Peter Everly. This morning she has a meeting with Pete to discuss which person to promote. Just before the meeting, Pete's golf buddy, Harold, a coworker of Susan's, tells Susan that Alice, Jerry, and Joe are favored by Pete. Susan had felt Darlene was the strongest candidate, but she goes into the meeting with Pete and suggests Alice, Jerry, and Joe as top candidates.
   Rule violation # _____

6. Sandy is a new supervisor for seven people. After several months Sandy is certain that Linda is marginally competent and frequently cannot produce any useful work. Looking over past appraisals Sandy sees all of Linda's evaluations were positive, and she is told that Linda "has problems" and not to be "too hard on her." Realizing this approach is not healthy, Sandy begins documenting Linda's inadequate performance. Several supervisors hint that she should "lighten up because we don't want Linda to feel hurt."
   Rule violation # _____

Sources: Marian S. Kellogg, *What to Do About Performance Appraisal*, AMACOM, a division of the American Management Association, New York, 1975; Marian S. Kellogg, *Personnel*, July–August 1965, American Management Association, New York; and Dorothy Marcic, *Organizational Behavior: Experiences and Cases*, 3rd ed. (West Publishing Company, 1992).

CASE STUDY

Porsche Shifts Gears

Porsche was a company going nowhere, which was, of course, a strange state of affairs for one of the world's most re-nowned sports car manufacturers. The firm was founded in 1929 by Ferdinand Porsche, an engineer who left Daimler-Benz with a vision to design and build racing cars. For several years, however, a lack of financial resources forced him to restrict his operation to making mass-market cars and trucks for the German military.

After World War II, the elder Porsche turned over the reins of the company to his son and a team of younger managers. These managers, in turn, decided the time was ripe to return to Ferdinand's original conception. Therefore, the firm began to design and build a line of sports cars that eventually became synonymous with status, speed, and mechanical precision—and, of course, extravagance, since the prices Porsche charged for its cars were far above those of mass-market cars like Fords, Nissans, and Volkswagens.

Because the market for such cars is relatively small, Porsche restricted its production and product lines, relying on large markups to generate cash flow and earn profits. Although this strategy had its ups and downs, Porsche was able to remain competitive and comfortable within its own relatively small niche.

But the automobile market changed dramatically during the early 1990s while Porsche stood still. Toyota launched its upscale Lexus line with an impressive sports coupe, the SC400. Mazda reawakened the roadster market with its popular Miata. And Chrysler launched its Viper, a direct competitor to Porsche's products. The entire approach to making cars also changed during this time, emphasizing lean production and just-in-time delivery cycles.

But Porsche remained rooted in the old ways. Staid German artisans, for example, still built each car by hand. And massive inventories remained stored in warehouses near the Porsche plant in Stuttgart. As a result, Porsche had to keep its prices high. But customers began to wonder why they needed to pay $80,000 or more for a Porsche when they could get an SC400 for $45,000 or a Miata for $25,000.

Porsche lost $270 million between 1992 and 1995 and was actually nearing bankruptcy. Almost out of desperation, a new CEO, Wendelin Wiedeking, was hired in an effort to save the firm. Within a few months Wiedeking shocked the automobile industry when he turned over the operational reins to a team of Japanese managers. These managers, in turn, set in motion a veritable cultural revolution that has both reshaped and saved the company.

The first acts were symbolic. When the new managers first entered the factory, one of them shouted, "We said bring us to the factory! This is a warehouse!" Wiedeking himself then took a circular saw and began cutting down the ten-foot shelving units that ran throughout the factory. The shelves had been used to store parts. But the Japanese managers knew that they also made the plant dark, foreboding, and inefficient.

Over the next few months, more substantive changes took place. The corporate staff was downsized, for example, and the firm cut its number of suppliers by two-thirds. The surviving suppliers were also forced to commit to the just-in-time delivery philosophy that virtually every other auto maker in the world had already adopted. Workplace clutter was also cut by 20 percent, and windows were installed all around the factory. Now each work area is light, open, and clean.

The workers themselves have also been reorganized into teams. Resistant to these changes at first, the German workers have now embraced them wholeheartedly. And the results have been impressive. The time required to produce the firm's mainstay, the Porsche 911, has been cut in half. Defect rates also plummeted. In 1994, for example, the first totally defect-free 911 rolled off the line.

Porsche is also looking ahead to the launch of a variety of new products. The first, the Boxster, is already such a big hit that customers are waiting nine months for their cars. A luxury sport utility vehicle is likely to be next. All told, Porsche has doubled its output since 1995. And most experts now believe that the company has indeed turned the corner and will regain its stature as a preeminent manufacturer of exclusive and high-quality sports cars and related vehicles.

Case Questions

1. Characterize the old and the new cultures at Porsche.
2. What role did multiculturalism play in changing the Porsche organization culture?
3. What organization culture and/or multicultural problems might Porsche have to face in the future?

Case References: "Porsche Calls 911, Boxster Japanese to the Rescue," *USA Today*, April 8, 1997, pp. B1, B2 and "The 25 Top Managers of the Year," *Business Week*, January 12, 1998, pp. 54–68.

CHAPTER NOTES

1. "'Off-the-Clock' Time: More Work for No Pay," *USA Today*, April 24, 1997, p. 1B (quote on p. 1B) and "So Much for the Minimum-Wage Scare," *Business Week*, July 21, 1997, p. 19.
2. See Jay B. Barney and William G. Ouchi (eds.), *Organizational Economics* (San Francisco: Jossey-Bass, 1986), for a detailed analysis of linkages between economics and organizations.
3. Susan Helper, "How Much Has Really Changed Between U.S. Automakers and Their Suppliers?" *Sloan Management Review*, Summer 1991, pp. 15–28.
4. Richard N. Osborn and John Hagedoorn, "The Institutionalization and Evolutionary Dynamics of Interorganizational Alliances and Networks," *Academy of Management Journal*, April 1997, pp. 261–278.
5. "Temporary Workers Getting Short Shrift," *USA Today*, April 11, 1997, pp. 1B, 2B.
6. See Thomas M. Garrett and Richard J. Klonoski, *Business Ethics*, 3rd ed. (Englewood Cliffs, N.J.: Prentice-Hall, 1990), for a review of the different meanings of the word *ethics*.
7. Thomas Donaldson and Thomas W. Dunfee, "Toward a Unified Conception of Business Ethics: An Integrative Social Contracts Theory," *Academy of Management Review*, Vol. 19, No. 2, 1994, pp. 252–284.
8. "Don't Look Now, but Bosses May Be Spying," *Honolulu Advertiser*, May 23, 1997, pp. A1, A9.
9. "How a Penney Buyer Made up to $1.5 Million on Vendors' Kickbacks," *Wall Street Journal*, February 7, 1995, pp. A1, A13.
10. Alan Richter and Cynthia Barnum, "When Values Clash," *HR Magazine*, September 1994, pp. 42–45.
11. Beth Rogers, "Serious About Its Code of Ethics," *HR Magazine*, September 1994, pp. 46–48 and Kate Walter, "Values Statements That Augment Corporate Success," *HRMagazine*, October 1995, pp. 87–92.
12. For discussions of this debate, see Jean B. McGuire, Alison Sundgren, and Thomas Schneeweis, "Corporate Social Responsibility and Firm Financial Performance," *Academy of Management Journal*, December 1988, pp. 854–872 and Margaret A. Stroup, Ralph L. Neubert, and Jerry W. An-

derson Jr., "Doing Good, Doing Better: Two Views of Social Responsibility," *Business Horizons*, March–April 1987, pp. 22–25.
13. "Is It Rainforest Crunch Time?" *Business Week*, July 15, 1996, pp. 70–71 and "Yo, Ben! Yo, Jerry! It's Just Ice Cream," *Fortune*, April 28, 1997, p. 374.
14. Lynn Sharp Paine, "Managing for Organizational Integrity," *Harvard Business Review*, March–April 1994, pp. 106–115.
15. "Giving—and Getting Something Back," *Business Week*, August 28, 1995, p. 81.
16. David M. Messick and Max H. Bazerman, "Ethical Leadership and the Psychology of Decision Making," *Sloan Management Review*, Winter 1996, pp. 9–22.
17. "Unfuzzing Ethics for Managers," *Fortune*, November 23, 1987, pp. 229–234.
18. See Janet P. Near and Marcia P. Miceli, "Whistle-Blowing: Myth and Reality," *Journal of Management*, 1996, Vol. 22, No. 3, pp. 507–526, for a recent review of the literature on whistle-blowing.
19. "Whistle-Blowers on Trial," *Business Week*, March 24, 1997, pp. 172–178.
20. "The *Fortune* Global 500—World's Largest Corporations," *Fortune*, August 3, 1998, p. 130.
21. "The *Fortune* Global 500 Ranked Within Industries," *Fortune*, August 3, 1998, pp. 135–136.
22. *Hoover's Handbook of American Business 1998* (Austin, Texas: Hoover's Business Press, 1998), pp. 214–215; 556–557.
23. "Creating a Worldwide Yen for Japanese Beer," *Financial Times*, October 7, 1994, p. 20.
24. Kenichi Ohmae, "The Global Logic of Strategic Alliances," *Harvard Business Review*, March–April 1989, pp. 143–154.
25. "Mercedes Bends Rules," *USA Today*, July 16, 1997, pp. B1, B2.
26. "Conditions Ripe for a Bonanza in Car-Building," *USA Today*, July 7, 1997, pp. B1, B2.
27. "What If There Weren't Any Clocks to Watch?" *Newsweek*, June 30, 1997, p. 14.
28. Deal and Kennedy, *Corporate Cultures*.
29. Stratford Sherman, "Levi's—As Ye Sew, So Shall Ye Reap," *Fortune*, May 12, 1997, pp. 104–116.

30. Jay B. Barney, "Organizational Culture: Can It Be a Source of Sustained Competitive Advantage?" *Academy of Management Review*, July 1986, pp. 656–665.

31. "Ford's Rebates Spell Trouble As New Models Fail to Excite Buyers," *Wall Street Journal*, January 10, 1996, pp. A1, A9.

32. "Why Wells Fargo Is Circling the Wagons," *Wall Street Journal*, June 9, 1997, pp. 92–93.

33. "At Arthur Andersen, The Accountants Face an Unlikely Adversary," *Wall Street Journal*, April 23, 1997, pp. A1, A13.

34. See Timothy Galpin, "Connecting Culture to Organizational Change," *HRMagazine*, March 1996, pp. 84–89.

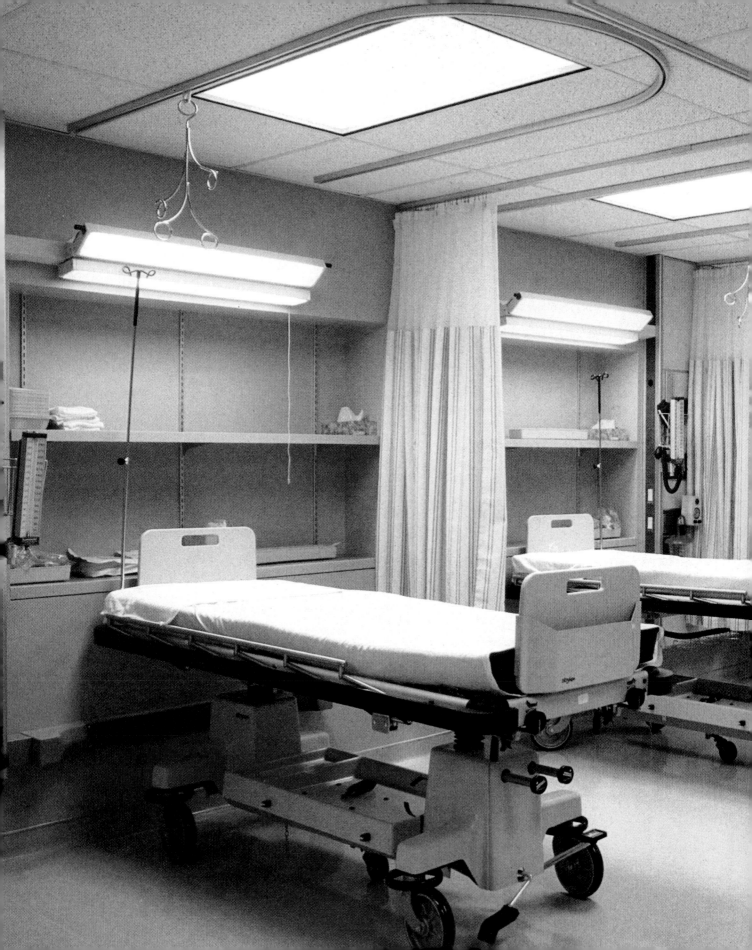

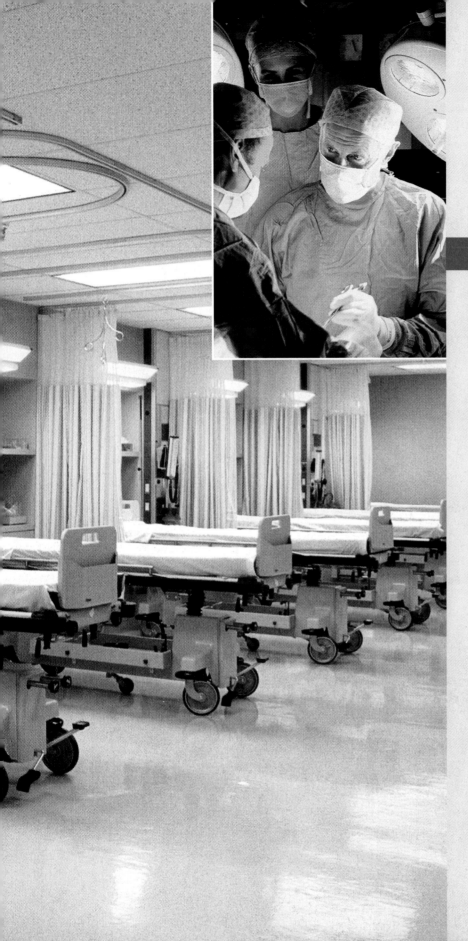

PART TWO

Planning

3

Planning and Strategic Management

OBJECTIVES

After studying this chapter, you should be able to:

- Summarize the planning process and describe organizational goals.
- Discuss the components of strategy and types of strategic alternatives.
- Describe how to use SWOT analysis in formulating strategy.
- Identify and describe various alternative approaches to business-level strategy formulation.
- Identify and describe various alternative approaches to corporate-level strategy formulation.
- Discuss how tactical plans are developed and executed.
- Describe the basic types of operational plans used by organizations.

Nike, of course, makes and sells more athletic shoes than any other company on earth. But the company has recently set its sights much higher and intends to become a truly global powerhouse across a wide spectrum of sports-related businesses. Indeed, Nike's lofty ambitions have earned it the spotlight throughout the sports equipment and apparel industries and in markets around the world.

In 1996, Nike was earning about $4 billion a year from its footwear business and another $2 billion from sports apparel and equipment. But Nike's CEO, Philip Knight, wants more. The company's managers understand, for example, that the footwear market has become so mature, especially in the United States, that significant new growth is unlikely. At the same time, however, Nike executives see untapped potential in many new markets.

Knight stunned Nike investors and competitors when he recently announced a goal of doubling the firm's annual revenues to a staggering $12 billion by the year 2001. Although many observers think Nike foolish to establish such a clear target—everyone will know whether or not the company reaches its lofty goal—insiders argue that the announcement sends an unambiguous message as to what they see as the firm's potential and underscores the company's commitment to fulfilling that potential. But Nike did more than simply toss out its revenue goals for people to debate. It also described in detail how it expects to achieve them. The firm actually has multiple plans to grow its revenues. One major plan relies on brand extension across a variety of sports-related equipment and apparel items. While some people equate Nike with basketball and running shoes and apparel, other products either currently offered or planned run the gamut from eyewear (sunglasses and swim goggles) to gloves (for golf, weightlifting, and batting) to skates (both in-line and hockey). Nike is also branching out into sports-related services, including sports management, and retailing, through its growing chain of Nike Town stores.

Foreign expansion, of course, is also a key part of Nike's plans. As already noted, the U.S. athletic shoe market has matured. But foreign markets are still growing rapidly, and Nike sees much of its future growth coming from abroad. Michael Jordan, of course, is the firm's best-known endorser in the United States. To help elevate the Nike name abroad, however, Nike has also enlisted a handball team in Germany, track and field stars in Kenya, and a women's basketball star in China.

Nike is focusing special attention on soccer. Adidas, a German sportswear company, dominates the soccer footwear and apparel markets. Given the worldwide popularity of soccer, however, Nike realizes that, to achieve its goals, it must establish a presence among aficionados of what everyone outside the U.S. calls "football." The company's first step in this direction was to outbid rival Adidas for sponsorship of the U.S. soccer team. Nike then followed suit with a similar deal with Brazil's national team, paying an unheard-of $200 million in sponsorship fees.

Nike has recently established another goal of becoming the world's number one supplier of soccer footwear, apparel, and equipment by the World Cup 2002 playoffs. But the going will be tough because Adidas—long content to sit back and rest on its long-standing connections—has awakened to Nike's threat and become more aggressive. Adidas still sponsors high-profile teams; has celebrity spokespersons in Germany, Spain, and France; and poses a major obstacle for Nike's ambitions, especially in Europe. Clearly, then, this face-off is shaping up to be a race to the goal.[1]

"There isn't any market outside the U.S. where we're anywhere near our ultimate goal."

Thomas E. Clarke, Nike's president

ike has set some ambitious targets for its future growth. These goals, in turn, serve to focus attention on what the firm anticipates doing and provide guidance and direction to managers throughout the firm with clear indicators of how they should manage their operations. In addition, the firm's plans for achieving its goals help guide day-to-day activities toward growth and expansion.

This chapter is the first of three that explore the planning process in more detail. We begin by examining the nature of planning and organizational goals. We then discuss strategic management, including its components and alternatives, and describe the kinds of analyses needed for firms to formulate their strategies. Next, we describe how organizations formulate business and corporate strategies. Finally, we examine how strategies are implemented via tactical and operational planning.

Planning and Organizational Goals

The planning process can best be thought of as a generic activity. All organizations engage in planning activities, but no two organizations plan in exactly the same fashion. Figure 3.1 is a general representation of the planning process that many organizations attempt to follow. But although most firms follow this general framework, each also has its own nuances and variations.

As Figure 3.1 shows, all planning occurs within an environmental context. With this context as a foundation, managers must then establish the organization's mission. The mission outlines the organization's purpose, premises, values, and directions. Flowing from the mission are parallel streams of goals and

FIGURE 3.1
The Planning Process

The planning process takes place within an environmental context. Managers must develop a complete and thorough understanding of this context to determine the organization's mission and develop its strategic, tactical, and operational goals and plans.

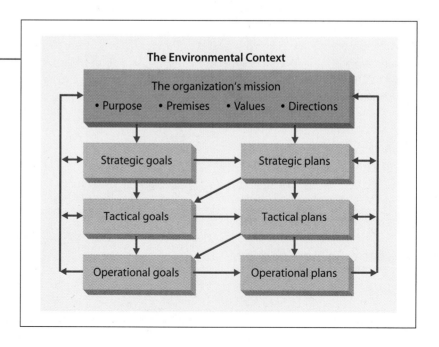

plans. Directly following the mission are strategic goals. These goals and the mission help determine strategic plans. Strategic goals and plans are primary inputs for developing tactical goals. Tactical goals and the original strategic plans help shape tactical plans. Tactical plans, in turn, combine with the tactical goals to shape operational goals. These goals and the appropriate tactical plans determine operational plans. Finally, goals and plans at each level can also be used as input for future activities at all levels.

■ Organizational Goals

Goals are critical to organizational effectiveness, and they serve a number of purposes. There are several kinds of goals. This section examines both the purposes and kinds of goals in organizations. (Note that some managers use the words *objective* and *goal* interchangeably.)

Purposes of Goals   Goals serve four important purposes.[2] First, they provide guidance and a unified direction for people in the organization. Nike's goal of doubling sales by the year 2001 helps everyone in the firm recognize the strong emphasis on growth and expansion that is driving the firm. Second, goal-setting practices strongly affect other aspects of planning: effective goal setting promotes good planning, and good planning facilitates future goal setting. The strong growth goal at Nike encourages managers to plan for expansion by looking for new market opportunities, for example. Similarly, they must also always be alert for competitive threats and new ideas that will help facilitate future expansion.

Third, goals can serve as a source of motivation to employees of the organization. Goals that are specific and moderately difficult can motivate people to work harder, especially if attaining the goal is likely to result in rewards.[3] The Italian furniture manufacturer Industrie Natuzzi SpA uses goals to motivate its workers. Each craftsperson has a goal for how long it should take to perform her or his job, such as sewing leather sheets together to make a sofa cushion or building wooden frames for chair arms. At the completion of assigned tasks, workers enter their ID numbers and job numbers into the firm's computer system. If they get a job done faster than their goal, a bonus is automatically added to their paycheck.[4] Finally, goals provide an effective mechanism for evaluation and control. Therefore, future performance can be assessed in terms of how successfully today's goals are accomplished.

Decision making and planning are critical parts of the management process. For example, managers at Sears recently made the decision to invest heavily in the firm's home services business by creating a nationwide network of repair and service providers. Jane Thompson, shown here on the back of this van, heads the business. Her goal is to reach $10 billion in sales. She and her management team have developed a variety of plans to help reach this goal.

mission A statement of an organization's fundamental purpose

strategic goal A goal set by and for top management of the organization

tactical goal A goal set by and for middle managers of the organization

operational goal A goal set by and for lower-level managers of the organization

Kinds of Goals Organizations establish many kinds of goals. The four basic levels of goals are the mission and strategic, tactical, and operational goals. An organization's **mission** is a statement of its "fundamental, unique purpose that sets a business apart from other firms of its type and identifies the scope of the business's operations in product and market terms."[5] **Strategic goals** are goals set by and for top management of the organization and focus on broad, general issues. For example, Nike's goal of doubling sales revenues is a strategic goal. **Tactical goals** are set by and for middle managers and focus on how to carry out the actions necessary to achieve the strategic goals. Tactical goals at Nike center on which foreign markets to enter, which new products to launch, and so forth. **Operational goals** are set by and for lower-level managers and concern shorter-term issues associated with the tactical goals. An operational goal for Nike might be a target number of new Nike Town retail outlets to be opened by the year 2000.

■ Kinds of Plans

Organizations establish many kinds of plans. At a general level, these include strategic, tactical, and operational plans.

strategic plan A general plan outlining decisions of resource allocation, priorities, and action steps necessary to reach strategic goals

Strategic Plans Strategic plans are the plans developed to achieve strategic goals. More precisely, a **strategic plan** is a general plan outlining decisions of resource allocation, priorities, and action steps necessary to reach strategic goals.[6] These plans are set by the board of directors and top management, generally have an extended time horizon, and address questions of scope, resource deployment, competitive advantage, and synergy. We discuss strategic planning in the next major section.

tactical plan A plan aimed at achieving tactical goals that is developed to implement parts of a strategic plan

Tactical Plans A **tactical plan**, aimed at achieving tactical goals, is developed to implement specific parts of a strategic plan. Tactical plans typically involve upper and middle management and, compared with strategic plans, have a somewhat shorter time horizon and a more specific and concrete focus. Thus, tactical plans are concerned more with actually getting things done than with deciding what to do. Tactical planning is covered after the discussion of strategic planning.

operational plan Focuses on carrying out tactical plans to achieve operational goals

Operational Plans An **operational plan** focuses on carrying out tactical plans to achieve operational goals. Developed by middle and lower-level managers, operational plans have a short-term focus and are relatively narrow in scope. Each one deals with a fairly small set of activities. We cover operational planning in the last section of this chapter.

The Nature of Strategic Management

strategy A comprehensive plan for accomplishing an organization's goals

A **strategy** is a comprehensive plan for accomplishing an organization's goals. **Strategic management**, in turn, is a way of approaching business opportunities and challenges—it is a comprehensive and ongoing management process aimed at formulating and implementing effective strategies. Finally, **effective strategies** are those that promote a superior alignment between the organization and its environment and the achievement of strategic goals.[7]

The Components of Strategy

In general, a well-conceived strategy addresses three areas: distinctive competence, scope, and resource deployment. A **distinctive competence** is something the organization does exceptionally well. The distinctive competence of The Limited, a large clothing chain, is the speed with which it moves inventory. The Limited tracks consumer preferences daily with point-of-sale computers, transmits orders to suppliers in Hong Kong electronically, charters 747s to fly products to the United States, and has products in stores forty-eight hours later. Because other retailers take weeks or sometimes months to accomplish the same things, The Limited relies on this distinctive competence to stay ahead of its competition.[8]

The **scope** of a strategy specifies the range of markets in which an organization will compete. Hershey Foods has essentially restricted its scope to the confectionery business, with a few related activities in other food-processing areas. In contrast, its biggest competitor, Mars, has adopted a broader scope by competing in the pet-food business and the electronics industry, among others. Some organizations, called *conglomerates*, compete in dozens or even hundreds of markets.

A strategy should also include an outline of the organization's projected **resource deployment**—how it will distribute its resources across the areas in which it competes. General Electric, for example, has been using profits from its highly successful U.S. operations to invest heavily in new businesses in Europe and Asia. Alternatively, the firm might have chosen to invest in different industries in its domestic market and/or to invest more heavily in Latin America. The choices it made as to where and how much to invest reflect issues of resource deployment.[9]

Types of Strategic Alternatives

Most businesses today also develop strategies at two distinct levels. These levels provide a rich combination of strategic alternatives for organizations. The two general levels are business strategies and corporate strategies. **Business-level strategy** is the set of strategic alternatives that an organization chooses from as it conducts business in a particular industry or a particular market. Such alternatives help the organization focus its competitive efforts for each industry or market in a targeted and focused manner.

Corporate-level strategy is the set of strategic alternatives that an organization chooses from as it manages its operations simultaneously across several industries and several markets.[10] As we discuss later, most large companies today compete in a variety of industries and markets. Thus, although the companies develop business-level strategies for each industry or market, they also develop an overall strategy that helps them define the appropriate mix of industries and markets that fit their overall strategic objectives.

strategic management A comprehensive and ongoing management process aimed at formulating and implementing effective strategies; it is a way of approaching business opportunities and challenges

effective strategy A strategy that promotes a superior alignment between the organization and its environment and the achievement of strategic goals

distinctive competence An organizational strength possessed by only a small number of competing firms

scope When applied to *strategy*, scope specifies the range of markets in which an organization will compete

resource deployment How an organization distributes its resources across the areas in which it competes

business-level strategy The set of strategic alternatives that an organization chooses from as it conducts business in a particular industry or market

corporate-level strategy The set of strategic alternatives that an organization chooses from as it manages its operations simultaneously across several industries and several markets

strategy formulation   The set of processes involved in creating or determining the strategies of the organization; it focuses on the content of strategies

strategy implementation   The methods by which strategies are put into operation or executed within the organization; it focuses on how strategies are achieved

Recognizing the distinction between strategy formulation and strategy implementation is also important. **Strategy formulation** is the set of processes involved in creating or determining the strategies of the organization, whereas **strategy implementation** is the methods by which strategies are put into operation or executed within the organization.[11] The primary distinction is along the lines of content versus process: the formulation stage determines what the strategy is, and the implementation stage focuses on how the strategy is achieved.

Using SWOT Analysis to Formulate Strategy

SWOT   An acronym that stands for strengths, weaknesses, opportunities, and threats

The starting point in formulating strategy is usually SWOT analysis. **SWOT** is an acronym that stands for strengths, weaknesses, opportunities, and threats. As shown in Figure 3.2, SWOT analysis is a careful evaluation of an organization's internal strengths and weaknesses as well as its environmental opportunities and threats.[12] In SWOT analysis, the best strategies accomplish an organization's mission by (1) exploiting an organization's opportunities and strengths while (2) neutralizing its threats and (3) avoiding (or correcting) its weaknesses.[13]

FIGURE 3.2
SWOT Analysis

SWOT analysis is one of the most important steps in formulating strategy. Using the organization's mission as a context, managers assess internal strengths (distinctive competencies) and weaknesses as well as external opportunities and threats. The goal is to then develop good strategies that exploit opportunities and strengths, neutralize threats, and avoid weaknesses.

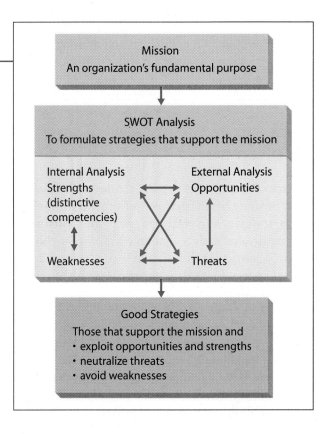

■ Evaluating an Organization's Strengths

Organizational strengths are skills and capabilities that enable an organization to conceive of and implement its strategies. Sears, for example, already has a national network of trained service personnel who repair Sears appliances. Jane Thompson, a Sears executive, recently conceived of a plan to consolidate repair and home-improvement services nationwide under the well-known Sears brand name and to promote the new service as a general repair operation for all appliances, not just those purchased from Sears. Thus, the firm is capitalizing on existing capabilities and the strength of its name to launch a new operation.[14]

A distinctive competence is a strength possessed by only a small number of competing firms. Distinctive competencies are rare among a set of competitors. George Lucas's well-known company Industrial Light and Magic (ILM), for example, has brought the cinematic art of special effects to new heights. No other organization has the ability to produce some of ILM's special effects, which are thus ILM's distinctive competencies. Organizations that exploit their distinctive competencies often obtain a competitive advantage and attain above-normal economic performance.[15]

> **organizational strengths** A skill or capability that enables an organization to conceive of and implement its strategies

■ Evaluating an Organization's Weaknesses

Organizational weaknesses are skills and capabilities that do not enable an organization to choose and implement strategies that support its mission. An organization has essentially two ways of addressing weaknesses. First, it may need to make investments to obtain the strengths required to implement strategies that support its mission. Second, it may need to modify its mission so that it can be accomplished with existing skills and capabilities.

In practice, organizations have a difficult time focusing on weaknesses, in part because organization members are often reluctant to admit that they do not possess all the skills and capabilities needed. Evaluating weaknesses also calls into question the judgment of managers who chose the organization's mission in the first place and who failed to invest in the skills and capabilities needed to accomplish it. Organizations that fail either to recognize or to overcome their weaknesses are likely to suffer from competitive disadvantages. An organization has a competitive disadvantage when it is not implementing valuable strategies that are being implemented by competing organizations. Organizations with a competitive disadvantage can expect to attain below-average levels of performance.

> **organizational weakness** A skill or capability that does not enable an organization to choose and implement strategies that support its mission

■ Evaluating an Organization's Opportunities and Threats

Whereas evaluating strengths and weaknesses focuses attention on the internal workings of an organization, evaluating opportunities and threats requires analyzing an organization's environment. **Organizational opportunities** are areas that may generate higher performance. **Organizational threats** are areas that increase the difficulty of an organization's performing at a high level.

> **organizational opportunity** An area in the environment that, if exploited, may generate high performance
>
> **organizational threat** An area in the environment that increases the difficulty an organization has achieving high performance

Formulating Business-Level Strategies

Implementing business-level strategy can be complicated, especially when it's necessary to make a change. A few years ago, Jeffrey Bezos launched Amazon.com, an Internet-based book retailer. Amazon.com built its business using a differentiation strategy, billing itself as "Earth's biggest bookstore," offering a huge selection of books, stressing ease-of-use, and relying on mail delivery service. But as other big firms, like Barnes & Noble and Amazon.com's own wholesaler, have launched Internet book-selling operations themselves, Bezos has found it necessary to shift to a cost leadership strategy to protect his marketshare and fend off these new competitors.

A number of frameworks have been developed for identifying the major strategic alternatives that organizations should consider when choosing their business-level strategies. Two important classification schemes are Porter's generic strategies and strategies based on the product life cycle.

■ Porter's Generic Strategies

According to Michael Porter, organizations may pursue a differentiation, overall cost leadership, or focus strategy at the business level.[16] An organization that pursues a **differentiation strategy** seeks to distinguish itself from competitors through the quality of its products or services. Firms that successfully implement a differentiation strategy are able to charge more than their competitors can charge because customers are willing to pay more to obtain the extra value they perceive.[17] Rolex pursues a differentiation strategy. Rolex watches are handmade of gold and stainless steel and are subjected to strenuous tests of quality and reliability. The firm's reputation enables it to charge thousands of dollars for its watches. Other firms that use differentiation strategies are Mercedes-Benz, Nikon, Cross, and Hewlett-Packard.

An organization implementing an **overall cost leadership strategy** attempts to gain a competitive advantage by reducing its costs below the costs of competing firms. By keeping costs low, the organization is able to sell its products at low prices and still make a profit. Timex uses an overall cost leadership strategy. For decades, this firm has specialized in manufacturing relatively simple, low-cost watches for the mass market. The price of Timex watches, starting around $29.95, is low because of the company's efficient high-volume manufacturing capacity. Other firms that implement overall cost leadership strategies are Hyundai, Eastman Kodak, Bic, and Texas Instruments.

A firm pursuing a **focus strategy** concentrates on a specific regional market, product line, or group of buyers. This strategy may have either a differentiation focus, whereby the firm differentiates its products in the focus market, or an overall cost leadership focus, whereby the firm manufactures and sells its products at low cost in the focus market. In the watch industry, Tag Heuer follows a focus differentiation strategy by emphasizing the rugged nature of its watches, rather than fashion and elegance, for those interested in outdoor and water sports. Fiat follows a focus cost leadership strategy by selling its automobiles only in Italy and in selected regions of Europe; Alpha Romeo uses focus differentiation to sell its high-performance cars in these same markets. And Edward Jones is making a big splash in the stock brokerage industry by focusing on small town settings and avoiding direct competition with Wall Street powerhouses like Merrill Lynch and Paine Webber in larger cities.[18]

■ Strategies Based on the Product Life Cycle

The **product life cycle** is a model that shows how sales volume changes over the life of products. Understanding the four stages in the product life cycle helps managers recognize that strategies need to evolve over time. As Figure 3.3 shows, the cycle begins when a new product or technology is introduced. In this *introduction stage*, demand may be very high and sometimes outpaces the firm's ability to supply the product. At this stage, managers need to focus their efforts on "getting product out the door" without sacrificing quality. Managing growth by hiring new employees and managing inventories and cash flow are also concerns during the introduction stage.

During the *growth stage*, more firms begin producing the product, and sales continue to grow. Important management issues include ensuring quality and delivery and beginning to differentiate an organization's product from competitors' products. New entries into the industry during the growth stage may threaten an organization's competitive advantages; thus strategies to slow the entry of competitors are important.

After a period of growth, products enter a third phase. During the *mature stage*, overall demand growth for a product begins to slow, and the number of new firms producing the product begins to decline. The number of established firms producing the product may also begin to decline. This period of maturity is essential if an organization is going to survive in the long run. Product differentiation concerns are still important during this stage, but keeping costs low and beginning the search for new products or services are also important strategic considerations.

In the *decline stage*, demand for the product or technology decreases, the number of organizations producing the product drops, and total sales drop. Demand often declines because all those who were interested in purchasing a particular product have already done so. Organizations that fail to anticipate

differentiation strategy A strategy in which an organization seeks to distinguish itself from competitors through the quality of its products or services

overall cost leadership strategy A strategy in which an organization attempts to gain a competitive advantage by reducing its costs below the costs of competing firms

focus strategy A strategy in which an organization concentrates on a specific regional market, product line, or group of buyers

product life cycle A model that portrays how sales volume for products changes over the life of products

FIGURE 3.3
The Product Life Cycle

Managers can use the framework of the product life cycle—introduction, growth, maturity, and decline—to plot strategy. For example, management may decide on a differentiation strategy for a product in the introduction stage and a prospector approach for a product in the growth stage. By understanding this cycle and where a particular product falls within it, managers can develop more effective strategies for extending product life.

the decline stage in earlier stages of the life cycle may go out of business. Those that differentiate their product, keep their costs low, or develop new products or services may do well during this stage. After Volkswagen stopped selling the original Beetle in the United States, the company continued to build the cars in Mexico and to sell them throughout Latin America for several more years, thus extending the product's life cycle.

Formulating Corporate-Level Strategies

strategic business unit (SBU)
A single business or set of businesses within a larger organization

Most large organizations are engaged in several businesses, industries, and markets. Each business or set of businesses within such an organization is frequently referred to as a **strategic business unit**, or **SBU**. An organization such as General Electric Co. operates hundreds of businesses, making and selling products as diverse as jet engines, nuclear power plants, and light bulbs. GE organizes these businesses into approximately twenty SBUs. Even organizations that sell only one product may operate in several distinct markets. McDonald's sells only fast food, but it competes in markets as diverse as the United States, Europe, Russia, Japan, and South Korea.

Decisions about which businesses, industries, and markets an organization will enter, and how to manage these different businesses, are based on an organization's corporate strategy. The most important strategic issue at the corporate level concerns the extent and nature of organizational diversification. **Diversification** describes the number of different businesses that an organization is engaged in and the extent to which these businesses are related to one another. There are three types of diversification strategies: single-product strategy, related diversification, and unrelated diversification.[19]

diversification The number of different businesses that an organization is engaged in and the extent to which these businesses are related to one another

■ Single-Product Strategy

single-product strategy A strategy in which an organization manufactures just one product or service and sells it in a single geographic market

An organization that pursues a **single-product strategy** manufactures just one product or service and sells it in a single geographic market. The WD-40 Company, for example, manufactures only a single product, WD-40 spray lubricant, and sells it in just one market, North America. WD-40 has considered broadening its market to Europe and Asia, but it continues to center all manufacturing, sales, and marketing efforts on one product.

The single-product strategy has one major strength and one major weakness. By concentrating its efforts so completely on one product and market, a firm is likely to be very successful in manufacturing and marketing the product. Because it has staked its survival on a single product, the organization works very hard to make sure that the product is a success. Of course, if the product is not accepted by the market or is replaced by a new one, the firm will suffer. This happened to slide-rule manufacturers when electronic calculators became widely available and to companies that manufactured only black-and-white televisions when low-priced color televisions were first mass marketed.

Related Diversification

Given the disadvantage of the single-product strategy, most large businesses today operate in several different businesses, industries, or markets.[20] If the businesses are somehow linked, that organization is implementing a strategy of **related diversification**. Virtually all larger businesses in the United States use related diversification.

Pursuing a strategy of related diversification has three primary advantages. First, it reduces an organization's dependence on any one of its business activities and thus reduces economic risk. Even if one or two of a firm's businesses lose money, the organization as a whole may still survive because the healthy businesses are likely to generate enough cash to support the others.[21] At The Limited, for example, sales declines at Lerners may be offset by sales increases at Victoria's Secret.

Second, by managing several businesses at the same time, an organization can reduce the overhead costs associated with managing any one business. In other words, if the normal administrative costs required to operate any business, such as legal services and accounting, can be spread over a large number of businesses, then the overhead costs *per business* will be lower than they would be if each business had to absorb all costs itself. Thus, the overhead costs of businesses in a related diversified firm are usually lower than those of similar businesses that are not part of a larger corporation.[22]

Third, related diversification allows an organization to exploit its strengths and capabilities in more than one business. Successful related diversification strategies enable organizations to capitalize on synergies, which are complementary effects that exist among their businesses. **Synergy** exists among a set of businesses when the businesses' economic value together is greater than their economic value separately. Disney is skilled at creating and exploiting synergies. Its hit movie *The Lion King* earned almost $300 million in box office revenues. In addition, Disney earned hundreds of millions more from the sales of licensed Lion King toys, clothing, and video games. *The Lion King* stage show at Disney World attracts more guests to the park, and the video earned millions more for the firm. A direct-to-video sequel was also successful, as was a television show and a recently opened Broadway stage version, each contributing more money to Disney coffers.

Unrelated Diversification

Firms that implement a strategy of **unrelated diversification** operate multiple businesses that are not logically associated with one another. At one time, for example, Quaker Oats owned clothing chains, toy companies, and a restaurant business. Unrelated diversification was a very popular strategy in the 1960s and early 1970s. During this time, several conglomerates like ITT and Transamerica grew by acquiring literally hundreds of other organizations and then running these numerous businesses as independent entities. Even if there are important potential synergies between their different businesses, organizations implementing a strategy of unrelated diversification do not attempt to exploit them.

related diversification A strategy in which an organization operates in several businesses that are somehow linked with one another

synergy Exists among a set of businesses when their economic value together is greater than the sum of their economic values separately

unrelated diversification A strategy in which an organization operates in several businesses that are not related to one another

In theory, unrelated diversification has two advantages. First, a business that uses this strategy should have stable performance over time. During any given period, if some businesses owned by the organization are in a cycle of decline, others may be in a cycle of growth. Unrelated diversification is also thought to have resource allocation advantages. Every year, when a corporation allocates capital, people, and other resources among its various businesses, it must evaluate information about the future of those businesses so that it can place its resources where they have the highest return potential. Given that it owns the businesses in question and thus has full access to information about the future of those businesses, a firm implementing unrelated diversification should be able to allocate capital to maximize corporate performance.

Despite these presumed advantages, evidence suggests that unrelated diversification usually does not lead to high performance. First, corporate-level managers in such a company usually do not know enough about the unrelated businesses to provide helpful strategic guidance or to allocate capital appropriately. To make strategic decisions managers must have complete and subtle understanding of a business and its environment. Because corporate managers often have difficulty fully evaluating the economic importance of investments for all the businesses under their wing, they tend to concentrate only on a business's current performance. This narrow attention at the expense of broader planning eventually hobbles the entire organization.

Second, because organizations that implement unrelated diversification fail to exploit important synergies, they are at a competitive disadvantage compared to organizations that use related diversification. Universal Studios has been at a competitive disadvantage relative to Disney because Universal's theme parks, movie studios, and licensing divisions are less integrated and therefore achieve less synergy.

For these reasons, almost all organizations have abandoned unrelated diversification as a corporate-level strategy. ITT and Transamerica have sold numerous businesses and now concentrate on a core set of related businesses and markets. Large corporations that have not concentrated on a core set of businesses eventually have been acquired by other companies and then broken up. Research suggests that these organizations are actually worth more when broken up into smaller pieces than when they are joined.[23]

■ Managing Diversification

portfolio management techniques
Methods that diversified organizations use to determine which businesses to engage in and how to manage these businesses to maximize corporate performance
BCG matrix A method of evaluating businesses relative to the growth rate of their market and the organization's share of the market

However an organization implements diversification, it must monitor and manage its strategy. **Portfolio management techniques** are methods that diversified organizations use to make decisions about what businesses to engage in and how to manage these multiple businesses to maximize corporate performance. Two important portfolio management techniques are the BCG matrix and the GE Business Screen.

BCG Matrix The **BCG** (for Boston Consulting Group) **matrix** provides a framework for evaluating the relative performance of businesses in which a diversified organization operates. The matrix also prescribes the preferred distribution of cash and other resources among these businesses.[24] The BCG matrix uses two factors to evaluate an organization's set of businesses: the growth rate of a particular market and the organization's share of that market. The matrix suggests that fast-growing markets in which an organization has the highest market share are more attractive business opportunities than slow-growing markets in which an organization has a small market share. Dividing market growth and market share into two categories (low and high) creates the simple matrix shown in Figure 3.4.

The matrix classifies the types of businesses that a diversified organization can engage in as dogs, cash cows, question marks, and stars. *Dogs* are businesses that have a very small share of a market that is not expected to grow. Because these businesses do not hold much economic promise, the BCG matrix suggests that organizations either should not invest in them or should consider selling them as soon as possible. *Cash cows* are businesses that have a large share of a market that is not expected to grow substantially. These businesses characteristically generate high profits that the organization should use to support question marks and stars. (Cash cows are "milked" for cash to support businesses in markets that have greater growth potential.) *Question marks* are businesses that have only a small share of a quickly growing market. The future performance of these businesses is uncertain. A question mark that is able to capture increasing amounts of this growing market may be very profitable. On the other hand, a question mark unable to keep up with market growth is likely to have low profits. The BCG matrix suggests that organizations should carefully invest in question marks. If their performance does not live up to expectations, question marks should be reclassified as dogs and divested. *Stars* are businesses that have the largest share of a rapidly growing market. Cash generated by cash cows should be invested in stars to ensure their pre-eminent position.

GE Business Screen   In response to criticisms aimed at the narrow focus of the BCG matrix, General Electric (GE) developed the **GE Business Screen**—a more sophisticated approach to managing diversified business units. The GE Business Screen is a portfolio management technique that can also be represented in the form of a matrix. Rather than focusing solely on market growth and market share, however, the GE Business Screen considers industry attractiveness and competitive position. These two factors are divided into three categories to make the nine-cell matrix shown in Figure 3.5.[25] These cells, in turn, classify business units as winners, question marks, average businesses, losers, or profit producers.

As Figure 3.5 shows, both market growth and market share appear in a broad list of factors that determine the overall attractiveness of an industry and the overall quality of a firm's competitive position. Other determinants of an industry's attractiveness (in addition to market growth) include market size,

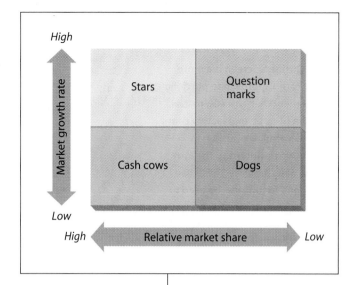

FIGURE 3.4
The BCG Matrix

The BCG matrix helps managers develop a better understanding of how different strategic business units contribute to the overall organization. By assessing each SBU on the basis of its market growth rate and relative market share, managers can make decisions about whether to commit further financial resources to the SBU or to sell or liquidate it.

Source: Perspectives, No. 66, "The Product Portfolio." Adapted by permission from The Boston Consulting Group, Inc., 1970.

GE Business Screen   A method of evaluating businesses along two dimensions: (1) industry attractiveness and (2) competitive position; in general, the more attractive the industry and the more competitive the position, the more an organization should invest in a business

FIGURE 3.5
The GE Business Screen

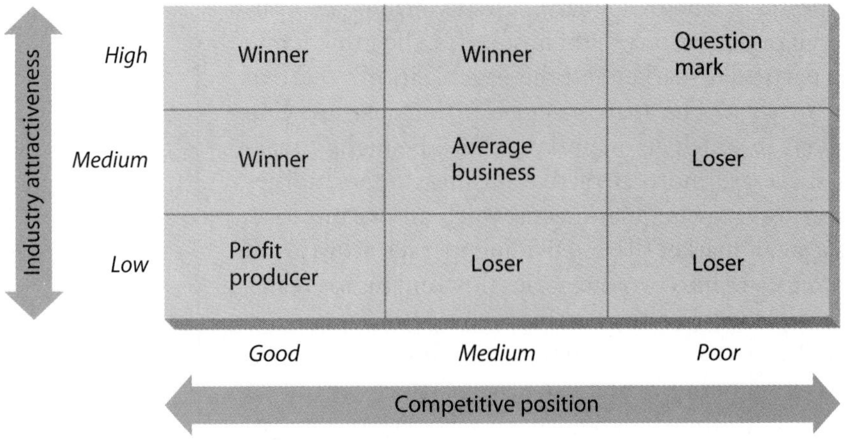

The GE Business Screen is a more sophisticated approach to portfolio management than the BCG matrix. As shown here, several factors combine to determine a business's competitive position and the attractiveness of its industry. These two dimensions, in turn, can be used to classify businesses as winners, question marks, average businesses, losers, or profit producers. Such a classification enables managers to more effectively allocate the organization's resources across various business opportunities.

From *Hofer Strategy Formulation: Analytical Concepts,* 1st edition, by C. W. Hofer and D. Schendel. © 1978. Reprinted with permission of South-Western College Publishing, a division of International Thomson Publishing. Fax 800-730-2215.

		Good	Medium	Poor
	High	Winner	Winner	Question mark
Industry attractiveness	Medium	Winner	Average business	Loser
	Low	Profit producer	Loser	Loser

Competitive position

Competitive position
1. Market share
2. Technological know-how
3. Product quality
4. Service network
5. Price competitiveness
6. Operating costs

Industry attractiveness
1. Market growth
2. Market size
3. Capital requirements
4. Competitive intensity

capital requirements, and competitive intensity. In general, the greater the market growth, the larger the market, the smaller the capital requirements, and the less the competitive intensity, the more attractive an industry will be. Other determinants of an organization's competitive position in an industry (besides market share) include technological know-how, product quality, service network, price competitiveness, and operating costs. In general, businesses with large market share, technological know-how, high product quality, a quality service network, competitive prices, and low operating costs are in a favorable competitive position.

Think of the GE Business Screen as a way of applying SWOT analysis to the implementation and management of a diversification strategy. The determinants of industry attractiveness are similar to the environmental opportunities and threats in SWOT analysis, and the determinants of competitive position are similar to organizational strengths and weaknesses. By conducting this type of SWOT analysis across several businesses, a diversified organization can decide how to invest its resources to maximize corporate performance.

In general, organizations should invest in winners and in question marks (where industry attractiveness and competitive position are both favorable), should maintain the market position of average businesses and profit producers (where industry attractiveness and competitive position are average), and should sell losers. For example, Unilever recently used a similar framework to assess its business portfolio and, as a result, decided to sell several specialty-chemical units that were not contributing to the firm's profitability as much as other businesses were.[26]

Tactical Planning

As we note earlier, tactical plans are developed to implement specific parts of a strategic plan. You have probably heard the saying about winning the battle but losing the war. **Tactical plans** are to battles what strategy is to a war: an organized sequence of steps designed to execute strategic plans. Strategy focuses on resources, environment, and mission, whereas tactics focus primarily on people and action.[27]

◼ Developing Tactical Plans

Although effective tactical planning depends on many factors that vary from one situation to another, we can identify some basic guidelines. First, the manager needs to recognize that tactical planning must address a number of tactical goals derived from a broader strategic goal.[28] An occasional situation may call for a stand-alone tactical plan, but most of the time tactical plans flow from and must be consistent with a strategic plan.

For example, several years ago top managers of Coca-Cola developed a strategic plan for carrying the firm into the twenty-first century. As part of developing the plan, these managers identified a critical environmental threat—considerable unrest and uncertainty among the independent bottlers who packaged and distributed Coca-Cola's products. To simultaneously counter this threat and strengthen the company's position, Coca-Cola bought several large independent bottlers and combined them into one new organization called Coca-Cola Enterprises. Selling half of the new company's stock reaped millions in profits while effectively keeping control of the enterprise in Coca-Cola's hands. Thus, the creation of the new business was a tactical plan developed to contribute to the achievement of an overarching strategic goal.[29]

Second, although strategies are often stated in general terms, tactics must specify resources and time frames. A strategy can call for being number one in a particular market or industry, but a tactical plan must specify precisely what activities will be undertaken to achieve that goal. Consider the Coca-Cola example again. Another element of its strategic plan involves increased worldwide market share. To facilitate additional sales in Europe, managers developed tactical plans for building a new plant in the south of France to make soft-drink concentrate and for building another canning plant in Dunkirk. Building these plants represents a concrete action involving measurable resources (funds to build the plants) and a clear time horizon (a target date for completion).[30]

Finally, tactical planning requires the use of human resources. Managers involved in tactical planning spend a great deal of time working with other people. These managers must be able to receive information from others in and outside the organization, process that information in the most effective way, and then pass it on to others who might make use of it. Coca-Cola executives have been intensively involved in planning the new plants, setting up the new bottling venture noted earlier, and exploring a joint venture with Cadbury

Schweppes in the United Kingdom. Each activity has required considerable time and effort from dozens of managers. One manager, for example, crossed the Atlantic twelve times while negotiating the Cadbury deal.

■ Executing Tactical Plans

Regardless of how well a tactical plan is formulated, its ultimate success depends on the way it is carried out. Successful implementation, in turn, depends on the astute use of resources, effective decision making, and insightful steps to ensure that the right things are done at the right time and in the right ways. A manager can see an absolutely brilliant idea fail because of improper execution.

Proper execution depends on a number of important factors. First, the manager needs to evaluate every possible course of action in light of the goal it is intended to reach. Next, he or she needs to make sure that each decision maker has the information and resources necessary to get the job done. Vertical and horizontal communication and integration of activities must be present to minimize conflict and inconsistent activities. And finally, the manager must monitor ongoing activities derived from the plan to make sure that they are achieving the desired results. Such monitoring typically occurs within the context of the organization's ongoing control systems.

Operational Planning

Another critical element in effective organizational planning is the development and implementation of operational plans. Operational plans are derived from tactical plans and are aimed at achieving operational goals. Thus operational plans tend to be narrowly focused, have relatively short time horizons, and involve lower-level managers. The two most basic forms of operational plans and specific types of each are summarized in Table 3.1.

■ Single-Use Plans

single-use plan Developed to carry out a course of action that is not likely to be repeated

program A single-use plan for a large set of activities

A **single-use plan** is developed to carry out a course of action that is not likely to be repeated. The two most common forms of single-use plans are programs and projects.

Programs   A **program** is a single-use plan for a large set of activities. It might consist of identifying procedures for introducing a new product line, opening a new facility, or changing the organization's mission. When Black & Decker bought General Electric's small-appliance business, the deal involved the largest brand-name switch in history: 150 products were converted from GE to the Black & Decker label. Each product went through 140 steps as it was carefully studied, redesigned, and reintroduced with an extended warranty. It took three years to convert all 150 products to Black & Decker. The total conversion of the product line was a program.

Projects   A **project** is similar to a program but is generally of less scope and complexity. A project may be a part of a broader program, or it may be a self-contained single-use plan. For Black & Decker, the conversion of each product was a separate project. Each product had its own manager, its own schedule, and so forth. Projects are also used to introduce a new product within an existing product line or to add a new benefit option to an existing salary package.

Plan	Description
Single-use plan	Developed to carry out a course of action not likely to be carried out in the future
Program	Single-use plan for a large set of activities
Project	Single-use plan of less scope and complexity than a program
Standing plan	Developed for activities that recur regularly over a period of time
Policy	Standing plan specifying the organization's general response to a designated problem or situation
Standard operating procedure	Standing plan outlining steps to be followed in particular circumstances
Rules and regulations	Standing plans describing exactly how specific activities are to be carried out

TABLE 3.1
Types of Operational Plans

Organizations develop various operational plans to help achieve operational goals. In general, there are two types of single-use plans and three types of standing plans.

■ Standing Plans

Whereas single-use plans are developed for nonrecurring situations, a **standing plan** is used for activities that recur regularly. Standing plans can greatly enhance efficiency by providing routines for decision making. Policies, standard operating procedures, and rules and regulations are three kinds of standing plans.[31]

Policies   As a general guide for action, a policy is the broadest form of standing plan. A **policy** specifies the organization's general response to a designated problem or situation. For example, McDonald's has a policy that it will not grant a franchise to an individual who already owns another fast-food restaurant. Similarly, Starbucks has a policy that it will not franchise at all, instead, retaining ownership of all Starbucks coffee shops. Likewise, a university admissions office might establish a policy that grants admission only to applicants with a minimum SAT score of 1,000 and a ranking in the top quarter of their high school classes. Admissions officers may routinely deny admission to applicants who fail to reach these minimums. A policy is also likely to describe how exceptions are to be handled. The university's policy statement, for example, might create an admissions appeals committee to evaluate applicants who do not meet minimum requirements but may warrant special consideration.

project   A single-use plan of less scope and complexity than a program
standing plan   Developed for activities that recur regularly over a period of time
policy   A standing plan that specifies the organization's general response to a designated problem or situation

Standard Operating Procedures   Another type of standing plan is the **standard operating procedure**, or **SOP**. An SOP is more specific than a policy in that the former outlines the steps to be followed in particular circumstances. The admissions clerk at the university, for example, might be told that when an application is received, he or she should (1) set up a file for the applicant; (2) add test-score records, transcripts, and letters of reference to the file as they are received; and (3) give the file to the appropriate admissions director when it is complete. Gallo Vineyards in California has a three-hundred-page manual

standard operating procedure (SOP)   A standing plan that outlines the steps to be followed in a particular circumstance

BEETLE BAILEY By Mort Walker

Standard operating procedures, rules, and regulations can all be useful methods for saving time, improving efficiency, and streamlining decision making and planning. But it is also helpful to periodically review SOPs, rules, and regulations to ensure that they remain useful. For example, as shown in this cartoon, a SOP for regularly ordering parts and supplies may become less effective if the demand for those parts and supplies changes.

rules and regulations Describe exactly how specific activities are to be carried out

of SOPs. This planning manual is credited with making Gallo one of the most efficient wine operations in the United States.[32] McDonald's has SOPs explaining exactly how Big Macs are to be cooked, how long they can stay in the warming rack, and so forth.

Rules and Regulations The narrowest of the standing plans, **rules and regulations** describe exactly how specific activities are to be carried out. Rather than guiding decision making, rules and regulations actually take the place of decision making in various situations. Each McDonald's restaurant has a rule prohibiting customers from using its telephones, for example. The university admissions office might have a rule stipulating that if an applicant's file is not complete two months before the beginning of a semester, the student cannot be admitted until the next semester. Of course, in most organizations a manager at a higher level can suspend or bend the rules. If the high school transcript of the child of a prominent university alumnus and donor arrives a few days late, the director of admissions would probably waive the two-month rule. Rules and regulations can become problematic if they are excessive or enforced too rigidly.

Rules and regulations and SOPs are similar in many ways. They are both relatively narrow in scope, and each can serve as a substitute for decision making. An SOP typically describes a sequence of activities, however, whereas rules and regulations focus on one activity. Recall our examples: the admissions-desk SOP consisted of three activities, whereas the two-month rule related to one activity only. In an industrial setting, the SOP for orienting a new employee could involve enrolling the person in various benefit options, introducing him or her to coworkers and supervisors, and providing a tour of the facilities. A pertinent rule for the new employee might involve when to come to work each day.

■ Contingency Planning

contingency planning The determination of alternative courses of action to be taken if an intended plan is unexpectedly disrupted or rendered inappropriate

Another important type of planning is **contingency planning**, or the determination of alternative courses of action to be taken if an intended plan of action is unexpectedly disrupted or rendered inappropriate.[33] Consider, for example, Nike's plans for growth. Philip Knight and his managers realize that a shift in the global economy might result in a different rate of expansion. Therefore, they might have two contingency plans based on extreme positive or negative economic shifts. First, if the economy begins to expand beyond some specific level (contingency event), then (contingency plan) the rate of the company's growth will increase. Second, if inflation increases substantially or the economy experiences a downturn, the growth rate may slow down a bit. Nike would therefore have specified two crucial contingencies (expansion or inflation in the economy outside the tolerable range) and two alternative plans (increased or decreased growth).

The mechanics of contingency planning are shown in Figure 3.6. In relation to an organization's other plans, contingency planning comes into play at four action points. At action point one, management develops the basic plans of the organization. These may include strategic, tactical, and operational plans. As part of this development process, managers usually consider various contingency events. Some management groups even assign someone the role of devil's advocate to ask "But what if . . ." about each course of action. Various contingencies are usually considered.

At action point two, the plan that management chooses is put into effect. The most important contingency events are also defined. Only the events that are likely to occur and whose effects will have a substantial impact on the organization are used in the contingency-planning process. Next, at action point three, the company specifies certain indicators or signs that suggest that a contingency event is about to take place. A bank might decide that a 2 percent drop in interest rates should be considered a contingency event. An indicator might be two consecutive months with a drop of .5 percent in each. As indicators of contingency events are being defined, the contingency plans themselves should also be developed. Examples of contingency plans for various situations are delaying plant construction, developing a new manufacturing process, and cutting prices.

After this stage, the managers of the organization monitor the indicators identified at action point three. If the situation dictates, a contingency plan is implemented. Otherwise, the primary plan of action continues in force. Finally, action point four marks the successful completion of either the original or a contingency plan.

FIGURE 3.6
Contingency Planning

Most organizations develop contingency plans. These plans specify alternative courses of action to be taken if an intended plan is unexpectedly disrupted or rendered inappropriate.

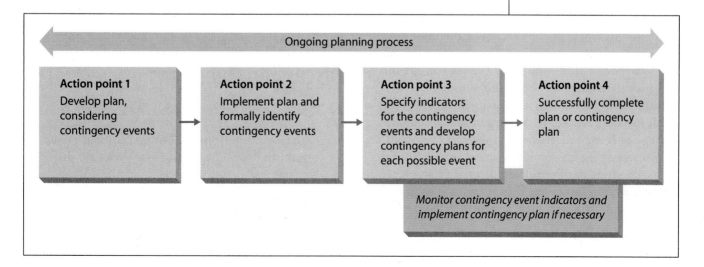

Ongoing planning process

Action point 1	Action point 2	Action point 3	Action point 4
Develop plan, considering contingency events	Implement plan and formally identify contingency events	Specify indicators for the contingency events and develop contingency plans for each possible event	Successfully complete plan or contingency plan

Monitor contingency event indicators and implement contingency plan if necessary

Contingency planning is becoming increasingly important for most organizations and especially for those operating in particularly complex or dynamic environments. Few managers have such an accurate view of the future that they can anticipate and plan for everything. Contingency planning is a useful technique for helping managers cope with uncertainty and change.[34]

Summary of Key Points

The planning process is the first basic managerial function that organizations must address. With an understanding of the environmental context, managers develop various types of goals and plans that serve different purposes. The major types of plans are strategic, tactical, and operational.

A strategy is a comprehensive plan for accomplishing the organization's goals. Strategic management is a comprehensive and ongoing process aimed at formulating and implementing effective strategies. Effective strategies address three organizational issues: distinctive competence, scope, and resource deployment. Most large companies have both business-level and corporate-level strategies.

SWOT analysis considers an organization's strengths, weaknesses, opportunities, and threats. Using SWOT analysis, an organization chooses strategies that support its mission and (1) exploit its opportunities and strengths, (2) neutralize its threats, and (3) avoid its weaknesses.

A business-level strategy is the plan an organization uses to conduct business in a particular industry or market. Porter suggests that, at this level, businesses may formulate a differentiation strategy, an overall cost leadership strategy, or a focus strategy. Business-level strategies may also take into account the stages in the product life cycle.

A corporate-level strategy is the plan an organization uses to manage its operations across several businesses. A firm that does not diversify is implementing a single-product strategy. An organization pursues a strategy of related diversification when it operates a set of businesses that are somehow linked. An organization pursues a strategy of unrelated diversification when it operates a set of businesses that are not logically associated with one another. Organizations usually manage diversification through portfolio management techniques. The BCG matrix classifies an organization's diversified businesses as dogs, cash cows, question marks, or stars according to market share and market growth rate. The GE Business Screen classifies businesses as winners, question marks, average businesses, losers, or profit producers according to industry attractiveness and competitive position.

After plans have been developed, the manager must address how they will be achieved. This step often involves tactical and operational plans. Tactical plans are at the middle of the organization, have an intermediate time horizon and moderate scope, and are developed to implement specific parts of a strategic plan. Tactical plans must flow from strategy, specify resource and time issues, commit human resources, and be executed effectively.

Operational plans are at the lower levels of the organization, have a shorter time horizon, and are narrower in scope. Operational plans are derived from a tactical plan and are aimed at achieving one or more operational goals. Two major types of operational plans are single-use and standing plans. Single-use plans carry out a course of action that is not likely to be repeated. Programs and projects are examples of single-use plans. Standing plans carry out a course of action that is likely to be repeated several times. Policies, standard operating procedures, and rules and regulations are all standing plans. Contingency planning is another important form of operational planning.

Discussion Questions

Questions for Review

1. Describe the purposes of organizational goals. Be certain to note how the purpose varies for different kinds of goals.

2. Identify and describe Porter's generic strategies.

3. What is the difference between a single-product strategy, a related diversification strategy, and an unrelated diversification strategy?

4. What is tactical planning? What is operational planning? What are the similarities and differences between them?

5. What is contingency planning? Is being flexible about your plans the same as contingency planning? Why or why not?

Questions for Analysis

1. Suppose that an organization does not have any distinctive competencies. If the organization is able to acquire some distinctive competencies, how long are these strengths likely to remain distinctive competencies? Why?

2. Suppose that an organization moves from a single-product strategy to a strategy of related diversification. How might the organization use SWOT analysis to select attributes of its current business to serve as bases of relatedness among its newly acquired businesses?

3. For decades now, Ivory Soap has advertised that it is 99 percent pure. Ivory has refused to add deodorants, facial creams, or colors to its soap. It also packages its soap in plain paper wrappers—no foil or fancy printing. Is Ivory implementing a product differentiation strategy, low-cost strategy, focus strategy, or some combination? Explain your answer.

4. Which kind of plan—tactical or operational—should an organization develop first? Why? Does the order of development really make a difference as long as plans of both types are made?

5. Identify examples of each type of operational plan you have used at work, in your school work, or even in your personal life.

Building Effective Communication Skills

EXERCISE OVERVIEW

Communication skills refer to the manager's abilities to both effectively convey ideas and information to others and effectively receive ideas and information from others. Communicating goals is an important part of management and requires strong communication skills.

EXERCISE BACKGROUND

Assume that you are the CEO of a large discount retailer. You have decided that your firm needs to change its strategy to survive. Specifically, you want the firm to move away from discount retailing and into specialty retailing.

To do so, you know that you will need to close four hundred of your twelve hundred discount stores within the next year. You also need to increase the expansion rate of your two existing specialty chains and to launch one new chain. Your tentative plans call for opening three hundred new specialty stores in one business and 150 in the other next year. You also want the basic concept for the new chain to be finalized and to have ten stores open next year as well. Finally, although you will be able to transfer some discount store employees to specialty retail jobs, a few hundred people will lose their jobs.

EXERCISE TASK

With the background information above as context, do the following:

1. Develop a press release that outlines these goals.

2. Determine the best way to communicate the goals to your employees.

3. Develop a contingency plan for dealing with problems.

Building Effective Decision-Making Skills

EXERCISE OVERVIEW

Decision-making skills refer to the manager's ability to correctly recognize and define problems and opportunities and to then select an appropriate course of action to solve problems and capitalize on opportunities. As noted in this chapter, many organizations use SWOT analysis as part of the process of strategy formulation. This exercise will help you better understand how managers obtain the information they need to perform such an analysis and use it as a framework for making decisions.

EXERCISE BACKGROUND

SWOT is an acronym for strengths, weaknesses, opportunities, and threats. Good strategies exploit an organization's opportunities and strengths while neutralizing threats and avoiding or correcting weaknesses.

Assume that you have just been hired to run a medium-size manufacturing company. The firm has been manufacturing electric motors, circuit breakers, and similar electronic components for industrial use. In recent years the firm's financial performance has gradually eroded. You have been hired to turn things around.

Meetings with both current and former top managers of the firm have convinced you that a new strategy is necessary. In earlier times the firm was successful in part because its products were of top quality. This factor allowed the company to charge premium prices. Recently, however, various cost-cutting measures have resulted in a decrease in quality. Moreover, competition has also increased. As a result, your firm no longer has a reputation for top-quality products, but your manufacturing costs are still relatively high. The next thing you want to do is to conduct a SWOT analysis.

EXERCISE TASK

With the situation described above as context, do the following:

1. List the sources you will use to obtain information about the firm's strengths, weaknesses, opportunities, and threats.

2. Rate each source in terms of its probable reliability.

3. Rate each source in terms of how easy or difficult it will be to access.

4. How confident should you be in making decisions based on the information you obtained?

Building Effective Conceptual Skills

EXERCISE OVERVIEW

Conceptual skills refer to the manager's ability to think in the abstract. This exercise gives you some experience in using your conceptual skills on real business opportunities and potential.

EXERCISE BACKGROUND

Many successful managers have at one time or another had an idea for using an existing product for new purposes or in new markets. For example, Arm &

Hammer Baking Soda (a food product used in cooking) is now also widely used to absorb odors in refrigerators. Commercials advise consumers to simply open a box of Arm & Hammer and place it in their refrigerator. This new approach has led to a big increase in sales of baking soda.

In other situations managers have extended the life cycles of products by moving them into new markets. The most common example today involves taking products that are becoming obsolete in more industrialized countries and introducing them in less industrialized countries.

EXERCISE TASK

Apply your conceptual skills to the following exercise:

1. Make a list of ten simple products that have relatively straightforward purposes (for example, a pencil, which is used for writing).

2. Try to identify two or three alternative uses for each product (a pencil can be used as an emergency splint for a broken finger).

3. Evaluate the market potential for each alternative product use as high, moderate, or low (the market potential for pencils as splints is low).

4. Form small groups of two or three members and pool your ideas. Each group should choose two or three ideas to present to the class.

You Make the Call

When Mark Spenser launched Sunset Landscape Services, he knew it was important to establish goals for his business. His first goal, of course, was survival. After the urgency of business start-up eased, however, he then found it useful to establish a clear and unambiguous set of business goals stressing the value of high-quality customer service and consistent business growth. Looking back, Mark believes that these goals have served him well on two important occasions.

By 1984, SLS was on reasonably secure financial footing, and Mark decided to expand his business. The firm initially consisted of two related but distinct businesses. One business was a retail nursery selling plants, pots, baskets, plant food, gardening supplies, and so forth. Mark's wife, Cynthia, managed this part of the operation. The other business was the actual landscape operation, which Mark managed. This business provided such services as planning new lawns and landscaping for local builders and owners of new homes. Mark also drew plans for decks and patios and worked with a local swimming-pool builder to jointly design and install pools and accompanying landscaping.

Mark then decided to expand his business into lawn-care services. This operation would handle routine mowing and related lawn-maintenance services for homeowners. He launched this new business in 1985. The initial start-up operation took a little longer than expected, however, and he ran into a financial crunch. Support from his suppliers and banker helped weather the storms so that within a year the new business was profitable. Today this business is as important to the overall operation as were the first two businesses.

The other time that Mark's goals were critical to his success was in 1990. A regional nursery chain, Lion Gardens, opened a store in Central City. Because of Lion's size, it was able to buy in bulk and sell at a discount. Mark knew that

Lion's prices would be lower than his, and he worried that he would lose customers to Lion. He initially considered cutting his own prices to meet those of Lion, but then realized that if he did so, he would not be able to provide the same level of customer support that he currently offered. For example, many customers sought advice on what kinds of plants would work best in different locations, how to best care for those plants, and so forth.

Mark eventually decided to not worry about Lion's prices. He realized that people who were only interested in price could already buy their plants at a discount at Wal-Mart, for example. Thus, he continued to stress quality customer service with reasonable prices. He was gratified to observe that, although his business took a bit of a hit during the first few months that Lion was open, his customers soon returned.

DISCUSSION QUESTIONS

1. How important have goals been to SLS?

2. What business strategy is SLS using? What corporate strategy is SLS using?

3. What business opportunities might Mark Spenser consider next?

Skills Self-Assessment Instrument

ARE YOU A GOOD PLANNER?

Introduction: Planning is an important skill for managers. The following assessment is designed to help you understand your planning skills.

Instructions: Answer either *yes* or *no* to each of the following questions.

	Yes	No
1. My personal objectives are clearly spelled out in writing.	_____	_____
2. Most of my days are hectic and disorderly.	_____	_____
3. I seldom make any snap decisions and usually study a problem carefully before acting.	_____	_____
4. I keep a desk calendar or appointment book as an aid.	_____	_____
5. I make use of "action" and "deferred action" files.	_____	_____
6. I generally establish starting dates and deadlines for all my projects.	_____	_____
7. I often ask others for advice.	_____	_____
8. I believe that all problems have to be solved immediately.	_____	_____

For interpretation, turn to page 457.

Source: From Stephen P. Robbins, *Management*, 4th ed. Copyright © 1994 by National Research Bureau. Reprinted by permission of National Resource Bureau, P.O. Box 1, Burlington, Iowa 52601-0001.

THE SWOT ANALYSIS

Purpose: SWOT analysis provides the manager with a cognitive model of the organization and its environmental forces. By developing this ability, the manager builds both process knowledge and a conceptual skill. This skill builder focuses on the *administrative management model*. It will help you develop the *coordinator role* of the administrative management model. One of the skills of the coordinator is the ability to plan.

Introduction: This exercise helps you understand the complex interrelationships between environmental opportunities and threats and organizational strengths and weaknesses.

Instructions:

Step 1: Study the exhibit below, Strategy Formulation at Marriott, and the text materials concerning the matching of organizations with environments.

Step 2: The instructor will divide the class into small groups. Each group will conduct a SWOT (strengths, weaknesses, opportunities, threats) analysis for Marriott and prepare group responses to the discussion questions. Marriott has been successful in its hotel and food services businesses but less than successful in its cruise ship, travel agency, and theme park businesses.

Strategy formulation is facilitated by a SWOT analysis. First the organization should study its internal operations in order to identify its strengths and weaknesses. Next the organization should scan the environment to identify existing and future opportunities and threats. Then the organization should identify the relationships that exist among the strengths, weaknesses, opportunities, and threats. Finally, major business strategies usually result from matching an organization's strengths with appropriate opportunities or from matching threats with weaknesses. To facilitate the environmental analysis in search of opportunities and threats, it is helpful to divide the environment into its major components—international, economic, political-legal, sociocultural, and technological.

Step 3: One representative from each group may be asked to report on the group's SWOT analysis and to report the group's responses to the discussion questions.

DISCUSSION QUESTIONS

1. What was the most difficult part of the SWOT analysis?

2. Why do most firms not develop major strategies for matches between threats and strengths?

3. Under what conditions might a firm develop a major strategy around a match between an opportunity and a weakness?

Source: From Burton, Gene E., *Exercises in Management*, 5th ed. Copyright © 1996 by Hougton Mifflin Company. Used with permission.

Strategy Formulation at Marriott

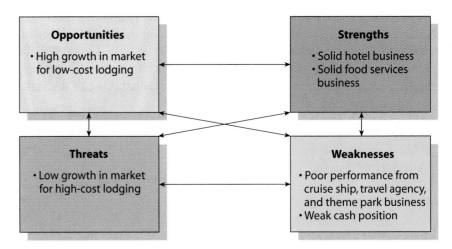

Source: Ricky Griffin, *Management*, 4th ed. Copyright © 1993 by Houghton Mifflin Co., p. 180. Reprinted by permission of the publisher.

Relationships Between Opportunities and Strengths

1. _____

2. _____

3. _____

Relationships Between Opportunities and Weaknesses

1. _____

2. _____

3. _____

Relationships Between Threats and Strengths

1. _____

2. _____

3. _____

Relationships Between Threats and Weaknesses

1. _____

2. _____

3. _____

Major Strategies Matching Opportunities with Strengths

1. _____

2. _____

3. _____

4. _____

Major Strategies Matching Threats with Weaknesses

1. _____

2. _____

3. _____

4. _____

Marriott SWOT Analysis Sheet

Environmental Analysis	**Organizational Analysis**

Opportunities
_____
_____
_____
_____
_____
_____
_____
_____
_____
_____
_____
_____
_____

Strengths
_____
_____
_____
_____
_____
_____
_____
_____
_____
_____
_____
_____
_____

Threats
_____
_____
_____
_____
_____
_____
_____
_____
_____
_____
_____
_____
_____

Weaknesses
_____
_____
_____
_____
_____
_____
_____
_____
_____
_____
_____
_____
_____

Volkswagen Shifts Its Strategy

The 1960s were turbulent years. The war in Vietnam, college campus protests, desegregation, and the emergence of the feminist movement contributed to a prevailing sense of unrest and social upheaval. But ubiquitous to the decade was a set of cultural icons that today are still associated with that era—hippies, tie-died shirts, bell-bottom jeans, and the two "Beatles"—the musical group (the Beatles) and the car (the venerable Volkswagen Beetle).

Volkswagen, a German firm, hoped to recapture some of the 1960s glory when it relaunched the Beetle in 1998. But this time the company sought an image far different from its earlier one. To best understand what Volkswagen wants to accomplish—and why—it's instructive to first examine the car's past.

Volkswagen began producing the car in 1938. The *New York Times* promptly dubbed it the Beetle because of its rounded shape and design. The first Beetles were actually shipped to the United States in 1949, selling for $800. The cars quickly became popular because of their low price and reputation for dependability. In 1968 U.S. sales of the Beetle peaked at 423,008, and four years later Beetle number 15,007,034 rolled off the assembly line, surpassing the Ford Model T as the most produced car in history.

But as sales declined, Volkswagen stopped selling the Beetle in 1979, deciding instead to concentrate on newer models. The last Beetle sold for $6,495 and was still one of the lowest priced cars in the country at the time. But the Beetle lived on in the hearts and minds of consumers, who remembered the car's low price and Volkswagen's dependable service.

Volkswagen's fortunes, meanwhile, began to slowly deteriorate. One model after another floundered in the U.S. market, and by 1970 the company's market share had dropped below 1 percent. In Europe, meanwhile, Volkswagen was undergoing a very successful renaissance. The same models that were rejected in the United States were catching on in other parts of the world. In addition, the firm acquired Audi, an upscale manufacturer known in Germany for high-quality, higher-priced automobiles.

Volkswagen used the technology it acquired with Audi to continue to upgrade the quality of its other products. And slowly but surely, the firm's image gravitated upward in Europe until it became almost as respected as BMW and Mercedes-Benz. And today Volkswagen's fortunes have improved to the point where it is both widely respected in its homeland and highly profitable throughout the world—except in the United States.

The firm is again turning its attention to the market where the Beetle once ruled. But this time Volkswagen wants a different image. Specifically, it wants to transplant its upscale image from Europe into the United States. If this plan is successful, Volkswagen will be able to charge higher prices for its cars and thus earn more profits. Of course, to hinge the new initiative on a car so long associated with low prices is a calculated risk. But Volkswagen believes that the Beetle's reputation will lure consumers from all walks of life into its showrooms, where they can then be impressed by the firm's high-quality product line.

Case Questions

1. From a strategic management perspective, explain Volkswagen's earlier problems and successes in the United States and in Europe.
2. Characterize the firm's current strategies from the standpoint of business- and corporate-level decisions and issues.
3. Identify and discuss the kinds of tactical and operational plans a firm like Volkswagen is likely to use.

Case References: "New Bug Goes Upscale But Draws on Nostalgia," *USA Today*, January 6, 1998, pp. 1B, 2B; "VW's U.S. Comeback Rides on Restyled Beetle," *Wall Street Journal,* May 6, 1997, pp. B1, B2; "Is VW Revving Too High?" *Business Week,* March 30, 1998, pp. 48–49; and "Hard-Driving Boss," *Business Week,* October 5, 1998, pp. 82–90.

CHAPTER NOTES

1. "Can Nike Get Unstuck?" *Time*, March 30, 1998, pp. 48–53; "The Swoosh Heard 'Round the World," *Business Week*, May 12, 1997, pp. 76–80 (quote on page 78); John Wyatt, "Is It Time to Jump on Nike?" *Fortune*, May 26, 1997, pp. 185–186; and "Tripped Up by too Many Shoes, Nike Regroups," *Wall Street Journal*, March 3, 1998, pp. B1, B12.

2. Max D. Richards, *Setting Strategic Goals and Objectives*, 2nd ed. (St. Paul, Minn.: West, 1986).

3. Kenneth R. Thompson, Wayne A. Hochwarter, and Nicholas J. Mathys, "Stretch Targets: What Makes Them Effective?" *Academy of Management Executive*, August 1997, pp. 48–57.

4. "A Methodical Man," *Forbes*, August 11, 1997, pp. 70–72.

5. John A. Pearce II and Fred David, "Corporate Mission Statements: The Bottom Line," *Academy of Management Executive*, May 1987, p. 109.

6. See Charles Hill and Gareth Jones, *Strategic Management*, 4th ed. (Boston: Houghton Mifflin, 1998).

7. For early discussions of strategic management, see Kenneth Andrews, *The Concept of Corporate Strategy*, rev. ed. (Homewood, Ill.: Dow Jones-Irwin, 1980) and Igor Ansoff, *Corporate Strategy* (New York: McGraw-Hill, 1965). For more recent perspectives, see Michael E. Porter, "What Is Strategy?" *Harvard Business Review*, November–December 1996, pp. 61–78.

8. *Hoover's Handbook of American Business 1998* (Austin, Texas: Hoover's Business Press, 1998), pp. 876–877.

9. Peter Koenig, "If Europe's Dead, Why Is GE Investing Billions There?" *Fortune*, September 9, 1996, pp. 114–118.

10. For a discussion of the distinction between business- and corporate-level strategies, see Charles Hill and Gareth Jones, *Strategic Management*, 4th ed. (Boston: Houghton Mifflin, 1998).

11. See David Barry and Michael Elmes, "Strategy Retold: Toward a Narrative View of Strategic Discourse," *Academy of Management Review*, April 1997, pp. 429–452 and Dennis P. Slevin and Jeffrey G. Covin, "Strategy Formation Patterns, Performance, and the Significance of Context," *Journal of Management*, Vol. 23, No. 2, 1997, pp. 189–209.

12. See W. Jack Duncan, Peter M. Ginter, and Linda E. Swayne, "Competitive Advantage and Internal Organizational Assessment," *Academy of Management Executive*, Vol. 12, No. 3, 1998, pp. 6–16.

13. For a recent discussion, see Elaine Mosakowski, "Strategy Making Under Causal Ambiguity: Conceptual Issues and Empirical Evidence," *Organization Science*, July–August 1997, pp. 414–423.

14. "If It's On the Fritz, Take It to Jane," *Business Week*, January 27, 1997, pp. 74–75.

15. Jay Barney, "Firm Resources and Sustained Competitive Advantage," *Journal of Management*, June 1991, pp. 99–120.

16. Porter, *Competitive Strategy*.

17. Ian C. MacMillan and Rita Gunther McGrath, "Discovering New Points of Differentiation," *Harvard Business Review*, July–August 1997, pp. 133–136.

18. Richard Teitelbaum, "The Wal-Mart of Wall Street," *Fortune*, October 13, 1997, pp. 128–130.

19. Alfred Chandler, *Strategy and Structure: Chapters in the History of the American Industrial Enterprise* (Cambridge, Mass.: MIT Press, 1962); Richard Rumelt, *Strategy, Structure, and Economic Performance* (Cambridge, Mass.: Division of Research, Graduate School of Business Administration, Harvard University, 1974); and Oliver Williamson, *Markets and Hierarchies* (New York: Free Press, 1975).

20. K. L. Stimpert and Irene M. Duhaime, "Seeing the Big Picture: The Influence of Industry, Diversification, and Business Strategy on Performance," *Academy of Management Journal*, Vol. 40, No. 3, 1997, pp. 560–583.

21. See Chandler, *Strategy and Structure*, and Yakov Amihud and Baruch Lev, "Risk Reduction as a Managerial Motive for Conglomerate Mergers," *Bell Journal of Economics*, 1981, pp. 605–617.

22. Chandler, *Strategy and Structure*, and Williamson, *Markets and Hierarchies*.

23. See Jay Barney and William G. Ouchi, *Organizational Economics* (San Francisco: Jossey-Bass, 1986), for a discussion of the limitations of unrelated diversification.

24. See Barry Hedley, "A Fundamental Approach to Strategy Development," *Long Range Planning*, December 1976, pp. 2–11, and Bruce Henderson, "The Experience Curve-Reviewed. IV: The Growth Share Matrix of the Product Portfolio," *Perspectives*, No. 135 (Boston: Boston Consulting Group, 1973).

25. Michael G. Allen, "Diagramming G.E.'s Planning for What's WATT," in Robert J. Allio and Malcolm W. Pennington (eds.), *Corporate Planning: Techniques and Applications* (New York: AMACOM, 1979). Limits of this approach are discussed in R. A. Bettis and W. K. Hall, "The Business Portfolio Approach: Where It Falls Down in Practice," *Long Range Planning*, March 1983, pp. 95–105.

26. "Unilever to Sell Specialty-Chemical Unit to ICI of the U.K. for About $8 Billion," *Wall Street Journal*, May 7, 1997, pp. A3, A12.

27. James Brian Quinn, Henry Mintzberg, and Robert M. James, *The Strategy Process* (Englewood Cliffs, N.J.: Prentice-Hall, 1988).

28. Vasudevan Ramanujam and N. Venkatraman, "Planning System Characteristics and Planning Effectiveness," *Strategic Management Journal*, Vol. 8, No. 2, 1987, pp. 453–468.

29. John Huey, "The World's Best Brand," *Fortune*, May 31, 1993, pp. 44–54.

30. J. Huey, "The World's Best Brand."

31. Thomas L. Wheelon and J. David Hunger, *Strategic Management and Business Policy*, 5th ed. (Reading, Mass.: Addison-Wesley, 1995).

32. Jaclyn Fierman, "How Gallo Crushes the Competition," *Fortune*, September 1, 1986, pp. 23–31.

33. K. A. Froot, D. S. Scharfstein, and J. C. Stein, "A Framework for Risk Management," *Harvard Business Review*, November–December 1994, pp. 91–102.

34. See Donald C. Hambrick and David Lei, "Toward an Empirical Prioritization of Contingency Variables for Business Strategy," *Academy of Management Journal*, December 1985, pp. 763–788.

4

Managing Decision Making

OBJECTIVES

After studying this chapter, you should be able to:

- Define decision making and discuss types of decisions and decision-making conditions.
- Discuss rational perspectives on decision making, including the steps in decision making.
- Describe the behavioral nature of decision making.
- Discuss group and team decision making, including the advantages and disadvantages of group and team decision making and how it can be managed more effectively.

Well-defined seminal moments in the history of most companies usually determine their future successes and failures. A good case in point is Kimberly-Clark Corporation. Indeed, two critical decisions coming twenty years apart have indelibly defined the company's current competitive strategies and its future directions.

In the mid-1970s Kimberly basically had its feet planted firmly in two disparate businesses. Its core businesses were forestry products—trees and paper—and pulp-making operations, and it was here that it had committed most of its capital. But most of the firm's profits came from its disposable-tissue business. Indeed, the name "Kleenex" was virtually synonymous with Kimberly-Clark and has almost become a generic term for facial tissues.

Company officials determined that their strategy was a barrier to future growth—low growth and low profits in the forestry businesses constrained expansion in those markets. Moreover, those businesses were requiring so much capital that there was not enough left to fuel growth in other areas. Consequently, Kimberly management made the decision to sell major portions of the forestry operations and use the proceeds to expand into consumer products such as disposable diapers and paper towels.

Over the next several years, therefore, Kimberly sold one forestry business after another and carefully and calculatedly launched a variety of new products. Unfortunately, however, Kimberly found it tough competing against the entrenched industry giant Procter & Gamble. Its vast size and sophisticated distribution network made it difficult for competitors like Kimberly to gain significant market share. At the same time, Procter & Gamble was also beginning to move into the facial tissue market, putting Kleenex in a vulnerable position.

The next major watershed event for Kimberly-Clark occurred in 1995 when its managers made the decision to buy Scott Paper Company for $9.4 billion. This acquisition gave Kimberly-Clark new market share in a number of markets. For example, Kimberly's share of the bathroom tissue market jumped from 5 percent to 31 percent, and its share of the home paper towel market more than tripled to 18 percent.

Even more important, the Scott acquisition gave Kimberly major positions in several foreign markets. Scott was the dominant tissue-product company in Mexico, for example, enjoying near-monopoly status. Kimberly was also now able to use its new clout to compete with Procter & Gamble on a more even basis. Indeed, the international competition between the two giants has produced some interesting twists and turns.

For example, when Kimberly entered the French market in 1994, ruthless price cutting between it and Procter & Gamble inadvertently pushed their largest French competitor, Peaudouce, to the edge of bankruptcy. Its savior? Kimberly-Clark. And the next year the same scenario was played out in Argentina, with Kimberly-Clark again landing the wounded domestic competitor. Although the winner has not yet been determined, Kimberly-Clark is clearly making its presence felt. And it all started with a decision to sell some trees and make more tissue.[1]

"Every morning I look in the mirror and ask how I can beat the hell out of P&G [Procter & Gamble]. And I want every one of my employees to do the same."

Wayne Sanders, Kimberly-Clark chief executive

The opening incident portrays two significant decisions made by Kimberly-Clark executives that have essentially reshaped the entire character of their firm. But in addition to the decisions highlighted here, Kimberly executives have made many, many more decisions, some also very important (such as which foreign markets to enter and how and when to do so), some of moderate importance (such as package design for tissue products and color choices for tissue products), and others of perhaps relatively low importance (such as the exact number of tissues to put in a box of Kleenex).

Some experts believe that decision making is the most basic and fundamental of all managerial activities.[2] Thus we discuss it here in the context of the first management function, planning. Keep in mind, however, that although decision making is perhaps most closely linked to the planning function, this activity is also part of organizing, leading, and controlling. We begin our discussion by exploring the nature of decision making. We then describe rational perspectives on decision making and behavioral aspects of decision making. We conclude with a discussion of group and team decision making.

The Nature of Decision Making

Managers at BMW recently made the decision to build a new manufacturing plant in South Carolina at a cost of more than $600 million. At about the same time, the manager at the BMW dealership in Bryan, Texas, made a decision to sponsor a local youth soccer team for $150. Each of these examples includes a decision, but the decisions differ in many ways. Thus as a starting point in understanding decision making, we must first explore the meaning of decision making as well as types of decisions and conditions under which decisions are made.[3]

■ Decision Making Defined

decision making The act of choosing one alternative from among a set of alternatives

decision-making process Recognizing and defining the nature of a decision situation, identifying alternatives, choosing the "best" alternative, and putting it into practice

Decision making can refer to either a specific act or a general process. **Decision making** per se is the act of choosing one alternative from among a set of alternatives. The decision-making process, however, is much more extensive. One step of the process, for example, requires the decision maker to recognize that a decision is necessary and to identify the set of feasible alternatives before selecting one. Hence, the **decision-making process** includes recognizing and defining the nature of a decision situation, identifying alternatives, choosing the "best" alternative, and putting it into practice.[4]

In this context the word "best" implies effectiveness. Effective decision making requires the decision maker to understand the situation driving the decision. Most people would consider an effective decision to be one that optimizes some set of factors such as profits, sales, employee welfare, and market share. In some situations, though, an effective decision may be one that minimizes loss, expenses, or employee turnover. It may even mean selecting the best method for going out of business, laying off employees, or terminating a contract.

We should also note that managers make decisions about both problems and opportunities. For example, making decisions about how to cut costs by 10 percent reflects a problem—an undesired situation that requires a solution. But decisions are also necessary in situations of opportunity. Learning that the firm is earning higher-than-projected profits, for example, requires a subsequent decision. Should the extra funds be used to increase shareholder dividends, reinvested in current operations, or used to expand into new markets?

Of course, it may take a long time before a manager can know whether he or she made the right decision. For example, when George Fisher took over as CEO of Kodak, he made several major decisions that will affect the company for decades. Among other things, for example, he sold off several chemical- and health-related businesses, reduced the firm's debt by $7 billion in the process, launched a major new line of advanced cameras and film called Advantix, and made major new investments in emerging technologies such as digital photography. But analysts believe that the payoffs from these decisions will not be known for at least ten years.[5]

■ Types of Decisions

Managers must make many types of decisions. In general, however, most decisions fall into one of two categories: programmed and nonprogrammed.[6] A **programmed decision** is one that is fairly structured or recurs with some frequency (or both). Kimberly-Clark uses programmed decisions to purchase new supplies of wood pulp, dyes and chemicals, and packaging materials for its tissue products. For example, a plant manager may need to keep a ten-day supply of packaging on hand, and knows that it takes three days to get the packaging from the supplier. Thus, whenever the on-hand supply of packaging reaches thirteen days, the manager places a new order. Likewise, the Bryan BMW dealer decided to sponsor a youth soccer team each year. Thus, when the soccer club president calls, the dealer already knows what to do. Many decisions regarding basic operating systems and procedures and standard organizational transactions can be programmed.

Nonprogrammed decisions, on the other hand, are relatively unstructured and occur much less often. Kimberly-Clark's earlier decision regarding its change of emphasis from wood products to consumer products and its more recent decision to acquire Scott Paper were both nonprogrammed decisions. Managers faced with such decisions must treat each one as unique and must

Decision making is a pervasive part of most managerial activities. Virtually everything that happens in a company involves making a decision or implementing a decision that has been made. Although some decisions are grand and significant in scope, others, such as the ones shown in the center panel of this cartoon, involve more routine, day-to-day activities. And still others, illustrated in the right panel, deal with what to have for lunch or when to take a break. Regardless of their goals, however, the people making the decisions need to take them seriously and do what they believe to be best for the company.

programmed decision A decision that is fairly structured or recurs with some frequency (or both)

nonprogrammed decision A decision that is relatively unstructured; occurs much less often than a programmed decision

invest enormous amounts of time, energy, and resources into exploring the situation from all perspectives. Intuition and experience are major factors in nonprogrammed decisions. Most of the decisions made by top managers involving strategy (including mergers, acquisitions, and takeovers) and organization design are nonprogrammed. So are decisions about new facilities, new products, labor contracts, and legal issues.

■ Decision-Making Conditions

state of certainty A condition in which the decision maker knows with reasonable certainty what the alternatives are and what conditions are associated with each alternative

state of risk A condition in which the availability of each alternative and its potential payoffs and costs are all associated with probability estimates

Just as there are different kinds of decisions, there are also different conditions in which decisions must be made. The managers who made Kimberly-Clark's decision to move from wood to consumer products had little idea what to expect. Alternatively, the managers who decided to buy Scott Paper knew details about Scott's current products, their market share, and so forth, and could thus estimate with reasonable assurance how the two firms together would stack up in the marketplace. Managers sometimes have an almost perfect understanding of conditions surrounding a decision, but at other times they have few clues about those conditions. In general, as shown in Figure 4.1, the circumstances that exist for the decision maker are conditions of certainty, risk, or uncertainty.[7]

Decision Making Under Certainty When the decision maker knows with reasonable certainty what the alternatives are and what conditions are associated with each alternative, a **state of certainty** exists. Suppose, for example, that Singapore Airlines needs to buy five new jumbo jets. The decision is from whom to buy them. Singapore has only two choices: Boeing (a U.S. firm) and Airbus (a European consortium). Each has proven products and will specify prices and delivery dates. The airline thus knows the alternative conditions associated with each. There is little ambiguity and relatively low chance of making a bad decision.

Few organizational decisions are made under conditions of true certainty.[8] The complexity and turbulence of the contemporary business world make such situations rare. In fact, even the airplane purchase decision we just considered has less certainty than it appears. The aircraft companies may not be able to guarantee delivery dates so they may write cost-increase or inflation clauses into contracts. Thus the airline may not be truly certain of the conditions surrounding each alternative.

Decision Making Under Risk A more common decision-making condition is a state of risk. Under a **state of risk**, the availability of each alternative and its potential payoffs and costs are associated with probability estimates.[9] Suppose, for example, that a labor contract negotiator for a company receives a "final" offer from the union just before a strike deadline. The negotiator has two alter-

FIGURE 4.1
Decision-Making Conditions

Most major decisions in organizations today are made under a state of uncertainty. Managers making decisions in these circumstances must be sure to learn as much as possible about the situation and approach the decision from a logical and rational perspective.

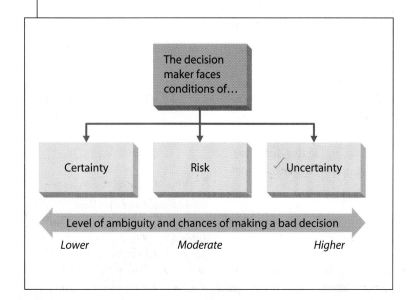

natives: to accept or to reject the offer. The risk centers on whether the union representatives are bluffing. If the company negotiator accepts the offer, she avoids a strike but commits to a costly labor contract. If the negotiator rejects the contract, she may get a more favorable contract if the union is bluffing; she may provoke a strike if it is not.

On the basis of past experiences, relevant information, the advice of others, and her own intuition, she may believe that there is about a 75 percent chance that the union is bluffing and about a 25 percent chance that it will back up its threats. Thus the company negotiator can base a calculated decision on the two alternatives (accept or reject the contract demands) and the probable consequences of each. When making decisions under a state of risk, managers must accurately determine the probabilities associated with each alternative. For example, if the union negotiators are committed to a strike if their demands are not met and the company negotiator rejects their demands because she guesses that the union will not strike, her miscalculation will prove costly. As indicated in Figure 4.1, decision making under conditions of risk is accompanied by moderate ambiguity and chances of a bad decision.[10] Kimberly-Clark's decision to acquire Scott Paper was made under conditions of risk.

Decision Making Under Uncertainty   Most of the major decision making in contemporary organizations is done under a **state of uncertainty**. The decision maker does not know all the alternatives, the risks associated with each, or the likely consequences of each alternative.[11] This uncertainty stems from the complexity and dynamism of contemporary organizations and their environments. Consider, for example, the decision that Kimberly-Clark made about moving from wood to consumer products. Because many of the alternatives, risks, and consequences were unknown, this decision was accompanied by considerable uncertainty. Indeed, many of the decisions already noted—BMW's decision to build a new plant and Kodak's decision to invest in digital photography—were made under conditions of uncertainty. To make effective decisions in these circumstances, managers must acquire as much relevant information as possible and approach the situation from a logical and rational perspective. Intuition, judgment, and experience always play major roles in the decision-making process under conditions of uncertainty. Even so, uncertainty is the most ambiguous condition for managers and the one most prone to error.

state of uncertainty   A condition in which the decision maker does not know all the alternatives, the risks associated with each, or the consequences each alternative is likely to have

Rational Perspectives on Decision Making

Most managers like to think of themselves as rational decision makers. And indeed, many experts argue that managers should try to be as rational as possible in making decisions.[12]

■ The Classical Model of Decision Making

The **classical decision model** is a prescriptive approach that tells managers how they should make decisions. It rests on the assumptions that managers

classical decision model   A prescriptive approach to decision making that tells managers how they should make decisions, assumes that managers are logical and rational, and assumes that their decisions will be in the best interests of the organization

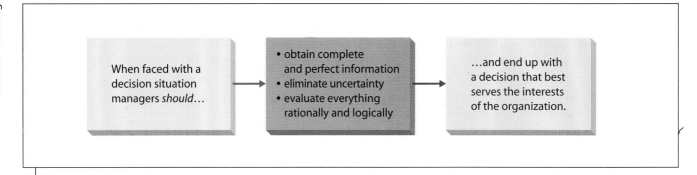

When faced with a decision situation managers *should*...

- obtain complete and perfect information
- eliminate uncertainty
- evaluate everything rationally and logically

...and end up with a decision that best serves the interests of the organization.

FIGURE 4.2

The Classical Model of Decision Making

The classical model of decision making assumes that managers are rational and logical. It attempts to prescribe how managers should approach decision situations.

steps in rational decision making
Recognize and define the decision situation; identify appropriate alternatives; evaluate each alternative in terms of its feasibility, satisfactoriness, and consequences; select the best alternative; implement the chosen alternative; follow up and evaluate the results of the chosen alternative

are logical and rational and that they make decisions that are in the best interests of the organization. Figure 4.2 shows how the classical model views the decision-making process: (1) Decision makers have complete information about the decision situation and possible alternatives. (2) They can effectively eliminate uncertainty to achieve a decision condition of certainty. (3) They evaluate all aspects of the decision situation logically and rationally. As we see later, these conditions rarely, if ever, actually exist.

∎ Steps in Rational Decision Making

A manager who really wants to approach a decision rationally and logically should try to follow the **steps in rational decision making**, as listed in Table 4.1. These steps in rational decision making help keep the decision maker focused on facts and logic and help guard against inappropriate assumptions and pitfalls.

Recognizing and Defining the Decision Situation   The first step in rational decision making is recognizing that a decision is necessary—that is, there must be some stimulus or spark to initiate the process. For many decisions and problem situations, the stimulus may occur without any warning. When equipment malfunctions, the manager must decide whether to repair or replace it. Or when a major crisis erupts the manager must quickly decide how to deal with it. As we already noted, the stimulus for a decision may be either positive or negative. A manager who must decide how to invest surplus funds, for example, faces a positive decision situation. A negative financial stimulus could involve having to trim budgets because of cost overruns.

Inherent in problem recognition is the need to define precisely what the problem is. The manager must develop a complete understanding of the problem, its causes, and its relationship to other factors. This understanding comes from careful analysis and thoughtful consideration of the situation. Consider the recent situation faced by Olin Pool Products. Even though Olin controlled half the market for chlorine-based pool treatment systems, its profits were slipping and it was rapidly losing market share to new competitors. These indicators provide clear evidence to General Manager Doug Cahill that something needed to be done. He went on to define the problem as a need to restore profitability and regain lost market share.[13]

Identifying Alternatives   Once the decision situation has been recognized and defined, the second step is to identify alternative courses of effective action.

Step	Detail	Example
1. Recognizing and defining the decision situation	Some stimulus indicates that a decision must be made. The stimulus may be positive or negative.	A plant manager sees that employee turnover has increased by 5 percent.
2. Identifying alternatives	Both obvious and creative alternatives are desired. In general, the more important the decision, the more alternatives should be generated.	The plant manager can increase wages, increase benefits, or change hiring standards.
3. Evaluating alternatives	Each alternative is evaluated to determine its feasibility, its satisfactoriness, and its consequences.	Increasing benefits may not be feasible. Increasing wages and changing hiring standards may satisfy all conditions.
4. Selecting the best alternative	Consider all situational factors and choose the alternative that best fits the manager's situation.	Changing hiring standards will take an extended period of time to cut turnover, so increase wages.
5. Implementing the chosen alternative	The chosen alternative is implemented into the organizational system.	The plant manager may need permission of corporate headquarters. The human resource department establishes a new wage structure.
6. Following up and evaluating the results	At some time in the future, the manager should ascertain the extent to which the alternative chosen in step four and implemented in step five has worked.	The plant manager notes that, six months later, turnover dropped to its previous level.

Developing both obvious, standard alternatives and creative, innovative alternatives is useful in most cases. In general, the more important the decision, the more attention is directed to developing alternatives. If the decision involves a multimillion-dollar relocation, a great deal of time and expertise will be devoted to identifying the best locations: J.C. Penney Company spent two years searching before selecting the Dallas-Fort Worth area for its new corporate headquarters. On the other hand, choosing a color for the company softball team uniform requires less managerial time and expertise.

Although managers should seek creative solutions, they must also recognize that various constraints often limit their alternatives. Common constraints include legal restrictions; moral and ethical norms; authority constraints; or constraints imposed by the power and authority of the manager, available technology, economic considerations, and unofficial social norms. Doug Cahill at Olin identified several alternatives that might help his firm: seek a bigger firm to take control of Olin and inject new resources, buy one or more competitors to increase Olin's own size, maintain the status quo and hope that competitors stubbed their toes, or overhaul the organization to become more competitive.

Evaluating Alternatives   The third step in the decision-making process is evaluating each alternative. Figure 4.3 presents a decision tree that can be used to judge different alternatives. The figure suggests that each alternative be evaluated in terms of its feasibility, its satisfactoriness, and its consequences. The first question to ask is whether an alternative is feasible. Is it

TABLE 4.1
Steps in the Rational Decision-Making Process

Although the presumptions of the classical decision model rarely exist, managers can approach decision making with rationality. By following the steps of rational decision making, managers ensure that they are learning as much as possible about the decision situation and its alternatives.

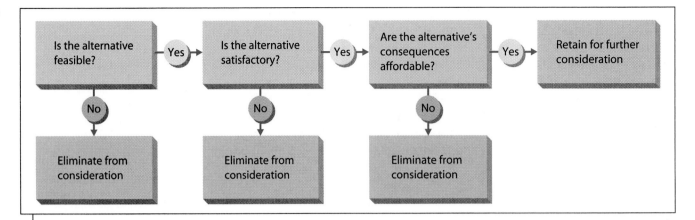

FIGURE 4.3
Evaluating Alternatives in the Decision-Making Process

Managers must thoroughly evaluate all the alternatives, which increases the chances that the alternative finally chosen will be successful. Failure to evaluate an alternative's feasibility, satisfactoriness, and consequences can lead to a wrong decision.

within the realm of probability and practicality? For a small, struggling firm, an alternative requiring a huge financial outlay is probably out of the question. Other alternatives may not be feasible because of legal barriers. And limited human, material, and information resources may make other alternatives impractical.

When an alternative has passed the test of feasibility, it must next be examined to see how well it satisfies the conditions of the decision situation. For example, a manager searching for ways to double production capacity might consider purchasing an existing plant from another company. If closer examination reveals that the new plant would increase production capacity by only 35 percent, this alternative may not be satisfactory. Finally, when an alternative has proven both feasible and satisfactory, its probable consequences must still be assessed. To what extent will a particular alternative influence other parts of the organization? What financial and nonfinancial costs will be associated with such influences? For example, a plan to boost sales by cutting prices may disrupt cash flows, need a new advertising program, and alter the behavior of sales representatives because it requires a different commission structure. The manager, then, must put "price tags" on the consequences of each alternative. Even an alternative that is both feasible and satisfactory must be eliminated if its consequences are too expensive for the total system. Cahill decided that being taken over would cause too great a loss of autonomy (consequences not affordable), that buying a competitor was too expensive (not feasible), and that doing nothing would not solve the problem (not satisfactory).

Selecting the Best Alternative Even though many alternatives fail to pass the triple tests of feasibility, satisfactoriness, and affordable consequences, two or more alternatives may remain. Choosing the best of these is the real crux of decision making. One approach is to choose the alternative with the highest combined level of feasibility, satisfactoriness, and affordable consequences. Even though most situations do not lend themselves to objective, mathematical analysis, the manager can often develop subjective estimates and weights for choosing an alternative.

Optimization is also a frequent goal. Because a decision is likely to affect several individuals or subunits, any feasible alternative will probably not maximize all the relevant goals. Suppose that the manager of the Kansas City Royals needs to select one new outfielder for the next baseball season. Bill hits .350 but is barely able to catch a fly ball; Joe hits only .175 but is outstanding in the field;

and Sam hits .290 and is a solid but not outstanding fielder. The manager would probably select Sam because of the optimal balance of hitting and fielding. Decision makers should also remember that finding multiple acceptable alternatives may be possible—selecting just one alternative and rejecting all the others may not be necessary. For example, the Royals' manager might decide that Sam will start each game, Bill will be retained as a pinch hitter, and Joe will be retained as a defensive substitute. In many hiring decisions the candidates remaining after evaluation are ranked. If the top candidate rejects the offer, it may be automatically extended to the number two candidate, and, if necessary, to the remaining candidates in order. The managers at Olin Pool Products selected the alternative of overhauling the organization to become more competitive.

Implementing the Chosen Alternative   After an alternative has been selected, the manager must put it into effect. In some decision situations implementation is fairly easy; in others it is more difficult. In the case of an acquisition, for example, managers must decide how to integrate all the activities of the new business, including purchasing, human resource practices, and distribution, into an ongoing organizational framework. For example, after Kimberly-Clark acquired Scott Paper, it took over a year to integrate the two firms into a single one. Operational plans, discussed in Chapter 3, are useful in implementing alternatives.

When managers implement decisions, they must also consider people's resistance to change. The reasons for such resistance include insecurity, inconvenience, and fear of the unknown. When Penney's managers decided to move the company's headquarters from New York to Texas, many employees chose to resign rather than to relocate. Managers should anticipate potential resistance at various stages of the implementation process. (Resistance to change is covered in Chapter 7.) Managers should also recognize that, even when all alternatives have been evaluated as precisely as possible and the consequences of each alternative weighed, unanticipated consequences are still likely. Any number of things—unexpected cost increases, a less-than-perfect fit with existing organizational subsystems, or unpredicted effects on cash flow or operating expenses, for example—could develop after implementation has begun. Doug Cahill eliminated several levels of management at Olin, combined fourteen departments into eight, gave new authority to every manager, and empowered employees to take greater control over their work.

Following Up and Evaluating the Results   The final step in the decision-making process requires managers to evaluate the effectiveness of their decision—that is, they should make sure that the chosen alternative has served its original purpose. If an implemented alternative appears not to be working, managers can respond in several ways. Another previously identified alternative (the second or third choice) could be adopted. Or the managers might recognize that the situation was not correctly defined to start with and begin the process all over again. Finally, they might decide that the original alternative is in fact appropriate but has not yet had time to work or should be implemented in a different way.

Failure to evaluate decision effectiveness may have serious consequences. The Pentagon spent $1.8 billion and eight years developing the Sergeant York antiaircraft gun. From the beginning, tests revealed major problems with the weapon system, but not until it was in its final stages, when it was demonstrated to be completely ineffective, was the project scrapped.[14] In a classic case of poor decision making, managers at Coca-Cola decided to change the formula for the soft drink. Consumer response was extremely negative. In contrast to the Pentagon, however, Coca-Cola immediately reacted: it reintroduced the old formula within three months as Coca-Cola Classic and quickly recovered from its mistake.[15] Had managers stubbornly stuck with their decision and failed to evaluate its effectiveness, the results would have been disastrous. Doug Cahill's decisions at Olin are paying big dividends—the firm's profits are back up and most of the market share it recently lost has been regained as well.

Behavioral Aspects of Decision Making

administrative model A decision-making model that argues that decision makers (1) have incomplete and imperfect information, (2) are constrained by bounded rationality, and (3) tend to satisfice when making decisions

If all decision situations were approached as logically as described in the previous section, more decisions would be successful. Yet decisions are often made with little consideration for logic and rationality. Some experts have estimated that U.S. companies use rational decision-making techniques less than 20 percent of the time.[16] And even when organizations try to be logical, they sometimes fail. For example, managers at Coca-Cola decided to change Coke's formula after four years of extensive marketing research, taste tests, and rational deliberation—but the decision was still wrong. On the other hand, sometimes when a decision is made with little regard for logic, it can still turn out to be correct. An important ingredient in how these forces work is the behavioral aspect of decision making. The administrative model better reflects these subjective considerations. Other behavioral aspects include political forces, intuition and escalation of commitment, risk propensity, and ethics.

FIGURE 4.4
The Administrative Model of Decision Making

The administrative model is based on behavioral processes that affect how managers make decisions. Rather than prescribing how decisions should be made, it focuses more on describing how they are made.

■ The Administrative Model

Herbert A. Simon was one of the first experts to recognize that decisions are not always made with rationality and logic.[17] Simon was subsequently awarded the Nobel Prize in economics. Rather than prescribing how decisions should be made, his view of decision making, now called the **administrative model**, describes how decisions often actually are made. As illustrated in Figure 4.4, the model holds that managers (1) have incomplete and imperfect information, (2) are constrained by bounded rationality, and (3) tend to satisfice when making decisions.

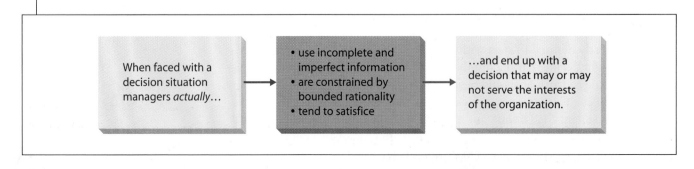

Bounded rationality suggests that decision makers are limited by their values and unconscious reflexes, skills, and habits. They are also limited by incomplete information and knowledge. Bounded rationality partially explains how U.S. auto executives allowed Japanese auto makers to get such a strong foothold in their domestic market. For years, executives at GM, Ford, and Chrysler compared their companies' performance to only one another and ignored foreign imports. The foreign "threat" wasn't acknowledged until the domestic auto market had been changed forever. If managers had gathered complete information from the beginning, they might have been better able to thwart foreign competitors. Essentially, then, the concept of bounded rationality suggests that although people try to be rational decision makers, their rationality has limits.

Another important part of the administrative model is **satisficing**. This concept suggests that rather than conducting an exhaustive search for the best possible alternative, decision makers tend to search only until they identify an alternative that meets some minimum standard of sufficiency. A manager looking for a site for a new plant, for example, may select the first site he finds that meets basic requirements for transportation, utilities, and price, even though further search might yield a better location. People satisfice for a variety of reasons. Managers may simply be unwilling to ignore their own motives (such as reluctance to spend time making a decision) and therefore not be able to continue searching after a minimally acceptable alternative is identified. The decision maker may be unable to weigh and evaluate large numbers of alternatives and criteria. Also, subjective and personal considerations often intervene in decision situations.

Because of the inherent imperfection of information, bounded rationality, and satisficing, a manager's decisions may or may not actually be in the best interests of the organization. A manager may choose a particular location for the new plant because it offers the lowest price and best availability of utilities and transportation. Or the manager may choose the location because it's in a community in which he or she wants to live.

In summary, then, the classical and administrative models paint quite different pictures of decision making. Which is more correct? Actually, each can be used to better understand how managers make decisions. The classical model is prescriptive: it explains how managers can at least attempt to be more rational and logical in their approach to decisions. Managers can use the administrative model to develop a better understanding of their inherent biases and limitations.[18] In the following sections, we describe more fully other behavioral forces that can influence decisions.

■ Political Forces in Decision Making

Political forces are another major element that contributes to the behavioral nature of decision making. Organizational politics is covered in Chapter 11, but one major element of politics, coalitions, is especially relevant to decision making. A **coalition** is an informal alliance of individuals or groups formed to achieve a common goal. This common goal is often a preferred decision alternative. For example, coalitions of stockholders frequently band together to force a board of directors to make a certain decision.

bounded rationality A concept suggesting that decision makers are limited by their values and unconscious reflexes, skills, and habits

satisficing The tendency to search for alternatives only until one is found that meets some minimum standard of sufficiency

coalition An informal alliance of individuals or groups formed to achieve a common goal

Coalitions led to the formation of Unisys Corporation, a large computer firm. Sperry, once a U.S. computer giant, was forced to the edge of bankruptcy by a series of poor decisions. Two major executives waged battle for three years over what to do. One wanted to get out of the computer business altogether, and the other wanted to stay in. Finally, the manager who wanted to remain in the computer business garnered enough support to earn promotion to the corporation's presidency. The other manager took early retirement. Shortly thereafter, Sperry agreed to be acquired by Burroughs Wellcome Co. The resulting combined company is called Unisys.[19]

The impact of coalitions can be either positive or negative. They can help astute managers get the organization on a path toward effectiveness and profitability, or they can strangle well-conceived strategies and decisions. Managers must recognize when to use coalitions, how to assess whether coalitions are acting in the best interests of the organization, and how to constrain their dysfunctional effects.

intuition An innate belief about something without conscious consideration

escalation of commitment A decision maker's staying with a decision even when it appears to be wrong

■ Intuition and Escalation of Commitment

Two other important decision processes that go beyond logic and rationality are intuition and escalation of commitment to a chosen course of action.

Intuition **Intuition** is an innate belief about something without conscious consideration. Managers sometimes decide to do something because it "feels right" or they have a hunch. This feeling is usually not arbitrary, however. Rather, it is based on years of experience and practice in making decisions in similar situations. An inner sense may help managers make an occasional decision without going through a full-blown rational sequence of steps. For example, the New York Yankees recently told three major sneaker manufacturers, Nike, Reebok, and Adidas, that the team was looking for a sponsorship deal. While Nike and Reebok were carefully and rationally assessing the possibilities, managers at Adidas quickly realized that a partnership with the Yankees made a lot of sense. Adidas responded very quickly to the idea and ended up hammering out a contract while the competitors were still analyzing details.[20] Of course, all managers, but most especially inexperienced ones, should be careful not to rely on intuition too heavily. If rationality and logic are continually flaunted for what "feels right," the odds are that disaster will strike one day.

Risk propensity is an important behavioral process that affects many decisions. When Harlem entrepreneur Melba Wilson was looking for new business opportunities, she could have pursued any number of relatively "safe" possibilities. Instead, however, she chose to gamble on a risky course of action—reopening Minton's Playhouse, a famous jazz club that had been shuttered for decades.

Escalation of Commitment Another important behavioral process that influences decision making is **escalation of commitment** to a chosen course of action. In particular, decision makers sometimes make decisions and then become so committed to the course of action suggested

by that decision that they stay with it, even when it appears to have been wrong.[21] For example, when people buy stock in a company, they sometimes refuse to sell it even after repeated drops in price. These investors choose a course of action—buying the stock in anticipation of making a profit—and then stay with it even in the face of increasing losses.

For years Pan American World Airways ruled the skies and used its profits to diversify into real estate and other businesses. But with the advent of deregulation, Pan Am began to struggle and lose market share to other carriers. When Pan Am managers finally realized how ineffective the airline operations had become, experts today point out that the "rational" decision would have been to sell off the remaining airline operations and concentrate on the firm's more profitable businesses. But because they still saw the company as being first and foremost an airline, they instead began to slowly sell off the firm's profitable holdings to keep the airline flying. Eventually, the company was left with nothing but an ineffective and inefficient airline and then had to sell off its more profitable routes before eventually being taken over by Delta. Had Pan Am managers made the more rational decision years earlier, chances are the firm could still be a profitable enterprise, albeit one with no involvement in the airline industry.[22]

Thus decision makers must walk a fine line. On the one hand, they must guard against sticking with an incorrect decision too long. To do so can bring about financial decline. On the other hand, managers should not bail out of a seemingly incorrect decision too soon, as Adidas did several years ago. Adidas once dominated the market for professional athletic shoes. It subsequently entered the market for amateur sports shoes and did well there also. But managers interpreted a sales slowdown as a sign that the boom in athletic shoes was over. They thought that they had made the wrong decision and ordered drastic cutbacks. The market took off again with Nike at the head of the pack, and Adidas never recovered. Fortunately, a new management team has changed the way Adidas makes decisions and, as illustrated earlier, the firm is again on its way to becoming a force in the athletic shoe and apparel markets.

■ Risk Propensity and Decision Making

The behavioral element of **risk propensity** is the extent to which a decision maker is willing to gamble when making a decision. Some managers are cautious about every decision they make. They try to adhere to the rational model and are extremely conservative in what they do. Such managers are more likely to avoid mistakes, and they infrequently make decisions that lead to big losses. Other managers are extremely aggressive in making decisions and are willing to take risks. They rely heavily on intuition, reach decisions quickly, and often risk big investments on their decisions. As in gambling, aggressive players are more likely than their conservative counterparts to achieve big successes with their decisions; they are also more likely to incur greater losses. The organization's culture is a prime ingredient in fostering different levels of risk propensity.

risk propensity The extent to which a decision maker is willing to gamble in making a decision

■ Ethics and Decision Making

As explained in Chapter 2, individual ethics are personal beliefs about right and wrong behavior. Ethics are clearly related to decision making in a number of ways. For example, suppose after careful analysis a manager realizes that her company could save money by closing her department and subcontracting with a supplier for the same services. But to recommend this course of action would result in the loss of several jobs, including her own. Her own ethical standards will clearly shape how she proceeds.[23] Indeed, each component of managerial ethics (relationships of the firm to its employees, of employees to the firm, and of the firm to other economic agents) involves numerous decisions, all of which are likely to have an ethical component. Managers must remember, then, that just as behavioral processes such as politics and risk propensity affect the decisions they make, so too do their ethical beliefs.

Group and Team Decision Making in Organizations

In more and more organizations today, important decisions are made by groups and teams rather than by individuals. Examples include the executive committee of General Motors, product design teams at Texas Instruments, and marketing planning groups at Compaq Computer. Managers can typically choose whether to have individuals or groups and teams make a particular decision. Thus knowing about forms of group and team decision making and their advantages and disadvantages is important.[24]

■ Forms of Group and Team Decision Making

The most common methods of group and team decision making are interacting groups, Delphi groups, and nominal groups.

interacting group or team A decision-making group or team in which members openly discuss, argue about, and agree on the best alternative

Interacting Groups and Teams **Interacting groups and teams** are the most common form of decision-making group. The format is simple—either an existing or a newly designated group or team is asked to make a decision. Existing groups or teams might be functional departments, regular work teams, or standing committees. Newly designated groups or teams can be ad hoc committees, task forces, or newly constituted work teams. The group or team members talk among themselves, argue, agree, argue some more, form internal coalitions, and so forth. Finally, after some period of deliberation, the group or team makes its decision. An advantage of this method is that the interaction between people often sparks new ideas and promotes understanding. A major disadvantage, though, is that political processes can play too big a role.

Delphi group A form of group decision making in which a group is used to achieve a consensus of expert opinion

Delphi Groups A **Delphi group** is sometimes used for developing a consensus of expert opinion. Developed by the Rand Corporation, the Delphi procedure solicits input from a panel of experts who contribute individually. Their opinions are combined and, in effect, averaged. Assume, for example, that the problem is to establish an expected date for a major technological breakthrough in converting coal into usable energy. The first step in using the Delphi procedure is to obtain the cooperation of a panel of experts. For this situation, experts might include various research scientists, university researchers, and executives in a relevant energy industry. At first the experts are asked to anonymously predict a time frame for the expected breakthrough. The Delphi group coordinators collect the responses, average them, and ask the experts for another prediction. In this round the experts who provided unusual or extreme predictions may be asked to justify them. These explanations may then be relayed to the other experts. When the predictions stabilize, the average prediction is taken to represent the decision of the "group" of experts. The time, expense, and logistics of the Delphi technique rule out its use for routine, everyday decisions, but it has been successfully used for forecasting technological breakthroughs at Boeing, market potential for new products at General Motors, research and development patterns at Eli Lilly, and future economic conditions by the U.S. government.[25]

Nominal Groups   Another useful group and team decision-making technique occasionally used is the **nominal group**. Unlike the Delphi method, where group members do not see one another, nominal group members are brought together. The members represent a group in name only, however; they do not talk to one another freely like the members of interacting groups. Nominal groups are used most often to generate creative and innovative alternatives or ideas. To begin, the manager assembles a group of knowledgeable people and outlines the problem to them. The group members are then asked to individually write down as many alternatives as they can think of. The members then take turns stating their ideas, which are recorded on a flip chart or board at the front of the room. Discussion is limited to simple clarification. After all alternatives have been listed, more open discussion takes place. Group members then vote, usually by rank-ordering the various alternatives. The highest-ranking alternative represents the decision of the group. Of course, the manager in charge may retain the authority to accept or reject the group decision.

More and more often these days, businesses are relying on groups and teams to make critical decisions. Hewlett-Packard recently announced an ambitious program to dramatically improve customer satisfaction with its products. HP assigned the program to two managers, Mei-Lin Cheng and Julie Anderson, and their team. But HP left all the details and major decisions associated with meeting its customer satisfaction goals in the hands of the team.

■ Advantages of Group and Team Decision Making

The advantages and disadvantages of group and team decision making relative to individual decision making are summarized in Table 4.2. One advantage is simply that more information is available in a group or team setting—as suggested by the old axiom "Two heads are better than one." A group or team represents a variety of education, experience, and perspective. Partly because of this increased information, groups and teams typically can identify and evaluate

nominal group   A structured technique used to generate creative and innovative alternatives or ideas

more alternatives than can one person.[26] The people involved in a group or team decision understand the logic and rationale behind it, are more likely to accept it, and are equipped to communicate the decision to their work groups or departments.[27] Finally, evidence suggests that group decisions may be better than individual decisions.[28]

■ Disadvantages of Group and Team Decision Making

groupthink   A situation that occurs when a group or team's desire for consensus and cohesiveness overwhelms its desire to reach the best possible decision

Perhaps the biggest drawback of group and team decision making is the additional time and hence the greater expense entailed. The increased time stems from interaction and discussion among group or team members. If a given manager's time is worth $50 an hour and the manager spends two hours making a decision, the decision "costs" the organization $100. For the same decision, a group of five managers might require three hours of time. At the same $50-an-hour rate, the decision "costs" the organization $750. Assuming the group or team decision is better, the additional expense may be justified, but the fact remains that group and team decision making is more costly.

Group or team decisions may also represent undesirable compromises.[29] For example, hiring a compromise top manager may be a bad decision in the long run because he or she may not be able to respond adequately to various subunits in the organization and may not have everyone's complete support. Sometimes one individual dominates the group process to the point where others cannot make a full contribution. This dominance may stem from a desire for power or from a naturally dominant personality. The problem is that what appears to emerge as a group decision may actually be the decision of one person.

Finally, a group or team may succumb to a phenomenon known as groupthink. **Groupthink** occurs when the desire for consensus and cohesiveness overwhelms the goal of reaching the best possible decision.[30] Under the influence of groupthink, the group may arrive at decisions that are not in the best interest of either the group or the organization but rather avoid conflict among group members. One of the clearest documented examples of groupthink involved the space shuttle *Challenger* disaster. As NASA was preparing to launch the shuttle, numerous problems and questions arose. At each step of the way, however, decision makers argued that there was no reason to delay and that everything would be fine. Shortly after the launch on January 28, 1986, the shuttle exploded, killing all seven crew members.

TABLE 4.2
Advantages and Disadvantages of Group and Team Decision Making

To increase the chances that a group or team decision will be successful, managers must learn how to manage the process of group and team decision making. Westinghouse, Federal Express, and IBM are increasingly using groups and teams in the decision-making process.

Advantages	Disadvantages
1. More information and knowledge are available.	1. The process takes longer than individual decision making, so it is costlier.
2. More alternatives are likely to be generated.	2. Compromise decisions resulting from indecisiveness may emerge.
3. More acceptance of the final decision is likely.	3. One person may dominate the group.
4. Enhanced communication of the decision may result.	4. Groupthink may occur.
5. Better decisions generally emerge.	

■ Managing Group and Team Decision-Making Processes

Managers can do several things to help promote the effectiveness of group and team decision making. One is simply being aware of the pros and cons of having a group or team make a decision. Time and cost can be managed by setting a deadline for making the decision. Dominance can be at least partially avoided if a special group is formed just to make the decision. An astute manager, for example, should know who in the organization may try to dominate and can either avoid putting that person in the group or put several strong-willed people together.

To avoid groupthink, each member of the group or team should critically evaluate all alternatives. To encourage members to present divergent viewpoints, the leader should not make his or her own position known too early. At least one member of the group or team might be assigned the role of devil's advocate. And, after reaching a preliminary decision, the group or team should hold a follow-up meeting wherein divergent viewpoints can be raised again if any group members wish to do so.[31] Gould Paper Company used these methods by assigning managers to two different teams. The teams then spent an entire day in a structured debate presenting the pros and cons of each side of an issue to ensure the best possible decision. Sun Microsystems makes most of its major decisions using this approach.

Summary of Key Points

Decisions are an integral part of all managerial activities, but they are perhaps most central to the planning process. Decision making is the act of choosing one alternative from among a set of alternatives. The decision-making process includes recognizing and defining the nature of a decision situation, identifying alternatives, choosing the best alternative, and putting it into practice. Two common types of decisions are programmed and nonprogrammed. Decisions may be made under states of certainty, risk, or uncertainty.

Rational perspectives on decision making rest on the classical model. This model assumes that managers have complete information and that they will behave rationally. The primary steps in rational decision making are (1) recognizing and defining the situation, (2) identifying alternatives, (3) evaluating alternatives, (4) selecting the best alternative, (5) implementing the chosen alternative, and (6) following up and evaluating the effectiveness of the alternative after it is implemented.

Behavioral aspects of decision making rely on the administrative model. This model recognizes that managers will have incomplete information and that they will not always behave rationally. The administrative model also recognizes the concepts of bounded rationality and satisficing. Political activities by coalitions, managerial intuition, and the tendency to become increasingly committed to a chosen course of action are all important. Risk propensity is also an important behavioral perspective on decision making. Finally, ethics also affect how managers make decisions.

To help enhance decision-making effectiveness, managers often use interacting, Delphi, or nominal groups or teams. Group and team decision making in general has several advantages as well as disadvantages relative to individual decision making. Managers can adopt a number of strategies to help groups and teams make better decisions.

Discussion Questions

Questions for Review

1. Describe the nature of decision making.

2. Identify and discuss the conditions under which most decisions are made.

3. What are the main features of the classical model of the decision-making process? What are the main features of the administrative model?

4. What are the steps in rational decision making? Which step do you think is the most difficult to carry out? Why?

5. Describe the behavioral nature of decision making. Be certain to provide some detail about political forces, risk propensity, ethics, and commitment in your description.

Questions for Analysis

1. Was your decision about what college or university to attend a rational decision? Did you go through each step in rational decision making? If not, why not?

2. Can any decision be purely rational, or are all decisions at least partially behavioral in nature? Defend your answer.

3. Think of an example for each condition for decision making. Then describe how conditions might change to alter the condition for each decision.

4. Is satisficing always a bad thing? Under what conditions, if any, might it be desirable?

5. Under what conditions would you expect group or team decision making to be preferable to individual decision making, and vice versa? Why?

Building Effective Decision-Making & Communication Skills

EXERCISE OVERVIEW

Decision-making skills refer to the manager's ability to correctly recognize and define problems and opportunities and to then select an appropriate course of action to solve problems and capitalize on opportunities. Communication skills refer to the manager's abilities to both effectively convey ideas and information to others and to effectively receive ideas and information from others. Not surprisingly, these skills can be highly interrelated. This exercise gives you insights into some of those interrelations.

EXERCISE BACKGROUND

Identify a decision that you will need to make sometime in the near future. If you work in a managerial position, you might select a real problem or issue to address. For example, you might use the selection or termination of an employee, the allocation of pay raises, or the selection of someone for a promotion.

If you do not work in a managerial position, you might instead select an upcoming decision related to your academic work. Example decisions might include what major to select, whether to attend summer school or to work, which job to select, or whether to live on or off campus next year. Be sure to select a decision that you have not yet made.

EXERCISE TASK

Using the decision selected above, do the following:

1. On a sheet of paper, list the kinds of information that you will most likely use in making your decision. Beside each item, make notes as to where you

can obtain the information, what form the information will be presented in, the reliability of the information, and other characteristics of the information that you deem to be relevant.

2. Assume that you have used the information obtained above and have now made the decision. (It might be helpful at this point to select a hypothetical decision and choice to frame your answers. For instance, you might choose selecting a new plant location as the decision, and St. Louis, Missouri as the choice.) On the other side of the paper, list the various communication consequences that come with your decision. For example, if your choice involves an academic major, you may need to inform your advisor and your family. List as many consequences as you can. Beside each entry, make notes as to how you would communicate with each party, the timeliness of your communication, and other factors that seem to be relevant.

3. What behavioral forces might play a role in your decision?

Building Effective Interpersonal Skills

EXERCISE OVERVIEW

Interpersonal skills refer to the manager's ability to understand and motivate individuals and groups. This exercise allows you to practice your interpersonal skills in a role-playing exercise.

EXERCISE BACKGROUND

You supervise a group of six employees who work in an indoor facility in a relatively isolated location. The company you work for has recently adopted an ambiguous policy regarding smoking. Essentially, the policy states that all company work sites are to be smoke free unless the employees at a specific site choose differently and at the discretion of the site supervisor.

Four members of the work group you supervise are smokers. They have come to you with the argument that because they constitute the majority, they should be allowed to smoke at work. The other two members of the group, both nonsmokers, have heard about this proposal and have also discussed the situation with you. They argue that the health-related consequences of secondary smoke should outweigh the preferences of the majority.

To compound the problem, your boss wrote the new policy and is quite defensive about it—numerous individuals have already criticized the policy. You know that your boss will get very angry with you if you also raise concerns about the policy. Finally, you are personally indifferent about the issue. You do not smoke yourself, but your spouse does smoke. Secondary smoke does not bother you, and you do not have strong opinions about it. Still, you have to make a decision. You see that your choices are to (1) mandate a smoke-free environment, (2) allow smoking in the facility, or (3) ask your boss to clarify the policy.

EXERCISE TASK

Based on the background presented above, assume that you are the supervisor and do the following:

1. Assume that you have chosen option one. Prepare an outline that you will use to announce your decision to the four smokers.

2. Assume that you have chosen option two. Prepare an outline that you will use to announce your decision to the two nonsmokers.

3. Assume that you have chosen option three. Prepare an outline that you will use when you meet with your boss.

4. Are there other alternatives?

5. What would you do if you were actually the group supervisor?

Building Effective Technical Skills

EXERCISE OVERVIEW

Technical skills are the skills necessary to accomplish or understand the specific kind of work being done in an organization. This exercise enables you to practice technical skills using the Internet to obtain information for making a decision.

EXERCISE BACKGROUND

Assume that you are a business owner seeking a location for a new factory. Your company makes products that are relatively "clean"—that is, they do not pollute the environment; in addition, your factory does not produce any dangerous waste products. Thus, most communities would welcome your plant.

You are seeking a place that has a stable and well-educated workforce, a good quality of life, good health care, and a good educational system. You have narrowed your choice to the following towns:

1. Columbia, Missouri

2. Madison, Wisconsin

3. Manhattan, Kansas

4. College Station, Texas

5. Baton Rouge, Louisiana

6. Athens, Georgia

EXERCISE TASK

With the background information above as context, do the following:

1. Use the Internet to learn about these cities.

2. Rank-order each city on the basis of the criteria noted above.

3. Select the best city for your new factory.

In 1992, Cynthia Spenser made an important decision that had a major effect on Sunset Landscape Services. Around the same time that SLS was built, a local developer had built a small shopping complex adjacent to the Spensers' site. This complex had an elegant ambiance and was named The Arbor. Its retail tenants included an interior decorator, a gourmet coffee shop, an upscale toy store, a bookstore, and a clothing store.

For years there had been considerable synergy between The Arbor and Sunset Landscape Services. The two establishments shared a parking lot, for example, and many customers could be observed strolling back and forth between SLS and The Arbor. Indeed, many people assumed that the two were actually one business.

The developer who had originally built The Arbor retired in 1992 and put the property on the market. The Spensers initially were quite concerned by this event. They feared that a new owner might revamp the shopping complex and alter the tenant mix in some way that might be to their disadvantage. Mark joked that it might be turned into a tattoo parlor or a video emporium.

But the Spensers soon decided that their fears were groundless. The current tenants of The Arbor all had long-term leases, and the property was in a location that would not work as well for other kinds of businesses. Mark put his concerns aside and went back to work on a big landscaping project. Cynthia, however, continued to think about the property.

She soon realized that she wanted to buy The Arbor herself. Aside from helping to protect the business interests of Sunset Landscape Services, The Arbor was an attractive investment. Its cash flow was strong, and the tenant base solid. And whenever a tenant left, the owner had been able to attract a replacement with little difficulty.

Cynthia also felt that The Arbor had additional possibilities. For example, the property behind the shopping complex was vacant, so the retail center could easily be expanded. Moreover, Cynthia was excited about the possibility of running her own business, rather than essentially managing one of Mark's businesses. Although she was the co-owner of SLS and obviously had considerable control over the nursery, the business itself had been conceptualized and planned by Mark. Cynthia also felt constrained by the overall landscape services environment. The Arbor, she realized, would represent something that she could put her own stamp on. The more she thought about it, the more she realized that she had made the decision to buy The Arbor.

DISCUSSION QUESTIONS

1. What perspectives on decision making are reflected in this case?

2. What role have various behavioral processes played in Cynthia's decision?

3. What challenges and hurdles does Cynthia face?

DECISION-MAKING STYLES

Introduction: Decision making is clearly important. However, individuals differ in their decision-making style, or the way that they approach decisions.

The following assessment is designed to help you understand your decision-making style.

Instructions: Respond to the following statements by indicating the extent to which they describe you. Circle the response that best represents your self-evaluation.

1. Overall, I'm _____ to act.
   1. quick   2. moderately fast   3. slow

2. I spend _____ amount of time making important decisions as/than I do making less important ones.
   1. about the same   2. a greater   3. a much greater

3. When making decisions, I _____ go with my first thought.
   1. usually   2. occasionally 3. rarely

4. When making decisions, I'm _____ concerned about making errors.
   1. rarely   2. occasionally 3. often

5. When making decisions, I _____ recheck my work more than once.
   1. rarely   2. occasionally 3. usually

6. When making decisions, I gather _____ information.
   1. little   2. some   3. lots of

7. When making decisions, I consider _____ alternatives.
   1. few   2. some   3. lots of

8. I usually make decisions _____ before the deadline.
   1. way   2. somewhat   3. just

9. After making a decision, I _____ look for other alternatives, wishing I had waited.
   1. rarely   2. occasionally 3. usually

10. I _____ regret having made a decision.
    1. rarely   2. occasionally 3. often

For interpretation, turn to page 457.

Source: Adapted from Lussier, Robert N. *Supervision: A Skill-Building Approach*, Second Edition, pp. 122–123, copyright 1994 by Richard D. Irwin, Inc. Reproduced with permission of The McGraw-Hill Companies.

Experiential Exercise

PROGRAMMED AND NONPROGRAMMED DECISION MAKING

Purpose: This exercise allows you to make decisions and helps you understand the difference between programmed and nonprogrammed decisions. You also learn how decision making by an individual differs from decision making by a group.

Introduction: You are asked to make decisions both individually and as a member of a group.

Instructions: Following is a list of typical organizational decisions. Your task is to determine whether they are programmed or nonprogrammed. Number your paper, and write P for programmed or N for nonprogrammed next to each number.

Next, your instructor will divide the class into groups of four to seven. All groups should have approximately the same number of members. Your task as a group is to make the decisions that you just made as individuals. In arriving at your decisions, do not use techniques such as voting or negotiating ("OK, I'll give in on this one if you'll give in on that one"). The group should discuss the difference between programmed and nonprogrammed decisions and each decision situation until all members at least partly agree with the decision.

Decision List:

1. Hiring a specialist for the research staff in a highly technical field

2. Assigning workers to daily tasks

3. Determining the size of the dividend to be paid to shareholders in the ninth consecutive year of strong earnings growth

4. Deciding whether to officially excuse an employee's absence for medical reasons

5. Selecting the location for another branch of a 150-branch bank in a large city

6. Approving the appointment of a new law school graduate to the corporate legal staff

7. Making the annual assignment of graduate assistants to the faculty

8. Approving the request of an employee to attend a local seminar in his or her special area of expertise

9. Selecting the appropriate outlets for print advertisements for a new college textbook

10. Determining the location for a new fast-food restaurant in a small but growing town on the major interstate highway between two very large metropolitan areas

Follow-up Questions:

1. To what extent did group members disagree about which decisions were programmed and which were nonprogrammed?

2. What primary factors did the group discuss in making each decision?

3. Were there any differences between the members' individual lists and the group lists? If so, discuss the reasons for the differences.

Source: From *Organizational Behavior,* 4th ed., by Gregory Moorhead and Ricky Griffin. Copyright © 1995 by Houghton Mifflin Company. Reprinted by permission.

CASE STUDY

The Path Not Taken

Sears, Roebuck and Company and Montgomery Ward were founded just a few years apart (Sears in 1893 and Ward in 1872) and together controlled the retailing landscape in the United States for more than half a century. For decades their growth and competitive strategies were mirror images. For example, their department stores dominated downtown areas and were often located within a city block of each other. Reading their mail-order catalogs became a ubiquitous part of American life. They even shared the same corporate headquarters location, Chicago. But after decades of parallel strategies and growth, critical decisions at each firm coming at just about the same time put them on dramatically different paths, one to fortune and success and one to the brink of ruin.

These decisions came immediately after the end of World War II. Executives at Sears looked carefully at demographic data and patterns and concluded that the citizens of the United States were on the verge of a massive exodus away from central downtown areas to the suburbs. These same executives decided to invest in this trend by moving along with the families who were becoming "suburbanites." Sears began opening its new stores in suburban locations, for example, usually as "anchors" in an emerging form of retailing—the enclosed shopping mall.

Montgomery Ward, however, followed a different course. Ward's CEO at the time, Sewell Avery, believed that the suburbs were a fad. More significantly, he also believed in a distorted view of economic history, which seemed to suggest that a major depression had followed every war since the time of Napoleon. Because World War II had just ended, Avery reasoned that a major depression was about to strike. And indeed, Sears was stretched so thin by its expansion that if a depression had occurred, the firm would have gone under.

But the depression never came, and Sears flourished. Between 1946, when its expansion started, and 1956, the company's revenues more than doubled, and it became the undisputed leader in the retailing industry. Although the firm hit some snags in the 1980s and was overtaken by Wal-Mart, Sears has remained a major force in the retailing industry and is still profitable and financially healthy.

But Ward never recovered from its decision to remain entrenched in the inner cities. Even worse, however, was Sewell Avery's steadfast commitment to his beliefs and his unwillingness to even consider that perhaps he was wrong. Amazingly, Montgomery Ward did not open a single new store between 1941 and 1957. And during this entire era, Avery clung to his beliefs that a depression was imminent, Sears would collapse, and Ward would be able to buy its competitor at a fraction of its worth!

Ward's board finally gave up on Avery's vision in 1955 and forced him out. But by then it was too late. Sears and J.C. Penney had sewn up the best suburban locations and established themselves in the minds of suburbanites as "the" department stores. And Ward was never really able to break back into the mix. The firm continued to stumble along but reached its nadir in 1997 when it was finally forced to file for bankruptcy protection from its creditors. Whether or not the venerable retailer will be able to figure out how to reinvent itself, of course, remains to be seen. But whatever the outcome, Ward's insiders can only think about what might have been if Avery Sewell had been willing to reconsider his decision a half a century earlier.

Case Questions

1. Describe the decision-making processes that likely took place at Sears and Ward in the 1940s.
2. Discuss how behavioral processes affected decisions at Ward.
3. Under what circumstances might group decision making at Ward have resulted in the same outcome? a better outcome?

Case References: "You Snooze, You Lose," *Newsweek,* July 21, 1997, p. 50; *Hoover's Handbook of American Business 1998* (Austin, Texas: Hoover's Business Press, 1998), pp. 946–947; 1198–1199.

CHAPTER NOTES

1. "Pulp Fiction at Kimberly-Clark," *Business Week*, February 23, 1998, pp. 90-91; "The Battle of the Bottoms," *Forbes*, March 24, 1997, pp. 98–103 (quote on page 100); "Strength Ahead?" *Barrons*, July 28, 1997, p. 13.

2. Richard Priem, "Executive Judgment, Organizational Congruence, and Firm Performance," *Organization Science*, August 1994, pp. 421–432.

3. Paul Nutt, "The Formulation Processes and Tactics Used in Organizational Decision Making," *Organization Science*, May 1993, pp. 226–240.

4. For recent reviews of decision making, see E. Frank Harrison, *The Managerial Decision-Making Process*, 4th ed. (Boston: Houghton Mifflin, 1995).

5. "Kodak Moment Came Early for CEO Fisher, Who Takes a Stumble," *Wall Street Journal*, July 25, 1997, pp. A1, A6.

6. George P. Huber, *Managerial Decision Making* (Glenview, Ill.: Scott, Foresman, 1980).

7. Huber, *Managerial Decision Making*. See also David W. Miller and Martin K. Starr, *The Structure of Human Decisions* (Englewood Cliffs, N.J.: Prentice-Hall, 1976); and Alvar Elbing, *Behavioral Decisions in Organizations*, 2nd ed. (Glenview, Ill.: Scott, Foresman, 1978).

8. Huber, *Managerial Decision Making*.

9. See Bart Nooteboom, Hans Berger, and Niels G. Noorderhaven, "Effects of Trust and Governance on Relational Risk," *Academy of Management Journal*, Vol. 40, No. 2, 1997, pp. 308–338. See also Avi Fiegenbaum and Howard Thomas, "Attitudes Toward Risk and the Risk-Return Paradox: Prospect Theory Explanations," *Academy of Management Journal*, March 1988, pp. 85–106; Jitendra V. Singh, "Performance, Slack, and Risk Taking in Organizational Decision Making," *Academy of Management Journal*, September 1986, pp. 562–585; and James G. March and Zur Shapira, "Managerial Perspectives on Risk and Risk Taking," *Management Science*, November 1987, pp. 1404–1418.

10. "Taking the Angst Out of Taking a Gamble," *Business Week*, July 14, 1997, pp. 52–53.

11. See Richard M. Cyert and Morris H. DeGroot, "The Maximization Process Under Uncertainty," in Patrick D. Larkey and Lee S. Sproull (eds.), *Information Processing in Organizations* (Greenwich, Conn.: JAI Press, 1984), pp. 47–61.

12. Glen Whyte, "Decision Failures: Why They Occur and How to Prevent Them," *Academy of Management Executive*, August 1991, pp. 23–31.

13. Thomas Stewart, "How to Lead a Revolution," *Fortune*, November 28, 1994, pp. 48–61.

14. Kenneth Labich, "Coups and Catastrophes," *Fortune*, December 23, 1985, p. 125.

15. "You Snooze, You Lose," *Newsweek*, July 21, 1997, p. 50.

16. "The Wisdom of Solomon," *Newsweek*, August 17, 1987, pp. 62–63.

17. Herbert A. Simon, *Administrative Behavior* (New York: Free Press, 1945). Simon's ideas have been recently refined and updated in Herbert A. Simon, *Administrative Behavior*, 3rd ed. (New York: Free Press, 1976) and Herbert A. Simon, "Making Management Decisions: The Role of Intuition and Emotion," *Academy of Management Executive*, February 1987, pp. 57–63.

18. Patricia Corner, Angelo Kinicki, and Barbara Keats, "Integrating Organizational and Individual Information Processing Perspectives on Choice," *Organization Science*, August 1994, pp. 294–302.

19. "Unisys: So Far, So Good—But the Real Test Is Yet to Come," *Business Week*, March 2, 1987, pp. 84–86 and "So Far, Married Life Seems to Agree With Unisys," *Business Week*, October 3, 1988, pp. 122–126.

20. Charles P. Wallace, "Adidas—Back in the Game," *Fortune*, August 18, 1997, pp. 176–182.

21. Barry M. Staw and Jerry Ross, "Good Money After Bad," *Psychology Today*, February 1988, pp. 30–33 and D. Ramona Bobocel and John Meyer, "Escalating Commitment to a Failing Course of Action: Separating the Roles of Choice and Justification," *Journal of Applied Psychology*, Vol. 79, No. 3, 1994, pp. 360–363.

22. "You Snooze, You Lose," *Newsweek*, July 21, 1997, p. 50.

23. Martha I. Finney, "The Catbert Dilemma—The Human Side of Tough Decisions," *HRMagazine*, February 1997, pp. 70–76.

24. Edwin A. Locke, David M. Schweiger, and Gary P. Latham, "Participation in Decision Making: When Should It Be Used?" *Organizational Dynamics*, Winter 1986, pp. 65–79 and Nicholas Baloff and Elizabeth M. Doherty, "Potential Pitfalls in Employee Participation," *Organizational Dynamics*, Winter 1989, pp. 51–62.

25. Andre L. Delbecq, Andrew H. Van de Ven, and David H. Gustafson, *Group Techniques for Program Planning* (Glenview, Ill.: Scott, Foresman, 1975) and Michael J. Prietula and Herbert A. Simon, "The Experts in Your Midst," *Harvard Business Review*, January–February 1989, pp. 120–124.

26. Norman P. R. Maier, "Assets and Liabilities in Group Problem Solving: The Need for an Integrative Function," in J. Richard Hackman, Edward E. Lawler III, and Lyman W. Porter (eds.), *Perspectives on Business in Organizations*, 2nd ed. (New York: McGraw-Hill, 1983), pp. 385–392.

27. Anthony L. Iaquinto and James W. Fredrickson, "Top Management Team Agreement About the Strategic Decision Process: A Test of Some of Its Determinants and Consequences," *Strategic Management Journal*, Vol. 18, 1997, pp. 63–75.

28. James H. Davis, *Group Performance* (Reading, Mass.: Addison-Wesley, 1969).

29. Richard A. Cosier and Charles R. Schwenk, "Agreement and Thinking Alike: Ingredients for Poor Decisions," *Academy of Management Executive*, February 1990, pp. 69–78.

30. Irving L. Janis, *Groupthink*, 2nd ed. (Boston: Houghton Mifflin, 1982).

31. Janis, *Groupthink*.

5

Entrepreneurship and New Venture Management

OBJECTIVES

After studying this chapter, you should be able to:

■ Discuss the nature of entrepreneurship.
■ Describe the roles of entrepreneurs in society.
■ Understand the major issues involved in choosing strategies for small firms.
■ Discuss the structural challenges unique to entrepreneurial firms.
■ Understand the determinants of the performance of small firms.

In 1984 James Koch was a high-flying management consultant pulling in $250,000 a year. To the surprise of his family and friends, however, he quit this job and invested his life's savings in starting a new business from scratch and going head-to-head with international competitors in a market that had not had a truly successful specialty product in decades. And to everyone's bigger surprise, he succeeded!

The company Koch founded is Boston Beer Co., and its flagship product is a premium beer called Samuel Adams. Koch's family had actually been brewing beer for generations, and he started with a recipe developed by his great-great-grandfather, who, in the 1870s, sold the beer in St. Louis under the name Louis Koch Lager. To fund the new operation, Koch used $100,000 in personal savings and another $300,000 invested by his friends.

Koch set up shop in an old warehouse in Boston, bought some surplus brewing equipment from a large brewery, and started operations. Because his beer used only the highest quality ingredients, he needed to price it at about $1 more per case than such premium imports as Heineken. Boston-area distributors, meanwhile, doubted that consumers would pay $6 per six-pack for an American beer, and most refused to carry it. Thus Koch was forced to begin selling the beer directly to retailers and bars.

But his big break came when he entered Samuel Adams Lager in the Great American Beer Festival, where it won the consumer preference poll—the industry's equivalent of the Oscar. Koch then started using this victory as his advertising mantra, proclaiming Samuel Adams as "The Best Beer in America." Sales began to take off, and national distributors began calling for the beer. To meet surging demand, Koch contracted part of the brewing to a nearly deserted Stroh's brewery in Pittsburgh.

During the early 1990s, sales of Samuel Adams products grew at an annual rate of more than 57 percent, and in 1996 sales topped $214 million. Koch, meanwhile, has retained controlling interests in the business and still oversees the day-to-day brewing operations. Indeed, he claims that he has sampled at least one of the firm's products every day since the business started, primarily as a way of monitoring quality.

But Koch's success has not gone unnoticed, especially by industry giant Anheuser Busch. Anheuser and other national brewers have recently seen their sales take a hit from so-called microbreweries, small regional or local companies that sell esoteric brews made in small quantities and deriving cache from their very scarcity. The Boston Beer Co. was the first microbrewery to make it big, and most others are trying to follow in its footsteps. Obviously, therefore, Anheuser Busch has a vested interest in not letting these smaller start-ups gain too much market share, most of which would come at its own expense.

Recently, for example, Koch learned that Anheuser had made inquiries about buying the entire crop from a German hops farmer that has an exclusive arrangement with Boston Beer. Had Anheuser succeeded, Koch says, he would have been put out of business. Anheuser has also complained that the labeling on Samuel Adams is misleading, hiding the fact that the beer made in Pittsburgh is actually being brewed under contract by Stroh's, not Boston Beer. And the industry giant has even tried to convince wholesalers, who are highly dependent on Anheuser products like Budweiser, to stop selling specialty beers like Samuel Adams. Koch, meanwhile, simply sees all this attention as a clear sign that he has made it.[1]

"You don't create a whole new national market in the beer business by being frightened."

James Koch, owner, Boston Beer Co.

Just like James Koch, thousands of people all over the world start new businesses each year. And like the Boston Beer Co., some of these businesses succeed; unfortunately, many others fail. Some of the people who fail in a new business try again, and sometimes it takes two or more failures before a successful business gets under way. Henry Ford, for example, went bankrupt twice before succeeding with the Ford Motor Co.

This process of starting a new business, sometimes failing and sometimes succeeding, is part of what is called entrepreneurship, the subject of this chapter. We begin by exploring the nature of entrepreneurship. We then examine the role of entrepreneurship in the business world and discuss strategies for entrepreneurial organizations. Finally, we describe the structure and performance of entrepreneurial organizations.

The Nature of Entrepreneurship

entrepreneurship The process of planning, organizing, operating, and assuming the risk of a business venture

entrepreneur Someone who engages in entrepreneurship

Entrepreneurship is the process of planning, organizing, operating, and assuming the risk of a business venture. An **entrepreneur**, in turn, is someone who engages in entrepreneurship. James Koch, as highlighted in the opening incident, fits this description. He put his own resources on the line and took a personal stake in the success or failure of his budding enterprise. Business owners who hire professional managers to run their businesses and then turn their attention to other interests are not entrepreneurs. Although these people are assuming the risk of the venture, they are not actively involved in organizing or operating it. Likewise, professional managers whose job is running someone else's business are not entrepreneurs, for they assume less-than-total personal risk for the success or failure of the business.

Entrepreneurs find new business through many different approaches. For example, take Dineh Mohajer. A few years ago, when she was studying pre-med at USC, she wanted some blue nail polish to wear to a party but couldn't find just the right shade, so she made it herself. She subsequently decided there is a market among Generation X-ers like herself for new approaches to cosmetics and toiletries. So, she dropped out of school and founded Hard Candy and started marketing nail polish with names like Pimp and Porno. Mohajer's firm now has twenty-five employees and sales of more than $10 million a year.

Entrepreneurs start small businesses. We define a **small business** as one that is privately owned by one individual or a small group of individuals and in which sales and assets are not large enough to influence its environment. A small two-person software development company with annual sales of $100,000 would clearly be a small business, whereas Microsoft Corp. is just as clearly a large business. But the boundaries are not always this clear-cut. For example, a regional retailing chain with twenty stores and annual revenues of $30 million may sound large, but is really very small when compared to such giants as Wal-Mart and Sears.

small business A business that is privately owned by one individual or a small group of individuals; it has sales and assets that are not large enough to influence its environment

The Role of Entrepreneurship in Society

The history of entrepreneurship, and of the development of new businesses, is in many ways the history of great wealth and of great failure. Some entrepreneurs have been very successful and have accumulated vast fortunes from their entrepreneurial efforts. For example, when Microsoft Corp. sold its stock to the public in 1986, Bill Gates, then just thirty years old, received $350 million for his share of Microsoft.[2] Today, his holdings—valued at more than $9 billion—make him one of the richest people in the world. But many other entrepreneurs have lost a great deal of money and fail within the first few years of running a new business. And many others succeed, but at much more modest levels—earning enough income to lead a comfortable life, but not accumulating substantial wealth.

Increasingly, women are spearheading small businesses in the United States.[3] There are many reasons for this trend, two of which we give here. First, some women, frustrated by what they see as limited promotion opportunities in large organizations, see starting their own business as the best route to success. Second, some women see owning their own business as a good way to increase their flexibility vis-à-vis child rearing. Figure 5.1 shows the dramatic increase in women-owned proprietorships in various industries between 1980 and 1990. Current projections for the year 2000 suggest that this trend is continuing.

The experiences of individuals who win (and lose) fortunes as a result of their entrepreneurial activities may make fascinating stories, but the vital role that entrepreneurship plays in our society and our economy is even more telling. More than 99 percent of the nation's sixteen million businesses are small. More than six hundred thousand new businesses are incorporated each year. Their vibrant, almost countless activities influence a number of economic areas, including innovation, job creation, and contributions to large businesses.[4]

■ Innovation

The resourcefulness and ingenuity typical of small business have spawned new industries and contributed a great many innovative ideas and technological breakthroughs to our society. Small businesses or individuals working alone invented, among other things, the personal computer, the transistor radio, the photocopying machine, the jet engine, and the instant photograph. They also gave us the pocket calculator, power steering, the automatic transmission, air conditioning, and even the nineteen-cent ballpoint pen. Some scholars believe that entrepreneurs and small businesses are the driving force behind innovation in a society. As entrepreneurs seek the income and wealth associated with successful innovation, they create new technologies and products that displace older technologies and products.[5]

■ Job Creation

Small businesses create more new jobs than do larger businesses. One study suggested that small businesses may account for as much as 66 percent of all new employment in the United States each year. In another study, the U.S. Department of Commerce found that small, young, high-technology businesses created new jobs at a much faster rate than did larger, older businesses. The new jobs created by small businesses come in small bites. When a new restaurant opens, it may employ fifteen persons. When a new retail specialty store opens, it may employ twenty persons. Because so many new businesses are created each year, however, the cumulative impact on employment is significant.

■ Contributions to Large Businesses

It is primarily small businesses that supply and distribute the products of large businesses. General Motors, for example, buys materials from more than twenty-five thousand suppliers, most of them small businesses. GM also distributes its products through small businesses—independent dealers. Likewise, an organization like Sony buys supplies from thousands of small businesses, distributes its electronic products through numerous small distributors and its movies through numerous independent movie theaters, and sells its records through independent record stores.

FIGURE 5.1
Trends in Women-Owned Small Business

The percentage of women-owned businesses in the United States continues to escalate dramatically. Although there are still relatively few women who own businesses in industries such as agriculture or forestry, their presence is quite large in other industries such as whole-saling, retailing, and services.

Source: Reprinted from April 18, 1994, issue of *Business Week* by special permission. Copyright © 1994 by The McGraw-Hill Companies.

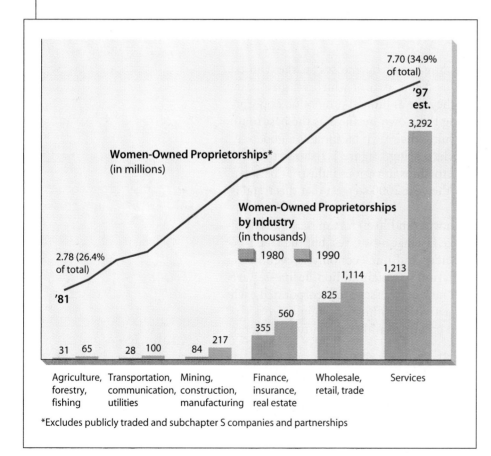

Women-Owned Proprietorships* (in millions)

7.70 (34.9% of total)
'97 est.

2.78 (26.4% of total)
'81

Women-Owned Proprietorships by Industry (in thousands)

1980   1990

	1980	1990
Agriculture, forestry, fishing	31	65
Transportation, communication, utilities	28	100
Mining, construction, manufacturing	84	217
Finance, insurance, real estate	355	560
Wholesale, retail, trade	825	1,114
Services	1,213	3,292

*Excludes publicly traded and subchapter S companies and partnerships

Strategy for Entrepreneurial Organizations

One of the most basic challenges facing an entrepreneurial organization is choosing a strategy. The three strategic challenges facing small firms, in turn, are choosing an industry in which to compete, emphasizing distinctive competencies, and writing a business plan.[6]

■ Choosing an Industry

Entrepreneurs seeking to begin small-business operations should generally look to industries with favorable industry attributes. Thus, for example, entrepreneurs who start a business based on a technology with few rivals or substitutes and a low threat of entry usually earn higher rates of return than entrepreneurs who start a business without these advantages.

Examples of small businesses that chose a high-potential industry are Microsoft and Quicken, two very successful software companies. These companies have developed personal computer software that dominates their respective market segments (Microsoft in operating systems and word processing applications, Quicken in personal financial planning and management). Because these firms are so dominant in their respective segments, rivalry in their industries is low. Because of the skills that computer users have developed in applying these particular software packages, there are few acceptable substitutes. And because of the reputation and success of these firms, entry into these software segments is unlikely (although certainly not impossible).

Examples of small businesses that operate in an industry with a lower return potential are independent video rental stores. Because of the large number of video rental stores and because all stores carry many of the same videos, rivalry in this industry is intense. Substitutes in the form of cable television, movie theaters, network television, and even books are common. Because the cost of entering this industry is relatively low (the cost of videos plus a lease and computer software), entry into the video rental business is easy. For these reasons, independent video rental operations are often marginal financial performers, although as members of national chains, video stores can be profitable.

Industries in Which Small Businesses Are Strong   Small businesses tend to do well in the service, retail, and wholesale industries. Service organizations are perhaps the most common type of entrepreneurial business because they require a fairly small capital investment to start up.[7] A certified public accountant, for example, can open a business simply by renting an office and hanging out a sign. The number of small businesses in the service industry, including video rental shops, hair salons, and tax preparation services, has significantly increased in recent years because the costs of the physical assets needed to start these businesses are relatively low.

Entrepreneurs are also effective in the area of specialty retailing. Specialty retailers cater to specific customer groups such as golfers, college students, and people who do their own automobile repairs. Often, the number of these special consumers is relatively small, and thus the dollar size of the market associated

FIGURE 5.2
Economies of Scale in Small Business Organizations

Small businesses sometimes find it difficult to compete in manufacturing-related industries because of the economies of scale associated with facilities, equipment, and technology. As shown in (a), firms that produce a large number of units (that is, larger businesses) can do so at a lower per unit cost. At the same time, however, new forms of technology occasionally cause the economies-of-scale curve to shift, as illustrated in (b). In this case, smaller firms may be able to compete more effectively with larger ones because of the drop in per unit manufacturing cost.

with these consumers is small. Although large organizations may be unwilling to enter a business where the market is so small, small businesses may be very successful in these industries.[8]

Wholesalers buy products from large manufacturers and resell them to retailers. Small businesses dominate the wholesale industry because they are often able to develop personal working relationships with several sellers and several buyers. A wholesale supplier of computer equipment may have to develop supply relationships with five or six floppy disk manufacturers, six or seven hard disk manufacturers, and five or six video screen manufacturers to have the inventory it needs to respond to the needs of its retail customers. If, instead of being an independent operation, this wholesaler belonged to a larger electronics company, the business would have supply relationships with only one supplier of floppy disks, one supplier of hard disks, and one maker of video screens. As long as end users want multiple supply options, the independent wholesaler can play an important economic role.

Industries in Which Small Businesses Are Weak   Small organizations have difficulty succeeding in certain other industries. Foremost among them are industries dominated by large-scale manufacturing and agriculture, which is an industry in transition from domination by small family farms to domination by large corporate farms.

Research has shown that manufacturing costs often fall as the number of units produced by an organization increases. This relationship between cost and production is called an *economy of scale*.[9] Small organizations usually cannot compete effectively on the basis of economies of scale. As depicted in the left panel of Figure 5.2, organizations with higher levels of production have a major cost advantage over those with lower levels of production. Given the cost positions of small and large firms when there are strong economies of scale in manufacturing, it is not surprising that small manufacturing organizations generally do not do as well as large ones.

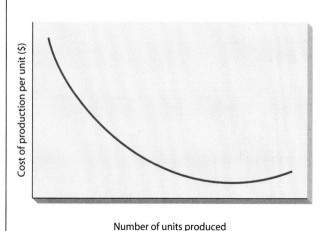

(a) Standard economies-of-scale curve

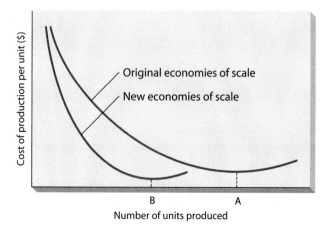

(b) Change in technology that shifts economies of scale and may make small business production possible

Interestingly, when technology in an industry changes, it often shifts the economies-of-scale curve, thereby creating opportunities for smaller organizations. For example, steel manufacturing was historically dominated by a few large companies that owned several huge facilities. With the development of mini-mill technology, however, extracting economies of scale at a much smaller level of production became possible. This type of shift is depicted in the right panel of Figure 5.2. Point A in this panel is the low-cost point with the original economies of scale. Point B is the low-cost point with the economies of scale brought on by the new technology. Notice that the number of units needed for low costs is considerably lower for the new technology. This factor has allowed the entry of numerous smaller firms into the steel industry. Such entry would not have been possible with the older technology.

Of course, not all manufacturing is capital-intensive. Some manufacturing can be done with minimal plant facilities and equipment. This kind of light industry is typical of some parts of the computer industry and some parts of the plastic fabrication industry, in printing, and elsewhere. Small organizations can excel in these industries.[10]

Agriculture is an industry in transition. Small family farms were among the first small businesses in the world, and until recently they were among the most successful. Economies of scale and high equipment prices, however, have forced many small farmers out of business. Giant agribusiness enterprises and corporate farms are gradually replacing them. These multifarm businesses own and farm millions of acres and are large enough to fully exploit economies of scale by purchasing and sharing the most modern farm equipment, applying the latest scientific methods in farming, and even influencing government policy to favor farmers.

■ Emphasizing Distinctive Competencies

As we define the term in Chapter 3, an organization's *distinctive competencies* are the aspects of business that the firm performs better than its competitors. The distinctive competencies of small business usually fall into three areas: the ability to identify new niches in established markets, the ability to identify new markets, and the ability to move quickly to take advantage of new opportunities.

Identifying Niches in Established Markets An **established market** is one in which several large firms compete according to relatively well-defined criteria. For example, throughout the 1970s the big computer companies—IBM, Digital Equipment, and Hewlett-Packard—competed according to three product criteria: computing power, service, and price. Over the years the computing power and quality of service delivered by these firms continued to improve while prices (especially relative to computing power) continued to drop.

Enter Apple Computer and the personal computer. For Apple, user friendliness, not computing power, service, and price, was to be the basis of competition. Apple targeted every manager, every student, and every household as the owner of a personal computer. The major entrepreneurial act of Apple was not to invent a new technology (indeed, the first Apple computers used all standard parts), but to recognize a new kind of computer and a new way to compete in the computer industry.

established market A market in which several large firms compete according to relatively well-defined criteria

niche A segment of a market not currently being exploited

Apple's approach to competition was to identify a new niche in an established market. A **niche** is simply a segment of a market that is not currently being exploited. In general, small entrepreneurial businesses are better at discovering these niches than are larger organizations. Large organizations usually have so many resources committed to older, established business practices that they may be unaware of new opportunities. Entrepreneurs can see these opportunities and move quickly to take advantage of them.[11]

Identifying New Markets Successful entrepreneurs also excel at discovering whole new markets. Discovery can happen in at least two ways. First, an entrepreneur can transfer a product or service that is well established in one geographic market to a second market. This is what Marcel Bich did with ballpoint pens, which occupied a well-established market in Europe before Bich introduced them to this country. Bich's company, Bic Corp., eventually came to dominate the U.S. market.

Second, entrepreneurs can sometimes create entire industries. Entrepreneurial inventions of the photocopying process and the semiconductor have created vast new industries. Not only have the first companies into these markets been very successful (Xerox and National Semiconductor, respectively), but their entrepreneurial activity has spawned the development of hundreds of other companies and hundreds of thousands of jobs. Again, because entrepreneurs are not encumbered with a history of doing business in a particular way, they are usually better at discovering new markets than are larger, more mature organizations.

first-mover advantage Any advantage that comes to a firm because it exploits an opportunity before any other firm does

First-Mover Advantages A **first-mover advantage** is any advantage that comes to a firm because it exploits an opportunity before any other firm does. Sometimes large firms discover niches within existing markets or new markets at just about the same time as small entrepreneurial firms do, but are not able to move as quickly as small companies to take advantage of these opportunities.

There are numerous reasons for this difference. For example, many large organizations make decisions slowly because each of their many layers of hierarchy has to approve an action before it can be implemented. Also, large organizations may sometimes put a great deal of their assets at risk when they take advantage of new opportunities. Every time Boeing decides to build a new model of a commercial jet, it is making a decision that could literally bankrupt the company if it does not turn out well. The size of the risk may make large organizations cautious. The dollar value of the assets at risk in a small organization, in contrast, is quite small. Managers may be willing to "bet the company" when the value of the company is only $100,000. They might be unwilling to place such a bet when the value of the company is $1 billion.

■ Writing a Business Plan

business plan A document that summarizes the business strategy and structure

Once an entrepreneur has chosen an industry to compete in and determined which distinctive competencies to emphasize, these choices are usually included in a document called a business plan. In a **business plan** the entrepreneur summarizes the business strategy and how that strategy is to be implemented. The very act of preparing a business plan forces prospective entrepreneurs to crystallize their thinking about what they must do to launch their business successfully and obliges them to develop their business on paper before investing time and money in it. The idea of a business plan is not new. What is new is the growing use of specialized business plans by entrepreneurs, mostly because creditors and investors demand them for use in deciding whether to help finance a small business.

The plan should describe the match between the entrepreneur's abilities and the requirements for producing and marketing a particular product or service. It should define strategies for production and marketing, legal aspects and organization, and accounting and finance. In particular, it should answer three questions: (1) What are the entrepreneur's goals and objectives? (2) What strategies will the entrepreneur use to obtain these goals and objectives? (3) How will the entrepreneur implement these strategies?

Some idea of the complexity of planning a new business may be gleaned from the PERT diagram in Figure 5.3. The diagram shows the major steps in planning the launch of a new business. Notice that the development of a business plan consists of a set of specific activities, perhaps the most pivotal of which is marketing research—the systematic and intensive study of all the facts, opinions, and judgments that bear on the successful marketing of a product or service.

FIGURE 5.3
A PERT Diagram for Business Planning

Business planning involves a number of very specific activities and events, as shown in this PERT diagram. Following a logical and systematic process such as the one shown here will enhance the chances for success.

Source: "A PERT Diagram for Business Planning," (figure 9.3) from Siropolis, Nicholas, *Small Business Management*, Fifth Edition. Copyright © 1994 by Houghton Mifflin Company. Adapted with permission.

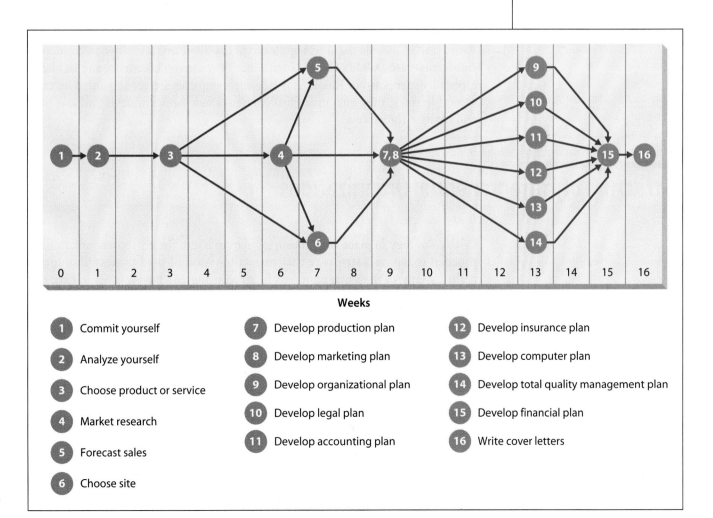

Weeks

1. Commit yourself
2. Analyze yourself
3. Choose product or service
4. Market research
5. Forecast sales
6. Choose site
7. Develop production plan
8. Develop marketing plan
9. Develop organizational plan
10. Develop legal plan
11. Develop accounting plan
12. Develop insurance plan
13. Develop computer plan
14. Develop total quality management plan
15. Develop financial plan
16. Write cover letters

Figure 5.3 also demonstrates the sequential nature of much strategic decision making in small businesses. For example, entrepreneurs cannot forecast sales revenues without first researching markets. The sales forecast itself is one of the most important elements in the business plan. Without such forecasts, it is all but impossible to estimate intelligently the size of a plant, store, or office or to determine how much inventory to carry or how many employees to hire.

Another important activity is financial planning, which translates all other activities into dollars. Generally, the financial plan is made up of a cash budget, an income statement, balance sheets, and a breakeven chart. The most important of these statements is the cash budget because it tells entrepreneurs how much money they need before they open for business and how much money they need to keep the business operating.

■ Entrepreneurship and International Management

Finally, although many people associate international management with big business, many smaller companies are also finding expansion and growth opportunities in foreign countries.[12] For example, Fuci Metals, a small but growing enterprise, buys metal from remote locations in areas such as Siberia and Africa and then sells them to big auto makers like Ford and Toyota. Similarly, California-based Gold's Gym is expanding into foreign countries, and has been especially successful in Russia.[13] While such ventures are accompanied by considerable risks, they also give entrepreneurs new opportunities and can be a real catalyst for success.

Structure of Entrepreneurial Organizations

With a strategy in place and a business plan in hand, the entrepreneur can then proceed to devise a structure that turns the vision of the business plan into a reality. Many of the same concerns in structuring any business, which are described in the next section of this book, are also relevant to small businesses. For example, entrepreneurs need to consider organization design and develop job descriptions, organization charts, and management control systems. Small businesses do have some special concerns relating to structure, however, including the form of ownership and sources of financing, methods for starting the business, and sources of management help.

■ Forms of Ownership and Sources of Financing

Ownership structure specifies who possesses legal title to all of an organization's assets and who has a claim on any economic profits generated by a firm. Financing a small business involves decisions concerning the sources of capital that will be used to start the business and what claims (if any) these sources have on the organization's profits. Numerous alternatives exist for both ownership structure and sources of financing, and each one has advantages and disadvantages.

Forms of Ownership A popular form of legal ownership for many new businesses is the **sole proprietorship,** in which one individual controls legal title to all assets and claims on all future economic profits. About 70 percent of all U.S. businesses are sole proprietorships. The major advantages of a sole proprietorship are that the individual entrepreneur has total freedom in conducting business, start-up is simple and inexpensive, and business profits are taxed as ordinary income to the proprietor. The disadvantages are that the proprietor has unlimited liability (his or her personal assets are at risk to cover business debts) and the business ends when the proprietor retires or dies.

Another form of ownership is the **partnership**, in which two or more persons agree to be partners in a business, share title to the firm's assets, be held jointly liable for a firm's debts, and share a firm's profits. Partnerships, the least common form of ownership, are often used by accounting, legal, and architectural firms. These types of organizations are highly dependent on the professional skills of individuals, and partnerships tend to foster the professional mutual respect that is essential in these business activities. Partnerships provide a larger pool of talent and capital to start a business than do sole proprietorships but are just as easy to form and offer the same tax benefits. The disadvantages are unlimited liability for the partners, no legal continuance if the partnership is dissolved, and possible conflict or tension between partners.

Most large organizations, and some smaller ones, use the corporation as the basis for ownership. A **corporation** is a legal entity that is independent of any single individual. Like an individual, a corporation can borrow money, enter into contracts, own property, sue, and be sued. Its owners are the stockholders. An advantage that distinguishes the corporation from sole proprietorships and partnerships is that it is responsible for its own liabilities, so the owners have limited liability. A corporation continues to exist despite the retirement or death of any of its owners, and it can often borrow money easily. Corporations have higher start-up costs than either sole proprietorships or partnerships and are subject to increased regulation and double taxation (the corporation pays taxes on its profits, and then stockholders pay taxes on their dividends).

A few other special forms of ownership exist. *Master limited partnerships* and *subchapter S corporations* provide many of the advantages of corporations without double taxation. *Cooperatives* enable a number of small organizations

Business ownership can take a variety of forms. For example, the Mississippi Band of Choctaw Indians owns and operates several successful businesses, including one that makes wire harnesses for automotive electronics and another, in partnership with American Greetings, that makes greeting cards. Indeed, the tribe's holdings have become so successful that they are the region's largest employer and rely on non-Indians to fill about half the jobs in the Choctaw's various enterprises.

sole proprietorship A form of ownership in which one individual controls legal title to all assets and claims on all future profits

partnership A form of ownership in which two or more persons agree to share title to the firm's assets, be held jointly liable for the firm's debts, and share the firm's profits

corporation A legal entity that is independent of any single individual for the sole purpose of business ownership and control

venture capitalist Someone who actively seeks to invest in new businesses

to pool resources and share markets. Ocean Spray Cranberries is a cooperative that is made up of seven hundred independent cranberry growers and one hundred citrus growers.

Sources of Financing An important issue confronting all entrepreneurs is locating the money necessary to open and operate the business. Personal resources (savings and money borrowed from friends or family) are the most common sources of new-business financing. Personal resources are often the most important source because they reinforce the entrepreneur's personal commitment to the venture. Many entrepreneurs also take advantage of various lending programs and assistance provided by lending institutions and government agencies.[14] Government programs are especially interested in helping women and minority entrepreneurs.

Another common source of funds is venture capitalists. A **venture capitalist** is someone who actively seeks to invest in new businesses. The advantage of this approach is that it gives entrepreneurs access to a large resource base with fewer restrictions than might be imposed by the government or by banks. In return, however, the entrepreneur must relinquish to the venture capitalist a portion of the profits or share ownership.[15]

■ Methods for Starting a New Business

Another set of questions that an entrepreneur must address when organizing a business is whether to buy an existing business, start a new one, or seek a franchising agreement.

Buying an Existing Business Buying an existing business has a strong set of advantages. Being able to examine the business's historical records to determine the pattern of revenue and profit and the type of cash flow eliminates much guesswork about what to expect. The entrepreneur also acquires existing supplier, distributor, and customer networks. On the negative side, the entrepreneur inherits whatever problems the business may already have and may be forced to accept existing contractual agreements. Howard Schultz bought Starbucks Corporation when it was a small, struggling outfit and turned it into a big successful company.

Starting a New Business Starting a business from scratch allows the owner to avoid the shortcomings of an existing business and to put his or her personal stamp on the enterprise. James Koch used this method to start the Boston Beer Co. The entrepreneur also has the opportunity to choose suppliers, bankers, lawyers, and employees without worrying about existing agreements or contractual arrangements.[16] More uncertainty is involved in starting a new business, however, than in taking over an existing one. The entrepreneur starts out with less information about projected revenues and cash flow, has to build a customer base from zero, and may be forced to accept unfavorable credit terms from suppliers. Because it is an unknown quantity, a new business may have difficulty borrowing money.

franchising agreement A contract between an entrepreneur (the

Franchising An alternative to buying an existing business or starting one from scratch is entering into a **franchising agreement**. The entrepreneur pays a parent company (the **franchiser**) a flat fee or a share of the income from the business. In return, the entrepreneur (the **franchisee**) is allowed to use the company's trademarks, products, formulas, and business plan. Industries that are heavily franchised include fast foods (for example, McDonald's), specialty retail clothing stores (for example, Benetton), personal computer stores (for example, ComputerLand), and local automobile dealerships.[17]

franchisee) and a parent company (the **franchiser**); the entrepreneur pays the parent company for the use of the trademarks, products, formulas, and business plans

Franchising may reduce the entrepreneur's financial risk because many parent companies provide advice and assistance. They also provide proven production, sales, and marketing methods; training; financial support; and an established identity and image. Some franchisers also allow successful individual franchisees to grow by opening multiple outlets.

On the negative side, franchises may cost a lot of money. A McDonald's franchise costs several hundred thousand dollars. Also, the parent company often restricts the franchisee to certain types of products. A McDonald's franchisee cannot change the formula for milk shakes, alter the preparation of Big Macs, or purchase supplies from any other company.[18] In addition, some franchise agreements are difficult to terminate.

Despite the drawbacks, franchising is growing by leaps and bounds. More than one-third of U.S. retail sales currently go through franchises, and that figure is expected to climb to one-half of sales by the end of this century.[19] Much of the attraction of franchising is that this approach to starting a new business involves limited risks. Nevertheless, no form of business is completely risk free.

■ Sources of Management Help

Since the 1950s, the idea that small businesses benefit from management assistance has grown widely. Many sources of management help are now offered at little or no cost to entrepreneurs, both before and after they embark on a new business. Because of the extent of management sophistication needed to launch a venture such as microcomputer manufacture, special services are available to entrepreneurs who go into a high-technology business.[20]

In addition to numerous federal programs, help is also available from sources such as community colleges and universities, the chambers of commerce, and other organizations made up of small businesses. Heading the list is the Small Business Administration (SBA). Many entrepreneurs have the mistaken view that the SBA only lends money or guarantees repayment of loans made by commercial banks. Even more important are SBA efforts to help entrepreneurs manage their businesses effectively and spend their money wisely.

The SBA offers entrepreneurs four major cost-free management-assistance programs: Service Corps of Retired Executives (SCORE), Active Corps of Executives (ACE), Small Business Institute (SBI), and Small Business Development Centers (SBDC). Under the SCORE and ACE programs, the SBA tries to match an expert to the need. If an entrepreneur needs a marketing plan but does not know how to put one together, the SBA pulls from its list of SCORE or ACE counselors someone with marketing knowledge and experience. The SBI program taps the talents available at colleges and universities. This program involves not only professors of business administration but also students working for advanced degrees. Under a professor's guidance, such students work with entrepreneurs to help solve their management problems.

Finally, the SBDC program brings resources and skills needed by entrepreneurs to a single location where entrepreneurs can go to receive instruction and training in management and technical skills.

The Performance of Entrepreneurial Organizations

The formulation and implementation of an effective strategy plays a major role in determining the overall performance of an entrepreneurial organization.[21] This section examines how entrepreneurial firms evolve and the attributes of these firms that enhance their chance for success.

■ The Life Cycle of Entrepreneurial Firms

The entrepreneurial life cycle is a series of predictable stages that small businesses pass through. A common pattern of evolution for entrepreneurial organizations is depicted in Figure 5.4. This pattern is similar to the product life cycle discussed in Chapter 3 but refers specifically to the challenges and changes in small entrepreneurial firms.

First comes the acceptance stage, in which the small business struggles to break even and survive. Entrepreneurial firms are usually small enough at this stage that they can spot obstacles to success and act quickly to remove them. Moreover, entrepreneurs usually have the skills needed to modify their products or services as required by customers during this stage. Such modifications are often necessary for small firms struggling to obtain enough cash from sales and other sources to continue operations. Many small organizations, despite the skill and effort of entrepreneurs, never emerge from the acceptance stage.

Next follows the breakthrough stage. In contrast to the acceptance stage, when the rate of growth is so slow that it is often unnoticed, in the breakthrough stage, growth is so fast and unpredictable that many entrepreneurs fail to keep pace with it. Caught unprepared, they blunder. Sales revenues spiral upward as problems begin to surface with cash flow, production, quality, and delivery. At the same time, competition may become more severe.[22]

In the face of these pressures, entrepreneurs may apply hasty, ill-conceived solutions to problems. For example, if sales begin to level off or slip, the owner may hire specialists such as an accountant, a quality-control analyst, or a customer services representative to relieve the problem. As a result, costs go up, squeezing profits further. The best way to become alerted to the problems presented by rapid growth is to continue updating the business plan. With a thorough, updated business plan in place, entrepreneurs are less likely to be surprised by breakthroughs.

In the mature stage the lack of control of the breakthrough stage is replaced by a more stable, balanced period of steady growth. Organizations that survive to this stage can continue to grow for many years. In this last stage, however, entrepreneurs often face another challenge. Although they

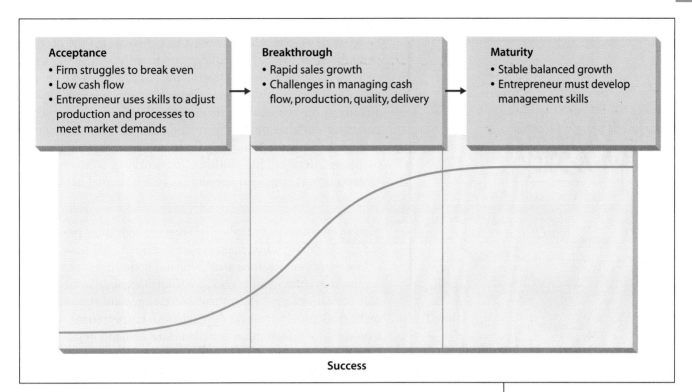

Acceptance
- Firm struggles to break even
- Low cash flow
- Entrepreneur uses skills to adjust production and processes to meet market demands

Breakthrough
- Rapid sales growth
- Challenges in managing cash flow, production, quality, delivery

Maturity
- Stable balanced growth
- Entrepreneur must develop management skills

Success

usually have the technical skills required during the acceptance stage, they often do not possess the managerial skills required during the mature stage. Entrepreneurs without these skills either have to develop them or turn the day-to-day operations of their organization over to professional managers and concentrate on new business opportunities or the creation of new organizations.

■ Reasons for Entrepreneurial Success

Many organizations successfully move through the stages listed in Figure 5.4 to become stable and mature organizations. Many factors contribute to this success, and six of the most common ones are described in the following sections.[23]

Hard Work, Drive, and Dedication   An individual must have a strong desire to work independently and be willing to put in long hours to succeed as an entrepreneur. Successful entrepreneurs tend to be reasonable risk takers, self-confident, hard working, goal setters, and innovators.[24] In addition, small businesses generally benefit if the owner attends well to detail. Some entrepreneurs fail because they neglect the details of business operations. They may open a business for the glamour and excitement of it, but as the concomitant drudgery of entrepreneurship builds, they may ignore essential areas such as inventory control and collections. They may also ignore customer dissatisfaction, worker unrest, or financial difficulties, preferring to think that problems will solve themselves. Over time, though, they rarely do.

FIGURE 5.4
Stages of Evolution for Entrepreneurial Firms

Entrepreneurial firms often follow a pattern of evolution that resembles this curve. After an initial period of acceptance, during which the firm struggles and experiences low cash flow, the breakthrough stage is achieved. During this period, the firm experiences rapid sales growth and must focus on managing growth. When the maturity stage is reached, growth becomes more stable and the entrepreneur must begin to focus more attention on the actual management of the enterprise.

THE FAR SIDE   By GARY LARSON

Early business failures

As noted in the text, successful entrepreneurs must choose an industry, emphasize their distinctive competencies, and develop an effective business plan. Unfortunately, entrepreneurs frequently misjudge or do not effectively implement one or more of these activities. As illustrated in this cartoon, for example, providing a product that people do not really want is almost certain to result in failure. Chocolate confections, sausages, and corn on the cob are popular treats served on sticks at athletic events, fairs, festivals, and carnivals—but cucumbers, peaches, and porcupines are not as well received!

Market Demand for Products or Services Provided   For any business to succeed, demand must be sufficient for the product or service it provides. If a college community of fifty thousand citizens and fifteen thousand students has one pizza parlor, demand for more is probably sufficient. If fifteen pizza parlors are already in operation, however, a new one will have to serve especially good pizza or offer something else unique if it is to succeed. Liz Claiborne's clothing business was successful because of unmet demand for clothing for working women; Apple Computer was initially successful because of unmet demand for personal computers.

Managerial Competence   The entrepreneur must possess basic managerial competence. He or she needs to know how to select business locations and facilities, acquire financing, and hire and evaluate employees. The entrepreneur must also be able to manage growth, control costs, negotiate contracts, and make difficult choices and decisions. An entrepreneur who has a product for which there is tremendous demand might be able to survive for a while without managerial skills. Over time, and especially in the mature stage of the life cycle, however, the entrepreneur who lacks these skills is unlikely to succeed.

Luck   Some small businesses succeed purely because of luck. There was an element of luck in Alan McKim's success with Clean Harbors, an environmental "clean up" organization based in New England. McKim formed this business just as the federal government committed $1.6 billion to help clean up toxic waste. Although McKim might have succeeded anyway, the extra revenue generated by the government Superfund no doubt contributed to this success.[25]

Strong Control Systems   Small businesses, like all organizations, need strong control systems. Small businesses can be ruined by weak control. For example, too many slow-paying customers can reduce a small business's cash flow to a trickle. Excess inventory, employee theft, poor-quality products, plummeting sales, and insufficient profit margins can have equally disastrous effects. If the control system either does not alert the entrepreneur to these problems or alerts the entrepreneur too late, recovery may be difficult or impossible. (Control systems are discussed more fully in Part V of this book.)

Sufficient Capitalization   Small businesses need sufficient funds to survive start-up and growth. One rule of thumb is that an entrepreneur should have sufficient personal funds when starting out to be able to live with no business income for a year. The entrepreneur needs to be able to maintain his or her personal life, cover all operating expenses, and still have an allowance for unexpected contingencies. An entrepreneur who is planning to pay next month's rent from a new business's profits may be courting disaster.

Summary of Key Points

Entrepreneurship is the process of planning, organizing, operating, and assuming the risk of a business venture. An entrepreneur is someone who engages in entrepreneurship. In general, entrepreneurs start small businesses. Small businesses are an important source of innovation, create numerous jobs, and contribute to the success of large businesses.

In choosing strategies, entrepreneurs have to consider the characteristics of the industry in which they are going to conduct business. A small business must also emphasize its distinctive competencies. Small businesses generally have several distinctive competencies that they should exploit in choosing their strategy. Small businesses are usually skilled at identifying niches in established markets, identifying new markets, and acting quickly to obtain first-mover advantages. Small businesses are usually not skilled at exploiting economies of scale. Once an entrepreneur has chosen a strategy, the strategy is normally written down in a business plan. Writing a business plan forces an entrepreneur to plan thoroughly and to anticipate problems that might occur.

With a strategy and business plan in place, entrepreneurs must choose a structure to implement them.

All of the structural issues summarized in the next three chapters of this book are relevant to the entrepreneur. In addition, the entrepreneur has some unique structural choices to make. In determining ownership and financial structure, the entrepreneur can choose between a sole proprietorship, a partnership, a corporation, a master limited partnership, a subchapter S corporation, and a cooperative. In determining financial structure, an entrepreneur has to decide how much personal capital to invest in an organization, how much bank and government support to obtain, and whether to encourage venture capital firms to invest. Finally, entrepreneurs have to choose among the options of buying an existing business, starting a new business from scratch, or entering into a franchising agreement.

Most small businesses pass through a three-phase life cycle: acceptance, breakthrough, and maturity. Several factors explain why successful small businesses are able to move through all three of these stages of development: hard work, drive, and dedication; market demand for products or services provided; managerial competence; luck; strong control systems; and sufficient capitalization.

Discussion Questions

Questions for Review

1. Why are entrepreneurs and small businesses important to society?

2. In which types of industries do small firms often excel? In which types of industries do small firms struggle?

3. List the ownership options available to entrepreneurs. What are the advantages and disadvantages of each?

4. What are the advantages and disadvantages of buying an existing business relative to starting a new one?

5. What are the elements of success for small businesses?

Questions for Analysis

1. Entrepreneurs and small businesses play a variety of important roles in society. If these roles are so important, do you think that the government should do more to encourage the development of small business? Why or why not?

2. Franchising agreements seem to be particularly popular ways of starting a new business in industries in which retail outlets are geographically widely spread and where the quality of goods or services purchased can be evaluated only after the purchase has occurred. For example, a hamburger may look tasty, but you know for sure that it is well made only after you buy it and eat it. By going to a McDonald's, you know exactly the kind and quality

of hamburger you will receive, even before you walk in the door. What makes franchise arrangements so popular under these conditions?

3. If employing family members can cause problems in a small organization, why is this practice so common?

4. What steps might an entrepreneur take before deciding to expand into a foreign market?

5. Are there any obvious market niches in your town or city where an entrepreneur might succeed with a new venture?

Building Effective Communication Skills

EXERCISE OVERVIEW

Communication skills refer to the manager's abilities to both effectively convey ideas and information to others and effectively receive ideas and information from others. Although communication skills are important to all organizations, some entrepreneurs argue that they are even more important in smaller organizations. This exercise helps you understand some of the complexities in communicating in smaller businesses.

EXERCISE BACKGROUND

Assume that you are the owner/manager of a small retail chain. Your company sells moderate-priced apparel for professional men and women. You have ten stores located in the Midwest. Each store has a general manager responsible for the overall management of that specific store. Each store also has one assistant manager.

In addition, a human resource manager, an advertising specialist, and two buyers staff your corporate office. In the past each store was managed at the total discretion of its local manager. As a result, each store had a different layout, a different culture, and different policies and procedures.

You want to begin opening more stores at a rapid pace. To expedite this process, you also want to standardize your stores. Unfortunately, however, you realize that many of your current managers will be unhappy by this decision. They will see standardization as a loss of authority and managerial discretion. Nevertheless, you believe that it is important to achieve standardization in all areas.

Your plans are to remodel all of your stores to fit a standard layout. You also intend to develop a policy and operations manual for each store. This manual will specify exactly how each store will be managed. You plan to inform your managers of this plan first in a memo and then in a follow-up meeting to discuss questions and concerns.

EXERCISE TASK

With the information described above as context, please do the following:

1. Draft a memo that explains your intentions to the store managers.

2. Make a list of the primary objections you anticipate.

3. Outline an agenda for the meeting in which you plan to address the managers' questions and concerns.

4. Do you personally agree with this communication strategy? Why or why not?

EXERCISE OVERVIEW

Technical skills are the skills necessary to accomplish or understand the specific work being done in an organization. This exercise allows you to gain insights into your own technical skills and the relative importance of technical skills in different kinds of organizations.

EXERCISE BACKGROUND

Some entrepreneurs have the technical skills that they need to open and run their business successfully. For example, a hair stylist who opens a hair salon, an architect who starts a residential design firm, and a chef who launches a new restaurant have the technical skills needed to do the work of the organization (hair styling, blueprint rendering, and cooking, respectively).

In other cases the entrepreneur who starts the organization may have general management skills but essentially "buy" required technical skills in the labor market. For example, an entrepreneur might start a new restaurant without knowing how to cook by hiring a professional chef to perform this function.

EXERCISE TASK

With the background information provided above as a context, do the following:

1. Listed below are examples of ten small businesses that an individual entrepreneur might conceivably launch. Spend a few minutes thinking about each business. (Hint: Try to conceptualize an existing local business that might generally fit the description.)

2. Make notes about the specific technical skills required for each business.

3. For each business, decide whether it is especially important for the entrepreneur to actually possess the technical skills or whether it is feasible to consider hiring others who possess the skills instead.

4. What are some major factors that determine the viability of buying technical skills in the labor market?

New Businesses:

a. Clothing retail store

b. Computer clone assembly business

c. Tavern

d. Sports card retail store

e. Aluminum recycling operation

f. Used compact disk retail store

g. Drop-in health care clinic

h. Gourmet coffee bean shop

i. Business services operation

j. Appliance repair shop

Building Effective Conceptual Skills

EXERCISE OVERVIEW

Conceptual skills refer to the manager's ability to think in the abstract. This exercise helps you relate conceptual skills to entrepreneurship.

EXERCISE BACKGROUND

Assume that you have made the decision to open a small business in the local business community when you graduate (the community where you are attending college, not your home). Assume that you have funds to start a business without having to worry about finding other investors.

Without regard to market potential, profitability, or similar considerations, list five businesses that you might want to open and operate based solely on your personal interests. For example, if you enjoy bicycling, you might enjoy opening a shop that caters to cyclists.

Next, without regard to personal attractiveness or interests, list five businesses that you might want to open and operate based solely on market opportunities. Evaluate the prospects for success of each of the ten businesses.

EXERCISE TASK

With the background information above as context, do the following:

1. Form a small group with three or four classmates and discuss your respective lists. Look for instances of where the same type of business appears on either the same or alternative lists. Also look for cases where the same business appears with similar or dissimilar prospects for success.

2. How important is personal interest in small business success?

3. How important is market potential in small business success?

You Make the Call

After Cynthia Spenser made the decision to buy The Arbor retail complex, she found it necessary to make a number of other decisions. One important decision involved financing for the purchase. She determined that she had three options. One option was to borrow the funds from a local bank. The second option was to borrow the money from the accumulated capital held by Sunset Landscape Services. The final option was to borrow a portion from the bank and use SLS resources for the remainder.

Discussions with the Spensers' accountant led Cynthia to choose the third option. Although she could borrow the total purchase price from SLS at an attractive interest rate, the loan would essentially reflect negatively on SLS's balance sheet, making it appear to be less solvent and putting more of the Spensers' personal funds at risk. Thus, she decided to borrow 50 percent of the purchase price from the bank and use personal funds for the remainder. The bank was amenable to this arrangement and agreed to the loan.

A second important decision was how to organize the new business. Mark suggested that they simply fold it into the SLS corporation, making it one more business owned and controlled by the existing company. Cynthia saw some merit to this plan, but she eventually decided to keep it as a separate business.

She knew that Mark's real interests were in horticulture and that he would have no involvement in The Arbor. She also recognized that managing a real-estate investment property was so different from managing a products-and-services retail operation that merging the two simply did not seem as logical as keeping them separate.

The final important decision she had to make involved her own role in SLS. Because Cynthia had a strong staff of sales associates, managing the retail nursery was not really a big job. She also felt that managing The Arbor would not require a great deal of time, at least at first. The retail complex already had a full tenant base, and she did not anticipate any major changes.

Thus, Cynthia and Mark agreed that she would retain her position as manager of the nursery for the time being. They also agreed that she would promote one of the sales associates to the position of assistant manager and give that person some additional responsibility and authority. If Cynthia found it necessary to devote more time to The Arbor, the Spensers could always make a management change at the nursery.

DISCUSSION QUESTIONS

1. What decision-making perspectives are reflected in this case?

2. What are the benefits and risks inherent in the plans that Cynthia has made?

3. Do you agree or disagree with Cynthia's decision to keep The Arbor as a separate business?

AN ENTREPRENEURIAL QUIZ

Skills Self-Assessment Instrument

Introduction: Entrepreneurs are starting ventures all the time. These new businesses are vital to the economy. The following assessment is designed to help you understand your readiness to start your own business—to be an entrepreneur.

Instructions: Place a checkmark or an X in the box next to the response that best represents your self-evaluation.

1. Are you a self-starter?
   - ☐ I do things on my own. Nobody has to tell me to get going.
   - ☐ If someone gets me started, I keep going all right.
   - ☐ Easy does it. I don't push myself until I have to.

2. How do you feel about other people?
   - ☐ I like people. I can get along with just about anybody.
   - ☐ I have plenty of friends—I don't need anybody else.
   - ☐ Most people irritate me.

3. Can you lead others?
   - ☐ I can get most people to go along when I start something.
   - ☐ I can give orders if someone tells me what we should do.
   - ☐ I let someone else get things moving. Then I go along if I feel like it.

4. Can you take responsibility?

☐ I like to take charge of things and see them through.

☐ I'll take over if I have to, but I'd rather let someone else be responsible.

☐ There are always eager beavers around wanting to show how smart they are. I let them.

5. How good an organizer are you?

☐ I like to have a plan before I start. I'm usually the one to get things lined up when the group wants to do something.

☐ I do all right unless things get too confused. Then I quit.

☐ You get all set and then something comes along and presents too many problems. So I just take things as they come.

6. How good a worker are you?

☐ I can keep going as long as I need to. I don't mind working hard for something I want.

☐ I'll work hard for a while, but when I've had enough, that's it.

☐ I can't see that hard work gets you anywhere.

7. Can you make decisions?

☐ I can make up my mind in a hurry if I have to. It usually turns out okay, too.

☐ I can if I have plenty of time. If I have to make up my mind fast, I think later I should have decided the other way.

☐ I don't like to be the one who has to decide things.

8. Can people trust what you say?

☐ You bet they can. I don't say things I don't mean.

☐ I try to be on the level most of the time, but sometimes I just say what's easiest.

☐ Why bother if the other person doesn't know the difference?

9. Can you stick with it?

☐ If I make up my mind to do something, I don't let *anything* stop me.

☐ I usually finish what I start—if it goes well.

☐ If it doesn't go well right away, I quit. Why beat your brains out?

10. How good is your health?

☐ I *never* run down!

☐ I have enough energy for most things I want to do.

☐ I run out of energy sooner than most of my friends.

Total the checks or Xs in each column here.

—— —— ——

For interpretation, turn to page 458.

Source: From *Business Startup Basics* by Donald Dible, pp. 9–10, © 1978. Adapted by permission of Prentice-Hall, Inc., Upper Saddle River, N.J.

NEGOTIATING A FRANCHISE AGREEMENT

Step One: Assume that you are the owner of a rapidly growing restaurant chain. In order to continue your current levels of growth, you are considering the option of selling franchises for new restaurants. Working alone, outline the major points that would be of most concern to you that you would want to have in a franchising agreement. Also note the characteristics you would look for in potential franchisees.

Step Two: Assume that you are an individual investor looking to buy a franchise in a rapidly growing restaurant chain. Again working alone, outline the major factors that might determine which franchise you elect to buy. Also note the characteristics you would look for in a potential franchiser.

Step Three: Now form small groups of four. Randomly select one member of the group to play the role of the franchiser; the other three members will play the roles of potential franchisees. Role-play a negotiation meeting. The franchiser should stick as closely as possible to the major points developed in step one. Similarly, the potential franchisees should do the same for points they developed in step two.

Follow-up Questions:

1. Did doing both step one and two in advance help or hinder your negotiations?

2. Can a franchising agreement be so one-sided so as to damage the interests of both parties? How so?

CASE STUDY

Many Young Entrepreneurs Seek Foreign Venues

In today's competitive business environment, more and more entrepreneurs are looking to foreign ports of call for business opportunities. Indeed, the U.S. Census Bureau estimates that as many as 250,000 U.S. citizens leave the country to live abroad each year, with many of them looking to start their own business when they arrive at their foreign destination.

For example, Michael Giles, a graduate of the Columbia law school, moved to a black township named Soweto, right outside of Johannesburg, South Africa. Giles determined that there were only four coin-operated laundries to serve the needs of 4.5 million residents. He arranged to get a loan from the U.S. government's Overseas Private Investment Corporation and has launched a chain of 198 laundromats throughout many of South Africa's black townships.

Mike DeNoma left a lucrative job at Kentucky Fried Chicken and launched his own chain of Chinese fast-food restaurants in Hong Kong. Eugene Matthews, another lawyer, has shipped twenty thousand cows to Vietnam and set up two modern dairy farms in that country. Lisa Frankenberg has started her own newspaper in Prague. Robert Brooker and Adam Haven-Weiss launched a chain of bagel shops in eastern Europe.

Of course, entrepreneurs from the United States are not the only ones seeking business opportunities abroad. Indeed, one of the most successful young international entrepreneurs is England's Matthew Stillman, the founder and owner of one of Europe's most successful film production companies, Stillking Productions. In 1992 Stillman spent a week in Prague on vacation. He had been trying to break into the movie business back home in London for years but had achieved only marginal success.

But in Prague, Stillman saw an opportunity that he couldn't pass up. He and a friend founded Stillking Productions with only $500 between them. They bought a used typewriter and answering machine and rented an abandoned office in a crumbling film studio for $150 a month. To support their fledgling enterprise, they worked in the evenings managing a local nightclub. When they had earned enough money for an airline ticket, Stillman took a trip to Los Angeles looking for customers. As it turned out, pop singer k.d. lang was looking for a central European location for her next music video and gave the contract to Stillman.

Stillking got its first big job making commercials for a Japanese firm. This job led to an even bigger contract making commercials to commemorate the fiftieth anniversary of the United Nations. Things continued to snowball, and Stillking quickly enlisted many large international clients all intent on selling products and making commercials in Europe. Today, the firm has a production schedule set more than a year in advance and is turning away business. Although commercials are still the bedrock of the company, Stillman eventually wants to break into the movie-making business.

Of course, there is no such thing as a sure thing. Many would-be entrepreneurs have also failed in their quest to launch new enterprises in foreign markets. And many others found success to be less than they had imagined, giving up and eventually returning home. The struggles of opening a business in a foreign country are indeed a challenge. Most emerging markets lack an effective infrastructure, for example, and getting even routine things done can take far longer than

one might expect. A four-month wait for a telephone hookup in many countries is not uncommon, for example.

People who want to try this route to success need to remember several important things. First, they must tailor their products and services to the local market. Second, they should not expect to get rich, but instead must be willing to work long and hard just to make ends meet. A certain degree of luck is also needed, as is a fair measure of perseverance. And market opportunities are where you find them—many successful entrepreneurs in foreign countries have found their market niche by providing products and services for other entrepreneurs.

Case Questions

1. What factors most likely contribute to success and failure in international start-up companies like Stillking Productions?
2. What countries or regions today do you think are most amenable to start-up operations by foreign entrepreneurs?
3. If you wanted to move to another country and start a business, where would you go, and what would you do?

Case References: "Turning Small into a Big Advantage, *Business Week*, July 13, 1998, pp. 42–44; "Go East," *Forbes*, December 2, 1996, pp. 80–82; William Echikson, "Young Americans Go Abroad to Strike It Rich," *Fortune*, October 17, 1994, pp. 185–195.

CHAPTER NOTES

1. Ronald B. Lieber, "Beating the Odds," *Fortune*, March 31, 1997, pp. 82–90 (quote on page 85); "Flashbacks," *Forbes*, April 7, 1997, p. 143; and "Those New Brews Have the Blues," *Business Week*, March 9, 1998, p. 40.
2. Bro Uttal, "Inside the Deal That Made Bill Gates $350,000,000," *Fortune*, July 21, 1986, pp. 23–33.
3. "Women Entrepreneurs," *Business Week*, April 18, 1994, pp. 104–110.
4. Scott Shane, "Explaining Variation in Rates of Entrepreneurship in the United States: 1899–1988," *Journal of Management*, Vol. 22, No. 5, 1996, pp. 747–781.
5. "Big vs. Small," *Time*, September 5, 1988, pp. 48–50 and J. A. Schumpeter, *Capitalism, Socialism, and Democracy*, 3rd ed. (New York: Harper & Row, 1950).
6. Amar Bhide, "How Entrepreneurs Craft Strategies That Work," *Harvard Business Review*, March–April 1994, pp. 150–163.
7. "Hot Growth Companies," *Business Week*, May 26, 1997, pp. 90–102.
8. See Faye Brookman, "Specialty Cosmetic Stores: A Hit with Frustrated Consumers," *Advertising Age*, March 4, 1991, p. 32 and Laurie Freeman, "Department Stores in Fight for Their Lives," *Advertising Age*, March 4, 1991, p. 29.
9. F. M. Scherer, *Industrial Market Structure and Economic Performance*, 2nd ed. (Boston: Houghton Mifflin, 1980).
10. Joel Kurtzman, "These Days, Small Manufacturers Can Play on a Level Field," *Fortune*, July 20, 1998, p. 156F.

11. The importance of discovering niches is emphasized in Charles Hill and Gareth Jones, *Strategic Management: An Integrative Approach*, 4th ed. (Boston: Houghton Mifflin, 1998).

12. "Turning Small Into a Big Advantage," *Business Week*, July 13, 1998, pp. 42–44.

13. Gregory Patterson, "An American in . . . Siberia?" *Fortune*, August 4, 1997, p. 63 and "Crazy for Crunchies," *Newsweek*, April 28, 1997, p. 49.

14. "Persistence Pays in Search of Funds," *USA Today*, May 11, 1987, p. 3E.

15. Daniel M. Cable and Scott Shane, "A Prisoner's Dilemma Approach to Entrepreneur-Venture Capitalist Relationships," *Academy of Management Review*, January 1997, pp. 142–176. See also "New Breed of Investor Brings More Than Cash to Hopeful Start-Ups," *Wall Street Journal*, August 25, 1997, pp. A1, A11.

16. Gary J. Castrogiovanni, "Pre Start-up Planning and the Survival of New Small Businesses: Theoretical Linkages," *Journal of Management*, Vol. 22, No. 6, 1996, pp. 801–822.

17. Faye Rice, "How to Succeed at Cloning a Small Business," *Fortune*, October 28, 1985, pp. 60–66 and "Franchising Tries to Divvy Up Risk," *USA Today*, May 11, 1987, p. 5E.

18. "McDonald's—Can it Regain Its Golden Touch?" *Business Week*, March 9, 1998, pp. 70–77.

19. Scott Shane and Chester Spell, "Factors for New Franchise Success," *Sloan Management Review*, Spring 1998, pp. 43–50.

20. "We Cure Small-Business Headaches," *Forbes*, October 20, 1997, pp. 168–169.

21. Charles Burck, "The Real World of the Entrepreneur," *Fortune*, April 5, 1993, pp. 62–80.

22. See Bethany McLean, "Investing Wisely in America's Fastest-Growing Companies," *Fortune*, September 28, 1998, pp. 216–248, for a discussion of firms currently going through this phase of growth.

23. John B. Miner, "The Expanded Horizon for Achieving Entrepreneurial Success," *Organizational Dynamics*, Winter 1997, pp. 54–67.

24. Amar Bhide, "The Questions Every Entrepreneur Must Answer," *Harvard Business Review*, November–December 1996, pp. 120–132. See also "'Career Opportunity: Long Hours, Good Pay,'" *Forbes*, May 19, 1997, pp. 102–103.

25. See Jay Barney, "Strategic Factor Markets: Expectations, Luck, and Business Strategy," *Management Science*, October 1986, pp. 1231–1241.

6

Organization Structure and Design

OBJECTIVES

After studying this chapter, you should be able to:

- Identify and describe the basic elements of organizations.
- Describe the bureaucratic perspective on organization design.
- Identify and explain several situational influences on organization design.
- Describe the basic forms of organization design that characterize many organizations.
- Describe emerging forms of organization design.

For decades Boeing has been the world's largest manufacturer of commercial aircraft. And almost since its inception in 1916, Boeing has been a hierarchical, bureaucratic firm bound by rules, regulations, and procedures. But as the twentieth century draws to a close, Boeing is remaking itself into a sleek and flexible organization that is in every way the antithesis of its former self.

Top managers at Boeing recognized several warning signals that changes were needed. For one thing, a long and bitter strike by the International Association of Machinists & Aerospace Workers revealed just how much distrust there was among the firm's workers and its managers. And for another, airline customers have become increasingly vocal in their criticism of the firm's delivery schedules and price structures.

As CEO Frank Shrontz was retiring, he named Philip Condit as his successor and challenged him to remake Boeing into a firm that would continue its legacy of engineering, technology, and industry leadership while simultaneously adopting many of the organization design features popularized by new high-technology companies like Microsoft and Compaq Computer.

Condit started by carefully analyzing every facet of how Boeing conducted its operations. He concluded that the firm's antiquated functional organization design was its biggest impediment. In a functional design, functional specialists in areas such as engineering, finance, and marketing are grouped together into departments. Each department, in turn, is responsible for its own unique functional area.

For example, at Boeing the work of design engineers was totally independent of production and operations people responsible for actually constructing airplanes and their component parts. That is, the engineer drew plans and then turned them over to the manufacturers who had no input whatsoever. Similarly, if tool builders found a problem in a design for a new part for an airplane, they had to report it to their supervisor, who took it up the ladder until the problem finally reached the senior engineer who had originally diagrammed the tools. The engineer would then respond to the question and pass the information laboriously back down the chain of command.

Condit decided that things needed to change. As a result, he threw out Boeing's old-fashioned functional design and replaced it with an organic and flexible model based on products. Under the new design, representatives from every relevant functional department work together from the inception of a project until its completion. Suppose, for example, that Boeing wanted to develop a new modular luggage storage compartment for its aircraft. Under the new arrangement, managers would create an organization within an organization to get the project completed. The group would have design engineers, manufacturing managers, industrial marketing managers, financial experts, and even a human resource specialist to provide employment services for the group.

By using the new approach, Boeing can move people and their talents where they need them. Moreover, organizational barriers are broken down as people communicate with one another more frequently and more directly. For example, if tool builders have a problem with a design now, they can pick up a telephone and call the engineer who designed the part. Or, just as likely, they will see the designer in a product meeting and can ask their question face to face. Boeing is still struggling with the last vestiges of its old ways of doing business, and the firm's financial performance is not what investors want. But overall, Boeing's managers think that with their new organization design in place, the sky's the limit![1]

"We're trying to destroy all of the old functional hierarchies."

Ron Woodard, Boeing executive

hilip Condit and his executive team at Boeing are remaking one of the largest major corporations in the world. The focus of their efforts is the structure and design of the company. One of the major ingredients in managing any business is the creation of an organization structure and design to link the various activities and elements that comprise the organization. As we will see, there is no one best structure and design, so managers have to assess various options as they carry out organizing activities, the second basic function of all managers.

This chapter discusses many of the critical elements of organization structure and design that managers can control and is the first of three devoted to organizing. We first elaborate on the meaning of organization structure and design. Then we explore the basic elements that managers use to create an organization. We conclude by introducing several current issues in organizing.

The Nature of Organizing

organization structure and design
The set of elements that can be used to configure an organization

The phrase **organization structure and design** refers to the overall set of structural elements and the relationships among those elements used to manage an organization.[2] This section introduces and describes these elements.

■ Job Specialization

job specialization The degree to which the overall task of the organization is broken down and divided into smaller component parts

The first element of organization structure is job specialization. **Job specialization** is the degree to which the overall task of the organization is broken into smaller component parts. Job specialization is a normal extension of organizational growth. For example, when Walt Disney started his company, he did everything himself—wrote cartoons, drew them, and then marketed them to theaters. As the business grew, he eventually hired others to perform many of these functions. As growth continued, so too did specialization. For example, animation artists working on Disney movies today may specialize in drawing only a single character. And today, The Walt Disney Company has thousands of specialized jobs.

Benefits and Limitations of Specialization   One benefit of job specialization is that workers performing small, simple tasks can become very proficient at that task.[3] Second, transfer time between tasks decreases. If employees perform several tasks, some time is lost as they stop doing the first task and start doing the next. Third, the more narrowly defined a job is, the easier it is to develop specialized equipment to assist with that job. Fourth, when an employee who performs a highly specialized job is absent or resigns, the manager is able to train someone new relatively quickly and at low costs.

The foremost criticism of job specialization is that workers who perform highly specialized jobs may become bored and dissatisfied. The job may be so specialized that it offers no challenge or stimulation. Boredom and monotony set in, absenteeism rises, and the quality of the work may suffer. Furthermore, the anticipated benefits of specialization do not always occur. For example, a study conducted at Maytag found that the time spent moving work-in-process from one worker to another was greater than the time needed for the same individual to change from job to job.[4] Thus, although some degree of specialization is necessary, it should not be carried to extremes because of the possible negative results. Managers must be sensitive to situations in which extreme specialization should be avoided. And indeed, several alternative approaches to designing jobs have been developed in recent years.

Alternatives to Specialization   To counter the problems associated with specialization, managers have sought other approaches to job design that achieve a better balance between organizational demands for efficiency and productivity and individual needs for creativity and autonomy. Five alternative approaches are job rotation, job enlargement, job enrichment, the job characteristics approach, and work teams.[5]

Job rotation involves systematically moving employees from one job to another. A worker in a warehouse might unload trucks on Monday, carry incoming inventory to storage on Tuesday, verify invoices on Wednesday, pull outgoing inventory from storage on Thursday, and load trucks on Friday. Thus the jobs do not change, but instead, workers move from job to job. Unfortunately, this factor explains why job rotation has not been very successful in enhancing employee motivation or satisfaction. Jobs that are amenable to rotation tend to be relatively standard and routine. Workers who are rotated to a "new" job may be more satisfied at first, but satisfaction soon wanes. Although many companies (among them Ford, Prudential Insurance, TRW, and Western Electric) have tried job rotation, it is most often used today as a training device to improve worker skills and flexibility.

Job enlargement was developed to increase the total number of tasks workers perform. As a result, all workers perform a wide variety of tasks, which presumably reduces the level of job dissatisfaction. Many organizations, including IBM, AT&T, and Maytag, have used job enlargement. Unfortunately, although job enlargement does have some positive consequences, training

job rotation   An alternative to job specialization that involves systematically moving employees from one job to another

job enlargement   An alternative to job specialization that involves giving employees more tasks to perform

Managers are always on the alert for new and better ways to design jobs for employees. One of the newest strategies is called cell manufacturing. Cell manufacturing is a flexible system that uses elements from job enrichment and the job characteristics theory to give workers more control over their jobs while simultaneously improving flexibility for the company by allowing it to more easily alter the products being made by a given worker. This employee is assembling computers for Compaq, a pioneer in cell manufacturing.

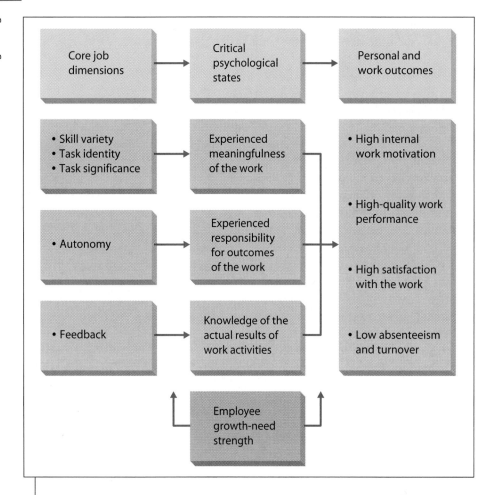

FIGURE 6.1
The Job Characteristics Approach

The job characteristics approach to job design provides a viable alternative to job specialization. Five core job dimensions may lead to critical psychological states that, in turn, may enhance motivation, performance, and satisfaction while also reducing absenteeism and turnover.

Source: J. R. Hackman and G. R. Oldham, "Motivation Through the Design of Work: Test of a Theory," *Organizational Behavior and Human Performance,* Vol. 16 (1976), pp. 250–279. Copyright © Academic Press, Inc. Reprinted by permission of Academic Press and the authors.

costs usually rise, unions have argued that pay should increase because the worker is doing more tasks, and in many cases the work remains boring and routine.

A more comprehensive approach, **job enrichment**, assumes that increasing the range and variety of tasks is not sufficient by itself to improve employee motivation.[6] To implement job enrichment, managers remove some controls from the job, delegate more authority to employees, and structure the work in complete, natural units. These changes increase subordinates' sense of responsibility. Another part of job enrichment is to continually assign new and challenging tasks, thereby increasing employees' opportunity for personal growth and advancement. AT&T, Texas Instruments, IBM, and General Foods have reported success with job enrichment. This approach, however, also has disadvantages. For example, work systems should be, but seldom are, thoroughly analyzed before enrichment, and managers rarely ask for employee preferences when enriching jobs.

The **job characteristics approach** is an alternative to job specialization that does take into account the work system and employee preferences.[7] As illustrated in Figure 6.1, the job characteristics approach suggests that jobs can be diagnosed and improved along five core dimensions:

1. *Skill variety:* the number of things a person does in a job
2. *Task identity:* the extent to which the worker does a complete or identifiable portion of the total job
3. *Task significance:* the perceived importance of the task
4. *Autonomy:* the degree of control the worker has over how the work is performed
5. *Feedback:* the extent to which the worker knows how well the job is being performed

Increasingly, the presence of these dimensions in a job presumably leads to higher motivation, performance, and satisfaction and to lower absenteeism and turnover. Numerous studies have been conducted to test the usefulness of this approach. The Southwestern Division of Prudential Insurance, for example, used it in its claims division. Results included moderate declines in turnover and a small but measurable improvement in work quality. Other research findings have not supported this approach as strongly. Thus, although the job characteristics approach is one of the most promising alternatives to job specialization, it is probably not the final answer.

Another alternative to job specialization is the **work team** approach. Under this arrangement, a group is given responsibility for designing the work system to be used in performing an interrelated set of jobs. In the typical assembly-line system, the work flows from one worker to the next, and each worker has a specified job to perform. In a work team, however, the group itself decides how to allocate jobs. For example, the work team assigns specific tasks to members, monitors and controls its own performance, and has autonomy over work scheduling.[8] We discuss work teams more fully in Chapter 13.

■ Departmentalization

The second building block of organization structure is **departmentalization**—the grouping of jobs according to some logical arrangement. When organizations are small, the owner-manager can personally oversee everyone who works there. As an organization grows, however, personally supervising all the employees becomes more and more difficult for the owner-manager. Consequently, new managerial positions are created to supervise the work of others. Employees are not assigned to particular managers randomly. Rather, jobs are grouped according to some plan. The logic embodied in such a plan is the basis for all departmentalization.[9]

Functional Departmentalization   The most common approach to departmentalization, especially among small organizations, is by function. **Functional departmentalization** groups together those jobs involving the same or similar activities. This approach has three primary advantages. First, each department can be staffed by experts in that functional area. Marketing experts can be hired to run the marketing function, for example. Second, supervision is facilitated because an individual manager needs to be familiar with only a relatively narrow set of skills. And third, coordinating activities inside each department is relatively easy.

On the other hand, decision making tends to become slower and more bureaucratic. Employees may also begin to concentrate too narrowly on their own units and lose sight of the total organizational system. Finally, accountability and performance become increasingly difficult to monitor. For example, determining whether a new product fails because of production deficiencies or a poor marketing campaign may not be possible.

Product Departmentalization   **Product departmentalization**—a second common approach to departmentalization—involves grouping and arranging activities around products or product groups. Most larger businesses adopt this form of departmentalization for grouping activities at the business or corporate level. Product departmentalization also has three major advantages. First, all activities associated with one product or product group can be easily integrated and coordinated. Second, the speed and effectiveness of decision making are enhanced. Third, the performance of individual products or product

job enrichment   An alternative to job specialization that involves increasing both the number of tasks the worker does and the control the worker has over the job

job characteristics approach   An alternative to job specialization that suggests that jobs should be diagnosed and improved along five core dimensions, taking into account both the work system and employee preferences

work team   An alternative to job specialization that allows an entire group to design the work system it will use to perform an interrelated set of tasks

departmentalization   The process of grouping jobs according to some logical arrangement

functional departmentalization
Grouping jobs involving the same or similar activities

product departmentalization
Grouping activities around products or product groups

groups can be assessed easily and objectively, thereby improving the accountability of departments for the results of their activities.

On the other hand, managers in each department may develop tendencies to focus on their own product or product group to the exclusion of the rest of the organization. That is, a marketing manager may see her or his primary duty as helping the group rather than helping the overall organization. Additionally, administrative costs rise because each department must have its own functional specialists for things like marketing research and financial analysis.

customer departmentalization
Grouping activities to respond to and interact with specific customers or customer groups

Customer Departmentalization   Under **customer departmentalization** the organization structures its activities to respond to and interact with specific customers or customer groups. The lending activities in most banks, for example, are usually tailored to meet the needs of different kinds of customers (for example, business, consumer, mortgage, and agricultural loans). The basic advantage of this approach is that the organization is able to use skilled specialists to deal with unique customers or customer groups. It takes one set of skills to evaluate a balance sheet and lend a business $500,000 for operating capital and a different set of skills to evaluate an individual's creditworthiness and lend a consumer $10,000 for a new car. However, a fairly large administrative staff is required to integrate the activities of the various departments. In banks, for example, coordination is necessary to make sure that the organization does not overcommit itself in any one area and to handle collections on delinquent accounts from a diverse set of customers.

location departmentalization
Grouping jobs on the basis of defined geographic sites or areas

Location Departmentalization   **Location departmentalization** groups jobs on the basis of defined geographic sites or areas. The defined sites or areas may range in size from a hemisphere to only a few blocks of a large city. The primary advantage of location departmentalization is that it enables the organization to respond easily to unique customer and environmental characteristics in the various regions. On the negative side, a larger administrative staff may be required if the organization must keep track of units in scattered locations.

■ Reporting Relationships

The third basic element of organizing is the establishment of reporting relationships among positions. The purpose of this activity is to clarify the chain of command and the span of management.

chain of command   A clear and distinct line of authority among the positions in an organization

Chain of Command   **Chain of command** is an old concept, first popularized early in this century. The chain of command actually has two components. The first, called *unity of command*, suggests that each person within an organization must have a clear reporting relationship to one and only one boss (as we see later, newer models of organization design successfully violate this premise). The second, called *the scalar principle*, suggests that a clear and unbroken line of authority must extend from the lowest to the highest position in the organization. The popular saying "The buck stops here" is derived from this idea—someone in the organization must ultimately be responsible for every decision.

The Span of Management   Another part of establishing reporting relationships is determining how many people will report to each manager. This defines the **span of management** (sometimes called the *span of control*). For years managers and researchers sought to determine the optimal span of management. For example, should it be relatively narrow (with few subordinates per manager) or relatively wide (with many subordinates)? Today we recognize that there are no universal, cut-and-dried prescriptions for an ideal or optimal span.[10] Instead, managers have to carefully assess their situation and context when making decisions about determining the span most suited for their needs.

span of management The number of people who report to a particular manager

Tall Versus Flat Organizations The span of management is also a primary determinant of whether the organization is relatively tall or flat. One early study at Sears found that a flat structure led to higher levels of employee morale and productivity.[11] It has also been argued that, compared to a flat structure, a tall structure is more expensive (because of the larger number of managers involved) and fosters more communication problems (because of the increased number of people through whom information must pass). On the other hand, a wide span of management in a flat organization may result in a manager's having more administrative responsibility (because of fewer managers) and more supervisory responsibility (because of more subordinates reporting to each manager). If these additional responsibilities become excessive, the flat organization may suffer.[12]

Many experts agree that businesses can function effectively with fewer layers of organization than they currently have. A few years ago the Franklin Mint, for example, reduced its number of management layers from six to four. At the same time, CEO Stewart Resnick increased his span of management from six to twelve. In similar fashion IBM has eliminated several layers of management. One additional reason for this trend is that improved organizational communication networks allow managers to stay in touch with a larger number of subordinates than was possible even just a few years ago.[13]

authority Power that has been legitimized by the organization

■ Authority

Another important building block in structuring organizations is the determination of how authority is to be distributed among positions. **Authority** is power that has been legitimized by the organization.[14] Two specific issues that managers must address when distributing authority are delegation and decentralization.[15]

Distributing authority is a key building block in creating an effective organization. Unfortunately, some managers prefer to avoid accountability for decisions and work to ensure that someone else can always be held responsible for mistakes and errors. This Dilbert cartoon, for instance, illustrates a whimsical view of a manager teaching others to avoid accountability and to pass the buck.

DILBERT reprinted by permission of United Feature Syndicate, Inc.

delegation The process by which a manager assigns a portion of his or her total workload to others

The Delegation Process Delegation is the establishment of a pattern of authority between a superior and one or more subordinates. Specifically, **delegation** is the process by which managers assign a portion of their total workload to others.[16] The delegation process involves three steps. First, the manager assigns responsibility, or gives the subordinate a job to do. The assignment of responsibility might range from instructing a subordinate to prepare a report to placing the person in charge of a task force. Along with the assignment the individual is also given the authority to do the job. The manager may give the subordinate the power to requisition needed information from confidential files or to direct a group of other workers. Finally, the manager establishes the subordinate's accountability—that is, the subordinate accepts an obligation to carry out the task assigned by the manager.

Decentralization and Centralization Just as authority can be delegated from one individual to another, organizations also develop patterns of authority across a wide variety of positions and departments. **Decentralization** is the process of systematically delegating power and authority throughout the organization to middle- and lower-level managers. Therefore, a decentralized organization is one in which decision-making power and authority are delegated as far down the chain of command as possible. It is important to remember that decentralization is actually one end of a continuum anchored at the other end by **centralization**, the process of systematically retaining power and authority in the hands of higher-level managers. Hence, in a centralized organization, decision-making power and authority are retained at the higher levels of management. No organization is ever completely decentralized or completely centralized: some firms position themselves toward one end of the continuum, and some lean the other way.[17]

decentralization The process of systematically delegating power and authority throughout the organization to middle- and lower-level managers

centralization The process of systematically retaining power and authority in the hands of higher-level managers

What factors determine an organization's position on the decentralization-centralization continuum? One common determinant is the organization's external environment. Usually, the greater the complexity and uncertainty of the environment, the greater the tendency to decentralize. Firms also have a tendency to do what they have done in the past, so there is likely to be some relationship between what an organization did in its early history and what it chooses to do today in terms of centralization or decentralization. The nature of the decisions being made is also considered. The costlier and riskier the decision, the greater the pressure to centralize. Hence, a manager has no clear-cut guidelines to determine whether to centralize or decentralize. Many successful organizations such as Sears and General Electric are quite decentralized. Equally successful firms, such as McDonald's and Kmart, have remained centralized.

■ Coordination

coordination The process of linking the activities of the various departments of the organization

A fifth major element of organizing is coordination. **Coordination** is the process of linking the activities of the various jobs and departments of the organization.[18] The primary reason for coordination is that departments and work groups are interdependent—they depend on each other for information and resources to perform their respective activities.

The Need for Coordination The greater the interdependence between departments, the more coordination the organization requires if departments are to be able to perform effectively. There are three major forms of interdependence: pooled, sequential, and reciprocal.[19] **Pooled interdependence** represents the lowest level of interdependence. Units with pooled interdependence operate with little interaction—the output of the units is pooled at the organizational level. The Gap clothing stores operate with pooled interdependence. Each store has its own operating budget, staff, and so forth. The profits or losses from each store are "added together" at the corporate level. The stores are interdependent to the extent that the final success or failure of one store affects the others, but they do not generally interact on a day-to-day basis.

In **sequential interdependence** the output of one unit becomes the input for another in a sequential fashion. This creates a moderate level of interdependence. At Nissan, for example, one plant assembles engines and then ships them to a final assembly site at another plant where the cars are completed. The plants are interdependent in that the final assembly plant must have the engines from engine assembly before it can perform its primary function of producing finished automobiles. But the level of interdependence is generally one-way—the engine plant is not necessarily dependent on the final assembly plant.

Reciprocal interdependence exists when activities flow both ways between units. This form is clearly the most complex. Within a Marriott Hotel, for example, the reservations department, front-desk check-in, and housekeeping are all reciprocally interdependent. Reservations has to provide front-desk employees with information about how many guests to expect each day, and housekeeping needs to know which rooms require priority cleaning. If any unit does not do its job properly, the other two will be affected.

Structural Coordination Techniques Because of the obvious coordination requirements that characterize most organizations, many techniques for achieving coordination have been developed. Organizations that use the *hierarchy* to achieve coordination place one manager in charge of interdependent departments or units. In Kmart distribution centers, major activities include receiving and unloading bulk shipments from railroad cars and loading other shipments onto trucks for distribution to retail outlets. The two groups (receiving and shipping) are interdependent in that they share the loading docks and some equipment. To ensure coordination and minimize conflict, one manager is in charge of the whole operation.

Routine coordination activities can be handled via *rules and standard procedures*. In the Kmart distribution center, an outgoing truck shipment has priority over an incoming rail shipment. Thus, when trucks are to be loaded, the shipping unit is given access to all of the center's auxiliary forklifts. This priority is specifically stated in a rule. But, as useful as rules and procedures often are in routine situations, they are not particularly effective when coordination problems are complex or unusual.

Liaisons also serve a coordination function. A manager in a liaison role coordinates interdependent units by acting as a common point of contact. This individual may not have any formal authority over the groups, but instead simply facilitates the flow of information between units. Two engineering groups

pooled interdependence When units operate with little interaction, their output is simply pooled

sequential interdependence When the output of one unit becomes the input of another in sequential fashion

reciprocal interdependence When activities flow both ways between units

working on component systems for a large project might interact through a liaison. The liaison maintains familiarity with each group as well as with the overall project. She can answer questions and otherwise serve to integrate the activities of all the groups.

A *task force* may be created when the need for coordination is acute. When interdependence is complex and several units are involved, a single liaison person may not be sufficient. Instead, a task force might be assembled by drawing one representative from each group. The coordination function is thus spread across several individuals, each of whom has special information about one of the groups involved. For example, several task forces comprised of members from both firms are planning the merger between Amoco and British Petroleum.

Integrating departments are occasionally used for coordination. These entities are somewhat similar to task forces but are more permanent. An integrating department generally has some permanent members as well as members who are assigned temporarily from units that are particularly in need of coordination. An integrating department usually has more authority than a task force and may even be given some budgetary control by the organization.

The Bureaucratic Model of Organization Design

bureaucracy A model of organization design based on a legitimate and formal system of authority

In Chapter 1 we made the distinction between contingency and universal approaches to solving management problems. Recall, for example, that universal perspectives try to identify the "one best way" to manage organizations, and contingency perspectives suggest that appropriate managerial behavior in a given situation depends on, or is contingent on, unique elements in that situation. The foundation of contemporary thinking about organization design can be traced back to an important early universal perspective called the *bureaucratic model*.

Max Weber, an influential German sociologist, was a pioneer of classical organization theory. At the core of his writings was the bureaucratic model of organizations.[20] The Weberian perspective suggests that a **bureaucracy** is a model of organization design based on a legitimate and formal system of authority. Many people associate bureaucracy with red tape, rigidity, and passing the buck. For example, how many times have you heard people refer disparagingly to "the federal bureaucracy"?

Weber viewed the bureaucratic form of organization as logical, rational, and efficient. He offered the model as a framework to which all organizations should aspire: the "one best way" of doing things. According to Weber, the ideal bureaucracy exhibits five basic characteristics:

1. The organization has a distinct division of labor, and an expert fills each position.
2. The organization has a consistent set of rules to ensure that task performance is uniform.
3. The organization has a hierarchy of positions or offices that create a chain of command from the top of the organization to the bottom.

4. Managers conduct business in an impersonal way and maintain an appropriate social distance between themselves and their subordinates.

5. Employment and advancement in the organization is based on technical expertise, and employees are protected from arbitrary dismissal.

Perhaps the best examples of bureaucracies today are government agencies and universities. Consider, for example, the steps you must go through and the forms you must fill out to apply for admission to college, request housing, register each semester, change majors, submit a degree plan, substitute a course, and file for graduation. The reason these procedures are necessary is that universities deal with large numbers of people who must be treated equally and fairly. Hence rules, regulations, and standard operating procedures are needed. Large labor unions are also usually organized as bureaucracies.[21] Some bureaucracies, such as the U.S. Postal Service (USPS), are trying to portray themselves as less mechanistic and impersonal. The strategy of the USPS is to become more service oriented as a way to fight back against competitors like Federal Express and United Parcel Service (UPS).

A primary strength of the bureaucratic model is that several of its elements (such as reliance on rules and employment based on expertise) do, in fact, often improve efficiency. Bureaucracies also help prevent favoritism (because everyone must follow the rules) and make procedures and practices very clear to everyone. Unfortunately, however, this approach also has several disadvantages. One major disadvantage is that the bureaucratic model results in inflexibility and rigidity. Once rules are created and put into place, making exceptions or changing them is often difficult. In addition, the bureaucracy often results in the neglect of human and social processes within the organization.

Situational Influences on Organization Design

The **situational view of organization design** is based on the assumption that the optimal design for any given organization depends on a set of relevant situational factors.[22] That is, situational factors play a role in determining the best organization design for any particular circumstance. The major factors—technology, environment, size, and organizational life cycle—are discussed here.

situational view of organization design Based on the assumption that the optimal design for any given organization depends on a set of relevant situational factors

Core Technology

Technology is the conversion processes used to transform inputs (such as materials or information) into outputs (such as products or services). Most organ-izations use multiple technologies, but an organization's most important one is called its *core technology*. Although most people visualize assembly lines and machinery when they think of technology, the term can also be applied to serv-ice organizations. For example, the brokerage firm Merrill Lynch uses technology to transform investment dollars into income in much the same way that Union Carbide uses natural resources to manufacture chemical products.

technology Conversion processes used to transform inputs into outputs

The link between technology and organization design was first recognized by Joan Woodward.[23] Woodward studied one hundred manufacturing firms in southern England. She collected information about such factors as the history of each organization, its manufacturing processes, its forms and procedures, and its financial performance. Woodward expected to find a relationship between the size of an organization and its design, but no such relationship emerged. As a result, she began to seek other explanations for differences. Close scrutiny of the firms in her sample led her to recognize a potential relationship between technology and organization design. This follow-up analysis led Woodward to first classify the organizations according to their technology. She identified three basic forms of technology:

1. *Unit or small-batch technology.* The product is custom-made to customer specifications or else it is produced in small quantities. Organizations using this form of technology include a tailor shop like Brooks Brothers (custom suits), a printing shop like Kinko's (business cards, company stationery), and a photography studio.

2. *Large-batch or mass-production technology.* The product is manufactured in assembly-line fashion by combining component parts into another part or finished product. Examples include automobile manufacturers like Subaru, washing-machine companies like Whirlpool Corporation, and electronics firms like Philips.

3. *Continuous-process technology.* Raw materials are transformed to a finished product by a series of machine or process transformations. The composition of the materials themselves is changed. Examples include petroleum refineries like Exxon and Shell and chemical refineries like Dow Chemical and Hoescht Celanese.

These forms of technology are listed in order of their assumed levels of complexity. That is, unit or small-batch technology is presumed to be the least complex and continuous-process technology the most complex. Woodward found that different configurations of organization design were associated with each technology.

Specifically, Woodward found that the two extremes (unit or small batch, and continuous process) tended to be relatively organic—less rigid and formal—whereas the middle-range organizations (large batch or mass production) were much more like bureaucracies. The large-batch and mass-production organizations also had a higher level of specialization.[24] Finally, Woodward found that organizational success was related to the extent to which organizations followed the typical pattern. For example, successful continuous-process organizations tended to be more organic, whereas less-successful firms with the same technology were more bureaucratic.

Small-batch technology can affect organization design in a number of ways. Shanghai Tang is a Hong Kong–based operation that makes custom suits and dresses. The firm's tailors use modern technology, rely on traditional styling, and have a reputation for high-quality work that has resulted in rapid growth. By using new flexible manufacturing methods, the company can deliver most custom-tailored apparel within twenty-four hours.

■ Environment

There are also a number of specific linkages between environmental elements and organization design. The first widely recognized analysis of environment-organization design linkages was provided by Tom Burns and G. M. Stalker.[25] Like Woodward, Burns and Stalker worked in England. Their first step was identifying two extreme forms of organizational environment: stable (one that remains relatively constant over time) and unstable (subject to uncertainty and rapid change). Next they studied the designs of organizations in each type of environment. Not surprisingly, they found that organizations in stable environments and organizations in unstable environments tended to have different kinds of designs. The two kinds of designs that emerged were called mechanistic and organic organization.

A **mechanistic organization** was most frequently found in stable environments. Free from uncertainty, organizations structured their activities in rather predictable ways by means of rules, specialized jobs, and centralized authority. Mechanistic organizations are also quite similar in nature to bureaucracies. Although no environment is completely stable, Kmart and Wendy's use mechanistic designs. Each Kmart store, for example, has prescribed methods for store design and merchandise-ordering processes. No deviations are allowed from these methods. An **organic organization**, on the other hand, was most often found in unstable and unpredictable environments, in which constant change and uncertainty usually dictate a much higher level of fluidity and flexibility. Motorola (facing rapid technological change) and The Limited (facing constant change in consumer tastes) use organic designs. A manager at Motorola, for example, has considerable discretion over how work is performed and how problems can be solved.

These ideas were extended in the United States by Paul R. Lawrence and Jay W. Lorsch.[26] They agreed that environmental factors influence organization design but believed that this influence varies between different units of the same organization. In fact, they predicted that each organizational unit has its own unique environment and responds by developing unique attributes. Lawrence and Lorsch suggested that organizations could be characterized along two primary dimensions.

One of these dimensions, **differentiation**, is the extent to which the organization is broken down into subunits. A firm with many subunits is highly differentiated; one with few subunits has a low level of differentiation. The second dimension, **integration**, is the degree to which the various subunits must work together in a coordinated fashion. For example, if each unit competes in a different market and has its own production facilities, they may need little integration. Lawrence and Lorsch reasoned that the degree of differentiation and integration needed by an organization depends on the stability of the environments that its subunits faced.[27]

mechanistic organization Similar to the bureaucratic model, most frequently found in stable environments

organic organization Very flexible and informal model of organization design, most often found in unstable and unpredictable environments

differentiation Extent to which the organization is broken into subunits

integration Degree to which the various subunits must work together in a coordinated fashion

■ Organizational Size and Life Cycle

The size of an organization and its life cycle are other factors that affect its design. **Organizational size** is the total number of full-time or full-time–equivalent employees.[28] A team of researchers at the University of Aston in

organizational size Total number of full-time or full-time–equivalent employees

Birmingham, England, believed that Woodward had failed to find a size-structure relationship (which was her original expectation) because almost all the organizations she studied were relatively small (three-fourths had fewer than five hundred employees).[29] Thus the Aston researchers decided to undertake a study of a wider array of organizations to determine how size and technology both individually and jointly affect an organization's design.

Their primary finding was that technology did in fact influence structural variables in small firms, probably because all their activities tended to be centered around their core technology. In large firms, however, the strong technology-design link broke down, most likely because technology is not as central to ongoing activities in large organizations. The Aston studies yielded a number of basic generalizations: when compared to small organizations, large organizations tend to be characterized by higher levels of job specialization, more standard operating procedures, more rules, more regulations, and a greater degree of decentralization.

Of course, size is not constant. As we note in Chapter 5, for example, some small businesses are formed but soon disappear. Others remain as small, independently operated enterprises as long as their owner-manager lives. A few, like Compaq Computer, Dell Computer, Liz Claiborne, and Reebok, skyrocket to become organizational giants. And occasionally large organizations reduce their size through layoffs or divestitures. For example, Navistar is now far smaller than it was in its previous incarnation as International Harvester Co. Although no clear pattern explains changes in size, many organizations progress through a four-stage **organizational life cycle**.[30]

organizational life cycle Progression through which organizations evolve as they grow and mature

The first stage is the *birth* of the organization. The second stage, *youth*, is characterized by growth and the expansion of organizational resources. *Midlife* is a period of gradual growth evolving eventually into stability. Finally, *maturity* is a period of stability, perhaps eventually evolving into decline. Montgomery Ward is an example of a mature organization—it is experiencing little or no growth and appears to be falling behind the rest of the retailing industry.

Managers must confront a number of organization design issues as the organization progresses through these stages. In general, as an organization passes from one stage to the next, it becomes bigger, more mechanistic, and more decentralized. It also becomes more specialized, devotes more attention to planning, and takes on an increasingly large staff component. Finally, coordination demands increase, formalization increases, organizational units become geographically more dispersed, and control systems become more extensive. Thus an organization's size and design are clearly linked, and this link is dynamic because of the organizational life cycle.[31]

Basic Forms of Organization Design

Because so many factors can influence organization design, it should come as no surprise that organizations adopt many different kinds of designs. Most designs, however, fall into one of four basic categories. Others are hybrids based on two or more of the basic forms.

■ Functional (U-Form) Design

The **functional design** is an arrangement based on the functional approach to departmentalization. This design has also been termed the **U-form** (for unitary).[32] Under the U-form arrangement the members and units in the organization are grouped into functional departments such as marketing and production. For the organization to operate efficiently in this design, considerable coordination must exist across departments. This integration and coordination are most commonly the responsibility of the CEO and members of senior management. Figure 6.2 shows the U-form design as applied to the corporate level of a small manufacturing company. In a U-form organization none of the functional areas can survive without the others. Marketing, for example, needs products from operations to sell and funds from finance to pay for advertising. The WD-40 Company, which makes a popular lubricating oil, and the McIlhenny Company, which makes Tabasco sauce, are both examples of firms that use the U-form design.

In general, this approach shares the basic advantages and disadvantages of functional departmentalization. Thus, it allows the organization to staff all important positions with functional experts and facilitates coordination and integration. On the other hand, it also promotes a functional, rather than an organizational, focus and tends to promote centralization. And as we noted earlier, functionally based designs are most commonly used in small organizations because an individual CEO can easily oversee and coordinate the entire organization. As an organization grows, the CEO finds that staying on top of all functional areas is increasingly difficult.

U-form or **functional design** Based on the functional approach to departmentalization

FIGURE 6.2

Functional U-Form Design for a Small Manufacturing Company

The U-form design is based on functional departmentalization. This small manufacturing firm uses managers at the vice-presidential level to coordinate activities within each functional area of the organization. Note that each functional area is dependent on the others.

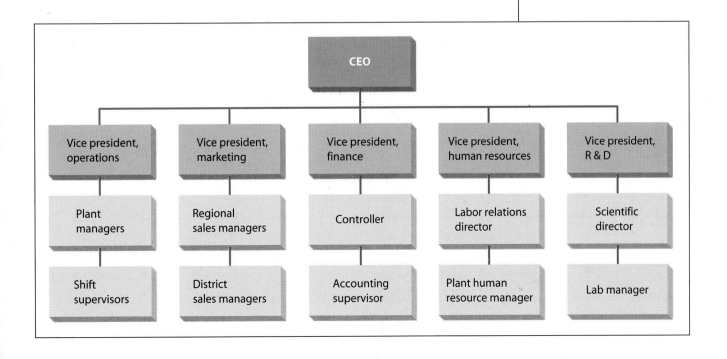

H-form or **conglomerate design**
Based on a set of unrelated businesses

M-form or **divisional design**   Based on multiple businesses in related areas operating within a larger organizational framework

■ Conglomerate (H-Form) Design

Another common form of organization design is the conglomerate, or **H-form**, approach.[33] The **conglomerate design** is used by an organization made up of a set of unrelated businesses. Thus, the H-form design is essentially a holding company that results from unrelated diversification. (The *H* in this term stands for "holding.") This approach is based loosely on the product form of departmentalization. A general manager independently operates each business or set of businesses and is responsible for its profits or losses. Pearson PLC, a British firm, uses the H-form design. As illustrated in Figure 6.3, Pearson consists of six business groups. Although its periodicals and publishing operations are related to one another, all of its other businesses are clearly unrelated. Other firms that use the H-form design include General Electric (aircraft engines, appliances, broadcasting, financial services, lighting products, plastics, and other unrelated businesses) and Tenneco (pipelines, auto parts, shipbuilding, financial services, and other unrelated businesses).

In an H-form organization a corporate staff usually evaluates the perform-ance of each business, allocates corporate resources across companies, and shapes decisions about buying and selling businesses. The basic shortcoming of the H-form design is the complexity associated with holding diverse and unrelated businesses. Managers usually find that comparing and integrating activities across a large number of diverse operations is difficult. Research suggests that many organizations following this approach achieve only average-to-weak financial performance.[34] Thus, although some U.S. firms are still using the H-form design, many have also abandoned it for other approaches.

■ Divisional (M-Form) Design

The divisional design also uses a product form of organization; in contrast to the H-form, however, the divisions are related. Thus, the **divisional design**, or **M-form** (for multidivisional), is based on multiple businesses in related areas operating within a larger organizational framework. This design results

FIGURE 6.3
Conglomerate (H-Form) Design at Pearson PLC

Pearson PLC, a British firm, uses the conglomerate form of organization design. This design, which results from a strategy of unrelated diversification, is complex to manage. Managers have trouble comparing and integrating activities among the dissimilar operations. Companies may abandon this design for another approach, such as the M-form design.

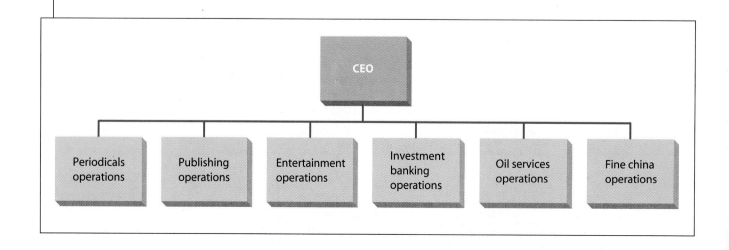

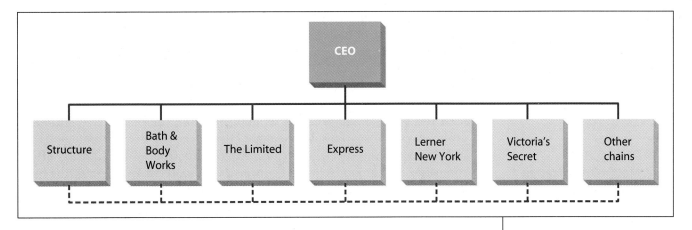

FIGURE 6.4
**Multidivisional (M-Form)
Design at The Limited, Inc.**

from a strategy of related diversification. Some activities are extremely decentralized down to the divisional level; others are centralized at the corporate level.[35] For example, as shown in Figure 6.4, The Limited uses this approach. A general manager heads each division and operates it with reasonable autonomy, but the divisions also coordinate their activities as is appropriate. Other firms that use this approach are The Walt Disney Company (theme parks, movies, and merchandising units, all interrelated) and Hewlett-Packard (computers, printers, scanners, electronic medical equipment, and other electronic instrumentation).

The opportunities for coordination and shared resources represent one of the biggest advantages of the M-form design. The Limited's marketing research and purchasing departments are centralized. Thus, a buyer can inspect a manufacturer's entire product line, buy some designs for The Limited chain, others for Express, and still others for Lerner New York. The M-form design's basic objective is to optimize internal competition and cooperation. Healthy competition among divisions for resources can enhance effectiveness, but cooperation should also be promoted. Research suggests that the M-form organization that can achieve and maintain this balance will outperform large U-form and all H-form organizations.[36]

The Limited, Inc., uses the multidivisional approach to organization design. Although each unit operates with relative autonomy, all units function in the same general market. This design resulted from a strategy of related diversification. Other firms that use M-form designs include PepsiCo and Woolworth Corporation.

■ Matrix Design

The **matrix design**, another approach to organization design, is based on two overlapping bases of departmentalization.[37] The foundation of a matrix is a set of functional departments. A set of product groups, or temporary departments, is then superimposed across the functional departments. Employees in a matrix are simultaneously members of a functional department (such as engineering) and of one or more project teams.

Figure 6.5 shows a basic matrix design. At the top of the organization are functional units headed by vice presidents of engineering, production, finance, and marketing. Each of these managers has several subordinates. Along the side of the organization are a number of positions called *project manager*. Each project manager heads a project group composed of representatives or workers from the functional departments. Note from the figure that a matrix reflects a

matrix design Based on two overlapping bases of departmentalization

multiple-command structure—any given individual reports to both a functional superior and one or more project managers.

The project groups, or teams, are assigned to designated projects or programs. For example, the company might be developing a new product. Representatives are chosen from each functional area to work as a team on the new product. They also retain membership in the original functional group. Ford used this approach in creating its popular Taurus automobile. It formed a group, named Team Taurus, made up of designers, engineers, production specialists, marketing specialists, and other experts from different areas of the company. This group facilitated getting a very successful product to the market at least a year earlier than would have been possible using Ford's previous approaches. More recently, the firm is using the same approach to create the newest version of the Thunderbird.

Both advantages and disadvantages are associated with the matrix design. Six primary advantages have been identified. First, a matrix design enhances flexibility because teams can be created, redefined, and dissolved as needed. Second, because they assume a major role in decision making, team members are likely to be highly motivated and committed to the organization. Third, employees in a matrix organization have considerable opportunity to learn new skills. A fourth advantage of a matrix design is that it provides an efficient way for the organization to take full advantage of its human resources. Fifth, team

FIGURE 6.5
A Matrix Organization

A matrix organization design is created by superimposing a product form of departmentalization onto an existing functional organization. Project managers coordinate teams of employees drawn from different functional departments. Thus, a matrix relies on a multiple-command structure.

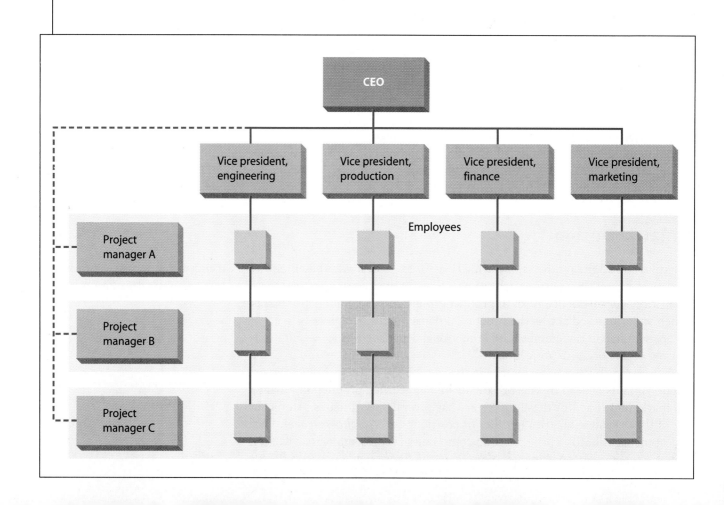

members retain membership in their functional unit so that they can serve as a bridge between the functional unit and the team, enhancing cooperation. Sixth, the matrix design gives top management a useful vehicle for decentralization. Once the day-to-day operations have been delegated, top management can devote more attention to areas such as long-range planning.

On the other hand, the matrix design also has some major disadvantages. Employees may be uncertain about reporting relationships, especially if they are simultaneously assigned to a functional manager and to several project managers. To complicate matters, some managers see the matrix as a form of anarchy in which they have unlimited freedom. Another set of problems is associated with the dynamics of group behavior. Groups take longer than individuals to make decisions, may be dominated by one individual, and may compromise too much. They may also get bogged down in discussion and not focus on their primary objectives. Finally, in a matrix more time may also be required for coordinating task-related activities.[38]

■ Hybrid Designs

Some organizations use a design that represents a hybrid of two or more of the common forms of organization design. For example, an organization may have five related divisions and one unrelated division, making its design a cross between an M-form and an H-form. Indeed, few companies use a design in its pure form: most firms have one basic organization design as a foundation to managing the business but maintain sufficient flexibility so that temporary or permanent modifications can be made for strategic purposes. Ford, for example, used the matrix approach to design the Taurus, but the company is basically a U-form organization showing signs of moving to an M-form design. As we noted earlier, any combination of factors may dictate the appropriate form of design for any particular company.

Emerging Forms of Organization Design

Finally, in today's complex and ever-changing environment, managers, unsurprisingly, continue to explore and experiment with new forms of organization design. This final section highlights some of the more important emerging approaches to organization design.[39]

■ The Team Organization

Some organizations today are using the **team organization**, an approach to organization design that relies almost exclusively on project-type teams with little or no underlying functional hierarchy. Within such an organization people float from project to project according to their skills and the demands of those projects. At Cypress Semiconductor, T. J. Rodgers refuses to allow the organization to grow so large that it can't function this way. Whenever a unit

team organization An approach to organization design that relies almost exclusively on project-type teams, with little or no underlying functional hierarchy

or group starts getting too large, he simply splits it into smaller units. Consequently, all units within the organization are small. This approach allows them to change direction, explore new ideas, and try new methods without dealing with a rigid bureaucratic organizational context.

■ The Virtual Organization

virtual organization One that has little or no formal structure

Closely related to the team organization is the virtual organization. A **virtual organization** is one that has little or no formal structure. Such an organization typically has only a handful of permanent employees and a very small staff and administrative headquarters facility. As the needs of the organization change, its managers bring in temporary workers, lease facilities, and outsource basic support services to meet the demands of each unique situation. As the situation changes, the temporary workforce changes in parallel, with some people leaving the organization and others entering. Facilities and the services subcontracted to others change as well. Thus, the organization exists only in response to its needs. For example, Global Research Consortium (GRC) is a virtual organization. GRC offers research and consulting services to firms doing business in Asia. As clients request various services, GRC's staff of three permanent employees subcontract the work to an appropriate set of several dozen independent consultants and/or researchers with whom it has relationships. At any given time, therefore, GRC may have several projects underway and twenty or thirty people working on projects. As the projects change, so does the composition of the organization.

■ The Learning Organization

learning organization One that works to facilitate the lifelong learning and personal development of all of its employees while continually transforming itself to respond to changing demands and needs

Another recent approach to organization design is the so-called learning organization. Organizations that adopt this approach work to integrate continuous improvement with continuous employee learning and development. Specifically, a **learning organization** is one that works to facilitate the lifelong learning and personal development of all of its employees while continually transforming itself to respond to changing demands and needs.[40] Although managers might approach the concept of a learning organization from a variety of perspectives, improved quality, continuous improvement, and performance measurement are frequent goals. The idea is that the most consistent and logical strategy for achieving continuous improvement is by constantly upgrading employee talent, skill, and knowledge.

In recent years many organizations have implemented this approach. For example, Shell Oil Company purchased an executive conference center north of its headquarters in Houston. The center boosts state-of-the-art classrooms and instructional technology; lodging facilities; a restaurant; and recreational amenities such as a golf course, swimming pool, and tennis courts. Line managers at the firm rotate through the Shell Learning Center, as the facility has been renamed, and serve as teaching faculty. Such teaching assignments last anywhere from a few days to several months. At the same time, all Shell employees routinely attend training programs, seminars, and related activities designed to teach them how to contribute more effectively to the firm. Recent seminar topics have ranged from time management to implications of the Americans with Disabilities Act, balancing work and family demands, and international trade theory.

Summary of Key Points

Organization structure and design are determined by five basic elements. These elements are job specialization, departmentalization, reporting relationships, authority, and coordination.

One early universal model of organization design was the bureaucratic model. This model was based on the presumed need for rational and logical rules, regulations, and procedures.

The situational view of organization design is based on the assumption that the optimal organization design is a function of situational factors. Four important situational factors are technology, environment, size, and organizational life cycle. Each of these factors plays a role in determining how an organization should be designed.

Many organizations today adopt one of four basic organization designs: functional (U-form), conglomerate (H-form), divisional (M-form), or matrix. Other organizations use a hybrid design derived from two or more of these basic designs.

Three emerging forms of organization design are the team organization, the virtual organization, and the learning organization.

Discussion Questions

Questions for Review

1. What is job specialization? What are its advantages and disadvantages?

2. What is meant by *departmentalization?* Why and how is departmentalization carried out?

3. In what general ways can organizations be shaped? What are the implications of each approach with regard to the distribution of authority within the organization?

4. What are the basic situational factors that affect an organization's design?

5. Describe the basic forms of organization design. Outline the advantages and disadvantages of each.

Questions for Analysis

1. Seeing how specialization can be utilized in manufacturing organizations is easy. How can it be used by other types of organizations such as hospitals, churches, schools, and restaurants? Should those organizations use specialization? Why or why not?

2. Try to develop a different way to departmentalize your college or university, a local fast-food restaurant, a manufacturing firm, or some other organization. What might be the advantages of your form of organization?

3. Can bureaucratic organizations avoid the problems usually associated with bureaucracies? If so, how? If not, why not? Do you think bureaucracies are still necessary? Why or why not? Is retaining the desirable aspects of bureaucracy and eliminating the undesirable ones possible? Why or why not?

4. The matrix organization design is complex and difficult to implement successfully. Why then do so many organizations use it?

5. Identify some problems in organization design that are common to both international and domestic businesses. Identify some problems that are unique to one or the other.

Building Effective Diagnostic Skills

EXERCISE OVERVIEW

Diagnostic skills enable a manager to visualize the most appropriate response to a situation. This exercise enables you to develop your diagnostic skills as they relate to issues of centralization and decentralization in an organization.

EXERCISE BACKGROUND

Managers often need to change the degree of centralization or decentralization in their organization. Begin this exercise by reflecting on two very different scenarios. In scenario A, assume that you are the top manager in a large organization. The organization has a long and well-known history of being very centralized. For valid reasons beyond the scope of this exercise, assume that you have made a decision to make the firm much more decentralized. For scenario B, assume the exact opposite situation. That is, you are the top manager of a firm that has always used decentralization but has now decided to become much more centralized.

EXERCISE TASK

With the background information above as context, do the following:

1. Make a list of the major barriers you see to implementing decentralization in scenario A.

2. Make a list of the major barriers you see to implementing centralization in scenario B.

3. Which scenario do you think would be easiest to actually implement? That is, is it likely to be easier to move from centralization to decentralization or from decentralization to centralization? Why?

4. Given a choice of starting your own career in a firm that is either highly centralized or highly decentralized, which do you think you would prefer? Why?

Building Effective Conceptual Skills

EXERCISE OVERVIEW

Conceptual skills are a manager's ability to think in the abstract. This exercise encourages you to apply your conceptual skills to the concepts associated with the situational influences on organization design.

EXERCISE BACKGROUND

As noted in this chapter, several factors affect the appropriate design of an organization. The key factors discussed in the text are core technology, the organization's environment, its size, and its life cycle. The chapter does not provide details, however, as to how the situational factors working together in different combinations might affect organization design. For example, how might a particular form of technology and certain environmental forces together influence organization design?

The text also notes several basic forms of organization design, such as the functional, conglomerate, divisional, and matrix approaches. Some implications are also drawn as to how situational factors relate to each design.

EXERCISE TASK

With these ideas in mind, do the following:

1. For each of the four basic forms of organization design, identify a firm that uses it. Assess the technology, environment, size, and life cycle of each firm.

2. Now relate each situational factor to the design used by each firm.

3. Form an opinion as to the actual relation between each factor and the design used by each firm. That is, do you think that each firm's design is directly determined by its environment, or are the relationships you observe coincidental?

4. Can you prioritize the relative importance of the situational factors across the firms? Does the rank-order importance of the factors vary in any systematic way?

EXERCISE OVERVIEW

Decision-making skills refer to the manager's ability to correctly recognize and define problems and opportunities and to then select an appropriate course of action to solve problems and capitalize on opportunities. The purpose of this exercise is to give you insights into how managers must make decisions within the context of creating an organization design.

EXERCISE BACKGROUND

Assume that you have decided to open a casual sportswear business in your local community. Your products will be athletic caps, shirts, shorts, and sweats emblazoned with the logos of your college and local high schools. You are a talented designer and have developed some ideas that will make your products unique and very popular. You also have inherited enough money to get your business up and running and to cover about one year of living expenses (that is, you do not need to pay yourself a salary).

You intend to buy sportswear in various sizes and styles from other suppliers. Your firm will then use silkscreen processes and add the logos and other decorative touches to the products. Local clothing store owners have seen samples of your products and have indicated a keen interest in selling them. You know, however, that you will still need to service accounts and keep your customers happy.

You are currently trying to determine how many people you need to get your business going and how to most effectively group them into an organization. You realize that you can start out quite small and then expand as sales warrant. However, you also worry that confusion and inefficiency will result if you are continually adding people and rearranging your organization.

Building Effective
**Decision-Making
Skills**

EXERCISE TASK

Step One: Under each of the following scenarios, decide how to best design your organization. Sketch a basic organization chart to show your thoughts.

Scenario 1—You will sell the products yourself, and you intend to start with a workforce of five people.

Scenario 2—You intend to oversee production yourself, and you intend to start with a workforce of nine people.

Scenario 3—You do not intend to handle any one function yourself, but will instead oversee the entire operation, and you intend to start with a workforce of fifteen people.

Step Two: Form small groups of four to five people each. Compare your various organization charts, focusing on similarities and differences.

Step Three: Working in the same group, assume that five years have passed and that your business is a big success. You have a large plant for making your products and are shipping them to fifteen states. You employ almost five hundred people. Create an organization design that you think best fits this organization.

Follow-up Questions

1. How clear or ambiguous were the decisions about organization design?

2. What are your thoughts about starting out large enough to maintain stability as opposed to starting small and then growing?

3. What basic factors did you consider in choosing a design?

You Make the Call

Within a few months of taking over The Arbor, Cynthia Spenser realized that this was indeed a full-time job. Even though she had an assistant manager to help run the retail nursery operation of Sunset Landscape Services, she felt that she really had no time at all to devote to SLS. To compound the problem, Mark was also having difficulty running SLS's other two operations, landscape services and the lawn-care business, by himself.

Thus, the Spensers decided to expand their organization and create a more distinct and formal organization design. The assistant manager of the retail nursery operation, Susan Turner, was promoted to manager of the business. Mark also promoted the senior and most reliable crew chief from his lawn-care services business, Manuel Hernandez, to manager of that operation. Mark would continue to run the landscape operation, as well as the overall business itself. Susan and Manuel would each report directly to Mark. Cynthia, meanwhile, would devote all of her time and attention to The Arbor.

Susan's total staff consists of six full-time and ten part-time employees. Manuel's staff consists of four lawn crews, each of which has a crew chief and three team members. The landscape operation consists of Mark, an assistant designer, and three installation employees.

The new organization looks like this:

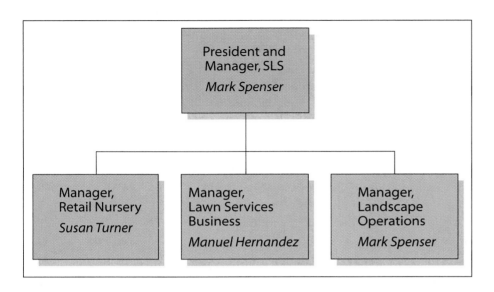

DISCUSSION QUESTIONS

1. Characterize SLS in terms of the major dimensions of organization structure.

2. What form of organization design is SLS using?

3. Can you anticipate any problems or weaknesses in the organization design?

HOW IS YOUR ORGANIZATION MANAGED?

Skills Self-Assessment Instrument

Introduction: Organizing is an important function of management. The following assessment helps you define how an organization is organized. This information enables you to determine whether this organization's design is consistent with the environmental forces it is facing.

Instructions: For this questionnaire focus on either an organization for which you are currently working or one for which you have worked in the past. This organization could be a club, sorority or fraternity, or the university you are attending. Please circle the response on the scale indicating the degree to which you agree or disagree with each statement. There is no right or wrong answer. Respond on the following scale to how you see your organization being managed:

Strongly Agree (SA)	Agree (A)	Don't Know (DK)	Disagree (D)	Strongly Disagree (SD)

1. If people believe that they have the right approach to carrying out their job, they can usually go ahead without checking with their superior.   SA   A   DK   D   SD

2. People in this organization don't always have to wait for orders from their superior on important matters.   **SA   A   DK   D   SD**

3. People in this organization share ideas with their superior.   **SA   A   DK   D   SD**

4. Different individuals play important roles in making decisions.   **SA   A   DK   D   SD**

5. People in this organization are likely to express their feelings openly on important matters.   **SA   A   DK   D   SD**

6. People in this organization are encouraged to speak their minds on important matters even if it means disagreeing with their superior.   **SA   A   DK   D   SD**

7. Talking to other people about the problems someone might have in making decisions is an important part of the decision-making process.   **SA   A   DK   D   SD**

8. Developing employees' talents and abilities is a major concern of this organization.   **SA   A   DK   D   SD**

9. People are encouraged to make suggestions before decisions are made.   **SA   A   DK   D   SD**

10. In this organization most people can have their point of view heard.   **SA   A   DK   D   SD**

11. Superiors often seek advice from their subordinates before decisions are made.   **SA   A   DK   D   SD**

12. Subordinates play an active role in running this organization.   **SA   A   DK   D   SD**

13. For many decisions the rules and regulations are developed as we go along.   **SA   A   DK   D   SD**

14. It is not always necessary to go through channels in dealing with important matters.   **SA   A   DK   D   SD**

15. The same rules and regulations are not consistently followed by employees.   **SA   A   DK   D   SD**

16. There are few rules and regulations for handling any kind of problem that may arise in making most decisions.   **SA   A   DK   D   SD**

17. People from different departments are often put together in task forces to solve important problems.   **SA   A   DK   D   SD**

18. For special problems we usually set up a temporary task force until we meet our objectives.   **SA   A   DK   D   SD**

19. Jobs in this organization are not clearly defined. **SA   A   DK   D   SD**

20. In this organization adapting to changes in the
    environment is important. **SA   A   DK   D   SD**

Copy your responses to the following table and then total each column at the bottom. Now add across the Total Score row to get an overall score in the lower right corner.

Question	Strongly Agree (SA)	Agree (A)	Don't Know (DK)	Disagree (D)	Strongly Disagree (SD)
1.	5	4	3	2	1
2.	5	4	3	2	1
3.	5	4	3	2	1
4.	5	4	3	2	1
5.	5	4	3	2	1
6.	5	4	3	2	1
7.	5	4	3	2	1
8.	5	4	3	2	1
9.	5	4	3	2	1
10.	5	4	3	2	1
11.	5	4	3	2	1
12.	5	4	3	2	1
13.	5	4	3	2	1
14.	5	4	3	2	1
15.	5	4	3	2	1
16.	5	4	3	2	1
17.	5	4	3	2	1
18.	5	4	3	2	1
19.	5	4	3	2	1
20.	5	4	3	2	1
Total Score:	__ +	__ +	__ +	__ +	__ = __

For interpretation, turn to page 458.

Source: From *Type of Management System* by Robert T. Keller. Copyright © 1988. Used by permission of the author.

Purpose: The purpose of this exercise is to help you better understand how new forms of technology can affect organization structure and design.

Experiential Exercise

Introduction: Amazon.com, Inc. is generally held up as one of the first—and best—examples of a new business created solely to capitalize on the potential of the Internet. Amazon.com started in 1991 as a supplier of hard-to-find books. It rapidly grew and soon began selling all kinds of books, often at significant discounts. Sales grew from $511,000 in 1995 to almost $16 million in 1996. Amazon.com went public in May 1997.

Amazon.com essentially serves as a book distributor. The firm receives orders from customers and fills those orders from one of several different wholesalers with whom it works. As a result, Amazon.com has little warehouse space, low distribution costs, and modest sales costs. In recent times, the firm has started to branch out and now sells CDs, videos, and DVDs as well.

Instructions:

Step One: Working alone, draw an organization chart of how you think Amazon.com is likely to be structured.

Step Two: Still working alone, draw an organization chart of how a firm like Amazon.com might look if the Internet did not exist.

Step Three: Now form small groups with three or four classmates and discuss similarities and differences in the two organization charts you each developed.

Follow-up Questions:

1. Even though Amazon.com has yet to make a profit, it's a darling among investors. How do you explain this?

2. How might the Internet affect the organization structure and design of an existing business?

3. Research Amazon.com and see if you can locate what its organization chart actually looks like.

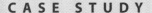

CASE STUDY

The Big Overhaul at American Express

As most people know, the ubiquitous phrase "Don't Leave Home Without It" refers to the American Express card. But American Express Company is really more than just a charge card business—it is an international financial services powerhouse with various businesses scattered around the world. And like other diversified global companies, American Express has to continually evaluate its operations and change how it does business to remain competitive.

A good case in point is a recent overhaul in the organization design of the firm's American Express Financial Advisors division, headquartered in Minneapolis. AEFA, as the division is known inside the company, is a network of financial planners who sell American Express products ranging from mutual funds to insurance and investment certificates to middle-income investors.

Until recently AEFA was organized in a functional design, just like most of its competitors. Planners were rewarded for bringing in new business (usually through cold calls to prospects and leads generated by mailing lists and referrals). Once new customers were signed up, they were passed on to the sales support staff, which was responsible for maintaining client records, answering questions, and handling routine transactions. Clear chains of command and a network of rules and procedures guided most of the firm's activities.

But in the mid-1990s, AEFA managers became concerned about the future of their business. Although the group was growing at a rate of more than 20 percent a year and generating huge profits for its corporate parent, key decision makers recognized that cold calling was becoming so widespread that a backlash from customers was emerging. Moreover, Internet-based competitors were beginning to emerge, and AEFA feared that these upstarts would so change the rules of business that an unprepared company might be blindsided.

As a result of these concerns and motivated to protect their business position, AEFA executives decided to overhaul their entire approach to business so as to be better prepared for new forms of competition. And their starting point was a new organization design intended to promote flexibility and responsiveness. AEFA started by eliminating the venerable position of general sales manager—one key executive ultimately responsible for all business sales and to whom all sales employees were accountable. After reorganization these responsibilities were spread across seven remaining positions.

Each of these seven key executives heads a vertical operation defined as a geographic region. For example, one manager might be responsible for the southeast part of the United States while another might be responsible for the northwest states. In addition, each executive has horizontal responsibility for one process that spans the entire company. For example, one of the seven key executives has companywide responsibility for client satisfaction. Another is responsible for companywide account management systems.

Below the level of these seven executives, 180 separate departments have also been reconfigured into forty-five clusters, each led by a vice president. Each cluster is also process oriented. For example, one cluster is responsible for training and integrating new planners into the company. Another is responsible for conducting customer satisfaction surveys and feeding the results back to relevant managers. The commission system for planners has also been changed. New business now provides only a portion of the individual planner's commission, with client satisfaction also providing a major portion. Thus, planners are motivated not only to generate new business but also to keep business after they get it.

So far, at least, the new system seems to be working quite well. The business is still growing, and its costs are down. In addition, most planners believe that they now have a better understanding of how to keep clients happy after they make their first purchase from AEFA. But there were a few rough spots during the transition as various individuals had to give up power or control over something they valued. And the new organization has not been particularly facilitative to international expansion. The current organization design seems to work well within existing markets but provides little incentive or catalyst for international growth.

Case Questions

1. Diagram AEFA's old and new organization designs. Compare and contrast them.
2. List the advantages and disadvantages of the old and new organization designs at AEFA.
3. Why does it appear that AEFA's new organization design is limiting the firm's international growth? How might this situation be changed?

Case References: *Hoover's Handbook of American Business 1998* (Austin, Texas: Hoover's Business Press, 1998), pp. 124–125; Rahul Jacob, "The Struggle to Create an Organization for the 21st Century," *Fortune,* April 3, 1995, pp. 90–99; and Raymond E. Miles, Charles C. Snow, John A. Mathews, Grant Miles, and Henry J. Coleman Jr., "Organizing in the Knowledge Age: Anticipating the Cellular Form," *Academy of Management Executive,* November 1997, pp. 7–24.

CHAPTER NOTES

1. Ronald Henkoff, "Boeing's Big Problem," *Fortune*, January 12, 1998, pp. 96–103; "Destroying the Old Hierarchies," *Forbes,* June 3, 1996, pp. 62–72 (quote on p. 64); "Behind Boeing's Woes: Clunky Assembly Line, Price War with Airbus," *Wall Street Journal*, April 24, 1998, pp. A1, A16; "Can a New Crew Buoy Boeing?" *Business Week,* September 14, 1998, p. 53.

2. Gareth Jones, *Organization Theory*, 2nd ed. (Reading, Mass.: Addison-Wesley, 1997).

3. Ricky W. Griffin, *Task Design* (Glenview, Ill.: Scott, Foresman, 1982).

4. M. D. Kilbridge, "Reduced Costs Through Job Enlargement: A Case," *Journal of Business*, Vol. 33, 1960, pp. 357–362.

5. Ricky W. Griffin and Gary C. McMahan, "Motivation Through Job Design," in Jerald Greenberg (ed.), *Organizational Behavior—The State of the Science* (Hillsdale, N.J.: Lawrence Erlbaum Associates, 1994), pp. 23–44.

6. Frederick Herzberg, *Work and the Nature of Man* (Cleveland: World Press, 1966).

7. J. Richard Hackman and Greg R. Oldham, *Work Redesign* (Reading, Mass.: Addison-Wesley, 1980).

8. "Some Plants Tear Out Long Assembly Lines, Switch to Craft Work," *Wall Street Journal*, October 24, 1994, pp. A1, A4.

9. Richard L. Daft, *Organization Theory and Design*, 6th ed. (St. Paul, Minn.: West, 1998).

10. David D. Van Fleet and Arthur G. Bedeian, "A History of the Span of Management," *Academy of Management Review*, 1977, pp. 356–372.

11. James C. Worthy, "Factors Influencing Employee Morale," *Harvard Business Review*, January 1950, pp. 61–73.

12. Dan R. Dalton, William D. Todor, Michael J. Spendolini, Gordon J. Fielding, and Lyman W. Porter, "Organization Structure and Performance: A Critical Review," *Academy of Management Review*, January 1980, pp. 49–64.

13. Brian Dumaine, "The Bureaucracy Busters," *Fortune*, June 17, 1991, pp. 36–50.

14. See Daft, *Organization Theory and Design*.

15. William Kahn and Kathy Kram, "Authority at Work: Internal Models and Their Organizational Consequences," *Academy of Management Review*, 1994, Vol. 19, No. 1, pp. 17–50.

16. Carrie R. Leana, "Predictors and Consequences of Delegation," *Academy of Management Journal*, December 1986, pp. 754–774.

17. "Remote Control," *HRMagazine*, August 1997, pp. 82–90.

18. Kevin Crowston, "A Coordination Theory Approach to Organizational Process Design," *Organization Science*, March–April 1997, pp. 157–166.

19. James Thompson, *Organizations in Action* (New York: McGraw-Hill, 1967). For a recent discussion, see Bart Victor and Richard S. Blackburn, "Interdependence: An Alternative Conceptualization," *Academy of Management Review*, July 1987, pp. 486–498.

20. Max Weber, *Theory of Social and Economic Organizations*, trans. by T. Parsons (New York: Free Press, 1947).

21. Paul Jarley, Jack Fiorito, and John Thomas Delany, "A Structural Contingency Approach to Bureaucracy and Democracy in U.S. National Unions," *Academy of Management Journal*, 1997, Vol. 40, No. 4, pp. 831–861.

22. For descriptions of situational factors, see Robert K. Kazanjian and Robert Drazin, "Implementing Internal Diversification: Contingency Factors for Organization Design Choices," *Academy of Management Review*, April 1987, pp. 342–354; Allen Bluedorn, "Pilgrim's Progress: Trends and Convergence in Research on Organizational Size and Environments," *Journal of Management*, Summer 1993, pp. 163–191; and Jones, *Organization Theory*.

23. Joan Woodward, *Industrial Organization: Theory and Practice* (London: Oxford University Press, 1965).

24. Joan Woodward, *Management and Technology, Problems of Progress Industry*, No. 3 (London: Her Majesty's Stationery Office, 1958).

25. Tom Burns and G. M. Stalker, *The Management of Innovation* (London: Tavistock, 1961).

26. Paul R. Lawrence and Jay W. Lorsch, *Organization and Environment* (Homewood, Ill.: Irwin, 1967).

27. For detailed discussions of the environment-organization design relationship, see Masoud Yasai-Ardekani, "Structural Adaptations to Environments," *Academy of Management Review*, January 1986, pp. 9–21; Christine S. Koberg and Geraldo R. Ungson, "The Effects of Environmental Uncertainty and Dependence on Organizational Performance: A Comparative Study," *Journal of Management*, Winter 1987, pp. 725–737; and Barbara W. Keats and Michael A. Hitt, "A Causal Model of Linkages Among Environmental Dimensions, Macro Organizational Characteristics, and Performance," *Academy of Management Journal*, September 1988, pp. 570–598.

28. Edward E. Lawler III, "Rethinking Organization Size," *Organizational Dynamics*, Autumn 1997, pp. 24–33.

29. Derek S. Pugh and David J. Hickson, *Organization Structure in Its Context: The Aston Program I* (Lexington, Mass.: D. C. Heath, 1976).

30. Robert H. Miles and Associates, *The Organizational Life Cycle* (San Francisco: Jossey-Bass, 1980). See also "Is Your Company Too Big?" *Business Week*, March 27, 1989, pp. 84–94.

31. Douglas Baker and John Cullen, "Administrative Reorganization and Configurational Context: The Contingent Effects of Age, Size, and Change in Size," *Academy of Management Journal*, 1993, Vol. 36, No. 6, pp. 1251–1277. See also Kevin Crowston, "A Coordination Theory Approach to Organizational Process Design," *Organization Science*, March–April 1997, pp. 157–175.

32. Oliver E. Williamson, *Markets and Hierarchies* (New York: Free Press, 1975).

33. Williamson, *Markets and Hierarchies*.

34. Michael E. Porter, "From Competitive Advantage to Corporate Strategy," *Harvard Business Review*, May–June 1987, pp. 43–59.

35. Williamson, *Markets and Hierarchies*.

36. Jay B. Barney and William G. Ouchi (eds.), *Organizational Economics* (San Francisco: Jossey-Bass, 1986), and Robert E. Hoskisson, "Multidivisional Structure and Performance: The Contingency of Diversification Strategy," *Academy of Management Journal*, December 1987, pp. 625–644. See also Bruce Lamont, Robert Williams, and James Hoffman, "Performance During 'M-Form' Reorganization and Recovery Time: The Effects of Prior Strategy and Implementation Speed," *Academy of Management Journal*, 1994, Vol. 37, No. 1, pp. 153–166.

37. Stanley M. Davis and Paul R. Lawrence, *Matrix* (Reading, Mass.: Addison-Wesley, 1977).

38. See Lawton Burns and Douglas Wholey, "Adoption and Abandonment of Matrix Management Programs: Effects of Organizational Characteristics and Interorganizational

Networks," *Academy of Management Journal*, Vol. 36, No. 1, pp. 106–138.

39. Raymond E. Miles, Charles C. Snow, John A. Mathews, Grant Miles, and Henry J. Coleman Jr., "Organizing in the Knowledge Age: Anticipating the Cellular Form," *Academy of Management Executive*, November 1997, pp. 7–24.

40. Peter Senge, *The Fifth Discipline* (New York: The Free Press, 1993). See also Alessandro Lomi, Erik R. Larsen, and Ari Ginsberg, "Adaptive Learning in Organizations: A Systems Dynamics-Based Exploration," *Journal of Management*, 1997, Vol. 23, No. 4, pp. 561–582.

7

Organization Change and Innovation

OBJECTIVES

After studying this chapter, you should be able to:

- Describe the nature of organization change, including forces for change and planned versus reactive change.
- Discuss models of organization change, how to overcome resistance to change, major areas of organization change, and the need for and approaches to reengineering.
- Discuss the assumptions, techniques, and effectiveness of organization development.
- Describe the innovation process, forms of innovation, the failure to innovate, and how organizations can promote innovation.

D aimler-Benz was long one of the most important industrial firms in Germany. The firm is best known among consumers for its line of luxury cars sold under the name Mercedes-Benz. Indeed, the Mercedes division is the world's oldest automaker. In addition to its pre-eminent passenger cars, Mercedes also manufactures commercial vans, trucks, buses, and industrial diesel engines.

A few years ago Daimler-Benz managers became concerned that the firm was perhaps too reliant on its Mercedes division and decided to diversify. Through an aggressive strategy based in part on acquiring new firms and in part on growing other existing Daimler-Benz businesses, the company was quickly transformed into a diversified conglomerate. One division consisted of various aerospace businesses. A second was created for financial services. A third included a variety of industrial and manufacturing units dealing with automation and rail systems. Mercedes-Benz comprised a fourth division.

Unfortunately, the diversified Daimler-Benz never lived up to its promise. Despite its major investments and managerial commitments, the firm continued to struggle as it attempted to bring each business up to an acceptable level of profitability. Especially problematic were the aerospace and financial services units, which continued to lose money at an alarming pace. Indeed, the losses in these two units were so great in 1995 that the entire corporation lost money for the first time in decades.

That same year, the board promoted Jurgen Schrempp to the position of CEO and gave him a mandate to turn things around—and quickly. One of his first major moves, in turn, also proved to be very controversial and ultimately cost the firm one of its most highly regarded executives. Up until that time, the Mercedes unit operated with virtual autonomy. Mercedes-Benz, for example, had its own CEO, Helmut Werner. And indeed, many observers had been surprised that Daimler's board had tapped Schrempp over Werner to take the top spot.

Schrempp decided almost immediately that to achieve his mandate, Mercedes would need to be folded into Daimler's corporate structure. His arguments were that the firm's other units needed to be better able to tap into Mercedes' managerial, technical, and operational expertise. In addition, costs could be lowered by consolidating administrative expenses. Not surprisingly, Werner opposed this move. Although he had several reasonable arguments for keeping Mercedes independent, it was also clearly the case that Schrempp's proposal would undermine Werner's authority in the company.

Each man had his own supporters on Daimler's board of directors, but Schrempp eventually prevailed. Although he tried to talk Werner into staying on as the number two executive in the company, the defeated Werner quickly left the firm. Schrempp, meanwhile, forged ahead at full speed. Carrying through on his plan, Mercedes was incorporated into Daimler, and several underperforming businesses were closed or sold.

Schrempp also supported the building of the first Mercedes factory outside of Germany (in the state of Alabama) and arranged for Daimler-Benz to become the first German firm to be listed on the New York Stock Exchange. He also made headlines around the world in 1998 when he announced that the firm was merging with Chrysler. After the merger was finalized in late 1998, the new firm became known as DaimlerChrysler AG. Schrempp's managerial moves have already started paying dividends. Profits are surging once more, and new Mercedes products became the talk of the industry. But to make these dreams a reality, Schrempp had to basically dismantle and then reassemble his firm so that it more closely resembles one of its high-powered roadsters than one of its buses.[1]

"In such a situation, you either run away or fix it yourself."

Jurgen Schrempp, CEO of Daimler-Benz

Managers at DaimlerChrysler have had to grapple with something all managers must eventually confront: the need for change. They first perceived that they needed to make certain changes aimed at fostered diversification. Later, they realized that this strategy was not working and that other changes were necessary to get the firm back on track. Making these changes, however, required the CEO to overcome internal corporate politics. And the changes were costly in a variety of ways. But they seem to be paying off now as the firm has regained its financial vitality.

Understanding when and how to implement change is a vital part of management. This chapter describes how organizations manage change. We first examine the nature of organization change and identify the basic issues of managing change. We then identify and describe major areas of change, including reengineering, a major type of change undertaken by many firms recently. We next examine organization development and conclude by discussing a related area, organizational innovation.

The Nature of Organization Change

organization change Any substantive modification to some part of the organization

Organization change is any substantive modification to some part of the organization. Thus change can involve virtually any aspect of an organization: work schedules, bases for departmentalization, span of management, machinery, organization design, people themselves, and so on. It is important to keep in mind that any change in an organization may have effects extending beyond the actual area where the change is implemented. For example, when Northrup Grumman recently installed a new computerized production system at one of its plants, employees were trained to operate new equipment, the compensation system was adjusted to reflect new skill levels, the span of management of supervisors was altered, and several related jobs were redesigned. Selection criteria for new employees were also changed, and a new quality control system was installed. In addition, it is quite common for multiple organization change activities to be going on simultaneously.[2]

■ Forces for Change

Why do organizations find change necessary? The basic reason is that something relevant to the organization either has changed or is going to change. The organization consequently has little choice but to change as well. Indeed, a primary reason for the problems that organizations often face is failure to anticipate or respond properly to changing circumstances. Forces for change may be external or internal to the organization.[3]

External Forces External forces for change derive from the organization's general and task environments. For example, in the late 1990s the Asian currency crisis and economic turmoil in numerous countries affected by those problems resulted in business downturns in numerous industries and companies. In the political area new laws, court decisions, and regulations affect organizations in a variety of ways. The technological dimension may yield new production techniques that the organization needs to explore. The economic dimension is affected by inflation, the cost of living, and money supplies. The sociocultural dimension, reflecting societal values, determines what products or services will be accepted in the market.

Because of its proximity to the organization, the task environment is an even more powerful force for change. Competitors influence an organization through their price structures and product lines. When Compaq lowers the prices it

charges for computers, Dell and IBM have little choice but to follow suit. Because customers determine what products can be sold at what prices, organizations must be concerned with consumer tastes and preferences. Suppliers affect organizations by raising or lowering prices or by changing product lines. Regulators can have dramatic effects on an organization. For example, if OSHA rules that a particular production process is dangerous to workers, the agency can force a firm to close a plant until it meets higher safety standards. Unions can force change when they negotiate for higher wages or strike.[4]

Internal Forces   Various forces inside the organization may cause change. If top management revises the organization's strategy, organization change is likely to result. A decision by an electronics company to enter the home computer market or a decision to increase a ten-year product sales goal by 3 percent would occasion many organization changes. Other internal forces for change may be reflections of external forces. As sociocultural values shift, for example, workers' attitudes toward their jobs may also shift—and workers may demand a change in working hours or working conditions. In such a case, even though the force is rooted in the external environment, the organization must respond directly to the internal pressure it generates.[5]

Change comes in all forms and fashions and affects organizations everywhere. For example, these Palestinian Boy Scouts from Hebron are having lunch with Israeli students in Haifa. As the world continues to become a global village, people everywhere will need to learn about new cultures and become more tolerant and open to new ideas. And managers will need to take this same path as they guide change in their own organizations as these social forces move into the workplace.

■ Planned Versus Reactive Change

Some change is planned well in advance; other change comes about as a reaction to unexpected events. **Planned change** is change that is designed and implemented in an orderly and timely fashion in anticipation of future events. **Reactive change** is a piecemeal response to events as they occur. Because reactive change may be hurried, the potential for poorly conceived and executed change is increased. Planned change is almost always preferable to reactive change.[6]

planned change   Change that is designed and implemented in an orderly and timely fashion in anticipation of future events

reactive change   A piecemeal response to circumstances as they develop

Panel 1: A NEW FOG IS ROLLING IN.

Panel 2: THIS CAN ONLY MEAN ONE THING.

Panel 3: CAROL, SCHEDULE A STAFF MEETING. IT'S TIME TO REORGANIZE THE DEPARTMENT.

Change is a common event in most organizations today. And although much of this change is necessary and beneficial, managers sometimes engage in change activities that are either unnecessary or poorly conceived. This situation increases the chances that employees will resist the change—they will experience uncertainty, threatened self-interests, different perceptions, and/or feelings of loss. Indeed, as shown in this cartoon, change can be so poorly managed that employees sense it before it even occurs and develop resistance without even knowing the details.

DILBERT reprinted by permission of United Feature Syndicate, Inc.

Georgia-Pacific, a large forest-products business, is an excellent example of a firm that recently went through a planned and well-managed change process. When the firm's current CEO, A. D. Correll, took over the firm's leadership in 1991, he quickly became alarmed at the firm's high accident rate—nine serious injuries per one hundred employees each year and twenty-six deaths during the most recent five-year period. Although the forest-products business is inherently dangerous, Correll believed that the accident rate was far too high and set out on a major change effort to improve safety conditions. He and other top managers developed a multistage change program intended to educate workers about safety, improve safety equipment in the plant, and eliminate a long-standing part of the firm's culture that made injuries almost a badge of courage. Today Georgia-Pacific has the best safety record in the industry, with relatively few injuries.[7]

A few years ago, on the other hand, Caterpillar was caught flat-footed by a worldwide recession in the construction industry, suffered enormous losses, and took several years to recover. Had managers at Caterpillar anticipated the need for change earlier, they might have been able to respond more quickly. More recently, Kodak announced plans to cut ten thousand jobs, a reaction to sluggish sales and profits.[8] Again, better anticipation might have forestalled these job cuts. The importance of approaching change from a planned perspective is reinforced by the frequency of organization change. Most companies or divisions of large companies implement some form of moderate change at least every year and one or more major changes every four to five years.[9] Managers who sit back and respond only when they have to are likely to spend a lot of time hastily changing and rechanging things. A more effective approach is to anticipate forces urging change and to plan ahead to deal with them.

Managing Change in Organizations

Organization change is a complex phenomenon. A manager cannot simply wave a wand and implement a planned change like magic. Instead, any change must be systematic and logical to have a realistic opportunity to succeed. To carry off a change, the manager needs to understand the steps of effective change and how to counter employee resistance to change.

■ Models of the Change Process

Researchers have developed a number of models or frameworks outlining steps for change.[10] The Lewin model was one of the first, although a more comprehensive approach is usually more useful.

The Lewin Model Kurt Lewin, a noted organizational theorist, suggested that every change requires three steps.[11] The first step is *unfreezing*—individuals who will be affected by the impending change must be led to recognize why the change is necessary. Next the *change itself* is implemented. Finally, *refreezing* involves reinforcing and supporting the change so that it becomes a part of the system. For example, one of the changes Caterpillar faced in response to the recession involved a massive workforce reduction. The first step (unfreezing) was convincing the United Auto Workers to support the reduction because of its importance to long-term effectiveness. After this unfreezing was accomplished, thirty thousand jobs were eliminated (implementation). Then Caterpillar worked to improve its damaged relationship with its workers (refreezing) by guaranteeing future pay hikes and promising no more cutbacks. As interesting as Lewin's model is, it unfortunately lacks operational specificity. Thus a more comprehensive perspective is often needed.

A Comprehensive Approach to Change The comprehensive approach to change takes a systems view and delineates a series of specific steps that often lead to successful change. This expanded model is illustrated in Figure 7.1. The first step is recognizing the need for change. Reactive change might be triggered by employee complaints, declines in productivity or turnover, court injunctions, sales slumps, or labor strikes. Recognition may simply be management awareness that change in a certain area is inevitable. For example, managers may be aware of the general frequency of organizational change undertaken by most organizations and recognize that their organization should probably follow the same pattern. The immediate stimulus might be the result of a forecast indicating new market potential, the accumulation of cash surplus for possible investment, or an opportunity to achieve and capitalize on a major technological breakthrough. Managers might also initiate change today because indicators suggest that it will be necessary in the near future.

Managers must next set goals for the change. To increase market share, to enter new markets, to restore employee morale, to settle a strike, and to identify investment opportunities might all be goals for change. Third, managers must diagnose what brought on the need for change. Turnover, for example, might be caused by low pay, poor working conditions, poor supervisors, or employee dissatisfaction. Thus, although turnover may be the immediate stimulus for change, managers must understand its causes to make the right changes.

The next step is to select a change technique that will accomplish the intended goals. If the cause of turnover is low pay, a new reward system may be needed. If the cause is poor supervision, interpersonal skills training may be called for. (Various change techniques are summarized later in this chapter.) After the appropriate technique has been chosen, its implementation must be planned. Issues to consider include the costs of the change, its effects on other areas of the organization, and the degree of employee

FIGURE 7.1
Steps in the Change Process

Managers must understand how and why to implement change. A manager who, when implementing change, follows a logical and orderly sequence such as the one shown here is more likely to succeed than a manager whose change process is haphazard and poorly conceived.

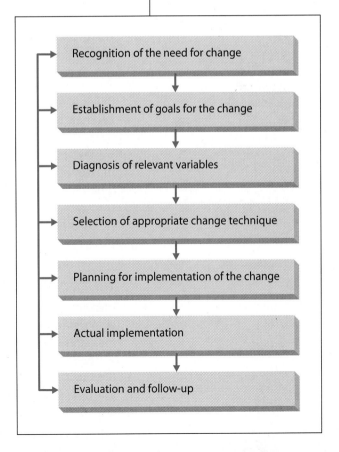

participation appropriate for the situation. If the change is implemented as planned, the results should then be evaluated. If the change was intended to reduce turnover, managers must check turnover after the change has been in effect for a while. If turnover is still too high, other changes may be necessary.[12]

■ Understanding Resistance to Change

Another element in the effective management of change is understanding the resistance that often greets change.[13] Managers need to know why people resist change and what can be done about their resistance. When Westinghouse replaced all its typewriters with personal computers several years ago, most people responded favorably. One manager, however, resisted the change to the point where he began leaving work every day at noon. It was some time before he began staying in the office all day again. Such resistance is common for a variety of reasons.

Uncertainty   Perhaps the biggest cause of employee resistance to change is uncertainty. In the face of impending change, employees may become anxious and nervous. They may worry about their ability to meet new job demands, they may think that their job security is threatened, or they may simply dislike ambiguity. RJR Nabisco was the target of an extended and confusing takeover battle a few years ago, and during the entire time employees were nervous about the impending change. The *Wall Street Journal* described them this way: "Many are angry at their leaders and fearful for their jobs. They are swapping rumors and spinning scenarios for the ultimate outcome of the battle for the tobacco and food giant. Headquarters staffers in Atlanta know so little about what's happening in New York that some call their office 'the mushroom complex,' where they are kept in the dark."[14]

Threatened Self-Interests   Many impending changes threaten the self-interests of some managers within the organization. A change might potentially diminish their power or influence within the company, so they fight it. Managers at Sears recently developed a plan calling for a new type of store. The new stores would be somewhat smaller than typical Sears stores and would not be located in large shopping malls. Instead, they would be located in smaller strip centers. They would carry clothes and other "soft goods" but not hardware, appliances, furniture, or automotive products. When executives in charge of the excluded product lines heard about the plan, they raised such strong objections that the plan was put on hold.

Different Perceptions   A third reason that people resist change is due to different perceptions. A manager may make a decision and recommend a plan for change on the basis of her own assessment of a situation. Others in the organization may resist the change because they do not agree with the manager's assessment or perceive the situation differently.[15] Executives at 7-Eleven are currently battling this problem as they attempt to enact a major organizational change. The corporation wants to take its convenience stores a bit up-scale and begin selling fancy fresh foods to go, the newest hardcover novels, and some gourmet products. But many franchisees are balking because they see this move as taking the firm away from its core blue-collar customers.[16]

Feelings of Loss Many changes involve altering work arrangements in ways that disrupt existing social networks. Because social relationships are important, most people resist any change that might adversely affect those relationships. Other intangibles threatened by change include power, status, security, familiarity with existing procedures, and self-confidence. As described in the opening incident of this chapter, Daimler-Benz recently lost a key executive because of a power struggle involving a change. And similar events will undoubtedly happen as the firm completes its merger with Chrysler.

◼ Overcoming Resistance to Change

Of course, a manager should not give up in the face of resistance to change. Although there are no sure-fire cures, several techniques have the potential to overcome resistance.[17]

Participation Participation is often the most effective technique for overcoming resistance to change. Employees who participate in planning and implementing a change are better able to understand the reasons for the change. Uncertainty is reduced, and self-interests and social relationships are less threatened. Having had an opportunity to express their ideas and assume the perspectives of others, employees are more likely to accept the change gracefully. A classic study of participation monitored the introduction of a change in production methods among four groups in a Virginia pajama factory.[18] The two groups that were allowed to fully participate in planning and implementing the change improved their productivity and satisfaction significantly, relative to the two groups that did not participate. 3M Company recently attributed $10 million in cost savings to employee participation in several organization change activities.[19]

Education and Communication Educating employees about the need for and the expected results of an impending change should reduce their resistance. If open communication is established and maintained during the change process, uncertainty can be minimized. For example, to reduce resistance during many of its cutbacks, Caterpillar used these methods: First, it educated UAW representatives about the need for and potential value of the planned changes. Then management told all employees what was happening, when it would happen, and how it would affect them individually.

Facilitation Several facilitation procedures are also advisable. For instance, making only necessary changes, announcing those changes well in advance, and allowing time for people to adjust to new ways of doing things can help reduce resistance to change.[20] One manager at a Prudential regional office spent several months systematically planning a change in work procedures and job design. He then became too hurried, coming in over the weekend with a work crew and rearranging the office layout. When employees walked in on

FIGURE 7.2
Force-Field Analysis for Plant Closing at Chrysler

A force-field analysis can help a manager facilitate change. A manager able to identify forces acting both for and against a change can see where to focus efforts to remove barriers to change (such as offering training and relocation to displaced workers). Removing the forces against the change can at least partially overcome resistance.

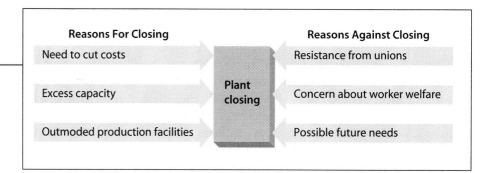

Reasons For Closing — Reasons Against Closing

Need to cut costs — Plant closing — Resistance from unions

Excess capacity — Concern about worker welfare

Outmoded production facilities — Possible future needs

Monday morning, they were hostile, anxious, and resentful. What was a promising change became a disaster, and the manager had to scrap the entire plan.

Force-Field Analysis   Although force-field analysis may sound like something out of a Star Trek movie, this technique can help overcome resistance to change. In almost any change situation, forces are acting for and against the change. To facilitate the change, managers start by listing each set of forces and then trying to tip the balance so that the forces facilitating the change outweigh those hindering the change. It is especially important to try to remove or at least minimize some of the forces acting against the change. Suppose, for example, that Chrysler is considering a plant closing as part of a change. As shown in Figure 7.2, three factors are reinforcing the change: Chrysler needs to cut costs, it has excess capacity, and the plant has outmoded production facilities. At the same time, there is resistance from the UAW, concern for workers being put out of their jobs, and a feeling that the plant might be needed again in the future. Chrysler might start by convincing the UAW that the closing is necessary by presenting profit and loss figures. It could then offer relocation and retraining to displaced workers. And it might shut down the plant and put it in "moth balls" so that it could be renovated later. The three major factors hindering the change are thus eliminated or reduced in importance.

■ Areas of Organization Change

Change can involve virtually any part of an organization. In general, however, most change interventions involve organization structure and design, technology and operations, or people.

Changing Structure and Design   Organization change might be focused on any of the basic components of organization structure or on the organization's overall design. Thus the organization might change the way it designs its jobs, or it might change reporting relationships, the distribution of authority, or the coordinating mechanisms it uses. On a larger scale the organization might change its overall design. For example, a growing business could decide to drop its functional design and adopt a divisional design. Or it might transform itself into a matrix. Finally, the organization might change any part of its human resource management system, such as its selection criteria, its performance appraisal methods, or its compensation package.[21]

Changing Technology and Operations Technology is the conversion process an organization uses to transform inputs into outputs. Because of the rapid rate of technological innovation, technological changes are becoming increasingly important to many organizations. One especially important area of change today revolves around information technology. The adoption and institutionalization of information technology innovations is almost constant in most firms today. Another important form of technological change involves equipment. To keep pace with competitors, firms periodically find that replacing existing machinery and equipment with newer models is necessary. And changes in work processes or work activities may be necessary if new equipment is introduced or new products are manufactured. Organizational control systems may also be targets of change.[22]

Changing People A third area of organization change has to do with human resources. For example, an organization might decide to change the skill level of its workforce, necessitating new training programs and new selection criteria. The organization might also decide to improve its workers performance level with a new incentive system or performance-based training. Perceptions and expectations are also a common focus of organization change. Workers in an organization might believe, for example, that their wages and benefits are not as high as they should be. But if managers have evidence that shows the firm is paying a competitive wage and providing a superior benefit package, they may undertake actions to alter their workers' perceptions. Change might also be directed at employee attitudes and values. In many organizations today, managers are trying to eliminate adversarial relationships with workers and to adopt a more collaborative relationship.

■ Reengineering in Organizations

Many organizations today have also gone through a massive and comprehensive change program involving all aspects of organization design, technology, and people. Although various terms are used, the term currently in vogue for these changes is *reengineering*. Specifically, **reengineering** is the radical redesign of all aspects of a business to achieve major gains in cost, service, or time.[23]

reengineering The radical redesign of all aspects of a business to achieve major gains in cost, service, or time

The Need for Reengineering Why are so many organizations finding it necessary to reengineer themselves? As we noted earlier, all systems, including organizations, are subject to entropy—a normal process leading to system decline. An organization is behaving most typically when it maintains the status quo, doesn't change in synch with its environment, and starts consuming its own resources to survive. In a sense that is what IBM did. The firm's managers grew complacent and assumed that IBM's historic prosperity would continue and that they need not worry about environmental shifts, foreign competition, and so forth—and entropy set in. The key is to recognize the

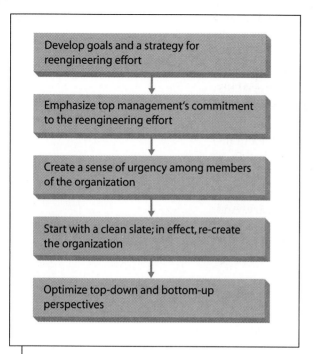

FIGURE 7.3
The Reengineering Process

Reengineering is a major redesign of all areas of an organization. To be successful, reengineering requires a systematic and comprehensive assessment of the entire organization. Goals, top management support, and a sense of urgency help the organization re-create itself and blend both top-down and bottom-up perspectives.

beginning of the decline and to immediately move toward reengineering. Major problems occur when managers don't recognize the onset of entropy until it is well advanced or else are complacent in taking steps to correct it.

Approaches to Reengineering Figure 7.3 shows general steps in reengineering. The first step is setting goals and developing a strategy for reengineering. The organization must know in advance what reengineering is supposed to accomplish and how those accomplishments will be achieved. Next, top managers must begin and direct the reengineering effort. If a CEO simply announces that reengineering is to occur but does nothing else, the program is unlikely to be successful. But if the CEO is constantly involved in the process, underscoring its importance and taking the lead, reengineering stands a much better chance of success.

Most experts also agree that successful reengineering is usually accompanied by a sense of urgency. People in the organization must see the clear and present need for the changes being implemented and appreciate their importance. In addition, most successful reengineering efforts start with a clean slate. That is, rather than assuming that the existing organization is a starting point and then trying to modify it, reengineering usually starts by asking questions such as how are customers best served and competitors best neutralized. New approaches and systems are then created and imposed in place of existing ones.

Finally, reengineering requires a careful blend of top-down and bottom-up involvement. On the one hand, strong leadership is necessary, but too much involvement by top management can make the changes seem autocratic. Similarly, employee participation is also important, but too little involvement by leaders can undermine the program's importance and create a sense that top managers don't care. Thus care must be taken to carefully balance these two countervailing forces.

Organization Development

organization development An effort that is planned, organization wide, and managed from the top; it is intended to increase organization effectiveness and health through planned interventions in the organization's process, using behavioral science knowledge

We note in several places the importance of people and change. A special area of interest that focuses almost exclusively on people is organization development.

■ OD Assumptions

Organization development (OD) is concerned with changing attitudes, perceptions, behaviors, and expectations. More precisely, **organization development** is a planned effort that is organization-wide and is managed from the top. It is intended to increase organization effectiveness and health through planned interventions in the organization's "process," using behavioral science knowledge.[24] The theory and practice of OD are based on several very important assumptions. The first is that employees have a desire to grow and develop. Another is that employees have a strong need to be accepted by others within the organization. Still another critical assumption of OD is that the total organization and the way it is designed will influence the way individuals and groups within the organization behave. Thus some form of collaboration between managers and their employees is necessary to (1) take advantage of the skills and abilities of the employees and (2) eliminate aspects of the organization that retard employee growth, development, and group acceptance. Because of the intense personal nature of many OD activities, many large organizations rely on one or more OD consultants (either full-time employees assigned to this function or outside experts hired specifically for OD purposes) to implement and manage their OD program.[25]

■ OD Techniques

Several kinds of interventions or activities are generally considered to be part of organization development.[26] Some OD programs may use only one or a few of these; other programs use several of them at once.

Diagnostic Activities   Just as a physician examines patients to diagnose their current condition, an OD diagnosis analyzes the current condition of an organization. To carry out this diagnosis managers use questionnaires, opinion or attitude surveys, interviews, archival data, and meetings to assess various characteristics of the organization. The results from this diagnosis may generate profiles of the organization's activities, which can then be used to identify problem areas in need of correction.

Team Building   Team-building activities are intended to enhance the effectiveness and satisfaction of individuals who work in groups or teams and to promote overall group effectiveness. Given the widespread use of teams today, these activities have taken on increased importance. An OD consultant might interview team members to determine how they feel about the group; then an off-site meeting could be held to discuss the issues that surfaced and to iron out any problem areas or member concerns. Caterpillar used team building as one method for changing the working relationships between workers and supervisors from confrontational to cooperative.[27]

Survey Feedback   In survey feedback each employee responds to a questionnaire intended to measure perceptions and attitudes (for example, satisfaction and supervisory style). Everyone involved, including the supervisor, receives the results of the survey. The aim of this approach is usually to change the behavior of supervisors by showing them how their subordinates view them. After the feedback has been provided, workshops may be conducted to evaluate results and suggest constructive changes.

■ Third-Party Peacemaking

Another approach to OD is through third-party peacemaking, which is most often used when substantial conflict exists within the organization. Third-party peacemaking can be appropriate on the individual, group, or organization level. The third party, usually an OD consultant, uses a variety of mediation or negotiation techniques to resolve any problems or conflicts between individuals or groups.

Technostructural Activities   Technostructural activities are concerned with the design of the organization, the technology of the organization, and the interrelationship of design and technology with people on the job. A structural change such as an increase in decentralization, a job design change such as an increase in the use of automation, and a technological change involving a modification in work flow all qualify as technostructural OD activities if their objective is to improve group and interpersonal relationships within the organization.

Process Consultation   In process consultation an OD consultant observes groups in the organization to develop an understanding of their communication patterns, decision-making and leadership processes, and methods of cooperation and conflict resolution. The consultant then provides feedback to the involved parties about the processes he or she has observed. The goal of this form of intervention is to improve the observed processes. A leader who is presented with feedback outlining deficiencies in his or her leadership style, for example, might be expected to change to overcome them.

Coaching and Counseling   Coaching and counseling provide nonevaluative feedback to individuals. The purpose is to help people both develop a better sense of how others see them and to learn behaviors that will assist others in achieving their work-related goals. The focus is not on how the individual is performing today; instead, it is on how the person can perform better in the future.

Planning and Goal Setting   More pragmatically oriented than many other interventions are activities designed to help managers improve their planning and goal setting. Emphasis still falls on the individual, however, because the intent is to help individuals and groups integrate themselves into the overall planning process. The OD consultant might use the same approach as in process consultation, but the focus is more technically oriented on the mechanics of planning and goal setting.

■ The Effectiveness of OD

Given the diversity of activities encompassed by OD, it is not surprising that managers report mixed results from various OD interventions. Organizations that actively practice some form of OD include American Airlines, Texas Instruments, Procter & Gamble, ITT Corporation, Polaroid, and B.F. Goodrich. Goodrich, for example, has trained sixty persons in OD processes and techniques. These trained experts have subsequently become internal OD consultants to assist other managers in applying the techniques.[28] Many other managers, in contrast, report that they have tried OD but discarded it.[29]

OD will probably remain an important part of management theory and practice. Of course, there are no sure things when dealing with social systems such as organizations, and the effectiveness of many OD techniques is difficult to evaluate. Because all organizations are open systems interacting with their environments, an improvement in an organization after an OD intervention may be attributable to the intervention, but it may also be attributable to changes in economic conditions, luck, or other factors.[30]

Organizational Innovation

A final element of organization change that we address is innovation. **Innovation** is the managed effort of an organization to develop new products or services or new uses for existing products or services. Innovation is clearly important because without new products or services, any organization will fall behind its competition.[31]

innovation The managed effort of an organization to develop new products or services or new uses for existing products or services

■ The Innovation Process

The organizational innovation process consists of developing, applying, launching, growing, and managing the maturity and decline of creative ideas.[32] This process is depicted in Figure 7.4.

Innovation Development   Innovation development involves the evaluation, modification, and improvement of creative ideas. Innovation development can transform a product or service with only modest potential into a product or service with significant potential. Parker Brothers, for example, decided during innovation development not to market an indoor volleyball game, but instead

FIGURE 7.4
The Innovation Process

Organizations actively seek to manage the innovation process. These steps illustrate the general life cycle that characterizes most innovations. Of course, as with creativity, the innovation process will suffer if it is approached too mechanically and rigidly.

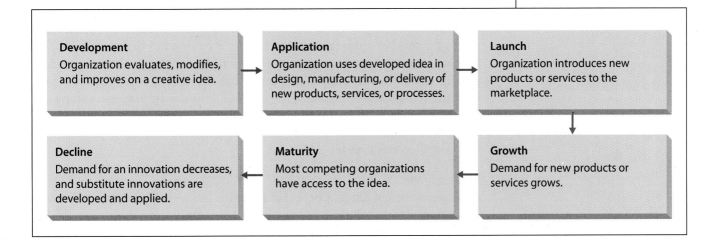

Development	Application	Launch
Organization evaluates, modifies, and improves on a creative idea.	Organization uses developed idea in design, manufacturing, or delivery of new products, services, or processes.	Organization introduces new products or services to the marketplace.

Decline	Maturity	Growth
Demand for an innovation decreases, and substitute innovations are developed and applied.	Most competing organizations have access to the idea.	Demand for new products or services grows.

MISSION: To design a new generation space launch vehicle that will dramatically reduce the cost and complexity of going into orbit. This will enable private companies to launch countless space-based businesses and take advantage of a whole new universe of opportunities in the century ahead — just as private enterprise helped the aviation industry take off during this century.

Quite possibly the most far-fetched idea since the airplane.

LOCKHEED MARTIN

SUCCESS: Lockheed Martin and our teammates have created an innovative yet practical design called VentureStar,™ a reusable, single-stage-to-orbit vehicle. The first step: we are building, and will soon fly, a 1/2-scale demonstrator—the X-33—to validate the vehicle's advanced technologies and capabilities. It's one way we, as a global technology leader, are helping to launch the future.
www.lmco.com

Innovation is the lifeblood of many companies. Lockheed Martin, for example, relies heavily on new products to remain strong and profitable. This potential product is called VentureStar. Managers at Lockheed Martin see VentureStar as a possible replacement for the space shuttle. At the present time, VentureStar is in the innovation development stage as a small-scale demonstrator is being constructed to validate the craft's basic design.

to sell separately the appealing little foam ball designed for the game. The firm will never know how well the volleyball game would have sold, but the Nerf ball and numerous related products have generated millions of dollars in revenues for Parker Brothers.[33]

Innovation Application Innovation application is the stage in which an organization takes a developed idea and uses it in the design, manufacturing, or delivery of new products, services, or processes. At this point the innovation emerges from the laboratory and is transformed into tangible goods or services. One example of innovation application is the use of radar-based focusing systems in Polaroid's instant cameras. The idea of using radio waves to discover the location, speed, and direction of moving objects was first applied extensively by Allied forces during World War II. As radar technology developed during the following years, the electrical components needed became smaller and more streamlined. Researchers at Polaroid applied this well-developed technology in a new way.[34]

Application Launch Application launch is the stage in which an organization introduces new products or services to the marketplace. The important question is not, Does the innovation work? but instead, Will customers want to purchase the innovative product and service? History is full of creative ideas that did not generate enough interest among customers to be successful. Some notable innovation failures include Sony's seat warmer, the Edsel automobile, and Polaroid's SX-70 instant camera (which cost $3 billion to develop, but never sold more than one hundred thousand units in a year).[35] Thus, despite development and application, new products and services can fail at the launch phase.

Application Growth Once an innovation has been successfully launched, it enters the stage of application growth. This is a period of high economic performance for an organization because the demand for the product or service is often greater than the supply. Organizations that fail to anticipate this stage may unintentionally limit their growth, as Gillette did by not anticipating demand for its Sensor razor blades. At the same time, overestimating demand for a new product can be just as detrimental to performance. Unsold products can sit in warehouses for years.

Innovation Maturity After a period of growing demand, an innovative product or service often enters a period of maturity. Innovation maturity is the stage in which most organizations in an industry have access to an innovation and are applying it in approximately the same way. The technological application of an innovation during this stage of the innovation process can be very sophisticated. Because most firms have access to the innovation, however, either as a result of developing the innovation on their own or copying the innovation of others, it no longer provides a competitive advantage to any one of them. The time that elapses between innovation development and innovation maturity varies notably depending on the particular product or service. Whenever an innovation involves the use of complex skills (such as a complicated manufacturing process or highly sophisticated teamwork), moving from the growth phase to the maturity phase will take longer. In addition, if the skills needed to implement these innovations are rare and difficult to imitate, then strategic imitation may be delayed and the organization may enjoy a period of sustained competitive advantage.

Innovation Decline   Every successful innovation bears its own seeds of decline. Because an organization does not gain a competitive advantage from an innovation at maturity, it must encourage its creative scientists, engineers, and managers to begin looking for new innovations. This continued search for competitive advantage usually leads new products and services to move from the creative process through innovation maturity, and finally to innovation decline. Innovation decline is the stage during which demand for an innovation decreases and substitute innovations are developed and applied.

■ Forms of Innovation

Each creative idea an organization develops poses a different challenge for the innovation process. Innovations can be radical or incremental, technical or managerial, and product or process.

Radical Versus Incremental Innovations   **Radical innovations** are new products or technologies developed by an organization that completely replace the existing products or technologies in an industry. **Incremental innovations** are new products or processes that modify existing ones. Firms that implement radical innovations fundamentally shift the nature of competition and the interaction of firms within their environments. Firms that implement incremental innovations alter, but do not fundamentally change, competitive interaction in an industry.

> **radical innovation**   A new product, service, or technology that completely replaces an existing one
>
> **incremental innovation**   A new product, service, or technology that modifies an existing one

Over the last several years, organizations have introduced many radical innovations. For example, compact disk technology has virtually replaced long-playing vinyl records in the recording industry, and high-definition television seems likely to replace regular television technology (both black-and-white and color) in the near future. Whereas radical innovations like these tend to be very visible and public, incremental innovations actually are more numerous. One example is Ford's sport utility vehicle, Explorer. Although other companies had similar products, Ford more effectively combined the styling and engineering that resulted in increased demand for all sport utility vehicles.

Technical Versus Managerial Innovations   **Technical innovations** are changes in the physical appearance or performance of a product or service or changes in the physical processes through which a product or service is manufactured or performed. Many of the most important innovations over the last

> **technical innovation**   A change in appearance or performance of products or services or the physical processes through which a product or service passes

managerial innovation A change in the management process in an organization

fifty years have been technical. For example, the serial replacement of the vacuum tube with the transistor, the transistor with the integrated circuit, and the integrated circuit with the microchip has greatly enhanced the power, ease of use, and speed of operation of a wide variety of electronic products. Not all innovations developed by organizations are technical, however. **Managerial innovations** are changes in the management process by which products and services are conceived, built, and delivered to customers. Managerial innovations do not necessarily affect the physical appearance or performance of products or services directly. In effect, reengineering represents a managerial innovation.

product innovation A change in the physical characteristics of a product or service or the creation of a new one

process innovation A change in the way a product or service is manufactured, created, or distributed

Product Versus Process Innovations   Perhaps the two most important types of technical innovations are product innovations and process innovations. **Product innovations** are changes in the physical characteristics or performance of existing products or services or the creation of brand-new products or services. **Process innovations** are changes in the way products or services are manufactured, created, or distributed. Whereas managerial innovations generally affect the broader context of development, process innovations directly affect manufacturing.

Japanese organizations have often excelled at process innovation. The market for 35mm cameras was dominated by German and other European manufacturers when, in the early 1960s, Japanese organizations such as Canon and Nikon began making cameras. Some of these early Japanese products were not very successful, but these companies continued to invest in their process technology and eventually were able to increase quality and decrease manufacturing costs. Now these Japanese organizations dominate the worldwide market for 35mm cameras, and the German companies, because they were not able to maintain the same pace of process innovation, are struggling to maintain market share and profitability.

■ The Failure to Innovate

To remain competitive in today's economy, organizations must be innovative. And yet many organizations that should be innovative are not successful at bringing out new products or services or do so only after innovations created by others are very mature. Organizations may fail to innovate for at least three reasons.

Lack of Resources   Innovation is expensive in terms of dollars, time, and energy. If a firm does not have sufficient money to fund a program of innovation, or does not currently employ the kinds of employees it needs to be innovative, it may lag behind in innovation. Even highly innovative organizations cannot become involved in every new product or service its employees think up. For example, numerous other commitments in the electronic instruments and computer industry forestalled Hewlett-Packard from investing in Steve Jobs and Steve Wozniak's idea for a personal computer. With infinite resources of money, time, and technical and managerial expertise, HP might have entered this market early. Because the firm did not have this flexibility, however, it had to make some difficult choices about which innovations to invest in.

Failure to Recognize Opportunities   Because firms cannot pursue all innovations, they need to develop the capability to carefully evaluate innovations and to select the ones that hold the greatest potential. To obtain a competitive advantage, an organization usually must make investment decisions before the innovation process reaches the mature stage. The earlier the investment, however, the greater the risk. If organizations are not skilled at recognizing and evaluating opportunities, they may be overly cautious and fail to invest in innovations that turn out later to be successful for other firms.

Resistance to Change   As we note earlier, many organizations tend to resist change. Innovation means giving up old products and old ways of doing things in favor of new products and new ways of doing things. These kinds of changes can be personally difficult for managers and other members of an organization. Thus, resistance to change can slow the innovation process.

■ Promoting Innovation in Organizations

Numerous ideas for promoting innovation in organizations have been developed over the years. Three specific ways for promoting innovation are through the reward system, through the organizational culture, and through a process called intrapreneurship.[36]

The Reward System   A firm's reward system is the means by which it encourages and discourages certain behaviors by employees. Major components of the reward system include salaries, bonuses, and perquisites. Using the reward system to promote innovation is a fairly mechanical but nevertheless effective management technique. The idea is to provide financial and nonfinancial rewards to people and groups that develop innovative ideas. Once the members of an organization understand that they will be rewarded for such activities, they are more likely to work creatively. With this end in mind, Monsanto Company gives a $50,000 award each year to the scientist or group of scientists that develops the biggest commercial breakthrough.

It is important for organizations to reward creative behavior, but it is vital to avoid punishing creativity when it does not result in highly successful innovations. It is the nature of the creative and innovative processes that many new product ideas will simply not work out in the marketplace. Each process is fraught with too many uncertainties to generate positive results every time. An individual may be prepared to be creative, but an insight may not be forthcoming. Or managers may attempt to apply a developed innovation, only to recognize that it does not work. Indeed, some organizations operate according to the assumption that if all their innovative efforts succeed, then they are probably not taking enough risks in research and development. At 3M, nearly 60 percent of the creative ideas suggested each year do not succeed in the marketplace.

Managers need to be very careful in responding to innovative failure. If innovative failure is due to incompetence, systematic errors, or managerial sloppiness, then a firm should respond appropriately; for example, by withholding raises or reducing promotion opportunities. People who act in good faith to develop an innovation that simply does not work out, however, should not be punished for failure. If they are, they will probably not be creative in the future. A punitive reward system will discourage people from taking risks and therefore reduce the organization's ability to obtain competitive advantages.

Organizational Culture As we discuss in Chapter 3, an organization's culture is the set of values, beliefs, and symbols that help guide behavior. A strong, appropriately focused organizational culture can be used to support innovative activity. A well-managed culture can communicate a sense that innovation is valued and will be rewarded and that occasional failure in the pursuit of new ideas is not only acceptable but even expected. In addition to reward systems and intrapreneurial activities, firms such as 3M, Corning, Monsanto, Procter & Gamble, Texas Instruments, Johnson & Johnson, and Merck are known to have strong, innovation-oriented cultures that value individual creativity, risk taking, and inventiveness.[37]

Intrapreneurship in Larger Organizations In recent years many large businesses have realized that the entrepreneurial spirit that propelled their growth becomes stagnant after they transform themselves from a small but growing concern into a larger one. To help revitalize this spirit, some firms today encourage what they call intrapreneurship. **Intrapreneurs** are similar to entrepreneurs except that the former develop a new business in the context of a large organization. There are three intrapreneurial roles in large organizations.[38] To successfully use intrapreneurship to encourage creativity and innovation, the organization must find one or more individuals to perform these roles.

The *inventor* is the person who actually conceives of and develops the new idea, product, or service by means of the creative process. Because the inventor may lack the expertise or motivation to oversee the transformation of the product or service from an idea into a marketable entity, however, a second role comes into play. A *product champion* is usually a middle manager who learns about the project and becomes committed to it. He or she helps overcome organizational resistance and convinces others to take the innovation seriously. The product champion may have only limited understanding of the technological aspects of the innovation. Nevertheless, product champions are skilled at knowing how the organization works, whose support is needed to push the project forward, and where to go to secure the resources necessary for successful development. A *sponsor* is a top-level manager who approves of and supports a project. This person may fight for the budget needed to develop an idea, overcome arguments against a project, and use organizational politics to ensure the project's survival. With a sponsor in place, the inventor's idea has a much better chance of being successfully developed.

Several firms have embraced intrapreneurship as a way to encourage creativity and innovation. Colgate-Palmolive has created a separate unit, Colgate Venture Company, staffed it with intrapreneurs who develop new products. General Foods developed Culinova Group as a unit to which employees can take their ideas for possible development. S.C. Johnson & Sons established a $250,000 fund to support new product ideas, and Texas Instruments refuses to approve a new innovative project unless it has an acknowledged inventor, champion, and sponsor.

intrapreneurs Similar to entrepreneurs except that intrapreneurs develop a new business in the context of a large organization

Summary of Key Points

Organization change is any substantive modification to some part of the organization. Change may be prompted by forces internal or external to the organization. In general, planned change is preferable to reactive change.

Managing the change process is very important. The Lewin model provides a general perspective on the steps involved in change, although a comprehensive model is usually more effective. People tend to resist change because of uncertainty, threatened self-interests, different perceptions, and feelings of loss. Participation, education and communication, facilitation, and force-field analysis are methods for overcoming this resistance.

Many change techniques or interventions are used. The most common ones involve changing organizational structure and design, technology, and people. There are several specific areas of change within each of these broad categories. Reengineering is the radical redesign of all aspects of a business to achieve major gains in cost, service, or time. It is occasionally needed to offset entropy. The basic steps are developing goals and strategies, conveying the involvement of top management, creating a sense of urgency, starting with a clean slate, and balancing top-down and bottom-up perspectives.

Organization development is concerned with changing attitudes, perceptions, behaviors, and expectations. Its effective use relies on an important set of assumptions. There are conflicting opinions about the effectiveness of several OD techniques.

The innovation process has six steps: development, application, launch, growth, maturity, and decline. Basic categories of innovation include radical, incremental, technical, managerial, product, and process innovations. Despite the importance of innovation, many organizations fail to innovate because they lack the required creative individuals, are committed to too many other creative activities, fail to recognize opportunities, or resist the change that innovation requires. Organizations can use a variety of tools to overcome these problems, including the reward system, organizational culture, and intrapreneurship.

Discussion Questions

Questions for Review

1. What forces or kinds of events lead to organization change? Identify each force or event as planned or reactive change.

2. How is each step in the process of organization change implemented? Are some of the steps likely to meet with more resistance than others? Why or why not?

3. What are the various areas of organization change? In what ways are they similar and in what ways do they differ?

4. What is reengineering? Why has it been so common in recent years?

5. What are the steps in the innovation process?

Questions for Analysis

1. Could reactive change of the type identified in question 1 above have been planned for ahead of time? Why or why not?

2. Should all organization change be planned? Why or why not? Is there a time when reactive change might actually be preferable? Why or why not?

3. A company has recently purchased equipment that, when installed, will do the work of one hundred employees. The workforce of the company is very concerned and is threatening to take some kind of action. If you were the human resource manager, how would you try to satisfy all parties concerned? Why?

4. Think of several examples to illustrate how changes in one area might dictate additional changes in other areas within an organization.

5. Think of several relatively new products or services that you use. What form of innovation was each?

Building Effective Time-Management Skills

EXERCISE OVERVIEW

Time-management skills refer to the manager's ability to prioritize work, to work efficiently, and to delegate appropriately. Using time-management skills wisely can change how a person works.

EXERCISE BACKGROUND

Almost every task we perform can theoretically be performed more efficiently. The next time you work on a particular task, such as studying for a test, writing a paper, or working on a project, take note of your work habits. You might even consider videotaping yourself while you work and reviewing the tape later.

Take special note of the things you do that do not seem to contribute to task performance. Examples might include going to the refrigerator and getting food, watching television while you are working, daydreaming, making an unnecessary telephone call, and so forth. Next, estimate how much of the total "work" time was actually spent on other activities.

EXERCISE TASK

With the background information above as context, do the following:

1. Assess the extent to which each nonwork activity was wasted effort or actually contributed in some way to task performance.

2. Describe how the work might have been completed had you not done any of the nonwork activities.

3. Assuming that you want to change your work habits to use your time more efficiently, describe a change approach that you might use.

Building Effective Interpersonal Skills

EXERCISE OVERVIEW

A manager's interpersonal skills are her or his ability to understand and motivate individuals and groups. These abilities are especially important during a period of change. This exercise helps you understand how to apply your interpersonal skills to a change situation.

EXERCISE BACKGROUND

Assume that you are the manager of a retail store in a local shopping mall. Your staff consists of seven full-time and ten part-time employees. The full-time employees have worked together as a team for three years. The part-timers are all local college students; several of them have worked in the store for more than a year, but there tends to be a lot of turnover among this group.

Your boss, the regional manager, has just informed you that the national chain that owns your store is planning to open a second store in the same mall. She has also informed you that you must plan and implement the following changes:

1. You will serve as manager of both stores until the sales volume of the new store warrants its own full-time manager.

2. You are to designate one of the full-time employees in your present store as the assistant manager, since you will be in the store less often now.

3. To have experienced workers in the new store, you are to select three of your current full-time workers to move to the new store, one of whom should also be appointed as assistant manager of that store.

4. You can hire three new people to replace those transferred from your present store and three new people to work at the new store.

5. You can decide for yourself how to deploy your part-timers, but you will need a total of ten in the present store and eight at the new store.

You realize that many of your employees will be unhappy with these changes. They know each other and work well together. However, the new store will be in a new section of the mall and will be a very nice place to work.

EXERCISE TASK

With this background information in mind, do the following:

1. Determine the likely reasons for resistance to this change among your workers.

2. Determine how you will decide about promotions and transfers (make whatever assumptions you think are warranted).

3. Outline how you will inform your employees about the change.

4. An alternative strategy that could be adopted would involve keeping the existing staff intact and hiring all new employees for the new store. Outline a persuasion strategy for trying to convince your boss to adopt this alternative.

EXERCISE OVERVIEW

Diagnostic skills help a manager visualize the most appropriate response to a situation. Diagnostic skills are especially important during a period of organization change.

Building Effective
Diagnostic
Skills

EXERCISE BACKGROUND

Assume that you are the general manager of a hotel located on a tropical island. The hotel, situated along a beautiful stretch of beach, is one of six large resorts in the area. The hotel is owned by a group of foreign investors and is one of the oldest on the island. For several years the hotel has been operated as a franchise unit of a large international hotel chain, as are all of the others on the island.

For the last few years, the hotel's owners have been taking most of the profits for themselves and putting relatively little back into the hotel. They also have let you know that their business is not in good financial health; the money earned from your hotel is being used to offset losses the owners are incurring elsewhere. Most of the neighboring hotels have recently been refurbished, and plans have just been announced to build two new hotels in the near future.

A team of executives from franchise headquarters has just visited your hotel. They expressed considerable disappointment in the property. They feel that it has not kept pace with the other resorts on the island. They also informed you that if the property is not brought up to their standards, the franchise agreement, up for review in a year, will be revoked. You see this as potentially disastrous, since you would lose the franchise's "brand name," access to its reservation system, and so forth.

Sitting alone in your office, you have identified a variety of alternatives that seem viable:

1. Try to convince the owners to remodel the hotel. You estimate that it will take $5 million to meet the franchiser's minimum standards, and another $5 million to bring the hotel up to the standards of the top resort on the island.

2. Try to convince the franchiser to give you more time and more options to upgrade the facility.

3. Allow the franchise agreement to terminate and try to succeed as an independent hotel.

4. Assume that the hotel is going to fail and start looking for another job. You have a good reputation, although you might have to start at a lower level with another firm (as an assistant manager perhaps).

EXERCISE TASK

With the background information presented above, do the following:

1. Rank-order the four alternatives in terms of their potential success (make assumptions as appropriate).

2. Identify other alternatives not noted above.

3. Can any alternatives be pursued simultaneously?

4. Develop an overall strategy for trying to save the hotel while also protecting yourself.

| You Make the **Call** |

With their new organization in place, the Spensers believed that their management difficulties were over. They assumed they would each have more time for their own work and that the organization itself would also function more efficiently. It wasn't long, however, before problems began to arise.

A few weeks after the changes were announced, Manuel Hernandez asked to meet with Mark one day after work. Mark was alarmed to learn that Manuel thought there were some major problems developing in the lawn-care business. Two of the crews, in particular, were of concern. Manuel reported that the two crews were having trouble completing their scheduled lawn work each day. It had been necessary for him to pitch in and help them finish, as well as to authorize overtime pay on a couple of occasions.

Manuel thought that the two crew chiefs might have something to do with the problem. They weren't as friendly toward him as they once had been, and they did not seem to be working as hard as before. Manuel believed that part of the problem was that they resented his promotion. While Manuel had more seniority than either of them, they had nonetheless worked for SLS for several years. Moreover, they and Manuel had been fairly close friends, sharing mutual interests in sports and local politics. Fortunately, the other two crews were functioning fine. One of them had a chief who had been on the job for several months, and the other was the crew formerly led by Manuel. His position had been taken over by one of the team members.

Mark asked Manuel how he wanted to proceed. Manuel indicated that he had already tried talking to his two former friends and had made no headway. After discussing various options, they decided that Mark should talk to the two crew chiefs who were causing problems. First, however, he wanted to discuss the situation with Cynthia. She was often able to come up with other alternatives that Mark had not considered.

In this case she had no other ideas about what to do. She did, however, suggest the cause of the problem. In particular, she pointed out that they had perhaps implemented the changes too quickly. Their strategy had been to do things with as little fuss as possible. They had simply drawn an organization chart, called a staff meeting one day after work, and announced the changes. In retrospect, she wondered whether they should have talked to key people in the organization before announcing the changes.

DISCUSSION QUESTIONS

1. Describe the change process that the Spensers could have used to plan and implement their changes.

2. Why might workers at SLS have resisted the changes?

3. What could the Spensers have done to overcome the resistance?

INNOVATIVE ATTITUDE SCALE

Skills Self-Assessment Instrument

Introduction: Change and innovation are important to organizations. The following assessment surveys your readiness to accept and participate in innovation.

Instructions: Indicate the extent to which each of the following statements is true of either your *actual* behavior or your *intentions* at work. That is, describe the way you are or the way you intend to be on the job. Use this scale for your responses:

Almost always true = **5**
Often true = **4**
Not applicable = **3**
Seldom true = **2**
Almost never true = **1**

____ 1. I openly discuss with my boss how to get ahead.
____ 2. I try new ideas and approaches to problems.
____ 3. I take things or situations apart to find out how they work.

_____ 4. I welcome uncertainty and unusual circumstances related to my tasks.

_____ 5. I negotiate my salary openly with my supervisor.

_____ 6. I can be counted on to find a new use for existing methods or equipment.

_____ 7. Among my colleagues and coworkers, I will be the first or nearly the first to try out a new idea or method.

_____ 8. I take the opportunity to translate communications from other departments for my work group.

_____ 9. I demonstrate originality.

_____10. I will work on a problem that has caused others great difficulty.

_____11. I provide critical input toward a new solution.

_____12. I provide written evaluations of proposed ideas.

_____13. I develop contacts with experts outside my firm.

_____14. I use personal contacts to maneuver myself into choice work assignments.

_____15. I make time to pursue my own pet ideas or projects.

_____16. I set aside resources for the pursuit of a risky project.

_____17. I tolerate people who depart from organizational routine.

_____18. I speak out in staff meetings.

_____19. I work in teams to try to solve complex problems.

_____20. If my coworkers are asked, they will say I am a wit.

For interpretation , turn to page 459.

Source: From J. E. Ettlie and R. D. O'Keefe, "Innovative Attitudes, Values, and Intentions in Organizations," _Journal of Management Studies_ 19 (1982), p. 176. Reprinted by permission of Blackwell Publishers.

Experiential Exercise

INNOVATION IN ACTION: EGG DROP

Purpose: Managers are continuously improving the work flow, the product, and the packaging of products. This is what Total Quality Management is all about. To do this means thinking creatively and acting innovatively. This skill builder focuses on the _open systems model_. It helps you develop the _innovator role_. One of the skills of the innovator is thinking creatively and acting innovatively.

Introduction: This activity is a practical and entertaining demonstration of creativity and innovation in action. The "Egg Drop" exercise provides practice in identifying, defining, or refining a problem or opportunity, developing options and alternatives, choosing the best option or alternative, actually launching the alternative into reality, and verifying the results within a specified time period. Your instructor will provide you with further instructions.

Source: Reproduced with permission from "Metaphorically Speaking," from _50 Activities on Creativity and Problem Solving_ by Geof Cox, Chuck DuFault, and Walt Hopkins, Gower, Aldershot, 1992.

CASE STUDY

Levi Strauss Hikes Up Its Pants

Levi Strauss & Co. and the ubiquitous denim blue jeans it sells around the world have been a virtual icon for years. The firm can trace its roots back to the mid-nineteenth century when its namesake immigrated to the U.S. from Bavaria. Shortly after arriving in San Francisco during the California gold rush, Levi Strauss decided that it was a safer bet to produce equipment for other miners than it was to set out with his own pick and shovel. Work pants crafted from heavy canvas proved to be his most successful product.

Strauss began coloring the pants with blue pigments and enlisted the aid of a friend to provide what would become the trademark rivets at key stress points. The firm grew slowly but surely for decades, always led by one of Strauss' direct descendants. But Levi's real growth started in the 1950s when its pants became an essential uniform for the youth of the United States.

The momentum continued into the 1960s as denim took its place alongside incense, tie-died shirts, and long hair as symbols of a rebellious youth. And as the baby boomers who were the youth of the 1950s and 1960s grew into adulthood, Levi's jeans became their fashion mainstay. Even the name Levi's became almost synonymous with blue jeans. During the 1970s through the 1990s, Levi Strauss & Co. also expanded rapidly overseas, and today its jeans are sold in more than seventy countries.

Under the leadership of Robert Hass (Levi Strauss' great-great-grandnephew), the company also forged an innovative relationship with its employees. High levels of job security, an innovative reward structure, and an open and participative approach to management created a loyal and dedicated workforce that helped keep the organization at the top of its industry.

But as the decade of the 1990s grew to a close, Levi Strauss seemed to hit a wall. And as a result, the firm has found it necessary to reexamine every aspect of its business operations while simultaneously redefining its relationship with its workforce. The catalyst for change was an almost-sudden drop in market share. For example, in 1990 Levi held 30.9 percent of the jeans market in the United States. But by 1997 that figure had plummeted to just 18.7 percent. Similarly, the firm's market share among fifteen- to nineteen-year-old consumers dropped from 33 percent in 1993 to 26 percent in 1997.

This alarming trend forced company executives to face an intense and detailed period of introspection to find out what was happening to the company. Their conclusion was that they had been so successful with their core baby-boomer consumers that they had essentially neglected younger consumers. As a result, top-end designers like Tommy Hilfiger and Ralph Lauren and discounted store brands sold at Sears and J.C. Penney had taken market share from Levi. Similarly, the jeans giant had also ignored emerging fashion trends like wide-legged and baggy jeans.

Once the company saw its problem, Levi Strauss took quick action along a number of fronts. Most painfully, it announced that it was closing eleven U.S. factories and laying off one-third of its North American workforce. This step served to dramatically and unalterably change the company's relationship with its workforce. The company also acknowledged that it needed to alter the composition of its executive team to boost creativity and market knowledge. Too many officials had come up through the ranks and knew only one way of doing things—the old tried-and-true Levi Strauss way. Thus, one goal now is to fill 30 percent of all new management jobs with outsiders. Experts agree that it will take the firm some time to get its act together again, but they also acknowledge that the changes seem to fit the situation as well as a pair of the firm's jeans fit after a long day at the office.

Case Questions

1. What forces led to the need for change at Levi Strauss?
2. What kinds of changes can you identify at Levi?
3. One mistake a firm can make is failing to change when it needs to; another is changing too quickly. How can managers like those at Levi best position themselves to change when they need to—not too quickly, but not too late either?

Case References: "Levi's Is Hiking Up Its Pants," *Business Week,* December 1, 1997, pp. 70–75; "Its Share Shrinking, Levi Strauss Lays Off 6,395," *Wall Street Journal,* November 4, 1997, pp. B1, B8; and "Levi's Gets the Blues," *Time,* November 17, 1997, p. 66.

CHAPTER NOTES

1. "Gentlemen, Start Your Engines," *Fortune*, June 8, 1998, pp. 138–146; Alex Taylor III, "'Neutron' Jurgen Ignites a Revolution at Daimler-Benz," *Fortune*, November 10, 1997, pp. 144–152 (quote on p. 146); and "Dustup at Daimler," *Business Week*, February 3, 1997, pp. 52–53.

2. Joel Cutcher-Gershenfeld, Ellen Ernst Kossek, and Heidi Sandling, "Managing Concurrent Change Initiatives," *Organizational Dynamics*, Winter 1997, pp. 21–38.

3. Thomas A. Stewart, "How to Lead a Revolution," *Fortune*, November 28, 1994, pp. 48–61.

4. See Warren Boeker, "Strategic Change: The Influence of Managerial Characteristics and Organizational Growth," *Academy of Management Journal*, 1997, Vol. 40, No. 1, pp. 152–170.

5. Alan L. Frohman, "Igniting Organizational Change from Below: The Power of Personal Initiative," *Organizational Dynamics*, Winter 1997, pp. 39–53.

6. Nandini Rajagopalan and Gretchen M. Spreitzer, "Toward a Theory of Strategic Change: A Multi-Lens Perspective and Integrative Framework," *Academy of Management Review*, 1997, Vol. 22, No. 1, pp. 48–79.

7. Anne Fisher, "Danger Zone," *Fortune*, September 8, 1997, pp. 165–167.

8. "Kodak to Cut 10,000 Jobs," Associated Press story reported in *The Bryan-College Station Eagle*, November 12, 1997, p. A6.

9. John P. Kotter and Leonard A. Schlesinger, "Choosing Strategies for Change," *Harvard Business Review*, March–April 1979, p. 106.

10. Erik Brynjolfsson, Amy Austin Renshaw, and Marshall Van Alstyne, "The Matrix of Change," *Sloan Management Review*, Winter 1997, pp. 37–54.

11. Kurt Lewin, "Frontiers in Group Dynamics: Concept, Method, and Reality in Social Science," *Human Relations*, June 1947, pp. 5–41.

12. See Connie J. G. Gersick, "Revolutionary Change Theories: A Multilevel Exploration of the Punctuated Equilibrium Paradigm," *Academy of Management Review*, January 1991, pp. 10–36.

13. See Gerald Andrews, "Mistrust, the Hidden Obstacle to Empowerment, *HRMagazine*, November 1994, pp. 66–74, for a good illustration of how resistance emerges.

14. "RJR Employees Fight Distraction Amid Buy-out Talks," *Wall Street Journal*, November 1, 1988, p. A8.

15. Arnon E. Reichers, John P. Wanous, and James T. Austin, "Understanding and Managing Cynicism About Organizational Change," *Academy of Management Executive*, February 1997, pp. 48–59.

16. "How Classy Can 7-Eleven Get?" *Business Week*, September 1, 1997, pp. 74–75.

17. See Paul R. Lawrence, "How to Deal with Resistance to Change," *Harvard Business Review*, January–February 1969, pp. 4–12, 166–176, for a classic discussion.

18. Lester Coch and John R. P. French Jr., "Overcoming Resistance to Change," *Human Relations*, August 1948, pp. 512–532.

19. Charles K. Day Jr., "Management's Mindless Mistakes," *Industry Week*, May 29, 1987, p. 42. See also "Inspection from the Plant Floor," *Business Week*, April 10, 1989, pp. 60–61.

20. Benjamin Schneider, Arthur P. Brief, and Richard A. Guzzo, "Creating a Climate and Culture for Sustainable Organizational Change," *Organizational Dynamics*, Spring 1996, pp. 7–19.

21. David A. Nadler, "The Effective Management of Organizational Change," in Jay W. Lorsch (ed.), *Handbook of Organizational Behavior* (Englewood Cliffs, N.J.: Prentice-Hall, 1987), pp. 358–369.

22. Jeffrey A. Alexander, "Adaptive Change in Corporate Control Practices," *Academy of Management Journal*, March 1991, pp. 162–193.

23. Thomas A. Stewart, "Reengineering—The Hot New Managing Tool," *Fortune*, August 23, 1993, pp. 41–48.

24. Richard Beckhard, *Organization Development: Strategies and Models* (Reading, Mass.: Addison-Wesley, 1969), p. 9.

25. W. Warner Burke, "The New Agenda for Organization Development," *Organizational Dynamics*, Summer 1997, pp. 7–20.

26. Wendell L. French and Cecil H. Bell Jr., *Organization Development: Behavioral Science Interventions for Organization Improvement*, 2nd ed. (Englewood Cliffs, N.J.: Prentice-Hall, 1978).

27. William G. Dyer, *Team Building Issues and Alternatives* (Reading, Mass.: Addison-Wesley, 1980).

28. Roger J. Hower, Mark G. Mindell, and Donna L. Simmons, "Introducing Innovation Through OD," *Management Review*, February 1978, pp. 52–56.

29. "Is Organization Development Catching On? A Personnel Symposium," *Personnel*, November–December 1977, pp. 10–22.

30. For a recent discussion on the effectiveness of various OD techniques in different organizations, see John M. Nicholas, "The Comparative Impact of Organization Development Interventions on Hard Criteria Measures," *Academy of Management Review*, October 1982, pp. 531–542.

31. Constantinos Markides, "Strategic Innovation," *Sloan Management Review*, Spring 1997, pp. 9–24.

32. L. B. Mohr, "Determinants of Innovation in Organizations," *American Political Science Review*, 1969, pp. 111–126; G. A. Steiner, *The Creative Organization* (Chicago: University of Chicago Press, 1965); R. Duncan and A. Weiss, "Organizational Learning: Implications for Organizational Design," in B. M. Staw (ed.), *Research in Organizational Behavior*, Vol. 1 (Greenwich, Conn.: JAI Press, 1979), pp. 75–123; and J. E. Ettlie, "Adequacy of Stage Models for Decisions on Adoption of Innovation," *Psychological Reports*, 1980, pp. 991–995.

33. Beth Wolfensberger, "Trouble in Toyland," *New England Business*, September 1990, pp. 28–36.

34. See Alan Patz, "Managing Innovation in High Technology Industries," *New Management*, September 1986, pp. 54–59.

35. "Flops," *Business Week*, August 16, 1993, pp. 76–82.

36. Dorothy Leonard and Jeffrey F. Rayport, "Spark Innovation Through Empathic Design," *Harvard Business Review*, November–December 1997, pp. 102–115.

37. See Steven P. Feldman, "How Organizational Culture Can Affect Innovation," *Organizational Dynamics*, Summer 1988, pp. 57–68.

38. See Gifford Pinchot III, *Intrapreneuring* (New York: Harper and Row, 1985).

8

Managing Human Resources

OBJECTIVES

After studying this chapter, you should be able to:

- Describe the environmental context of human resource management, including its strategic importance and its relationship with legal factors.
- Discuss how organizations attract human resources, including human resource planning, recruiting, and selecting.
- Describe how organizations develop human resources, including training and development, performance appraisal, and performance feedback.
- Discuss how organizations maintain human resources, including the determination of compensation and benefits.
- Discuss the nature of diversity, including its meaning, associated trends, and impact.
- Discuss labor relations, including how employees form unions and the mechanics of collective bargaining.

Cisco Systems is one of the hottest companies in California's fabled Silicon Valley. Founded in 1984 by two enterprising Stanford University employees, Cisco specializes in technology to link networks. By 1997 the firm's annual sales exceeded $6 billion, and it was selling its products in seventy-five countries.

To maintain its phenomenal growth level, Cisco has had to add new employees at a steady pace. For example, the company recently doubled the size of its workforce in an eighteen-month period. In some areas and in some industries, this level of growth would be easy. But in the Silicon Valley and in the world of high technology, finding and keeping bright and talented people is difficult even during periods of normal growth. But the pace of growth experienced by Cisco is dizzying.

Nevertheless, Cisco has been able to identify, hire, and—most important of all—retain the best employees through the use of a well-developed and executed recruiting strategy. The strategy began when top managers at Cisco clearly defined the kinds of employees they wanted to hire. In particular, they set a goal of hiring only from among the top 15 percent of the people working in the industry.

Next, Cisco's managers studied exactly how this caliber of person goes about looking for a job. For example, Cisco prefers to hire high-caliber employees who are relatively content with their present jobs but are willing to consider challenging, exciting, and rewarding alternatives. These people often dislike actually looking for new jobs and, instead, are more likely to be enticed by web sites with interesting graphics. That is, these people may not be actively looking for a new job, but frequently surf the Web and look at interesting sites.

And finally, they developed innovative hiring procedures for getting these people interested in Cisco. For example, interested recruits can actually indicate their interest in Cisco via e-mail and electronic submission of résumés. And the firm will reply electronically and provide answers to many common questions, such as pay and benefits.

Of course, after the firm hires these employees, it must still work to keep them. Thus Cisco's salaries are among the highest in the industry. The firm also provides an exhaustive set of leading-edge benefits for its employees and maintains a casual and relaxing corporate culture in which employees like to work. As a result, the company also has one of the lowest turnover rates in its industry. Cisco managers believe that these loyal and talented employees will help keep the firm on top for a long time to come.[1]

"Our philosophy is very simple—if you get the best people in the industry to fit into your culture and you motivate them properly, then you're going to be an industry leader."

John Chambers, Cisco CEO

Cisco Systems is one of the most successful businesses around these days. And its human resources are clearly an integral part of Cisco's success. From its earliest days, the firm's managers made a strategic commitment to identify, hire, and retain the best and brightest people available. Moreover, the firm has been able to maintain this strategy and today is still the employer of choice for many talented people in California's Silicon Valley.

This chapter is about how organizations manage people. This set of processes is called human resource management, or HRM. We start by describing the environmental context of HRM. We then discuss how organizations attract human resources. Next we describe how organizations seek to further develop the capacities of their human resources. We also examine how organizations maintain high-quality human resources. Diversity in organizations is examined next, and we conclude by discussing labor relations.

The Environmental Context of Human Resource Management

human resource management (HRM) The set of organizational activities directed at attracting, developing, and maintaining an effective workforce

Human resource management (HRM) is the set of organizational activities directed at attracting, developing, and maintaining an effective workforce.[2] Human resource management takes place within a complex and ever-changing environmental context.

■ The Strategic Importance of HRM

Human resources are critical for effective organizational functioning.[3] Most managers realize that the effectiveness of their HR function has a substantial impact on the bottom-line performance of the firm. Poor human resource planning can result in spurts of hiring followed by layoffs—costly in terms of unemployment compensation payments, training expenses, and morale. Haphazard compensation systems do not attract, keep, and motivate good employees, and outmoded recruitment practices can expose the firm to expensive and embarrassing discrimination lawsuits. Consequently, the chief human resource executive of most large businesses is a vice president directly accountable to the CEO, and many firms are developing strategic HR plans and are integrating those plans with other strategic planning activities.[4]

Even organizations with as few as two hundred employees usually have a human resource manager and a human resource department charged with overseeing these activities. Responsibility for HR activities, however, is shared between the HR department and line managers. The HR department may recruit and initially screen candidates, but managers in the department where the new employee will work usually make the final selection. Similarly, although the HR department may establish performance appraisal policies and procedures, the actual evaluating and coaching of employees is done by their immediate superiors.

The Legal Environment of HRM

A number of laws regulate various aspects of employee-employer relations, especially in the areas of equal employment opportunity, compensation and benefits, labor relations, and occupational safety and health. The major laws are summarized in Table 8.1.

Equal Employment Opportunity **Title VII of the Civil Rights Act of 1964** forbids discrimination in all areas of the employment relationship. The intent of Title VII is to ensure that employment decisions are made on the basis of an individual's qualifications rather than personal biases. The law has reduced both direct forms of discrimination (refusing to hire blacks, for example) and indirect forms of discrimination (using employment tests that whites pass at a higher rate than blacks, for example). Selection requirements have an **adverse impact** on minorities and women when such individuals meet or pass the requirement at a rate less than 80 percent of the rate of majority group members. Criteria that have an adverse impact on protected groups can be used only when there is solid evidence that those criteria effectively identify individuals who are better

TABLE 8.1
The Legal Environment of Human Resource Management

As much as any area of management, HRM is subject to wide-ranging laws and court decisions. These laws and decisions affect the human resource function in many areas. For example, AT&T was once fined several million dollars for violating Title VII of the Civil Rights Act of 1964.

Equal Employment Opportunity

Title VII of the Civil Rights Act of 1964 (as amended by the *Equal Employment Opportunity Act of 1972*): forbids discrimination in all areas of the employment relationship

Age Discrimination in Employment Act: outlaws discrimination against people older than forty years

Various executive orders, especially *Executive Order 11246* in 1965: requires employers with government contracts to engage in affirmative action

Pregnancy Discrimination Act: specifically outlaws discrimination on the basis of pregnancy

Vietnam Era Veterans Readjustment Assistance Act: extends affirmative action mandate to military veterans who served during the Vietnam War

Americans with Disabilities Act: specifically outlaws discrimination against disabled persons

Civil Rights Act of 1991: makes it easier for employees to sue an organization for discrimination but limits punitive damage awards if they win

Compensation and Benefits

Fair Labor Standards Act: establishes minimum wage and mandated overtime pay for work in excess of forty hours per week

Equal Pay Act of 1963: requires that men and women be paid the same amount for doing the same jobs

Employee Retirement Income Security Act of 1974: regulates how organizations manage their pension funds

Family and Medical Leave Act of 1993: requires employers to provide up to twelve weeks of unpaid leave for family and medical emergencies

Labor Relations

National Labor Relations Act: spells out procedures by which employees can establish labor unions and requires organizations to bargain collectively with legally formed unions; also known as the *Wagner Act*

Labor-Management Relations Act: limits union power and specifies management rights during a union-organizing campaign; also known as the *Taft-Hartley Act*

Health and Safety

Occupational Safety and Health Act of 1970: mandates the provision of safe working conditions.

Title VII of the Civil Rights Act of 1964 Forbids discrimination on the basis of sex, race, color, religion, or national origin in all areas of the employment relationship

adverse impact When minority group members pass a selection standard at a rate less than 80 percent of the pass rate of majority group members

Equal Employment Opportunity Commission Charged with enforcing Title VII of the Civil Rights Act of 1964

Age Discrimination in Employment Act Outlaws discrimination against people older than forty years; passed in 1967, amended in 1978 and 1986

affirmative action Intentionally seeking and hiring qualified or qualifiable employees from racial, sexual, and ethnic groups that are underrepresented in the organization

Americans with Disabilities Act Prohibits discrimination against people with disabilities

Civil Rights Act of 1991 Amends the original Civil Rights Act, making it easier to bring discrimination lawsuits while also limiting punitive damages

Fair Labor Standards Act Sets a minimum wage and requires overtime pay for work in excess of forty hours per week; passed in 1938 and amended frequently since then

Equal Pay Act of 1963 Requires that men and women be paid the same amount for doing the same jobs

Employee Retirement Income Security Act of 1974 (ERISA) Sets standards for pension plan management and provides federal insurance if pension funds go bankrupt

Family and Medical Leave Act of 1993 Requires employers to provide up to twelve weeks of unpaid leave for family and medical emergencies

National Labor Relations Act Passed in 1935 to set up procedures for employees to vote whether to have a union; also known as the Wagner Act

able than others to do the job. The **Equal Employment Opportunity Commission** is charged with enforcing Title VII as well as several other employment-related laws.

The **Age Discrimination in Employment Act**, passed in 1967, amended in 1978, and amended again in 1986, is an attempt to prevent organizations from discriminating against older workers. This act outlaws discrimination against people older than forty years. Both the Age Discrimination Act and Title VII require passive nondiscrimination, or equal employment opportunity. Employers are not required to seek out and hire minorities, but they must treat fairly all who apply.

Several executive orders, however, require that employers holding government contracts engage in **affirmative action**—intentionally seeking and hiring employees from groups that are underrepresented in the organization. These organizations must have a written affirmative action plan that spells out employment goals for underutilized groups and how those goals will be met. These employers are also required to act affirmatively in hiring Vietnam-era veterans and qualified handicapped individuals.

In 1990 Congress passed the **Americans with Disabilities Act** that forbids discrimination on the basis of disabilities and requires employers to provide reasonable accommodations for disabled employees. More recently, the **Civil Rights Act of 1991** amended the original Civil Rights Act as well as other related laws by making it easier to bring discrimination lawsuits while simultaneously limiting the amount of punitive damages that can be awarded in those lawsuits.

Compensation and Benefits The **Fair Labor Standards Act**, passed in 1938 and amended frequently since then, sets a minimum wage (currently $5.15 an hour) and requires the payment of overtime rates for work in excess of forty hours per week. Salaried professional, executive, and administrative employees are exempt from the minimum hourly wage and overtime provisions. The **Equal Pay Act of 1963** requires that men and women be paid the same amount for doing the same jobs.

The provision of benefits is also regulated in some ways by state and federal laws. Certain benefits are mandatory—for example, worker's compensation insurance for employees who are injured on the job. Employers who provide a pension plan for their employees are regulated by the **Employee Retirement Income Security Act of 1974 (ERISA)**. The purpose of this act is to help ensure the financial security of pension funds by regulating how they can be invested. The **Family and Medical Leave Act of 1993** requires employers to provide up to twelve weeks of unpaid leave for family and medical emergencies.

Labor Relations The **National Labor Relations Act** (also known as the Wagner Act), passed in 1935, sets up a procedure for employees of a firm to vote on whether to have a union. If they vote for a union, management is required to bargain collectively with the union. The **National Labor Relations Board** was established by the Wagner Act to enforce its provisions. The **Labor-Management Relations Act** (also known as the *Taft-Hartley Act*) was passed in 1947 to limit union power and to increase management's rights during an organizing campaign. The Taft-Hartley Act also contains the *National*

Employee safety and health have become major issues for organizations and their human resource managers. For example, Karen Vanderstoep's job at Hormel requires that she lift heavy pieces of meat and operate dangerous equipment. Note that she is wearing a hard hat, ear protectors, and a heavy apron and gloves. She also stands on a springy rubber mat to reduce fatigue and strain on her knees. These and myriad other improvements have dramatically reduced injuries at the Hormel facility.

Emergency Strike provision, which allows the president of the United States to prevent or end a strike that endangers national security. Taken together, those laws balance union and management power. Employees can be represented by a properly constituted union, and management can make non-employee-related business decisions without interference.

Health and Safety   The **Occupational Safety and Health Act of 1970** directly mandates the provision of safe working conditions. It requires that employers (1) provide a place of employment that is free from hazards that may cause death or serious physical harm and (2) obey the safety and health standards established by the *Occupational Safety and Health Administration* (OSHA). Safety standards are intended to prevent accidents, whereas occupational health standards are concerned with preventing occupational disease. For example, standards limit the concentration of cotton dust in the air because this contaminant has been associated with lung disease in textile workers. OSHA inspections, which are conducted when an employee files a complaint of unsafe conditions or when a serious accident occurs, enforce the standards. OSHA also makes spot inspections of plants in especially hazardous industries such as mining and chemicals. Employers who fail to meet OSHA standards may be fined.

National Labor Relations Board Established by the Wagner Act to enforce its provisions

Labor-Management Relations Act Passed in 1947 to limit union power; also known as the Taft-Hartley Act

Occupational Safety and Health Act of 1970   Directly mandates the provision of safe working conditions

Attracting Human Resources

With an understanding of the environmental context of human resource management as a foundation, we are now ready to address its first substantive concern—attracting qualified people who are interested in employment with the organization.

■ Human Resource Planning

The starting point in attracting qualified human resources is planning. HR planning, in turn, involves job analysis and forecasting the demand and supply of labor.

job analysis A systematized procedure for collecting and recording information about jobs

Job Analysis   **Job analysis** is a systematic analysis of jobs within an organization and results in two things. The *job description* lists the duties of a job, the job's working conditions, and the tools, materials, and equipment used to perform it. The *job specification* lists the skills, abilities, and other credentials needed to do the job.

Forecasting Human Resource Demand and Supply   After managers fully understand the jobs to be performed within the organization, they can start planning for the organization's future human resource needs. Figure 8.1 summarizes the steps most often followed. The manager starts by assessing trends in past human resources usage, future organizational plans, and general economic trends. A good sales forecast is often the foundation, especially for smaller organizations. Large organizations use more complicated models to predict future human resource needs.

Forecasting the supply of labor is really two tasks: forecasting the internal supply (the number and type of employees who will be in the firm at some future date) and forecasting the external supply (the number and type of people who will be available for hiring in the labor market at large). The simplest approach merely adjusts present staffing levels for anticipated turnover and promotions. Again, though, large organizations use extremely sophisticated models to make these forecasts. Union Oil Company of California, for example, has a complex forecasting system for keeping track of present and future distributions of professionals and managers. The system can spot areas where there will eventually be too many qualified professionals competing for too few promotions or, conversely, too few good people available to fill important positions.

At higher levels of the organization, managers plan for specific people and positions. The technique most commonly used is the **replacement chart**, which lists each important managerial position, who occupies it, how long he or she will probably stay

FIGURE 8.1
Human Resource Planning

Attracting human resources cannot be left to chance if an organization expects to function at peak efficiency. Human resource planning involves assessing trends, forecasting supply and demand of labor, and then developing appropriate strategies for addressing any differences.

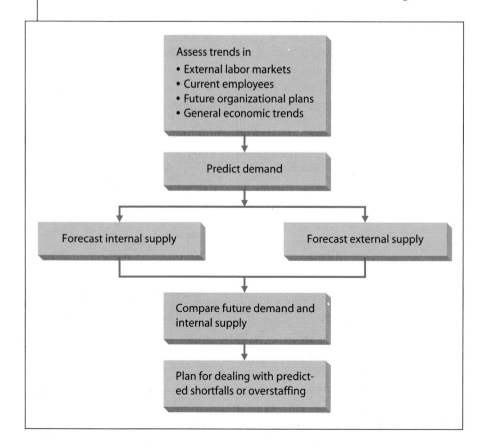

in it before moving on, and who (by name) is now qualified or soon will be qualified to move into the position. This technique allows ample time to plan developmental experiences for persons identified as potential successors to critical managerial jobs. Charles Knight, CEO of Emerson Electric Co., has an entire room dedicated to posting the credentials of his top seven hundred executives.

To facilitate both planning and identifying persons for current transfer or promotion, some organizations also have an **employee information system**, or **skills inventory**. Such systems are usually computerized and contain information on each employee's education, skills, work experience, and career aspirations. Such a system can quickly locate all the employees in the organization who are qualified to fill a position requiring, for instance, a degree in chemical engineering, three years of experience in an oil refinery, and fluency in Spanish.

Forecasting the external supply of labor is a different problem altogether. How does a manager, for example, predict how many electrical engineers will be seeking work in Georgia three years from now? To get an idea of the future availability of labor, planners rely on information from outside sources such as state employment commissions, government reports, and figures supplied by colleges on the number of students in major fields.

Matching Human Resource Supply and Demand After comparing future demand and internal supply, managers can make plans to manage predicted shortfalls or overstaffing. If a shortfall is predicted, new employees can be hired, present employees can be retrained and transferred into the understaffed area, individuals approaching retirement can be convinced to stay on, or labor-saving or productivity-enhancing systems can be installed. If overstaffing is expected to be a problem, the main options are transferring the extra employees, not replacing individuals who quit, encouraging early retirement, and laying off people.[5]

■ Recruiting Human Resources

Once an organization has an idea of its future human resource needs, the next phase is usually recruiting new employees. **Recruiting** is the process of attracting qualified persons to apply for the jobs that are open. Some recruits are found internally; others come from outside of the organization.

Internal recruiting means considering present employees as candidates for openings. Promotion from within can help build morale and keep high-quality employees from leaving the firm. In unionized firms the procedures for notifying employees of internal job change opportunities are usually spelled out in the union contract. For higher-level positions, a skills inventory system may be used to identify internal candidates, or managers may be asked to recommend individuals who should be considered. One disadvantage of internal recruiting, however, is its "ripple effect." When an employee moves to a different job, someone else must be found to take his or her old job. In one organization, 454 job movements were necessary as a result of filling 195 initial openings![6]

External recruiting involves attracting persons from outside the organization to apply for jobs. External recruiting methods include advertising, campus interviews, employment agencies or executive search firms, union hiring

replacement chart Lists each important managerial position in the organization, who occupies it, how long he or she will probably remain in the position, and who is or will be a qualified replacement

employee information system (skills inventory) Contains information on each employee's education, skills, experience, and career aspirations; usually computerized

recruiting The process of attracting individuals to apply for jobs that are open

internal recruiting Considering current employees as applicants for higher-level jobs in the organization

external recruiting Getting people from outside the organization to apply for jobs

realistic job preview (RJP) Provides the applicant with a real picture of what a particular job is like

validation Determining the extent to which a selection device is really predictive of future job performance

halls, referrals by present employees, and hiring "walk-ins" or "gate hires" (people who show up without being solicited). Private employment agencies can be a good source of clerical and technical employees, and executive search firms specialize in locating top-management talent. Newspaper ads are often used because they reach a wide audience and thus allow minorities "equal opportunity" to find out about and apply for job openings.

When hiring externally, most experts suggest providing what is called a **realistic job preview (RJP)** for recruits. As the term suggests, the RJP involves providing a real picture of what the job is like. For example, AT&T used to have very high turnover among its long-distance operators because the firm described the job as being more exciting and rewarding than was really the case. People would accept the job, become disillusioned, and then leave. Now, though, AT&T gives a more realistic description and actually has applicants watch a video showing exactly what an operator does. As a result, turnover is much lower, in part because people who take the job know what to expect.

■ Selecting Human Resources

Once the recruiting process has attracted a pool of applicants, the next step is to select whom to hire. The intent of the selection process is to gather from applicants information that will predict their job success and then to hire the candidates likely to be most successful. Of course, the organization can only gather information about factors that are predictive of future performance. The process of determining the predictive value of information is called **validation**.

Application Blanks   The first step in selection is usually asking the candidate to fill out an application blank. Application blanks are an efficient method of gathering information about the applicant's previous work history, educational background, and other job-related demographic data. They should not contain questions about areas not related to the job, such as gender, religion, or national origin. This information is generally used to decide whether a candidate merits further evaluation, and interviewers use the applications to familiarize themselves with candidates before interviewing them.

Tests   Tests of ability, skill, aptitude, or knowledge that is relevant to the particular job are usually the best predictors of job success, although tests of general intelligence or personality are occasionally useful as well. In addition to being validated, tests should be administered and scored consistently. All candidates should be given the same directions, should be allowed the same amount of time, and should experience the same testing environment (temperature, lighting, distractions).[7]

Interviews   Although interviews are a popular selection device, they are sometimes poor predictors of job success. For example, biases inherent in the way people perceive and judge others on first meeting affect subsequent evaluations by the interviewer. Interview validity can be improved by training interviewers to be aware of potential biases and by increasing the structure of the interview. In a structured interview, questions are written in advance, and all interviewers follow the same question list with each candidate they interview. This procedure introduces consistency into the interview procedure and allows the organization to validate the content of the questions.[8] For interviewing managerial or professional candidates, a somewhat less structured approach can be used. Question areas and information-gathering objectives are still planned in advance, but the specific questions vary with the candidates' backgrounds. Trammell Crow Real Estate Investors uses a novel approach in hiring managers. Each applicant is interviewed not only by two or three other managers but also by a secretary or young leasing agent. This technique provides information about how the prospective manager relates to nonmanagers.[9]

Assessment Centers Assessment centers are a popular method used to select managers and are particularly good for selecting current employees for promotion. A typical center lasts two to three days, with groups of six to twelve persons participating in a variety of managerial exercises. Centers may also include interviews, public speaking, and standardized ability tests. Candidates are assessed by several trained observers, usually managers several levels above the job for which the candidates are being considered. Assessment centers are quite valid if properly designed and are fair to members of minority groups and women.[10] AT&T pioneered the assessment center concept. For years the firm has used centers to make virtually all of its selection decisions for management positions.

Other Techniques Organizations also use other selection techniques depending on the circumstances. Polygraph tests, once popular, are declining in popularity. On the other hand, more and more organizations are requiring that applicants in whom they are interested take physical exams. Organizations are also increasingly using drug tests, especially in situations in which drug-related performance problems could create serious safety hazards.[11] For example, applicants for jobs in a nuclear power plant would likely be tested for drug use. And some organizations today even run credit checks on prospective employees.

Developing Human Resources

Regardless of how effective a selection system is, however, most employees need additional training if they are to grow and develop in their jobs. Evaluating their performance and providing feedback are also necessary.

■ Training and Development

In HRM, **training** usually refers to teaching operational or technical employees how to do the job for which they were hired. **Development** refers to teaching managers and professionals the skills needed for both present and future jobs. Most organizations provide regular training and development programs for managers and employees.[12] For example, Shell spends more than $500 million annually on programs and has a vice president in charge of employee education. U.S. businesses spend more than $35 billion annually on training and development programs away from the workplace. And this figure doesn't include compensation paid to employees while they are in such programs.[13]

training Teaching operational or technical employees how to do the job for which they were hired

development Teaching managers and professionals the skills needed for both present and future jobs

Training and developing people is an important part of human resource management. Canon, for example, invests heavily in training its employees as part of its goal to remain a leading manufacturer of photography equipment. One of its biggest problems has been trying to balance the trend toward moving production to cheaper labor markets while maintaining high performance levels. One tactic Canon uses is to send its newly hired Malaysian workers to one of its plants in Japan for training. After these workers have gained proficiency, they are sent back to Malaysia to work in Canon's factory there.

Assessing Training Needs

The first step in developing a training plan is to determine what needs exist. For example, if employees do not know how to operate the machinery necessary to do their jobs, a training program on how to operate the machinery is clearly needed. On the other hand, when a group of office workers is performing poorly, training may not be the answer. The problem could be motivation, aging equipment, poor supervision, inefficient work design, or a deficiency of skills and knowledge. Only the last could be remedied by training. As training programs are developed, the manager should set specific and measurable goals specifying what participants are to learn. Managers should also plan to evaluate the training program after employees complete it.

Common Training Methods   Many training and development methods are available. Selection of methods depends on many considerations, but perhaps the most important is training content. When the training content is factual material (such as company rules or explanations of how to fill out forms), assigned reading, programmed learning, and lecture methods work well. When the content is interpersonal relations or group decision making, however, firms must use a method that allows interpersonal contact such as role-playing or case discussion groups. When employees must learn a physical skill, methods allowing practice and the actual use of tools and material are needed, as in on-the-job training. CD-ROM, Web-based, and distance-learning programs are also becoming popular. Xerox, Federal Express, and Ford have reported tremendous success with these methods.[14] In addition, most training programs actually rely on a mix of methods. Boeing, for example, sends managers to an intensive two-week training seminar involving tests, simulations, role-playing exercises, and CD-ROM flight simulation exercises.[15]

Evaluation of Training   Training and development programs should always be evaluated. Typical evaluation approaches include measuring one or more relevant criteria (such as attitudes or performance) before and after the training and determining whether the criteria changed. Evaluation data collected at the end of training are easy to get, but actual performance measures collected when the trainee is on the job are more important. Trainees may say that they enjoyed the training and learned a lot, but the true test is whether their performance improves after their training.

■ Performance Appraisal

When employees are trained and settled into their jobs, one of management's next concerns is performance appraisal. **Performance appraisal** is a formal assessment of how well employees are doing their job. Employees' performance should be evaluated regularly for many reasons. For example, appraisals may be necessary for validating selection devices or assessing the impact of training programs; to aid in making decisions about pay raises, promotions, and training; and to provide feedback to employees to help them improve their present performance and plan future careers. Because performance evaluations often help determine wages and promotions, they must be fair and nondiscriminatory.

performance appraisal A formal assessment of how well an employee is doing his or her job

Common Appraisal Methods   Two basic categories of appraisal methods commonly used in organizations are objective methods and judgmental methods. Objective measures of performance include actual output, such as the number of units produced, dollar volume of sales, and number of claims processed. Another type of objective measure, the special performance test, is a method in which each employee is assessed under standardized conditions. For example, operators at GTE Southwest Inc. are graded on their speed, accuracy, and courtesy in handling a series of prerecorded test calls. Performance tests measure ability but do not measure the extent to which one is motivated to use that ability on a daily basis. (A high-ability person may be a lazy performer except when being tested.) Special performance tests must therefore be supplemented by other appraisal methods to provide a complete picture of performance.

Judgmental methods, including ranking and rating techniques, are the most common way to measure performance. Ranking compares employees directly with each other and orders them from best to worst. Rating differs from ranking in that the former compares each employee with a fixed standard rather than with other employees, with a rating scale providing the standard. Figure 8.2 gives examples of three graphic rating scales for a bank teller. Each consists of a performance dimension to be rated (punctuality, congeniality, and accuracy) followed by a scale on which to make the rating. In constructing graphic rating scales,

FIGURE 8.2
Graphic Rating Scales for a Bank Teller

Graphic rating scales are a very common method for evaluating employee performance. The manager who is doing the rating circles the point on each scale that best reflects her or his assessment of the employee on that scale. Graphic rating scales are widely used for many different kinds of jobs.

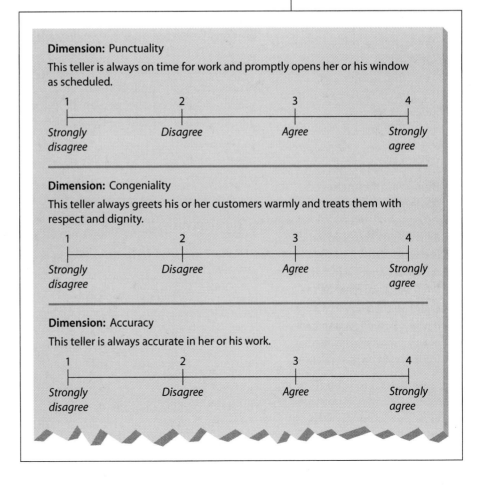

Behaviorally Anchored Rating Scale (BARS) A sophisticated rating method in which supervisors construct a rating scale associated with behavioral anchors

only dimensions that are relevant to performance must be selected. In particular, they should focus on job behaviors and results rather than on personality traits or attitudes.

The **Behaviorally Anchored Rating Scale (BARS)** is a sophisticated and useful rating method. Supervisors construct rating scales with associated behavioral anchors. Supervisors first identify relevant performance dimensions and then generate anchors—specific, observable behaviors typical of each performance level. Figure 8.3 shows an example of a behaviorally anchored rating scale for the dimension "inventory control."

Errors in Performance Appraisal Errors or biases can occur in any kind of rating or ranking system. One common problem is recency error—the tendency to base judgments on the subordinate's most recent performance because it is most easily recalled. Other errors include overuse of one part of the scale—being too lenient, being too severe, or giving everyone a rating of "average." Halo error is allowing the assessment of an employee on one dimension to "spread" to ratings of that employee on other dimensions. For instance, if an employee is outstanding on quality of output, a rater might tend to give that employee higher marks than deserved on other dimensions. Errors can also occur because of race, sex, or age discrimination, intentionally or unintentionally. The best way to offset these errors is to ensure that a valid rating system is developed at the outset and then to train managers in how to use it.

■ Performance Feedback

The last step in most performance appraisal systems is giving feedback to subordinates about their performance. Feedback is usually provided in a private meeting between the person being evaluated and the person's supervisor. The discussion should generally be focused on the facts—the assessed level of

FIGURE 8.3
Behaviorally Anchored Rating Scale

Behaviorally anchored rating scales help overcome some of the limitations of standard rating scales. Each point on the scale is accompanied by a behavioral anchor—a summary of an employee behavior that fits that spot on the scale.

Job: Specialty store manager
Dimension: Inventory control

7 Always orders in the right quantities and at the right time

6 Almost always orders at the right time but occasionally orders too much or too little of a particular item

5 Usually orders at the right time and almost always in the right quantities

4 Often orders in the right quantities and at the right time

3 Occasionally orders at the right time but usually not in the right quantities

2 Occasionally orders in the right quantities but usually not at the right time

1 Never orders in the right quantities or at the right time

performance, how and why that assessment was made, and how it can be improved in the future. Feedback interviews are not easy to conduct. Many managers are uncomfortable with the task, especially if feedback is negative and subordinates are disappointed by what they hear. Proper training can help managers conduct more effective feedback interviews.[16]

A recent innovation in performance appraisal used in many organizations today is called "360 degree" feedback: managers are evaluated by everyone around them—their boss, their peers, and their subordinates. Such a complete and thorough approach provides people with a far richer array of information about their performance than does a conventional appraisal given just by the boss. Of course, such a system also takes considerable time and must be handled to not breed fear and mistrust in the workplace.[17]

Maintaining Human Resources

After organizations have attracted and developed an effective workforce, they must also make every effort to maintain that workforce. To do so requires effective compensation and benefits as well as career planning.

■ Determining Compensation

Compensation is the financial remuneration given by the organization to its employees in exchange for their work. Basic compensation is necessary to provide employees with the means to maintain a reasonable standard of living. Beyond this, however, compensation also provides a tangible measure of the value of the individual to the organization. If employees do not earn enough to meet their basic economic goals, they will seek employment elsewhere. Likewise, if they believe that their contributions are undervalued by the organization, they may leave or exhibit poor work habits, low morale, and little commitment to the organization. Thus, designing an effective compensation system is clearly in the organization's best interests.[18] A good compensation system can help attract qualified applicants, retain present employees, and stimulate high performance at a cost reasonable for one's industry and geographic area. Determining compensation requires decisions regarding wage levels, the wage structure, and individual wages within that structure.

compensation The financial remuneration given by the organization to its employees in exchange for their work

Wage-Level Decision The wage-level decision is a management policy decision about whether the firm wants to pay above, at, or below the going rate for labor in the industry or the geographic area.[19] Most firms choose to pay near the average. Large, successful firms may like to cultivate the image of being "wage leaders" by intentionally paying more than average and thus attracting and keeping high-quality employees. IBM, for example, pays top dollar to get the new employees it wants. McDonald's, on the other hand, often pays close to the minimum wage. Once managers make the wage-level decision, they need information to help set actual wage rates. Managers need to know what the maximum, minimum, and average wages are for particular jobs in the appropriate labor market. This information is collected by means of a wage survey. Area wage surveys are conducted by individual firms or by local HR or business associations.

Wage-Structure Decision   Wage structures are usually set up through a procedure called **job evaluation**—an attempt to assess the worth of each job relative to other jobs.[20] The simplest method for creating a wage structure is to rank jobs from those that should be paid the most (for example, the president) to those that should be paid the least (for example, a mail clerk or a janitor). At Ben & Jerry's Homemade, company policy dictates that the highest-paid employee in the firm cannot make more than seven times what the lowest-paid employee earns. Larger firms with a greater array of jobs usually require more sophisticated methods and use complex methods of job evaluation.

Individual Wage Decisions   After wage-level and wage-structure decisions are made, individual wage decisions must be addressed. This decision concerns how much to pay each employee in a particular job. Although the easiest decision is to pay a single rate for each job, more typically a range of pay rates is associated with each job. For example, the pay range for an individual job might be $6.85 to $8.39 per hour, with different employees earning different rates within the range. Individual rates within this range may then be set on the basis of seniority (enter the job at $6.85, for example, and increase 10 cents per hour every six months on the job), of initial qualifications (inexperienced people start at $6.85, more experienced start at a higher rate), or merit (raises above the entering rate are given for good performance).

job evaluation   An attempt to assess the worth of each job relative to other jobs

■ Determining Benefits

Benefits are things of value other than compensation that the organization provides to its workers. The average company spends an amount equal to more

benefits   Things of value other than compensation that an organization provides to its workers

Organizations offer a wide array of compensation and benefits to their employees. Many also provide extra incentives for key employees who remain with the company for an extended time. Longevity pay, for example, is used in some settings, whereas other organizations reward their more senior employees with pins, plaques, watches, or even cash bonuses. But as illustrated in this cartoon, such rewards are meaningful and effective only if they provide something of real value to the employee. Trivial or meaningless tokens or rewards can even backfire, causing employees to feel unappreciated.

"Your thirty-five years of hard work, sacrifice, and devotion
to duty won't go unrewarded, Erickson —
go ahead and pick a duck."

than one-third of its cash payroll on employee benefits. Thus an average employee who is paid $18,000 per year averages about $6,588 more per year in benefits. Benefits come in several forms, including pay for time not worked (sick leave, vacation, holidays, and unemployment compensation), insurance (life and health insurance for employees and their dependents), workers' compensation (a legally required insurance benefit that provides medical care and disability income for employees injured on the job), and Social Security (a government pension plan to which both employers and employees contribute). Many employers also provide a private pension plan to which they and their employees contribute. Employee service benefits include such things as tuition reimbursement and recreational opportunities.

Some organizations have instituted "cafeteria benefit plans," whereby basic coverage is provided for all employees but employees are then allowed to choose which additional benefits they want (up to a cost limit based on salary). Such flexible systems are expected to encourage people to stay in the organization and even help the company attract new employees.[21] Some companies have also started offering even more innovative benefits as a way of accommodating different needs. On-site childcare, mortgage assistance, and generous paid leave programs are becoming popular.[22]

Managing Workforce Diversity

Workforce diversity has become a very important issue in many organizations. The management of diversity is often seen as a key human resource function today.

■ The Meaning of Diversity

Diversity exists in a group or organization when its members differ from one another along one or more important dimensions.[23] Especially important dimensions of diversity include gender, age, and ethnicity. For example, the average age of the U.S. workforce is gradually increasing and will continue to do so for the next several years. Similarly, as more females have entered the workforce, organizations have experienced changes in the relative proportions of male and female employees. And within the United States, most organizations reflect varying degrees of ethnicity with workforces comprising whites, African Americans, Hispanics, and Asians.[24] Other groups such as single parents, dual-career couples, same-sex couples, and the physically challenged are also important.

diversity Exists in a group or organization when its members differ from one another along one or more important dimensions

■ The Impact of Diversity

There is no question that organizations are becoming ever more diverse. This diversity provides both opportunities and challenges for organizations.

Diversity as a Competitive Advantage   Many organizations are finding that diversity can be a source of competitive advantage in the marketplace.[25] For example, businesses that manage diversity effectively will generally have higher levels of productivity and lower levels of turnover and absenteeism, thus lowering costs. Ortho Pharmaceuticals estimates that it has saved $500,000 by lowering turnover among women and ethnic minorities.[26] In addition, organizations that manage diversity effectively will become known among women and minorities as good places to work, thus attracting qualified employees from among these groups. Moreover, organizations with diverse workforces may have the edge in being able to understand different market segments. For example, a cosmetics firm like Avon that wants to sell its products to African-American women can better understand how to create such products and to effectively market them if African-American women managers are available to provide inputs into product development, design, packaging, advertising, and so forth.[27] Finally, organizations with diverse workforces will generally be more creative and innovative compared to organizations in which the workforce is less diverse.

Diversity as a Source of Conflict   Unfortunately, diversity can also become a major source of conflict. One potential avenue for conflict is when an individual thinks that someone has been hired, promoted, or fired because of her or his diversity status.[28] Another source of conflict stemming from diversity is through misunderstood, misinterpreted, or inappropriate interactions between people of different groups. Conflict may also arise as a result of fear, distrust, or individual prejudice. Members of the dominant group in an organization may worry that newcomers from other groups pose a personal threat to their own position in the organization. For example, when U.S. firms have been taken over by Japanese firms, U.S. managers have sometimes been resentful or hostile to Japanese managers assigned to work with them. Employees may also be unwilling to accept people who are different from themselves. And personal bias and prejudices are still very real among some people today and can lead to potentially harmful conflict.[29]

■ Managing Diversity in Organizations

Because of the tremendous potential that diversity holds for competitive advantage, as well as the possible consequences of diversity-related conflict, much attention has been focused in recent years on how individuals and organizations can better manage diversity.[30]

Individual Strategies   One key element of managing diversity consists of things that individuals can do.[31] Understanding, of course, is the starting point. While people need to be treated fairly and equitably, managers must understand that differences do, in fact, exist among people. People should also try to understand the perspective of others. Tolerance is also important. Even though managers learn to understand diversity and even though they may try to empathize with others, the fact remains that they may still not accept or enjoy some aspect of behavior on the part of others. Communication is also important. Problems often get magnified over diversity issues because people are afraid or otherwise unwilling to openly discuss issues that relate to diversity. For example, suppose a younger employee has a habit of making jokes about the age of an elderly colleague. Perhaps the younger colleague means no harm and is just engaging in what she sees as good-natured kidding. But the older employee may find the jokes offensive. If there is no communication between the two, the jokes will continue and the resentment will grow. Eventually, what started as a minor problem may erupt into a much bigger one.

Organizational Approaches to Managing Diversity   While individuals can play an important role in managing diversity, the organization itself must also play a fundamental role.[32] The starting point in managing diversity is the policies that an organization adopts that affect how it treats people. Another aspect of organizational policies that affects diversity is how the organization addresses and responds to problems that arise from diversity. For example, consider the example of a manager charged with sexual harassment. If the organization puts an excessive burden of proof on the individual being harassed and invokes only minor sanctions against the guilty party, it is sending a clear signal as to the importance of such matters. But the organization that has a balanced set of policies for addressing questions like sexual harassment sends its employees a different message as to the importance of diversity and individual rights and privileges.

Organizations can also help manage diversity through a variety of ongoing practices and procedures. Avon has created networks for various groups within the firm. Benefit packages can be structured to better accommodate individual situations. Differences in family arrangements, religious holidays, cultural events, and so forth may dictate that employees have some degree of flexibility in when they work. Many organizations are finding that diversity training is an effective means for managing diversity and minimizing its associated conflict. More specifically, *diversity training* is training that is specifically designed to better enable members of an organization to function in a diverse workplace. The ultimate test of an organization's commitment to managing diversity, however, is its culture.[33] Regardless of what managers say or put in writing, unless there is a basic and fundamental belief that diversity is valued, it cannot ever become a truly integral part of an organization.

Managing Labor Relations

Labor relations is the process of dealing with employees who are represented by a union.[34] Managing labor relations is an important part of HRM.

labor relations   The process of dealing with employees when they are represented by a union

■ How Employees Form Unions

For employees to form a new local union, several things must occur. First, employees must become interested in having a union. Non-employees who are professional organizers employed by a national union (such as the Teamsters or United Auto Workers) may generate interest by making speeches and distributing literature outside the workplace. Inside, employees who want a union try to convince other workers of the benefits of a union.

The second step is to collect employees' signatures on authorization cards. These cards state that the signer wishes to vote to determine whether the union will represent him or her. Thirty percent of the employees in the potential bargaining unit must sign these cards to show the National Labor Relations Board (NLRB) that interest is sufficient to justify holding an election. Before an election can be held, however, the bargaining unit must be defined. The bargaining unit consists of all employees who will be eligible to vote in the election and to join and be represented by the union if one is formed.

The election is supervised by an NLRB representative (or, if both parties agree, the American Arbitration Association—a professional association of arbitrators) and is conducted by secret ballot. If a simple majority of those voting (not of all those eligible to vote) votes for the union, then the union becomes certified as the official representative of the bargaining unit.[35] The new union then organizes itself by officially signing up members and electing officers; it will soon be ready to negotiate the first contract. The union-organizing process is diagrammed in Figure 8.4. If workers become disgruntled with their

FIGURE 8.4
The Union-Organizing Process

If employees of an organization want to form a union, the law prescribes a specific set of procedures that both employees and the organization must follow. Assuming that these procedures are followed and the union is approved, the organization must engage in collective bargaining with the new union.

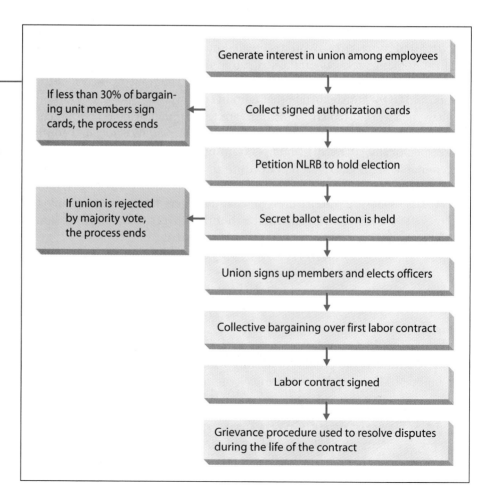

union or if management presents strong evidence that the union is not representing workers appropriately, the NLRB can arrange a decertification election. The results of such an election determine whether the union remains certified.

Organizations usually prefer that employees not be unionized because unions limit management's freedom in many areas. Management may thus wage its own campaign to convince employees to vote against the union. "Unfair labor practices" are often committed at this point. For instance, it is an unfair labor practice for management to promise to give employees a raise (or any other benefit) if the union is defeated. Experts agree that the best way to avoid unionization is to practice good employee relations all the time—not just when threatened by a union election. Providing absolutely fair treatment with clear standards in the areas of pay, promotion, layoff, and discipline; having a complaint or appeal system for persons who feel unfairly treated; and avoiding any kind of favoritism will help make employees feel that a union is unnecessary.

■ Collective Bargaining

The intent of **collective bargaining** is to agree on a labor contract between management and the union that is satisfactory to both parties. The contract contains agreements about issues such as wages and hours; conditions of employment, promotion, and layoff; discipline; benefits; methods of allocating overtime, vacations, and rest periods; and the grievance procedure. The process of bargaining may go on for weeks, months, or longer, with representatives of management and the union meeting to make proposals and counterproposals. The resulting agreement must be ratified by the union membership. If it is not approved, the union may strike to put pressure on management, or it may choose not to strike and simply continue negotiating until a more acceptable agreement is reached.

The **grievance procedure** is the means by which the contract is enforced. Most of what is in a contract concerns how management will treat employees. When employees feel that they have not been treated fairly under the contract, they file a grievance to correct the problem. The first step in a grievance procedure is for the aggrieved employee to discuss the alleged contract violation with her immediate superior. Often the grievance is resolved at this stage. If the employee still believes that she is being mistreated, however, the grievance can be appealed to the next level. A union official can help an aggrieved employee present her case. If the manager's decision is also unsatisfactory to the employee, additional appeals to successively higher levels are made, until finally all in-company steps are exhausted. The final step is to submit the grievance to binding arbitration. An arbitrator is a labor-law expert who is paid jointly by the union and management. The arbitrator studies the contract, hears both sides of the case, and renders a decision that both parties must obey. The grievance system for resolving disputes about contract enforcement heads off any need to strike during the term of the contract.[36]

collective bargaining The process of agreeing on a satisfactory labor contract between management and a union

grievance procedure The means by which a labor contract is enforced

Summary of Key Points

Human resource management is concerned with acquiring, developing, and maintaining the human resources an organization needs. Its environmental context consists of its strategic importance and the legal and social environments that affect human resource management.

Attracting human resources is an important part of the HRM function. Human resource planning starts with job analysis and then focuses on forecasting the organization's future need for employees, forecasting the availability of employees both within and outside the organization, and planning programs to ensure that the proper number and type of employees will be available when needed. Recruitment and selection are the processes by which job applicants are attracted, assessed, and hired. Methods for assessing applicants include application blanks, tests, interviews, and assessment centers. Any method used for selection should be properly validated.

Organizations must also work to develop their human resources. Training and development enable employees to perform their present jobs well and to prepare for future jobs. Performance appraisals are important for determining training needs, deciding pay raises and promotions, and providing helpful feedback to employees. Both objective and judgmental methods of appraisal can be applied, and a good system usually includes several methods. The validity of appraisal information is always a concern because it is difficult to accurately evaluate the many aspects of a person's job performance.

Maintaining human resources is also important. Compensation rates must be fair compared with rates for other jobs within the organization and with rates for the same or similar jobs in other organizations in the labor market. Properly designed incentive or merit pay systems can encourage high performance, and a good benefits program can help attract and retain employees. Career planning is also a major aspect of HRM.

Diversity exists in a group or organization when its members differ from one another along one or more important dimensions. Three of the more important dimensions of diversity are age, gender, and ethnicity. Diversity affects organizations in many different ways. Managing diversity in organizations can be done by both individuals and the organization itself.

If a majority of a company's nonmanagement employees so desire, they have the right to be represented by a union. Management must engage in collective bargaining with the union in an effort to agree on a contract. While the contract is in effect, the grievance system is used to settle labor disputes.

Discussion Questions

Questions for Review

1. Describe recruiting and selection. What are the major sources for recruits? What are the common selection techniques?

2. What is the role of compensation and benefits in organizations? How should the amount of compensation and benefits be determined?

3. Identify the major dimensions of diversity and discuss recent trends for each.

4. Summarize the basic impact of diversity on organizations.

5. What are the basic steps that employees can follow if they wish to create a union?

Questions for Analysis

1. What are the advantages and disadvantages of internal and external recruiting? Which do you feel is best in the long term? Why? Be sure to think about this issue from the standpoint of both the organization and individuals (whether inside or outside of the organization) who might be considered for positions.

2. How do you know if a selection device is valid? What are the possible consequences of using invalid selection methods? How can an organization ensure that its selection methods are valid?

3. Are benefits more important than compensation to an organization? to an individual? Why?

4. The text outlines many different advantages of diversity in organizations. Can you think of any disadvantages?

5. When you finish school and begin your career, what should you be prepared to do to succeed in a diverse workforce?

EXERCISE OVERVIEW

Technical skills refer to the manager's abilities to accomplish or understand work done in an organization. Many managers must have technical skills to hire appropriate people to work in the organization. This exercise helps you use technical skills as part of the selection process.

Building Effective
Technical
Skills

EXERCISE BACKGROUND

Variation one: If you currently work full-time, or have worked full-time in the past, select two jobs with which you have some familiarity. One job should be relatively low in skill level, responsibility, required education, and pay; the other should be relatively high in skill level, responsibility, required education, and pay. The exercise will be more useful to you if you use real jobs that you can relate to at a personal level.

Variation two: If you have never worked full-time or if you are not personally familiar with an array of jobs, assume that you are a manager for a small manufacturing facility. You need to hire individuals to fill two jobs. One job is for the position of plant custodian. This individual will sweep floors, clean bathrooms, empty trash cans, and so forth. The other person will be office manager. This individual will supervise a staff of three clerks and secretaries, administer the plant payroll, and coordinate the administrative operations of the plan.

EXERCISE TASK

With the information above as background, do the following:

1. Identify the most basic skills that you think are necessary for someone to perform each job effectively.

2. Identify the general indicators or predictors of whether or not a given individual can perform each job.

3. Develop a brief set of interview questions that you might use to determine whether or not an applicant has the qualifications to perform each job.

4. How important is it for a manager hiring employees to perform a job to have the technical skills to do that job him- or herself?

EXERCISE OVERVIEW

All managers must be able to effectively communicate with others in the organization. Communication is especially important in the human resource area, since people are the domain of HRM.

Building Effective
Communication
Skills

EXERCISE BACKGROUND

Many companies provide various benefits to their workers. These benefits may include such things as pay for time not worked, insurance coverage, pension plans, and so forth. These benefits are often very costly to the organization. As noted in the text, for example, benefits often equal around one-third of what employees are paid in wages and salaries. In some countries, such as Germany, the figures are even higher.

Yet, many employees often fail to appreciate the actual value of the benefits their employers provide. For example, employees frequently underestimate the dollar value of their benefits. And when comparing their income to that of others or when comparing alternative job offers, many people focus almost entirely on direct compensation—wages and salaries directly paid to the individual.

For example, consider a college graduate who has two offers. One job offer is for $20,000 a year, and the other is for $22,000. The individual is likely to see the second offer as being more attractive even if the first offer has sufficiently more attractive benefits to make the total compensation packages equivalent to one another.

EXERCISE TASK

With this information as context, respond to the following:

1. Why do you think most people focus on pay when assessing their compensation?

2. If you were the human resource manager for a firm, how would you go about communicating benefit value to your employees?

3. Suppose an employee comes to you and says that he is thinking about leaving for a "better job." You then learn that he is defining "better" only in terms of higher pay. How might you help him compare total compensation (including benefits)?

4. Some firms today are cutting their benefits. How would you communicate a benefit cut to your employees?

**Building Effective
Decision-Making
Skills**

EXERCISE OVERVIEW

Decision-making skills include the manager's ability to correctly recognize and define problems and opportunities and to then select an appropriate course of action to solve problems and capitalize on opportunities. This exercise helps you develop decision-making skills by applying them to a human resource problem. Managers must frequently select one or more employees from a pool of employees for termination, layoff, special recognition, training, or promotion. Each such selection represents a decision.

EXERCISE TASK

Your company recently developed a plan to identify and train top hourly employees for promotion to first-line supervisor. As part of this program, your boss has requested a ranking of the six hourly employees who report to you with respect to their promotion potential. Given their biographical data, rank them in the order in which you would select them for promotion to first-line supervisor; that is, the person ranked number one would be first in line for promotion. Repeat this process in a group with three or four of your classmates.

Biographical Data

1. *Sam Nelson:* White male, age forty-five, married, with four children. Sam has been with the company for five years, and his performance evaluations have been average to above average. He is well liked by the other employees in the department. He devotes his spare time to farming and plans to farm after retirement.

2. *Ruth Hornsby:* White female, age thirty-two, married, with no children; husband has a management-level job with a power company. Ruth has been with the company for two years and has received above-average performance evaluations. She is very quiet and keeps to herself at work. She says she is working to save for a down payment on a new house.

3. *Joe Washington:* Black male, age twenty-six, single. Joe has been with the company for three years and has received high performance evaluations. He is always willing to take on new assignments and to work overtime. He is attending college in the evenings and someday wants to start his own business. He is well liked by the other employees in the department.

4. *Ronald Smith:* White male, age thirty-five, recently divorced, with one child, age four. Ronald has received excellent performance evaluations during his two years with the company. He seems to like his present job but has removed himself from the line of progression. He seems to have personality conflicts with some of the employees in the department.

5. *Betty Norris:* Black female, age forty-four, married, with one grown child. Betty has been with the company for ten years and is well liked by fellow employees. Her performance evaluations have been average to below-average, and her advancement has been limited by a lack of formal education. She has participated in a number of technical training programs conducted by the company.

6. *Roy Davis:* White male, age thirty-six, married, with two teenage children. Roy has been with the company for ten years and has received excellent performance evaluations until last year. His most recent evaluation was average. He is friendly and well liked by his fellow employees. One of his children has had a serious illness for over a year, resulting in a number of large medical expenses. Roy is working a second job on weekends to help with these expenses. He has expressed a serious interest in promotion to first-line supervisor.

Source: From *Supervisory Management,* 3rd edition, by D.C. Mosley, L.C. Megginson, and P.H. Pietri. ©1993. Reprinted with permission of South-Western College Publishing, a division of International Thomson Publishing. Fax 800-730-2215.

You Make the Call

Mark Spenser decided that rather than talking to the two crew chiefs together, it might be more productive to meet with them individually. Thus, he asked one of them, Betty Bickham, to come by after work on Tuesday and the other one, Jason Taber, to come by on Wednesday.

His conversation with Betty was a bit tense to begin with. She had been the first woman he had hired for his lawn-care business, and she had worked hard to prove that she could perform the physically challenging work as well as anyone. She had worked hard enough, she believed, that she should have been promoted instead of Manuel Hernandez. Mark assured her that he recognized and appreciated her hard work. He pointed out, however, that Manuel had worked for SLS three years longer than Betty and that he, too, had an exemplary performance record.

Mark also pointed out that because of her strong performance record she was being paid more than any of the other three crew chiefs. He assured her that if she got her crew back on track and kept up her strong performance, she would be next in line for a promotion. After thinking things over for a few minutes, Betty decided that Mark was right. She indicated that she had, indeed, not been working very hard or pushing her crew but that she would turn things around starting the very next day.

On Wednesday, Mark was pleased to see that Betty's crew was the first one finished and back at the warehouse. Jason Taber's crew came in last, but Mark was optimistic that his meeting with Jason would also be productive. Unfortunately, however, Mark's optimism was ill-founded. During their meeting, Mark was both surprised and disappointed to realize that Jason was prejudiced against ethnic minorities. Although he had had no trouble working with Manuel when they were both crew chiefs, he indicated that he had trouble taking orders from Manuel and seeing him in a position of authority.

Mark asked Jason point-blank if he could set his prejudices aside and get his performance back to where it needed to be. Jason said that he could not and that he assumed that he would have to resign. Mark indicated that he was sorry that Jason felt as he did but that it would indeed be necessary for Jason to leave.

The next day Mark and Manuel met and decided to promote one of the regular crew members from Jason's team to the position of crew chief. Manuel placed a help-wanted ad in the newspaper and called the local office of the Texas Employment Commission to inform them of the new job opening. Within a few days, a new lawn-care team member had been hired and things were under control again.

DISCUSSION QUESTIONS

1. Evaluate how Mark handled this situation.

2. If Jason had said that, even though he was prejudiced, he could "hide it" and still work effectively, should Mark still have fired him?

3. What recruiting and selection approaches are most likely to be used in a business like SLS?

DIAGNOSING POOR PERFORMANCE AND ENHANCING MOTIVATION

Introduction: Formal performance appraisal and feedback are part of assuring proper performance in an organization. The following assessment is designed to help you understand how to detect poor performance and overcome it.

Instructions: Please respond to these statements by entering a number from the following rating scale. Your answers should reflect your attitudes and behaviors as they are *now*.

Rating Scale

6 Strongly agree   3 Slightly disagree

5 Agree   2 Disagree

4 Slightly agree   1 Strongly disagree

When another person needs to be motivated:

_____ 1. I always approach a performance problem by first establishing whether it is caused by a lack of motivation or ability.

_____ 2. I always establish a clear standard of expected performance.

_____ 3. I always offer to provide training and information, without offering to do the task myself.

_____ 4. I am honest and straightforward in providing feedback on performance and assessing advancement opportunities.

_____ 5. I use a variety of rewards to reinforce exceptional performances.

_____ 6. When discipline is required, I identify the problem, describe its consequences, and explain how it should be corrected.

_____ 7. I design task assignments to make them interesting and challenging.

_____ 8. I determine what rewards are valued by the person and strive to make those available.

_____ 9. I make sure that the person feels fairly and equitably treated.

_____10. I make sure that the person gets timely feedback from those affected by task performance.

_____11. I carefully diagnose the causes of poor performance before taking any remedial or disciplinary actions.

_____12. I always help the person establish performance goals that are challenging, specific, and timebound.

_____13. Only as a last resort do I attempt to reassign or release a poor performing individual.

_____14. Whenever possible I make sure that valued rewards are linked to high performance.

_____15. I consistently discipline when effort is below expectations and capabilities.

_____16. I try to combine or rotate assignments so that the person can use a variety of skills.

_____17. I try to arrange for the person to work with others in a team, for the mutual support of all.

_____18. I make sure that the person is using realistic standards for measuring fairness.

_____19. I provide immediate compliments and other forms of recognition for meaningful accomplishments.

_____20. I always determine whether the person has the necessary resources and support to succeed in the task.

For interpretation, turn to page 459.

Source: D. Whetten/K. Cameron, *Developing Management Skills,* 3rd ed. (pages 358–359). © 1995 Addison-Wesley Educational Publishers Inc. Reprinted by permission of Addison Wesley Longman.

Experiential Exercise

CHOOSING A COMPENSATION STRATEGY

Purpose: This exercise helps you better understand how internal and external market forces affect compensation strategies.

Introduction: Assume that you are the head of a large academic department in a major research university. Your salaries are a bit below external market salaries. For example, your assistant professors make between $45,000 and $55,000 a year, your associate professors make between $57,000 and $65,000 a year, and your full professors make between $67,000 and $75,000 a year.

Faculty who have been in your department for a long time enjoy the work environment and appreciate the low cost of living in the area. They know that they are somewhat underpaid, but offset this against the advantages of being in your department. Recently, however, external market forces have caused salaries for people in your field to escalate rapidly. Unfortunately, while your university acknowledges this problem, you have also been told that no additional resources can be made available to your department.

You currently have four vacant positions that need to be filled. One of these is at the rank of associate professor, and the other three are at the rank of assistant professor. You have surveyed other departments in similar universities, and realize that to hire the best new assistant professors you will need to offer at least $58,000 a year, and to get a qualified associate professor you will need to pay at least $70,000. You have been given the budget to hire new employees at more competitive salaries, but cannot do anything to raise the salaries of faculty currently in your department. You have identified the following options:

1. You can hire new faculty from lower-quality schools that pay salaries that are below market rate.

2. You can hire the best people available, pay market salaries, and deal with internal inequities later.

3. You can hire fewer new faculty, use the extra money to boost the salaries of your current faculty, and cut class offerings in the future.

Instructions:

Step One: Working alone, decide how you will proceed.

Step Two: Form small groups with your classmates and compare solutions.

Step Three: Identify the strengths and weaknesses of each option.

Follow-up Questions:

1. Are there other options that might be pursued?

2. Assume that you chose option 2. How would you go about dealing with the internal equity problems?

3. Discuss with your instructor the extent to which this problem exists at your school.

CASE STUDY

The Labor Standoff at UPS

The ubiquitous brown trucks that make up the fleet of United Parcel Service, or UPS, have become a common scene on the U.S. landscape. The huge parcel delivery service has dominated its industry for years, moving millions of packages every day. One key ingredient to UPS's long-standing success has been a strong and loyal relationship with its employees. The firm has a history of promoting from within, paying well, and treating its employees fairly and justly. Even though the firm's drivers have long been organized by the Teamsters Union, labor relations have been generally calm and amicable.

But all that changed in 1997 when UPS drivers walked out on strike, bringing the company to its knees and allowing UPS competitors like Federal Express and the U.S. Postal Service to seize market share that would be hard for UPS to recapture. The story of what prompted the strike and how it ended provides useful and interesting insights into an array of HRM practices and issues.

The wedge between UPS and the Teamsters was created by two fundamental issues. One was the firm's growing reliance on part-time workers. UPS had started using more and more part-time workers, often replacing a retired employee with two or more part-timers. This plan allowed the firm to have greater flexibility while also holding down wage and benefits costs. For example, its full-time employees were paid $19.95 an hour, whereas part-timers received half that amount. The Teamsters, meanwhile, argued that this practice was actually intended to undercut the job security of the firm's full-time employees and weaken the power of the union itself. At the time of the strike, UPS employed 105,000 part-time workers.

The other issue related to the firm's pension plan. At the time of the strike, the Teamsters had managed to create a "standard" pension plan for several larger companies whose employees the union represented. UPS, meanwhile, wanted to pull out of the multi-employer plan and create its own plan just for UPS workers. Again, the firm argued that it could provide a comparable plan at a lower price; in contrast, the union contended that UPS was taking the first step toward a reduced plan for retired employees.

The two sides bargained extensively for months and nearly reached agreement on several occasions. But one or another problem always came up, and the two sides eventually became more and more antagonistic. Finally, UPS workers went out on strike on October 3, 1997. The strike had immediate and dramatic effects, not only on UPS but all across the country. The firm itself tried to maintain operations with managers and nonunion employees, but could only handle about 5 percent of the volume. And other businesses—especially small ones—complained long and loudly that the strike was putting them out of business. President Clinton considered intervening but eventually decided to stay out of the fray.

Meanwhile, much to the firm's dismay, surveys showed that there was dramatic public support for the striking workers. In addition, many long-standing and loyal customers were transferring their business to other carriers. Finally, two weeks after the strike started, UPS essentially threw in the towel, and the striking workers went back to work. Among the concessions the firm made were an agreement to convert ten thousand part-time jobs into full-time ones and to double the pay, to drop plans to pull out of the Teamsters multi-employer pension plan, and to boost employee pay over a five-year period by an average of 15 percent for full-time employees and 35 percent for part-timers. The Teamsters, meanwhile, agreed to a five-year contract instead of their preferred three-year deal.

But even after the striking workers returned to work, UPS still faced an uphill battle. For one thing, its public image had been irreparably tarnished. For another, it had lost 10 percent of its market share, and those customers who had switched showed no indication of returning to a firm that some felt had betrayed them. And finally, managers had to figure out how to cover more than $1 billion in additional costs the new contract would add to the company's income statement.

Case Questions

1. Identify as many human resource issues as possible in this case.

2. How might the UPS strike have been averted? Which side "won" the strike? Why?

3. Are strikes always bad? Under what circumstances might a strike be beneficial to a company?

Case References: "A Wake-up Call for Business," *Business Week*, September 1, 1997, pp. 28–29; "This Package Is a Heavy One for the Teamsters," *Business Week*, August 25, 1997, pp. 40–41; "UPS Pact Fails to Shift Balance of Power Back Toward U.S. Workers," *Wall Street Journal*, August 20, 1997, pp. A1, A6.

CHAPTER NOTES

1. "Cisco Embraces 'Internet Economy'," *USA Today*, September 23, 1998, p. 3B; Andrew Kupfer, "The Real King of the Internet," *Fortune*, September 7, 1998, pp. 84–90; Patricia Nakache, "Cisco's Recruiting Edge," *Fortune*, September 29, 1997, pp. 275–276 (quote on p. 275); and "The Corporation of the Future," *Business Week*, August 31, 1998, pp. 102–106.

2. For a complete review of human resource management, see Cynthia D. Fisher, Lyle F. Schoenfeldt, and James B. Shaw, *Human Resource Management*, 4th ed. (Boston: Houghton Mifflin, 1999).

3. David Terpstra and Elizabeth Rozell, "The Relationship of Staffing Practices to Organizational Level Measures of Performance," *Personnel Psychology*, Spring 1993, pp. 27–38.

4. Patrick Wright and Scott Snell, "Toward a Unifying Framework for Exploring Fit and Flexibility in Strategic Human Resource Management," *Academy of Management Review*, 1998, Vol. 23, No. 4, pp. 756–772; see also Augustine Lado and Mary Wilson, "Human Resource Systems and Sustained Competitive Advantage: A Competency-Based Perspective," *Academy of Management Review*, 1994, Vol. 19, No. 4, pp. 699–727.

5. Leonard Greenhalgh, Anne T. Lawrence, and Robert I. Sutton, "Determinants of Work Force Reduction Strategies in Declining Organizations," *Academy of Management Review*, April 1988, pp. 241–254.

6. Michael R. Carrell and Frank E. Kuzmits, *Personnel: Human Resource Management*, 3rd ed. (New York: Merrill, 1989).

7. Frank L. Schmidt and John E. Hunter, "Employment Testing: Old Theories and New Research Findings," *American Psychologist*, October 1981, 1128–1137; see also "New Test Quantifies the Way We Work," *Wall Street Journal*, February 7, 1990, p. B1.

8. Robert Liden, Christopher Martin, and Charles Parsons, "Interviewer and Applicant Behaviors in Employment Interviews," *Academy of Management Journal*, 1993, Vol. 36, No. 2, pp. 372–386.

9. Brian Dumaine, "The New Art of Hiring Smart," *Fortune*, August 17, 1987, pp. 78–81.

10. Paul R. Sackett, "Assessment Centers and Content Validity: Some Neglected Issues," *Personnel Psychology*, Vol. 40, 1987, pp. 13–25.

11. Abby Brown, "To Test or Not to Test," *Personnel Administrator*, March 1987, pp. 67–70.

12. See Bernard Keys and Joseph Wolfe, "Management Education and Development: Current Issues and Emerging Trends," *Journal of Management*, June 1988, pp. 205–229, for a recent review.

13. Michael Brody, "Helping Workers to Work Smarter," *Fortune*, June 8, 1987, pp. 86–88.

14. "Videos Are Starring in More and More Training Programs," *Business Week*, September 7, 1987, pp. 108–110.

15. "'Boeing U': Flying by the Book," *USA Today*, October 6, 1997, pp. 1B, 2B.

16. Barry R. Nathan, Allan Mohrman, and John Milliman, "Interpersonal Relations as a Context for the Effects of Appraisal Interviews on Performance and Satisfaction: A Longitudinal Study," *Academy of Management Journal*, June 1991, pp. 352–369.

17. Brian O'Reilly, "360 Feedback Can Change Your Life," *Fortune*, October 17, 1994, pp. 93–100.

18. Jaclyn Fierman, "The Perilous New World of Fair Pay," *Fortune*, June 13, 1994, pp. 57–64.

19. Caroline L. Weber and Sara L. Rynes, "Effects of Compensation Strategy on Job Pay Decisions," *Academy of Management Journal*, March 1991, pp. 86–109.

20. Peter Cappelli and Wayne F. Cascio, "Why Some Jobs Command Wage Premiums: A Test of Career Tournament and Internal Labor Market Hypotheses," *Academy of Management Journal*, December 1991, pp. 848–868.

21. "To Each According to His Needs: Flexible Benefits Plans Gain Favor," *Wall Street Journal*, September 16, 1986, p. 29.

22. "The Future Look of Employee Benefits," *Wall Street Journal*, September 7, 1988, p. 21.

23. Marlene G. Fine, Fern L. Johnson, and M. Sallyanne Ryan, "Cultural Diversity in the Workplace," *Public Personnel Management*, Fall 1990, pp. 305–319.

24. *Occupational Outlook Handbook* (Washington D.C.: U.S. Bureau of Labor Statistics, 1990–1991).

25. Based on Taylor H. Cox and Stacy Blake, "Managing Cultural Diversity: Implications for Organizational Competitiveness," *Academy of Management Executive*, August 1991, pp. 45–56.

26. Cox and Taylor, "Managing Cultural Diversity: Implications for Organizational Competitiveness."

27. For an example, see "Get to Know the Ethnic Market," *Marketing*, June 17, 1991, p. 32.

28. "As Population Ages, Older Workers Clash with Younger Bosses," *Wall Street Journal*, June 13, 1994, pp. A1, A8.

29. Patti Watts, "Bias Busting: Diversity Training in the Workforce," *Management Review*, December 1987, pp. 51–54.

30. See Stephenie Overman, "Managing the Diverse Work Force," *HRMagazine*, April 1991, pp. 32–36.

31. Lennie Copeland, "Making the Most of Cultural Differences at the Workplace," *Personnel*, June 1988, pp. 52–60.

32. Sara Rynes and Benson Rosen," What Makes Diversity Programs Work?" *HRMagazine*, October 1994, pp. 67–75.

33. Anthony Carneville and Susan Stone, "Diversity—Beyond the Golden Rule," *Training & Development*, October 1994, pp. 22–27.

34. Barbara Presley Nobel, "Reinventing Labor," *Harvard Business Review*, July–August 1993, pp. 115–125.

35. John A. Fossum, "Labor Relations: Research and Practice in Transition," *Journal of Management*, Summer 1987, pp. 281–300.

36. For recent research on collective bargaining, see Wallace N. Davidson III, Dan L. Worrell, and Sharon H. Garrison, "Effect of Strike Activity on Firm Value," *Academy of Management Journal*, June 1988, pp. 387–394; John M. Magenau, James E. Martin, and Melanie M. Peterson, "Dual and Unilateral Commitment Among Stewards and Rank-and-File Union Members," *Academy of Management Journal*, June 1988, pp. 359–376; and Brian E. Becker, "Concession Bargaining: The Meaning of Union Gains," *Academy of Management Journal*, June 1988, pp. 377–387.

9

Managing Individual Behavior

OBJECTIVES

After studying this chapter, you should be able to:

- Explain the nature of the individual-organization relationship.
- Define personality and describe personality attributes that affect behavior in organizations.
- Discuss individual attitudes in organizations and how they affect behavior.
- Describe basic perceptual processes and the role of attributions in organizations.
- Discuss the causes and consequences of stress and describe how it can be managed.
- Describe creativity and its role in organizations.
- Explain how workplace behaviors can directly or indirectly influence organizational effectiveness.

Delta Air Lines has long been one of the flagships of the U.S. air industry. Delta's image has been based on clean planes, plush amenities, and a distinctly warm and highly personalized service. Its employees have been treated exceptionally well, paid among the highest wages in the industry, and provided high-levels of job security. As a result, the firm has had a proud and stable workforce which, in turn, was pleased to deliver high-quality service to Delta passengers.

In response to competition from low-cost carriers like Air-Tran and Southwest Airlines, executives at Delta launched a dramatic three-year cost-cutting program. One area that received major attention was the workforce as the firm shrunk by approximately eighty thousand employees. Many of these employees had twenty-five years or more experience with the firm. The airline then hired outside contractors to handle such things as airplane cleaning, maintenance and ground support, equipment, and baggage loading.

As a consequence of these steps, Delta's profit picture has improved immensely. At the same time, however, its image has been tarnished and many of the remaining employees feel resentful and bitter. For example, prior to cost cutting, Delta maintained one full-time mechanic at each gate. This mechanic was ready to immediately solve any routine problem that existed on an arriving aircraft. Now, however, the firm has one mechanic for every three or four gates. Thus, the individual mechanic must often move quickly between gates. As a result, some flights are delayed, some problems go uncorrected, and the mechanics complain about their workload.

To make matters worse, many of the new contract employees do not have the level of commitment to Delta as did their full-time predecessors. For example, during East Coast winter storms in 1995, many newly hired contract workers at Delta's primary hub, Atlanta, simply didn't show up for work. To make matters worse, the airline's reduced staff of baggage handlers was totally overwhelmed by their job. At one point, more than five thousand bags were sitting in Atlanta when they needed to be somewhere else. Meanwhile, inside the airport, long lines of angry passengers stood impatiently waiting for someone to help them. In the old days, experienced, loyal Delta employees would have gone out of their way to make these passengers more comfortable while they tried to deal with their disrupted travel plans. At the new Delta, part-time employees, with no understanding of the organization's heritage, stood in their place and often offered curt and/or incorrect suggestions to people.

Even the level of in-flight service has been reduced. Delta has eliminated one flight attendant from virtually every aircraft it flies. For example, whereas the firm once used three flight attendants in coach on its Boeing 727s, the standard staffing is now two flight attendants, the FAA minimum. Similarly, in earlier times cabin cleaning was the job of in-house employees who earned almost $8 an hour and enjoyed full health benefits and travel privileges. Outside contractors now do the work, and many customers have started to complain about poor-quality cleaning, soiled carpets, and sticky tray tables.

Will Delta be able to overcome these problems? The firm's CEO acknowledges that the cost-cutting program has been anything but smooth. Moreover, he also acknowledges that the firm may have cut too deeply and eliminated people that it should have retained. Nevertheless, he says, the old days of high-cost benevolent operations are past. The firm has to remain cost focused and bottom-line oriented if it's to survive.[1]

"This has tested our people. There have been some morale problems. But so be it."

Ronald Allen, Delta CEO

Delta AirLines and its employees are in the process of redefining their relationship. To do so, they are having to each assess how well their respective needs and capabilities match. And the many unique characteristics that reside in each and every employee affect how he or she feels about these changes, shapes the individual's attitudes about the firm, and dictates how the employee performs on the job. These characteristics reflect the basic elements of individual behavior in organizations.

This chapter describes several of these basic behavioral elements and is the first of five chapters designed to develop a more complete perspective on the leading function of management. In the first section we investigate the psychological nature of individuals in organizations. Subsequent sections discuss personality and important personality attributes that can influence behavior in organizations, attitudes and their role in organizations, stress in the workplace, and individual creativity. Finally, we describe a number of basic individual behaviors that are important to organizations.

psychological contract The overall set of expectations held by an individual with respect to what he or she will contribute to the organization and what the organization will provide to the individual

Understanding Individuals in Organizations

contributions What the individual provides to the organization

inducements What the organization provides to the individual

As a starting point in understanding human behavior in the workplace, we must consider the basic nature of the relationship between individuals and organizations. We must also gain an appreciation of the nature of individual differences.

FIGURE 9.1
The Psychological Contract

Psychological contracts are the basic assumptions that individuals have about their relationships with their organization. Such contracts are defined in terms of contributions by the individual relative to inducements from the organization.

▪ The Psychological Contract

Most people have a basic understanding of a contract. Whenever we buy a car or sell a house, for example, both buyer and seller sign a contract that specifies the terms of the agreement. A psychological contract is similar in some ways to a standard legal contract, but is less formal and not as well defined. In particular, a **psychological contract** is the overall set of expectations held by an individual with respect to what he or she will contribute to the organization and what the organization will provide in return.[2] Thus, a psychological contract is not written on paper nor are all of its terms explicitly negotiated.

The essential nature of a psychological contract is illustrated in Figure 9.1. The individual makes a variety of **contributions** to the organization—effort, skills, ability, time, loyalty, and so forth. These contributions presumably satisfy various needs and requirements of the organization. That is, since the organization may have hired the person because of her skills, it is reasonable for the organization to expect that she will subsequently display those skills in the workplace.

In return for these contributions, the organization provides **inducements** to the individual.

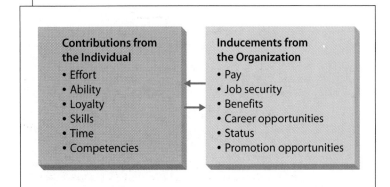

Contributions from the Individual	Inducements from the Organization
• Effort	• Pay
• Ability	• Job security
• Loyalty	• Benefits
• Skills	• Career opportunities
• Time	• Status
• Competencies	• Promotion opportunities

Some inducements, like pay and career opportunities, are tangible rewards. Others, like job security and status, are more intangible. Just as the contributions available from the individual must satisfy needs of the organization, the inducements offered by the organization must serve the needs of the individual. That is, if a person accepts employment with an organization because he thinks he will earn an attractive salary and have an opportunity to advance, he will expect those rewards to actually be forthcoming.

If both the individual and organization perceive that the psychological contract is fair and equitable, they will be satisfied with the relationship and will likely continue it. On the other hand, if either party sees an imbalance or inequity in the contract, that party may initiate a change. For example, the individual may request a pay raise or promotion, decrease her contributed effort, or look for a better job elsewhere. Similarly, the organization may ask the employee to attend a training program, transfer the person to another job, or terminate the person's employment altogether.

A basic challenge faced by the organization, then, is to manage psychological contracts. The organization must ensure that it is getting value from its employees. At the same time, it must also be sure that it is providing employees with appropriate inducements. If the organization is underpaying its employees for their contributions, for example, they may perform poorly or leave for better jobs elsewhere. On the other hand, if they are being overpaid relative to their contributions, the organization is incurring unnecessary costs.[3]

person-job fit The extent to which the contributions made by the individual match the inducements offered by the organization

The person-job fit is an important relationship in any organizational setting. For example, many people would balk at the idea of cleaning the outside windows on the top of a skyscraper, of cutting logs in harsh weather, or, as shown here, trying to train a white tiger. But for Gregg Lee, the animal trainer at Marine World Africa USA in California, it's just all in a day's work!

■ The Person-Job Fit

One specific aspect of managing psychological contracts is managing the person-job fit. **Person-job fit** is the extent to which the contributions made by the individual match the inducements offered by the organization. In theory, each employee has a specific set of needs that he or she wants fulfilled and a set of job-related behaviors and abilities to contribute. Thus, if the organization can take perfect advantage of those behaviors and abilities and exactly fulfill the employee's needs, it will have achieved a perfect person-job fit.

Of course, such a precise level of person-job fit is seldom achieved for several reasons. For one thing, organizational selection procedures are imperfect. Organizations can make approximations of employee skill levels when making hiring decisions and can improve those skills through training. But even simple performance dimensions are hard to measure objectively and validly.

Another reason for imprecise person-job fits is that both people and organizations change. An individual who finds a new job stimulating and exciting may find the same job boring and monotonous after a few years of performing it. And when the organization adopts new technology, it needs different skills from its employees. Still another reason for imprecision in the person-job fit is that each individual is unique. Measuring skills and performance is difficult enough. Assessing needs,

attitudes, and personality is far more complex. Individual differences complicate the process of matching individuals with jobs.

■ The Nature of Individual Differences

individual differences Personal attributes that vary from one person to another

Individual differences are personal attributes that vary from one person to another. Individual differences may be physical, psychological, and emotional. Taken together, the attributes that characterize a specific person make that individual unique. Much of the remainder of this chapter is devoted to the topic of individual differences. Before proceeding, however, we must also note the importance of the situation in assessing the behavior of individuals.

Are specific differences that characterize a given individual good or bad? Do they contribute to or detract from performance? The answer, of course, is that it depends on the circumstances. One person may be very dissatisfied, withdrawn, and negative in one job setting but very satisfied, outgoing, and positive in another. Working conditions, coworkers, and leadership are all important ingredients in determining how well a given person will fit into a particular job or organization.

Thus, whenever an organization attempts to assess or account for individual differences among its employees, it must also be sure to consider the situation in which behavior occurs. Individuals who are satisfied or productive workers in one context may prove to be dissatisfied or unproductive workers in another context. Attempting to consider both individual differences and contributions in relation to inducements and contexts, then, is a major challenge for organizations as they attempt to establish effective psychological contracts with their employees and achieve optimal fits between people and jobs.

Personality and Individual Behavior

personality The relatively permanent set of psychological and behavioral attributes that distinguish one person from another

Personality traits represent some of the most fundamental sets of individual differences in organizations. **Personality** is the relatively stable set of psychological attributes that distinguish one person from another.[4] Managers should strive to understand basic personality attributes and the ways they can affect people's behavior in organizational situations, not to mention their perceptions of and attitudes toward the organization.

■ The "Big Five" Personality Traits

"big five" personality traits A popular personality framework based on five key traits

Psychologists have identified literally thousands of personality traits and dimensions that differentiate one person from another. But in recent years, researchers have identified five fundamental traits that are especially relevant to organizations. Because these five traits, shown in Figure 9.2, are so important and because they are the subject of so much attention, they are commonly referred to now as the **"big five" personality traits**.[5]

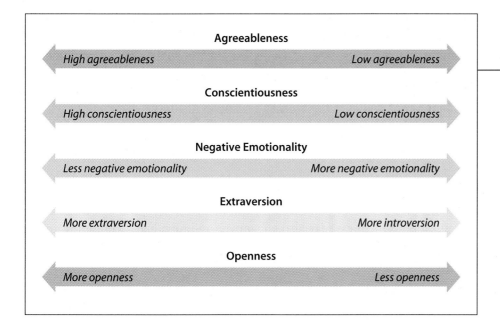

FIGURE 9.2
The "Big Five" Model of Personality

The "big five" personality model represents an increasingly accepted framework for understanding personality traits in organizational settings. In general, experts tend to agree that personality traits toward the left end of each dimension, as illustrated in this figure, are more positive in organizational settings, whereas traits closer to the right are less positive.

Agreeableness refers to a person's ability to get along with others. Agreeableness causes some people to be gentle, cooperative, forgiving, understanding, and good-natured in their dealings with others. But it results in others being irritable, short-tempered, uncooperative, and generally antagonistic toward other people. Highly agreeable people may be better able to develop good working relationships with coworkers, subordinates, and higher-level managers, whereas less agreeable people may not have particularly good working relationships. This pattern might also extend to relationships with customers, suppliers, and other key organizational constituents.

Conscientiousness refers to the number of goals on which a person focuses. People who focus on relatively few goals at one time are likely to be organized, systematic, careful, thorough, responsible, and self-disciplined as they work to pursue those goals. Others, however, tend to take on a wider array of goals, and, as a result, to be more disorganized, careless, and irresponsible, as well as less thorough and self-disciplined. People who are more conscientious tend to be higher performers than their less conscientious counterparts across a variety of jobs. This pattern seems logical, of course, because more-conscientious people generally take their jobs seriously and perform them in a highly responsible fashion.

The third of the big five personality dimensions is **negative emotionality**. People with less negative emotionality are relatively poised, calm, resilient, and secure. But people with more negative emotionality are more excitable, insecure, reactive, and subject to extreme mood swings. People with less negative emotionality might be expected to better handle job stress, pressure, and tension. Their stability might also lead them to be seen as being more reliable than their less stable counterparts.

Extraversion refers to a person's comfort level with relationships. People who are called extraverts are sociable, talkative, assertive, and open to establishing new relationships. But introverts are much less sociable, talkative, assertive, and less open to establishing new relationships. Extraverts may tend

agreeableness A person's ability to get along with others

conscientiousness The number of goals on which a person focuses

negative emotionality Extent to which a person is poised, calm, resilient, and secure

extraversion a person's comfort level with relationships

openness A person's rigidity of beliefs and range of interests

locus of control The degree to which an individual believes that behavior has a direct impact on the consequences of that behavior

self-efficacy An individual's beliefs about her or his capabilities to perform a task

to be higher overall job performers than introverts and are more likely to be attracted to jobs based on personal relationships, such as sales and marketing positions.

Finally, **openness** refers to a person's rigidity of beliefs and range of interests. People with high levels of openness are willing to listen to new ideas and to change their own ideas, beliefs, and attitudes as a result of new information. These people also tend to have broad interests and to be curious, imaginative, and creative. On the other hand, people with low levels of openness tend to be less receptive to new ideas and less willing to change their minds; they tend to have fewer and narrower interests and to be less curious and creative. People with more openness might be expected to be better performers, owing to their flexibility and the likelihood that they will be better accepted by others in the organization. Openness may also encompass an individual's willingness to accept change. For example, people with high levels of openness may be more receptive to change, whereas people with low levels of openness may be more likely to resist change.

The big five framework continues to attract the attention of both researchers and managers. The potential value of this framework is that it encompasses an integrated set of traits that appear to be valid predictors of certain behaviors in certain situations. Thus, managers who can develop both an understanding of the framework and the ability to assess these traits in their employees will be in a good position to understand how and why they behave as they do.[6] On the other hand, managers must also be careful to not overestimate their ability to assess the big five traits in others. Even assessment using the most rigorous and valid measures, for instance, is still likely to be somewhat imprecise.

■ Other Personality Traits at Work

In addition to the big five, several other personality traits influence behavior in organizations. Among the most important are locus of control, self-efficacy, authoritarianism, Machiavellianism, self-esteem, and risk propensity.

Locus of control is the extent to which people believe that their behavior has a real affect on what happens to them.[7] Some people, for example, believe that if they work hard, they will succeed. They also may believe that people who fail do so because they lack ability or motivation. People who believe that individuals are in control of their lives are said to have an *internal locus of control*. Other people think that fate, chance, luck, or other people's behavior determines what happens to them. For example, an employee who fails to get a promotion may attribute that failure to a politically motivated boss or just bad luck, rather than to her or his own lack of skills or poor performance record. People who think that forces beyond their control dictate what happens to them are said to have an *external locus of control*.

Self-efficacy is a person's beliefs about his or her capabilities to perform a task.[8] People with high self-efficacy believe that they can perform well on a specific task, whereas people with low self-efficacy tend to doubt their ability to perform a specific task. Although self-assessments of ability contribute to self-efficacy, so does the individual's personality. Some people simply have more self-confidence than others have. This confidence, in turn, results in their being more self-assured and more able to focus their attention on performance.

Another important personality characteristic is **authoritarianism**, the extent to which an individual believes that power and status differences are appropriate within hierarchical social systems like organizations.[9] For example, a person who is highly authoritarian may accept directives or orders from someone with more authority purely because the other person is "the boss." On the other hand, although a person who is not highly authoritarian may still carry out normal directives from the boss, that employee is also more likely to question things, disagree with the boss, and even refuse to carry out orders if they are for some reason objectionable. A highly authoritarian manager may be autocratic and demanding, and highly authoritarian subordinates will be more likely to accept this behavior from their leader. On the other hand, a less authoritarian manager may allow subordinates a bigger role in making decisions, and less authoritarian subordinates will respond positively to this behavior.

Machiavellianism, named after Niccolo Machiavelli, a sixteenth-century author, is another important personality trait. In his book entitled *The Prince*, Machiavelli explained how the nobility could more easily gain and use power. Machiavellianism is now used to describe behavior directed at gaining power and controlling the behavior of others. Research suggests that Machiavellianism is a personality trait that varies from person to person. More Machiavellian individuals tend to be rational and nonemotional, may be willing to lie to attain their personal goals, put little weight on loyalty and friendship, and enjoy manipulating others' behavior. Less Machiavellian individuals are more emotional, less willing to lie to succeed, value loyalty and friendship highly, and get little personal pleasure from manipulating others.

Self-esteem is the extent to which a person believes that he or she is a worthwhile and deserving individual.[10] A person with high self-esteem is more likely to seek higher status jobs, be more confident in his ability to achieve higher levels of performance, and derive greater intrinsic satisfaction from his accomplishments. In contrast, a person with less self-esteem may be more content to remain in a lower-level job, be less confident of her ability, and focus more on extrinsic rewards.

Risk propensity is the degree to which an individual is willing to take chances and make risky decisions. A manager with a high risk propensity, for example, might be expected to experiment with new ideas and gamble on new products. She might also lead the organization in new and different directions and be a catalyst for innovation. On the other hand, the same individual might also jeopardize the continued well-being of the organization if the risky decisions prove to be bad ones. A manager with low risk propensity might lead to a stagnant and overly conservative organization, or help the organization successfully weather turbulent and unpredictable times by maintaining stability and calm. Thus, the potential consequences of risk propensity to an organization are heavily dependent on the environment.

authoritarianism The extent to which an individual believes that power and status differences are appropriate within hierarchical social systems like organizations

Machiavellianism Behavior directed at gaining power and controlling the behavior of others

self-esteem The extent to which a person believes that he or she is a worthwhile and deserving individual

risk propensity The degree to which an individual is willing to take chances and make risky decisions

Attitudes and Individual Behavior

attitudes Complexes of beliefs and feelings that people have about specific ideas, situations, or other people

Another important element of individual behavior in organizations is attitudes. **Attitudes** are complexes of beliefs and feelings that people have about specific ideas, situations, or other people. Attitudes are important because they are the mechanism through which most people express their feelings. An employee's statement that he feels underpaid by the organization reflects his feelings about his pay. Similarly, when a manager says that she likes the new advertising campaign, she is expressing her feelings about the organization's marketing efforts.

Attitudes have three components. The *affective component* reflects feelings and emotions an individual has toward a situation. The *cognitive component* is derived from knowledge an individual has about a situation. It is important to note that cognition is subject to individual perceptions. Thus, one person might "know" that a certain political candidate is better than another, whereas someone else may "know" just the opposite. Finally, the *intentional component* reflects how an individual expects to behave toward or in the situation.

To illustrate these three components, consider the case of a manager who places an order for some supplies for his organization from a new office supply firm. Suppose many of the items he orders are out of stock, others are overpriced, and still others arrive damaged. When he calls someone at the supply firm for assistance, he is treated rudely and gets disconnected before his claim is resolved. When asked how he feels about the new office supply firm, he might respond, "I don't like that company (affective component). It is the worst office supply firm I've ever dealt with (cognitive component). I'll never do business with them again (intentional component)."

cognitive dissonance Caused when an individual has conflicting attitudes

People try to maintain consistency among the three components of their attitudes as well as among all their attitudes. However, circumstances sometimes arise that lead to conflicts. The conflict individuals may experience among their own attitudes is called **cognitive dissonance**.[11] Say, for example, an individual who has vowed never to work for a big, impersonal corporation intends instead to open her own business and be her own boss. Unfortunately, some financial setbacks force her to take a job with a large company. Thus, cognitive dissonance occurs: the affective and cognitive components of the individual's attitude conflict with intended behavior. To reduce cognitive dissonance, which is usually an uncomfortable experience for most people, the individual described above might tell herself the situation is only temporary and that she can go back out on her own in the near future. Or she might revise her cognitions and decide that working for a large company is more pleasant than she expected.

■ Work-Related Attitudes

People in organizations form attitudes about many different things. For example, employees are likely to have attitudes about their salary, promotion possibilities, their boss, employee benefits, the food in the company cafeteria, and the color of the company softball team uniforms. Of course, some of these attitudes are more important than others. Especially important attitudes are job satisfaction or dissatisfaction and organizational commitment.[12]

Job Satisfaction or Dissatisfaction **Job satisfaction** or **dissatisfaction** is an attitude that reflects the extent to which an individual is gratified by or fulfilled in his or her work. Extensive research conducted on job satisfaction has indicated that personal factors such as an individual's needs and aspirations determine this attitude, along with group and organizational factors such as relationships with coworkers and supervisors and working conditions, work policies, and compensation.[13]

A satisfied employee also tends to be absent less often, to make positive contributions, and to stay with the organization. In contrast, a dissatisfied employee may be absent more often, may experience stress that disrupts coworkers, and may be continually looking for another job. Contrary to what a lot of managers believe, however, high levels of job satisfaction do not necessarily lead to higher levels of performance.

Organizational Commitment **Organizational commitment** is an attitude that reflects an individual's identification with and attachment to the organization itself. A person with a high level of commitment is likely to see herself as a true member of the organization (for example, referring to the organization in personal terms: "We make high-quality products"), to overlook minor sources of dissatisfaction with the organization, and to see herself remaining a member of the organization. In contrast, a person with less organizational commitment is more likely to see himself as an outsider (for example, referring to the organization in less personal terms: "They don't pay their employees very well"), to express more dissatisfaction about things, and to not see himself as a long-term member of the organization.

Research suggests that commitment strengthens with an individual's age, years with the organization, sense of job security, and participation in decision making.[14] Employees who feel committed to an organization have highly reliable habits, plan a long tenure with the organization, and muster more effort in performance. Although there are few definitive things that organizations can do to promote commitment, a few specific guidelines are available. For one thing, if the organization treats its employees fairly and provides reasonable rewards and job security, those employees will more likely be satisfied and committed. Allowing employees to have a say in how things are done can also promote both attitudes.

■ Affect and Mood in Organizations

Researchers have recently started to focus renewed interest on the affective component of attitudes. Recall from our earlier discussion that the affect component of an attitude reflects feelings and emotions. Whereas managers once believed that a person's emotions and feelings varied from day to day, research now suggests that although some short-term fluctuation does indeed occur, there are also underlying stable predispositions toward fairly constant and predictable moods and emotional states.[15]

Some people, for example, tend to have a higher degree of **positive affectivity**. They are relatively upbeat and optimistic, have an overall sense of well-being, and usually see things in a positive light. Thus, they always seem to be in a good mood. Other people, those with more **negative affectivity**, are just

job satisfaction or **dissatisfaction** An attitude that reflects the extent to which an individual is gratified by or fulfilled in his or her work

organizational commitment An attitude that reflects an individual's identification with and attachment to the organization

positive affectivity A relatively stable tendency to be upbeat and optimistic, to have a sense of well-being, and to see things in a positive light

negative affectivity A relatively stable tendency to be downbeat and pessimistic and to see things in a negative light

perception The set of processes by which an individual becomes aware of and interprets information about the environment

selective perception The process of screening out information that we are uncomfortable with or that contradicts our beliefs

the opposite. They are generally downbeat and pessimistic and usually see things in a negative way. They seem to be in a bad mood most of the time.

Of course, as noted above, short-term variations can occur among even the most extreme types. People with a lot of positive affectivity, for example, may be in a bad mood if they have just received some bad news—being passed over for a promotion or being laid off or fired, for instance. Similarly, those with negative affectivity may be in a good mood—at least for a short time—if they have just been promoted or received very positive performance feedback. After the initial impact of these events wears off, however, those with positive affectivity will generally return to their normal positive mood, whereas those with negative affectivity will gravitate back to their normal bad mood.

Perception and Individual Behavior

FIGURE 9.3
Perceptual Processes

Two of the most basic perceptual processes are selective perception and stereotyping. As shown here, selective perception occurs when we screen out information (represented by the – symbols) that causes us discomfort or that contradicts our beliefs. Stereotyping occurs when we categorize or label people on the basis of a single attribute, illustrated here by color.

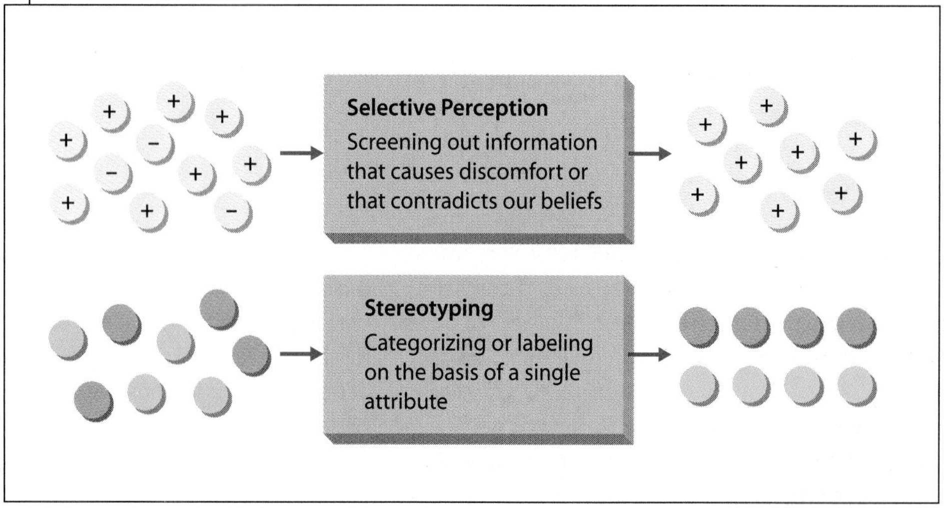

As noted earlier, an important element of an attitude is the individual's perception of the object about which the attitude is formed. Since perception plays a role in a variety of other workplace behaviors, managers need to have a general understanding of basic perceptual processes.[16] The role of attributions is also important.

■ Basic Perceptual Processes

Perception is the set of processes by which an individual becomes aware of and interprets information about the environment. As shown in Figure 9.3, basic perceptual processes that are particularly relevant to organizations are selective perception and stereotyping.

Selective Perception **Selective perception** is the process of screening out information that we are uncomfortable with or that contradicts our beliefs. For example, suppose a manager is exceptionally fond of a particular worker. The manager has a very positive attitude about the worker and thinks he is a top performer. One day the manager notices that the worker seems to be goofing off. Selective perception may cause the manager to quickly forget the incident. Similarly, suppose a manager has formed a very negative image of a particular worker. She thinks this worker is a poor performer and never

Selective Perception
Screening out information that causes discomfort or that contradicts our beliefs

Stereotyping
Categorizing or labeling on the basis of a single attribute

does a good job. When she happens to observe an example of high performance from the worker, she, too, may not remember it for very long. In one sense, selective perception is beneficial because it allows us to disregard minor bits of information. Of course, this benefit holds true only if our basic perception is accurate. If selective perception causes us to ignore important information, however, it can become quite detrimental.

Stereotyping   **Stereotyping** is the process of categorizing or labeling people on the basis of a single attribute. Common attributes from which people often stereotype are race and sex. Of course, stereotypes along these lines are inaccurate and can be harmful. For example, suppose a manager forms the stereotype that women can perform only certain tasks and that men are best suited for other tasks. To the extent that this stereotype affects the manager's hiring practices, the manager is (1) costing the organization valuable talent for both sets of jobs, (2) violating federal law, and (3) behaving unethically. On the other hand, certain forms of stereotyping can be useful and efficient. Suppose, for example, that a manager believes that communication skills are important for a particular job and that speech communication majors tend to have exceptionally good communication skills. As a result, whenever he interviews candidates for jobs, he pays especially close attention to speech communication majors. To the extent that communication skills truly predict job performance and that majoring in speech communication does indeed provide those skills, this form of stereotyping can be beneficial.

stereotyping   The process of categorizing or labeling people on the basis of a single attribute

■ Perception and Attribution

Perception is also closely linked with another process called attribution. **Attribution** is a mechanism through which we observe behavior and then attribute causes to it.[17] The behavior that is observed may be our own or that of others. For example, suppose someone realizes one day that she is working fewer hours than before, that she talks less about her work, and that she calls in sick more frequently. She might conclude from this that she has become disenchanted with her job and subsequently decide to quit. Thus, she observed her own behavior, attributed a cause to it, and developed a consistent response.

attribution   The process of observing behavior and attributing causes to it

More common is attributing cause to the behavior of others. For example, if the manager of the individual described above has observed the same behavior, he might form exactly the same attribution. On the other hand, he might instead decide that she has a serious illness, that he is driving her too hard, that she is experiencing too much stress, that she has a drug problem, or that she is having family problems.

The basic framework around which we form attributions is *consensus* (the extent to which other people in the same situation behave the same way), *consistency* (the extent to which the same person behaves in the same way at different times), and *distinctiveness* (the extent to which the same person behaves in the same way in other situations). For example, suppose a manager observes that an employee is late for a meeting. The manager might further realize that the individual is the only one who is late (low consensus), recall that he is often late for other meetings (high consistency), and subsequently realize that the same employee is sometimes late for work and returning from lunch (low distinctiveness). This pattern of attributions might cause the manager to decide that the individual's behavior is something that should be changed. As a result, the manager might meet with the subordinate and establish some punitive consequences for future tardiness.

Stress and Individual Behavior

stress An individual's response to a strong stimulus, which is called a **stressor**

General Adaptation Syndrome General cycle of the stress process

Another important element of behavior in organizations is stress. **Stress** is an individual's response to a strong stimulus.[18] This stimulus is called a **stressor**. Stress generally follows a cycle referred to as the **General Adaptation Syndrome**, or GAS,[19] shown in Figure 9.4. According to this view, when an individual first encounters a stressor, the GAS is initiated and the first stage, alarm, is activated. He may feel panic, may wonder how to cope, and may feel helpless. For example, suppose a manager is told to prepare a detailed evaluation of a plan by his firm to buy one of its competitors. His first reaction may be to say, "How will I ever get this done by tomorrow?"

If the stressor is too intense, the individual may feel unable to cope and never really try to respond to its demands. In most cases, however, after a short period of alarm, the individual gathers some strength and starts to resist the negative effects of the stressor. For example, the manager with the evaluation to write may calm down, call home to say he's working late, roll up his sleeves, order out for coffee, and get to work. Thus, at stage two, the person is resisting the effects of the stressor.

In many cases, the resistance phase may end the GAS. If the manager is able to complete the evaluation earlier than expected, he may drop it in his briefcase, smile to himself, and head home tired but satisfied. On the other hand, prolonged exposure to a stressor without resolution may bring on stage three of the GAS—exhaustion. At this stage, the individual literally gives up and can no longer resist the stressor. The manager, for example, might fall asleep at his desk at 3 A.M. and never finish the evaluation.

We should note that stress is not all bad. In the absence of stress, we may experience lethargy and stagnation. An optimal level of stress, on the other hand, can result in motivation and excitement. Too much stress, however, can have negative consequences. Another feature of stress is that it can be caused by "good" as well as "bad" things. Excessive pressure, unreasonable demands on our time, and bad news can all cause stress. But receiving a bonus and then having to decide what to do with the money can be stressful. So, too, can receiving a promotion, gaining recognition, and similar positive events.

FIGURE 9.4
The General Adaptation Syndrome

The General Adaptation Syndrome represents the normal process by which we react to stressful events. At stage one—alarm—we feel panic and alarm and our level of resistance to stress drops. Stage two—resistance—represents our efforts to confront and control the stressful circumstance. If we fail, we may eventually reach stage three—exhaustion—and just give up or quit.

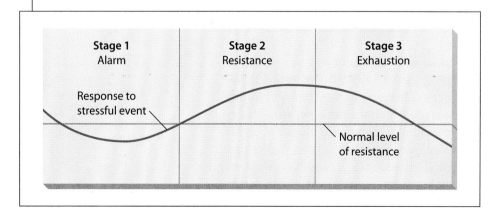

| Stage 1 Alarm | Stage 2 Resistance | Stage 3 Exhaustion |

Response to stressful event

Normal level of resistance

One important line of thinking about stress focuses on **Type A** and **Type B** personalities.[20] Type A individuals are extremely competitive, very devoted to work, and have a strong sense of time urgency. They are likely to be aggressive, impatient, and very work oriented. They have a lot of drive and want to accomplish as much as possible as quickly as possible. Type B individuals are less competitive, less devoted to work, and have a weaker sense of time urgency. Such individuals are less likely to experience conflict with other people and more likely to have a balanced, relaxed approach to life. They are able to work at a constant pace without time urgency. Type B people are not necessarily more or less successful than are Type A people. But Type Bs are less likely to experience stress.

Type A Individuals who are extremely competitive, very devoted to work, and have a strong sense of time urgency

Type B Individuals who are less competitive, less devoted to work, and have a weaker sense of time urgency

■ Causes and Consequences of Stress

Stress is obviously not a simple phenomenon. As shown in Figure 9.5, various factors can cause stress. Note that this list includes only work-related conditions—stress can also result from personal circumstances.[21]

Causes of Stress Work-related stressors fall into four categories—task, physical, role, and interpersonal demands. *Task demands* are associated with the task itself. Some occupations are inherently more stressful than others. Having to make fast decisions, decisions with less than complete information, or decisions that have relatively serious consequences are some of the things that can make some jobs stressful. The jobs of surgeon, airline pilot, and stockbroker are relatively more stressful than the jobs of general practitioner, airplane baggage loader, and office receptionist. Although a general practitioner makes important decisions, he is also likely to have time to make a considered diagnosis and fully explore a number of different treatments. But during surgery, the surgeon must make decisions quickly while realizing that the wrong one may endanger her patient's life.

Physical demands are stressors associated with the job setting. Working outdoors in extremely hot or cold temperatures, or even in an improperly heated or cooled office, can lead to stress. A poorly designed office, which may make it difficult for people to have privacy or promotes too little social interaction, can result in stress, as can poor lighting and inadequate work surfaces. Even

FIGURE 9.5
Causes of Work Stress

There are several causes of work stress in organizations. Four general sets of organizational stressors are task demands, physical demands, role demands, and interpersonal demands.

Psychological contracts help define mutual understandings between people and their employers in terms of what inducements the organization will provide in return for contributions from individuals. In general, the higher the inducements, the greater the contributions that are expected, and vice versa. Psychological contracts are often more central to people than to organizations, however. As illustrated in this cartoon, managers often take their work home—sometimes tangible work and other times things that are more intangible. If they feel they are being properly rewarded, these managers will continue to provide this extra level of support. But if they feel their extra efforts are not appreciated, they are inclined to cut back on these extra contributions.

more severe are actual threats to health. Examples include jobs like coal mining, poultry processing, and toxic-waste handling.

Role demands can also cause stress. (Roles are discussed more fully in Chapter 13.) A role is a set of expected behaviors associated with a position in a group or organization. Stress can result from either role ambiguity or role conflict that people can experience in groups. For example, an employee who is feeling pressure from her boss to work longer hours while also being asked by her family for more time at home will almost certainly experience stress. Similarly, a new employee experiencing role ambiguity because of poor orientation and training practices by the organization will also suffer from stress.

Interpersonal demands are associated with relationships that confront people in organizations. For example, group pressures regarding restriction of output and norm conformity can lead to stress. Leadership style may also cause stress. An employee who feels a strong need to participate in decision making may feel stress if his boss refuses to allow participation. And individuals with conflicting personalities may experience stress if required to work too closely together. A person with an internal locus of control might be frustrated when working with someone who prefers to wait and just let things happen.

Consequences of Stress   As noted earlier, the results of stress may be positive or negative. The negative consequences may be behavioral, psychological, or medical. Behaviorally, for example, stress may lead to detrimental or harmful actions, such as smoking, alcoholism, overeating, and drug abuse. Other stress-induced behaviors are accident proneness, violence toward self or others, and appetite disorders.

Psychological consequences of stress interfere with an individual's mental health and well-being. These outcomes include sleep disturbances, depression, family problems, and sexual dysfunction. Managers are especially prone to sleep disturbances when they experience stress at work.[22] Medical consequences of stress affect an individual's physiological well-being. Heart disease and stroke have been linked to stress, as have headaches, backaches, ulcers, and skin conditions such as acne and hives.

Individual stress also has direct consequences for businesses. For an operating employee, stress may translate into poor quality work and lower productivity. For a manager, it may mean faulty decision making and disruptions in working relationships. Withdrawal behaviors can also result from stress. People who are having difficulties with stress in their jobs are more likely to call in sick or to leave the organization. More subtle forms of withdrawal may also occur. A manager may start missing deadlines, for example, or taking longer lunch breaks. Employees may also withdraw by developing feelings of indifference. The irritation displayed by people under great stress can make them difficult to get along with. Job satisfaction, morale, and commitment can all suffer as a result of excessive levels of stress. So, too, can motivation to perform.

Another consequence of stress is **burnout**—a feeling of exhaustion that may develop when someone experiences too much stress for an extended period of time. Burnout results in constant fatigue, frustration, and helplessness. Increased rigidity follows, as does a loss of self-confidence and psychological withdrawal. The individual dreads going to work, often puts in longer hours but gets less accomplished than before, and exhibits mental and physical exhaustion. Because of the damaging effects of burnout, some firms are taking steps to help avoid it. For example, British Airways provides all of its employees with training designed to help them recognize the symptoms of burnout and develop strategies for avoiding it.

burnout A feeling of exhaustion that may develop when someone experiences too much stress for an extended period of time

■ Managing Stress

Given the potential consequences of stress, it follows that both people and organizations should be concerned about how to limit its more damaging effects. Numerous ideas and approaches have been developed to help manage stress. Some are strategies for individuals, and others are strategies for organizations.[23]

One way people manage stress is through exercise. People who exercise regularly feel less tension and stress, are more self-confident, and more optimistic. Their better physical condition also makes them less susceptible to many common illnesses. People who don't exercise regularly, on the other hand, tend to feel more stress and are more likely to be depressed. They are also more likely to have heart attacks. And because of their physical condition, they are more likely to contract illnesses.

Another method people use to manage stress is relaxation. Relaxation allows individuals to adapt to, and therefore better deal with, their stress. Relaxation comes in many forms, such as taking regular vacations. A recent study found that people's attitudes toward a variety of workplace characteristics improved significantly following a vacation. People can also learn to relax while on their jobs. For example, some experts recommend that people take regular rest breaks during their normal workday.

People can also use time management to control stress. The idea behind time management is that many daily pressures can be reduced or eliminated if individuals do a better job of managing time. One approach to time management is to make a list every morning of things to do that day. The items on the list are then grouped into three categories: critical activities that must be performed, important activities that should be

Stress can be a powerful force in organizations. Dr. Madan Kataria has founded thirty-seven "laughing clubs" to help people in high-stress jobs cope with pressure and tension. His approach includes deep breathing exercises and yoga, but also relies heavily on laughter.

performed, and optional or trivial things that can be delegated or postponed. The individual performs the items on the list in their order of importance.

Finally, people can manage stress through support groups. A support group can be as simple as a group of family members or friends to enjoy leisure time with. Going out after work with a few coworkers—to a basketball game or a movie, for example—can help relieve stress built up during the day. Family and friends can help people cope with stress on an ongoing basis and during times of crisis. For example, an employee who has just learned that she did not get the promotion she has been working toward for months may find it helpful to have a good friend to lean on, to talk to, or to yell at. People also may make use of more elaborate and formal support groups. Community centers or churches, for example, may sponsor support groups for people who have recently gone through a divorce, the death of a loved one, or some other tragedy.

Organizations are also beginning to realize that they should be involved in helping employees cope with stress. One reason is that because the business is at least partially responsible for stress, it should also help relieve it. Another is that stress-related insurance claims by employees can cost the organization considerable sums of money. Still another is that workers experiencing lower levels of detrimental stress will be able to function more effectively. AT&T has initiated a series of seminars and workshops to help its employees cope with the stress they face in their jobs. The firm was prompted to develop these seminars for all three of the reasons noted above.

A wellness program is a special program created to help employees deal with health and stress issues. Organizations have implemented stress management programs, health promotion programs, and other kinds of wellness programs for this purpose. The AT&T seminar program noted earlier is similar in nature to a wellness program, but true wellness programs are ongoing activities that have a number of components. They commonly include exercise-related activities as well as classroom instruction programs dealing with smoking cessation, weight reduction, and general stress management.

Some companies are developing their own programs or using existing programs of this type. Johns-Manville, for example, has a gym at its corporate headquarters. Other firms negotiate discounted health club membership rates with local establishments. For the instructional part of the program the organization can again either sponsor its own training or perhaps jointly sponsor seminars with a local YMCA, civic organization, or church. Organization-based fitness programs facilitate employee exercise, a very positive consideration, but such programs are also quite costly. Still, more and more companies are developing fitness programs for employees.

Creativity in Organizations

creativity The ability of an individual to generate new ideas or to conceive of new perspectives on existing ideas

Creativity is yet another important component of individual behavior in organizations. **Creativity** is the ability of an individual to generate new ideas or to conceive of new perspectives on existing ideas. Examining a few general patterns can help us understand the sources of individual creativity within organizations.[24]

■ The Creative Individual

Numerous researchers have focused their efforts on attempting to describe the common attributes of creative individuals. These attributes generally fall into three categories: background experiences, personal traits, and cognitive abilities.

Background Experiences and Creativity   Researchers have observed that many creative individuals were raised in an environment in which creativity was nurtured. Mozart was raised in a family of musicians and began composing and performing music at age six, and Pierre and Marie Curie, great scientists in their own right, also raised a daughter, Irene, who won the Nobel Prize in chemistry. However, people with background experiences very different from theirs have also been creative. The African-American abolitionist and writer Frederick Douglass was born into slavery and had very limited opportunities for education. Nonetheless, his powerful oratory and creative thinking helped lead to the Emancipation Proclamation, which outlawed slavery in the United States.

Personal Traits and Creativity   Certain personal traits have also been linked to creativity in individuals. The traits shared by most creative people are openness; an attraction to complexity; high levels of energy, independence and autonomy; strong self-confidence; and a strong belief that one is, in fact, creative. Individuals who possess these traits are more likely to be creative than are those who do not have them.

Cognitive Abilities and Creativity   Cognitive abilities are an individual's power to think intelligently and to analyze situations and data effectively. Intelligence may be a precondition for individual creativity—although most creative people are highly intelligent, not all intelligent people necessarily are creative. Creativity is also linked with the ability to think divergently and convergently. *Divergent thinking* is a skill that allows people to see differences between situations, phenomena, or events. *Convergent thinking* is a skill that allows people to see similarities between situations, phenomena, or events. Creative people are generally very skilled at both divergent and convergent thinking.

■ The Creative Process

Although creative people often report that ideas seem to come to them "in a flash," individual creative activity actually tends to progress through a series of stages. Not all creative activity has to follow these four stages, but much of it does.

Preparation   The creative process normally begins with a period of *preparation*. Formal education and training are usually the most efficient ways of becoming familiar with this vast amount of research and knowledge. To make a creative contribution to business management or business services, individuals must usually receive formal training and education in business. Experiences that managers have on the job after their formal training has finished can also contribute to the creative process. In an important sense, the education and training of creative people never really ends. It continues as long as they remain interested in the world and curious about the way things work.

Incubation   The second phase of the creative process is *incubation*—a period of less intense conscious concentration during which the knowledge and ideas acquired during preparation mature and develop. A curious aspect of incubation is that it is often helped along by pauses in concentrated rational thought. Some creative people rely on physical activity such as jogging or swimming to provide a break from thinking. Others may read or listen to music. Sometimes sleep may even supply the needed pause. While out rowing one day, David Morse, a research scientist at Corning, hit on the answer to a difficult product improvement. Morse had a special interest in a new line of cookware called Visions. These glass pots and pans had many advantages over traditional cookware, but no one at Corning had yet succeeded in putting a nonstick surface on the glass. Looking for a solution to this problem, Morse put in many long days in the laboratory, but it was during his hours of rowing that the ideas and concepts that would enable him to devise a nonstick coating began to come together and mature. Morse may never have been able to solve this technical problem if he had not taken the time to let his ideas incubate.

Insight   Usually occurring after preparation and incubation, insight is a spontaneous breakthrough in which the creative person achieves a new understanding of some problem or situation. *Insight* represents a coming together of all the scattered thoughts and ideas that were maturing during incubation. It may occur suddenly or develop slowly over time. Insight can be triggered by some external event, such as a new experience or an encounter with new data that forces the individual to think about old issues and problems in new ways, or it can be a completely internal event in which patterns of thought finally coalesce in ways that generate new understanding. One manager's key insight led to a complete restructuring of Citibank's back-room operations—the enormous avalanche of paperwork that a bank must process to serve its customers: listing checks and deposits, updating accounts, and preparing bank statements. Historically, these operations at Citibank had been managed as if they were part of the regular banking operation. When a young executive named John Reed arrived on the scene, he realized that back-room operations had less to do with banking and more to do with manufacturing. Reed's insight was that the operations could be managed more efficiently as a paper-manufacturing process. On this basis, he hired former manufacturing managers from outside the banking industry. By reconceptualizing the nature of the operation, Reed was able to substantially reduce the costs of these operations.

Verification   Once an insight has occurred, *verification* determines the validity or truthfulness of the insight. For many creative ideas, verification includes scientific experiments to determine whether or not the insight actually leads to the results expected. In David Morse's case, the insight concerning how to apply a nonstick coating on glass pots was verified in several important experiments and practical trials. Verification may also include the development of a product or service prototype. A *prototype* is one (or a very small number) of products built just to see whether the ideas behind this new product actually work. Product prototypes are rarely sold to the public but are very valuable in verifying the insights developed in the creative process. Once the new product or service is developed, verification in the marketplace is the ultimate test of the creative idea behind it.

Enhancing Creativity in Organizations

Managers who want to enhance and promote creativity can do so in a variety of ways.[25] One important method for enhancing creativity is to make it a part of the organization's culture, often through explicit goals. Firms that truly want to stress creativity, such as 3M and Rubbermaid, state goals that some percentage of future revenues are to be gained from new products. This goal clearly communicates that creativity and innovation are valued.

Another important part of enhancing creativity is to reward creative successes while being careful to not punish creative failures. Many ideas that seem worthwhile on paper fail to pan out in reality. If the first person to come up with an idea that fails is fired or otherwise punished, others in the organization will become more cautious in their own work. And as a result, fewer creative ideas will emerge.

Types of Workplace Behavior

Now that we have looked closely at how individual differences can influence behavior in organizations, let's turn our attention to the subject of workplace behavior. **Workplace behavior** is a pattern of action by the members of an organization that directly or indirectly influences organizational effectiveness. Important workplace behaviors include performance and productivity, absenteeism and turnover, and organizational citizenship.

workplace behavior A pattern of action by the members of an organization that directly or indirectly influences organizational effectiveness

Performance Behaviors

Performance behaviors are the total set of work-related behaviors that the organization expects the individual to display. Thus, they derive from the psychological contract. For some jobs, performance behaviors can be narrowly defined and easily measured. For example, an assembly line worker who sits by a moving conveyor and attaches parts to a product as it passes by has relatively few performance behaviors. He or she is expected to remain at the work station and correctly attach the parts. Performance can often be assessed quantitatively by counting the percentage of parts correctly attached.

For many other jobs, however, performance behaviors are more diverse and much more difficult to assess. For example, consider the case of a research and development scientist at Merck. The scientist works in a lab trying to find new scientific breakthroughs that have commercial potential. The scientist must apply knowledge learned in graduate school with experience gained from previous research. Intuition and creativity are also important elements. And

performance behaviors The total set of work-related behaviors that the organization expects the individual to display

the desired breakthrough may take months or even years to accomplish. As we discuss in Chapter 8, organizations rely on a number of different methods for evaluating performance. The key, of course, is to match the evaluation mechanism with the job being performed.

■ Withdrawal Behaviors

absenteeism When an individual does not show up for work

Another important type of work-related behavior is that which results in withdrawal—absenteeism and turnover. **Absenteeism** occurs when an individual does not show up for work. The cause may be legitimate (illness, jury duty, death in the family, and so on) or feigned (reported as legitimate but actually just an excuse to stay home). When an employee is absent, her or his work does not get done at all or a substitute must be hired to do it. In either case, the quantity or quality of actual output is likely to suffer. Obviously, some absenteeism is expected. The key concern of organizations is to minimize feigned absenteeism and reduce legitimate absences as much as possible. High absenteeism may be a symptom of other problems as well, such as job dissatisfaction and low morale.

turnover When people quit their jobs

Turnover occurs when people quit their jobs. An organization usually incurs costs in replacing individuals who have quit, but if turnover involves especially productive people, it is even more costly. Turnover seems to result from a number of factors including aspects of the job, the organization, the individual, the labor market, and family influences. In general, a poor person-job fit is also a likely cause of turnover.

Efforts to directly manage turnover are frequently fraught with difficulty, even in organizations that concentrate on rewarding good performers. Of course, some turnover is inevitable and in some cases it may even be desirable. For example, if the organization is trying to cut costs by reducing its staff, having people voluntarily choose to leave is preferable to having to terminate them. And if the people who choose to leave are low performers or express high levels of job dissatisfaction, the organization may also benefit from turnover.

■ Organizational Citizenship

organizational citizenship The behavior of individuals that makes a positive overall contribution to the organization

Organizational citizenship refers to the behavior of individuals that makes a positive overall contribution to the organization.[26] Consider, for example, an employee who does work that is acceptable in terms of both quantity and quality. However, she refuses to work overtime, she won't help newcomers learn the ropes, and she is generally unwilling to make any contribution to the organization beyond the strict performance of her job. Although this person may be seen as a good performer, she is not likely to be seen as a good organizational citizen.

Another employee may exhibit a comparable level of performance. In addition, however, he always works late when the boss asks him to, he takes time to help newcomers learn their way around, and he is perceived as being helpful and committed to the organization's success. Although his level of performance may be seen as equal to that of the first worker, he is also likely to be seen as a better organizational citizen.

The determinant of organizational citizenship behaviors is likely to be a complex mosaic of individual, social, and organizational variables. For example, the personality, attitudes, and needs of the individual have to be consistent with citizenship behaviors. Similarly, the social context, or work group, in which the individual works needs to facilitate and promote such behaviors (we discuss group dynamics in Chapter 13). And the organization itself, especially its culture, must be capable of promoting, recognizing, and rewarding these types of behaviors if they are to be maintained. Although the study of organizational citizenship is still in its infancy, preliminary research suggests that it may play a powerful role in organizational effectiveness.[27]

Summary of Key Points

Understanding individuals in organizations is an important consideration for all managers. A basic framework that can be used to facilitate this understanding is the psychological contract—the set of expectations held by people with respect to what they will contribute to the organization and what they expect to get in return. Organizations strive to achieve an optimal person-job fit, but this process is complicated by the existence of individual differences.

Personality is the relatively stable set of psychological and behavioral attributes that distinguish one person from another. The "big five" personality traits are agreeableness, conscientiousness, negative emotionality, extraversion, and openness. Other important traits are locus of control, self-efficacy, authoritarianism, Machiavellianism, self-esteem, and risk propensity.

Attitudes are based on emotion, knowledge, and intended behavior. Whereas personality is relatively stable, some attitudes can be formed and changed easily. Others are more constant. Job satisfaction or dissatisfaction and organizational commitment are important work-related attitudes.

Perception is the set of processes by which an individual becomes aware of and interprets information about the environment. Basic perceptual processes include selective perception and stereotyping. Perception and attribution are also closely related.

Stress is an individual's response to a strong stimulus. The General Adaptation Syndrome outlines the basic stress process. Stress can be caused by task, physical, role, and interpersonal demands. Consequences of stress include organizational and individual outcomes, as well as burnout. Various stress management techniques are available.

Creativity is the capacity to generate new ideas. Creative people tend to have certain profiles of background experiences, personal traits, and cognitive abilities. The creative process itself includes preparation, incubation, insight, and verification.

Workplace behavior is a pattern of action by the members of an organization that directly or indirectly influences organizational effectiveness. Performance behaviors are the set of work-related behaviors the organization expects the individual to display to fulfill the psychological contract. Basic withdrawal behaviors are absenteeism and turnover. Organizational citizenship refers to behavior that makes a positive overall contribution to the organization.

Discussion Questions

Questions for Review

1. What is a psychological contract? Why is it important?

2. Identify and describe five basic personality attributes.

3. What are the basic causes and consequences of stress in organizations?

4. Identify and discuss the steps in the creative process.

5. Identify and describe several important workplace behaviors.

Questions for Analysis

1. An individual was heard to describe someone else as having "no personality." What is wrong with this statement? What did the individual actually mean?

2. Describe a circumstance in which you formed a new attitude about something.

3. Identify the basic causes of stress in your life. How might you go about reducing or eliminating them?

4. Identify a person who you consider to be especially creative. What evidence can you cite to support your choice? What factors do you think most clearly led to this person being so creative?

5. As a manager, how would you go about trying to make someone a better organizational citizen?

Building Effective Diagnostic & Conceptual Skills

EXERCISE OVERVIEW

Conceptual skills refer to a manager's ability to think in the abstract, and diagnostic skills focus on responses to situations. These skills must frequently be used together to better understand the behavior of others in the organization, as illustrated by this exercise.

EXERCISE BACKGROUND

Human behavior is a complex phenomenon in any setting, but especially so in organizations. Understanding how and why people choose particular behaviors can be difficult and frustrating, but quite important. Consider, for example, the following scenario.

Sandra Buckley has worked in your department for several years. Until recently, she has been a "model" employee. She was always on time, or early, for work, and stayed late whenever necessary to get her work done. She was upbeat, cheerful, and worked very hard. She frequently said that the company was the best place she had ever worked and that you were the perfect boss.

About six months ago, however, you began to see changes in Sandra's behavior. She began to occasionally come in late, and you cannot remember the last time she agreed to work past 5:00. She also complains a lot. Other workers have started to avoid her because she is so negative all the time. You also suspect that she may be looking for a new job.

EXERCISE TASK

Using the scenario described above as background, do the following:

1. Assume that you have done some background work to find out what has happened. Write a brief case with more information that explains why Sandra's behavior has changed (for example, your case might note that you recently promoted someone else when Sandra might have expected to get the job). Make the case as descriptive as possible.

2. Relate elements of your case to the various behavioral concepts discussed in this chapter.

3. Decide whether or not you might be about to resolve things with Sandra to overcome whatever issues have arisen.

4. Which behavioral process or concept discussed in this chapter is easiest to change? Which is the most difficult to change?

EXERCISE OVERVIEW

Time-management skills help people prioritize work, work more efficiently, and delegate appropriately. Poor time management, in turn, may result in stress. This exercise helps you relate time-management skills to stress reduction.

EXERCISE BACKGROUND

Make a list of several major causes of stress for you. Stressors might involve school (hard classes, too many exams, and so on), work (financial pressures or a demanding work schedule, for example), and/or personal circumstances (friends, romance, family, and so on). Try to be as specific as possible. Also, try to identify at least ten different stressors.

EXERCISE TASK

Using the list developed above, do each of the following:

1. Evaluate the extent to which poor time management on your part plays a role in how each stressor affects you. For example, do exams cause stress because you delay studying?

2. Develop a strategy for using time more efficiently in relation to each stressor that relates to time.

3. Note interrelationships among different kinds of stressors and time. For example, financial pressures may cause you to work, but work may interfere with school. Can any of these interrelationships be more effectively managed vis-à-vis time?

4. How do you manage the stress in your life? Is it possible to manage stress in a more time-effective manner?

EXERCISE OVERVIEW

Interpersonal skills refer to the ability to communicate with, understand, and motivate individuals and groups. Implicit in this definition is the notion that a manager should try to understand important characteristics of others, including their personalities. This exercise gives you insights into the importance of personality in the workplace as well as some of the difficulties associated with assessing personality traits.

EXERCISE BACKGROUND

You will first try to determine which personality traits are most relevant for different jobs. You will then write a series of questions that you think may help assess or measure those traits in prospective employees. First, read the following job descriptions:

Sales representative: This position involves calling on existing customers to ensure that they continue to be happy with your firm's products. It also requires the sales representative to try to get those customers to buy more of your products, as well as to attract new customers. A sales representative should be aggressive but not pushy.

Office manager: The office manager oversees the work of a staff of twenty secretaries, receptionists, and clerks. The manager hires them, trains them, evaluates their performance, and sets their pay. The manager also schedules working hours and, when necessary, disciplines or fires workers.

Warehouse worker: Warehouse workers unload trucks and carry shipments to shelves for storage. They also pull orders for customers from shelves and take products for packing. The job requires workers to follow orders precisely and has little room for autonomy or interaction with others during work.

EXERCISE TASK

Working alone, identify a single personality trait that you think is especially important for a person to effectively perform each job. Next, write five questions which, when answered by a job applicant, will help you assess how that applicant scores on that particular trait. These questions should be of the type that can be answered on a five-point scale (for example, strongly agree, agree, neither agree or disagree, disagree, strongly disagree).

Exchange questions with a classmate. Then pretend you are a job applicant. Provide honest and truthful answers to each question. Next, discuss the traits each of you identified for each position and how well you think the questions actually measure those traits.

Conclude by considering the following questions:

1. How easy is it to measure personality?

2. How important do you believe it is for organizations to consider personality in hiring decisions?

3. Do perception and attitudes affect how people answer personality questions?

You Make the Call

The day Susan Turner was promoted to the position of manager of Sunset Landscape Service's retail nursery operation, she felt as though her feet were not touching the ground. She could hardly wait to get home that evening and share her good news with her husband, Will Larson.

As the two of them prepared dinner together that evening and talked about her work, Susan said, "You know, it's really amazing to have just the perfect job. I've always loved watching things grow. Being outside most of the time is just too good to be true. And getting to wear casual clothes at work is also nice. I know that I'm going to be a great manager. I really appreciate this opportunity.

"I think there are going to be some more opportunities in the future, too. I think the Spensers really know what they're doing. Sunset is already the most successful nursery business in town. I wouldn't be surprised to see them start expanding even more, and maybe even open a new nursery across town."

Will shared his wife's happiness with her work, although he clearly had different preferences. He was a stockbroker in the local office of a national firm. He said, "I know what you mean about liking your work. Well, you know how much I've always liked mine. I guess everyone is different, though. While being outside is okay some of the time, I really like my air-conditioned office. The thought of being outside on hot days or when it's raining just doesn't sound good to me. And I guess that I sorta like getting dressed up every morning."

Later that evening, Susan received a telephone call from her sister, Elaine Turner. Elaine had just moved to California for a new job. It was her fourth new job in the past five years. She never seemed to find a job that she really liked. Each new job seemed great at first, but within just a few weeks, Elaine was usually grumbling about something and saying that it didn't suit her in some way or another. And sure enough, after Susan and Elaine had talked for awhile, Elaine said, "I hope that the work gets more exciting soon, though. I thought it was going to be a lot of fun, but so far about the only real fun I'm having is fighting traffic on the way home each evening."

DISCUSSION QUESTIONS

1. Describe the elements of person-job fit as they apply to Susan, Will, and Elaine.

2. What inferences about individual differences can be drawn from these people?

3. How do you see the attitudes of Susan, Will, and Elaine affecting their workplace behaviors?

ASSESSING YOUR MENTAL ABILITIES

Skills Self-Assessment Instrument

Introduction: Mental abilities are important to job performance, especially in this information age. The following assessment surveys your judgments about your personal mental abilities.

Instructions: Judge how accurately each of the following statements describes you. In some cases, making a decision may be difficult, but you should force a choice. Record your answers next to each statement according to the following scale:

Rating Scale

5 Very descriptive of me   **2** Not very descriptive of me
4 Fairly descriptive of me   **1** Not descriptive of me at all
3 Somewhat descriptive of me

____ 1. I am at ease learning visually. I readily take in and hold in mind visual precepts.

____ 2. I can produce remotely associated, clever, or uncommon responses to statements or situations.

_____ 3. I can formulate and test hypotheses directed at finding a principle of relationships among elements of a case or problem.

_____ 4. I am able to remember bits of unrelated material and can recall parts of such material.

_____ 5. I can recall perfectly for immediate reproduction a series of items after only one presentation of the series.

_____ 6. I can manipulate numbers in arithmetical operations rapidly.

_____ 7. I am fast in finding figures, making comparisons, and carrying out other very simple tasks involving visual perception.

_____ 8. I can reason from stated premises to their necessary conclusion.

_____ 9. I can perceive spatial patterns or maintain orientation with respect to objects in space. I can manipulate or transform the image of spatial patterns into other visual arrangements.

_____ 10. I have a large knowledge of words and their meanings and am able to apply this knowledge in understanding connected discourse.

For interpretation, turn to page 460.

Source: Adapted from M. D. Dunnette, "Aptitudes, Abilities, and Skills," in M. D. Dunnette (ed.), *Handbook of Industrial and Organizational Psychology* (Chicago: Rand McNally, 1976), pp. 481–483. Copyright © 1976 by Rand McNally. Reprinted by permission of the author.

Experiential Exercise

ASSUMPTIONS THAT COLOR PERCEPTIONS

Purpose: Perceptions rule the world. In fact, everything we know or think we know is filtered through our perceptions. Our perceptions are rooted in past experiences and socialization by significant others in our life. This exercise is designed to help you become aware of how much our assumptions influence our perceptions and evaluations of others. It also illustrates how we compare our perceptions with others to find similarities and differences.

Instructions:

1. Read the descriptions of the four individuals provided in the personal descriptions below.

2. Decide which occupation is most likely for each person and place the name by the corresponding occupation in the occupations list. Each person is in a different occupation, and no two people hold the same one.

Personal Descriptions:

R. B. Red is a trim, attractive woman in her early thirties. She holds an undergraduate degree from an eastern woman's college and is active in several professional organizations. She is an officer (on the national level) of Toastmistress International. Her hobbies include classical music, opera, and jazz. She is an avid traveler who is planning a sojourn to China next year.

W. C. White is a quiet, meticulous person. W. C. is tall and thin with blond hair and wire-framed glasses. Family, friends, and church are very important, and W. C. devotes any free time to community activities. W. C. is a wizard with figures but can rarely be persuaded to demonstrate this ability to do mental calculations.

G. A. Green grew up on a small farm in rural Indiana. He is an avid hunter and fisherman. In fact, he and his wife joke about their "deer-hunting honeymoon" in Colorado. One of his primary goals is to "get back to the land," and he hopes to be able to buy a small farm before he is fifty. He drives a pickup truck and owns several dogs.

B. E. Brown is the child of wealthy professionals who reside on Long Island. B. E.'s father is a "self-made" financial analyst who made it a point to stress the importance of financial security as B. E. grew up. B. E. values the ability to structure one's use of time and can often be found on the golf course on Wednesday afternoons. B. E. dresses in a conservative upper-class manner and professes to be "allergic to polyester."

Occupations: Choose the occupations that seem most appropriate for each person described. Place the correct names in the spaces next to the corresponding occupations.

_____ Banker   _____ Clerk

_____ Labor negotiator   _____ Army general

_____ Production manager   _____ Salesperson

_____ Travel agent   _____ Physician

_____ Accountant   _____ Truck driver

_____ Teacher   _____ Financial analyst

_____ Computer
operations manager

Source: Jerri L. Frantzve, *Behaving in Organizations* (Boston: Allyn & Bacon, 1983), pp. 63–65.

CASE STUDY

Hard Work or Dead End?

People everywhere seem to be working longer hours. Sometimes they do it to survive, sometimes because they want to, and sometimes because they see it as a means to an end. Consider, for example, Julie Herendeen, Richard Thibeault, and Josh McIntyre. Ms. Herendeen has an MBA from Harvard and is considered one of the best and the brightest young managers at Netscape. Herendeen's workday starts at 6:30 A.M. when she checks her e-mail from her home computer.

By 8:30, Julie is in her office cubicle. She immediately turns on her computer and discovers a new string of e-mails that have arrived since she last checked. She eats a fast-food breakfast at her computer while she answers these messages. Throughout the day Herendeen attends various meetings and conferences. Finally, around 5:00 P.M. when many workers in other industries are headed home, Julie escapes

the endless litany of meetings and conversations and finally makes it to her own desk again where she sits and begins to work. At 8:30 that evening, she's still working. During the last three and a half hours, she has continued to respond to e-mail and voice mail. She also developed an outline of a sales presentation. Finally, at 9:00 she leaves her office. Ms. Herendeen says she loves her work and can't see doing anything else.

Richard Thibeault also works long hours. Thibeault manages an Au Bon Pain bakery cafe in Boston. But much of what he has to do doesn't seem like management at all. Like many other businesses, Au Bon Pain has cut back on its workforce and is holding store managers strictly accountable for keeping costs in line. Thus, Richard does a lot of work himself that he once had employees to do. For example, he is often at work at 3:00 A.M. to start baking rolls and pastries. During the day he also empties trash, fills in at the cash register when his employees take a lunch break, and cleans tables.

Because Au Bon Pain does little evening business, Richard can often get off around 4:00 or so in the afternoon during the week. He also works long hours on Saturday and Sunday. Mr. Thibeault recently calculated that he was working around seventy hours a week and earning the equivalent of $7.83 an hour—scarcely more than the wages his part-time workers make. But he is under constant pressure from the home office to keep shaving costs while also boosting revenues. He doesn't know how much longer he can keep it up, though. His doctor is already telling him he needs to quit before he suffers serious health problems.

Finally, Josh McIntyre works at a small electronics factory in California. He has a law degree, and started out as an attorney with a major law firm in a big city. But from the day he started, he was miserable. Although the pay was good, the pressure was unrelenting. He routinely worked seventy or more hours a week, and sometimes exceeded one hundred. Josh was doing very well; he received regular feedback that the partners were very pleased with his work and that big things were on the horizon.

One night, however, as he was walking to his car at 10:00, he suddenly realized that it was his birthday. No one had known it, and it had passed without fanfare. Indeed, he had not talked to anyone outside his law practice for weeks—had not watched television, had not exercised, had not read a novel. In short, all he

was doing was working. The next day he tendered his resignation and moved to a small town near his family home. Josh's brother helped him get a job assembling electrical components. He makes an hourly wage, but works only forty hours a week.

McIntyre says that he is happier now than he's ever been in his life. He isn't making much money, but has plenty of personal time to do the things he enjoys in life. For example, he has learned to play the guitar and is taking up gardening. He still thinks about the law, however, and intends to get back into it soon. However, his plan is to start a small practice in a rural community where he can avoid the big-city pressures and stress that drove him away.

Case Questions

1. What individual differences might explain the three people discussed in this case?

2. Why do you think these three individuals have made certain choices but not others?

3. Identify causes and consequences of stress that might be relevant for each of these three people.

Case References: Stratford Sherman, "A Day in the Life of a Netscape Exec," *Fortune*, May 13, 1996, pp. 124–130; "For Richard Thibeault, Being a 'Manager' Is a Blue-Collar Life," *Wall Street Journal*, October 1, 1996, pp. A1, A12; "When Money Isn't Enough," *Forbes*, November 18, 1996, pp. 164–170.

CHAPTER NOTES

1. "Cost Cutting at Delta Raises the Stock Price But Lowers the Service," *Wall Street Journal*, June 20, 1996, pp. A1, A8 (quote on p. A8); and *Hoover's Handbook of American Business 1998* (Austin, Texas: The Reference Press, 1998), pp. 478–479.

2. Lynn McGarlane Shore and Lois Tetrick, "The Psychological Contract as an Explanatory Framework in the Employment Relationship," in C. L. Cooper and D. M. Rousseau (eds.), *Trends in Organizational Behavior* (London: John Wiley & Sons Ltd., 1994), pp. 99–110.

3. Elizabeth Wolfe Morrison and Sandra L. Robinson, "When Employees Feel Betrayed: A Model of How Psychological Contract Violation Develops," *Academy of Management Review*, January 1997, pp. 226–256.

4. Lawrence Pervin, "Personality" in Mark Rosenzweig and Lyman Porter (eds.), *Annual Review of Psychology*, Vol. 36 (Palo Alto, Calif.: Annual Reviews, 1985), pp. 83–114 and S. R. Maddi, *Personality Theories: A Comparative Analysis*, 4th ed. (Homewood, Ill: Dorsey, 1980).

5. L. R. Goldberg, "An Alternative Description of Personality: The Big Five Factor Structure," *Journal of Personality and Social Psychology*, Vol. 59, 1990, pp. 1216–1229.

6. Michael K. Mount, Murray R. Barrick, and J. Perkins Strauss, "Validity of Observer Ratings of the Big Five Personality Factors," *Journal of Applied Psychology*, Vol. 79, No. 2, 1994, pp. 272–280 and Timothy A. Judge, Joseph J. Martocchio, and Carl J. Thoreson, "Five-Factor Model of Personality and Employee Absence," *Journal of Applied Psychology*, Vol. 82, No. 5, 1997, pp. 745–755.

7. J. B. Rotter, "Generalized Expectancies for Internal vs. External Control of Reinforcement," *Psychological Monographs*, Vol. 80, 1966, pp. 1–28.

8. Marilyn E. Gist and Terence R. Mitchell, "Self-Efficacy: A Theoretical Analysis of Its Determinants and Malleability," *Academy of Management Review*, April 1992, pp. 183–211.

9. T. W. Adorno, E. Frenkel-Brunswick, D. J. Levinson, and R. N. Sanford, *The Authoritarian Personality* (New York: Harper & Row, 1950).

10. Jon L. Pierce, Donald G. Gardner, and Larry L. Cummings, "Organization-Based Self-Esteem: Construct Definition, Measurement, and Validation," *Academy of Management Journal*, Vol. 32, 1989, pp. 622–648.

11. Leon Festinger, *A Theory of Cognitive Dissonance* (Palo Alto, Calif.: Stanford University Press, 1957).

12. Linda Grant, "Happy Workers, High Returns," *Fortune*, January 12, 1998, p. 81.

13. Patricia C. Smith, L. M. Kendall, and Charles Hulin, *The Measurement of Satisfaction in Work and Behavior* (Chicago: Rand-McNally, 1969).

14. Richard M. Steers, "Antecedents and Outcomes of Organizational Commitment," *Administrative Science Quarterly*, Vol. 22, 1977, pp. 46–56.

15. For research work in this area, see Jennifer M. George and Gareth R. Jones, "The Experience of Mood and Turnover Intentions: Interactive Effects of Value Attainment, Job Satisfaction, and Positive Mood," *Journal of Applied Psychology*, Vol. 81, No. 3, 1996, pp. 318–325 and Larry J. Williams, Mark B. Gavin, and Margaret Williams, "Measurement and Nonmeasurement Processes with Negative Affectivity and Employee Attitudes," *Journal of Applied Psychology*, Vol. 81, No. 1, 1996, pp. 88–101.

16. Kathleen Sutcliffe, "What Executives Notice: Accurate Perceptions in Top Management Teams," *Academy of Management Journal*, Vol. 37, No. 5, 1994, pp. 1360–1378.

17. See H. H. Kelley, *Attribution in Social Interaction* (Morristown, N.J.: General Learning Press, 1971), for a classic treatment of attribution.

18. For a recent overview of the stress literature, see Frank Landy, James Campbell Quick, and Stanislav Kasl, "Work, Stress, and Well-Being," *International Journal of Stress Management*, Vol. 1, No. 1, 1994, pp. 33–73.

19. Hans Selye, *The Stress of Life* (New York: McGraw-Hill, 1976).

20. M. Friedman and R. H. Rosenman, *Type A Behavior and Your Heart* (New York: Alfred A. Knopf, 1974).

21. "Work & Family," *Business Week*, June 28, 1993, pp. 80–88.

22. "Breaking Point," *Newsweek*, March 6, 1995, pp. 56–62.

23. Richard DeFrank and John Ivancevich, "Stress on the Job: An Executive Update," *Academy of Management Executive*, Vol. 12, No. 3, 1998, pp. 55–66. See also John M. Kelly, "Get a Grip on Stress," *HRMagazine*, February 1997, pp. 51–58.

24. See Richard W. Woodman, John E. Sawyer, and Ricky W. Griffin, "Toward a Theory of Organizational Creativity," *Academy of Management Review*, April 1993, pp. 293–321.

25. Filiz Tabak, "Employee Creative Performance: What Makes It Happen?" *Academy of Management Executive*, Vol. 11, No. 1, 1997, pp. 119–122.

26. See Dennis W. Organ, "Personality and Organizational Citizenship Behavior," *Journal of Management*, Vol. 20, No.2, 1994, pp. 465–478, for recent findings regarding this behavior.

27. Mary Konovsky and S. Douglas Pugh, "Citizenship Behavior and Social Exchange," *Academy of Management Journal*, Vol. 37, No. 3, 1994, pp. 656–669 and Philip M. Podsakoff, Michael Ahearne, and Scott B. MacKenzie, "Organizational Citizenship Behavior and the Quantity and Quality of Work Group Performance," *Journal of Applied Psychology*, Vol. 82, No. 2, pp. 262–270.

10

Motivating Employee Performance

OBJECTIVES

After studying this chapter, you should be able to:

■ Characterize the nature of motivation, including its importance and basic historical perspectives.

■ Identify and describe the major content perspectives on motivation.

■ Identify and describe the major process perspectives on motivation.

■ Describe reinforcement perspectives on motivation.

■ Identify and describe popular motivational strategies.

■ Describe the role of organizational reward systems in motivation.

Changing the work-related needs, motives, and values of an individual in an organization is, on its own merits, a daunting challenge. Consider, then, the difficulties inherent in trying to change the needs, motives, and values of an entire population. This is exactly the task being confronted by businesses in Saudi Arabia. For decades Saudi Arabia relied heavily on so-called guest workers to perform most of its menial and service-oriented jobs. People from Pakistan, Egypt, and the Philippines, for example, found it easy to gain access to Saudi Arabia and to find steady work performing jobs that were unattractive to locals. And companies in Saudi Arabia took advantage of this situation by routinely hiring these guest workers for less attractive jobs and paying them relatively low wages. Most guest workers found jobs in restaurants, as security guards, as custodians and maintenance people, and as package couriers.

Recently, however, the government of Saudi Arabia has had to change its liberal guest worker policy. For one thing, a huge baby boom of Saudis is now reaching employment age, and there aren't enough jobs to go around. For another, the government, a large employer itself, is in the midst of downsizing and has fewer jobs to offer citizens. Officials are now taking a much harder stance regarding guest workers. For example, few new guest workers are being admitted. And as current workers' visas expire, they are not being renewed, forcing those workers to leave the country. One new law bans foreign workers from owning cars. In some cities in Saudi Arabia, a retail store can be closed down automatically if someone other than a Saudi national is working behind the counter. And the government has ordered all companies to increase the native workforce 5 percent each year.

A problem, however, arises from the prevailing work ethic reflected by the motivational needs of Saudi workers. Because most of them have grown up in a privileged setting and have had autonomy over where and when they worked, they have trouble adjusting to more regimented and routine work situations. For example, a typical Saudi trying to cope with a new job situation has difficulty understanding why he can't come to work at 9:00 instead of 8:00 and make up the time by simply working an hour longer in the evening. Although some companies are making progress, others still face major challenges. For example, McDonald's is having trouble attracting enough qualified Saudis to hold management positions in its restaurants because most Saudis consider all restaurant work demeaning.

And even though many workers are trying, they still have a difficult time adjusting to a traditional work environment. For example, when beginning higher-level business dealings in Saudi Arabia, it is typical to spend a considerable amount of time exchanging information and asking questions about one another's families. Many young Saudis who are now working in lower-level positions still adhere to this practice and may trade pleasantries with one another before getting down to business. Saudi workers are also prone to showing unfailing hospitality to visitors. Although this approach is desirable in some situations, in others it can be quite dysfunctional. For example, some Saudi workers have been known to walk off their job at a busy airline counter to have tea with a friend who has strolled up—Saudis consider it rude to not be sociable with visitors, regardless of the circumstance![1]

"If I'm supposed to be here at 8 and I come in at 9, why can't I stay until 3:30 instead of 2:30?"

Khalid Al Sharif, Saudi worker fired for coming to work late

ike employees throughout the world, workers in Saudi Arabia are motivated by fundamental needs, motives, and values. But as society changes, these workers are also having to change. These dynamics—the needs of the employees and how organizations can and cannot satisfy them—are fundamental concepts in employee motivation. Virtually any organization is capable of having a motivated workforce. The trick is figuring out how to create a system in which employees can receive rewards that they genuinely want by performing in ways that fit the organization's goals and objectives.

In most settings, people can choose how hard they work and how much effort they expend. Thus, managers need to understand how and why employees make different choices regarding their own performance. The key ingredient behind this choice is motivation, the subject of this chapter. We first examine the nature of employee motivation and then explore the major perspectives on motivation. Newly emerging approaches are then discussed. We conclude with a description of rewards and their role in motivation.

The Nature of Motivation

motivation The set of forces that cause people to behave in certain ways

Motivation is the set of forces that cause people to behave in certain ways.[2] On any given day, an employee may choose to work as hard as possible at a job, to work just hard enough to avoid a reprimand, or to do as little as possible. The goal for the manager is to maximize the likelihood of the first behavior and minimize the likelihood of the last one. This goal becomes all the more significant when we understand the importance of motivation in the workplace.

People can be motivated by a wide array of factors, some of them obvious (such as money or prestige), but others more subtle. For example, Scott Coleman is an air-traffic controller and an amateur pilot. He is one of more than eight hundred volunteer pilots across the United States who donate their time, planes, and fuel to transport patients to hospitals. Coleman is shown here preparing to take young Erika Carlson and her mother to a hospital in Boston where Erika will undergo a week of medical tests and treatment. Coleman is motivated simply by his desire to help others.

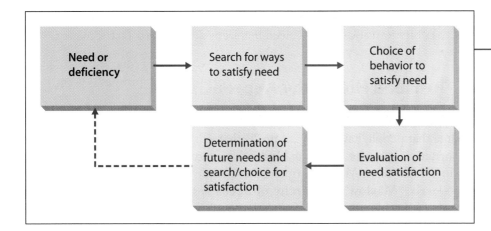

FIGURE 10.1
The Motivation Framework

The motivation process progresses through a series of discrete steps. Content, process, and reinforcement perspectives on motivation address different parts of this process.

Individual performance is generally determined by three factors: motivation (the desire to do the job), ability (the capability to do the job), and the work environment (the resources needed to do the job). If an employee lacks ability, the manager can provide training or replace the worker. If resources are a problem, the manager can correct it. But if motivation is the problem, the task for the manager is more challenging. Individual behavior is a complex phenomenon, and the manager may be hard-pressed to figure out the precise nature of the problem and how to solve it. Thus, motivation is important because of its significance as a determinant of performance and because of its intangible character.

The motivation framework in Figure 10.1 is a good starting point for understanding how motivated behavior occurs. The motivation process begins with a need deficiency. For example, when a worker feels that she is underpaid, she experiences a need for more income. In response, the worker searches for ways to satisfy the need, such as working harder to try to earn a raise or seeking a new job. Next, she chooses an option to pursue. After carrying out the chosen option—working harder and putting in more hours for a reasonable period of time, for example—she then evaluates her success. If her hard work resulted in a pay raise, she probably feels good about things and will continue to work hard. But if no raise has been provided, she is likely to try another option.

Content Perspectives on Motivation

Content perspectives on motivation deal with the first part of the motivation process—needs and need deficiencies. More specially, **content perspectives** address the question: "What factors in the workplace motivate people?" Labor leaders often argue that workers can be motivated by more pay, shorter working hours, and improved working conditions. Meanwhile, some experts suggest that motivation can be enhanced by providing employees with more autonomy and greater responsibility. Both of these views represent content views of motivation. The former asserts that motivation is a function of pay, working hours, and working conditions; the latter suggests that autonomy and

content perspectives Approaches to motivation that try to answer the question: "What factor or factors motivate people?"

Maslow's hierarchy of needs
Suggests that people must satisfy five groups of needs in order—physiological, security, belongingness, esteem, and self-actualization

FIGURE 10.2
Maslow's Hierarchy of Needs

Maslow's hierarchy suggests that human needs can be classified into five categories and that these categories can be arranged in a hierarchy of importance. A manager should understand that an employee may not be satisfied with only a salary and benefits; he or she may also need challenging job opportunities to experience self-growth and satisfaction.

Source: Adapted from Abraham H. Maslow, "A Theory of Human Motivation," *Psychological Review,* Vol. 50, 1943, pp. 370–396.

responsibility are the causes of motivation. Two widely known content perspectives on motivation are the need hierarchy and the two-factor theory.

■ The Need Hierarchy Approach

Many theorists have advanced the need hierarchy approach. Need hierarchies assume that people have different needs that can be arranged in a hierarchy of importance. The best known is Maslow's hierarchy of needs. Pioneering psychologist Abraham Maslow argued that people are motivated to satisfy five need levels.[3] **Maslow's hierarchy of needs** is shown in Figure 10.2. At the bottom of the hierarchy are *physiological needs*—things like food, sex, and air that represent basic issues of survival and biological function. In organizations, these needs are generally satisfied by adequate wages and the work environment itself, which provides restrooms, adequate lighting, comfortable temperatures, and ventilation.

Next are *security needs* for a secure physical and emotional environment. Examples include the desire for housing and clothing and the need to be free from worry about money and job security. These needs can be satisfied in the workplace by job continuity (no layoffs), a grievance system (to protect against arbitrary supervisory actions), and an adequate insurance and retirement benefit package (for security against illness and provision of income in later life). Even today, however, depressed industries and economic decline can put people out of work and restore the primacy of security needs.

Belongingness needs relate to social processes. They include the need for love and affection and the need to be accepted by one's peers. These needs are satisfied for most people by family and community relationships outside of work and friendships on the job. A manager can help satisfy these needs by allowing social interaction and by making employees feel like part of a team or work group.

Esteem needs actually comprise two different sets of needs: the need for a positive self-image and self-respect and the need for recognition and respect from others. A manager can help address these needs by providing a variety of extrinsic symbols of accomplishment such as job titles, nice offices, and similar rewards as appropriate. At a more intrinsic level, the manager can provide challenging job assignments and opportunities for the employee to feel a sense of accomplishment.

At the top of the hierarchy are *self-actualization needs*. These involve realizing one's potential

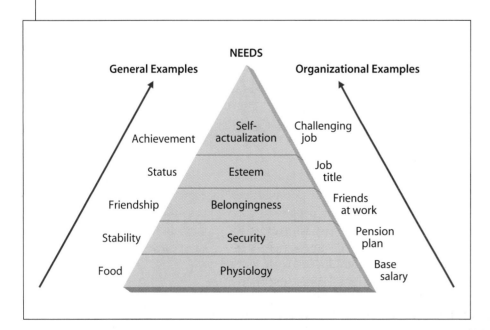

NEEDS

General Examples — Organizational Examples

General Examples	Needs	Organizational Examples
Achievement	Self-actualization	Challenging job
Status	Esteem	Job title
Friendship	Belongingness	Friends at work
Stability	Security	Pension plan
Food	Physiology	Base salary

for continued growth and individual development. The self-actualization needs are perhaps the most difficult for a manager to address. In fact, it can be argued that these needs must be met entirely from within the individual. But a manager can help by promoting a culture wherein self-actualization is possible. For instance, a manager could give employees a chance to participate in making decisions about their work and the opportunity to learn new things.

Maslow suggests that the five need categories constitute a hierarchy. An individual is motivated first and foremost to satisfy physiological needs. As long as they remain unsatisfied, the individual is motivated only to fulfill them. When satisfaction of physiological needs is achieved, they cease to act as primary motivational factors and the individual moves "up" the hierarchy and becomes concerned with security needs. This process continues until the individual reaches the self-actualization level. Maslow's concept of the need hierarchy has a certain intuitive logic and has been accepted by many managers. But research has revealed certain shortcomings and defects in the theory. Some research has found that five levels of need are not always present and that the order of the levels is not always the same as postulated by Maslow.[4] In addition, people from different cultures are likely to have different need categories and hierarchies.

▮ The Two-Factor Theory

Another popular content perspective on motivation is the **two-factor theory**.[5] Frederick Herzberg developed his theory by interviewing two hundred accountants and engineers. He asked them to recall occasions when they had been satisfied and motivated and occasions when they had been dissatisfied and unmotivated. Surprisingly, he found that different sets of factors were associated with satisfaction and with dissatisfaction—that is, a person might identify "low pay" as causing dissatisfaction, but would not necessarily mention "high pay" as a cause of satisfaction. Instead, different factors—such as recognition or accomplishment—were cited as causing satisfaction and motivation.

two-factor theory of motivation
Suggests that people's satisfaction and dissatisfaction are influenced by two independent sets of factors— motivation factors and hygiene factors

This finding led Herzberg to conclude that the traditional view of job satisfaction was incomplete. That view assumed that satisfaction and dissatisfaction are at opposite ends of a single continuum. People might be satisfied, dissatisfied, or somewhere in between. But Herzberg's interviews had identified two different dimensions altogether: one ranging from satisfaction to no satisfaction and the other ranging from dissatisfaction to no dissatisfaction. This perspective, along with several examples of factors that affect each continuum, is shown in Figure 10.3. Note that the factors influencing the satisfaction continuum— called motivation factors—are related specifically to the work content. The factors presumed to cause dissatisfaction—called hygiene factors—are related to the work environment.

Based on these findings, Herzberg argues that the process of motivating employees comprises two stages. First, managers must ensure that the hygiene factors are not deficient. Pay and security must be appropriate, working conditions must be safe, technical supervision must be acceptable, and so on. By providing hygiene factors at an appropriate level, managers do not stimulate motivation but merely ensure that employees are "not dissatisfied."

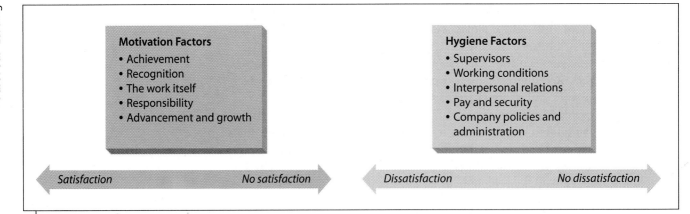

Motivation Factors
- Achievement
- Recognition
- The work itself
- Responsibility
- Advancement and growth

Satisfaction — No satisfaction

Hygiene Factors
- Supervisors
- Working conditions
- Interpersonal relations
- Pay and security
- Company policies and administration

Dissatisfaction — No dissatisfaction

FIGURE 10.3
The Two-Factor Theory of Motivation

The two-factor theory suggests that job satisfaction has two dimensions. A manager who tries to motivate an employee using only hygiene factors such as pay and good working conditions will likely not succeed. To motivate employees and produce a high level of satisfaction, managers must also offer factors such as responsibility and the opportunity for advancement (motivation factors).

need for achievement The desire to accomplish a goal or task more effectively than in the past

need for affiliation The desire for human companionship and acceptance

Employees whom managers attempt to "satisfy" through hygiene factors alone will usually do just enough to get by. Thus, managers should proceed to stage two—giving employees the opportunity to experience motivation factors such as achievement and recognition. The result is predicted to be a high level of satisfaction and motivation. Herzberg also goes a step further than most theorists and describes exactly how to use the two-factor theory in the workplace. Specifically, he recommends job enrichment, as discussed in Chapter 6. He argues that jobs should be redesigned to provide higher levels of the motivation factors.

Although widely accepted by many managers, Herzberg's two-factor theory is not without its critics. One criticism is that the findings in Herzberg's initial interviews are subject to different explanations. Another charge is that his sample was not representative of the general population and that subsequent research often failed to uphold the theory.[6] At the present time, researchers in the field do not hold Herzberg's theory in high esteem. The theory has had a major impact on managers, however, and has played a key role in increasing their awareness of motivation and its importance in the workplace.

■ Individual Human Needs

In addition to these theories, research has also focused on specific individual human needs that are important in organizations. The three most important individual needs are achievement, affiliation, and power.[7]

The **need for achievement**, the best known of the three, is the desire to accomplish a goal or task more effectively than in the past. People with a high need for achievement have a desire to assume personal responsibility, a tendency to set moderately difficult goals, a desire for specific and immediate feedback, and a preoccupation with their task. David C. McClelland, the psychologist who first identified this need, argues that only about 10 percent of the U.S. population has a high need for achievement. In contrast, almost 25 percent of the workers in Japan have a high need for achievement.

The **need for affiliation** is less well understood. Like Maslow's belongingness need, the need for affiliation is a desire for human companionship and acceptance. People with a strong need for affiliation are likely to prefer (and perform better in) a job that entails a lot of social interaction and offers opportunities to make friends. The need for power has also received considerable attention as an important ingredient in managerial success.

The **need for power** is the desire to be influential in a group and to control one's environment. Research has shown that people with a strong need for power are likely to be superior performers, have good attendance records, and occupy supervisory positions. One study found that managers as a group tend to have a stronger power motive than the general population and that successful managers tend to have stronger power motives than less successful managers.[8]

need for power The desire to be influential in a group and to control one's environment

Process Perspectives on Motivation

Process perspectives are concerned with how motivation occurs. Rather than attempting to identify motivational stimuli, **process perspectives** focus on why people choose certain behavioral options to satisfy their needs and how they evaluate their satisfaction after they have attained these goals. Three useful process perspectives on motivation are the expectancy, equity, and goal-setting theories.

process perspectives Approaches to motivation that focus on why people choose certain behavioral options to fulfill their needs and how they evaluate their satisfaction after they have attained these goals

■ Expectancy Theory

Expectancy theory suggests that motivation depends on two things—how much we want something and how likely we think we are to get it.[9] Assume that you are approaching graduation and looking for a job. You see in the want ads that Exxon is seeking a new vice president with a starting salary of $350,000 per year. Even though you might want the job, you will not apply because you realize that you have little chance of getting it. The next ad you see is for someone to scrape bubble gum from underneath theater seats for $5.15 an hour. Even though you could probably get this job, you do not apply because you do not want it. Then you see an ad for a management trainee for a big company with a starting salary of $30,000. You will probably apply for this job because you want it and because you think you have a reasonable chance of getting it.

expectancy theory Suggests that motivation depends on two things—how much we want something and how likely we think we are to get it

Expectancy theory rests on four basic assumptions. First, it assumes that behavior is determined by a combination of forces in the individual and in the environment. Second, it assumes that people make decisions about their own behavior in organizations. Third, it assumes that different people have different types of needs, desires, and goals. Fourth, it assumes that people make choices from among alternative plans of behavior based on their perceptions of the extent to which a given behavior will lead to desired outcomes.

Figure 10.4 summarizes the basic expectancy model. The model suggests that motivation leads to effort and that effort, combined with employee ability and environmental factors, results in performance. Performance, in turn, leads to various outcomes, each of which has an associated value called its valence. The most important parts of the expectancy model cannot be shown in the

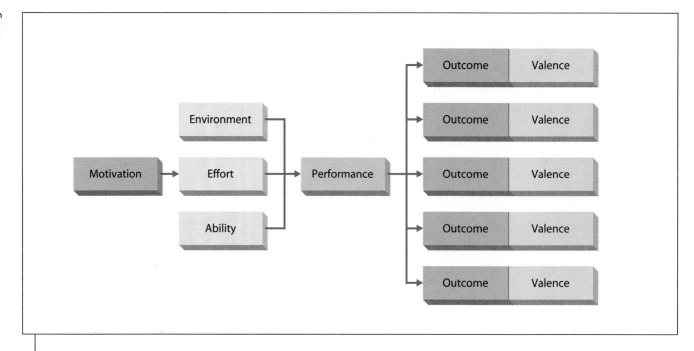

FIGURE 10.4
The Expectancy Model of Motivation

The expectancy model of motivation is a complex but relatively accurate portrayal of how motivation occurs. According to this model, a manager must understand what employees want (such as pay, promotions, or status) to begin to motivate them.

effort-to-performance expectancy
The individual's perception of the probability that his or her effort will lead to high performance

performance-to-outcome expectancy The individual's perception that her or his performance will lead to a specific outcome

outcomes Consequences of behaviors in an organizational setting, usually rewards

valence An index of how much an individual desires a particular outcome; it is the attractiveness of the outcome to the individual

figure, however. These are the individual's expectation that effort will lead to high performance, that performance will lead to outcomes, and that each outcome will have some kind of value.

Effort-to-Performance Expectancy The **effort-to-performance expectancy** is the individual's perception of the probability that effort will lead to high performance. When the individual believes that effort will lead directly to high performance, expectancy will be quite strong (close to 1.00). When the individual believes that effort and performance are unrelated, the effort-to-performance expectancy is very weak (close to 0). The belief that effort is somewhat but not strongly related to performance carries with it a moderate expectancy (somewhere between 0 and 1).

Performance-to-Outcome Expectancy The **performance-to-outcome expectancy** is the individual's perception that performance will lead to a specific outcome. For example, if the individual believes that high performance will result in a pay raise, the performance-to-outcome expectancy is high (approaching 1.00). The individual who believes that high performance may lead to a pay raise has a moderate expectancy (between 1.00 and 0). The individual who believes that performance has no relationship with rewards has a low performance-to-outcome expectancy (close to 0).

Outcomes and Valences Expectancy theory recognizes that an individual's behavior results in a variety of **outcomes**, or consequences, in an organizational setting. A high performer, for example, may get bigger pay raises, faster promotions, and more praise from the boss. On the other hand, she may also be subject to more stress and incur resentment from coworkers. Each of these outcomes also has an associated value, or **valence**—an index of how much an individual values a particular outcome. If the individual wants the outcome, its valence is positive; if the individual does not want the outcome, its valence is negative; and if the individual is indifferent to the outcome, its valence is zero.

This part of expectancy theory goes beyond the content perspectives on motivation. Different people have different needs, and they will try to satisfy these needs in different ways. For an employee who has a high need for achievement and a low need for affiliation, the pay raise and promotions cited above as outcomes of high performance might have positive valences, the praise and resentment zero valences, and the stress a negative valence. For a different employee with a low need for achievement and a high need for affiliation, the pay raise, promotions, and praise might all have positive valences, whereas both resentment and stress could have negative valences.

For motivated behavior to occur, three conditions must be met. First, the effort-to-performance must be greater than zero (the individual must believe that if effort is expended, high performance will result). The performance-to-outcome expectancy must also be greater than zero (the individual must believe that if high performance is achieved, certain outcomes will follow). And the sum of the valences for the outcomes must be greater than zero. (One or more outcomes may have negative valences if they are more than offset by the positive valences of other outcomes. For example, the attractiveness of a pay raise, a promotion, and praise from the boss may outweigh the unattractiveness of more stress and resentment from coworkers.) Expectancy theory suggests that when these conditions are met, the individual is motivated to expend effort.

Starbucks credits its unique stock ownership program with maintaining a dedicated and motivated workforce. Based on the fundamental concepts of expectancy theory, Starbucks employees earn stock as a function of their seniority and performance. Thus, their hard work helps them earn shares of ownership in the company.[10]

The Porter-Lawler Extension   An interesting extension of expectancy theory has been proposed by Porter and Lawler.[11] Recall from Chapter 1 that the human relationists assumed that employee satisfaction causes good performance. We also noted that research has not supported such a relationship. Porter and Lawler suggest that there may indeed be a relationship between satisfaction and performance but that it goes in the opposite direction—that is, high performance may lead to high satisfaction. Figure 10.5 summarizes Porter and Lawler's logic. Performance results in rewards for an individual. Some of these are extrinsic (such as pay and promotions); others are intrinsic (such as self-esteem and accomplishment). The individual evaluates the equity,

FIGURE 10.5
The Porter-Lawler Extension of Expectancy Theory

The Porter-Lawler extension of expectancy theory suggests that if performance results in equitable rewards, people will be more satisfied. Thus, performance can lead to satisfaction. Managers must therefore be sure that any system of motivation includes rewards that are fair, or equitable, for all.

Source: Edward E. Lawler III and Lyman W. Porter, "The Effect of Performance on Job Satisfaction," *Industrial Relations,* October 1967, p. 23. Permission granted courtesy of Blackwell Publishers, Inc.

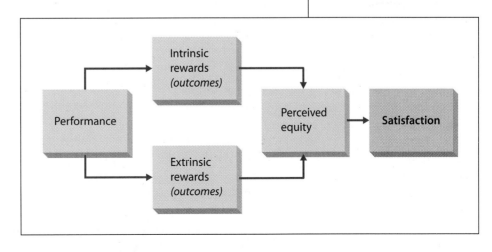

or fairness, of the rewards relative to the effort expended and the level of performance attained. If the rewards are perceived to be equitable, the individual is satisfied.

■ Equity Theory

equity theory Suggests that people are motivated to seek social equity in the rewards they receive for performance

After needs have stimulated the motivation process and the individual has chosen an action that is expected to satisfy those needs, the individual assesses the fairness, or equity, of the resultant outcome. **Equity theory** contends that people are motivated to seek social equity in the rewards they receive for performance.[12] Equity is an individual's belief that the treatment he or she is receiving is fair relative to the treatment received by others. According to equity theory, outcomes from a job include pay, recognition, promotions, social relationships, and intrinsic rewards. To get these rewards, the individual makes inputs to the job, such as time, experience, effort, education, and loyalty. The theory suggests that people view their outcomes and inputs as a ratio and then compare it to the ratio of someone else. This other "person" may be someone in the work group or some sort of group average or composite. The process of comparison looks like this:

$$\frac{\text{outcomes (self)}}{\text{inputs (self)}} = \frac{\text{outcomes (other)}}{\text{inputs (other)}}$$

Both the formulation of the ratios and comparisons between them are very subjective and are based on individual perceptions. As a result of comparisons, three conditions may occur: the individual may feel equitably rewarded, under-rewarded, or over-rewarded. A feeling of equity will result when the two ratios are equal. However, this outcome may occur even though the other person's outcomes are greater than the individual's own outcomes—provided that the other's inputs are also proportionately greater. Suppose that Mark has a high school education and earns $25,000. He may still feel equitably treated relative to Susan, who earns $30,000, because she has a college degree.

People who feel under-rewarded try to reduce the inequity. Such an individual might decrease her inputs by exerting less effort, increase her outcomes by asking for a raise, distort the original ratios by rationalizing, try to get the other person to change her or his outcomes or inputs, leave the situation, or change the object of comparison. An individual may also feel over-rewarded relative to another person. This situation is not likely to be terribly disturbing to most people, but research suggests that some people who experience inequity under these conditions are somewhat motivated to reduce it. Under such a circumstance, the person might increase his inputs by exerting more effort, reduce his outcomes by producing fewer units (if paid on a per unit basis), distort the original ratios by rationalizing, or try to reduce the inputs or increase the outcomes of the other person.

■ Goal-Setting Theory

The goal-setting theory of motivation assumes that behavior is a result of conscious goals and intentions.[13] Therefore, by setting goals for people in the organization, a manager should be able to influence their behavior. Given this premise, the challenge is to develop a thorough understanding of the processes by which people set goals and then work to reach them. In the original version of goal-setting theory, two specific goal characteristics—goal difficulty and goal specificity—were expected to shape performance.

Goal Difficulty *Goal difficulty* is the extent to which a goal is challenging and requires effort. If people work to achieve goals, it is reasonable to assume they will work harder to achieve more difficult goals. But a goal must not be so difficult that it is unattainable. If a new manager asks her sales force to increase sales by 300 percent, the group may become disillusioned. A more realistic but still difficult goal—perhaps a 30 percent increase—would be a better incentive. A substantial body of research supports the importance of goal difficulty. In one study, for example, managers at Weyerhaeuser set difficult goals for truck drivers hauling loads of timber from cutting sites to wood yards. Over a nine-month period, the drivers increased the quantity of wood they delivered by an amount that would have required $250,000 worth of new trucks at the previous per truck average load.[14]

Goal Specificity *Goal specificity* is the clarity and precision of the goal. A goal of "increasing productivity" is not very specific; a goal of "increasing productivity by 3 percent in the next six months" is quite specific. Some goals, such as those involving costs, output, profitability, and growth are readily amenable to specificity. Other goals, however, such as improving employee job satisfaction, morale, company image and reputation, ethics, and socially responsible behavior may be much harder to state in specific terms. Like difficulty, specificity is consistently related to performance. The study of timber truck drivers mentioned above, for example, also examined goal specificity. The initial loads the truck drivers were carrying were found to be 60 percent of the maximum weight each truck could haul. The managers set a new goal for drivers of 94 percent, which the drivers were soon able to reach. Thus, the goal was both specific and difficult.

Because the theory attracted so much widespread interest and research support from researchers and managers alike, an expanded model of the goal-setting process was eventually proposed. The expanded model, shown in Figure 10.6, attempts to capture more fully the complexities of goal setting in organizations.

FIGURE 10.6
The Expanded Goal-Setting Theory of Motivation

One of the most important emerging theories of motivation is goal-setting theory. This theory suggests that goal difficulty, specificity, acceptance, and commitment combine to determine an individual's goal-directed effort. This effort, when complemented by appropriate organizational support and individual abilities and traits, results in performance. Finally, performance is seen as leading to intrinsic and extrinsic rewards, which, in turn, result in employee satisfaction.

Source: Adapted from "A Motivational Technique That Works" by Gary P. Latham and Edwin A. Locke. Reprinted from *Organizational Dynamics*, Autumn 1979. Copyright © 1979 American Management Association International. Reprinted by permission of American Management Association International, New York, NY. All rights reserved. (http://www.amanet.org)

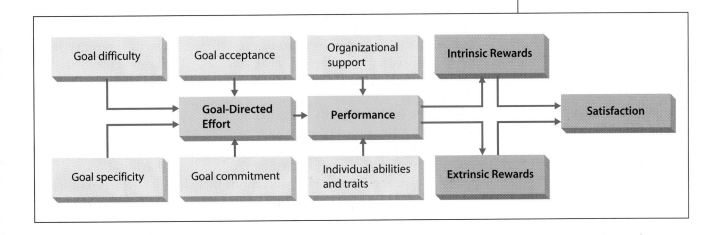

The expanded theory argues that goal-directed effort is a function of four goal attributes: difficulty and specificity, as already discussed, and acceptance and commitment. *Goal acceptance* is the extent to which a person accepts a goal as his or her own. *Goal commitment* is the extent to which she or he is personally interested in reaching the goal. The manager who vows to take whatever steps are necessary to cut costs by 10 percent has made a commitment to achieve the goal. Factors that can foster goal acceptance and commitment include participating in the goal-setting process, making goals challenging but realistic, and believing that goal achievement will lead to valued rewards.

The interaction of goal-directed effort, organizational support, and individual abilities and traits determine actual performance. Organizational support is whatever the organization does to help or hinder performance. Positive support might mean making available adequate personnel and a sufficient supply of raw materials; negative support might mean failing to fix damaged equipment. Individual abilities and traits are the skills and other personal characteristics necessary for doing a job. As a result of performance, a person receives various intrinsic and extrinsic rewards, which in turn influence satisfaction. Note that the latter stages of this model are quite similar to the Porter and Lawler expectancy model discussed earlier.

Reinforcement Perspectives on Motivation

A third element of the motivational process addresses why some behaviors are maintained over time and why other behaviors change. As we have seen, content perspectives deal with needs, whereas process perspectives explain why people choose various behaviors to satisfy needs and how they evaluate the equity of the rewards they get for those behaviors. Reinforcement perspectives explain the role of those rewards as they cause behavior to change or remain the same over time. Specifically, **reinforcement theory** argues that behavior that results in rewarding consequences is likely to be repeated, whereas behavior that results in punishing consequences is less likely to be repeated.[15]

reinforcement perspective
Approach to motivation that explains the role of rewards as they cause behavior to change or remain the same over time

■ Kinds of Reinforcement in Organizations

Four basic kinds of reinforcement can result from behavior—positive reinforcement, avoidance, punishment, and extinction.[16] Two kinds of reinforcement strengthen or maintain behavior, whereas the other two weaken or decrease behavior.

positive reinforcement A method of strengthening behavior with rewards or positive outcomes after a desired behavior is performed

Positive reinforcement, one method of strengthening behavior, is a reward or a positive outcome after a desired behavior is performed. When a manager observes an employee doing an especially good job and offers praise, the praise serves to positively reinforce the behavior of good work. Other positive reinforcers in organizations include pay raises, promotions, and awards. Employees who work at General Electric's customer service center receive clothing, sporting goods, and even trips to Disney World as rewards for outstanding performance. The other method of strengthening desired behavior is through **avoidance**. An employee may come to work on time to avoid a reprimand. In this instance, the employee is motivated to perform the behavior of punctuality to avoid an unpleasant consequence that is likely to follow tardiness.

Some managers use **punishment** to weaken undesired behaviors. When an employee is loafing, coming to work late, doing poor work, or interfering with the work of others, the manager might resort to reprimands, discipline, or fines. The logic is that the unpleasant consequence will reduce the likelihood that the employee will choose that particular behavior again. Given the counterproductive side effects of punishment (such as resentment and hostility), it is often advisable to use the other kinds of reinforcement if at all possible. **Extinction** can also be used to weaken behavior, especially behavior that has previously been rewarded. When an employee tells an off-color joke and the boss laughs, the laughter reinforces the behavior and the employee may continue to tell off-color jokes. By simply ignoring this behavior and not reinforcing it, the boss can cause the behavior to subside and eventually become "extinct."

avoidance Used to strengthen behavior by avoiding unpleasant consequences that would result if the behavior were not performed

punishment Used to weaken undesired behaviors by using negative outcomes or unpleasant consequences when the behavior is performed

extinction Used to weaken undesired behaviors by simply ignoring or not reinforcing that behavior

■ Providing Reinforcement in Organizations

Not only is the kind of reinforcement important, but so is when or how often it occurs. Various strategies are possible for providing reinforcement. The **fixed-interval schedule** provides reinforcement at fixed intervals of time, regardless of behavior. A good example of this schedule is the weekly or monthly paycheck. This method provides the least incentive for good work, though, because employees know they will be paid regularly regardless of their effort. A **variable-interval schedule** also uses time as the basis for reinforcement, but the time interval varies from one reinforcement to the next. This schedule is appropriate for praise or other rewards based on visits or inspections. When employees do not know when the boss is going to drop by, they tend to maintain a reasonably high level of effort all the time.

A **fixed-ratio schedule** gives reinforcement after a fixed number of behaviors, regardless of the time that elapses between behaviors. This results in an even higher level of effort. For example, when Sears is recruiting new credit-card customers, salespersons get a small bonus for every fifth application returned from their department. Under this arrangement, motivation will be high because each application gets the person closer to the next bonus. The **variable-ratio schedule**, the most powerful schedule in terms of maintaining desired behaviors, varies the number of behaviors needed for each reinforcement. A supervisor who praises an employee for her second order, the seventh order after that, the ninth after that, then the fifth, and then the third is using a variable-ratio schedule. The employee is motivated to increase the frequency of the desired behavior because each performance increases the probability of receiving a reward. Of course, a variable-ratio schedule is difficult (if not impossible) to use for formal rewards such as pay because it would be too complicated to keep track of who was rewarded when.

fixed-interval schedules Provide reinforcement at fixed intervals of time, such as regular weekly pay checks

variable-interval schedules Provide reinforcement at varying intervals of time, such as occasional visits by the supervisor

fixed-ratio schedules Provide reinforcement after a fixed number of behaviors regardless of the time interval involved, such as a bonus for every fifth sale

variable-ratio schedules Provide reinforcement after varying numbers of behaviors are performed, such as the use of compliments by a supervisor on an irregular basis

behavior modification or **OB Mod**
Method for applying the basic elements of reinforcement theory in an organizational setting

Managers wanting to explicitly use reinforcement theory to motivate their employees generally do so with a technique call **behavior modification**, or **OB Mod**.[17] An OB Mod program starts by specifying behaviors that are to be increased (such as producing more units) or decreased (such as coming to work late). These target behaviors are then tied to specific forms of kinds of reinforcement. Although many organizations (such as Procter & Gamble and Ford) have used OB Mod, the best-known application has been at Emery Air Freight. Management felt that the containers used to consolidate small shipments into fewer, larger shipments were not being packed efficiently. Through a system of self-monitored feedback and rewards, Emery increased container usage from 45 percent to 95 percent and saved more than $3 million during the first three years of the program.[18]

Popular Motivational Strategies

Although these theories provide a solid explanation for motivation, managers must use various techniques and strategies to actually apply them. Among the most popular motivational strategies today are empowerment and participation and alternative forms of work arrangements.

■ Empowerment and Participation

empowerment The process of enabling workers to set their own work goals, make decisions, and solve problems within their sphere of responsibility and authority
participation The process of giving employees a voice in making decisions about their own work

Empowerment and participation represent important methods that managers can use to enhance employee motivation. **Empowerment** is the process of enabling workers to set their own work goals, make decisions, and solve problems within their sphere of responsibility and authority. **Participation** is the process of giving employees a voice in making decisions about their own work. Thus, empowerment is a somewhat broader concept that promotes participation in a wide variety of areas, including but not limited to work itself, work context, and work environment.[19]

The role of participation and empowerment in motivation can be expressed in terms of both the content perspectives and the expectancy theory. Employees who participate in decision making may be more committed to executing decisions properly. Furthermore, the successful process of making a decision, executing it, and then seeing the positive consequences can help satisfy one's need for achievement, provide recognition and responsibility, and enhance self-esteem. Simply being asked to participate in organizational decision making also may enhance an employee's self-esteem. In addition, participation should help clarify expectancies; that is, by participating in decision making, employees may better understand the linkage between their performance and the rewards they want most.

■ New Forms of Working Arrangements

Many organizations today are also experimenting with a variety of alternative work arrangements. These alternative arrangements are generally intended to enhance employee motivation and performance by providing them with greater flexibility in how and when they work. Among the more popular alternative work arrangements are compressed work schedules, flexible work schedules, job sharing, and telecommuting.[20]

Compressed work schedules generally involve working a full forty-hour week in fewer than the traditional five days.[21] One approach involves working ten hours a day for four days, leaving an extra day off. Another alternative is for employees to work slightly less than ten hours a day but to complete the forty hours by lunch time on Friday. And a few firms have tried having employees work twelve hours a day for three days, followed by four days off. One problem with this schedule is that when employees put in too much time in a single day, they tend to get tired and perform at a lower level later in the day.

A schedule that some organizations today are beginning to use is what they call a "nine eighty" schedule. Under this arrangement, an employee works a traditional schedule one week and a compressed schedule the next, getting every other Friday off. That is, employees work eighty hours (the equivalent of two weeks of full-time work) in nine days. By alternating the regular and compressed schedules across half of its workforce, the organization can be fully staffed at all times and still give employees two full days off each month. Shell Oil and Amoco Chemicals currently use this schedule.

Another promising alternative work arrangement is the **flexible work schedule**, sometimes called *flexitime*. Flexitime gives employees more personal control over the times they work. The workday is broken down into two categories, flexible time and core time. All employees must be at their workstations during core time, but they can choose their own schedules during flexible time. Thus, one employee may choose to start work early in the morning and leave in midafternoon; another to start in the late morning and work until late afternoon; and still another to start early in the morning, take a long lunch break, and work until late afternoon. Organizations that have

compressed work schedule Working a full forty-hour week in fewer than the traditional five days

flexible work schedules Allowing employees to select, within broad parameters, the hours they work

Flexible work schedules can be a powerful motivational strategy. Consider, for example, Tina Willford and her employer, First Tennessee Bank. The bank allows Willford to leave work early each day so that she can spend time with her young children. She makes up the time after her children are in bed. First Tennessee considers Willford to be a rising star, and is interested in doing whatever it can to both motivate her and keep her satisfied.

job sharing   When two part-time employees share one full-time job.

telecommuting   Allowing employees to spend part of their time working off-site, usually at home

reward systems   The formal and informal mechanisms by which employee performance is defined, evaluated, and rewarded

used the flexible work schedule method for arranging work include Control Data Corporation, DuPont, Metropolitan Life, Texaco, and some offices within the U.S. government.

Yet another potentially useful alternative work arrangement is job sharing. In **job sharing**, two part-time employees share one full-time job. One person may perform the job from 8:00 A.M. to noon and the other from 1:00 P.M. to 5:00 P.M. Job sharing may be desirable for people who want to work only part-time or when job markets are tight. For its part, the organization can accommodate the preferences of a broader range of employees and may benefit from the talents of more people.

A relatively new approach to alternative work arrangements is **telecommuting**—allowing employees to spend part of their time working off-site, usually at home. By using e-mail, the Internet, and other forms of information technology, many employees can maintain close contact with their organization and still get just as much work done at home as they do at the office. The increased power and sophistication of modern communication technology is making telecommuting easier and easier.

Using Reward Systems to Motivate Performance

Aside from these types of motivational strategies, an organization's reward system is its most basic tool for managing employee motivation. An organizational **reward system** is the formal and informal mechanisms by which employee performance is defined, evaluated, and rewarded.

■ Effects of Organizational Rewards

Organizational rewards can affect attitudes, behaviors, and motivation. Thus, it is important for managers to clearly understand and appreciate their importance.[22]

Effect of Rewards on Attitudes   Although employee attitudes such as satisfaction are not a major determinant of job performance, they are nonetheless important. They contribute to (or discourage) absenteeism, affect turnover, and help establish the culture of the organization. We can draw four major generalizations about employee attitudes and rewards.[23] First, employee satisfaction is influenced by how much is received and how much the individual thinks should be received. Second, employee satisfaction is affected by comparisons with what happens to others. Third, employees often misperceive the rewards of others. When an employee believes that someone else is making more money than that person really makes, the potential for dissatisfaction increases. Fourth, overall job satisfaction is affected by how satisfied employees are with both the extrinsic and the intrinsic rewards they derive from their jobs. Drawing from the content theories and expectancy theory, this conclusion suggests that a variety of needs may cause behavior and that behavior may be channeled toward a variety of goals.

Effect of Rewards on Behaviors An organization's primary purpose in giving rewards is to influence employee behavior. Extrinsic rewards affect employee satisfaction, which, in turn, plays a major role in determining whether an employee will remain on the job or seek a new job. Reward systems also influence patterns of attendance and absenteeism; and, if rewards are based on actual performance, employees tend to work harder to earn those rewards.

Effect of Rewards on Motivation Reward systems are clearly related to the expectancy theory of motivation. The effort-to-performance expectancy is strongly influenced by the performance appraisal that is often a part of the reward system. An employee is likely to put forth extra effort if he or

"I think I should warn you that the flip side of our generous bonus-incentive program is capital punishment."

she knows that performance will be measured, evaluated, and rewarded. The performance-to-outcome expectancy is affected by the extent to which the employee believes that performance will be followed by rewards. Finally, as expectancy theory predicts, each reward or potential reward has a somewhat different value for each individual. One person may want a promotion more than benefits; someone else may want just the opposite.

■ Designing Effective Reward Systems

What are the elements of an effective reward system? Experts agree that they have four major characteristics.[24] First, the reward system must meet the needs of the individual for basic necessities. Next, the rewards should compare favorably with those offered by other organizations. Unfavorable comparisons with people in other settings could result in feelings of inequity. Third, the distribution of rewards within the organization must be equitable. And fourth, the reward system must recognize that different people have different needs and choose different paths to satisfy those needs. Both content theories and expectancy theory contribute to this conclusion. Insofar as possible, a variety of rewards and a variety of methods for achieving them should be available to all employees.

Organizations provide rewards and incentives that can serve as positive reinforcement to desired behavior. Similarly, most also have various forms of punishment that can be used to weaken or eliminate undesired behaviors. Although not as extreme as the humorous example shown here, positive reinforcement and punishment that are clearly linked to desired and undesired behaviors can play a major role in boosting employee performance and organizational effectiveness.

■ New Approaches to Rewarding Employees

Organizational reward systems have traditionally been of two kinds: a fixed hourly or monthly rate or an incentive system. Fixed-rate systems are familiar to most people. Hourly employees are paid a specific wage (based on job demands, experience, or other factors) for each hour they work. Salaried employees receive a fixed sum of money on a weekly or monthly basis. Although some reductions may be made for absences, the amount is usually the same regardless of whether the individual works less than or more than a normal amount of time.[25]

merit system A reward system whereby people get different pay raises at the end of the year depending on their overall job performance

incentive system A reward system whereby people get different pay amounts at each pay period in proportion to what they do

From a motivational perspective, such rewards can be tied more directly to performance through merit pay raises. A **merit system** is one whereby people get different pay raises at the end of the year, depending on their overall job performance.[26] When the organization's performance appraisal system is appropriately designed, merit pay is a good system for maintaining long-term performance. Increasingly, however, organizations are experimenting with various kinds of incentive systems. **Incentive systems** attempt to reward employees in proportion to what they do. A piece-rate pay plan is a good example of an incentive system. In a luggage-manufacturing factory, for example, each worker may be paid fifty cents for each handle and set of locks installed on a piece of luggage. Hence, there is incentive for the employee to work hard: the more units produced, the higher the pay. Four increasingly popular incentive systems are profit sharing, gain sharing, lump-sum bonuses, and pay-for-knowledge.

Profit sharing provides a varying annual bonus to employees based on corporate profits. This system unites workers and management toward the same goal—higher profits. Ford, USX, and Alcoa have profit-sharing plans. Gain sharing is a group-based incentive system in which all group members get bonuses when predetermined performance levels are exceeded. The lump-sum bonus plan gives each employee a one-time cash bonus, rather than a base salary increase. Finally, pay-for-knowledge systems focus on paying the individual rather than the job.

Summary of Key Points

Motivation is the set of forces that cause people to behave in certain ways. Motivation is an important consideration for managers because it, along with ability and environmental factors, determines individual performance.

Content perspectives on motivation are concerned with what factor or factors cause motivation. Popular content theories include Maslow's need hierarchy and Herzberg's two-factor theory. Other important needs are the needs for achievement, affiliation, and power.

Process perspectives on motivation deal with how motivation occurs. Expectancy theory suggests that people are motivated to perform if they believe that their effort will result in high performance, that this performance will lead to rewards, and that the positive aspects of the outcomes outweigh the negative aspects. Equity theory is based on the premise that people are motivated to achieve and maintain social equity. Goal-setting theory helps to put both expectancy and equity theory into operation.

The reinforcement perspective focuses on how motivation is maintained. Its basic assumption is that behavior that results in rewarding consequences is likely to be repeated, whereas behavior resulting in negative consequences is less likely to be repeated. Reinforcement contingencies can be arranged in the form of positive reinforcement, avoidance, punishment, and extinction, and they can be provided on fixed-interval, variable-interval, fixed-ratio, or variable-ratio schedules.

Among the most popular motivational strategies today are empowerment and participation and alternative forms of work arrangements.

Organizational reward systems are the primary mechanisms managers have for managing motivation. Properly designed systems can improve attitudes, motivation, and behaviors. Effective reward systems must provide sufficient rewards on an equitable basis at the individual level. Contemporary reward systems include merit systems and various kinds of incentive systems.

Discussion Questions

Questions for Review

1. Summarize the basic motivation process.

2. What are the differences between the motivation and hygiene factors in the two-factor theory?

3. Compare and contrast content, process, and reinforcement perspectives on motivation.

4. In what ways do empowerment and participation and alternative forms of work arrangements rely on the content, process, and reinforcement perspectives?

5. What are the similarities and differences between the motivational strategies described in this chapter?

Questions for Analysis

1. Compare and contrast the different content theories. Can you think of any ways in which the theories are contradictory?

2. Expectancy theory seems to make a great deal of sense, but it is complicated. Some people argue that its complexity reduces its value to practicing managers. Do you agree or disagree?

3. Under what circumstances might a famous athlete earning $3 million a year feel underpaid?

4. Offer examples other than those from this chapter to illustrate positive reinforcement, avoidance, punishment, and extinction.

5. Think of examples of when you have been motivated by the various theories in this chapter.

EXERCISE OVERVIEW

Interpersonal skills—the ability to understand and motivate individuals and groups—are especially critical when managers attempt to deal with issues associated with equity and justice in the workplace. This exercise provides you with insights into how these skills may be used.

Building Effective
Interpersonal Skills

EXERCISE BACKGROUND

You are the manager of a group of professional employees in the electronics industry. One of your employees, David Brown, has asked to meet with you. You think you know what David wants to discuss, and you are unsure as to how to proceed.

You hired David about ten years ago. During his time in your group, he has been a solid, but not outstanding, employee. His performance, for example, has been satisfactory in every respect, but seldom outstanding. As a result, he has consistently received average performance evaluations, pay increases, and so forth. Indeed, he actually makes somewhat less today than do a couple of people with less tenure in the group but with stronger performance records.

The company has just announced an opening for a team leader position in your group, and you know that David wants the job. He believes that he has earned the opportunity to have the job on the basis of his consistent efforts. Unfortunately, you see things a bit differently. You really want to appoint another individual, Becky Thomas, to the job. Becky has worked for the firm for only six years but is your top performer. You want to reward her performance and think that she will do an excellent job. On the other hand, you do not want to lose David because he is a solid member of the group.

EXERCISE TASK

Using the information above, respond to the following:

1. Using equity theory as a framework, how are David and Becky likely to see the situation?

2. Outline a conversation with David in which you will convey your decision to him.

3. What advice might you offer Becky, in her new job, about interacting with David?

4. What other rewards might you offer David to keep him motivated?

Building Effective Decision-Making Skills

EXERCISE OVERVIEW

Decision-making skills include the manager's ability to correctly recognize and define situations and to select courses of action. This exercise allows you to use expectancy theory as part of a hypothetical decision-making situation.

EXERCISE BACKGROUND

Assume that you are about to graduate from college and have received three job offers, as summarized below:

1. Offer number one is an entry-level position in a large company. The salary offer is for $22,000, and you will begin work in a very attractive location. However, you also see promotion prospects as being relatively limited, and you know that you are likely to have to move frequently.

2. Offer number two is a position with a new start-up company. The salary offer is $19,000. You know that you will have to work especially long hours. If the company survives for a year, however, opportunities there are unlimited. You may need to move occasionally, but not for a few years.

3. Offer number three is a position in a business owned by your family. The salary is $25,000, and you start as a middle manager. You know that you can control your own transfers, but you also know that some people in the company may resent you because of your family ties.

EXERCISE TASK

Using the three job offers as a framework, do the following:

1. Use expectancy theory as a framework to assess your own personal valence for each outcome in selecting a job.

2. Evaluate the three jobs in terms of their outcomes and associated valences.

3. Decide which of the three jobs you would select.

4. Determine what other outcomes will be important to you in selecting a job.

EXERCISE OVERVIEW

Conceptual skills refer to the manager's ability to think in the abstract. This exercise enables you to develop your conceptual skills by relating theory to reality in a personal way.

EXERCISE BACKGROUND

First, you will develop a list of things you want from life. Then you will categorize them according to one of the theories in the chapter. Next, you will discuss your results with a small group of classmates.

EXERCISE TASK

1. Prepare a list of approximately fifteen things you want from life. These can be very specific (such as a new car) or very general (such as a feeling of accomplishment in school). Try to include some things you want right now and other things you want later in life. Next, choose the one motivational theory discussed in this chapter that best fits your set of needs. Classify each item from your "wish list" in terms of the need or needs it might satisfy.

2. Your instructor will then divide the class into groups of three. Spend a few minutes in the group discussing each person's list and its classification according to needs.

3. After the small-group discussions, your instructor will reconvene the entire class. Discussion should center on the extent to which each theory can serve as a useful framework for classifying individual needs. Students who found that their needs could be neatly categorized or those who found little correlation between their needs and the theories are especially encouraged to share their results.

4. As a result of this exercise, do you now place more or less trust in the need theories as viable management tools?

5. Could a manager use some form of this exercise in an organizational setting to enhance employee motivation?

Building Effective
Conceptual Skills

You Make the Call

At first, Mark Spenser was at a loss. Michael Chou, his assistant landscape designer, had just given his two-week notice. Mark hated to see Michael leave because he was a good, hard-working employee. But even more troubling was that Michael was the third assistant designer to leave in the last two years. During their conversation, Michael had indicated some vague things about wanting to do something different and try some new things in his life. But he had offered nothing concrete in terms of problems or things that were wrong with his job.

Finally, Mark began to understand. It was perhaps a problem of motivation. Perhaps the job of assistant landscape designer wasn't providing the right kinds of rewards. The nursery employees, for example, had a clear incentive system. Each nursery employee received a direct sales commission on her or his monthly sales figures, and all nursery employees shared in another end-of-year bonus that was tied to total nursery sales.

The lawn-care teams also had an incentive system, albeit a different type. Each morning the teams were given a list of jobs to complete that day. Each day's assignments could be finished in about eight hours, with a one-hour lunch break figured in. If the day's work was not finished, those jobs were either delayed until the next day or done on an overtime basis. But if the crew finished its jobs early, its members were still paid for eight hours of time and were free to go home early.

The job of assistant landscape designer, however, had no incentives. Mark assumed that designers such as himself were motivated more by intrinsic satisfaction than by money. As a result, he paid his assistant a straight monthly salary. But Mark began to realize that, although perhaps his assumptions were partially true, he was guilty of not providing enough sources of intrinsic satisfaction for the individuals he hired. It slowly began to dawn on him that, although he believed them capable of greater responsibility, he treated them like his hourly workers. In particular, he assigned their jobs, carefully told them how to do their work, and often looked over their shoulders.

He suddenly recognized that he would certainly be frustrated and disappointed in his work if someone else limited him in the same way that he limited his own assistants. He resolved, therefore, to give his next assistant more responsibility. For example, he would let his new assistant do some simple jobs without any supervision at all. And if this approach worked out, Mark would let the assistant designer have more and more authority to design projects independently.

DISCUSSION QUESTIONS

1. Which motivation theories does this situation illustrate?

2. Evaluate the incentives that SLS uses in its retail nursery and lawn-care businesses.

3. Do you agree or disagree with Mark's assessment of motivation for his landscape design assistant?

Skills Self-Assessment Instrument

ASSESSING YOUR NEEDS

Introduction: Needs are one factor that influences motivation. The following assessment surveys your judgments about your personal needs that might be partially shaping your motivation.

Instructions: Judge how descriptively accurate each of the following statements is about you. You may find making a decision difficult in some cases, but you should force a choice. Record your answers next to each statement according to the following scale:

Rating Scale

5 Very descriptive of me   **2** Not very descriptive of me

4 Fairly descriptive of me   **1** Not descriptive of me at all

3 Somewhat descriptive of me

_____ 1. I aspire to accomplish difficult tasks, maintain high standards, and am willing to work toward distant goals.

_____ 2. I enjoy being with friends and people in general and accept people readily.

_____ 3. I am easily annoyed and am sometimes willing to hurt people to get my way.

_____ 4. I try to break away from restraints or restrictions of any kind.

_____ 5. I want to be the center of attention and enjoy having an audience.

_____ 6. I speak freely and tend to act on the "spur of the moment."

_____ 7. I assist others whenever possible, giving sympathy and comfort to those in need.

_____ 8. I believe in the saying that "there is a place for everything and everything should be in its place." I dislike clutter.

_____ 9. I express my opinions forcefully, enjoy the role of leader, and try to control my environment as much as I can.

_____10. I want to understand many areas of knowledge and value synthesizing ideas and generalization.

For interpretation, turn to page 460.

AN EXERCISE IN THEMATIC APPERCEPTION

> **Experiential Exercise**

Purpose: All people have needs, and those needs make people pursue different goals. This exercise introduces one of the tools by which managers can identify both their own needs and those of their employees.

Introduction: Over the last thirty years, behaviorists have researched the relationship between a person's fantasies and his or her motivation. One popular instrument used to establish this relationship is the Thematic Apperception Test (TAT).

Instructions

Step 1:

1. Examine each picture (provided by your instructor) for about one minute. Then cover the picture.

2. Using the picture as a guide, write a story that could be used in a TV soap opera. Make your story continuous, dramatic, and interesting. Do not just answer the questions. Try to complete the story in less than ten minutes.

3. Do not be concerned about obtaining negative results from this instrument. There are no right or wrong stories.

4. After finishing one story, repeat the same procedure until all six stories are completed.

Step 2: Conduct a story interpretation in groups of three persons each. Taking turns reading one story at a time, each person will read a story out loud to the other two people in the group. Then all three will examine the story for statements that fall into one of the following three categories:

- Category AC—Statements that refer to:
    High standards of excellence
    A desire to win, do well, succeed
    Unique accomplishments
    Long-term goals
    Careers

- Category PO—Statements that refer to:
    Influencing others
    Controlling others
    The desire to instruct others
    The desire to dominate others
    The concern over weakness, failure, or humiliation
    Superior-subordinate relationships or status relationship

- Category AF—Statements that refer to:
    Concern over establishing positive emotional relationships
    Warm friendships or their loss
    A desire to be liked
    One person liking another
    Parties, reunions, or visits
    Relaxed small talk
    Concern for others when not required by social custom

To assist in the interpretation of the test results, assign ten points to each story. Divide the ten points among the three categories based on the frequency of statements that refer to AC, PO, and AF behaviors in the story. Once the allocation of the ten points is determined, record the results in the following scoring table:

Divide ten points among the following categories:

Number of Story Scored	AC		PO		AF		TOTAL
1	____	+	____	+	____	=	__10__
2	____	+	____	+	____	=	__10__
3	____	+	____	+	____	=	__10__
4	____	+	____	+	____	=	__10__
5	____	+	____	+	____	=	__10__
6	____	+	____	+	____	=	__10__
TOTAL	____	+	____	+	____	=	__60__

Divide totals by ten times number of stories scored ____ + ____ + ____

Category percentages ____ % ____ % ____ %=__100%__

Your Thematic Apperception Test values of AC, PO, and AF indicate your mix of needs for achievement (AC), power (PO), and affiliation (AF), respectively. Due to the circumstances under which this exercise was conducted, your values should be considered as only rough estimates. If you feel uncomfortable with your results, it is suggested that you consult with your instructor.

Step 3: In small groups/discuss the following questions:
Do you agree with your TAT results?
Can you cite specific behaviors to substantiate your opinions?
Do other members of your group perceive you as having the needs indicated by your TAT results?
Can they cite specific behaviors to substantiate their opinions?
What interpersonal problems might exist between a manager and an employee who had different need mixes?
In what type of job would you place an employee with a high need for achievement? A high need for power? A high need for affiliation?

Source: From *Motives in Fantasy, Action and Society: Methods of Assessment and Study*, John W. Atkinson, ed. (Princeton, NJ: D. Van Nostrand Co., Inc., 1958.)

CASE STUDY

Gambling with Motivation

People who frequent gambling casinos usually do so because they enjoy the activity of wagering. These people often forget, however, that gambling itself is a big business, a business that must be effectively managed if its owners are to remain in operation. Just as any business relies on people to carry out its work, casinos need employees to manage and work in hotel operations, entertainment venues, gift shops, parking operations, and the gaming areas. Moreover, casino owners rely on managers to oversee their marketing, financial, and human resource functions. Although people may debate the morality of legalized gambling, there is no question as to its profitability.

One of the most successful businesses in the gambling industry today is Mirage Resorts, Incorporated. Stephen Wynn is the primary owner and chief executive officer of Mirage Resorts. The company is best known for its elaborate Mirage and Treasure Island Resorts in Las Vegas. The Mirage Resort, for example, has 3,030 hotel rooms, a 95,000-square-foot casino, and features such attractions as Siegfried and Roy's white tigers and a dolphin exhibit. The Treasure Island resort includes full-size replicas of a British frigate and a pirate ship that engage in live sea battles.

The company also owns the Golden Nugget casinos in Las Vegas and Laughlin and has a 50 percent stake in the Casino Iguazu in Argentina. In addition, Mirage has new projects under development for other areas in Nevada as well as in New Jersey and Mississippi. Most industry observers credit the success of Mirage directly to Wynn and to his innovative management practices. Wynn, for example, has all the characteristics of a charismatic and inspirational leader. He is interesting and well informed and can inspire others to follow his lead.

Another integral part of Mirage's success has been Wynn's approach to dealing with his employees. For example, he recently observed, "I have found that you can never go wrong indulging your employees." Thus, throughout his company he regularly strives for ways to recognize superior performance. One routine part of this management system is what Wynn calls his "Gotcha" awards. These awards can be handed out at the discretion of a first-line supervisor to any employee observed doing his or her job in an exceptionally competent manner. The most common Gotcha awards are an extra day off with pay or a gift certificate good for merchandise at one of Mirage's gift shops or restaurants.

Employees and supervisors of the year at each Mirage casino are treated to Hawaiian vacations and a banquet that costs the company about $400,000. In addition, although entertainment operations like hotels commonly give employees

Part Four Leading

free food, most competitors use leftovers from the guest buffet to feed their employees. Mirage workers, however, enjoy fresh and free meals in gleaming new cafeterias.

Another management innovation pioneered by Wynn is what he calls planned insubordination. Essentially, managers at Mirage Resorts are required to explain why any given task needs to be accomplished. If subordinates find the explanation to be unconvincing, they are not required to perform the task. This arrangement causes managers to carefully consider the reasons behind their decisions before announcing them and helps subordinates more fully understand how the business is being managed.

And what are the effects of these benevolent human resource strategies? For one thing, Mirage's annual turnover rate of 12 percent is less than half the industry average. Moreover, despite the fact that almost half of Mirage's workers belong to unions, no grievances have been filed against the firm for more than four years. Because the company is seen as such an attractive place to work, Mirage can attract good employees and pay them at or even sometimes below market rates.

Case Questions

1. Which motivational theories and techniques are being used by Wynn?

2. How well do you think Wynn's management style would work in other settings?

3. If you were one of Wynn's competitors, how would you deal with the fact that his casinos seem to be the preferred places to work in Las Vegas today?

Case References: "Picasso Among the High Rollers," *Forbes*, May 19, 1997, pp. 44–46; Kenneth Labich, "Gambling's Kings," *Fortune*, July 22, 1996, pp. 80–88; and Patrick J. Spain and James R. Talbot (eds.), *Hoover's Handbook of American Business 1998* (Austin, Texas: The Reference Press, 1998), pp. 1008–1009.

CHAPTER NOTES

1. "Certain Work Is Foreign to Saudis, But That's Changing," *Wall Street Journal*, September 12, 1996, pp. A1, A4 (quote on p. A1) and Ricky W. Griffin and Michael W. Pustay, *International Business—A Managerial Perspective*, 2nd ed., Chapter 14 (Reading, Mass.: Addison-Wesley), 1999.

2. Richard M. Steers and Lyman W. Porter, *Motivation and Work Behavior*, 5th ed. (New York: McGraw-Hill, 1991).

3. Abraham H. Maslow, "A Theory of Human Motivation," *Psychological Review*, Vol. 50, 1943, pp. 370–396; Abraham H. Maslow, *Motivation and Personality* (New York: Harper & Row, 1954).

4. For a review, see Craig Pinder, *Work Motivation* (Glenview, Ill.: Scott, Foresman, 1984). See also Steers and Porter, *Motivation and Work Behavior*.

5. Frederick Herzberg, Bernard Mausner, and Barbara Snyderman, *The Motivation to Work* (New York: Wiley, 1959) and Frederick Herzberg, "One More Time: How Do You Motivate Employees?" *Harvard Business Review*, January–February 1987, pp. 109–120.

6. Robert J. House and Lawrence A. Wigdor, "Herzberg's Dual-Factor Theory of Job Satisfaction and Motivation: A Review of the Evidence and a Criticism," *Personnel Psychology*, Winter 1967, pp. 369–389 and Victor H. Vroom, *Work and Motivation* (New York: Wiley, 1964). See also Pinder, *Work Motivation*.

7. David C. McClelland, *The Achieving Society* (Princeton, N.J.: Van Nostrand, 1961) and David C. McClelland, *Power: The Inner Experience* (New York: Irvington, 1975).

8. David McClelland and David H. Burnham, "Power Is the Great Motivator," *Harvard Business Review*, March–April 1976, pp. 100–110.

9. Vroom, *Work and Motivation*.

10. "Starbucks' Secret Weapon," *Fortune*, September 29, 1997, p. 268.

11. Lyman W. Porter and Edward E. Lawler III, *Managerial Attitudes and Performance* (Homewood, Ill.: Dorsey Press, 1968).

12. J. Stacy Adams, "Towards an Understanding of Inequity," *Journal of Abnormal and Social Psychology*, November 1963, pp. 422–436 and Richard T. Mowday, "Equity Theory Predictions of Behavior in Organizations" in Steers and Porter, *Motivation and Work Behavior*, pp. 91–113.

13. See Edwin A. Locke, Toward a Theory of Task Performance and Incentives," *Organizational Behavior and Human Performance*, Vol. 3, 1968, pp. 157–189.

14. Gary P. Latham and J. J. Baldes, "The Practical Significance of Locke's Theory of Goal Setting," *Journal of Applied Psychology*, Vol. 60, 1975, pp. 187–191.

15. B. F. Skinner, *Beyond Freedom and Dignity* (New York: Knopf, 1971).

16. Fred Luthans and Robert Kreitner, *Organizational Behavior Modification and Beyond: An Operant and Social Learning Approach* (Glenview, Ill.: Scott, Foresman, 1985).

17. Luthans and Kreitner, *Organizational Behavior Modification and Beyond* and W. Clay Hamner and Ellen P. Hamner, "Behavior Modification on the Bottom Line," *Organizational Dynamics*, Spring 1976, pp. 2–21.

18. "At Emery Air Freight: Positive Reinforcement Boosts Performance," *Organizational Dynamics*, Winter 1973, pp. 41–50; for a recent update, see Alexander D. Stajkovic and Fred Luthans, "A Meta-Analysis of the Effects of Organizational Behavior Modification on Task Performance, 1975–95," *Academy of Management Journal*, Vol. 40, No. 5, 1997, pp. 1122–1149.

19. David J. Glew, Anne M. O'Leary-Kelly, Ricky W. Griffin, and David D. Van Fleet, "Participation in Organizations: A Preview of the Issues and Proposed Framework for Future Analysis," *Journal of Management*, Vol. 21, No. 3, 1995, pp. 395–421.

20. Baxter W. Graham, "The Business Argument for Flexibility, *HRMagazine*, May 1996, pp. 104–110.

21. A. R. Cohen and H. Gadon, *Alternative Work Schedules: Integrating Individual and Organizational Needs* (Reading, Mass.: Addison-Wesley, 1978).

22. Michelle Neely Martinez, "Rewards Given the Right Way," *HRMagazine*, May 1997, pp. 109–118.

23. Edward E. Lawler III, *Pay and Organizational Development* (Reading, Mass.: Addison-Wesley, 1981). See also Edward E. Lawler III, *Pay and Organizational Effectiveness: A Psychological View* (New York: McGraw-Hill, 1971).

24. Lawler, *Pay and Organizational Development*.

25. Bill Leonard, "New Ways to Pay Employees," *HRMagazine*, February 1994, pp. 61–69.

26. "Grading 'Merit Pay,'" *Newsweek*, November 14, 1988, pp. 45–46; Frederick S. Hills, K. Dow Scott, Steven E. Markham, and Michael J. Vest, "Merit Pay: Just or Unjust Desserts," *Personnel Administrator*, September 1987, pp. 53–59.

11

Leadership and Influence Processes

OBJECTIVES

After studying this chapter, you should be able to:

■ Describe the nature of leadership and distinguish leadership from management.

■ Discuss and evaluate the trait approach to leadership.

■ Discuss and evaluate models of leadership focusing on behaviors.

■ Identify and describe the major situational approaches to leadership.

■ Identify and describe three related perspectives on leadership.

■ Discuss political behavior in organizations and how it can be managed.

Even though Compaq Computer was formed less than two decades ago, the firm seems to have already had two distinct lives. The first started when Rod Canion and two other former Texas Instruments engineers launched the firm in 1982. Their first product design was sketched on a paper place mat in a restaurant where they agreed to go into business together. Led by Canion's rational and deliberate decision-making style, Compaq did all the right things and became the youngest firm to enter the *Fortune* 500 in 1988.

It appeared for awhile that the firm's management could do no wrong. But, unfortunately, things have a way of changing in the computer business. Canion's strategy for Compaq was to sell primarily to big businesses and to be relatively slow and deliberate to avoid mistakes. When Compaq began to falter in 1991, Canion was at a loss as to how to proceed and was eventually forced out by the firm's board of directors.

To get the firm back on track, the board tapped Eckhard Pfeiffer, a German marketing specialist who had previously headed Compaq's very successful European operations. Pfeiffer wasted little time in revamping how the firm did business. In short order he mandated that the firm develop and launch dozens of new products, that manufacturing become more efficient so that costs could be lowered, and that the dealer network selling Compaq computers be enlarged. He also announced new initiatives directed at selling computers to individual consumers and to schools, domains previously controlled by Dell and Apple, respectively.

Even the wildest optimist could not have predicted how successful Pfeiffer's approach would turn out to be. Since he took over, for example, Compaq has more than tripled its share of the PC market, moving from 3.8 percent to 12 percent. Moreover, its profits in 1996 exceeded those of IBM and Apple combined. But Pfeiffer does not believe in standing still. Indeed, his ideas and strategies are keeping the firm in a constant state of flux. He continues to push for ever lower costs, ever greater productivity, and constant increases in market share, sales, and profits.

More recently, he has taken Compaq into new markets and still encourages managers to constantly be on the alert for new market opportunities. Indeed, in every business where it competes, Compaq is growing at a faster pace than the market itself. Pfeiffer recently announced a goal of transforming Compaq into a $40-billion Goliath by the turn of the century.

How does he do it? His colleagues believe that Pfeiffer has two qualities that allowed him to first turn things around and then set forth in bold new directions at Compaq. The first is that he was able to clearly communicate his vision for the company to each of its managers and employees. The second is that he is able to impart a sense of urgency—a feeling that things have to be done now.

This latter characteristic has facilitated the ongoing sense of change that he believes must drive Compaq in the years to come. And he sees plenty of changes on the horizon—lower prices, more powerful machines, and technology unheard of today are right around the corner. And many experts believe that Pfeiffer will lead Compaq to that corner first.[1]

"We've seen the long-term potential. It's stronger than we had anticipated, much stronger than others have recognized."

Eckhard Pfeiffer, Compaq CEO

ckhard Pfeiffer has a relatively rare combination of skills that sets him apart from many others: he is both an astute leader and a fine manager, and he recognizes many of the challenges necessary to play both roles. He knows when to make tough decisions, when to lead and encourage his employees, and when to stand back and let them do their jobs. And thus far, Compaq is reaping big payoffs from his efforts.

This chapter examines people like Pfeiffer more carefully—by focusing on leadership and its role in management. We characterize the nature of leadership and trace through the three major approaches to studying leadership—traits, behaviors, and situations. After examining other perspectives on leadership, we conclude by describing another approach to influencing others—political behavior in organizations.

The Nature of Leadership

In Chapter 10 we described various models and perspectives on employee motivation. From the manager's standpoint, trying to motivate people is an attempt to influence their behavior. In many ways, leadership, too, is an attempt to influence the behavior of others. In this section we first define leadership, then differentiate it from management, and conclude by relating it to power.

■ The Meaning of Leadership

leadership As a process, the use of noncoercive influence to shape the group's or organization's goals, motivate behavior toward the achievement of those goals, and help define group or organization culture; as a property, the set of characteristics attributed to individuals who are perceived to be leaders

leaders People who can influence the behaviors of others without having to rely on force; those accepted by others as leaders

Leadership is both a process and a property.[2] As a process—focusing on what leaders actually do—leadership is the use of noncoercive influence to shape the group's or organization's goals, motivate behavior toward the achievement of those goals, and help define group or organization culture.[3] As a property, leadership is the set of characteristics attributed to individuals who are perceived to be leaders. Thus, **leaders** are people who can influence the behaviors of others without having to rely on force; leaders are people whom others accept as leaders.

■ Leadership Versus Management

These definitions show that although leadership and management are related, they are not the same. A person can be a manager, a leader, both, or neither.[4] Some of the basic distinctions between leaders and managers are summarized in Table 11.1. At the left side of the table are four elements that differentiate leadership from management. The two columns show how each element differs when considered from a management and a leadership point of view. For example, when executing plans, managers focus on monitoring results, comparing them with goals, and correcting deviations. In contrast, the leader focuses on energizing people to overcome bureaucratic hurdles to help reach

Activity	Management	Leadership
Creating an agenda	**Planning and budgeting.** Establishing detailed steps and timetables for achieving needed results; allocating the resources necessary to make those needed results happen.	**Establishing direction.** Developing a vision of the future, often the distant future, and strategies for producing the changes needed to achieve that vision.
Developing a human network for achieving the agenda	**Organizing and staffing.** Establishing some structure for accomplishing plan requirements, staffing that structure with individuals, delegating responsibility and authority for carrying out the plan, providing policies and procedures to help guide people, and creating methods or systems to monitor implementation.	**Aligning people.** Communicating the direction by words and deeds to everyone whose cooperation may be needed to influence the creation of teams and coalitions that understand the vision and strategies and accept their validity.
Executing plans	**Controlling and problem solving.** Monitoring results versus planning in some detail, identifying deviations, and then planning and organizing to solve these problems.	**Motivating and inspiring.** Energizing people to overcome major political, bureaucratic, and resource barriers by satisfying very basic, but often unfulfilled, human needs.
Outcomes	Produces a degree of predictability and order and has the potential to consistently produce major results expected by various stakeholders (for example, for customers, always being on time; for stockholders, being on budget).	Produces change, often to a dramatic degree, and has the potential to produce extremely useful change (for example, new products that customers want and new approaches to labor relations that help make a firm more competitive).

TABLE 11.1
Distinctions Between Management and Leadership

Management and leadership are related, but distinct, constructs. Managers and leaders differ in how they go about creating an agenda, developing a rationale for achieving the agenda, and executing plans, as well as in the types of outcomes they achieve.
Source: Reprinted with the permission of The Free Press, a Division of Simon & Schuster, Inc. from *A Force for Change: How Leadership Differs from Management* by John P. Kotter. Copyright © 1990 by John P. Kotter, Inc.

goals. Thus, when Eckhard Pfeiffer monitors the performance of his employees, he is playing the role of manager. But when he inspires them to work harder at achieving their goals, he is a leader.

To be effective, organizations need both management and leadership. Leadership is necessary to create change, and management is necessary to achieve orderly results. Management in conjunction with leadership can produce orderly change, and leadership in conjunction with management can keep the organization properly aligned with its environment. An excellent example of an individual who is clearly both an excellent manager and an exemplary leader is Kenneth Chenault, president of American Express. Chenault excels at the more routine tasks of a senior manager, but also inspires great confidence and motivation in his followers.[5]

■ Power and Leadership

To fully understand leadership, it is necessary to understand power. **Power** is the ability to affect the behavior of others. One can have power without actually using it. For example, a football coach has the power to bench a player who is not performing up to par. The coach seldom has to use this power because players recognize that the power exists and work hard to keep their starting positions. In organizational settings, there are usually five kinds of power: legitimate, reward, coercive, referent, and expert power.[6]

Legitimate Power **Legitimate power** is power granted through the organizational hierarchy; it is the power accorded people occupying a particular position as defined by the organization. A manager can assign tasks to a subordinate,

power The ability to affect the behavior of others

legitimate power Power granted through the organizational hierarchy; it is the power defined by the organization that is to be accorded people occupying particular positions

and a subordinate who refuses to do them can be reprimanded or even fired. Such outcomes stem from the manager's legitimate power as defined and vested in her or him by the organization. Legitimate power, then, is authority. All managers have legitimate power over their subordinates. The mere possession of legitimate power, however, does not by itself make someone a leader. Some subordinates follow only orders that are strictly within the letter of organizational rules and policies. If asked to do something not in their job description, they refuse or do a poor job. The manager of such employees is exercising authority but not leadership.

reward power The power to give or withhold rewards, such as salary increases, bonuses, promotions, praise, recognition, and interesting job assignments

Reward Power   **Reward power** is the power to give or withhold rewards. Rewards that a manager may control include salary increases, bonuses, promotion recommendations, praise, recognition, and interesting job assignments. In general, the greater the number of rewards a manager controls and the more important the rewards are to subordinates, the greater is the manager's reward power. If the subordinate sees as valuable only the formal organizational rewards provided by the manager, then he or she is not a leader. If the subordinate also wants and appreciates the manager's informal rewards like praise, gratitude, and recognition, however, then the manager is also exercising leadership.

coercive power The power to force compliance by means of psychological, emotional, or physical threat

Coercive Power   **Coercive power** is the power to force compliance by means of psychological, emotional, or physical threat. In the past physical coercion in organizations was relatively common. In most organizations today, however, coercion is limited to verbal reprimands, written reprimands, disciplinary layoffs, fines, demotion, and termination. Some managers occasionally go so far as to use verbal abuse, humiliation, and psychological coercion in an attempt to manipulate subordinates. (Of course, most people would agree that these are not appropriate managerial behaviors.) James Dutt, former CEO of Beatrice Company, once told a subordinate that if his wife and family got in the way of his working a twenty-four-hour day, seven days a week, he should get rid of them.[7] The more punitive the elements under a manager's control and the more important they are to subordinates, the more coercive power the manager possesses. On the other hand, the more a manager uses coercive power, the more likely he is to provoke resentment and hostility and the less likely he is to be seen as a leader.

referent power The personal power that accrues to someone based on identification, imitation, loyalty, or charisma

Referent Power   Compared with legitimate, reward, and coercive power, which are relatively concrete and grounded in objective facets of organizational life, **referent power** is abstract. It is based on identification, imitation, loyalty, or charisma. Followers may react favorably because they identify in some way with a leader, who may be like them in personality, background, or attitudes. In other situations, followers might choose to imitate a leader with referent power by wearing the same kinds of clothes, working the same hours, or espousing the same management philosophy. Referent power may also take the form of charisma, an intangible attribute of the leader that inspires loyalty and enthusiasm. Thus a manager might have referent power, but it is more likely to be associated with leadership.

expert power The personal power that accrues to someone based on the information or expertise that the person possesses

Expert Power   **Expert power** is derived from information or expertise. A manager who knows how to interact with an eccentric but important customer, a scientist who is capable of achieving an important technical breakthrough that no other company has dreamed of, and a secretary who knows how to unravel bureaucratic red tape all have expert power over anyone who needs that information. The more important the information and the fewer the people who have access to it, the greater is the degree of expert power possessed by any one individual. In general, people who are both leaders and managers tend to have a lot of expert power.

The Search for Leadership Traits

The first organized approach to studying leadership analyzed the personal, psychological, and physical traits of strong leaders. The trait approach assumed that some basic trait or set of traits existed that differentiated leaders from nonleaders. If those traits could be defined, potential leaders could be identified. Researchers thought that leadership traits might include intelligence, assertiveness, above-average height, good vocabulary, attractiveness, self-confidence, and similar attributes.[8]

During the first several decades of this century, hundreds of studies were conducted in an attempt to identify important leadership traits. For the most part, the results of the studies were disappointing. For every set of leaders who possessed a common trait, a long list of exceptions was also found, and the list

The trait approach to leadership assumes that some basic trait or traits differentiates leaders from nonleaders. For example, many people in Great Britain assume that members of the royal family will be great leaders simply by virtue of their lineage. Thus, they expect Prince Charles to be a strong and effective leader, and publically express their dismay or outrage whenever he makes a mistake or fails to meet their expectations.

of suggested traits soon grew so long that it had little practical value. Alternative explanations usually existed even for relations between traits and leadership that initially appeared valid. For example, it was observed that many leaders have good communication skills and are assertive. Rather than those traits being the cause of leadership, however, successful leaders may begin to display those traits after they have achieved leadership positions.

Although most researchers gave up trying to identify traits as predictors of leadership ability, many people still explicitly or implicitly adopt a trait orientation.[9] For example, politicians are all too often elected on the basis of personal appearance, speaking ability, or an aura of self-confidence. In addition, traits like honesty and integrity may very well be fundamental leadership traits that serve an important purpose.

Leadership Behaviors

Spurred on by their lack of success in identifying useful leadership traits, researchers soon began to investigate other variables, especially the behaviors or actions of leaders. The new hypothesis was that effective leaders somehow behaved differently than less-effective leaders. Thus the goal was to develop a fuller understanding of leadership behaviors.

■ Michigan Studies

Researchers at the University of Michigan, led by Rensis Likert, began studying leadership in the late 1940s.[10] Based on extensive interviews with both leaders (managers) and followers (subordinates), this research identified two basic forms of leader behavior: job centered and employee centered. Managers using **job-centered leader behavior** pay close attention to subordinates' work, explain work procedures, and are keenly interested in performance. Managers using **employee-centered leader behavior** are interested in developing a cohesive work group and ensuring that employees are satisfied with their jobs. Their primary concern of these managers is the welfare of subordinates. The two styles of leader behavior were presumed to be at the ends of a single continuum. Although this approach suggests that leaders may be extremely job centered, extremely employee centered, or somewhere in between, Likert studied only the two end styles for contrast. He argued that employee-centered leader behavior generally tended to be more effective.

job-centered leader behavior The behavior of leaders who pay close attention to the job and work procedures involved with that job

employee-centered leader behavior The behavior of leaders who develop cohesive work groups and ensure employee satisfaction

■ Ohio State Studies

At about the same time that Likert was beginning his leadership studies at the University of Michigan, a group of researchers at Ohio State also began studying leadership.[11] The extensive questionnaire surveys conducted during the Ohio State studies also suggested that there are two basic leader behaviors or styles: initiating-structure behavior and consideration behavior.

When using **initiating-structure behavior,** the leader clearly defines the leader-subordinate role so that everyone knows what is expected, establishes formal lines of communication, and determines how tasks will be performed. Leaders using **consideration behavior** show concern for subordinates and attempt to establish a friendly and supportive climate. The behaviors identified at Ohio State are similar to those described at Michigan, but there are important differences. One major difference is that the Ohio State researchers did not interpret leader behavior as being one-dimensional: each behavior was assumed to be independent of the other. Presumably, then, a leader could exhibit varying levels of initiating structure and at the same time varying levels of consideration.

At first, the Ohio State researchers thought that leaders who exhibit high levels of both behaviors would tend to be more effective than other leaders. A study at International Harvester Co. (now Navistar International Corp.), however, suggested a more complicated pattern.[12] The researchers found that employees of supervisors who ranked high on initiating structure were high performers but expressed low levels of satisfaction and had a higher absence rate. Conversely, employees of supervisors who ranked high on consideration had low performance ratings but high levels of satisfaction and few absences from work. Later research isolated other variables that make consistent prediction difficult and determined that situational influences also occurred. (This body of research is discussed in the section on situational approaches to leadership.)

■ Leadership Grid®

Yet another behavioral approach to leadership is the Leadership Grid®.[13] The Leadership Grid® provides a means for evaluating leadership styles and then training managers to move toward an ideal style of behavior. The Leadership Grid® is shown in Figure 11.1. The horizontal axis represents **concern for production** (similar to job-centered and initiating-structure behaviors), and the vertical axis represents **concern for people** (similar to employee-centered and consideration behavior). Note the five extremes of managerial behavior: the 1,1 manager (impoverished management) who exhibits minimal concern for both production and people; the 9,1 manager

FIGURE 11.1
The Leadership Grid®

The Leadership Grid® is a method of evaluating leadership styles. The overall objective of an organization using the Grid® is to train its managers using OD techniques so that they are simultaneously more concerned for both people and production (9, 9 style on the Grid®).
Source: From *Leadership Dilemmas-Grid Solutions,* p. 29 by Robert R. Blake and Anne Adams McCanse. Copyright © 1991 by Robert R. Blake and Estate of Jane S. Mouton. Used with permission. All rights reserved.

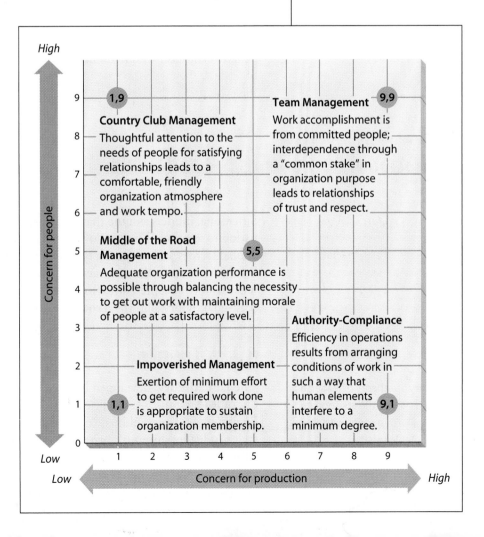

initiating-structure behavior The behavior of leaders who define the leader-subordinate role so that everyone knows what is expected, establish formal lines of communication, and determine how tasks will be performed

consideration behavior The behavior of leaders who show concern for subordinates and attempt to establish a warm, friendly, and supportive climate

concern for production That part of the Leadership Grid® that deals with the job and task aspects of leader behavior

concern for people That part of the Leadership Grid® that deals with the human aspects of leader behavior

(authority-compliance) who is highly concerned about production but exhibits little concern for people; the 1,9 manager (country club management) whose concerns are the exact opposite of the 9,1 manager's concerns; the 5,5 manager (middle-of-the-road management) who maintains adequate concern for both people and production; and the 9,9 manager (team management) who exhibits maximum concern for both people and production.

According to this approach, the ideal style of managerial behavior is 9,9. There is a six-phase program to assist managers in learning how to exhibit this style of behavior. A.G. Edwards, Westinghouse, FAA, Equicor, and other companies have used the Leadership Grid® with reasonable success. However, little published scientific evidence proves its true effectiveness.

The leader-behavior theories have played an important role in the development of contemporary thinking about leadership. In particular, they urge us not to be preoccupied with what leaders are (the trait approach) but to concentrate on what leaders do (their behaviors). Unfortunately, these theories also make universal prescriptions about what constitutes effective leadership. When we are dealing with complex social systems composed of complex individuals, few if any relationships are consistently predictable, and certainly no formulas for success are infallible. Yet the behavior theorists tried to identify consistent relationships between leader behaviors and employee responses in the hope of finding a dependable prescription for effective leadership. As we might expect, they often failed. Other approaches to understanding leadership were therefore needed. The catalyst for these new approaches was the realization that, although interpersonal and task-oriented dimensions might be useful to describe the behavior of leaders, they were not useful for predicting or prescribing it. The next step in the evolution of leadership theory was the creation of situational models.

Situational Approaches to Leadership

Situational models assume that appropriate leader behavior varies from one situation to another. The goal of a situational theory, then, is to identify key situational factors and to specify how they interact to determine appropriate leader behavior. In the following sections, we describe the three most important and most widely accepted situational theories of leadership: the LPC theory, the path-goal theory, and the Vroom-Yetton-Jago model.

▮ LPC Theory

LPC theory A theory of leadership that suggests that the appropriate style of leadership varies with situational favorableness

The **LPC theory**, developed by Fred Fiedler, was the first true situational theory of leadership.[14] As we discuss later, LPC stands for *least preferred coworker*. Beginning with a combined trait and behavior approach, Fiedler identified two styles of leadership: task oriented (analogous to job-centered and initiating-structure behavior) and relationship oriented (similar to employee-centered and consideration behavior). He went beyond the earlier behavioral approaches by arguing that the style of behavior is a reflection of the leader's personality, and that most personalities fall into one of his two categories, task oriented or relationship oriented by nature. Fiedler measures leader style by means of a controversial questionnaire called the **least preferred coworker (LPC)** measure. To use the measure, a manager or leader is asked to describe the specific person with whom he or she is able to work least well—the LPC—by filling in a set of sixteen scales anchored at each end by a positive or negative adjective. Three of the sixteen scales follow.

least preferred coworker (LPC) The measuring scale that asks leaders to describe the person with whom he or she is able to work least well

Helpful __ __ __ __ __ __ __ __ Frustrating
         8 7 6 5 4 3 2 1

Tense __ __ __ __ __ __ __ __ Relaxed
     1 2 3 4 5 6 7 8

Boring __ __ __ __ __ __ __ __ Interesting
      1 2 3 4 5 6 7 8

The leader's LPC score is then calculated by adding up the numbers below the line checked on each scale. Note in these three examples that the higher numbers are associated with the positive qualities (helpful, relaxed, and interesting), whereas the negative qualities (frustrating, tense, and boring) have low point values. A high total score is assumed to reflect a relationship orientation and a low score a task orientation on the part of the leader. The LPC measure is controversial because researchers disagree about its validity. Some question exactly what an LPC measure reflects and whether the score is an index of behavior, personality, or some other factor.[15]

Favorableness of the Situation The underlying assumption of situational models of leadership is that appropriate leader behavior varies from one situation to another. According to Fiedler, the key situational factor is the favorableness of the situation from the leader's point of view. This factor is determined by leader-member relations, task structure, and position power. *Leader-member relations* refer to the nature of the relationship between the leader and the work group. If the leader and the group have a high degree of mutual trust, respect, and confidence, and if they like one another, relations are assumed to be good. If there is little trust, respect, or confidence and if they do not like each other, relations are poor. Naturally, good relations are more favorable.

Task structure is the degree to which the group's task is well defined. The task is structured when it is routine, easily understood, and unambiguous and when the group has standard procedures and precedents to rely on. An unstructured task is nonroutine, ambiguous, and complex, with no standard procedures or precedents. You can see that high structure is more favorable for the leader, whereas low structure is less favorable. For example, if the task is unstructured, the group will not know what to do and the leader will have to play a major role in guiding and directing its activities. If the task is structured, the leader will not have to get so involved and can devote time to nonsupervisory activities. *Position power* is the power vested in the leader's position. If the leader has the power to assign work and to reward and punish employees, position power is assumed to be strong. But if the leader must get job assignments approved by someone else and does not administer rewards and punishment, position power is weak and it is more difficult to accomplish goals. From the leader's point of view, strong position power is clearly preferable to weak position. However, position power is not as important as task structure and leader-member relations.

Favorableness and Leader Style Fiedler and his associates conducted numerous studies linking the favorableness of various situations to leader style and the effectiveness of the group.[16] The results of these studies—and the overall framework of the theory—are shown in Figure 11.2. To interpret the model, look first at the situational factors at the top of the figure: good or bad leader-member relations, high or low task structure, and strong or weak leader-position power can be combined to yield eight unique situations. For example, good leader-member relations, high task structure, and strong leader-position power (at the far left) are presumed to define the most favorable situation; bad leader-member relations, low task structure, and weak leader-power (at the far right) are the least favorable. The other combinations reflect intermediate levels of favorableness.

Below each set of situations are the degree of favorableness and the form of leader behavior found to be most strongly associated with effective group performance for those situations. When the situation is most and least favorable, Fiedler has found that a task-oriented leader is most effective. When the situation is only moderately favorable, however, a relationship-oriented leader is predicted to be most effective.

Flexibility of Leader Style Fiedler argued that, for any given individual, leader style is essentially fixed and cannot be changed: leaders cannot change their behavior to fit a particular situation because it is linked to their particular personality traits. Thus, when a leader's style and the situation do not match, Fiedler argued that the situation should be changed to fit the leader's style. When leader-member relations are good, task structure low, and position power weak, the leader style most likely to be effective is relationship oriented.

FIGURE 11.2
The Least-Preferred Coworker Theory of Leadership

Fiedler's LPC theory of leadership suggests that appropriate leader behavior varies as a function of the favorableness of the situation. Favorableness, in turn, is defined by task structure, leader-member relations, and the leader's position power. According to LPC theory, the most and least favorable situations call for task-oriented leadership, whereas moderately favorable situations suggest the need for relationship-oriented leadership.

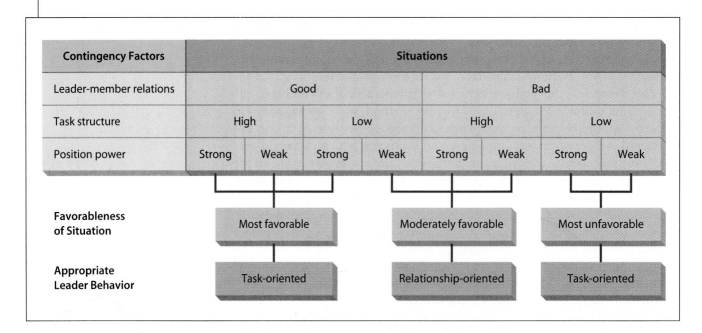

If the leader is task oriented, a mismatch exists. According to Fiedler, the leader can make the elements of the situation more congruent by structuring the task (by developing guidelines and procedures, for instance) and increasing power (by requesting additional authority or by other means).

Fiedler's contingency theory has been criticized on the grounds that it is not always supported by research, that his findings are subject to other interpretations, that the LPC measure lacks validity, and that his assumptions about the inflexibility of leader behavior are unrealistic.[17] However, Fiedler's theory was one of the first to adopt a situational perspective on leadership. It has helped many managers recognize the important situational factors they must contend with, and it has fostered additional thinking about the situational nature of leadership. Moreover, in recent years Fiedler has attempted to address some of the concerns about his theory by revising it and adding elements such as cognitive resources.

■ Path-Goal Theory

The path-goal theory of leadership—associated most closely with Martin Evans and Robert House—is a direct extension of the expectancy theory of motivation discussed in Chapter 10.[18] Recall that the primary components of expectancy theory included the likelihood of attaining various outcomes and the value associated with those outcomes. The **path-goal theory** of leadership suggests that the primary functions of a leader are to make valued or desired rewards available in the workplace and to clarify for the subordinate the kinds of behavior that will lead to goal accomplishment and valued rewards—that is, the leader should clarify the paths to goal attainment.

path-goal theory A theory of leadership suggesting that the primary functions of a leader are to make valued or desired rewards available in the workplace and to clarify for the subordinate the kinds of behavior that will lead to those rewards

Leader Behavior The most fully developed version of path-goal theory identifies four kinds of leader behavior. *Directive leader behavior* is letting subordinates know what is expected of them, giving guidance and direction, and scheduling work. *Supportive leader behavior* is being friendly and approachable, showing concern for subordinate welfare, and treating members as equals. *Participative leader behavior* is consulting subordinates, soliciting suggestions, and allowing participation in decision making. *Achievement-oriented leader behavior* is setting challenging goals, expecting subordinates to perform at high levels, encouraging subordinates, and showing confidence in subordinates' abilities.

In contrast to Fiedler's theory, path-goal theory assumes that leaders can change their style or behavior to meet the demands of a particular situation. For example, when encountering a new group of subordinates and a new project, the leader may be directive in establishing work procedures and in outlining what needs to be done. Next, the leader may adopt supportive behavior to foster group cohesiveness and a positive climate. As the group becomes familiar with the task and as new problems are encountered, the leader may exhibit participative behavior to enhance group members' motivation. Finally, achievement-oriented behavior may be used to encourage continued high performance.

Situational Factors Like other situational theories of leadership, path-goal theory suggests that appropriate leader style depends on situational factors. Path-goal theory focuses on the situational factors of the personal characteristics of subordinates and environmental characteristics of the workplace.

Most effective leaders demonstrate sincere interest in the personal welfare of their followers. This interest can extend to concern about their families and personal lives as well. When the interest is real, employees may feel more valued and appreciated by their leader and develop stronger job satisfaction and dedication. But if the leader's interest is superficial and is an obvious ploy to show interest, employees will likely see what's going on and come to resent and lose respect for the leader.

DILBERT reprinted by permission of United Feature Syndicate, Inc.

Important personal characteristics include the subordinates' perception of their own ability and their locus of control. If people perceive that they are lacking in ability, they may prefer directive leadership to help them understand path-goal relationships better. If they perceive themselves to have a lot of ability, however, employees may resent directive leadership. Locus of control is a personality trait. People who have an internal locus of control believe that what happens to them is a function of their own efforts and behavior. Those who have an external locus of control assume that fate, luck, or "the system" determines what happens to them. A person with an internal locus of control may prefer participative leadership, whereas a person with an external locus of control may prefer directive leadership. Managers can do little or nothing to influence the personal characteristics of subordinates, but they can shape the environment to take advantage of these personal characteristics by providing rewards and structuring tasks, for example.

Environmental characteristics include factors outside the subordinate's control. Task structure is one such factor. When structure is high, directive leadership is less effective than when structure is low. Subordinates do not usually need their boss to continually tell them how to do an extremely routine job. The formal authority system is another important environmental characteristic. Again, the higher the degree of formality, the less directive is the leader behavior that subordinates will accept. The nature of the work group also affects appropriate leader behavior. When the work group provides the employee with social support and satisfaction, supportive leader behavior is less critical. When social support and satisfaction cannot be derived from the group, the worker may look to the leader for this support.

The basic path-goal framework as illustrated in Figure 11.3 shows that different leader behaviors affect subordinate's motivation to perform. Personal and environmental characteristics are seen as defining which behaviors lead to which outcomes. The path-goal theory of leadership is a dynamic and incomplete model. The original intent was to state the theory in general terms so that future research could explore a variety of interrelationships and modify the theory. Research suggests that the path-goal theory is a reasonably good description of the leadership process and that future investigations along these lines should enable us to discover more about the link between leadership and motivation.[19]

■ Vroom-Yetton-Jago Model

The **Vroom-Yetton-Jago (VYJ) model** predicts what kinds of situations call for what degrees of group participation. The VYJ model, then, sets norms or standards for including subordinates in decision making. The model was first proposed by Victor Vroom and Philip Yetton in 1973 and was revised and expanded in 1988 by Vroom and Arthur G. Jago.[20] The VYJ model is somewhat narrower than the other situational theories in that it focuses on only one part of the leadership process—how much decision-making participation to allow subordinates.

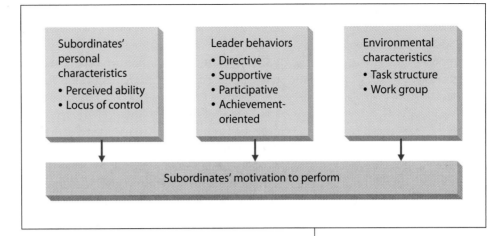

FIGURE 11.3
The Path-Goal Framework

The path-goal theory of leadership suggests that managers can use four types of leader behavior to clarify subordinates' paths to goal attainment. Both personal characteristics of the subordinate and environmental characteristics within the organization must be taken into account when determining which style of leadership will work best for a particular situation.

Basic Premises The VYJ model argues that decision effectiveness is best gauged by the quality of the decision and by employee acceptance of the decision. Decision quality is the objective effect of the decision on performance. Decision acceptance is the extent to which employees accept and are committed to the decision. To maximize decision effectiveness, the VYJ model suggests that, depending on the situation, managers adopt one of five decision-making styles. As summarized in Table 11.2, there are two autocratic styles (AI and AII), two consultative styles (CI and CII), and one group style (GII).

The situation that is presumed to dictate an appropriate decision-making style is defined by a series of questions about the characteristics or attributes of the problem under consideration. To address the questions, the manager uses

Decision Style	Definition
AI	Manager makes the decision alone.
AII	Manager asks for information from subordinates but makes the decision alone. Subordinates may or may not be informed about what the situation is.
CI	Manager shares the situation with individual subordinates and asks for information and evaluation. Subordinates do not meet as a group, and the manager alone makes the decision.
CII	Manager and subordinates meet as a group to discuss the situation, but the manager makes the decision.
GII	Manager and subordinates meet as a group to discuss the situation, and the group makes the decision.

A = autocratic; C = consultative; G = group

TABLE 11.2
Decision Styles in the Vroom-Yetton-Jago Model

The difference between these styles is the degree of participation they provide for subordinates. The extreme forms are purely autocratic (AI) and total participation (GII). The other three styles fall between these extremes.

Source: Reprinted with permission of the University of Pittsburgh Press from *Leadership and Decision-Making* by Victor H. Vroom and Philip H. Yetton. Copyright © 1973 by the University of Pittsburgh Press.

Vroom-Yetton-Jago (VYJ) model
Predicts what kinds of situations call for what degrees of group participation

one of four decision trees. Two of the trees are used when the problem affects the entire group, and the other two are appropriate when the problem relates to an individual. One of each is to be used when the time necessary to reach a decision is important, and the others are to be used when time is less important but the manager wants to develop subordinates' decision-making abilities.

Figure 11.4 shows the tree for time-driven group problems. The problem attributes defining the situation are arranged along the top of the tree and are expressed as questions. To use the tree, the manager starts at the left side and asks the first question. Thus, the manager first decides whether the problem involves a quality requirement—that is, whether there are quality differences in the alternatives and whether they matter. The answer determines the path to the second node, where the manager asks another question. The manager continues in this fashion until a terminal node is reached and an appropriate decision style is indicated. Each prescribed decision style is designed to protect the original goals of the process (decision quality and subordinate acceptance) within the context of the group versus individual and time versus development framework.

Evaluation The original version of the VYJ model has been widely tested. Indeed, one recent review concluded that it had received more scientific support than any other leadership theory.[21] The inherent complexity of the model presents a problem for many managers, however. Even the original version was criticized because of its complexity, and the revised VYJ model is far more complex than the original. To aid managers, computer software has been developed to facilitate their ability to define their situation, answer the questions about problem attributes, and develop a strategy for decision-making participation.[22]

■ Other Situational Approaches

In addition to the major theories, other situational models have been developed in recent years. We discuss the leader-member exchange model and the life cycle model.

leader-member exchange (LMX) model Stresses that leaders have different kinds of relationships with different subordinates

The Leader-Member Exchange Model The **leader-member exchange (LMX) model** stresses that leaders have different kinds of relationships with different subordinates.[23] Each manager-subordinate relationship represents one vertical dyad. The model suggests that leaders establish special working relationships with a handful of subordinates called the in-group. Other subordinates remain in the out-group. Those in the in-group receive more of the manager's time and attention and also tend to be better performers. Early research on this model is quite promising.[24]

life cycle theory A model suggesting that appropriate leader behavior depends on the maturity of the follower

Life Cycle Theory Another well-known situational theory is the **life cycle theory**, which suggests that appropriate leader behavior depends on the maturity of the followers.[25] In this context, maturity includes motivation, competence, and experience. The theory suggests that as followers become more mature, the leader needs to gradually move from a high level of task orientation to a low level. Simultaneously, employee-oriented behavior should start low, increase at a moderate rate, and then decline again. This theory is well known among practicing managers, but it has received little scientific support from researchers.[26]

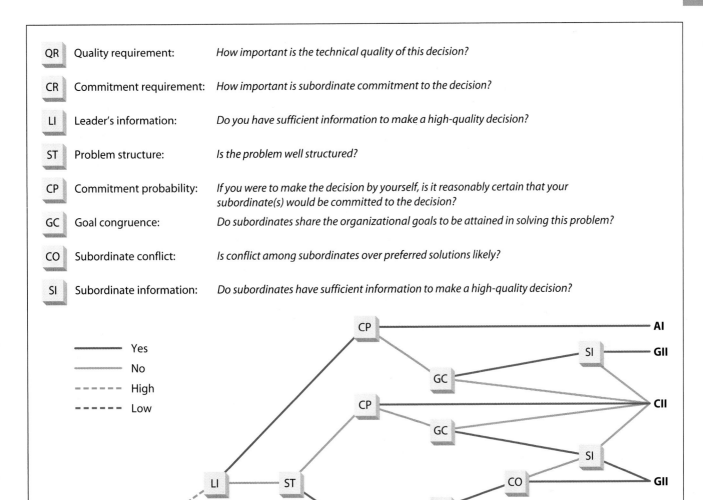

QR	Quality requirement:	*How important is the technical quality of this decision?*
CR	Commitment requirement:	*How important is subordinate commitment to the decision?*
LI	Leader's information:	*Do you have sufficient information to make a high-quality decision?*
ST	Problem structure:	*Is the problem well structured?*
CP	Commitment probability:	*If you were to make the decision by yourself, is it reasonably certain that your subordinate(s) would be committed to the decision?*
GC	Goal congruence:	*Do subordinates share the organizational goals to be attained in solving this problem?*
CO	Subordinate conflict:	*Is conflict among subordinates over preferred solutions likely?*
SI	Subordinate information:	*Do subordinates have sufficient information to make a high-quality decision?*

FIGURE 11.4
Time-Driven Group Problem Decision Tree for VYJ Model

To use this decision tree, the manager asks a series of questions about the problem situation. The answers lead the manager through the tree. The recommended decision style (see Table 11.2) at each endpoint is predicted to enhance decision quality and acceptance.

Adapted and reprinted from *Leadership and Decision-Making* by Victor H. Vroom and Philip H. Yetton, by permission of the University of Pittsburgh Press. Copyright © 1973 by University of Pittsburgh Press.

Related Perspectives on Leadership

Because of its importance to organizational effectiveness, leadership continues to be the focus of a great deal of research and theory building. New approaches that have attracted much attention are the concepts of substitutes for leadership and transformational leadership.

■ Substitutes for Leadership

substitutes for leadership A concept that identifies situations in which leader behaviors are neutralized or replaced by characteristics of subordinates, the task, and the organization

The concept of **substitutes for leadership** was developed because existing leadership models and theories do not account for situations in which leadership is not needed.[27] They simply try to specify what kind of leader behavior is appropriate. The substitute concepts, however, identify situations in which leader behaviors are neutralized or replaced by characteristics of the subordinate, the task, and the organization. For example, when a patient arrives at a hospital emergency room, the professionals on duty do not wait for a leader to tell them what to do. Nurses, doctors, and attendants all go into action without waiting for directive or supportive leader behavior from the emergency-room supervisor.

Characteristics of the subordinate that may serve to neutralize leader behavior include ability, experience, need for independence, professional orientation, and indifference toward organizational rewards. For example, employees with a high level of ability and experience may not need to be told what to do. Similarly, a subordinate's strong need for independence may render leader behavior ineffective. Task characteristics that may substitute for leadership include routineness, the availability of feedback, and intrinsic satisfaction. When the job is routine and simple, the subordinate may not need direction. When the task is challenging and intrinsically satisfying, the subordinate may not need or want social support from a leader.

Organizational characteristics that may substitute for leadership include formalization, group cohesion, inflexibility, and a rigid reward structure. Leadership may not be necessary when policies and practices are formal and inflexible, for example. Similarly, a rigid reward system may rob the leader of reward power and thereby decrease the importance of the role. Preliminary research has provided support for the concept of substitutes for leadership.[28]

■ Charismatic Leadership

charismatic leadership Assumes that charisma is an individual characteristic of the leader

charisma A form of interpersonal attraction that inspires support and acceptance

The concept of **charismatic leadership**, like trait theories, assumes that charisma is an individual characteristic of the leader. **Charisma** is a form of interpersonal attraction that inspires support and acceptance. All else being equal, then, someone with charisma is more likely to be able to influence others than is someone without charisma. For example, compared to a supervisor who lacks charisma, a highly charismatic supervisor will be more successful in influencing subordinate behavior. Thus, influence is again a fundamental element of this perspective.

Robert House first proposed a theory of charismatic leadership in 1977, based on research findings from a variety of social science disciplines.[29] His theory suggests that charismatic leaders are likely to have a lot of self-confidence, a firm conviction in their beliefs and ideals, and a strong need to influence people. They also tend to communicate high expectations about follower performance and express confidence in followers. Donald Trump is an excellent example of a charismatic leader. Even though he has made his share of mistakes and generally is perceived as only an "average" manager, many people view him as larger than life.[30]

There are three elements of charismatic leadership in organizations that most experts acknowledge today.[31] First, the leader needs to be able to envision the future, to set high expectations, and to model behaviors consistent with meeting those expectations. Next, the charismatic leader must be able to energize others through a demonstration of personal excitement, personal confidence, and patterns of success. And finally, the charismatic leader enables others by supporting them, by empathizing with them, and by expressing confidence in them.

Charismatic leadership ideas are quite popular among managers today and are the subject of numerous books and articles. Unfortunately, few studies have specifically attempted to test the meaning and impact of charismatic leadership. In addition, lingering ethical issues about charismatic leadership trouble some people.

■ Transformational Leadership

Another new perspective on leadership has been called by a number of labels: charismatic leadership, inspirational leadership, symbolic leadership, and transformational leadership. We use the term **transformational leadership** and define it as leadership that goes beyond ordinary expectations by transmitting a sense of mission, stimulating learning experiences, and inspiring new ways of thinking.[32] Because of rapid change and turbulent environments, transformational leaders are increasingly being seen as vital to the success of business.

A recent popular-press article identified seven keys to successful leadership: trusting one's subordinates, developing a vision, keeping cool, encouraging risk, being an expert, inviting dissent, and simplifying things.[33] Although this list was the result of a simplistic survey of the leadership literature, it is nevertheless consistent with the premises underlying transformational leadership. So, too, are recent examples cited as effective leadership. Take, for example, the case of General Electric. When Jack Welch assumed the position of CEO, GE was a lethargic behemoth composed of more than one hundred businesses. Decision making was slow, and bureaucracy stifled individual initiative. Welch stripped away

transformational leadership Leadership that goes beyond ordinary expectations by transmitting a sense of mission, stimulating learning experiences, and inspiring new ways of thinking

Jackie Thomas, Nike's associate director of sports marketing, is a charismatic leader. She is a fierce competitor, both in the executive suite and, as shown here, on the basketball court. Ms. Thomas leads by example, inspires loyalty and dedication from her subordinates, and is very effective at planning and implementing new programs and initiatives. She is recognized throughout Nike as one of the firm's strongest and most capable managers and leaders.

the bureaucracy, streamlined the entire organization, sold dozens of businesses, and bought many new ones. He literally re-created the organization, and today GE is one of the most admired and profitable firms in the world. Transformational leadership was the basis for all of Welch's changes.

Political Behavior in Organizations

political behavior The activities carried out for the specific purpose of acquiring, developing, and using power and other resources to obtain one's preferred outcomes

Another common influence on behavior is politics and political behavior. **Political behavior** describes activities carried out for the specific purpose of acquiring, developing, and using power and other resources to obtain one's preferred outcomes.[34] Political behavior may be undertaken by managers dealing with their subordinates, subordinates dealing with their managers, and managers and subordinates dealing with others at the same level. In other words, it may be directed upward, downward, or laterally. Decisions ranging from where to locate a manufacturing plant to where to put the company coffeepot are subject to political action. In any situation, individuals may engage in political behavior to further their own ends, to protect themselves from others, to further goals they sincerely believe to be in the organization's best interest, or to simply acquire and exercise power. And power may be sought by individuals, by groups of individuals, or by groups of groups.[35]

Although political behavior is difficult to study because of its sensitive nature, one early survey found that many managers believed that politics influenced salary and hiring decisions in their firms. Many also believed that the incidence of political behavior was greater at the upper levels of their organizations and less at the lower levels. More than one-half of the respondents felt that organizational politics are bad, unfair, unhealthy, and irrational, but most suggested that successful executives have to be good politicians and be political to "get ahead."[36]

■ Common Political Behaviors

Research has identified four basic forms of political behavior widely practiced in organizations.[37] One form is *inducement*, which occurs when a manager offers to give something to someone else in return for that individual's support. For example, a product manager might suggest to another product manager that she will put in a good word with his boss if he supports a new marketing plan that she has developed. A second tactic is *persuasion*, which relies on both emotion and logic. An operations manager wanting to construct a new plant on a certain site might persuade others to support his goal on grounds that are objective and logical (it is less expensive, taxes are lower) as well as subjective and personal.

A third political behavior involves the *creation of an obligation*. For example, one manager might support a recommendation made by another manager for a new advertising campaign. Although he may really have no opinion on the new campaign, he may think that by going along, he is incurring a debt from the other manager and will be able to "call in" that debt when he wants to get something done and needs additional support. *Coercion* is the use of force to get one's way. For example, a manager may threaten to withhold support, rewards, or other resources as a way to influence someone else.

Impression management is a subtle form of political behavior that deserves special mention. **Impression management** is a direct and intentional effort by someone to enhance his or her image in the eyes of others. People engage in impression management for a variety of reasons. For one thing, they may do so to further their own career. By making themselves look good, they think they are more likely to receive rewards, to be given attractive job assignments, and to receive promotions. They may also engage in impression management to boost their self-esteem. When people have a solid image in an organization, others make them aware of it through compliments, respect, and so forth. Still another reason people use impression management is in an effort to acquire more power, and hence more control.

People attempt to manage how others perceive them through a variety of mechanisms. Appearance is one of the first things people think of. Hence, a person motivated by impression management will pay close attention to choice of attire, selection of language, and the use of manners and body posture. People interested in impression management are also likely to jockey to be associated only with successful projects. By being assigned to high-profile projects led by highly successful managers, a person can begin to link his or her own name with such projects in the minds of others.

Sometimes people too strongly motivated by impression management become obsessed by it and may resort to dishonest and/or unethical means. For example, some people have been known to take credit for others' work in an effort to make themselves look better. People have also been known to exaggerate or even falsify their personal accomplishments in an effort to build an enhanced image.[38]

impression management A direct and intentional effort by someone to enhance his or her image in the eyes of others

■ Managing Political Behavior

By its very nature, political behavior is tricky to approach in a rational and systematic way. But managers can handle political behavior so that it does not do excessive damage. First, managers should be aware that even if their actions are not politically motivated, others may assume that they are. Second, by providing subordinates with autonomy, responsibility, challenge, and feedback, managers reduce the likelihood of political behavior by subordinates. Third, managers should avoid using power if they want to avoid charges of political motivation. Fourth, managers should get disagreements out in the open so that subordinates will have less opportunity for political behavior, using conflict for their own purposes. Finally, managers should avoid covert activities. Behind-the-scene activities give the impression of political intent even if none really exists.[39] Other guidelines include clearly communicating the bases and processes for performance evaluation, tying rewards directly to performance, and minimizing competition among managers for resources.[40]

Of course, those guidelines are a lot easier to list than they are to implement. The well-informed manager should not assume that political behavior does not exist or, worse yet, attempt to eliminate it by issuing orders or commands. Instead, the manager must recognize that political behavior exists in virtually all organizations and that it cannot be ignored or stamped out. It can, however, be managed in such a way that it will seldom inflict serious damage on the organization. It may even play a useful role in some situations.[41] For example, a manager may be able to use his or her political influence to stimulate a greater sense of social responsibility or to heighten awareness of the ethical implications of a decision.

Summary of Key Points

As a process, leadership is the use of noncoercive influence to shape the group's or organization's goals, motivate behavior toward the achievement of those goals, and help define group or organization culture. As a property, leadership is the set of characteristics attributed to those who are perceived to be leaders. Leadership and management are often related but are also different. Managers and leaders use legitimate, reward, coercive, referent, and expert power.

The trait approach to leadership assumes that some basic trait or set of traits differentiate leaders from nonleaders. The leadership-behavior approach to leadership assumes that the behavior of effective leaders is somehow different from the behavior of nonleaders. Research at the University of Michigan and Ohio State identified two basic forms of leadership behavior—one concentrating on work and performance and the other concentrating on employee welfare and support. The Leadership Grid® attempts to train managers to exhibit high levels of both forms of behavior.

Situational approaches to leadership recognize that appropriate forms of leadership behavior are not universally applicable and attempt to specify situations in which various behaviors are appropriate. The LPC theory suggests that a leader's behaviors should be either task oriented or relationship oriented, depending on the favorableness of the situation. The path-goal theory suggests that directive, supportive, participative, or achievement-oriented leader behaviors may be appropriate, depending on the personal characteristics of subordinates and the environment. The Vroom-Yetton-Jago model maintains that leaders should vary the extent to which they allow subordinates to participate in making decisions as a function of problem attributes. The vertical-dyad linkage model and the life cycle theory are two new situational theories.

Related leadership perspectives are the concept of substitutes for leadership, charismatic leadership, and the role of transformational leadership in organizations.

Political behavior is another influence process frequently used in organizations. Impression management, one especially important form of political behavior, is a direct and intentional effort by someone to enhance his or her image in the eyes of others. Managers can take steps to limit the effects of political behavior.

Discussion Questions

Questions for Review

1. Could someone be a manager but not a leader? a leader but not a manager? both a leader and a manager? Explain.

2. What were the major findings of the Michigan and Ohio State studies of leadership behaviors? Briefly describe each group of studies and compare and contrast their findings.

3. What are the situational approaches to leadership? Briefly describe each and compare and contrast their findings.

4. Describe charismatic and transformation perspectives on leadership. How can they be integrated with existing approaches to leadership?

5. What are the most common forms of political behavior in organizations? How can political behavior be managed?

Questions for Analysis

1. What traits best seem to describe student leaders? military leaders? business leaders? political leaders? religious leaders? What might account for the similarities and differences in your lists of traits?

2. How is it possible for a leader to be both task oriented and employee oriented at the same time? Can you think of other forms of leader behavior that would be important to a manager? If so, share your thoughts with your class.

3. Think about a decision that would affect you as a student. Use the Vroom-Yetton-Jago model to decide whether the administrator making that decision should involve students in the decision. Which parts of the model seem most important in making that decision? Why?

4. When all or most of the leadership substitutes are present, does the follower no longer need a leader? Why or why not?

5. Why should members of an organization be aware that political behavior may be going on within the organization? What might occur if they were not aware?

EXERCISE OVERVIEW

Diagnostic skills help a manager visualize appropriate responses to a situation. One situation managers often face is whether to use power to solve a problem. This exercise helps you develop your diagnostic skills as they relate to using different types of power in different situations.

Building Effective Diagnostic Skills

EXERCISE BACKGROUND

Several methods have been identified for using power. These include:

1. legitimate request—The manager requests that the subordinate comply because the subordinate recognizes that the organization has given the manager the right to make the request. Most day-to-day interactions between manager and subordinate are of this type.

2. instrumental compliance—In this form of exchange, a subordinate complies to get the reward the manager controls. Suppose that a manager asks a subordinate to do something outside the range of the subordinate's normal duties, such as working extra hours on the weekend, terminating a relationship with a long-standing buyer, or delivering bad news. The subordinate complies and, as a direct result, reaps praise and a bonus from the manager. The next time the subordinate is asked to perform a similar activity, that subordinate will recognize that compliance will be instrumental in her getting more rewards. Hence, the basis of instrumental compliance is clarifying important performance-reward contingencies.

3. coercion—This form of power is used when the manager suggests or implies that the subordinate will be punished, fired, or reprimanded if he does not do something.

4. rational persuasion—This form of power is used when the manager can convince the subordinate that compliance is in the subordinate's best interest. For example, a manager might argue that the subordinate should accept a transfer because it would be good for the subordinate's career. In

some ways, rational persuasion is like reward power except that the manager does not really control the reward.

5. personal identification—This use of power occurs when a manager who recognizes that she has referent power over a subordinate can shape the behavior of that subordinate by engaging in desired behaviors. The manager consciously becomes a model for the subordinate and exploits personal identification.

6. inspirational appeal—This use of power occurs when a manager can induce a subordinate to do something consistent with a set of higher ideals or values through inspirational appeal. For example, a plea for loyalty represents an inspirational appeal.

EXERCISE TASK

With these ideas in mind, do the following:

1. Relate each use of power listed above to the five types of power identified in the chapter. That is, indicate which type(s) of power are most closely associated with each use of power, which type(s) may be related to each use of power, and which type(s) are unrelated to each use of power.

2. Consider whether a manager is more likely to be using multiple forms of power at the same time or a single type of power.

3. Identify other methods and approaches to using power.

4. Describe some of the dangers and pitfalls associated with using power.

Building Effective Decision-Making Skills

EXERCISE OVERVIEW

The Vroom-Yetton-Jago (VYJ) model of leadership is an effective method for determining how much participation a manager might allow his or her subordinates in making a decision. This exercise enables you to refine your decision-making skills by applying the VYJ model to a hypothetical situation.

EXERCISE BACKGROUND

Assume that you are the branch manager of the West Coast region of the United States for an international manufacturing and sales company. The company is making a major effort to control costs and boost efficiency. As part of this effort, the firm recently installed a networked computer system linking sales representatives, customer service employees, and other sales support staff. The goal of this network was to increase sales while cutting sales expenses.

Unfortunately, just the opposite has resulted—sales are down slightly, whereas expenses are increasing. You have looked into this problem and believe that although the computer hardware in use is fine, the software is flawed. It is too hard to use and provides less than complete information.

Your employees disagree with your assessment, however. They believe that the entire system is fine. They attribute the problems to poor training in how to use the system and a lack of incentive for using it to solve many problems that they already know how to handle using other methods. Some employees also think that their colleagues are just resisting change.

Your boss has just called and instructed you to "solve the problem." She indicated that she has complete faith in your ability to do so, will let you decide how you proceed, and wants a report suggesting a course of action in five days.

EXERCISE TASK

Using the information presented above, do the following:

1. Using your own personal preferences and intuition, describe how you think you would proceed.

2. Now use the VYJ model to determine a course of action.

3. Compare and contrast your initial approach and the approach suggested by the VYJ model.

EXERCISE OVERVIEW

Conceptual skills refer to the manager's ability to think in the abstract. This exercise enables you to apply your conceptual skills to the identification of leadership qualities in others.

Building Effective
Conceptual
Skills

EXERCISE TASK

1. Working alone, list the names of ten people you think of as leaders. Note that the names should not necessarily be confined to "good" leaders, but instead should identify "strong" leaders.

2. Form small groups with three or four classmates and compare lists. Focus on common and unique examples, as well as the kinds of individuals listed (for example, male versus female, contemporary versus historical, business versus nonbusiness).

3. From all the lists, choose two leaders whom most people in the group consider to be the most successful and least successful.

4. Identify similarities and differences between the two successful leaders and between the two less successful leaders.

5. Relate the successes and failures to at least one theory or perspective discussed in the chapter.

6. Select one group member to report your findings to the rest of the class.

When Susan Turner hired Gordon Jackson to work in the retail nursery operation at Sunset Landscape Services (SLS), she thought that he would be a strong addition to the staff. He had just graduated from college with a major in

You Make the **Call**

horticulture and had exceptional knowledge of certain rare and delicate flowers that she wanted to start selling in the nursery.

For a while, things were great. Gordon helped determine the specific plants to be carried, arranged for the purchase of a special display case, investigated different suppliers, and placed the first order. As he and Susan expected, SLS customers loved the plants. Gordon would spend almost an hour with each customer, demonstrating how to prune the plants, what kind of plant food to use, and so forth.

Gradually, Gordon stopped doing anything other than talking with customers about the plants. Susan saw this shift in job focus as a problem for two reasons. First, Gordon was sometimes needed in other areas of the nursery. He refused to answer pages, however, claiming that he was busy with customers. Second, although sales of the new plants were strong, they were not nearly enough to justify the salary of a full-time employee who did nothing but help sell them.

One day Susan called Gordon into her office for a conference. She said, "Gordon, you've done an excellent job with the new line of plants. However, I need you to start spending more time working in other parts of the nursery. I never intended for these plants to take all of your time. I guess I let you concentrate on them at first, but now that the new line is established, you need to get involved in other areas. And I would like you to teach some of the rest of us how to sell these plants."

To Susan's surprise, Gordon replied, "Well, I really don't want to do that. I'm the only one here who knows about these plants, and I don't think anyone else should be messing with them. I also don't think that I should be expected to work in other areas. I've built this part of the business by myself and really think that I should get to concentrate on it now. I hope you understand my position, but if not, I guess I'll start looking for another job."

DISCUSSION QUESTIONS

1. Identify the types of power reflected in this situation.

2. What do you think Susan should do?

3. Could she have foreseen this turn of events and kept it from happening?

Skills Self-Assessment Instrument

MANAGERIAL LEADER BEHAVIOR QUESTIONNAIRE

Introduction: Leadership is now recognized as being an important set of characteristics for everyone in an organization to develop. The following assessment surveys your leadership practices or beliefs in a management role, that is, managerial leadership.

Instructions: The following statements refer to the possible ways in which you might behave in a managerial leadership role. Indicate how you do behave or how you think that you would behave for each statement. Describing yourself may be difficult in some cases, but you should force a selection. Record your answers next to each statement according to the following scale:

Rating Scale

5 Very descriptive of me   **2** Not very descriptive of me

4 Fairly descriptive of me   **1** Not descriptive of me at all

3 Somewhat descriptive of me

_____ 1. I emphasize the importance of performance and encourage everyone to make a maximum effort.

_____ 2. I am friendly, supportive, and considerate toward others.

_____ 3. I offer helpful advice to others on how to advance their careers and encourage them to develop their skills.

_____ 4. I stimulate enthusiasm for the work of the group and say things to build the group's confidence.

_____ 5. I provide appropriate praise and recognition for effective performance and show appreciation for special efforts and contributions.

_____ 6. I reward effective performance with tangible benefits.

_____ 7. I inform people about their duties and responsibilities, clarify rules and policies, and let people know what is expected of them.

_____ 8. Either alone or jointly with others, I set specific and challenging but realistic performance goals.

_____ 9. I provide any necessary training and coaching or arrange for others to do it.

_____10. I keep everyone informed about decisions, events, and developments that affect their work.

_____11. I consult with others before making work-related decisions.

_____12. I delegate responsibility and authority to others and allow them discretion in determining how to do their work.

_____13. I plan in advance how to efficiently organize and schedule the work.

_____14. I look for new opportunities for the group to exploit, propose new undertakings, and offer innovative ideas.

_____15. I take prompt and decisive action to deal with serious work-related problems and disturbances.

_____16. I provide subordinates with supplies, equipment, support services, and other resources necessary to work effectively.

_____17. I keep informed about the activities of the group and check on its performance.

_____18. I keep informed about outside events that have important implications for the group.

_____19. I promote and defend the interests of the group and take appropriate action to obtain necessary resources for the group.

_____20. I emphasize teamwork and try to promote cooperation, cohesiveness, and identification with the group.

_____21. I discourage unnecessary fighting and bickering within the group and help settle conflicts and disagreements in a constructive manner.

_____22. I criticize specific acts that are unacceptable, find positive things to say, and provide an opportunity for people to offer explanations.

_____23. I take appropriate disciplinary action to deal with anyone who violates a rule, disobeys an order, or has consistently poor performance.

For interpretation, turn to page 461.

Source: Adapted from David D. Van Fleet and Gary A. Yukl, _Military Leadership: An Organizational Behavior Perspective_, 1986, pp. 38–39. Copyright © 1986 by JAI Press. Used with permission of the publisher.

Experiential Exercise

THE LEADERSHIP/MANAGEMENT INTERVIEW EXPERIMENT

Purpose: Leadership and management are in some ways the same, but more often they are different. This exercise allows you to develop a conceptual framework for leadership and management.

Introduction: Because most management behaviors and leadership behaviors are a product of individual work experience, each leader/manager tends to have a unique leadership/management style. An analysis of leadership/management styles and a comparison of such styles with different organizational experiences are often rewarding experiences in learning.

Instructions: *Fact-Finding and Execution of the Experiment*

1. Develop a list of questions relating to issues studied in this chapter that you want to ask a practicing manager and leader during a face-to-face interview. Prior to the actual interview, submit your list of questions to your instructor for approval.

2. Arrange to interview a practicing manager and a practicing leader. For purposes of this assignment, a manager or leader is a person whose job priority involves supervising the work of other people. The leader/manager may work in a business or in a public or private agency.

3. Interview at least one manager and one leader, using the questions you developed. Take good notes on their comments and on your own observations. Do not take more than one hour of each leader's/manager's time.

Oral Report

Prepare an oral report using the questions here and your interview information. Complete the following report after the interview. (Attach a copy of your interview questions.)

The Leadership/Management Interview Experiment Report

1. How did you locate the leaders/managers you interviewed? Describe your initial contacts.

2. Describe the level and responsibilities of your leaders/managers. Do not supply names—their responses should be anonymous.

3. Describe the interview settings. How long did the interview last?

4. In what ways were the leaders/managers similar or in agreement about issues?

5. What were some of the major differences between the leaders/managers and the ways in which they approached their jobs?

6. In what ways would the managers agree or disagree with ideas presented in this course?

7. Describe and evaluate your own interviewing style and skills.

8. How did your managers feel about having been interviewed? How do you know that?

9. Overall, what were the most important things you learned from this experience?

Source: Adapted from Stephen C. Iman, "The Management Interview Experiment" in *Introducing Organizational Behavior: Exercises and Experiments* 2nd ed., by Peter P. Dawson and Stephen C. Iman, 1981, pp. 135–138, Ginn and Co.

CASE STUDY

Big Turnaround at Adidas

For years Adidas ruled the market for athletic sportswear. But bumbling management allowed Nike to swoop in and take control. Under new leadership, however, Adidas is beginning to bounce back and shows signs of making the sneaker wars a real battle. Adidas was founded in 1948 by Adi Dassler, a brilliant Bavarian shoe designer. Virtually every athlete who competed in the 1956 Olympics wore Adidas shoes during the competition. And no less a player than Kareem Abdul-Jabbar wore Adidas shoes when he dominated the NBA.

But internal problems seriously weakened the firm. First, Adi's brother Rudolf left and started his own firm, Puma. Adi's son Horst also split from the family and started another competing manufacturer. Horst later returned to the fold and took over the firm's management in 1985. Neglect and the onslaught of Nike and Reebok had taken their toll. When Horst died in 1987, Adidas's market share had fallen from a high of 70 percent to just 2 percent. And no one in the family was prepared to step in and take over.

Horst's sisters sold the company to a French financier named Bernard Tapie in 1989 for a paltry $320 million. Tapie professed to have big plans for the firm and promised to bring in $100 million in new investment to get the firm back on its feet. Unfortunately, Tapie became so involved in politics that he, too, paid the firm little attention. He subsequently became embroiled in a soccer-fixing scandal while serving as France's Urban Affairs Minister, was sentenced to prison, declared bankruptcy, and turned Adidas over to his creditors.

The creditors, in turn, turned to Robert Louis-Dreyfuss, another French financier, and asked him to take control of the company. Louis-Dreyfuss had no experience in the shoe or sportswear businesses, but did have a sterling reputation as a turnaround artist. As soon as he moved into the president's office, he was astonished to be asked to personally approve a sales representative's expense account for $300. He knew at that moment that his challenges centered around bureaucracy and old-fashioned business practices.

Over the next few weeks, Louis-Dreyfuss replaced the entire top management team at Adidas, all of whom were German. He brought in new executives from other countries and designated English as the firm's official language. He also renegotiated the firm's manufacturing contracts to get costs in line with those of Nike and Reebok. And as he got costs under control, he then turned to marketing.

Louis-Dreyfuss doubled the firm's marketing budget and instructed managers in that department to get busy with new, innovative, and aggressive ideas for taking back market share previously lost to competitors. These managers, in turn, enlisted the endorsements of sports stars like Steffi Graf and Kobe Bryant. Their biggest coup, however, was getting the New York Yankees to strike a deal that all of their players would wear Adidas shoes.

Adidas still faces an uphill battle. But Louis-Dreyfuss has shown remarkable acumen for managing in a highly competitive industry. Among his more recent victories have been signing up the several major national soccer teams and acquiring Salomon, a major ski equipment manufacturer. Moreover, he believes that the firm will continue its renaissance and will one day soon take what he sees as its rightful place alongside Nike—and ahead of Reebok and other competitors—atop the athletic apparel industry.

Case Questions

1. What leadership theory or concept best explains Louis-Dreyfuss's success at Adidas?
2. What can other leaders learn from Louis-Dreyfuss?
3. Do you think Adidas can overtake Nike? Why or why not?

Case References: "An Adrenaline Rush at Adidas," *Business Week*, September 29, 1997, p. 136; Charles P. Wallace, "Adidas—Back in the Game," *Fortune*, August 18, 1997, pp. 176–182; and "Adidas Is Dropping the Other Shoes," *International Herald Tribune*, March 20, 1998, pp. 15, 19.

CHAPTER NOTES

1. "Compaq: There's No End to Its Drive," *Business Week*, February 17, 1997, pp. 72–73 (quote on p. 72); Stephanie Losee, "How Compaq Keeps the Magic Going," *Fortune*, February 21, 1994, pp. 90–92; and *Hoover's Handbook of American Business 1998* (Austin, Texas: Hoover's Business Press, 1998), pp. 398–399.

2. See Ronald A. Heifetz and Donald L. Laurie, "The Work of Leadership," *Harvard Business Review*, January–February 1997, pp. 124–134. See also Arthur G. Jago, "Leadership: Perspectives in Theory and Research," *Management Science*, March 1982, pp. 315–336.

3. Gary A. Yukl, *Leadership in Organizations*, 3rd ed. (Englewood Cliffs, N.J.: Prentice-Hall, 1994), p. 5.

4. See John P. Kotter, "What Leaders Really Do," *Harvard Business Review*, May–June 1990, pp. 103–111.

5. "Leader, Not Boss," *Forbes*, December 1, 1997, pp. 52–54.

6. John R. P. French and Bertram Raven, "The Bases of Social Power," in Dorwin Cartwright (ed.), *Studies in Social Power* (Ann Arbor, Mich.: University of Michigan Press, 1959), pp. 150–167.

7. Hugh D. Menzies, "The Ten Toughest Bosses," *Fortune*, April 21, 1980, pp. 62–73.

8. Bernard M. Bass, *Bass & Stogdill's Handbook of Leadership*, 3rd ed. (Riverside, N.J.: Free Press, 1990).

9. Shelley A. Kirkpatrick and Edwin A. Locke, "Leadership: Do Traits Matter?" *Academy of Management Executive*, May 1991, pp. 48–60; see also Robert J. Sternberg, "Managerial Intelligence: Why IQ Isn't Enough," *Journal of Management*, Vol. 23, No. 3, 1997, pp. 475–493.

10. Rensis Likert, *New Patterns of Management* (New York: McGraw-Hill, 1961) and Rensis Likert, *The Human Organization* (New York: McGraw-Hill, 1967).

11. The Ohio State studies stimulated many articles, monographs, and books. A good overall reference is Ralph M. Stogdill and A. E. Coons (eds.), *Leader Behavior: Its Description and Measurement* (Columbus, Ohio: Bureau of Business Research, Ohio State University, 1957).

12. Edwin A. Fleishman, E. F. Harris, and H. E. Burt, *Leadership and Supervision in Industry* (Columbus, Ohio: Bureau of Business Research, Ohio State University, 1955).

13. Robert R. Blake and Jane S. Mouton, *The Managerial Grid* (Houston: Gulf Publishing, 1964) and Robert R. Blake and Jane S. Mouton, *The Versatile Manager: A Grid Profile* (Homewood, Ill.: Dow Jones-Irwin, 1981).

14. Fred E. Fiedler, *A Theory of Leadership Effectiveness* (New York: McGraw-Hill, 1967).

15. Chester A. Schriesheim, Bennett J. Tepper, and Linda A. Tetrault, "Least Preferred Co-Worker Score, Situational Control, and Leadership Effectiveness: A Meta-Analysis of Contingency Model Performance Predictions," *Journal of Applied Psychology*, Vol. 79, No. 4, 1994, pp. 561–573.

16. Fiedler, *A Theory of Leadership Effectiveness* and Fred E. Fiedler and M. M. Chemers, *Leadership and Effective Management* (Glenview, Ill.: Scott, Foresman, 1974).

17. For recent reviews and updates, see Lawrence H. Peters, Darrell D. Hartke, and John T. Pohlmann, "Fiedler's Contingency Theory of Leadership: An Application of the Meta-Analysis Procedures of Schmidt and Hunter," *Psychological Bulletin*, Vol. 97, pp. 274–285 and Fred E. Fiedler, "When to Lead, When to Stand Back," *Psychology Today*, September 1987, pp. 26–27.

18. Martin G. Evans, "The Effects of Supervisory Behavior on the Path-Goal Relationship," *Organizational Behavior and Human Performance*, May 1970, pp. 277–298 and Robert J. House and Terence R. Mitchell, "Path-Goal Theory of Leadership," *Journal of Contemporary Business*, Autumn 1974, pp. 81–98. See also Yukl, *Leadership in Organizations*.

19. For a recent review, see J.C. Wofford and Laurie Z. Liska, "Path-Goal Theories of Leadership: A Meta-Analysis," *Journal of Management*, Vol. 19, No. 4, 1993, pp. 857–876.

20. Victor H. Vroom and Philip H. Yetton, *Leadership and Decision-Making* (Pittsburgh: University of Pittsburgh Press, 1973) and Victor H. Vroom and Arthur G. Jago, *The New Leadership* (Englewood Cliffs, N.J.: Prentice-Hall, 1988).

21. Yukl, *Leadership in Organizations*.

22. Vroom and Jago, *The New Leadership*.

23. Fred Dansereau, George Graen, and W. J. Haga, "A Vertical-Dyad Linkage Approach to Leadership Within Formal Organizations: A Longitudinal Investigation of the Role-Make Process," *Organizational Behavior and Human Performance*, Vol. 15, 1975, pp. 46–78 and Chester A. Schreisheim, Linda L. Neider, and Terri A. Scandura, "Delegation and Leader-Member Exchange: Main Effects, Moderators, and Measurement Issues," *Academy of Management Journal*, Vol. 41, No. 3, 1998, pp. 298–318.

24. Antoinette Phillips and Arthur Bedeian, "Leader-Follower Exchange Quality: The Role of Personal and Interpersonal Attributes," *Academy of Management Journal*, Vol. 37, No. 4, 1994, pp. 990–1001.

25. Paul Hersey and Kenneth H. Blanchard, *Management of Organizational Behavior*, 3rd ed. (Englewood Cliffs, N.J.: Prentice-Hall, 1977).

26. Yukl, *Leadership in Organizations*.

27. Steven Kerr and John M. Jermier, "Substitutes for Leadership: Their Meaning and Measurement," *Organizational Behavior and Human Performance*, December 1978, pp. 375–403.

28. See Charles C. Manz and Henry P. Sims Jr., "Leading Workers to Lead Themselves: The External Leadership of Self-Managing Work Teams," *Administrative Science Quarterly*, March 1987, pp. 106–129.

29. See Robert J. House, "A 1976 Theory of Charismatic Leadership," in J. G. Hunt and L. L. Larson (eds.), *Leadership: The Cutting Edge* (Carbondale, Ill.: Southern Illinois University Press, 1977), pp. 189–207. See also Jay A. Conger and Rabindra N. Kanungo, "Toward a Behavioral Theory of Charismatic Leadership in Organizational Settings," *Academy of Management Review*, October 1987, pp. 637–647.

30. Stratford P. Sherman, "Donald Trump Just Won't Die," *Fortune*, August 13, 1990, pp. 75–79.

31. David A. Nadler and Michael L. Tushman, "Beyond the Charismatic Leader: Leadership and Organizational

Change," *California Management Review*, Winter 1990, pp. 77–97.

32. James MacGregor Burns, *Leadership* (New York: Harper & Row, 1978). See also Badrinarayan Shankar Pawar and Kenneth K. Eastman, "The Nature and Implications of Contextual Influences on Transformational Leadership: A Conceptual Examination," *Academy of Management Review*, Vol. 22, No. 1, 1997, pp. 80–109.

33. Labich, "The Seven Keys to Business Leadership."

34. Jeffrey Pfeffer, *Power in Organizations* (Marshfield, Mass.: Pitman Publishing, 1981), p. 7.

35. Timothy Judge and Robert Bretz, "Political Influence Behavior and Career Success," *Journal of Management*, Vol. 20, No. 1, 1994, pp. 43–65.

36. Victor Murray and Jeffrey Gandz, "Games Executives Play: Politics at Work," *Business Horizons*, December 1980, pp. 11–23 and Jeffrey Gandz and Victor Murray, "The Experience of Workplace Politics," *Academy of Management Journal*, June 1980, pp. 237–251.

37. Don R. Beeman and Thomas W. Sharkey, "The Use and Abuse of Corporate Power," *Business Horizons*, March–April 1987, pp. 26–30.

38. See William L. Gardner, "Lessons in Organizational Dramaturgy: The Art of Impression Management," *Organizational Dynamics*, Summer 1992, pp. 51–63 and Elizabeth Wolf Morrison and Robert J. Bies, "Impression Management in the Feedback-Seeking Process: A Literature Review and Research Agenda," *Academy of Management Review*, July 1991, pp. 522–541.

39. Murray and Gandz, "Games Executives Play."

40. Beeman and Sharkey, "The Use and Abuse of Corporate Power."

41. Stefanie Ann Lenway and Kathleen Rehbein, "Leaders, Followers, and Free Riders, An Empirical Test of Variation in Corporate Political Involvement," *Academy of Management Journal*, December 1991, pp. 893–905.

12

Communication in Organizations

OBJECTIVES

After studying this chapter, you should be able to:

- Describe the role and importance of communication in the manager's job.
- Identify the basic forms of communication in organizations.
- Describe electronic communication in organizations.
- Discuss informal communication, including its various forms and types.
- Describe how the communication process can be managed so as to recognize and overcome barriers.

Kmart had its brief moment in the spotlight and then seemed to fade from the scene. But a new CEO is bent on restoring the firm's luster and its status both as a name respected by customers and as an industry powerhouse to be reckoned with by competitors. Unfortunately, he has quite a challenge ahead.

Kmart was the first big retailer to successfully take the plunge into discounting. During the 1970s, Kmart was opening more than one hundred stores a year and was clearly and unambiguously focused on passing Sears to become the biggest retailer in the world. But the firm was so fixated on who was ahead of it—Sears, Penney, and Ward—that it paid too little attention to who was behind it—Sam Walton and Wal-Mart. Kmart did indeed pass the "big three" retailers and take the top spot, but only for a short time.

Even as Wal-Mart was moving past Kmart to become the largest retailer, the firm's managers essentially chose to ignore this formidable competitor and to instead embark on a diversification program into other areas of retailing. Kmart allowed its core discounting business to drift and flounder while it invested in retailing outfits such as OfficeMax, Borders Bookstores, the Sports Authority, Builders Square, and others. But the poorly managed amalgam began to fall apart almost as quickly as it was built, and one CEO after another failed to get things turned around.

Finally, however, the firm may have found the right person for the job. As the firm bordered on bankruptcy, its board knew it had to find a real superstar to run the business. Floyd Hall was named to the top spot at Kmart in 1995 and given a sweeping mandate to restore the firm's long-lost competitiveness. His previous jobs included stints as manager of a Montgomery Ward store, president of B. Dalton bookstores, president of Target, a rival discount chain, and founder of his own retail chain, The Museum Company. He came in as one of the most respected executives in retailing.

According to his supporters, Hall seems to have brought two great strengths to his new job. First, he is known as an excellent listener. Many top managers are too impatient to really listen to others, or they believe they already have the answers to everything. Hall, however, will listen to anybody who has something meaningful to say. He calls it "filling up his knowledge jar." During his first year on the job, he held weekly meetings with employees, customers, and suppliers, listening intently as they described what they liked and disliked about Kmart.

In addition to being an effective listener, Hall is excellent in communicating his ideas to others. He has the capacity to select just the right words to capture what he wants to say and to know just how and when to say them for maximum impact. For example, after one early briefing with stock market analysts, several brokers who had previously discouraged their clients from investing in retailing stocks started to encourage investment in Kmart stock. But Hall is far more than talk. He quickly sold several underperforming units, for example, and is frantically converting many old and run-down Kmart stores into modern, bright, and efficient operations. Although Kmart has a long way to go, it does appear, at least for now, that its stores will remain "open for business."[1]

"I see no reason why Kmart can't be as good a retailer as anybody in the country."

Floyd Hall, Kmart CEO

Floyd Hall seems to have what is a surprisingly rare combination of communication skills and managerial acumen. Communication is a vital part of managerial work. Indeed, managers around the world agree that communication is one of their most important tasks. It is important for them to communicate their vision and goals for the organization to others. And it is important for others to communicate with managers so that they will better understand what's going on in their environment and how they and their organizations can become more effective.

This chapter begins by examining communication in the context of the manager's job. We then identify and discuss forms of interpersonal, group, and organizational communication. Electronic communication is also discussed. After discussing informal methods of communication, we describe effective ways to manage organizational communication.

Communication and the Manager's Job

A typical day for a manager includes doing desk work, attending scheduled meetings, placing and receiving telephone calls, reading correspondence, answering correspondence, attending unscheduled meetings, and tours.[2] Most of these activities involve communication. In fact, managers usually spend more than half of their time on some form of communication. Communication always involves two or more people, so other behavioral processes such as motivation, leadership, and group and team processes come into play. Top executives must handle communication effectively if they are to be true leaders.

■ A Definition of Communication

Imagine three managers working in an office building. The first is all alone but is nevertheless yelling for a subordinate to come help. No one appears, but he continues to yell. The second is talking on the telephone to a subordinate, but static on the line causes the subordinate to misunderstand some important numbers being provided by the manager. As a result, the subordinate sends 1,500 crates of eggs to 150 Fifth Street, when he should have sent 150 crates of eggs to 1500 Fifteenth Street. The third manager is talking in her office with a subordinate who clearly hears and understands what is being said. Each of these managers is attempting to communicate but with different results.

communication The process of transmitting information from one person to another

effective communication The process of sending a message so that the message received is as close in meaning as possible to the message intended

Communication is the process of transmitting information from one person to another. Did any of our three managers communicate? The last did and the first did not. How about the second? In fact, she did communicate. She transmitted information and information was received. The problem was that the message transmitted and the message received were not the same. The words spoken by the manager were distorted by static and noise. **Effective communication**, then, is the process of sending a message so that the message received is as close in meaning as possible to the message intended. Although the second manager engaged in communication, it was not effective.

A key element in effective communication is the distinction between data and information. **Data** are raw figures and facts reflecting a single aspect of reality. The facts that a plant has thirty-five machines, that each machine is capable of producing a thousand units of output per day, that current and projected future demand for the units is thirty thousand per day, and that workers sufficiently skilled to run the machines make $15 an hour are data. **Information** is data presented in a way or form that has meaning. Thus, summarizing the preceding four pieces of data provides information—the plant has excess capacity and is therefore incurring unnecessary costs. Information has meaning to a manager and provides a basis for action. The plant manager might use the information and decide to sell four machines (keeping one as a backup) and transfer five operators to other jobs.

data Raw figures and facts reflecting a single aspect of reality

information Data presented in a way or form that has meaning

■ Characteristics of Useful Information

What factors differentiate information that is useful from information that is not? In general, information is useful if it is accurate, timely, complete, and relevant.

Accurate   For information to be of real value to a manager, it must be accurate. Accuracy means that the information must provide a valid and reliable reflection of reality. A Japanese construction company once bought information from a consulting firm about a possible building site in London. The Japanese were told that the land, which would be sold in a sealed bid auction, would attract bids of close to $250 million. They were also told that the land currently held an old building that could easily be demolished. Thus, the Japanese bid $255 million—which ended up being $90 million more than the next-highest bid. A few days later the British government declared the building historic, preempting any thought of demolition. Clearly, the Japanese acted on information that was less than accurate.[3]

Timely   Information also needs to be timely. Timeliness does not necessarily mean speediness; it means only that information needs to be available in time for appropriate managerial action. Timeliness is a function of the situation facing the manager. When Marriott was gathering information for its Fairfield Inn project, managers projected a six-month window for data collection because there was no urgency to their plans. In contrast, Marriott's computerized reservation and accounting system can provide a manager with the previous night's occupancy level at any Marriott facility.[4]

Complete   Information must tell a complete story for it to be useful to a manager. If it is less than complete, the manager is likely to get an inaccurate or distorted picture of reality. For example, managers at Kroger used to think that house-brand products were more profitable than were national brands because house brands yielded higher unit profits. On the basis of this information, the managers gave house brands a lot of shelf space and centered a lot of promotional activities on them. As Kroger's managers became more sophisticated in understanding their information, however, they realized that national brands were actually more profitable over time because national brands outsold house brands during any given period. Although a store might sell ten cans of Kroger coffee in a day with a profit of twenty-five cents per can (total profit of $2.50), it would also sell fifteen cans of Maxwell House coffee with a profit of twenty cents per can (total profit of $3.00).

Relevant Finally, information must be relevant if it is to be useful to managers. Relevance, like timeliness, is defined according to the needs and circumstances of a particular manager. Operations managers need information on costs and productivity; human resource managers need information on hiring needs and turnover rates; and marketing managers need information on sales projections and advertising rates. As Wal-Mart contemplates countries for possible expansion opportunities, it gathers information about local regulations, customs, and so forth. But the information about any given country isn't really relevant until managers decide to enter that market.

■ The Communication Process

Figure 12.1 illustrates how communication generally takes place between people. The process of communication begins when one person (the sender) wants to transmit a fact, idea, opinion, or other information to someone else (the receiver). This fact, idea, or opinion has meaning to the sender, whether it be simple and concrete or complex and abstract. The next step is to encode the meaning into a form appropriate to the situation. The encoding might take the form of words, facial expressions, gestures, or even artistic expressions and physical actions.

After the message has been encoded, it is transmitted through the appropriate channel or medium. The channel by which the present encoded message is being transmitted to you is the printed page. Common channels in organizations include meetings, e-mail, memos, letters, reports, and telephone calls. Next, it is decoded back into a form that has meaning for the receiver. As noted earlier, the consistency of this meaning can vary dramatically. In many cases, the meaning prompts a response, and the cycle is continued when a new message is relayed by the same steps to the original sender.

"Noise" may disrupt communication anywhere along the way. Noise can be the sound of someone coughing, a truck driving by, or two people talking close at hand. It can also include disruptions such as a letter being lost in the mail, a telephone line

FIGURE 12.1
The Communication Process

As the figure shows, noise can disrupt the communication process at any step. Managers must therefore understand that a conversation in the next office, a fax machine out of paper, and the receiver's worries may all thwart the manager's best attempts to communicate.

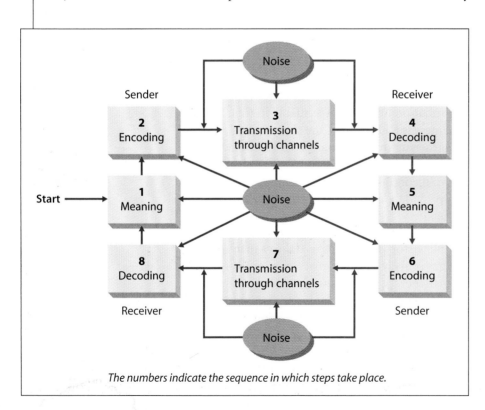

The numbers indicate the sequence in which steps take place.

going dead, an e-mail getting misrouted, or one of the participants in a conversation being called away before the communication process is completed.

Forms of Communication in Organizations

Managers need to understand several kinds of communication that are common in organizations today. These include interpersonal communication, communication in networks and teams, organizational communication, and electronic communication.

oral communication Face-to-face conversation, group discussions, telephone calls, and other circumstances in which the spoken word is used to transmit meaning

■ Interpersonal Communication

Interpersonal communication generally takes two forms, oral and written. As we will see, each has clear strengths and weaknesses.

Oral Communication **Oral communication** takes place in face-to-face conversation, group discussions, telephone calls, and other circumstances in which the spoken word is used to express meaning. Indeed, early research suggests that most managers spend between 50 percent and 90 percent of their time talking to people.[5] Oral communication is so prevalent for several reasons. The primary advantage of oral communication is that it promotes prompt feedback and interchange in the form of verbal questions or agreement, facial expressions, and gestures. Oral communication is also easy (all the sender needs to do is talk), and it can be done with little preparation (though careful preparation is advisable in certain situations). The sender does not need pencil and paper, typewriter, or other equipment. In one survey, 55 percent of the executives sampled felt that their own written communication skills were fair or poor, so they chose oral communication to avoid embarrassment![6]

However, oral communication also has drawbacks. It may suffer from problems of inaccuracy if the speaker chooses the wrong words to convey meaning or leaves out pertinent details, if noise disrupts the process, or if the receiver forgets part or all of the message. In a two-way discussion, there is seldom time for a thoughtful, considered response or for introducing many new facts, and there is no permanent record of what has been said. In addition, although most managers are comfortable talking to people individually or in small groups, fewer enjoy speaking to larger audiences.[7]

People communicate with one another in a variety of ways and in many different settings. Consider this team of Netscape employees. They are using oral communication as they talk while they eat lunch. They are also using written communication from the papers stacked on the table and electronic communication in the form of e-mail. Moreover, they are using nonverbal communication with their body language and facial expressions.

written communication Memos, letters, reports, notes, and other situations in which the written word is used to transmit meaning

Written Communication   "Putting it in writing" can solve many of the problems inherent in oral communication. Nevertheless, and perhaps surprisingly, **written communication** is not as common as one might imagine, nor is it a mode of communication much respected by managers. One sample of managers indicated that only 13 percent of the mail they received was of immediate use to them.[8] More than 80 percent of the managers who responded to another survey indicated that the written communication they received was of fair or poor quality.[9]

The biggest single drawback of written communication is that it inhibits feedback and interchange. When one manager sends another manager a letter, it must be written or dictated, typed, mailed, received, routed, opened, and read. If there is a misunderstanding, it may take several days for it to be recognized, let alone rectified. A phone call could settle the whole matter in just a few minutes. Thus, written communication often inhibits feedback and interchange and is usually more difficult and time-consuming than is oral communication.

Of course, written communication offers some advantages. It is often quite accurate and provides a permanent record of the exchange. The sender can take the time to collect and assimilate the information and can draft and revise it before it is transmitted. The receiver can take the time to read it carefully and can refer to it repeatedly, as needed. For these reasons, written communication is generally preferable when important details are involved. At times it is important to one or both parties to have a written record available as evidence of exactly what took place.

Choosing the Right Form   Which form of interpersonal communication should the manager use? The best medium will be determined by the situation. Oral communication is often preferred when the message is personal, nonroutine, and brief. Written communication is usually best when the message is more impersonal, routine, and longer. The manager can also combine media to capitalize on the advantages of each. For example, a quick telephone call to set up a meeting is easy and gets an immediate response. Following up the call with a reminder note helps ensure that the recipient will remember the meeting, and it provides a record of the meeting having been called. Electronic communication, discussed more fully later, blurs the differences between oral and written communication and can help each be more effective.

■ Communication in Networks and Work Teams

Although communication among team members in an organization is clearly interpersonal, substantial research focuses specifically on how people in networks and work teams communicate with one another. A **communication network** is the pattern through which the members of a group or team communicate. Researchers studying group dynamics have discovered several typical networks in groups and teams consisting of three, four, and five members. Representative networks among members of five-member teams are shown in Figure 12.2.[10]

In the wheel pattern, all communication flows through one central person who is probably the group's leader. In a sense the wheel is the most centralized network because one person receives and disseminates all information. The Y

communication network The pattern through which the members of a group communicate

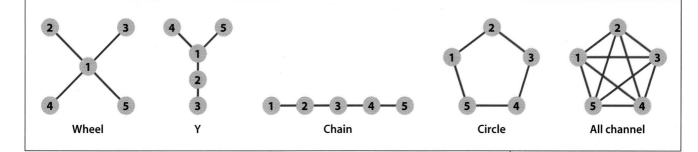

| Wheel | Y | Chain | Circle | All channel |

FIGURE 12.2
Types of Communication Networks

pattern is slightly less centralized—two people are close to the center. The chain offers a more even flow of information among members, although two people (the ones at each end) interact with only one other person. This path is closed in the circle pattern. Finally, the all-channel network, the most decentralized, allows a free flow of information among all group members. Everyone participates equally, and the group's leader, if there is one, is not likely to have excessive power.

Research conducted on networks suggests some interesting connections between the type of network and group performance. For example, when the group's task is relatively simple and routine, centralized networks tend to perform with greatest efficiency and accuracy. The dominant leader facilitates performance by coordinating the flow of information. When a group of accounting clerks is logging incoming invoices and distributing them for payment, for example, one centralized leader can coordinate things efficiently. When the task is complex and nonroutine, such as making a major decision about organizational strategy, decentralized networks tend to be most effective because open channels of communication permit more interaction and a more efficient sharing of relevant information. Managers should recognize the effects of communication networks on group and organizational performance and should try to structure networks appropriately.

Research on communication networks has identified five basic networks for five-person groups. These vary in terms of information flow, position of the leader, and effectiveness for different types of tasks. Managers might strive to create centralized networks when group tasks are simple and routine. Alternatively, managers can foster decentralized groups when group tasks are complex and nonroutine.

■ Organizational Communication

Other forms of communication in organizations flow among and between organizational units or groups. Each of these involves oral or written communication, but each also extends to broad patterns of communication across the organization.[11] As shown in Figure 12.3, two of these forms of communication follow vertical and horizontal linkages in the organization.

Vertical Communication **Vertical communication** is communication that flows both up and down the organization, usually along formal reporting lines—that is, it is the communication that takes place between managers and their superiors and subordinates. Vertical communication may involve only two people, or it may flow through several different organizational levels.

Upward communication consists of messages from subordinates to superiors. This flow is usually from subordinates to their direct superior, then to that person's direct superior, and so on up the hierarchy. Occasionally, a message might bypass a particular superior. The typical content of upward communication is requests, information that the lower-level manager thinks is of

vertical communication Communication that flows up and down the organization usually along formal reporting lines; it takes place between managers and their subordinates and may involve several different levels of the organization

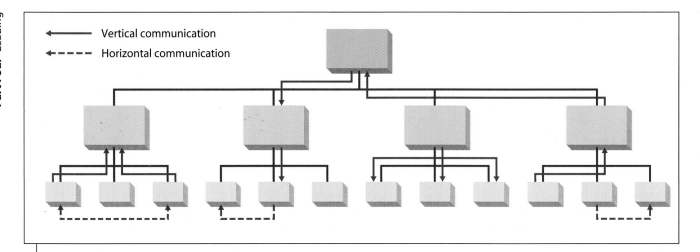

Vertical communication

Horizontal communication

FIGURE 12.3
Formal Communication in Organizations

Formal communication in organizations follows official reporting relationships and/or prescribed channels. For example, vertical communication, shown here with dashed lines, flows between levels in the organization and involves subordinates and their managers. Horizontal communication flows between people at the same level and is usually used to facilitate coordination.

horizontal communication
Communication that flows laterally within the organization; it involves colleagues and peers at the same level of the organization and may involve individuals from several different organizational units

importance to the higher-level manager, responses to requests from the higher-level manager, suggestions, complaints, and financial information. Research has shown that upward communication is more subject to distortion than is downward communication. Subordinates are likely to withhold or distort information that makes them look bad. The greater the degree of difference in status between superior and subordinate and the greater the degree of distrust, the more likely the subordinate is to suppress or distort information.[12] For example, when Harold Geneen was CEO of ITT, subordinates routinely withheld information about problems from him if they thought the news would make him angry and if they thought they could solve the problem themselves without his ever knowing about it.[13]

Downward communication occurs when information flows down the hierarchy from superiors to subordinates. The typical content of these messages is directives on how something is to be done, the assignment of new responsibilities, performance feedback, and general information that the higher-level manager thinks will be of value to the lower-level manager. Vertical communication can, and usually should, be two-way in nature. That is, give-and-take communication with active feedback is generally likely to be more effective than one-way communication.[14]

Horizontal Communication Whereas vertical communication involves a superior and a subordinate, **horizontal communication** involves colleagues and peers at the same level of the organization. For example, an operations manager might communicate to a marketing manager that inventory levels are running low and that projected delivery dates should be extended by two weeks. Horizontal communication probably occurs more among managers than among nonmanagers.

This type of communication serves a number of purposes. It facilitates coordination among interdependent units. For example, a manager at Motorola was once researching the strategies of Japanese semiconductor firms in Europe. He found a great deal of information that was relevant to his assignment. He also uncovered some additional information that was potentially important to another department, so he passed it along to a colleague in that department, who used it to improve his own operations.[15] Horizontal communication can also be used for joint problem solving, as when two plant managers at Northrup

Grumman got together to work out a new method to improve productivity. Finally, horizontal communication plays a major role in work teams with members drawn from several departments.

Electronic Communication

An increasingly important form of organization communication relies on electronic communication technology. **Information technology**, or **IT**, refers to the resources used by an organization to manage information that it needs to carry out its mission. IT may consist of computers, computer networks, telephones, facsimile machines, and other pieces of hardware. In addition, IT involves software that facilitates the system's capabilities to manage information in a way that is useful for managers.[16] Both formal information systems and personal information technology have reshaped how managers communicate with one another.

information technology or **IT** The resources an organization uses to manage information that it needs to carry out its mission

■ Formal Information Systems

Organizations can use various kinds of information systems. The six most general kinds of information systems are transaction-processing systems, basic management information systems, decision support systems, executive information systems, intranets, and expert systems.

Transaction-Processing Systems A **transaction-processing system**, or **TPS**, handles routine and recurring transactions within the business. Visa uses a TPS to record charges to individual credit accounts, credit payments made on the accounts, and send monthly bills to customers. In general, a TPS is most useful when the organization has a large number of highly similar transactions to process. Thus, most forms of customer billings, bank transactions, and point-of-sale records are amenable to this form of information system. The automated scanners at Kroger that record each unit sold and its price are a form of TPS.

transaction-processing system or **TPS** A system that handles a business's routine and recurring information transactions

Management Information Systems Another popular form of information management is generally called the **management information system**, or **MIS**. An MIS gathers more comprehensive data, organizes and summarizes it in a form that is of value to functional managers, and then provides those same managers with the information they need to do their work. An MIS for a manufacturing firm might develop a computerized inventory system that keeps track of both anticipated orders and inventory on hand. A marketing representative talking to a customer about anticipated delivery dates can "plug into the system" and get a good idea of when an order can be shipped. Likewise, the plant manager can use the system to help determine how much of each of the firm's products to manufacture next week or next month. Seminole Manufacturing Co. uses a variation on the standard MIS called electronic data exchange (EDE). Seminole supplies Wal-Mart with men's pants. The EDE system ties

management information system or **MIS** A system that gathers more comprehensive data, organizes and summarizes it in a form of value to managers, and provides those managers with the information they need to do their work

Seminole directly into Wal-Mart's computerized inventory system to check current sales levels and stock on hand. Wal-Mart can then transmit new orders directly into Seminole's system—and managers there are already geared up to start working on it. As a result, delivery times have been cut in half and sales are up 31 percent.[17]

decision support system or DSS
A system that automatically searches for, manipulates, and summarizes information needed by managers for use in making specific decisions

Decision Support Systems An increasingly common information system is called a **decision support system**, or **DSS**. A DSS is both very elaborate and quite powerful. Such a system can automatically search for, manipulate, and summarize information needed by managers for specific decisions. A DSS is much more flexible than a traditional MIS and can help cope with nonroutine problems and decisions. A manager might be interested in knowing the likely effects of a price increase for a particular product sold by the firm. Thus, she might decide to query the DSS to determine the potential outcomes for price increases of 5, 7, and 10 percent. The DSS already knows the pricing history for the product, the prices charged by competitors, their most recent price changes, the effects of price on sales, seasonal variations in demand and price, inflation rates, and virtually any other relevant piece of information that might have already been determined. The system then calculates projected sales, market share, and profit profiles for each of the potential price-increase levels and provides them to the manager.

executive information system or
EIS A system that meets the special information-processing needs of top managers

Executive Information Systems Executive information systems are among the newest forms of information system. An **executive information system**, or **EIS**, meets the special information-processing needs of top managers. Because many top managers lack basic computer skills and because they need highly specialized information not readily available in conventional systems, many executives were reluctant to use their organizations' information systems. An EIS is constructed to be very user-friendly. That is, technical knowledge is not necessary to use it. Instead, such systems generally use icons and symbols and require very few commands. The information they provide allows managers to bypass details and get directly to overall trends and patterns that may affect strategic decision making. The EIS summarizes information for managers; it does not provide specific details. It also tailors the information to the specific needs of the manager.[18]

intranet A communication network similar to the Internet but operating within the boundaries of a single organization

Intranets Many larger organizations today are also developing **intranets**, communication networks similar to the Internet but operating within the boundaries of a single organization. Such systems enable every business unit or division within the organization to compile information about itself and to make it available to employees in the business units or divisions. Specific functional groups can use an intranet for communication. For example, human resources can post job openings and describe benefit options, and marketing can outline details of upcoming promotional activities. Interest groups can use an intranet to post announcements. In addition, rather than print company newsletters on paper, the material can be made available electronically.[19]

expert system An information system created to duplicate or imitate the thought processes of a human expert

Expert Systems Expert systems are also becoming more and more practical. An **expert system** is an information system created to duplicate, or at least imitate, the thought processes of a human being. The starting point in developing an expert system is to identify all the "if then" contingencies that pertain to a given situation. These contingencies form the knowledge base for the system. For example, Campbell's developed an expert system to re-create the thought processes of one of its key employees, a manager who knew everything about the seven-story soup kettles used to cook soup. The manager, Aldo Cimino, knew so much about how the kettles worked that the company feared no one else could learn the job as well as he. So it hired Texas Instruments to study his job, interview him and observe his work, and create an expert system that could mimic his experience. The resulting system, containing more than 150 if-then rules, helps operate the kettles today.[20]

■ Personal Electronic Technology

The nature of organizational communication continues to change dramatically, mainly because of breakthroughs in personal electronic communication technology, and the future promises even more change. Electronic typewriters and photocopying machines were early breakthroughs. The photocopier, for example, enables a manager to distribute a typed report to many people in an extremely short time. Personal computers have accelerated the process even more. E-mail systems, the Internet, and corporate intranets promise to carry communication technology even further in the years to come.[21]

It is now possible to have teleconferences in which managers stay at their own locations (such as offices in different cities) and "meet" via television monitors. A manager in New York can keyboard a letter or memorandum at her personal computer, point and click with a mouse, and have it delivered to hundreds or even thousands of colleagues around the world in a second. Highly detailed information can be retrieved with ease from large electronic databanks. Electronic technology has given rise to a new version of an old work arrangement—*telecommuting* is the label given to a new electronic cottage industry. In a cottage industry, people work at home (in their cottages) and periodically deliver the product of their labor to the company. In telecommuting, people work at home on their computers and transmit their work to the company by means of telephone modems.

For example, David L. Hoffman, a partner in a Chicago law firm, lives in Telluride, Colorado. He consults with clients over the phone, sends them reports through the telephone lines with his modem or by Federal Express, and has calls to his Chicago office electronically routed to Telluride. Recent estimates suggest that as many as fifteen million Americans use telephones, computers, and couriers to work outside their conventional offices.

Cellular telephones and facsimile machines have made it even easier for managers to communicate with one another. Many now use cellular phones to make calls while commuting to and from work and carry them in briefcases so they can receive calls at lunch. Facsimile machines make it easy for people to send documents that contain text and graphics and get rapid feedback.

Psychologists, however, are beginning to associate some problems with these communication advances. For one thing, managers who are seldom in their "real" offices are likely to fall behind in their fields and to be victimized by organizational politics because they are not present to keep in touch with what's going on and to protect themselves. They drop out of the organizational grapevine and miss out on much of the informal communication that takes place. Moreover, the use of electronic communication at the expense of face-to-face meetings and conversations makes it hard to build a strong culture, develop solid working relationships, and create a mutually supportive atmosphere of trust and cooperativeness.[22]

Informal Communication in Organizations

The various forms of organizational communication discussed in the preceding two sections represent planned, formal communication mechanisms. However, in many cases much of the communication that takes place in an organization transcends these formal channels and instead follows any of several informal methods. Figure 12.4 illustrates numerous paths of informal communication. Common forms of informal communication in organizations include the grapevine, management by wandering around, and nonverbal communication.

grapevine An informal communication network among people in an organization

■ The Grapevine

The **grapevine** is an informal communication network that can permeate an entire organization. Grapevines are found in all organizations except the very smallest, but they do not always follow the same patterns as, nor do they necessarily coincide with, formal channels of authority and communication. There is some disagreement about the accuracy of information carried by the grapevine, but research is increasingly finding it to be fairly accurate, especially when the information is based on fact rather than speculation. One study found that the grapevine may be between 75 percent and 95 percent accurate.[23] That same study also found that informal communication is increasing in many organizations for two basic reasons. One contributing factor is the recent increase in merger, acquisition, and takeover activity. Because such activity can greatly affect the people within an organization, they are likely to spend more

FIGURE 12.4
Informal Communication in Organizations

Informal communication in organizations may or may not follow official reporting relationships and/or prescribed channels. It may cross different levels and different departments or work units, and may or may not have anything to do with official organizational business.

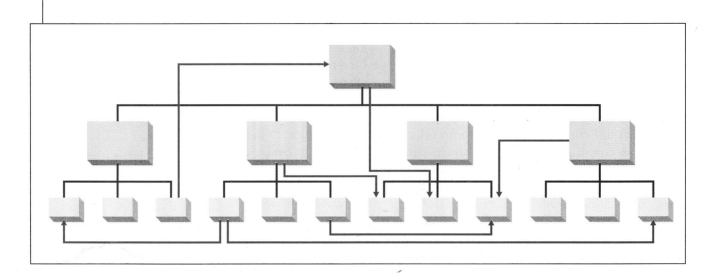

time talking about it.[24] The second contributing factor is that as more and more corporations move facilities from inner cities to suburbs, employees tend to talk less and less to others outside the organization and more and more to each other.

Attempts to eliminate the grapevine are fruitless, but fortunately the manager does have some control over it. By maintaining open channels of communication and responding vigorously to inaccurate information, the manager can minimize the damage the grapevine can do. The grapevine can actually be an asset. By learning who the key people in the grapevine are, for example, the manager can partially control the information they receive and use the grapevine to sound out employee reactions to new ideas such as a change in human resource policies or benefit packages. The manager can also get valuable information from the grapevine and use it to improve decision making.

■ Management by Wandering Around

Another increasingly popular form of informal communication is called **management by wandering around**.[25] The basic idea is that some managers keep in touch with what's going on by wandering around and talking with people—immediate subordinates, subordinates far down the organizational hierarchy, delivery people, customers, or anyone else who is involved with the company in some way. Bill Marriott, for example, frequently visits the kitchens, loading docks, and custodial work areas whenever he tours a Marriott hotel. He claims that by talking with employees throughout the hotel, he gets new ideas and has a better feel for the entire company.

management by wandering around An approach to communication that involves the manager literally wandering around and engaging in spontaneous conversations with others

A related form of organizational communication that really has no specific term is the informal interchange that takes place outside the normal work setting. Employees attending the company picnic, playing on the company softball team, or taking fishing trips together will almost always spend part of their time talking about work. For example, Texas Instruments engineers at TI's Lewisville, Texas, facility often frequent a local bar in town after work. On any given evening, they talk about the Dallas Cowboys, the newest government contract received by the company, the weather, their boss, the company's stock price, local politics, and problems at work. There is no set agenda, and the key topics of discussion vary from group to group and from day to day. Still, the social gatherings serve an important role. They promote a strong culture and enhance understanding of how the organization works.

■ Nonverbal Communication

Nonverbal communication is a communication exchange that does not use words or that uses words to carry more meaning than the strict definition of the words themselves. Nonverbal communication is a powerful but little-understood form of communication in organizations. It often relies on facial expression, body movements, physical contact, and gestures. One study found that as much as 55 percent of the content of a message is transmitted by facial expression and body posture and that another 38 percent derives

nonverbal communication Any communication exchange that does not use words or that uses words to carry more meaning than the strict definition of the words themselves

Communication is a powerful force in organizations. Nonverbal communication can be especially important. As shown in this cartoon, some organizations are experimenting with meetings in rooms with no furniture. The logic is twofold: without status symbols like traditional seating arrangements, better communication may result (leaders usually sit at the head of the table), and meetings may be more efficient if people can't get too comfortable (because they have no place to sit). But some managers might still attempt to circumvent the goals of this approach by seeking other ways to maintain their status.

from inflection and tone. Words themselves account for only 7 percent of the content of the message.[26]

Research has identified three kinds of nonverbal communication practiced by managers—images, settings, and body language.[27] In this context, *images* are the kinds of words people elect to use. "Damn the torpedoes, full speed ahead" and "Even though there are some potential hazards, we should proceed with this course of action" may convey the same meaning. Yet the person who uses the first expression may be perceived as a maverick, a courageous hero, an individualist, or a reckless and foolhardy adventurer. The person who uses the second might be described as aggressive, forceful, diligent, or narrow-minded and resistant to change. In short, our choice of words conveys much more than just the strict meaning of the words themselves.

The setting for communication also plays a major role in nonverbal communication. Boundaries, familiarity, the home turf, and other elements of the setting are all important. Much has been written about the symbols of power in organizations. The size and location of an office, the kinds of furniture in the office, and the accessibility of the person in the office communicate useful information. For example, H. Ross Perot positions his desk so that it is always between him and a visitor. This arrangement keeps him in charge. When he wants a less formal dialogue, he moves around to the front of the desk and sits beside his visitor.

A third form of nonverbal communication is body language.[28] The distance we stand from someone as we speak has meaning. In the U.S., standing very close to someone you are talking to generally signals either familiarity or aggression. The English and Germans stand farther apart than Americans when talking, whereas the Arabs, Japanese, and Mexicans stand closer together.[29] Eye contact is another effective means of nonverbal communication. For example, prolonged eye contact might suggest either hostility or romantic interest. Other kinds of body language include body and arm movement, pauses in speech, and mode of dress.

The manager should be aware of the importance of nonverbal communication and recognize its potential impact. Giving an employee good news about a reward with the wrong nonverbal cues can destroy the reinforcement value of the reward. Likewise, reprimanding an employee but providing inconsistent nonverbal cues can limit the effectiveness of the sanctions. The tone of the message, where and how the message is delivered, facial expressions, and gestures can amplify or weaken the message or change its meaning altogether.

Managing Organizational Communication

In view of the importance and pervasiveness of communication in organizations, it is vital for managers to understand how to manage the communication process.[30] Managers should understand how to maximize the potential benefits of communication and minimize the potential problems. We begin our discussion of communication management by considering the factors that might disrupt effective communication and identifying ways to deal with them.

■ Barriers to Communication

Several factors may disrupt the communication process or serve as barriers to effective communication.[31] As shown in Table 12.1, these may be divided into two classes: individual barriers and organizational barriers.

Individual Barriers Several individual barriers may disrupt effective communication. One common problem is conflicting or inconsistent signals. Another is lack of credibility. A manager is sending conflicting signals when she says on Monday that things should be done one way but then prescribes an entirely different procedure on Wednesday. Similarly, a manager is sending inconsistent signals when he says he has an "open door" policy and wants his subordinates to drop by but keeps his door closed and becomes irritated whenever someone stops in. Credibility problems arise when the sender is not considered a reliable source of information. He may not be trusted or may not be perceived as knowledgeable about the subject at hand. When a politician is caught withholding information or when a manager makes a series of bad decisions, the extent to which he or she will be listened to and believed thereafter diminishes. In extreme cases, people may talk about something they obviously know little or nothing about. Some people are simply reluctant to initiate a communication exchange. This reluctance may occur for a variety of reasons. A manager may be reluctant to tell subordinates about an impending budget cut because he knows they will be unhappy about it. Likewise, a subordinate may be reluctant to transmit information

Individual Barriers	Organizational Barriers
Conflicting or inconsistent cues	Semantics
Credibility about the subject	Status or power differences
Reluctance to communicate	Different perceptions
Poor listening skills	Noise
Predispositions about the subject	Overload

TABLE 12.1
Barriers to Effective Communication

Numerous barriers can disrupt effective communication. Some of these barriers involve individual characteristics and processes. Others are a function of the organizational context in which communication is taking place.

upward for fear of reprisal or because she feels that such an effort would be futile.

Two other individual barriers to effective communication are poor listening habits and predispositions about the subject at hand. Some people are poor listeners. When someone is talking to them, they may be daydreaming, looking around, reading, or listening to another conversation. Because they are not concentrating on what is being said, they may not comprehend part or all of the message. They may even think that they really are paying attention, only to realize later that they cannot remember parts of the conversation. Receivers may also bring certain predispositions to the communication process. They may already have their minds made up, firmly set in a certain way. For example, a manager may have heard that his new boss is unpleasant and hard to work with. When she calls him in for an introductory meeting, he may go into that meeting predisposed to dislike her and discount what she has to say.

Organizational Barriers   Other barriers to effective communication involve the organizational context in which the communication occurs. Semantics problems arise when words have different meanings for different people. Words and phrases such as *profit*, *increased output*, and *return on investment* may have positive meanings for managers but less positive meanings for labor. Communication problems may arise when people of different power or status try to communicate with each other. The company president may discount a suggestion from an operating employee, thinking, "How can someone at that level help me run my business?" Or when the president goes out to inspect a new plant, workers may be reluctant to offer suggestions because of their lower status. The marketing vice president may have more power than the human resource vice president and consequently may not pay much attention to a staffing report submitted by the human resource department. If people perceive a situation differently, they may have difficulty communicating with one another. When two managers observe that a third manager has not spent much time in her office lately, one may believe that she has been to several important meetings while the other may think she is "hiding out." If they need to talk about her in some official capacity, problems may arise because one has a positive impression and the other a negative impression.

Environmental factors may also disrupt effective communication. As mentioned earlier, noise may affect communication in many ways. Similarly, overload may be a problem when the receiver is being sent more information than he or she can effectively handle. When the manager gives a subordinate many jobs on which to work and at the same time the subordinate is being told by family and friends to do other things, overload may result and communication effectiveness diminish.

■ Improving Communication Effectiveness

Considering how many factors can disrupt communication, it is fortunate that managers can resort to several techniques for improving communication effectiveness.[32] As shown in Table 12.2, these techniques include both individual and organizational skills.

Individual Skills   The most important individual skill for improving communication effectiveness is learning to be a good listener. Being a good listener requires that the individual be prepared to listen, not interrupt the speaker, concentrate on both the words and the meaning being conveyed, be patient, and ask questions as appropriate.[33] So important are good listening skills that companies like Delta, IBM, and Unisys conduct programs to train their managers to be better listeners. Figure 12.5 illustrates the characteristics of poor listeners versus good listeners.

In addition to being a good listener, several other individual skills can promote effective communication. Feedback, one of the most important, is facilitated by two-way communication. Two-way communication allows the receiver to ask questions, request clarification, and express opinions that let the sender know whether he or she has been understood. In general, the more complicated the message, the more useful two-way communication is. In addition, the sender should be aware of the meanings that different receivers might attach to various words. For example, when addressing stockholders, a manager might frequently use the word *profits*. When addressing labor leaders, however, she may choose to use *profits* less often.

Furthermore, the sender should try to maintain credibility. Some ways to maintain credibility are by not pretending to be an expert when one is not, by

Individual Skills	Organizational Skills
Develop good listening skills	Follow up
Encourage two-way communication	Regulate information flows
Be aware of language and meaning	Understand the richness of media
Maintain credibility	
Be sensitive to receiver's perspective	
Be sensitive to sender's perspective	

TABLE 12.2
Overcoming Barriers to Communication

Because communication is so important, managers have developed a number of methods for overcoming barriers to effective communication. Some of these methods involve individual skills, whereas others are based on organizational skills.

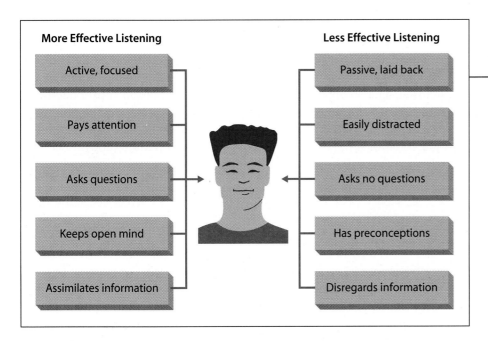

FIGURE 12.5
More and Less Effective Listening Skills

Effective listening skills are a vital part of communication in organizations. Several factors can contribute to poor listening skills by individuals in organizations. Fortunately, people can learn to improve their listening skills.

Managing organizational communication takes a variety of innovative forms. For example, managers at Interim Services, a Florida-based temp company, believe that they should know all their employees. To facilitate this, all new employees are given a "passport" when they start work at Interim. They are expected to visit all the firm's department managers during their first month at work. Each manager "stamps" the employee's passport after they have met. Employees turn their passports in when they are completed and then proceed to the next stage in their orientation program, a series of workshops.

doing one's homework and checking facts, and by otherwise being as accurate and honest as possible. The sender should also try to be sensitive to the receiver's perspective. A manager who must tell a subordinate that she has not been recommended for a promotion should recognize that the subordinate will be frustrated and unhappy. The content of the message and its method of delivery should be chosen accordingly. The manager should be primed to accept a reasonable degree of hostility and bitterness without getting angry in return.[34] Finally, the receiver should also try to be sensitive to the sender's point of view. Suppose that a manager has just received some bad news—for example, that his position is being eliminated next year. Others should understand that he may be disappointed, angry, or even depressed for a while. Thus, they might make a special effort not to take too much offense if he snaps at them, and they might look for signals that he needs someone to talk to.

Organizational Skills   Three useful organizational skills can also enhance communication effectiveness for both the sender and the receiver—following up, regulating information flow, and understanding the richness of different media.

Following up simply involves checking at a later time to be sure that a message has been received and understood. After a manager mails a report to a colleague, she might call a few days later to make sure the report has arrived. If it has, the manager might ask whether the colleague has any questions about it.

Regulating information flow means that the sender or receiver takes steps to ensure that overload does not occur. For the sender, preventing overflow could mean not passing too much information through the system at one time. For the receiver, it might mean calling attention to the fact that he is being asked to do too many things at once. Many managers limit the influx of information by periodically weeding out the list of journals and routine reports they receive, or they train a secretary to screen phone calls and visitors.

Both parties should also understand the richness associated with different media. When a manager is going to lay off a subordinate temporarily, the message should be delivered in person. A face-to-face channel of communication gives the manager an opportunity to explain the situation and answer questions. When the purpose of the message is to grant a pay increase, written communication may be appropriate because it can be more objective and precise. The manager could then follow up the written notice with personal congratulations.

Summary of Key Points

Communication is the process of transmitting information from one person to another. Effective communication is the process of sending a message so that the message received is as close in meaning as possible to the message intended. Data and information are key ingredients of effective communication.

Communication is a pervasive and important part of the manager's world. The communication process consists of a sender encoding meaning and transmitting it to one or more receivers, who receive the message and decode it into meaning. In two-way communication the process continues with the roles reversed. Noise can disrupt any part of the overall process.

Several forms of organizational communication exist. Interpersonal communication focuses on communication among a small number of people. Two important forms of interpersonal communication, oral and written, offer unique advantages and disadvantages. Thus, the manager should weigh the pros and cons of each method when choosing a medium for communication. Communication networks are recurring patterns of communication among members of a group or work team. Vertical communication between superiors and subordinates may flow upward or downward. Horizontal communication involves peers and colleagues at the same level in the organization.

Electronic communication is having a profound effect on managerial and organizational communication. The kinds of information systems are transaction-processing systems, basic management information systems, decision support systems, executive information systems, intranets, and expert systems. Each provides certain types of information and is most valuable for specific types of managers.

Informal communication also occurs in organizations. The grapevine is the informal communication network among people in an organization. Management by wandering around is also a popular informal method of communication. Nonverbal communication includes facial expressions, body movement, physical contact, gestures, and inflection and tone.

Managing the communication process necessitates recognizing the barriers to effective communication and understanding how to overcome them. Barriers can be identified at both the individual and organizational level. Likewise, both individual and organizational skills can be used to overcome these barriers.

Discussion Questions

Questions for Review

1. Define communication. What are the components of the communication process?

2. Which form of interpersonal communication is best for long-term retention? Why? Which form is best for getting across subtle nuances of meaning? Why?

3. Describe three different communication networks. Which type of network seems to most accurately describe the grapevine? Why?

4. Identify and describe the basic kinds of information systems commonly used in organizations today.

5. What are the informal methods of communication? Identify five examples of nonverbal communication that you have recently observed.

Questions for Analysis

1. Is it possible for an organization to function without communication? Why or why not?

2. At what points in the communication process can problems occur? Give examples of communication problems and indicate how they might be prevented or alleviated.

3. How are electronic communication devices likely to affect the communication process in the future? Why?

4. Do you participate in one or more grapevines? Would you say they are relatively accurate?

5. In terms of the barriers most likely to be encountered, what are the differences between horizontal and vertical communication in an organization? How might a formal information system be designed to reduce such barriers?

Building Effective Technical Skills

EXERCISE OVERVIEW

Technical skills are the skills necessary to perform the work of the organization. This exercise helps you develop and apply technical skills involving the Internet and its potential for gathering information relevant to making important decisions.

EXERCISE BACKGROUND

Assume that you are a manager for a large national retailer. You have been assigned the responsibility for identifying potential locations for the construction of a warehouse and distribution center. The idea behind such a center is that the firm can use its enormous purchasing power to buy many products in large, bulk quantities at relatively low prices. Individual stores can then order specific quantities they need from the warehouse.

The location will need an abundance of land. The warehouse itself, for example, will occupy more than four square acres of land. In addition, the location needs to be close to railroads and major highways; shipments will be arriving by both rail and trucks, although outbound shipments will be exclusively by truck. Other important variables are that land prices and the cost of living should be relatively low and that weather conditions should be mild (to minimize disruptions to shipments).

The firm's general experience is that small to midsize communities work best. Moreover, warehouses are already in place in the western and eastern parts of the United States, so this new one will most likely be in the central or south-central area. Your boss has asked you to identify three or four potential sites.

EXERCISE TASK

With the information above as a framework, do the following:

1. Use the Internet to identify up to ten possible locations.

2. Use additional information from the Internet to narrow the set of possible locations to three or four.

3. Finally, use the Internet to find out as much as possible about the potential locations.

Building Effective Communication Skills

EXERCISE OVERVIEW

Communication skills refer to a manager's ability to both effectively convey ideas and information to others and to effectively receive ideas and information from others. This exercise focuses on communication skills as they involve deciding on the best way to convey information.

EXERCISE BACKGROUND

Assume that you are a middle manager for a large electronics firm. People in your organization generally use one of three means for communicating with one another. The most common way is verbal communication, either face to face or by telephone. Electronic mail is also widely used. Finally, a surprisingly large amount of communication is still paper based, such as memos, reports, or letters.

On a typical day you receive and send a variety of messages and other communication, and you generally use some combination of all of the communication methods noted above. Here are some of the communication tasks on your to-do list for today:

1. You need to schedule a meeting with five subordinates.

2. You need to congratulate a coworker who just had a baby.

3. You need to reprimand a staff assistant who has been coming in to work late for the last several days.

4. You need to inform the warehouse staff that several customers have recently complained because their shipments were not packed properly.

5. You need to schedule a meeting with your boss.

6. You need to announce two promotions.

7. You need to fire someone who has been performing poorly for some time.

8. You need to inform several individuals about a set of new government regulations that will soon affect them.

9. You need to inform a supplier that your company will soon be cutting back on its purchases because a competing supplier has lowered its prices and you plan to shift more of your business to that supplier.

10. You need to resolve a disagreement between two subordinates who want to take their vacation at the same time.

EXERCISE TASK

Using the information presented above, do the following:

1. Indicate which methods of communication would be appropriate for each situation.

2. Rank-order the methods for each communication situation from best to worst.

3. Compare your rankings with those of a classmate and discuss any differences.

EXERCISE OVERVIEW

Time-management skills refer to the manager's ability to prioritize work, to work efficiently, and to delegate appropriately. This exercise helps you develop your time-management skills as they relate to communication.

**Building Effective
Time-Management
Skills**

EXERCISE BACKGROUND

Communication is a vital and necessary part not only of management but also of our daily lives. We benefit when communication takes place in effective ways. But ineffective communication can be a major source of wasted time and energy.

EXERCISE TASK

With this idea as context, do the following:

1. Reflect back on your communication for one day. Recall who you talked to, when, for how long, and about what subjects.

2. Do the same for mail you received and mail you sent.

3. Evaluate each communication exchange as being more valuable or less valuable.

4. Estimate how much time you spent on less valuable communication.

5. Decide how you could have either avoided those less valuable communication exchanges or made them more valuable.

6. Consider how much control we really have over our communication.

You Make the Call

Mark Spenser didn't realize that he was asking for trouble. A professional football player who had attended the local university had retired recently and moved back to town. He bought a large house and hired Mark to install a pool, decks, and extensive landscaping in the backyard. Mark subcontracted the construction of the pool and decks but kept the landscaping part of the contract for his own business. It was still a huge job, however, and Mark's staff of three installers was having a tough time getting the project done on schedule.

One Thursday afternoon after four weeks of work, Mark realized that with some extra effort he could finish the job the next day and not have to run it into the next week. He wrote the following note to Betty Bickham, one of the lawn-care crew chiefs:

Betty—
I need some extra help tomorrow at the Johnson home. Please send your crew over there to work. I'll ask Manny to get some volunteers to take care of your Friday lawn jobs on Saturday and pay them time-and-a-half.

—Mark

Sure enough, with the extra help the project was finished the next day. Mark went home tired but satisfied and relieved that they were finished.

On Monday morning, however, Mark was met by a visibly upset Manuel Hernandez. Manuel told him that several customers had called to complain that their yards weren't done. He had confronted Betty, who told him the story. As he listened, Mark realized to his horror that he had totally forgotten to tell Manuel what was going on and to schedule extra help on Saturday.

Mark had little choice but to apologize to Manuel, both for not consulting him about using Betty's crew and for forgetting to have the work rescheduled.

Manuel accepted Mark's apology graciously but also indicated that he thought they needed to figure out a way to keep each other better informed.

DISCUSSION QUESTIONS

1. Why did the problem described above happen?

2. What could Mark have done differently to avoid the problem?

3. Was Manuel justified in being angry?

4. What could Manuel and Betty have done to avoid this problem?

SEX TALK QUIZ

Skills Self-Assessment Instrument

Introduction: As more women enter the workforce, communication between men and women will increase. Research shows that men and women frequently have difficulty in communicating effectively with one another because of differences in their beliefs and values about each sex. The following assessment surveys your beliefs and values about each sex.

Instructions: Mark each statement as either true or false. In some cases, you may find making a decision difficult, but you should force a choice.

	True	False
1. Women are more intuitive than men. They have a sixth sense, which is typically called "women's intuition."	[]	[]
2. At business meetings, coworkers are more likely to listen to men than they are to women.	[]	[]
3. Women are the "talkers." They talk much more than men in group conversations.	[]	[]
4. Men are the "fast talkers." They talk much quicker than women.	[]	[]
5. Men are more outwardly open than women. They use more eye contact and exhibit more friendliness when first meeting someone than do women.	[]	[]
6. Women are more complimentary and give more praise than men.	[]	[]
7. Men interrupt more than women and will answer a question even when it is not addressed to them.	[]	[]
8. Women give more orders and are more demanding in the way they communicate than are men.	[]	[]

9. In general, men and women laugh at the
same things. [ ] [ ]

10. When making love, both men and women
want to hear the same things from their partner. [ ] [ ]

11. Men ask for assistance less often than do women. [ ] [ ]

12. Men are harder on themselves and blame
themselves more often than do women. [ ] [ ]

13. Through their body language, women make
themselves less confrontational than men. [ ] [ ]

14. Men tend to explain things in greater detail
when discussing an incident than do women. [ ] [ ]

15. Women tend to touch others more often
than men. [ ] [ ]

16. Men appear to be more attentive than women
when they are listening. [ ] [ ]

17. Women and men are equally emotional when
they speak. [ ] [ ]

18. Men are more likely than women to discuss
personal issues. [ ] [ ]

19. Men bring up more topics of conversation than
do women. [ ] [ ]

20. Today we tend to raise our male children the
same way we do our female children. [ ] [ ]

21. Women tend to confront problems more
directly and are likely to bring up the problem
first. [ ] [ ]

22. Men are livelier speakers who use more body
language and facial animation than do women. [ ] [ ]

23. Men ask more questions than women. [ ] [ ]

24. In general, men and women enjoy talking about
similar things. [ ] [ ]

25. When asking whether their partner has had an
AIDS test or when discussing safe sex, a woman
will likely bring up the topic before a man. [ ] [ ]

For interpretation, turn to page 462.

Source: From *He Says, She Says* by Lillian Glass, Ph.D. Copyright © 1992 by Lillian Glass, Ph.D. Used by permission of Putnam Berkley, a division of Penguin Putnam Inc., and the author.

DEVELOPING COMMUNICATION SKILLS

Purpose: Some ways of giving instructions to people are quicker or more accurate than others. Some generate more satisfaction in or greater compliance by the recipient. It is important for you to recognize different communication models with their resulting costs and benefits. This exercise identifies the types of behaviors that assist or interfere with effective transmission of instructions. It also illustrates forms of communication and investigates the differing outcomes as well as the processes resulting from these means of communication. The exercise allows you to explore possible techniques for dealing with dysfunctional communication behaviors.

Instructions: Your instructor will provide further instructions.

Source: From Ritchie, *Organization and People: Readings, Cases, and Exercises in Organizational Behavior,* 3d ed., by J.B. Ritchie and Paul Thompson. © 1984. Reprinted with permission of South-Western College Publishing, a division of International Thomson Publishing. Fax: 1-800-730-2215.

CASE STUDY

Exxon's Communication Failure

Exxon Corporation is one of the oldest businesses in the United States, tracing its roots back to 1863 when John D. Rockefeller opened an oil refinery that would eventually become Standard Oil Company. The U.S. Justice Department broke up Standard Oil under antitrust legislation in 1911. One surviving piece eventually became Exxon, which is now the largest U.S. oil company and one of the largest industrial companies in the U.S. But just because it is large and successful does not mean that it handles crisis communication well.

In 1989 an Exxon oil tanker, the *Exxon Valdez,* ran aground in Prince William Sound, Alaska, spilling nearly eleven million barrels of oil and causing tremendous environmental damage. Exxon's poor handling of the crisis sent a message to corporations worldwide that they needed to have better and more effective crisis-communication plans.

After the *Valdez* incident Exxon was attacked for being too slow to respond, for being too slow to accept its responsibility, and for providing inadequate cleanup efforts. In a crisis situation such as the *Valdez* disaster, the primary task of management is to inform the public—through the media—about what has happened. Exxon's then-CEO, Lawrence Rawl, however, made no comment for nearly a week after the incident and instead relied on his staff to handle early communications. When he finally did make a public appearance, he seemed uninformed and unsure of the details of what was happening, which further fueled negative reactions.

For example, while Exxon was claiming that the damage was minimal, newscasts were showing pictures of oil-covered beaches and rocks covered with thousands of dead birds and fish. The media essentially suggested that Exxon was not being completely honest and candid in its statements and public relations releases. Differences between accounts provided by Exxon and as covered by the media led to a negative public reaction and distrust of Exxon.

Delays, errors, and contradictions seemed to demonstrate that Exxon was arrogant, uncaring, and unaware of the environment in which it operated. The public quickly became outraged. Customers threatened a boycott, and thousands of them even returned their credit cards (the actual impact of these actions, however, was virtually negligible). Nevertheless, in a full-page newspaper advertisement ten days after the crisis, Rawl claimed that the company had acted swiftly and competently.

Unfortunately, Exxon's crisis-communication problems were compounded by internal problems of its own making. As it was still dealing with its environmental disaster, Exxon laid off more than seventy-five thousand workers and reduced training for those that remained. Employees were asked to take early retirement or to relocate when Exxon moved to Texas. Consequently, many Exxon employees were unhappy or worried about their own future. As a result, they were not particularly motivated or excited about helping the company overcome its problems.

Thus, while the press coverage of the *Valdez* crisis emphasized Rawl's difficulties in responding to the public outcry over the oil spill, morale and attitude problems among its employees also played a role. Exxon seemed to have image problems both within and without the company and was having communication problems of varying kinds.

Has Exxon ever learned its lesson? It does appear to finally be getting the message. For example, its crisis-communication plan now involves having video and telecommunications resources, senior executives trained in dealing with a hostile media, contacts with print and broadcast media, and a clear spokesperson, the new CEO, Lee Raymond, all in place and prepared to deal with any situation imaginable. In the event of another disaster, the crisis team will meet every hour after a disaster occurs until it is resolved. The plan has also been tested in mock disaster drills and simulations. Had Exxon had such a plan ten years ago, most of its problems from the *Valdez* crisis could have been averted.

Case Questions

1. In what ways did Exxon not handle the communication process very well in the *Valdez* crisis?

2. What barriers to communication seemed to be involved in your response to question one above? Why or in what way?

3. What unintended messages did Exxon send as a result of the way it handled the *Valdez* crisis? How might it prevent any negative communication problems from such crises in the future?

Case References: *Hoover's Handbook of American Business 1999* (Austin, Texas: Hoover's Business Press, 1999), pp. 566–567; Daniel G. Johnson, "Crisis Management: Forewarned Is Forearmed," *Journal of Business Strategy*, March–April 1993, pp. 58–64; "Exxon Stops the Flow," *Time,* March 25, 1991, p. 51; Peter Nulty, "Exxon's Problem: Not What You Think," *Fortune,* April 23, 1990, pp. 202–204; and Sue Stephenson, "The Media and You," *HRMagazine*, June 1997, pp. 146–155.

CHAPTER NOTES

1. "Shoppers Get Kmart's Attention," *USA Today*, April 9, 1997, pp. 1B, 2B (quote on p. 1B); "Kmart Chief Known for Plain Talk, Bold Action," *USA Today*, April 9, 1997, p. 2B; and *Hoover's Handbook of American Business 1999* (Austin, Texas: Hoover's Business Press, 1999), pp. 834–835.

2. Henry Mintzberg, *The Nature of Managerial Work* (New York: Harper & Row, 1973).

3. Carla Rapoport, "Great Japanese Mistakes," *Fortune*, February 13, 1989, pp. 108–111.

4. Edward W. Desmond, "How Your Data May Soon Seek You Out," *Fortune*, September 1997, pp. 149–154.

5. Mintzberg, *The Nature of Managerial Work*.

6. Walter Kiechel III, "The Big Presentation," *Fortune*, July 26, 1982, pp. 98–100.

7. "Executives Who Dread Public Speaking Learn to Keep Their Cool in the Spotlight," *Wall Street Journal*, May 4, 1990, pp. B1, B6.

8. Mintzberg, *The Nature of Managerial Work*.

9. Kiechel, "The Big Presentation."

10. A. Vavelas, "Communication Patterns in Task-Oriented Groups," *Journal of the Acoustical Society of America*, Vol. 22, 1950, pp. 725–730 and Jerry Wofford, Edwin Gerloff, and Robert Cummins, *Organizational Communication* (New York: McGraw-Hill, 1977).

11. Nelson Phillips and John Brown, "Analyzing Communications in and Around Organizations: A Critical Hermeneutic Approach," *Academy of Management Journal*, Vol. 36, No. 6, 1993, pp. 1547–1576.

12. "Walter Kiechel III, "Breaking Bad News to the Boss," *Fortune*, April 9, 1990, pp. 111–112.

13. Myron Magnet, "Is ITT Fighting Shadows—or Raiders?" *Fortune*, November 11, 1985, pp. 25–28.

14. Mary Young and James Post, "How Leading Companies Communicate with Employees," *Organizational Dynamics*, Summer 1993, pp. 31–43.

15. Brian Dumaine, "Corporate Spies Snoop to Conquer," *Fortune*, November 7, 1988, pp. 68–76.

16. Christopher P. Holland and A. Geoffrey Lockett, "Mixed Mode Network Structures: The Strategic Use of Electronic Communication by Organizations," *Organization Science*, September–October 1997, pp. 475–488.

17. "Believe in Yourself, Believe in the Merchandise," *Forbes*, September 8, 1997, pp. 118–124.

18. Jeremy Main, "At Last, Software CEOs Can Use," *Fortune*, March 13, 1989, pp. 77–83.

19. "Get What You Want from the Web," *Fortune*, October 27, 1997, pp. 283–284.

20. "Turning an Expert's Skills into Computer Software," *Business Week*, October 7, 1985, pp. 104–108.

21. "Here Comes the Intranet," *Business Week*, February 26, 1996, pp. 76–84.

22. Walter Kiechel III, "Hold for the Communicaholic Manager," *Fortune*, January 2, 1989, pp. 107–108.

23. "Spread the Word: Gossip Is Good," *Wall Street Journal*, October 4, 1988, p. B1.

24. See David M. Schweiger and Angelo S. DeNisi, "Communication with Employees Following a Merger: A Longitudinal Field Experiment," *Academy of Management Journal*, March 1991, pp. 110–135.

25. See Tom Peters and Nancy Austin, *A Passion for Excellence* (New York: Random House, 1985).

26. Albert Mehrabian, *Non-verbal Communication* (Chicago: Aldine, 1972).

27. Michael B. McCaskey, "The Hidden Messages Managers Send," *Harvard Business Review*, November–December 1979, pp. 135–148.

28. David Givens, "What Body Language Can Tell You That Words Cannot," *U.S. News & World Report*, November 19, 1984, p. 100.

29. Edward J. Hall, *The Hidden Dimension* (New York: Doubleday, 1966).

30. For a detailed discussion of improving communication effectiveness, see Courtland L. Bove and John V. Thill, *Business Communication Today*, 3rd ed. (New York: McGraw-Hill, 1992).

31. See Otis W. Baskin and Craig E. Aronoff, *Interpersonal Communication in Organizations* (Glenview, Ill.: Scott, Foresman, 1980).

32. Joseph Allen and Bennett P. Lientz, *Effective Business Communication* (Santa Monica, Calif.: Goodyear, 1979).

33. Boyd A. Vander Houwen, "Less Talking, More Listening," *HRMagazine*, April 1997, pp. 53–58.

34. For a recent discussion of these and related issues, see Eric M. Eisenberg and Marsha G. Witten, "Reconsidering Openness in Organizational Communication," *Academy of Management Review*, July 1987, pp. 418–426.

13

Managing Groups and Teams

OBJECTIVES

After studying this chapter, you should be able to:

- Define and identify types of groups and teams in organizations, discuss reasons people join groups and teams, and describe the stages of group and team development.
- Identify and discuss four essential characteristics of groups and teams.
- Discuss interpersonal and intergroup conflict in organizations.
- Describe how organizations manage conflict.

Few people have ever heard of a small company called Fastener Supply. The twenty-year-old, sixteen-employee company based in Reading, Massachusetts, distributes eighteen thousand different types of metal, rubber, and nylon fasteners—devices used to hold together the parts that make up everything from automobiles to personal computers to bug zappers. Motorola, Polaroid, and Lucent Technologies are among the company's 350 or so biggest customers.

No one at Fastener Supply believed that the firm had a quality problem. However, John Jenkins, the company president, was aware of recent trends and concerns in quality management and knew that his firm needed to be ahead of the industry, not behind it. A small firm like Fastener Supply can really suffer from the loss of only one big customer, so Jenkins decided to be proactive with regard to quality.

An initial quality audit revealed no significant customer complaints. And on a percentage basis, things seemed to be fine. For example, less than 1 percent of the firm's fasteners failed to meet customer standards. But in absolute terms, the numbers didn't look quite so good. Each year the firm ships more than seventy million products, and of those, about 112,000 fasteners (a very small percentage of the total, but still a very large number nevertheless!) were returned because of a quality problem. Jenkins decided to cut that rate to five hundred per million.

To tackle this problem, Jenkins created a team of three employees, one each from purchasing, sales, and quality control. The group was named the Continuous Improvement Team, or CIT, and charged with reducing the customer rejection rate by 50 percent. The team members were initially concerned about meeting such an ambitious goal but quickly set to work.

They decided to focus their efforts on three areas: supplier quality, customer feedback, and training. Fastener Supply doesn't actually make fasteners at all, but instead buys them from a variety of fastener manufacturers. The CIT instructed each supplier to improve its quality for production and delivery or risk losing business. Some suppliers did indeed balk, and thirty-seven were dropped from Fastener Supply's supplier network. The remaining 250 or so did meet the new standards and continue to have a strong relationship with the firm.

The CIT also sought feedback about areas where customers were not unhappy, but where there was still room for improvement. Almost forty useful suggestions were received and implemented. For example, one suggestion was that a Fastener Supply representative inform customers in advance when a shipment was going to be delayed for even a day or two. Because the firm was already notifying customers about extended delays, it was easy enough to begin doing so routinely. Finally, the CIT also suggested that all employees at Fastener Supply receive more training in every phase of the operation, ranging from packing and loading boxes to logging inventory in computers. As a result, virtually all phases of the firm's operations improved. For example, the year after shipping employees received better training, only two of the seven thousand boxes shipped were returned with parts damaged from bad packing.

By virtually any measure, the CIT has been a big success for Fastener Supply. It actually beat its lofty quality-improvement goal by driving down defects to only 216 per million, a phenomenally low level. In addition, the firm's business has been increasing at a rapid pace as word of its quality spreads throughout the industry. But neither the firm nor the CIT are finished. Indeed, the mantra heard throughout Fastener Supply today is achieving the ultimate—zero defects. Although this ideal may never truly be reached, Fastener Supply's CIT vows to keep working toward it.[1]

"Staying still wasn't going to cut it anymore."

John Jenkins, president of Fastener Supply

John Jenkins at Fastener Supply recognized and took advantage of what many experts are increasingly seeing as a tremendous resource for all organizations—the power of groups and teams. When he needed some changes made at his firm, Jenkins could have just mandated them himself. Or he could have hired an outside consulting firm to tell his employees how to improve. Instead, he created a team of employees and allowed them to figure it out themselves.

This chapter is about processes that lead to and follow from groups and teams in organizations. We first introduce and discuss basic concepts of group and team dynamics. Subsequent sections explain the characteristics of groups and teams in organizations. We then describe interpersonal and intergroup conflict. Finally, we conclude with a discussion of how conflict can be managed.

Groups and Teams in Organizations

Groups are a ubiquitous part of organizational life. They are the basis for much of the work that gets done, and they evolve both inside and outside the normal structural boundaries of the organization. We will define a **group** as two or more people who interact regularly to accomplish a common purpose or goal.[2] The purpose of a group or team may range from preparing a new advertising campaign to informally sharing information to making important decisions to fulfilling social needs.

group Consists of two or more people who interact regularly to accomplish a common purpose or goal

■ Types of Groups and Teams

In general, three basic kinds of groups are found in organizations—functional groups, task groups and teams, and informal or interest groups.[3] These types of groups are illustrated in Figure 13.1.

functional group A group created by the organization to accomplish a number of organizational purposes with an indefinite time horizon

Functional Group A **functional group** is a permanent group created by the organization to accomplish a number of organizational purposes with an unspecified time horizon. The marketing department of Kmart, the management department of the University of North Texas, and the nursing staff of the Mayo Clinic are functional groups. The marketing department at Kmart, for example, seeks to plan effective advertising campaigns, increase sales, run in-store promotions, and develop a unique identity for the company. It is assumed that the functional group will remain in existence after it attains its current objectives—those objectives will be replaced by new ones.

informal or **interest group** Created by its members for purposes that may or may not be relevant to those of the organization

Informal or Interest Groups An **informal** or **interest group** is created by its own members for purposes that may or may not be relevant to organizational goals. It also has an unspecified time horizon. A group of employees who eat lunch together everyday may be discussing how to improve productivity, how to embezzle money, or local politics and sports. As long as the group members enjoy eating together, they will probably continue to do so.

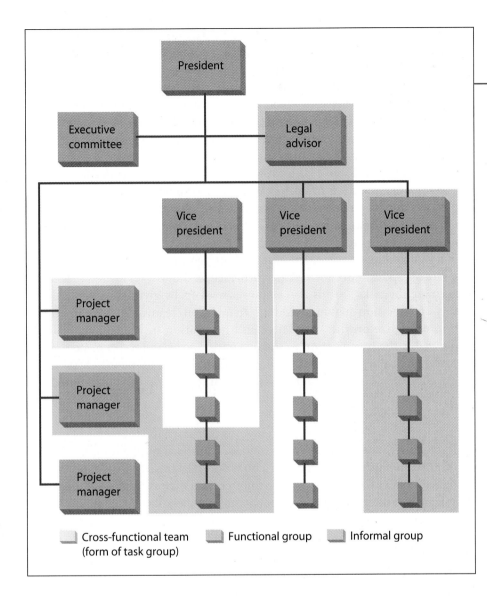

FIGURE 13.1
Types of Groups in Organizations

Every organization has many different types of groups. In this hypothetical organization, a functional group is shown within the blue area, a cross-functional group within the yellow area, and an informal group within the green area.

President

Executive committee

Legal advisor

Vice president

Vice president

Vice president

Project manager

Project manager

Project manager

Cross-functional team (form of task group)   Functional group   Informal group

When lunches cease to be pleasant, participants will seek other company or a different activity. Informal groups can be a powerful force that managers cannot ignore. One writer described how a group of employees at a furniture factory subverted the boss's efforts to increase production. They tacitly agreed to produce a reasonable amount of work but not to work too hard. One man kept a stockpile of completed work hidden as a backup in case he got too far behind. In another example, auto workers described how they left out gaskets and seals and put soft-drink bottles inside doors.[4] Of course, informal groups can also be a positive force, as demonstrated recently when Continental Airline's employees worked together to buy a new motorcycle for Gordon Bethune, the company's CEO, to show their support and gratitude for his excellent leadership.

Task Groups   A **task group** is a group created by the organization to accomplish a relatively narrow range of purposes within a stated or implied time horizon. Most committees and task forces are task groups. The organization

task group   A group created by the organization to accomplish a relatively narrow range of purposes within a stated or implied time horizon

team A group of workers that functions as a unit, often with little or no supervision, to carry out work-related tasks, functions, and activities

specifies group membership and assigns a relatively narrow set of goals, such as developing a new product or evaluating a proposed grievance procedure. The time horizon for accomplishing these purposes is either specified (a committee may be asked to make a recommendation within sixty days) or implied (the project team will disband when the new product is developed).

Teams are a special form of task group that have become increasingly popular. In the sense used here, a **team** is a group of workers who function as a unit, often with little or no supervision, to carry out work-related tasks, functions, and activities. Table 13.1 lists and defines some of the types of teams that are being used today. Earlier forms of teams included autonomous work groups and quality circles. Today teams are also sometimes called *self-managed teams*, *cross-functional teams*, or *high-performance teams*. In many firms teams routinely carry out most of the daily operations.[5]

Organizations create teams for various reasons. For one thing, teams give more responsibility for task performance to the workers who are actually performing the tasks. Teams also empower workers by giving them greater authority and decision-making freedom. In addition, teams allow the organization to capitalize on the knowledge and motivation of its workers. Finally, teams enable the organization to shed its bureaucracy and to promote flexibility and responsiveness.[6] Ford used a team to design its new F-150 pickup truck.[7] Similarly, General Motors used a team to develop the newest model of the Chevrolet Malibu.[8]

When an organization decides to use teams, it is essentially implementing a major form of organization change, as discussed in Chapter 7. Thus, it's important to follow a logical and systematic approach to planning and implementing teams into an existing organization design. It's also important to recognize that resistance may be encountered. This resistance is most likely from first-line managers who will be giving up much of their authority to the team. Many organizations find that they must change the whole management philosophy of such managers from being a supervisor to being a coach or facilitator.[9]

After teams are in place, managers should continue to monitor the teams' contributions and effectiveness. In the best circumstance, teams will become very cohesive groups with high performance norms. To achieve this state, the

TABLE 13.1
Types of Teams

Source: "Types of Teams" adapted from Brian Dumaine, "The Trouble with Teams," *Fortune,* September 5, 1994, page 87. Copyright © 1994 Time Inc. All rights reserved.

Problem-solving team Most popular type of team; comprises knowledge workers who gather to solve a specific problem and then disband

Management team Consists mainly of managers from various functions like sales and production; coordinates work among other teams

Work team An increasingly popular type of team, work teams are responsible for the daily work of the organization; when empowered, they are self-managed teams

Virtual team A new type of work team that interacts by computer; members enter and leave the network as needed and may take turns serving as leader

Quality circle Declining in popularity, quality circles, comprising workers and supervisors, meet intermittently to discuss workplace problems

"We work 24 hours a day."

Advanced Systems Development Corporation (ASDC)
Beijing, China

IBM emerging markets software development team
Seattle, Washington

manager can use any or all of the techniques described later in this chapter for enhancing cohesiveness. If implemented properly, and with the support of the workers themselves, performance norms will likely be relatively high. That is, if the change is properly implemented, the team participants will understand the value and potential of teams and the rewards they may expect as a result of their contributions. On the other hand, poorly designed and implemented teams will do a less effective job and may detract from organizational effectiveness.[10]

■ Why People Join Groups and Teams

People join groups and teams for many reasons. They join functional groups simply by virtue of joining organizations. People accept employment to earn money or to practice their chosen profession. Once inside the organization, they are assigned to jobs and roles and thus become members of functional groups. People in existing functional groups are told, are asked, or volunteer to serve on committees, task forces, and teams. People join informal or interest groups for various reasons, most of them quite complex.[11]

Interpersonal Attraction   One reason people choose to form informal or interest groups is that they are attracted to each other. Many factors contribute to interpersonal attraction. When people see a lot of each other, pure proximity increases the likelihood that interpersonal attraction will develop. Attraction is increased when people have similar attitudes, personality, or economic standing.

Teams in organizations are used to create products, to provide customer service, to solve problems, and for myriad other purposes. In the late 1990s, IBM used a global system of interrelated teams to establish Java as the standard for network applications. The software development team shown on the right was based in Seattle. When its workday ended, the project was electronically transmitted to a counterpart team in Beijing, shown on the left. They continued work on the project and transmitted it back to Seattle in time for the next workday.

Group Activities   Individuals may also be motivated to join a group because the activities of the group appeal to them. For example, people enjoy jogging, playing bridge, bowling, discussing poetry, playing war games, and flying model airplanes. Many of these activities lend themselves to group participation, and, in fact, most require more than one person. Many large firms like Exxon and Apple have a league of football, softball, or bowling teams. A person may join a bowling team not because of any noticeable attraction to other group members, but simply because being a member of the group allows that person to participate in a pleasant activity. Of course, if the level of interpersonal attraction of the group is very low, a person may choose to forgo the activity rather than join the group.

Group Goals   The goals of a group may also motivate people to join. The Sierra Club, which is dedicated to environmental conservation, is a good example of this kind of interest group. Various fund-raising groups are another illustration. Members may or may not be personally attracted to the other fundraisers, and they probably do not enjoy the activity of knocking on doors asking for money, but they join the group because they subscribe to its goal. Workers join unions like the United Auto Workers because they support its goals.

Need Satisfaction   Still another reason for joining a group is to satisfy the need for affiliation. New residents in a community may join the Newcomers Club partially as a way to meet new people and partially just to be around other people. Likewise, newly divorced individuals often join support groups as a way to have companionship.

Instrumental Benefits   A final reason people join groups is that membership is sometimes seen as instrumental in providing other benefits to the individual. For example, college seniors often join several professional clubs or associations because listing such memberships on a resume is thought to enhance the chances of getting a good job. Similarly, a manager might join a certain racquet club not because she is attracted to its members (although she might be) and not because of the opportunity to play tennis (although she may enjoy it). The club's goals are not relevant and her affiliation needs may be satisfied in other ways. However, she may feel that being a member of this club will lead to important and useful business contacts. The racquet club membership is instrumental in establishing those contacts. Membership in civic groups such as Kiwanis and Rotary may be solicited for similar reasons.

■ Stages of Group and Team Development

Imagine the differences between a collection of five people who have just been brought together to form a group or team and a group or team that has functioned like a well-oiled machine for years. Members of a new group or team are unfamiliar with how they will function together and are tentative in their interactions. In a group or team with considerable experience, members are familiar with one another's strengths and weaknesses and are more secure in their role in the group. The former group or team is generally considered to be immature; the latter, mature. To progress from the immature phase to the mature phase, a group or team must go through certain stages of development, as shown in Figure 13.2.[12]

The first stage of development is called *forming*. The members of the group or team get acquainted and begin to test which interpersonal behaviors are acceptable and which are unacceptable to the other members. The members are very dependent on others at this point to provide cues about what is acceptable. The basic ground rules for the group or team are established and a tentative group structure may emerge. At Reebok, for example, a merchandising team was created to handle its sportswear business. The team leader and his members were barely acquainted and had to spend a few weeks getting to know one another.

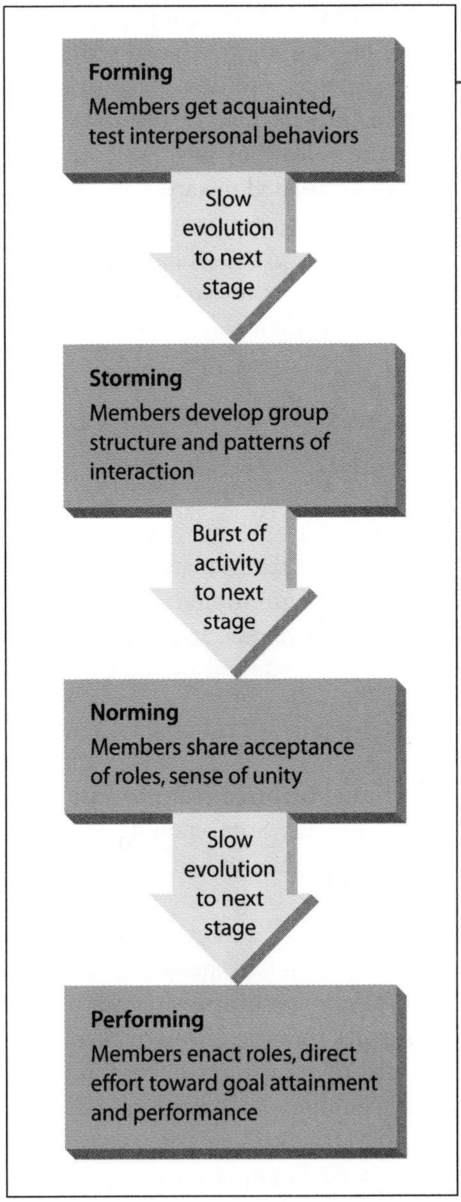

The second stage of development, often slow to emerge, is *storming*. During this stage there may be a general lack of unity and uneven interaction patterns. At the same time, some members of the group or team may begin to exert themselves to become recognized as the group leader or at least to play a major role in shaping the group's agenda. In Reebok's team some members advocated a rapid expansion into the marketplace; others argued for a slower entry. The first faction won, with disastrous results. Because of the rush, product quality was poor and deliveries were late. As a result, the team leader was fired and a new manager was placed in charge.

The third stage of development, called *norming*, usually begins with a burst of activity. During this stage each person begins to recognize and accept her or his role and to understand the roles of others. Members also begin to accept one another and to develop a sense of unity. There may also be temporary regressions to the previous stage. For example, the group or team might begin to accept one particular member as the leader. If this person later violates important norms and otherwise jeopardizes his or her claim to leadership, conflict might reemerge as the group rejects this leader and searches for another. Reebok's new leader transferred several people away from the team and set up

FIGURE 13.2
Stages of Group Development

As groups mature, they tend to evolve through four distinct stages of development. Managers must understand that group members need time to become acquainted, accept each other, develop a group structure, and become comfortable with their roles in the group before they can begin to work directly to accomplish goals.

Forming
Members get acquainted, test interpersonal behaviors

Slow evolution to next stage

Storming
Members develop group structure and patterns of interaction

Burst of activity to next stage

Norming
Members share acceptance of roles, sense of unity

Slow evolution to next stage

Performing
Members enact roles, direct effort toward goal attainment and performance

a new system and structure for managing things. The remaining employees accepted his new approach and settled into doing their jobs.

Performing, the final stage of group or team development, is again slow to develop. The team really begins to focus on the problem at hand. The members enact the roles they have accepted, interaction occurs, and the efforts of the group are directed toward goal attainment. The basic structure of the group or team is no longer an issue but has become a mechanism for accomplishing the purpose of the group. Reebok's sportswear business is now growing consistently and has successfully avoided the problems that plagued it at first.

Characteristics of Groups and Teams

As groups and teams mature and pass through the four basic stages of development, they begin to take on four important characteristics—a role structure, norms, cohesiveness, and informal leadership.[13]

■ Role Structures

roles The parts individuals play in groups in helping the group reach its goals

Each individual in a team has a part—or **role**—to play in helping the group reach its goals. Some people are leaders, some do the work, some interface with other teams, and so on. Indeed, a person may take on a *task-specialist role* (concentrating on getting the group's task accomplished) or a *socioemotional role* (providing social and emotional support to others on the team). A few people, usually the leaders, perform both roles; a few others may do neither. The group's **role structure** is the set of defined roles and interrelationships among those roles that the group or team members define and accept. Each of us belongs to many groups and therefore plays multiple roles—in work groups, classes, families, and social organizations.[14]

FIGURE 13.3
The Development of a Role

Roles and role structures within a group generally evolve through a series of role episodes. The first two stages of role development are group processes as the group members let individuals know what is expected of them. The other two parts are individual processes as the new group members perceive and enact their roles.

Role structures emerge as a result of role episodes, as shown in Figure 13.3. The process begins with the expected role—what other members of the team expect the individual to do. The expected role gets translated into the sent role—the messages and cues that team members use to communicate the expected role to the individual. The perceived role is what the individual perceives the sent role to mean. Finally, the enacted role is what the individual actually does in the role. The enacted role, in turn, influences future expectations of the team. Of course, role episodes seldom unfold this easily. When major disruptions occur, individuals may experience role ambiguity, conflict, or overload.

Role Ambiguity **Role ambiguity** arises when the sent role is unclear. If your instructor tells you to write a term paper but refuses to provide more information, you will probably experience role ambiguity. You

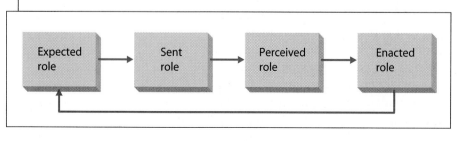

do not know what the topic is, how long the paper should be, what format to use, or when the paper is due. In work settings, role ambiguity can stem from poor job descriptions, vague instructions from a supervisor, or unclear cues from coworkers. The result is likely to be a subordinate who does not know what to do. Role ambiguity can be a significant problem for both the individual who must contend with it and the organization that expects the employee to perform.

Role Conflict   **Role conflict** occurs when the messages and cues composing the sent role are clear but contradictory or mutually exclusive.[15] One common form is *interrole conflict*—conflict between roles. For example, if a person's boss says that to get ahead one must work overtime and on weekends, and the same person's spouse says that more time is needed at home with the family, conflict may result. In a matrix organization, interrole conflict often arises between the roles one plays in different teams as well as between team roles and one's permanent role in a functional group.

Intrarole conflict may occur when the person gets conflicting demands from different sources within the context of the same role. A manager's boss may tell her that she needs to put more pressure on subordinates to follow new work rules. At the same time, her subordinates may indicate that they expect her to get the rules changed. Thus, the cues are in conflict, and the manager may be unsure about which course to follow. *Intrasender conflict* occurs when a single source sends clear but contradictory messages. This situation might arise if the boss says one morning that there can be no more overtime for the next month but after lunch tells someone to work late that same evening. *Person-role conflict* results from a discrepancy between the role requirements and the individual's personal values, attitudes, and needs. If a person is told to do something unethical or illegal, or if the work is distasteful (for example, firing a close friend), person-role conflict is likely. Role conflict is of particular concern to managers. Research has shown that conflict may occur in a variety of situations and lead to a variety of adverse consequences, including stress, poor performance, and rapid turnover.

Role Overload   A final consequence of a weak role structure is **role overload**, which occurs when expectations for the role exceed the individual's capabilities. When a manager gives an employee several major assignments at once while increasing the person's regular workload, the employee will probably experience role overload. Role overload may also result when an individual takes on too many roles at one time. For example, a person trying to work extra hard at his job, run for election to the school board, serve on a church committee, coach Little League baseball, maintain an active exercise program, and be a contributing member to his family will probably encounter role overload.

Implications   In a functional group or team, the manager can take steps to avoid role ambiguity, conflict, and overload. Having clear and reasonable expectations and sending clear and straightforward cues go a long way toward eliminating role ambiguity. Consistent expectations that take into account the employee's other roles and personal value system may minimize role conflict. Role overload can be avoided simply by recognizing the individual's capabilities and limits. In friendship and interest groups, role structures are likely to

role structure   The set of defined roles and interrelationships among those roles that the group members define and accept

role ambiguity   Arises when the sent role is unclear and the individual does not know what is expected of him or her

role conflict   Occurs when the messages and cues making up the sent role are clear but contradictory or mutually exclusive

role overload   Occurs when expectations for the role exceed the individual's capabilities to perform

be less formal; hence, the possibility of role ambiguity, conflict, or overload may not be so great. However, if one or more of these problems do occur, they may be difficult to handle. Because roles in friendship and interest groups are less likely to be partially defined by a formal authority structure or written job descriptions, the individual cannot turn to these sources to clarify a role.

■ Behavioral Norms

norms Standards of behavior that the group accepts and expects of its members

Norms are standards of behavior that the group or team accepts for its members. Most committees, for example, develop norms governing their discussions. A person who talks too much is perceived as doing so to make a good impression or to get his or her own way. Other members may not talk much to this person, may not sit nearby, may glare at the person, and may otherwise "punish" the individual for violating the norm. Norms, then, define the boundaries between acceptable and unacceptable behavior.[16] Some groups develop norms that limit the upper bounds of behavior to "make life easier" for the group. In general, these norms are counterproductive—don't make more than two comments in a committee discussion or don't produce any more than you have to. Other groups may develop norms that limit the lower bounds of behavior. These norms tend to reflect motivation, commitment, and high performance—don't come to meetings unless you've read the reports to be discussed or produce as much as you can. Managers can sometimes use norms for the betterment of the organization. For example, Kodak has successfully used group norms to reduce injuries in some of its plants.[17]

Norm Generalization   The norms of one group cannot always be generalized to another group. Some academic departments, for example, have a norm that suggests that faculty members dress up on teaching days. People who fail to observe this norm are "punished" by sarcastic remarks or even formal reprimands. In other departments the norm may be casual clothes, and the person unfortunate enough to wear dress clothes may be punished just as vehemently. Even within the same work area, similar groups or teams can develop different norms. One team may strive always to produce above its assigned quota; another may maintain productivity just below its quota. The norm of one team may be to be friendly and cordial to its supervisor; that of another team may be to remain aloof and distant. Some differences are due primarily to the composition of the teams.

Norm Variation   In some cases there can also be norm variation within a group or team. A common norm is that the least senior member of a group is expected to perform unpleasant or trivial tasks for the rest of the group. These tasks might be to wait on customers who are known to be small tippers (in a restaurant), to deal with complaining customers (in a department store), or to handle the low-commission line of merchandise (in a sales department). Another example is when certain individuals, especially informal leaders, may violate some norms. If the team is going to meet at eight o'clock, anyone arriving late will be chastised for holding things up. Occasionally, however, the informal leader may arrive a few minutes late. As long as this behavior does not occur too often, the group will probably not do anything.

Norm Conformity Four sets of factors contribute to norm conformity. First, factors associated with the group are important. For example, some groups or teams may exert more pressure for conformity than others. Second, the initial stimulus that prompts behavior can affect conformity. The more ambiguous the stimulus (for example, news that the team is going to be transferred to a new unit), the more pressure there is to conform.

THE FAR SIDE By GARY LARSON

Third, individual traits determine the individual's propensity to conform (for example, more intelligent people are often less susceptible to pressure to conform). Finally, situational factors such as team size and unanimity influence conformity. As an individual learns the group's norms, he can do several different things. The most obvious is to adopt the norms. For example, the new male professor who notices that all the other men in the department dress up to teach can also start wearing a suit. A variation is to try to obey the "spirit" of the norm while retaining individuality. The professor may recognize that the norm is actually to wear a tie; thus, he might succeed by wearing a tie with his sport shirt, jeans, and sneakers.

The individual may also ignore the norm. When a person does not conform, several things can happen. At first the group may increase its communication with the deviant individual to try to bring her back in line. If this approach does not work, communication may decline. Over time, the group may begin to exclude the individual from its activities and, in effect, ostracize the person.

Finally, we need to briefly consider another aspect of norm conformity—socialization. **Socialization** is generalized norm conformity that occurs as a person makes the transition from being an outsider to being an insider. A newcomer to an organization, for example, gradually begins to learn the norms about such things as dress, working hours, and interpersonal relations. As the newcomer adopts these norms, she is being socialized into the organizational culture. Some organizations, like Texas Instruments, work to actively manage the socialization process; others leave it to happenstance.

■ Cohesiveness

A third important team characteristic is cohesiveness. **Cohesiveness** is the extent to which members are loyal and committed to the group. In a highly cohesive team, the members work well together, support and trust one another, and are generally effective at achieving their chosen goal.[18] In contrast, a team that lacks cohesiveness is not very coordinated, and its members do not necessarily support one another fully and may have a difficult time reaching goals. Of particular interest are the factors that increase and reduce cohesiveness and the consequences of team cohesiveness. These are listed in Table 13.2.

Groups and teams are powerful forces in many organizations. People working together in a coordinated and integrated way can often accomplish far more than they could working alone. One problem that can arise, however, is called "free-riding." Free-riding occurs when someone in a group or team fails to carry out his or her responsibilities and lets others do all the work. As illustrated in this cartoon, the Viking in the back of the boat is neglecting his work, letting the rest of the group carry his weight. Thus, he is a free rider!

socialization Generalized norm conformity that occurs as a person makes the transition from being an outsider to being an insider in the organization

cohesiveness The extent to which members are loyal and committed to the group; the degree of mutual attractiveness within the group

TABLE 13.2
Factors That Influence Group Cohesiveness

Several different factors can potentially influence the cohesiveness of a group. For example, a manager can establish intergroup competition, assign compatible members to the group, create opportunities for success, establish acceptable goals, and foster interaction to increase cohesiveness. Other factors can be used to decrease cohesiveness.

Factors That Increase Cohesiveness	Factors That Reduce Cohesiveness
Intergroup competition	Group size
Personal attraction	Disagreement on goals
Favorable evaluation	Intragroup competition
Agreement on goals	Domination
Interaction	Unpleasant experiences

Factors That Increase Cohesiveness   Five factors can increase the level of cohesiveness in a group or team. One of the strongest is intergroup competition. When two or more groups are in direct competition (for example, three sales groups competing for top sales honors or two football teams competing for a conference championship), each group is likely to become more cohesive. Second, just as personal attraction plays a role in causing a group to form, so too does attraction seem to enhance cohesiveness. Third, favorable evaluation of the entire group by outsiders can increase cohesiveness. Thus, a group's winning a sales contest or a conference title or receiving recognition and praise from a superior will tend to increase cohesiveness.

Similarly, if all the members of the group or team agree on their goals, cohesiveness is likely to increase.[19] And the more frequently members of the group interact with each other, the more likely the group is to become cohesive. A manager who wants to foster a high level of cohesiveness in a team might do well to establish some form of intergroup competition, assign members to the group who are likely to be attracted to one another, provide opportunities for success, establish goals that all members are likely to accept, and allow ample opportunity for interaction.

Factors That Reduce Cohesiveness   There are also five factors that are known to reduce team cohesiveness. First of all, cohesiveness tends to decline as a group increases in size. Second, when members of a team disagree on what the goals of the group should be, cohesiveness may decrease. For example, when some members believe the group should maximize output and others think output should be restricted, cohesiveness declines. Third, intragroup competition reduces cohesiveness. When members are competing among themselves, they focus more on their own actions and behaviors than on those of the group.

Fourth, domination by one or more persons in the group or team may cause overall cohesiveness to decline. Other members may feel that they are not being given an opportunity to interact and contribute and may become less attracted to the group. Finally, unpleasant experiences that result from group membership may reduce cohesiveness. A sales group that comes in last in a sales contest, an athletic team that sustains a long losing streak, and a work group reprimanded for poor-quality work may all become less cohesive as a result of their unpleasant experience.

Consequences of Cohesiveness   In general, as teams become more cohesive their members tend to interact more frequently, conform more to norms, and become more satisfied with the team. Cohesiveness may also influence team performance. However, performance is also influenced by the team's performance norms. Figure 13.4 shows how cohesiveness and performance norms interact to help shape team performance.

When both cohesiveness and performance norms are high, high performance should result because the team wants to perform at a high level (norms) and its members are working together toward that end (cohesiveness). When norms are high and cohesiveness is low, performance will be moderate. Although the team wants to perform at a high level, its members are not necessarily working well together. When norms are low, performance will be low, regardless of whether group cohesiveness is high or low. The least desirable situation occurs when low performance norms are combined with high cohesiveness. In this case all team members embrace the standard of restricting performance (owing to the low performance norm), and the group is united in its efforts to maintain that standard (owing to the high cohesiveness). If cohesiveness is low, the manager might be able to raise performance norms by establishing high goals and rewarding goal attainment or by bringing in new group members who were high performers. But a highly cohesive group is likely to resist these interventions.[20]

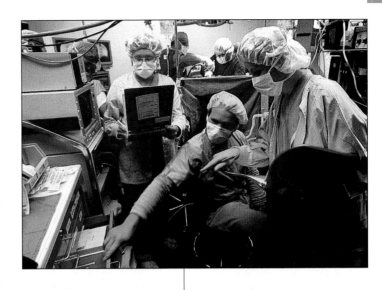

Cohesive teams can be highly effective contributors to the success of any organization. This team, for example, consists of doctors and nurses working together to lower costs at Methodist Healthcare System in San Antonio. The team members share the same performance norms, and their close personal relationships have led the team to become more cohesive as they find new answers and help reach their goal. To date, the overall cost reduction program to which they belong has yielded savings of more than $60 million.

■ Formal and Informal Leadership

Most functional groups and teams have a formal leader—that is, one appointed by the organization or chosen or elected by the members of the group. Because friendship and interest groups are formed by the members themselves, however,

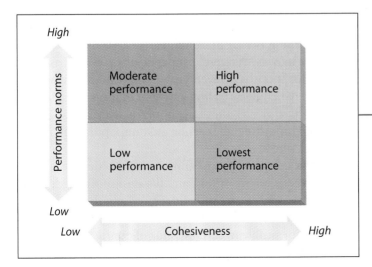

FIGURE 13.4

The Interaction Between Cohesiveness and Performance Norms

Group cohesiveness and performance norms interact to determine group performance. From the manager's perspective, high cohesiveness combined with high performance norms is the best situation, and high cohesiveness with low performance norms is the worst situation. Managers who can influence the level of cohesiveness and performance norms can greatly improve the effectiveness of a work group.

informal leader A person who engages in leadership activities but whose right to do so has not been formally recognized by the organization or group

any formal leader must be elected or designated by the members. Although some groups do designate such a leader (a softball team may elect a captain, for example), many do not. Moreover, even when a formal leader is designated, the group or team may also look to others for leadership. An **informal leader** is a person who engages in leadership activities but whose right to do so has not been formally recognized. The formal and the informal leader in any group or team may be the same person, or they may be different people. We noted earlier the distinction between the task-specialist and socioemotional roles within groups. An informal leader is likely to be a person capable of carrying out both roles effectively. If the formal leader can fulfill one role but not the other, an informal leader often emerges to supplement the formal leader's functions. If the formal leader cannot fill either role, one or more informal leaders may emerge to carry out both sets of functions.

Is informal leadership desirable? In many cases informal leaders are quite powerful because they draw from referent or expert power. When they are working in the best interest of the organization, they can be a tremendous asset. Notable athletes such as Brett Favre and Rebecca Lobo are classic examples of informal leaders. However, when informal leaders work counter to the goals of the organization, they can cause significant difficulties. Such leaders may lower performance norms, instigate walkouts or wildcat strikes, or otherwise disrupt the organization.

Interpersonal and Intergroup Conflict

Of course, when people work together in an organization, things do not always go smoothly. Indeed, conflict is an inevitable element of interpersonal relationships in organizations. In this section we look at how conflict affects overall performance. We also explore the causes of conflict between individuals, between groups, and between an organization and its environment.

■ The Nature of Conflict

conflict A disagreement between two or more individuals or groups

Conflict is a disagreement among two or more individuals, groups, or organizations. This disagreement may be relatively superficial or very strong. It may be short-lived or exist for months or even years, and it may be work related or personal. Conflict may manifest itself in a variety of ways. People may compete with one another, glare at one another, shout, or withdraw. Groups may band together to protect popular members or oust unpopular members. Organizations may seek legal remedy.

Most people assume that conflict is something to be avoided because it connotes antagonism, hostility, unpleasantness, and dissension. Indeed, managers and management theorists have traditionally viewed conflict as a problem to be avoided.[21] In recent years, however, we have come to recognize that although conflict can be a major problem, certain kinds of conflict may also be beneficial.[22] For example, when two members of a site selection committee disagree over the best location for a new plant, each may be forced to more thoroughly study and defend his or her preferred alternative. As a result of more systematic analysis and discussion, the committee may make a better decision and be better prepared to justify it to others than if everyone had agreed from the outset and accepted an alternative that was perhaps less well analyzed.

As long as conflict is being handled in a cordial and constructive manner, it is probably serving a useful purpose in the organization. On the other hand, when working relationships are being disrupted and the conflict reaches destructive levels, it has likely become dysfunctional and needs to be addressed.[23] We discuss ways of dealing with such conflict later in this chapter.

Figure 13.5 depicts the general relationship between conflict and performance for a group or organization. If there is absolutely no conflict in the group or organization, its members may become complacent and apathetic. As a result, group or organizational performance and innovation may begin to suffer. A moderate level of conflict among group or organizational members, on the other hand, can spark motivation, creativity, innovation, and initiative and raise performance. Too much conflict, though, can produce such undesirable results as hostility and lack of cooperation, which lower performance. The key for managers is to find and maintain the optimal amount of conflict that fosters performance. Of course, what constitutes optimal conflict varies according to the situation and the people involved.[24]

■ Causes of Conflict

Conflict may arise in both interpersonal and intergroup relationships. Occasionally, particular organizational strategies and practices may cause conflict between individuals and groups. A third arena for conflict is between an organization and its environment.

Interpersonal Conflict   Conflict between two or more individuals is almost certain to occur in any organization, given the great variety in perceptions, goals, attitudes, and so forth among its members. William Gates, founder and CEO of Microsoft, and Kazuhiko Nishi, a former business associate from Japan, ended a long-term business relationship because of interpersonal conflict. Nishi accused Gates of becoming too political, and Gates charged that Nishi became to unpredictable and erratic in his behavior.[25]

A frequent source of interpersonal conflict in organizations is what many people call a personality clash—when two people distrust each others' motives, dislike one another, or for some other reason simply can't get along.[26] Conflict also may arise between people who have different beliefs or perceptions about some aspect of their work or their organization. For example, one manager may want the organization to require all employees to use Microsoft Office software to promote standardization. Another manager may believe a variety of software packages should be

FIGURE 13.5
The Nature of Organizational Conflict

Either too much or too little conflict can be dysfunctional for an organization. In either case performance may be low. However, an optimal level of conflict that sparks motivation, creativity, innovation, and initiative can result in higher levels of performance. T. J. Rodgers, CEO of Cypress Semiconductor, maintains a moderate level of conflict in his organization as a way of keeping people energized and motivated.

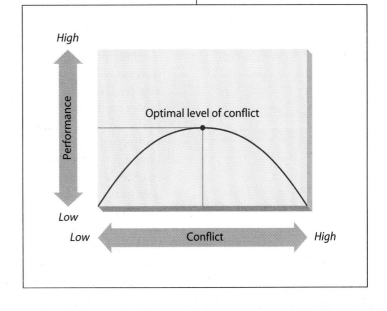

allowed in order to recognize individuality. Similarly, a male manager may disagree with his female colleague over whether the organization is guilty of discriminating against women in promotion decisions.

Conflict also can result from excess competitiveness among individuals. Two people vying for the same job, for example, may resort to political behavior in an effort to gain an advantage. If either competitor sees the other's behavior as inappropriate, accusations are likely to result. Even after the "winner" of the job is determined, such conflict may continue to undermine interpersonal relationships, especially if the reasons given in selecting one candidate are ambiguous or open to alternative explanation. Robert Allen recently resigned as CEO of Delta Air Lines because he disagreed with other key executives over how best to reduce the carrier's costs. After he began looking for a replacement for one of his rivals without the approval of the firm's board of directors, the resultant conflict and controversy left him no choice but to leave.[27]

Intergroup Conflict   Conflict between two or more organizational groups is also quite common. For example, the members of a firm's marketing group may disagree with the production group over product quality and delivery schedules. Two sales groups may disagree over how to meet sales goals, and two groups of managers may have different ideas about how best to allocate organizational resources.

Many intergroup conflicts arise more from organizational causes than interpersonal causes. In Chapter 6, we described three forms of group interdependence—pooled, sequential, and reciprocal. Just as increased interdependence makes coordination more difficult, it also increases the potential for conflict. For example, in sequential interdependence, work is passed from one unit to another. Intergroup conflict may arise if the first group turns out too much work (the second group will fall behind), too little work (the second group will not meet its own goals), or poor-quality work.

At a J.C. Penney department store, conflict recently arose between stockroom employees and sales associates. The sales associates claimed that the stockroom employees were slow in delivering merchandise to the sales floor so that it could be priced and shelved. The stockroom employees, in turn, claimed that the sales associates were not giving them enough lead time to get the merchandise delivered and failed to understand that they had additional duties besides carrying merchandise to the sales floor.

Just like people, different departments often have different goals. Further, these goals may often be incompatible. A marketing goal of maximizing sales, achieved partially by offering many products in a wide variety of sizes, shapes, colors, and models, probably conflicts with a production goal of minimizing costs, achieved partially by long production runs of a few items. Reebok recently confronted this very situation. One group of managers wanted to introduce a new sportswear line as quickly as possible, while other managers wanted to expand more deliberately and cautiously. Because the two groups were not able to reconcile their differences effectively, conflict between the two factions led to quality problems and delivery delays that plagued the firm for months.

Competition for scarce resources can also lead to intergroup conflict. Most organizations—especially universities, hospitals, government agencies, and businesses in depressed industries—do not have unlimited resources. In one New England town, for example, the public works department and the library recently battled over funds from a federal construction grant. The Oldsmobile, Pontiac, and Chevrolet divisions of General Motors have frequently fought over the rights to manufacture various new products developed by the company.

Conflict Between Organization and Environment   Conflict that arises between one organization and another is called interorganizational conflict. A moderate amount of interorganizational conflict resulting from business competition is, of course, expected, but sometimes conflict becomes more extreme. For example, the owners of Jordache Enterprises Inc. and Guess? Inc. have been battling in court for years over ownership of the Guess label, allegations of design theft, and several other issues.[28] Similarly, General Motors and Volkswagen only recently resolved a bitter four-year conflict that started when a key GM executive, Jose Ignacio Lopez de Arriortua, left for a position at Volkswagen. The U.S. company claimed that he took with him key secrets that could benefit its German competitor. After the messy departure, dozens of charges and countercharges were made by the two firms, and only a court settlement was able to put the conflict to an end.[29]

Conflict can also arise between an organization and other elements of its environment. For example, an organization may conflict with a consumer group over claims it makes about its products. McDonald's faced this problem a few years ago when it published nutritional information about its products that omitted details about fat content. A manufacturer might conflict with a governmental agency such as OSHA. For example, the firm's management may believe it is in compliance with OSHA regulations, whereas agency officials believe that the firm is not in compliance. Or a firm might conflict with a supplier over the quality of raw materials. The firm may think the supplier is providing inferior materials, although the supplier thinks the materials are adequate. Finally, individual managers may obviously have disagreements with groups of workers. For example, a manager may think her workers are doing poor-quality work and that they are unmotivated. The workers, on the other hand, may believe they are doing a good job and that the manager is doing a poor job of leading them.

Managing Conflict in Organizations

How do managers cope with all this potential conflict? Fortunately, as Table 13.3 shows, there are ways to stimulate conflict for constructive ends, to control conflict before it gets out of hand, and to resolve it if it does. Below we look at ways of managing conflict.

■ Stimulating Conflict

In some situations, an organization may stimulate conflict by placing individual employees or groups in competitive situations. Managers can establish sales contests, incentive plans, bonuses, or other competitive stimuli to spark competition. As long as the ground rules are equitable and all participants perceive the contest as fair, the conflict created by the competition is likely to be

TABLE 13.3
Methods for Managing Conflict

Conflict is a powerful force in organizations and has both negative and positive consequences. Managers can draw on several techniques to stimulate, control, resolve, or eliminate conflict, depending on their unique circumstances.

Stimulating conflict
  Increase competition among individuals and teams
  Hire outsiders to shape things up
  Change established procedures

Controlling conflict
  Expand resource base
  Enhance coordination of interdependence
  Set supraordinate goals
  Match personalities and work habits of employees

Resolving and eliminating conflict
  Avoid conflict
  Convince conflicting parties to compromise
  Bring conflicting parties together to confront and negotiate conflict

because each participant will work hard to win (thereby enhancing some aspect of organizational performance).

Another useful method for stimulating conflict is to bring in one or more outsiders who will shake things up and present a new perspective on organizational practices. Outsiders may be new employees, current employees assigned to an existing work group, or consultants or advisers hired on a temporary basis. Of course, this action can also provoke resentment from insiders who feel they were qualified for the position. The Beecham Group, a British company, once hired an executive from the United States for its CEO position expressly to change how the company did business. His arrival brought with it new ways of doing things and a new enthusiasm for competitiveness. Unfortunately, some valued employees also chose to leave Beecham because they resented some of the changes that were made.

Changing established procedures, especially procedures that have outlived their usefulness, can also stimulate conflict. Such actions cause people to reassess how they perform their jobs and whether they perform them correctly. For example, one university president announced that vacant staff positions could be filled only after written justification received his approval. Conflict arose between the president and the department heads who felt they were having to do more paperwork than was necessary. Most requests were approved, but because department heads now had to think through their staffing needs, a few unnecessary positions were appropriately eliminated.

■ Controlling Conflict

One method of controlling conflict is to expand the resource base. Suppose a top manager receives two budget requests for $100,000 each. If she has only $180,000 to distribute, the stage is set for conflict because each group will feel its proposal is worth funding and will be unhappy if it is not fully funded. If both proposals are indeed worthwhile, it may be possible for her to come up with the extra $20,000 from some other source and thereby avoid difficulty.

As noted in Chapter 6, pooled, sequential, and reciprocal interdependence can all result in conflict. If managers use an appropriate technique for enhancing coordination, they can reduce the probability that conflict will arise. Techniques for coordination include making use of the managerial hierarchy, relying on rules and procedures, enlisting liaison persons, forming task forces, and integrating departments. At the J.C. Penney store mentioned earlier, the conflict was addressed by providing sales people with clearer forms on which to specify the merchandise they needed and in what sequence. If one coordination technique does not have the desired effect, a manager might shift to another.

Competing goals can also be a potential source of conflict among individuals and groups. Managers can sometimes focus employee attention on higher-level, or superordinate, goals as a way of eliminating lower-level conflict. When labor unions such as the United Auto Workers make wage concessions to ensure survival of the automobile industry, they are responding to a superordinate goal. Their immediate goal may be higher wages for members, but they realize that without the automobile industry, their members would not even have jobs.

Finally, managers should try to match the personalities and work habits of employees to avoid conflict between individuals. For instance, two valuable subordinates, one a chain smoker and the other a vehement antismoker, should probably not be required to work together in an enclosed space. If conflict does arise between incompatible individuals, a manager might seek an equitable transfer for one or both of them to other units.

■ Resolving and Eliminating Conflict

Despite everyone's best intentions, conflict will sometimes flare up. If it is disrupting the workplace, creating too much hostility and tension, or otherwise harming the organization, attempts must be made to resolve it. Some managers who are uncomfortable dealing with conflict choose to avoid the conflict and hope it will go away. Avoidance may sometimes be effective in the short run for some kinds of interpersonal disagreements, but it does little to resolve long-run or chronic conflict. Even more unadvisable, though, is "smoothing"—minimizing the conflict and telling everyone that things will "get better." Often the conflict will only worsen as people continue to brood over it.

Compromise is striking a middle-range position between two extremes. This approach can work if it is used with care, but in most compromise situations someone wins and someone loses. Budget problems are one of the few areas amenable to compromise because of their objective nature. Assume, for example, that additional resources are not available to the manager mentioned earlier. She has $180,000 to divide, and each of two groups claims to need $100,000. If the manager believes that both projects warrant funding, she can allocate $90,000 to each. The fact that the two groups have at least been treated equally may minimize the potential conflict.

The confrontation approach to conflict resolution—also called interpersonal problem solving—consists of bringing the parties together to confront the conflict. The parties discuss the nature of their conflict and attempt to reach an agreement or a solution. Confrontation requires a reasonable degree of maturity on the part of the participants, and the manager must structure the situation carefully. If handled well, this approach can be an effective means of resolving conflict. In recent years, many organizations have experimented with a technique called alternative dispute resolution, using a team of employees to arbitrate conflict in this way.[30]

Regardless of the approach, organizations and their managers must realize that conflict must be addressed if it is to serve constructive purposes and be prevented from bringing about destructive consequences. Conflict is inevitable in organizations, but its effects can be constrained with proper attention. For example, Union Carbide once sent two hundred of its managers to a three-day workshop on conflict management. The managers engaged in a variety of exercises and discussions to learn with whom they were most likely to come into conflict and how they should try to resolve it. As a result, managers at the firm later reported that hostility and resentment in the organization had been greatly diminished and that people in the firm reported more pleasant working relationships.[31]

Summary of Key Points

A group is two or more people who interact regularly to accomplish a common purpose or goal. General kinds of groups in organizations are functional groups, task groups and teams, and informal or interest groups. A team is a group of workers who function as a unit, often with little or no supervision, to carry out organizational functions.

People join functional groups and teams to pursue a career. Their reasons for joining informal or interest groups include interpersonal attraction, group activities, group goals, need satisfaction, and potential instrumental benefits. The stages of team development include testing and dependence, resolving intragroup conflict and hostility, developing group cohesion, and focusing on the problem at hand.

Four important characteristics of teams are role structures, behavioral norms, cohesiveness, and informal leadership. Role structures define task and socioemotional specialists and may be victimized by role ambiguity, role conflict, or role overload. Norms are standards of behavior for group members. Cohesiveness is the extent to which members are loyal and committed to the team and to one another. Several factors can increase or reduce team cohesiveness. The relationship between performance norms and cohesiveness is especially important. Informal leaders are those leaders whom the group members themselves choose to follow.

Conflict is a disagreement between two or more people, groups, and/or organizations. Too little or too much conflict may hurt performance, but an optimal level of conflict may improve performance. Interpersonal and intergroup conflict in organizations may be caused by personality differences or by particular organizational strategies and practices.

Organizations may encounter conflict with one another and with various elements of the environment. Three methods of managing conflict are to stimulate it, control it, or resolve and eliminate it.

Discussion Questions

Questions for Review

1. What is a group? Describe the several different types of groups and indicate the similarities and differences between them.

2. Why do people join groups? Do all teams develop through all the stages discussed in this chapter? Why or why not?

3. Describe the characteristics of teams. How might the management of a mature team differ from the management of teams that are not yet mature?

4. Identify and summarize the causes and consequences of group cohesiveness.

5. Describe the nature and causes of conflict in organizations. Is conflict always bad? Why or why not?

Questions for Analysis

1. Is it possible for a group to be of more than one type at a time? If so, under what circumstances? If not, why not?

2. Think of several groups of which you have been a member. Why did you join each? Did each group progress through the stages of development discussed in this chapter? If not, why not?

3. Do you think teams are a valuable new management technique that will endure, or are they just a fad that will be replaced with something else in the near future?

4. Suppose you were the manager of a highly cohesive group with low performance norms. What would you do?

5. Would a manager ever want to stimulate conflict in his or her organization? Why or why not?

Building Effective Interpersonal Skills

EXERCISE OVERVIEW

A manager's interpersonal skills refer to her or his ability to understand and motivate individuals and groups. Clearly, then, interpersonal skills play a major role in determining how well a manager can interact with others in a group setting. This exercise allows you to practice your interpersonal skills in relation to just such a setting.

EXERCISE BACKGROUND

You have just been transferred to a new position supervising a group of five employees. The small business you work for has few rules and regulations. Unfortunately, the lack of rules and regulations is creating a problem that you must now address.

Specifically, two of the group members are nonsmokers. They are becoming increasingly vocal about the fact that two other members of the group smoke at work. The nonsmokers believe that the secondary smoke in the workplace is endangering their health and want to establish a no-smoking policy like that of many large businesses today.

The two smokers, however, argue that because the firm did not have such a policy when they started working there, it would be unfair to impose such a policy on them now. One of them, in particular, says that he turned down an attractive job with another company because he wanted to work in a place where he could smoke.

The fifth worker is also a nonsmoker, but says that she doesn't care if others smoke. Her husband smokes at home anyway, and she says she is used to being around smokers. You suspect that if the two vocal nonsmokers are not appeased, they may leave. At the same time, you also think that the two smokers will leave if you mandate a no-smoking policy. All five workers do good work, and you do not want any of them to leave. [Note: Several states and many cities regulate smoking in public places to varying degrees. For purposes of this exercise, assume that no such regulations exist for your location.]

EXERCISE TASK

With this information as context, do the following:

1. Explain the nature of the conflict that exists in this work group.

2. Develop a course of action for dealing with the situation.

Building Effective Conceptual Skills

EXERCISE OVERVIEW

Groups and teams are becoming ever more important in organizations. This exercise allows you to practice your conceptual skills as they apply to work teams in organizations.

EXERCISE BACKGROUND

Many highly effective groups exist outside the boundaries of typical business organizations, as described in the preceding case study. For example, each of the following represents a team:

1. A basketball team

2. An elite military squadron

3. A government policy group such as the presidential cabinet

4. A student planning committee

EXERCISE TASK

1. Identify an example of a real team, such as one of the above. Choose one that (1) is not part of a normal business, (2) you can argue is highly effective, and (3) was not discussed in the case study.

2. Determine the reasons for the team's effectiveness.

3. Determine how a manager can learn from this particular team and use its success determinants in a business setting.

Building Effective Time-Management Skills

EXERCISE OVERVIEW

Time-management skills refer to the manager's ability to prioritize work, to work efficiently, and to delegate appropriately. This exercise enables you to develop time-management skills as they relate to running team meetings.

EXERCISE BACKGROUND

While teams and team meetings are becoming more and more common, some managers worry that they waste too much time. Listed below are several suggestions that experts have made for being more efficient in a meeting:

1. Have an agenda.

2. Meet only when there is a reason.

3. Set a clear starting and ending time.

4. Put a clock in front of everyone.

5. Take away all the chairs and make people stand.

6. Lock the door at starting time to "punish" latecomers.

7. Give everyone a role in the meeting.

8. Use visual aids.

9. Have a recording secretary to document what transpires.

10. Have a one-day-a-week meeting "holiday"—a day on which no one can schedule a meeting.

EXERCISE TASK

With the information above as context, do the following:

1. Evaluate the likely effectiveness of each of these suggestions.

2. Rank-order the suggestions in terms of their likely value.

3. Identify at least three other suggestions that you think might improve the efficiency of a team meeting.

One day Mark Spenser and Manuel Hernandez decided to see whether they could improve the work performance of Sunset Landscape Service's lawn-care operation. Under the current arrangement, each of the four lawn-care teams, consisting of a crew chief and three team members, is given a set of lawns to work on a daily basis. The assignments are chosen so that the crew should have no trouble completing the work in eight hours. If a crew finishes early, however, its members are free to leave while still getting paid for a full day.

You Make the Call

Mark and Manuel noticed, however, that the crews seldom finished very early, because, in part, they were given enough work to take most of the day. Getting done in much less than eight hours was not easy.

Mark and Manuel decided to hold a contest to see which crew could finish its work the fastest. The contest called for each team to log the exact time it worked each day for a three-month period. To ensure equity, various lawn assignments would be rotated across the teams. The winning team members would receive an extra week of paid vacation as their prize.

Within a couple of weeks, Mark and Manuel began to notice some interesting things. First, one group began showing up in matching T-shirts. Next, another group also got matching T-shirts, but with a team name printed on the back. Soon each team had its own team name, logo, and set of T-shirts to wear.

In addition, absenteeism was down. If a team member did not work one day, the remaining team members still had to do the same amount of work. And, of course, it took them somewhat longer to complete their work. Now employees were taking a day off only when it was absolutely necessary.

When the contest was over, Mark and Manuel felt so good about how it had worked that they gave the three losing teams each one extra day off with pay. Within a matter of days, employees began asking if the contest was going to be repeated.

DISCUSSION QUESTIONS

1. Explain what happened in terms of group/team characteristics.

2. Should Mark and Manuel run the same contest again? Why or why not?

3. What risks did they run with the contest?

Skills Self-Assessment Instrument

USING TEAMS

Introduction: The use of groups and teams is becoming more common in organizations throughout the world. The following assessment surveys your beliefs about the effective use of teams in work organizations.

Instructions: You will agree with some of the statements and disagree with others. In some cases you may find making a decision difficult, but you should force a choice. Record your answers next to each statement according to the following scale:

Rating Scale

4 Strongly agree   **2** Somewhat disagree

3 Somewhat agree   **1** Strongly disagree

_____ 1. Each individual in a work team should have a clear assignment so that individual accountability can be maintained.

_____ 2. For a team to function effectively, the team must be given complete authority over all aspects of the task.

_____ 3. One way to get teams to work is to simply assemble a group of people, tell them in general what needs to be done, and let them work out the details.

_____ 4. Once a team gets going, management can turn its attention to other matters.

_____ 5. To ensure that a team develops into a cohesive working unit, managers should be especially careful not to intervene in any way during the initial start-up period.

_____ 6. Training is not critical to a team because the team will develop any needed skills on its own.

_____ 7. It's easy to provide teams with the support they need because they are basically self-motivating.

_____ 8. Teams need little or no structure to function effectively.

_____ 9. Teams should set their own direction with managers determining the means to the selected end.

_____10. Teams can be used in any organization.

For interpretation, turn to page 465.

Source: Adapted from J. Richard Hackman (ed.), _Groups That Work (and Those That Don't)_ (San Francisco: Jossey-Bass Publishers, 1990) pp. 493–504.

Experiential Exercise

INDIVIDUAL VERSUS GROUP PERFORMANCE

Purpose: This exercise demonstrates the benefits a group can bring to accomplishing a task.

Introduction: You will be asked to do the same task both individually and as part of a group.

Instructions: Part 1: You will need a pen or pencil and an 8 ½"× 11" sheet of paper. Working alone, do the following:

1. Write the letters of the alphabet in a vertical column down the left side of the paper: A–Z.

2. Your instructor will randomly select a sentence from any written document and read out loud the first twenty-six letters in that sentence. Write these letters in a vertical column immediately to the right of the alphabet column. Everyone should have identical sets of 26 two-letter combinations.

3. Working alone, think of a famous person whose initials correspond to each pair of letters, and write the name next to the letters, for example, "MT Mark Twain." You will have ten minutes. Only one name per set is allowed. One point is awarded for each legitimate name, so the maximum score is twenty-six points.

4. After time expires, exchange your paper with another member of the class and score each other's work. The instructor will settle disputes about the legitimacy of names. Keep your score for use later in the exercise.

Part 2: Your instructor will divide the class into groups of five to ten. All groups should have approximately the same number of members. Each group now follows the procedure given in part one. Again write the letters of the alphabet down the left side of the sheet of paper, this time in reverse order: Z–A. Your instructor will dictate a new set of letters for the second column. The time limit and scoring procedure are the same. The only difference is that the groups will generate the names.

Part 3: Each team identifies the group member who came up with the most names. The instructor places these "best" students into one group. Then all groups repeat part two, but this time the letters from the reading will be in the first column and the alphabet letters will be in the second column.

Part 4: Each team calculates the average individual score of its members on part one and compares it with the team score from parts two and three. Your instructor will put the average individual score and team scores for each group on the board.

Follow-up Questions:

1. Do the average individual scores and the team scores differ? What are the reasons for the difference, if any?

2. Although the team scores in this exercise usually are higher than the average individual scores, under what conditions might individual averages exceed group scores?

CASE STUDY

Elite Teams

Some managers believe that work teams are a new concept in the workplace and that the first work teams were the "quality circles" that became popular in U.S. businesses in the early 1980s. In reality, however, teams have been around in many work settings for years. And managers can learn a great deal about teams in their own organizations by observing how other organizations create and manage their own elite teams. These teams can be found in a wide variety of settings and doing a wide variety of work.

Take the Navy Seals, for example. This elite group demands absolute and total commitment to the group. A grueling and exhausting training camp culminates with hell week— a five-day period during which recruits run endless miles over wet sand wearing combat boots, swim countless miles carrying a full backpack, run obstacles courses over and over again, and perform rigorous calisthenics while instructors yell insults at them. They get perhaps four hours of sleep during this entire period. But after three months of training, those who remain have been molded into a highly cohesive group in which every member is totally committed to the others. Although only three out of ten make it, those who do have accomplished something special.

Or take the Tokyo String Quartet, universally recognized as one of the best musical performing groups in the world. Its members have played together for decades, and each one knows exactly how the moods, talents, and preferences of the others will affect the decisions the group makes and the performances they create. While each member is a musical virtuoso in his own right, each person is also willing—indeed, even anxious—to make his own ego and recognition secondary to the good of the group.

Another shining example of teamwork in action is the University of North Carolina women's soccer team. The team coach, Anson Dorrance, has learned the importance of understanding each individual member of the team and what motivates her to perform at her best. He builds individual self-confidence by constant practice and encouragement, yet melds his charges into a well-oiled machine by teaching them to depend on one another. The results have been remarkable: UNC is the most dominant college athletic program in history, with a winning percentage of .945 and twelve national titles in the last twenty years.

Yet another exemplary example of teamwork is the emergency room staff at Massachusetts General Hospital in Boston. Considered one of the best teaching hospitals in the world, the emergency room team is one of Mass General's strengths. Around two hundred patients show up for emergency treatment every day. A team of doctors, nurses, and technicians, each with a role to play, flows to the gurney of every patient brought in for emergency surgery. One team member starts an IV, one cuts away clothing from wounds or burns, one tries to soothe the patient, and others begin to take stock of the damage and figure out what to do. The lead role may be played by an attending physician or senior resident, but everyone is free to offer suggestions and point out alternative treatment options. The result is an impressive survival rate and recognition from other hospitals that Mass General's emergency team is the best.

Managers can also learn valuable lessons from other elite teams. For example, the top NBA basketball teams function flawlessly as they run fast breaks or a full-court pressure defense. Members of police SWAT teams have to depend on one another and have a clear understanding of their roles. The offensive linemen of a football team must learn different blocking schemes and be able to help one another pick up a blitz or double team an especially effective rusher. And the engineers at Houston's Boots & Coots who travel the world to extinguish oil-well fires must have absolute confidence and trust in one another as they undertake their hazardous jobs in conditions that are often dangerous and far removed from the comforts of home.

Case Questions

1. What can managers learn from each of the elite teams identified in this case?

2. Can you identify other kinds of elite teams that managers might learn from?

3. What characteristics and elements of these teams cannot be generalized to organizations?

Case References: Kenneth Labich, "Elite Teams," *Fortune,* February 19, 1996, pp. 90–99 and Gregory Moorhead and Ricky W. Griffin, *Organizational Behavior,* 5th ed. (Boston: Houghton Mifflin, 1998), Chapter 12.

CHAPTER NOTES

1. "Fastener's 3-Prong Plan Yields Perfection," *USA Today,* May 2, 1997, p. 9B (quote on p. 9B). Based on "Winners Triumph Through Teamwork/Fastener's 3-Prong Plan Yields Perfection," *USA Today,* May 2, 1997. Copyright 1997, *USA Today.* Reprinted with permission.

2. See Gregory Moorhead and Ricky W. Griffin, *Organizational Behavior,* 5th ed. (Boston: Houghton Mifflin, 1998), for a review of definitions of groups.

3. Dorwin Cartwright and Alvin Zander (eds.), *Group Dynamics: Research and Theory,* 3rd ed. (New York: Harper & Row, 1968).

4. Robert Schrank, *Ten Thousand Working Days* (Cambridge, Mass.: MIT Press, 1978) and Bill Watson, "Counter Planning on the Shop Floor," in Peter Frost, Vance Mitchell, and Walter Nord (eds.), *Organizational Reality*, 2nd ed. (Glenview, Ill.: Scott, Foresman, 1982), pp. 286–294.

5. Brian Dumaine, "Payoff from the New Management," *Fortune*, December 13, 1993, pp. 103–110.

6. Glenn Parker, "Cross-Functional Collaboration," *Training & Development*, October 1994, pp. 49–58.

7. "How Ford's F-150 Lapped the Competition," *Business Week*, July 29, 1996, pp. 74–76.

8. "Struggle to Remake the Malibu Says a Lot About Remaking GM," *Wall Street Journal*, March 27, 1997, pp. A1, A8.

9. "Why Teams Fail," *USA Today*, February 25, 1997, pp. 1B, 2B.

10. Brian Dumaine, "The Trouble with Teams," *Fortune*, September 5, 1994, pp. 86–92. See also Susan G. Cohen and Diane E. Bailey, "What Makes Teams Work: Group Effectiveness Research from the Shop Floor to the Executive Suite," *Journal of Management*, Vol. 23, No. 3, 1997, pp. 239–290.

11. Marvin E. Shaw, *Group Dynamics—The Psychology of Small Group Behavior*, 4th ed. (New York: McGraw-Hill, 1985).

12. See Connie Gersick, "Marking Time: Predictable Transitions in Task Groups," *Academy of Management Journal*, June 1989, pp. 274–309.

13. See Michael Campion, Gina Medsker, and A. Catherine Higgs, "Relations Between Work Group Characteristics and Effectiveness: Implications for Designing Effective Work Groups," *Personnel Psychology*, Winter 1993, pp. 823–850 for a review of other team characteristics.

14. David Katz and Robert L. Kahn, *The Social Psychology of Organizations*, 2nd ed. (New York: Wiley, 1978), pp. 187–221.

15. Robert L. Kahn, D. M. Wolfe, R. P. Quinn, J. D. Snoek, and R. A. Rosenthal, *Organizational Stress: Studies in Role Conflict and Role Ambiguity* (New York: Wiley, 1964).

16. Daniel C. Feldman, "The Development and Enforcement of Group Norms," *Academy of Management Review*, January 1984, pp. 47–53.

17. "Companies Turn to Peer Pressure to Cut Injuries as Psychologists Join the Battle," *Wall Street Journal*, March 29, 1991, pp. B1, B3.

18. James Wallace Bishop and K. Dow Scott, "How Commitment Affects Team Performance," *HRMagazine*, February 1997, pp. 107–115.

19. Anne O'Leary-Kelly, Joseph Martocchio, and Dwight Frink, "A Review of the Influence of Group Goals on Group Performance," *Academy of Management Journal*, Vol. 37, No. 5, 1994, pp. 1285–1301.

20. Philip M. Podsakoff, Michael Ahearne, and Scott B. MacKenzie, "Organizational Citizenship Behavior and the Quantity and Quality of Work Group Performance," *Journal of Applied Psychology*, Vol. 82, No. 2, 1997, pp. 262–270.

21. Clayton P. Alderfer, "An Intergroup Perspective on Group Dynamics," in Jay W. Lorsch (ed.), *Handbook of Organizational Behavior* (Englewood Cliffs, N.J.: Prentice-Hall, 1987), pp. 190–222. See also Eugene Owens and E. Leroy Plumlee, "Intraorganizational Competition and Interorganizational Conflict: More Than a Matter of Semantics," *Business Review*, Winter 1988, pp. 28–32 and Dina Lynch, "Unresolved Conflicts Affect the Bottom Line," *HRMagazine*, May 1997, pp. 49–55.

22. Kathleen M. Eisenhardt, Jean L. Kahwajy, and L. J. Bourgeois III, "How Management Teams Can Have a Good Fight," *Harvard Business Review*, July–August 1997, pp. 77–89.

23. Thomas Bergmann and Roger Volkema, "Issues, Behavioral Responses and Consequences in Interpersonal Conflicts," *Journal of Organizational Behavior*, Vol. 15, 1994, pp. 467–471.

24. Robin Pinkley and Gregory Northcraft, "Conflict Frames of Reference: Implications for Dispute Processes and Outcomes," *Academy of Management Journal*, Vol. 37, No. 1, 1994, pp. 193–205.

25. "How 2 Computer Nuts Transformed Industry Before Messy Breakup," *Wall Street Journal*, August 27, 1986, pp. 1, 10.

26. Bruce Barry and Greg L. Stewart, "Composition, Process, and Performance in Self-Managed Groups: The Role of Personality," *Journal of Applied Psychology*, Vol. 82, No. 1, 1997, pp. 62–78.

27. "Delta CEO Resigns After Clashes with Board," *USA Today*, May 13, 1997, p. B1.

28. "A Blood War in the Jeans Trade," *Business Week*, November 13, 1989, pp. 74–81.

29. Peter Elkind, "Blood Feud," *Fortune*, April 14, 1997, pp. 90–102.

30. "Solving Conflicts in the Workplace Without Making Losers," *Wall Street Journal*, May 27, 1997, p. B1.

31. "Teaching How to Cope with Workplace Conflicts," *Business Week*, February 18, 1980, pp. 136, 139.

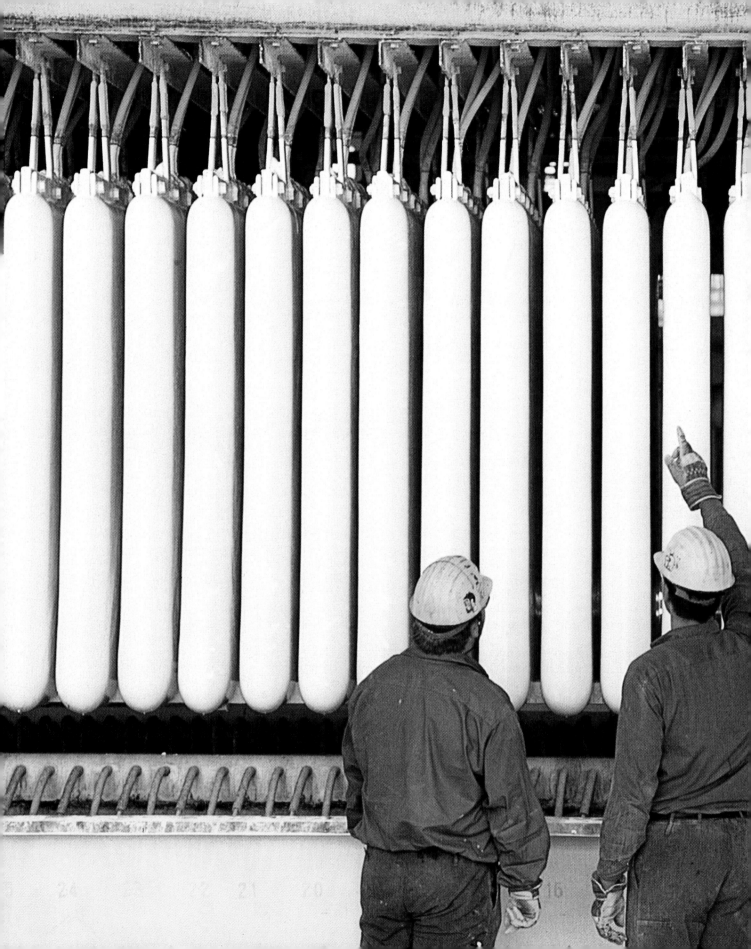

14

Managing the Control Process

OBJECTIVES

After studying this chapter, you should be able to:

- Explain the purpose of control, identify different types of control, and describe the steps in the control process.
- Identify and explain the three forms of operations control.
- Describe budgets and other tools of financial control.
- Identify and distinguish between two opposing forms of structural control.
- Identify characteristics of effective control, explain why people resist control, and describe how managers can overcome this resistance.

The name "Abercrombie & Fitch" goes back to the days when Teddy Roosevelt and Admiral Byrd chose the small Manhattan emporium to outfit their expeditions. Its more recent incarnation, however, has been in the form of a thriving specialty retailer under the umbrella of retailing giant Limited, Inc. Limited acquired the twenty-five-store chain in 1988 and planned to use it to gain entree into the men's fashion market. The corporation's own Limited, Express, Lerner, Victoria's Secret, and Lane Bryant had a strong presence in different segments of the women's fashion market, so the firm was looking to the men's market for future growth.

Limited appointed Sally Frame Kasaks to head up Abercrombie & Fitch. She set the firm on its expansion path and developed its basic product mix before leaving Limited in 1992 to take over Ann Taylor Stores. Limited recruited Mike Jeffries from another retailer to take her place. He modified the basic concepts Ms. Kasaks had envisioned and then implemented them throughout all Abercrombie & Fitch stores. He also put into place his own near-fanatical control orientation.

For example, each week the company's home office sends each store a detailed "time line" that specifies minute tasks to be performed each day, including how to arrange clothes on racks and how many hours and store employees each such task should require. Merchandise display techniques are also spelled out in detail. For example, sweaters are not to be stacked higher than four to a pile. Moreover, men's sweaters are to be arranged with larger sizes on top, whereas women's sweaters have the smaller sizes on top. Blouses displayed on hangers are to have the top button undone, but if the blouse is folded, then the top two buttons are to be kept undone.

Mr. Jeffries' fashion design team at headquarters also dispatches detailed plans and layouts for each table on the sales floor, along with specific weekly sales and profit goals. For example, a merchandise table by the door or in the center of the sales floor is supposed to generate, on average, $2,800 in sales each week.

But Abercrombie & Fitch management doesn't stop with merchandise. Jeffries also has a twenty-nine-page "look book"—detailed specifications for dress and appearance of the firm's sales staff. For example, men cannot wear necklaces or have facial hair. Women can wear nail polish only in "natural colors," and the nails themselves cannot extend more than a quarter inch beyond the fingertip. The only "piercing" allowed is for earrings—men can wear one, and women can wear two. But no earring can be larger than a dime.

So far, at least, Jeffries' efforts have been paying off in a big way. Since he took over, for example, the number of Abercrombie & Fitch stores has quadrupled. And his chain is by far the most profitable of the Limited's holdings. Although it remains to be seen whether or not his plans can weather the next wave of fickle fashion trends, for the time being, at least, Jeffries clearly has Abercrombie & Fitch on the right path—a path that he has blazed and from which he doesn't intend to stray.[1]

"This is very much a military operation. It is very disciplined and very controlled."

Mike Jeffries, CEO of Abercrombie & Fitch

Mike Jeffries is relying on one of the four fundamental functions of management to keep Abercrombie & Fitch on its path to growth and profitability—control. He decided where he wanted the business to go, pointed it in that direction, and created systems to keep it on track. Any business can enhance its financial health by taking the same steps, although each organization must work with its own particular configuration of revenues and costs. The general framework for achieving and maintaining financial health is control.

As we discuss in Chapter 1, control is one of the four basic managerial functions that provide the organizing framework for this book. In the first section of this chapter, we explain the purpose of control. We then look at types of control and the steps in the control process. Operations, financial, and structural control are then examined in detail. We conclude by discussing the characteristics of effective control, noting why some people resist control, and describing what organizations can do to overcome this resistance.

The Nature of Control in Organizations

control The regulation of organizational activities so as to facilitate goal attainment

Control is the regulation of organizational activities so that some targeted element of performance remains within acceptable limits. Without this regulation, organizations have no indication of how well they perform in relation to their goals. At any point in time, the control system compares where the organization is in terms of performance to where it is supposed to be. Like a ship's rudder, control provides an organization with a mechanism for adjusting its course if performance falls outside acceptable boundaries. For example, Federal Express has a performance goal of delivering 99 percent of its packages on time. If on-time deliveries fall to 97 percent, control systems will signal the problem to managers so they can make necessary adjustments in operations to regain the target level of performance.

■ The Purpose of Control

As Figure 14.1 illustrates, control provides an organization with ways to adapt to environmental change, to limit the accumulation of error, to cope with organizational complexity, and to minimize costs.

Adapting to Environmental Change   In today's complex and turbulent business environment, all organizations must contend with change.[2] A properly designed control system can help managers anticipate, monitor, and respond to changing circumstances.[3] In contrast, an improperly designed system can result in organizational performance that falls far below acceptable levels. Michigan-based Metalloy, a forty-three-year-old, family-run, metal-casting company, signed a contract to make engine-seal castings for NOK, a big Japanese auto-parts maker. Metalloy was satisfied when its first 5,000-unit production run yielded 4,985 acceptable castings and only 15 defective ones.

NOK, however, was quite unhappy with this performance and insisted that Metalloy raise its standards. In short, global quality standards had shifted so dramatically that managers at Metalloy had lost touch with how high their own standards had to be to remain competitive. A properly designed control system, on the other hand, would have kept Metalloy's managers better attuned to rising standards.

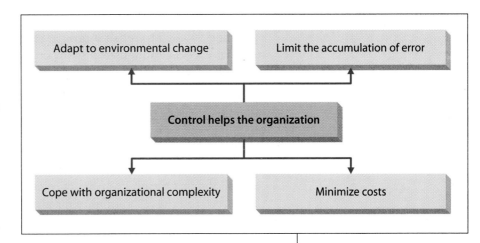

FIGURE 14.1
The Purpose of Control

Control is one of the four basic management functions in organizations. The control function, in turn, has four basic purposes. Properly designed control systems are able to fulfill each of these purposes.

Limiting the Accumulation of Error   Small mistakes and errors do not often seriously damage the financial health of an organization. Over time, however, small errors may accumulate and become very serious. Whistler Corporation, a large radar-detector manufacturer, once faced such rapidly escalating demand that it essentially stopped worrying about quality. The defect rate rose from 4 percent to 9 percent to 15 percent and eventually reached 25 percent. One day a manager realized that 100 of the firm's 250 employees were spending all their time fixing defective units and that $2 million worth of inventory was awaiting repair. Had the company adequately controlled quality as it responded to increased demand, the problem would have never reached such proportions.

Coping with Organizational Complexity   When a firm purchases only one raw material, produces one product, has a simple organization design, and enjoys constant demand for its product, its managers can maintain control with a very basic and simple system. But a business that produces many products from myriad raw materials and has a large market area, a complicated organization design, and many competitors needs a sophisticated system to maintain adequate control. Emery Air Freight was quite profitable until it bought Purolator Courier Corporation. The new Emery that resulted from the acquisition was much bigger and more complex, but no new controls were added to operations. Consequently, Emery began to lose money and market share, costs increased, and service deteriorated until the company was on the verge of bankruptcy. Only when more elaborate controls were developed did the company turn itself around.

Minimizing Costs   When control is practiced effectively, it can also help reduce costs and boost output. For example, Georgia-Pacific Corporation, a large wood-products company, learned of a new technology that could be used to make thinner blades for its saws. The firm's control system was used to calculate the amount of wood that could be saved from each cut made by the thinner blades relative to the costs used to replace the existing blades. The results have been impressive—the wood that the new blades save each year fills eight hundred railcars. As Georgia-Pacific discovered, effective control systems can eliminate waste, reduce labor costs, and improve output per unit of input. Similarly, the CEO of Travelers' Insurance recently decided that spending $60,000 to repair a broken fountain in front of company headquarters was excessive and instead spent only $20,000 to have it filled and planted with a low-maintenance tree.[4]

▮ Types of Control

The preceding examples of control illustrate the regulation of several organizational activities, from producing quality products to coordinating complex organizations. Organizations practice control in a number of areas and at various levels, and the responsibility for managing control is widespread.

Areas of Control   Control can focus on any area of an organization. Most organizations define areas of control in terms of the four basic types of resources they use: physical, human, information, and financial resources.[5] Control of physical resources includes inventory management (stocking neither too few nor too many units in inventory), quality control (maintaining appropriate levels of output quality), and equipment control (supplying the necessary facilities and machinery). Control of human resources includes selection and placement, training and development, performance appraisal, and compensation. Control of information resources includes sales and marketing forecasting, environmental analysis, public relations, production scheduling, and economic forecasting. Financial control involves managing the organization's debt so that it does not become excessive, ensuring that the firm always has enough cash on hand to meet its obligations but that it does not have excess cash in a checking account, and that receivables are collected and bills paid on a timely basis.

In many ways, the control of financial resources is the most important area because financial resources are related to the control of all the other resources in an organization. Too much inventory leads to storage costs; poor selection of personnel leads to termination and rehiring expenses; inaccurate sales forecasts lead to disruptions in cash flows and other financial effects. Financial issues tend to pervade most control-related activities. Indeed, financial issues are the basic problem faced by Emery Air Freight. Various inefficiencies and operating blunders put the company in a position where it lacked the money to service its debt (make interest payments on loans), had little working capital (cash to cover daily operating expenses), and was too heavily leveraged (excessive debt) to borrow more money.

operations control Focuses on the processes the organization uses to transform resources into products or services

financial control Concerned with the organization's financial resources

structural control Concerned with how the elements of the organization's structure are serving their intended purpose

Levels of Control   Just as control can be broken down by area, it can also be broken down by level within the organizational system. **Operations control** focuses on the processes the organization uses to transform resources into products or services (quality control is one type of operations control).[6] **Financial control** is concerned with the organization's financial resources (monitoring receivables to make sure customers are paying their bills on time is an example of financial control). **Structural control** is concerned with how the elements of the organization's structure are serving their intended purposes (monitoring the administrative ratio to make sure staff expenses do not become excessive is an example of structural control).

Responsibilities for Control Traditionally, managers have been responsible for overseeing the wide array of control systems and concerns in organizations. Managers decide which types of control the organization will use, and they implement control systems and take actions based on the information provided by control systems. Thus, ultimate responsibility for control rests with all managers throughout an organization. Most larger organizations also have one or more specialized managerial positions called controller. A **controller** is responsible for helping line managers with their control activities, for coordinating the organization's overall control system, and for gathering and assimilating relevant information. Many businesses that use an H-form or M-form organization design have several controllers: one for the corporation and one for each division. The job of controller is especially important in organizations where control systems are complex.[7]

In addition, many organizations are also beginning to use operating employees to help maintain effective control. Indeed, employee participation is often used as a vehicle for allowing operating employees an opportunity to help facilitate organizational effectiveness. For example, Whistler Corporation increased employee participation in an effort to turn its quality problems around. As a starting point, the quality control unit, formerly responsible for checking product quality at the end of the assembly process, was eliminated. Next, all operating employees were encouraged to check their own work and told that they would be responsible for correcting their own errors. As a result, Whistler has eliminated its quality problems and is again a highly profitable business.

controller A position in organizations that helps line managers with their control activities

control standard A target against which subsequent performance will be compared

■ Steps in the Control Process

Regardless of the type or levels of control systems an organization needs, there are four fundamental steps in any control process.[8] These are illustrated in Figure 14.2.

Establish Standards The first step in the control process is establishing standards. A **control standard** is a target against which subsequent performance

FIGURE 14.2
Steps in the Control Process

Having an effective control system can help ensure that an organization achieves its goals. Implementing a control system, however, is a systematic process that generally proceeds through four interrelated steps.

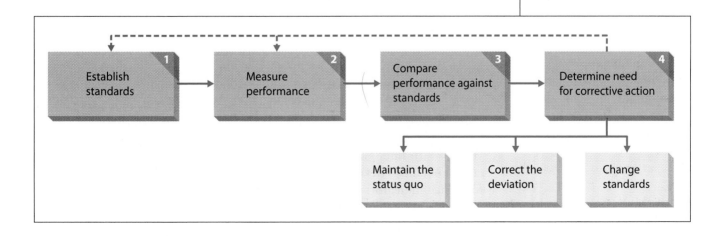

will be compared.[9] Employees at Taco Bell fast-food restaurant, for example, work toward the following service standards:

1. A minimum of 95 percent of all customers will be greeted within three minutes of their arrival.
2. Preheated tortilla chips will not sit in the warmer more than thirty minutes before they are served to customers.
3. Empty tables will be cleaned within five minutes after being vacated.

Standards established for control purposes should be expressed in measurable terms. Note that standard one above has a time limit of three minutes and an objective target of 95 percent of all customers. In standard three the objective target is implied: "all" empty tables.

Control standards should also be consistent with the organization's goals. Taco Bell has organizational goals involving customer service, food quality, and restaurant cleanliness. A control standard for a retailer like Home Depot should be consistent with its goal of increasing its annual sales volume by 25 percent within five years. A hospital trying to shorten the average hospital stay will have control standards that reflect current averages. A university reaffirming its commitment to academics might adopt a standard of graduating 80 percent of its student athletes within five years of their enrollment. Control standards can be as narrow or as broad as the level of activity to which they apply and must follow logically from organizational goals and objectives.

A final aspect of establishing standards is to identify performance indicators. Performance indicators are measures of performance that provide information that is directly relevant to what is being controlled. For example, suppose an organization is following a tight schedule in building a new plant. Relevant performance indicators could be buying a site, selecting a building contractor, and ordering equipment. Monthly sales increases are not, however, directly relevant. On the other hand, if control is being focused on revenue, monthly sales increases are relevant, whereas buying land for a new plant is less relevant.

Measure Performance   The second step in the control process is measuring performance. Performance measurement is a constant, ongoing activity for most organizations. For control to be effective, performance measures must be valid. Daily, weekly, and monthly sales figures measure sales performance, and production performance may be expressed in terms of unit cost, product quality, or volume produced. Employees performance often may be measured in terms of quality or quantity of output, but for many jobs measuring performance is not so straightforward.

A research and development scientist at Merck, for example, may spend years working on a single project before achieving a breakthrough. A manager who takes over a business on the brink of failure may need months or even years to turn things around. Valid performance measurement, however difficult to obtain, is nevertheless vital in maintaining effective control, and performance indicators usually can be developed. The scientist's progress, for example, may be partially assessed by peer review, and the manager's success may be evaluated by her ability to convince creditors that she will eventually be able to restore profitability.

Compare Performance Against Standards The third step in the control process is comparing measured performance against established standards. Performance may be higher than, lower than, or identical to the standard. In some cases comparison is easy. The goal of each product manager at General Electric is to make the product either number one or number two (on the basis of total sales) in its market. Because this standard is clear and total sales are easy to calculate, determining whether this standard has been met is relatively simple. Sometimes, however, comparisons are less clear-cut. If performance is lower than expected, the question is how much deviation from standards to allow before taking remedial action. For example, is increasing sales by 7.9 percent when the standard was 8 percent close enough?

The timetable for comparing performance to standards depends on a variety of factors, including the importance and complexity of what is being controlled. For longer-run and higher-level standards, annual comparisons may be appropriate. Other circumstances may require more-frequent comparisons. For example, a business with a cash shortage may need to monitor its on-hand cash reserves daily. We noted earlier the cash-flow problems Emery Air Freight faced after it purchased Purolator Courier. As part of their efforts to improve the firm's control, Emery's managers eventually started monitoring their cash reserves weekly.

Consider Corrective Action The final step in the control process is determining the need for corrective action. Decisions regarding corrective actions draw heavily on a manager's analytic and diagnostic skills. After comparing performance against control standards, one of three actions is appropriate: maintain the status quo (do nothing); correct the deviation; or change the standard. Maintaining the status quo is preferable when performance essentially matches the standard, but it is more likely that some action will be needed to correct a deviation from the standard.

Performance that is higher than expected may also cause problems for organizations. For example, when Chrysler first introduced both the Viper and the Prowler, demand was so strong that there were waiting lists and many customers were willing to pay more than the suggested retail price to obtain a car. The company was reluctant to increase production, primarily because it feared demand would eventually drop. At the same time, however, it didn't want to alienate potential customers. Consequently, Chrysler decided to simply reduce its advertising. This curtailed demand a bit and limited customer frustration.

Changing an established standard usually is necessary if it was set too high or too low at the outset. This condition is apparent if large numbers of employees routinely beat the standard by a wide margin or if no employees ever meet the standard. Also, standards that seemed perfectly appropriate when they were established may need to be adjusted because circumstances have changed.

Operations Control

preliminary control Attempts to monitor the quality or quantity of financial, physical, human, and information resources before they actually become part of the system

screening control Relies heavily on feedback processes during the transformation process

FIGURE 14.3
Forms of Operations Control

Most organizations develop multiple control systems that incorporate all three basic forms of control. For example, the publishing company that produced this book screens inputs by hiring only qualified persons, typesetters, and printers (preliminary control). In addition, quality is checked during the transformation process such as after the manuscript is typeset (screening control), and the outputs—printed and bound books—are checked before they are shipped from the bindery (postaction control).

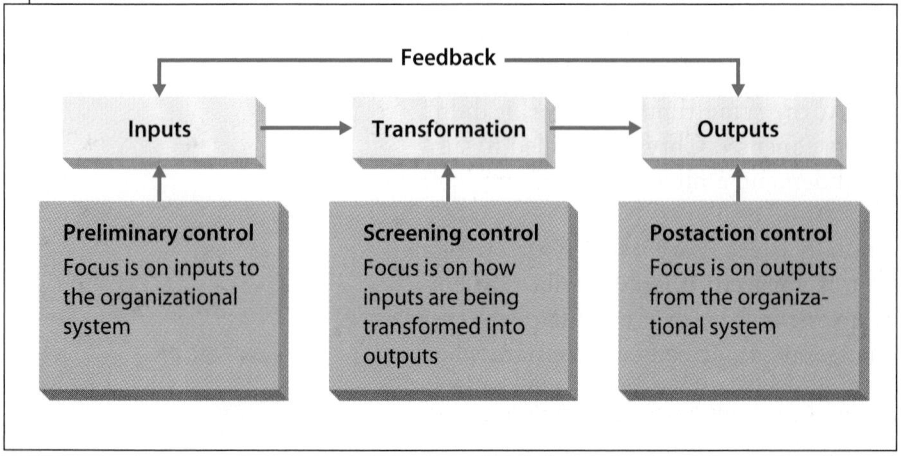

One of the three levels of control practiced by most organizations, operations control, is concerned with the processes the organization uses to transform resources into products or services. As Figure 14.3 shows, the three forms of operations control—preliminary, screening, and postaction—occur at different points in relation to the transformation processes used by the organization.

■ Preliminary Control

Preliminary control concentrates on the resources—financial, material, human, and information—the organization brings in from the environment. Preliminary control attempts to monitor the quality or quantity of these resources before they enter the organization. Firms like PepsiCo and General Mills hire only college graduates for their management-training program—and only after applicants satisfy several interviewers and selection criteria. In this way the firms control the quality of the human resources entering the organization. When Sears orders merchandise to be manufactured under its own brand name, it specifies rigid standards of quality, thereby controlling physical inputs. Organizations also control financial and information resources. For example, privately held companies like UPS and Mars limit the extent to which outsiders can buy their stock, and television networks verify the accuracy of news stories before they are broadcast.

■ Screening Control

Screening control focuses on meeting standards for product and/or service quality or quantity during the actual transformation process. Screening control relies heavily on feedback processes. For example, in a Compaq Computer factory, computer system components are checked periodically as each unit is being assembled. This type of control ensures that all the components that have been assembled up to that point are working properly. The periodic quality checks provide feedback to workers so they know what, if any, corrective actions to take. Because they are useful in identifying the cause of problems, screening controls tend to be used more often than other forms of control.

Feedback

Inputs → Transformation → Outputs

Preliminary control
Focus is on inputs to the organizational system

Screening control
Focus is on how inputs are being transformed into outputs

Postaction control
Focus is on outputs from the organizational system

Companies use various forms of operations control. Manchester Plastics, for example, makes instrument panels for the Ford Taurus and Mercury Sable. This worker is inspecting what are called cluster trim appliqués—plastic-based components that are combined to create the external surface of the instrument panels. Because her inspection is taking place within the overall assembly process, it represents screening control. Meanwhile, Ford requires its suppliers to meet exacting quality standards. Therefore, Manchester's efforts also serve as a preliminary control for Ford, since the auto maker knows that the instrument panels it receives from Manchester will meet or exceed the standards that Ford has imposed.

More and more companies are adopting screening controls because they are an effective way to promote employee participation and catch problems early in the overall transformation process. For example, Corning recently adopted screening controls for use in manufacturing television glass. In the past, television screens were inspected only after they were finished. Unfortunately, more than 4 percent of them were later returned by customers because of defects. Now the glass screens are inspected at each step in the production process rather than at the end, and the return rate from customers has dropped to .03 percent.

■ Postaction Control

Postaction control focuses on the outputs of the organization after the transformation process is complete. Corning's old system was postaction control—final inspection after the product is completed. Although Corning abandoned its postaction control system, this method of control may still be effective, primarily if a product can be manufactured in only one or two steps or if the service is fairly simple and routine. Although postaction control alone may not be as effective as preliminary or screening control, the former can provide management with information for future planning. For example, if a quality check of finished goods indicates an unacceptably high defective rate, the production manager knows that he or she must identify the causes and take steps to eliminate them. Postaction control also provides a basis for rewarding employees. Recognizing that an employee has exceeded personal sales goals by a wide margin, for example, may alert the manager that a bonus or promotion is in order.

Most organizations use more than one form of operations control. For example, Honda's preliminary control includes hiring only qualified employees and specifying strict quality standards when ordering parts from other manufacturers.

postaction control Monitors the outputs or results of the organization after the transformation process is complete

Honda uses numerous screening controls in checking the quality of components during assembly of cars. A final inspection and test drive as each car rolls off the assembly line are part of the company's postaction control. Organizations employ a wide variety of techniques to facilitate operations control.

Financial Control

Financial control is the control of financial resources as they flow into the organization (for example, revenues, shareholder investments), are held by the organization (for example, working capital, retained earnings), and flow out of the organization (for example, pay expenses). Businesses must manage their finances so that revenues are sufficient to cover expenses and still return a profit to the firm's owners. Not-for-profit organizations such as universities have the same concerns: their revenues (from tax dollars or tuition) must cover operating expenses and overhead. Dickson Poon is a Chinese investor who has profited by relying heavily on financial control. He buys distressed upscale retailers like Britain's Harvey Nichols and the U.S.'s Barney's, imposes strict financial controls, and begins generating hefty profits.[10] A complete discussion of financial management is beyond the scope of this book, but we will examine the control provided by budgets and other financial control tools.

■ Budgetary Control

budget A plan expressed in numerical terms

A **budget** is a plan expressed in numerical terms.[11] Organizations establish budgets for work groups, departments, divisions, and the whole organization. The usual time period for a budget is one year, although breakdowns of budgets by the quarter or month are also common. Budgets are generally expressed in financial terms, but they may occasionally be expressed in units of output, time, or other quantifiable factors.

Because of their quantitative nature, budgets provide yardsticks for measuring performance and facilitate comparisons across departments, between levels in the organization, and from one time period to another. Budgets serve four primary purposes. They help managers coordinate resources and projects (because they use a common denominator, usually dollars.) They help define the established standards for control. They provide guidelines about the organization's resources and expectations. Finally, budgets enable the organization to evaluate the performance of managers and organizational units.

Types of Budgets   Most organizations develop and make use of three different kinds of budgets—financial, operating, and nonmonetary. Table 14.1 summarizes the characteristics of each of these.

A financial budget indicates where the organization expects to get its cash for the coming time period and how the organization plans to use the money. Because financial resources are critically important, the organization needs to

Type of Budget	What Budget Shows
Financial budget	**Sources and uses of cash**
Cash-flow or cash budget	All sources of cash income and cash expenditures in monthly, weekly, or daily periods
Capital expenditures budget	Costs of major assets such as a new plant, machinery, or land
Balance sheet budget	Forecast of the organization's assets and liabilities in the event all other budgets are met
Operating budget	**Planned operations in financial terms**
Sales or revenue budget	Income the organization expects to receive from normal operations
Expense budget	Anticipated expenses for the organization during the coming time period
Profit budget	Anticipated differences between sales or revenues and expenses
Nonmonetary budget	**Planned operations in nonfinancial terms**
Labor budget	Hours of direct labor available for use
Space budget	Square feet or meters of space available for various functions
Production budget	Number of units to be produced during the coming time period

TABLE 14.1
Types of Budgets

Organizations use various types of budgets to help manage their control function. The three major categories of budgets are financial, operating, and nonmonetary budgets. There are several different types of budgets in each category. Each budget must be carefully matched with the specific function being controlled to be most effective.

know where those resources will be coming from and how they are to be used. The financial budget provides answers to both these questions. Usual sources of cash include sales revenue, short- and long-term loans, the sale of assets, and the issuance of new stock.

For years Exxon has been very conservative in its capital budgeting. As a result, the firm has amassed a huge financial reserve but has been overtaken in sales by Royal Dutch/Shell. More recently Exxon has decided to loosen its purse strings and begin budgeting more for capital expenditures. For example, whereas Exxon's capital budget was less than $8 billion in 1994, managers increased this budget to $9.2 billion in 1996 and plan to increase to around $11 billion by the year 2000.[12]

An operating budget is concerned with planned operations within the organization. It outlines what quantities of products and/or services the organization intends to create and what resources will be used to create them. IBM creates an operating budget that specifies how many of each model of its personal computer will be produced each quarter.

A nonmonetary budget is simply a budget expressed in nonfinancial terms, such as units of output, hours of direct labor, machine hours, or square-foot allocations. Nonmonetary budgets are most commonly used by managers at the lower levels of an organization. For example, a plant manager can schedule work more effectively knowing that he or she has eight thousand labor hours to allocate in a week, rather than trying to determine how to best spend $76,451 in wages in a week.

Developing Budgets   Traditionally, budgets were developed by top management and the controller and then imposed on lower-level managers. Although some organizations still follow this pattern, many contemporary organizations now allow all managers to participate in the budget process. As a starting point, top management generally issues a call for budget requests, accompanied by an indication of overall patterns the budgets may take. For example, if sales are expected to drop in the next year, managers may be told up front to prepare for cuts in operating budgets.

The heads of each operating unit typically submit budget requests to the head of their division. An operating-unit head might be a department manager in a manufacturing or wholesaling firm or a program director in a social service agency. The division heads might include plant managers, regional sales managers, or college deans. The division head integrates and consolidates the budget requests from operating-unit heads into one overall division budget request. A great deal of interaction among managers usually takes place at this stage, as the division head coordinates the budgetary needs of the various departments.

Division budget requests are then forwarded to a budget committee. The budget committee is usually composed of top managers. The committee reviews budget requests from several divisions and, once again, duplications and inconsistencies are corrected. Finally, the budget committee, the controller, and the CEO review and agree on the overall budget for the organization as well as specific budgets for each operating unit. These decisions are then communicated back to each manager.

Strengths and Weaknesses of Budgeting   Budgets offer a number of advantages, but they have weaknesses as well. On the plus side, budgets facilitate effective control. Placing dollar values on operations enables managers to monitor operations better and pinpoint problem areas. Budgets also facilitate coordination and communication between departments because they express diverse activities in a common denominator (dollars). Budgets help maintain records of organizational performance and are a logical complement to planning. That is, managers should develop plans and consider control measures to accompany them at the same time. Organizations can use budgets to link plans and control by first developing budgets as part of the plan and then using those budgets as a part of control.

On the other hand, some managers apply budgets too rigidly. Budgets are intended to serve as frameworks, but managers sometimes fail to recognize that changing circumstances may warrant budget adjustments. The process of developing budgets can also be very time-consuming. Finally, budgets may limit innovation and change. When all available funds are allocated to specific operating budgets, it may be impossible to procure additional funds to take advantage of an unexpected opportunity. Indeed, for these very reasons, some organizations are working to scale back their budgeting system. Although most organizations are likely to continue to use budgets, the goal is to make them less confining and rigid. For example, Xerox, 3M, and Digital Equipment have all cut back on their budgeting systems by reducing the number of budgets they generate and by injecting more flexibility into the budgeting process.[13]

Well-established and monitored financial regulations in most of today's developed economies ensure that financial control systems can be easily followed and readily interpreted and evaluated. But less certainty exists in some of today's developing economies. The Almaty stock exchange in Kazakhstan is subject to few rules and has no operating procedures. Not surprisingly, the exchange has had difficulty in attracting foreign investors. But as these economies mature and continue to develop, new controls will be created and investors can have more faith in the financial information they are given.

■ Other Tools of Financial Control

Although budgets are the most common means of financial control, other useful tools are financial statements, ratio analysis, and financial audits.

Financial Statements   A **financial statement** is a profile of some aspect of an organization's financial circumstances. Financial statements are prepared and presented according to commonly accepted and required accounting standards.[14] The two most basic financial statements prepared and used by virtually all organizations are a balance sheet and an income statement.

The **balance sheet** lists the assets and liabilities of the organization at a specific point in time, usually the last day of an organization's fiscal year. For example, the balance sheet may summarize the financial condition of an organization on December 31, 1999. Most balance sheets are divided into current assets (assets that are relatively liquid, or easily convertible into cash), fixed assets (assets that are longer-term and, therefore, less liquid), current liabilities (debts and other obligations that must be paid in the near future), long-term liabilities (payable over an extended period of time), and stockholders' equity (the owners' claim against the assets).

Whereas the balance sheet reflects a snapshot profile of an organization's financial position at a single point in time, the **income statement** summarizes financial performance over a period of time, usually one year. For example, the income statement might be for the period January 1, 1999 through December 31, 1999. The income statement summarizes the firm's revenues less its expenses to report net income (that is, profit or loss) for the period. Information from the balance sheet and income statement is used in computing important financial ratios.

Ratio Analysis   Financial ratios compare different elements of a balance sheet and/or income statement to one another. **Ratio analysis** is the calculation of

financial statement   A profile of some aspect of an organization's financial circumstances

balance sheet   List of assets and liabilities of an organization at a specific point in time

income statement   A summary of financial performance over a period of time

ratio analysis   The calculation of one or more financial ratios to assess some aspect of the organization's financial health

one or more financial ratios to assess some aspect of the financial health of an organization. Organizations use various financial ratios as part of financial control. For example, *liquidity ratios* indicate how liquid (easily converted into cash) an organization's assets are. *Debt ratios* reflect the ability to meet long-term financial obligations. *Return ratios* show managers and investors how much return the organization is generating relative to its assets. *Coverage ratios* help estimate the organization's ability to cover interest expenses on borrowed capital. *Operating ratios* indicate the effectiveness of specific functional areas rather than the total organization. The Walt Disney Company relies heavily on financial ratios to keep its financial operations on track.[15]

audits An independent appraisal of an organization's accounting, financial, and operational systems

Financial Audits   **Audits** are independent appraisals of an organization's accounting, financial, and operational systems. The two major types of financial audit are the external audit and the internal audit.

External audits are financial appraisals conducted by experts who are not employees of the organization.[16] External audits are typically concerned with determining that the organization's accounting procedures and financial statements are compiled in an objective and verifiable fashion. The organization contracts with certified public accountants (CPAs) for this service. The CPA's main objective is to verify for stockholders, the IRS, and other interested parties that the methods by which the organization's financial managers and accountants prepare documents and reports are legal and proper. External audits are so important that publicly held corporations are required by law to have external audits regularly, as assurance to investors that the financial reports are reliable. An external audit at U.S. Shoe Corporation once discovered some significant accounting irregularities in one of the firm's divisions. As a result, the firm was fined and had to revamp its entire accounting system.[17]

Some organizations are also starting to employ external auditors to review other aspects of their financial operations. For example, there are now auditing firms that specialize in checking corporate legal bills. An auditor for the Fireman's Fund Insurance Corporation uncovered several thousands of dollars in legal fee errors. Other auditors are beginning to specialize in real estate, employee benefits, and pension plan investments.[18]

Whereas external audits are conducted by outside accountants, an *internal audit* is handled by employees of the organization. The objective of an internal audit is the same as that of an external audit—to verify the accuracy of financial and accounting procedures used by the organization. Internal audits also examine the efficiency and appropriateness of financial and accounting procedures. Because the staff members who conduct them are a permanent part of the organization, internal audits tend to be more expensive than external audits. But employees, who are more familiar with the organization's practices, may also point out significant aspects of the accounting system besides its technical correctness. Large organizations such as Dresser Industries and Ford have internal auditing staffs that spend all their time conducting audits of different divisions and functional areas of the organizations. Smaller organizations may assign accountants to an internal audit group on a temporary or rotating basis.

Structural Control

Organizations can create designs for themselves that result in very different approaches to control. Two major forms of structural control, bureaucratic control and clan control, represent opposite ends of a continuum, as shown in Figure 14.4.[19] The six dimensions shown in the figure represent perspectives adopted by the two extreme types of structural control. That is, they have different goals, degrees of formality, performance focus, organization designs, reward systems, and levels of participation. Although a few organizations fall precisely at one extreme or the other, most tend toward one end but may have specific characteristics of either.

bureaucratic control   A form of organizational control characterized by formal and mechanistic structural arrangements

■ Bureaucratic Control

Bureaucratic control is an approach to organization design characterized by formal and mechanistic structural arrangements. As the term suggests, it follows the bureaucratic model. The goal of bureaucratic control is employee compliance. Organizations that use this type of control rely on strict rules and a rigid hierarchy, insist that employees meet minimally acceptable levels of performance, and often have a tall structure. They focus their rewards on individual performance and allow only limited and formal employee participation.

Abercrombie & Fitch's approach to control is clearly bureaucratic in nature. In another example, a large oil company recently decided to allow employees to

FIGURE 14.4
Organizational Control

Organizational control generally falls somewhere between the two extremes of bureaucratic and clan control. NBC Television uses bureaucratic control, whereas Levi Strauss uses clan control.

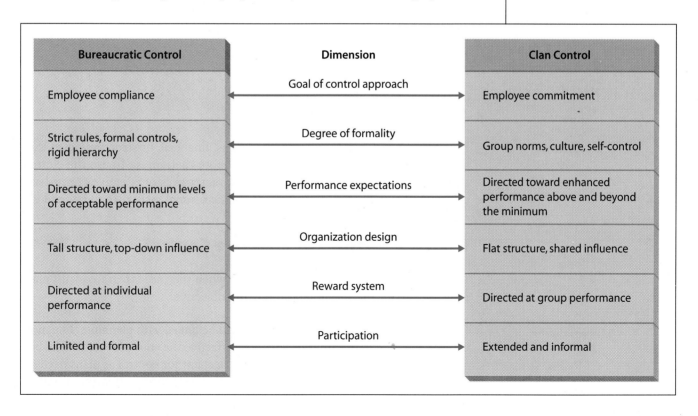

Bureaucratic Control	Dimension	Clan Control
Employee compliance	Goal of control approach	Employee commitment
Strict rules, formal controls, rigid hierarchy	Degree of formality	Group norms, culture, self-control
Directed toward minimum levels of acceptable performance	Performance expectations	Directed toward enhanced performance above and beyond the minimum
Tall structure, top-down influence	Organization design	Flat structure, shared influence
Directed at individual performance	Reward system	Directed at group performance
Limited and formal	Participation	Extended and informal

wear casual attire to work. But a committee then spent weeks developing a twenty-page set of guidelines on what was and was not acceptable. For example, denim pants are not allowed. Similarly, athletic shoes may be worn as long as they are not white, and all shirts must have a collar.

■ Clan Control

clan control An approach to organizational control based on informal and organic structural arrangements

Clan control, in contrast, is an approach to organizational design characterized by informal and organic structural arrangements. As Figure 14.4 shows, its goal is employee commitment to the organization. Accordingly, clan control relies heavily on group norms, has a strong corporate culture, and gives employees the responsibility for controlling themselves. Employees are encouraged to perform beyond minimally acceptable levels. Organizations using this approach are usually relatively flat. They direct rewards at group performance and favor widespread employee participation.

Levi Strauss is a firm that practices clan control. The firm's managers use groups as the basis for work and have created a culture wherein group norms help facilitate high performance. Rewards are subsequently provided to the higher performing groups and teams. The company's culture also reinforces contributions to the overall team effort, and employees have a strong sense of loyalty to the organization. Levi's has a flat structure, and power is widely shared. Employee participation is encouraged in all areas of operation. Another company that uses this approach is Southwest Airlines. When Southwest made the decision to "go casual," the firm resisted the temptation to develop dress guidelines. Instead, managers decided to allow employees to exercise discretion over their attire, and to deal with clearly inappropriate situations on a case-by-case basis as they arise.

Managing Control in Organizations

Effective control, whether at the operations, financial, or structural level, successfully regulates and monitors organizational activities. To use the control process, managers must recognize the characteristics of effective control and understand how to identify and overcome occasional resistance to control.[20]

■ Characteristics of Effective Control

Control systems tend to be most effective when they are integrated with planning and are flexible, accurate, timely, and objective.

Integration with Planning   Control should be linked with planning. The more explicit and precise this linkage, the more effective the control system. The best way to integrate planning and control is to account for control as plans develop. In other words, as goals are set during the planning process, attention should be paid to developing standards that will reflect how well the plan is realized. Managers at Champion Spark Plug Company decided to broaden their product line to include a full range of automotive accessories—a total of twenty-one new products. As a part of this plan, managers decided in advance what level of sales they wanted to realize from each product for each of the next five years. They established these sales goals as standards against which actual sales would be compared. Thus, by accounting for their control system as they developed their plan, managers at Champion did an excellent job of integrating planning and control.

Flexibility   The control system itself must be flexible enough to accommodate change. The alternative—designing and implementing a new control system—is an avoidable expense. Champion's control system includes a mechanism that automatically shipped products to major customers to keep their inventory at predetermined levels. The firm had to adjust this system when one of its biggest customers, Montgomery Ward & Company, decided not to stock the full line of Champion products. Because the control system was flexible, modifying it for Montgomery Ward was relatively simple.

Accuracy   Managers make a surprisingly large number of decisions based on inaccurate information. Field representatives may hedge their sales estimates to make themselves look better. Production managers may hide costs to meet their targets. Human resource managers may overestimate their minority recruiting prospects to meet affirmative action goals. In each case the information other managers receive is inaccurate, and the results of inaccurate information may be quite dramatic. If sales projections are inflated, a manager might cut advertising (thinking it is no longer needed) or increase advertising (to further build momentum). Similarly, a production manager unaware of hidden costs may quote a sales price much lower than desirable. Or a human resources manager may speak out publicly on the effectiveness of the company's minority recruiting, only to find out later that these prospects have been overestimated. In each case the result of inaccurate information is inappropriate managerial action.

Timeliness   Timeliness does not necessarily mean quickness. Rather, it describes a control system that provides information as often as necessary. Because Champion has a wealth of historical data on its sparkplug sales, it does not need information on sparkplugs as frequently as it needs sales feedback for its newer products. Retail organizations usually need sales results daily so that they can manage cash flow and adjust advertising and promotion. In contrast, they may require information about physical inventory only quarterly or annually. In general, the more uncertain and unstable the circumstances, the more frequently measurement is needed.

Objectivity   The control system should provide information that is as objective as possible. To appreciate this statement, imagine the task of a manager responsible for controlling his organization's human resources. He asks two plant managers to submit reports. One manager notes that morale at his plant is "okay," that grievances are "about where they should be," and that turnover is "under control." The other reports that absenteeism at her plant is running at 4 percent, that sixteen grievances have been filed this year (compared to twenty-four last year), and that turnover is 12 percent. The second report will almost always be more useful than the first. Of course, managers also need to look beyond the numbers when assessing performance. For example, a plant manager may be boosting productivity and profit margins by putting too much pressure on workers and using poor-quality materials. As a result, impressive short-run gains may be overshadowed by longer-run increases in employee turnover and customer complaints.

■ Resistance to Control

Managers may sometimes make the mistake of assuming that the value of an effective control system is self-evident to employees. This situation is not always so, however. Many employees resist control, especially if they feel overcontrolled, if they think that control is inappropriately focused or that it rewards inefficiency, or if they are uncomfortable with accountability.

Overcontrol   Occasionally, organizations try to control too many things. This situation becomes especially problematic when the control directly affects employee behavior. An organization that instructs its employees when to come to work, where to park, when to have morning coffee, and when to leave for the day exerts considerable control over people's daily activities. Yet many organizations attempt to control not only these but other aspects of work behavior as well. Troubles arise when employees perceive these attempts to limit their behavior as being unreasonable. A company that tells its employees how to dress, how to arrange their desks, and how to wear their hair may meet with considerable resistance. Employees at Chrysler used to complain because anyone driving a non-Chrysler vehicle to work was forced to park in a distant parking lot. People felt that these efforts to control their personal behavior (in this case, what kind of car to drive) were excessive. Managers eventually removed these controls and now allow open parking. Some employees at Abercrombie & Fitch might also feel that the firm is guilty of overcontrol.

Inappropriate Focus   The control system may be too narrow or it may focus too much on quantifiable variables and leave no room for analysis or interpretation. A sales standard that encourages high-pressure tactics to maximize short-run sales may do so at the expense of goodwill from long-term customers. Such a standard is too narrow. A university reward system that encourages faculty members to publish large numbers of articles but fails to consider the quality of the work is also inappropriately focused. Employees resist the intent of the control system by focusing their efforts only at the performance indicators being used.

Rewards for Inefficiency   Imagine two operating departments that are approaching the end of the fiscal year. Department one expects to have $5,000 of its budget left over; department two is already $3,000 in the red. As a result, department one is likely to have its budget cut for the next year ("They had money left, so they obviously got too much to begin with"), and department two is likely to get a budget increase ("They obviously haven't been getting enough money"). Thus, department one is punished for being efficient, and department two is rewarded for being inefficient. (No wonder departments commonly hasten to deplete their budgets as the end of the year approaches!) As with inappropriate focus, people resist the intent of this control and behave in ways that run counter to the organization's intent.

Too Much Accountability Effective controls allow managers to determine whether or not employees successfully discharge their responsibilities. If standards are properly set and performance accurately measured, managers know when problems arise and which departments and individuals are responsible. People who do not want to be answerable for their mistakes or who do not want to work as hard as their boss might like therefore resist control. For example, American Express has a system that provides daily information on how many calls each operator handles. If one operator works at a slower pace and handles fewer calls than the others, that individual's deficient performance is fairly easy to pinpoint.

■ Overcoming Resistance to Control

Perhaps the best way to overcome resistance to control is to create effective control to begin with. If control systems are properly integrated with organizational planning and if the controls are flexible, accurate, timely, and objective, the organization will be less likely to overcontrol, to focus on inappropriate standards, or to reward inefficiency. Two other ways to overcome resistance are to encourage participation and to develop verification procedures.

Encourage Employee Participation Chapter 7 notes that participation can help overcome resistance to change. By the same token, when employees are involved with planning and implementing the control system, they are less likely to resist it. For instance, employee participation in planning, decision making, and quality control at the Chevrolet Gear Axle plant in Detroit has resulted in increased employee concern for quality and a greater commitment to meeting standards.

Develop Verification Procedures Multiple standards and information systems provide checks and balances in control and allow the organization to verify the accuracy of performance indicators. Suppose a production manager argues that she failed to meet a certain cost standard because of increased prices of raw materials. A properly designed inventory control system will either support or contradict her explanation. Suppose that an employee who was fired for excessive absences argues that he was not absent "for a long time." An effective human resource control system should have records that support the termination. Resistance to control declines because these verification procedures protect both employees and management. If the inventory control records support the production manager's claim about the rising cost of raw materials, she will not be held solely accountable for failing to meet the cost standard and some action will probably be taken to lower the cost of raw materials.

In recent years, many organizations have sought ways to lower their costs through cost-cutting programs. They have reduced their workforces, eliminated perquisites, and outsourced services that independent contractors can do for a lower price. But some experts worry that many organizations have cut too much, increasing pressure and stress on the employees who are left. Although it is doubtful that any organization has gone to the lengths illustrated in this cartoon, many employees nevertheless are feeling the consequences of these cutbacks.

"You've got to really wonder just how many more cut-backs this department can absorb!"

Summary of Key Points

Control is the regulation of organizational activities so that some targeted element of performance remains within acceptable limits. Control provides ways to adapt to environmental change, to limit the accumulation of errors, to cope with organizational complexity, and to minimize costs. Control can focus on financial, physical, information, and human resources and includes operational, financial, and structural levels. Control is the function of managers, the controller, and, increasingly, of operating employees.

Steps in the control process are (1) establish standards of expected performance, (2) measure actual performance, (3) compare performance to the standards, and (4) evaluate the comparison and take appropriate action.

Operations control focuses on the processes the organization uses to transform resources into products or services. Preliminary control is concerned with the resources that serve as inputs to the system. Screening control is concerned with the transformation processes used by the organization. Postaction control is concerned with the outputs of the organization. Most organizations need multiple control systems because no one system can provide adequate control.

Financial control focuses on controlling the organization's financial resources. The foundation of financial control is budgets, plans expressed in numerical terms. Most organizations rely on financial, operating, and nonmonetary budgets. Financial statements, various kinds of ratios, and external and internal audits are also important tools organizations use as part of financial control.

Structural control addresses how well an organization's structural elements serve their intended purpose. Two basic forms of structural control are bureaucratic and clan control. Bureaucratic control is relatively formal and mechanistic, whereas clan control is informal and organic. Most organizations use a form of organizational control somewhere between these two extremes.

One way to increase the effectiveness of control is to fully integrate planning and control. The control system should also be flexible, accurate, timely, and as objective as possible. Employees may resist organizational controls because of overcontrol, inappropriate focus, rewards for inefficiency, and a desire to avoid accountability. Managers can overcome this resistance by improving the effectiveness of controls and by allowing employee participation and developing verification procedures.

Discussion Questions

Questions for Review

1. What is the purpose of organizational control? Why is it important?

2. What are the steps in the control process? Which step is likely to be the most difficult to perform? Why?

3. What are the similarities and differences between the various forms of operations control? What are the costs and benefits of each form?

4. What are the basic differences and similarities between bureaucratic and clan control?

5. How can a manager understand and overcome resistance and make control effective?

Questions for Analysis

1. How is the controlling process related to the functions of planning, organizing, and leading?

2. Are the differences in bureaucratic control and clan control related to differences in organization structure? If so, how? If not, why not? (The terms do sound similar to those used to discuss the organizing process.)

3. Do you use a budget for your personal finances? Relate your experiences with budgeting to the discussion in the chapter.

4. Have you ever resisted control? Why?

5. Why might control in an international business be more complex and difficult than control in a domestic business?

EXERCISE OVERVIEW

Time-management skills—a manager's abilities to prioritize work, to work efficiently, and to delegate appropriately—play a major role in the control function. That is, a manager can use time-management skills to more effectively control his or her own work. This exercise helps demonstrate the relationship between time management skills and control.

EXERCISE BACKGROUND

You are a middle manager in a small manufacturing plant. Today is Monday and you have just returned from a one-week vacation. The first thing you discover is that your secretary will not be in today. His aunt died, and he is out of town at the funeral. He did, however, leave you the following note:

Dear Boss:
Sorry about not being here today. I will be back tomorrow. In the meantime, here are some things you need to know about:

1. *Ms. Glinski [your boss] wants to see you today at 4:00.*

2. *The shop steward wants to see you ASAP about a labor problem.*

3. *Mr. Bateman [one of your big customers] has a complaint about a recent shipment.*

4. *Ms. Ferris [one of your major suppliers] wants to discuss a change in the delivery schedule.*

5. *Mr. Prescott from the chamber of commerce wants you to attend a breakfast meeting on Wednesday and discuss our expansion plans.*

6. *The legal office wants to discuss our upcoming OSHA inspection.*

7. *Human resources wants to know when you can interview someone for the new supervisor's position.*

8. *Jack Williams, the machinist you fired last month, has been hanging around the parking lot.*

EXERCISE TASK

With the information above as a framework, do the following:

1. Prioritize the work that needs to be done into three categories: very timely, moderately timely, and less timely.

2. Explain whether importance and timeliness are the same thing.

3. Determine what additional information you need before you can really begin to prioritize this work.

4. Consider how your approach would differ if your secretary had come in today.

Building Effective Diagnostic Skills

EXERCISE OVERVIEW

Diagnostic skills enable managers to visualize responses to situations. Given that control focuses on regulating organizational activities, diagnostic skills are clearly important to the determination of what activities should be regulated, how to best assess activities, and how to respond to deviations. This exercise helps demonstrate the nature of this relationship.

EXERCISE BACKGROUND

You are the manager of a popular, locally owned restaurant that competes with chains such as Chili's, Bennigan's, and Applebee's. You have been able to maintain your market share in light of increased competition from these outlets by providing exceptional service.

Recently, you have become aware of three trends that concern you. First, your costs are increasing. Monthly charges for food purchases seem to be growing at an exceptionally rapid pace. Second, customer complaints are also increasing. Although the actual number of complaints is still quite small, complaints are nevertheless increasing. And finally, turnover among your employees is also increasing. Although turnover in the restaurant business is usually very high, the recent increase is in marked contrast to your historical pattern of turnover.

EXERCISE TASK

Using the information presented above, do the following:

1. Identify as many potential causes as possible for each of the three problem areas.

2. Group the causes into two categories: more likely and less likely.

3. Develop at least one potential action that you might take to address each cause.

Building Effective Decision-Making Skills

EXERCISE OVERVIEW

Decision-making skills refer to the manager's ability to correctly recognize and define problems and opportunities and to then select an appropriate course of action to solve problems and capitalize on opportunities. This exercise enables you to practice your decision-making skills in relation to organizational control.

EXERCISE BACKGROUND

Assume that you are the top manager of a medium-sized, family-owned manufacturing company. Family members work in several managerial positions. Because of your own special skills and abilities, you have just been brought in from the outside to run the company. The company has a long-standing tradition of avoiding debt and owns several smaller businesses in related industries.

Over the last few years, the company has lagged in productivity and efficiency and now finds itself in desperate straits. Profits have just about disappeared, and one of your bigger competitors may be planning an attempt to take over the business. You have hired a consulting firm to help you identify alternatives for turning things around. The primary options are as follows:

1. Issue a public stock offering (IPO) to raise funds.

2. Borrow money from a bank to finance a turnaround.

3. Sell several of the smaller operations to fund a turnaround.

4. Seek a buyer for the entire firm.

EXERCISE TASK

With the background information above as context, do the following:

1. Evaluate each option from a strategic standpoint.

2. Explain how each option relates to control?

3. Select the option that appeals most to you.

4. Describe the barriers you are likely to encounter with the option you have chosen.

You Make the **Call**

As Cynthia Spenser began to devote all of her time to managing The Arbor, she was dismayed to find what she believed to be a fairly haphazard management system. While the developer of the retail complex was clearly an astute entrepreneur, she began to feel that he had not paid enough attention to detail in the course of day-to-day operating procedures.

She and Mark had learned a lot about management from their experience with SLS. Mark, for example, had found that the most effective way of running the business involved buying only from reputable suppliers, keeping all plants well fertilized and pruned while they were in inventory, and checking with customers after landscaped jobs had been completed to ensure that they were satisfied.

When she bought The Arbor, Cynthia talked with a friend who managed a store at the regional shopping mall in town. Her friend explained how the mall development company had elaborate rules and procedures for its tenants. These rules and procedures dictated store hours, appearance standards, lease terms, promotional and advertising policies, and just about everything else imaginable.

The Arbor, however, was a different story. There were no written policies for tenants. As a result, there was considerable variation in how they were managed. Some stores opened on Sunday or in the evening, for example, while others did not; some tenants had long-term leases while others had no current lease at all.

To address these and other issues, Cynthia called a meeting of all the tenants and expressed her concerns. To her surprise, she found that they already were aware of each of her issues, as well as some others that she had not yet had time to consider. They argued, however, that the current system was really best for The Arbor. As a smaller operation, each tenant knew all the others, and they worked together to keep things in good order. They thought it was fine that they kept different hours—few customers came to The Arbor just to walk around and shop. Customers usually came to visit specific stores and were aware of those stores' hours. The tenants even thought the lease situation was fine. Some wanted the security afforded by a lease, whereas others preferred the flexibility of no lease.

DISCUSSION QUESTIONS

1. What kinds of control examples are illustrated in this situation?

2. What kinds of control systems might be most useful for retailers?

3. What does this situation illustrate regarding the situational nature of control?

Skills Self-Assessment Instrument

UNDERSTANDING CONTROL

Introduction: Control systems must be carefully constructed for all organizations regardless of their goals. The following assessment surveys your ideas about and approaches to control.

Instructions: You will agree with some of the statements and disagree with others. In some cases, making a decision may be difficult, but you should force a choice. Record your answers next to each statement according to the following scale:

Rating Scale

4 Strongly agree   **2** Somewhat disagree

3 Somewhat agree   **1** Strongly disagree

____ 1. Effective controls must be unbending if they are to be used consistently.

____ 2. The most objective form of control is one that uses measures such as stock prices and rate of return on investment (ROI).

____ 3. Control is restrictive and should be avoided if at all possible.

____ 4. Controlling through rules, procedures, and budgets should not be used unless measurable standards are difficult or expensive to develop.

____ 5. Overreliance on measurable control standards is seldom a problem for business organizations.

____ 6. Organizations should encourage the development of individual self-control.

____ 7. Organizations tend to try to establish behavioral controls as the first type of control to be used.

____ 8. The easiest and least costly form of control is output or quantity control.

____ 9. Short-run efficiency and long-run effectiveness result from the use of similar control standards.

____10. ROI and stock prices are ways of ensuring that a business organization is responding to its external market.

____11. Self-control should be relied on to replace other forms of control.

____12. Controls such as ROI are more appropriate for corporations and business units than they are for small groups or individuals.

_____13. Control is unnecessary in a well-managed organization.

_____14. The use of output or quantity controls can lead to unintended or unfortunate consequences.

_____15. Standards of control do not depend on which constituency is being considered.

_____16. Controlling through the use of rules, procedures, and budgets can lead to rigidity and a loss of creativity in an organization.

_____17. Different forms of control cannot be used at the same time. An organization must decide how it is going to control and just do it.

_____18. Setting across-the-board output or quantity targets for divisions within a company can lead to destructive results.

_____19. Control through rules, procedures, and budgets are generally not very costly.

_____20. Individual self-control can lead to integration and communication problems.

For interpretation, turn to page 465.

Source: Adapted from Chapter 12 (especially pp. 380–395) in Charles W. L. Hill and Gareth R. Jones, _Strategic Management,_ Fourth Edition. Copyright © 1998 by Houghton Mifflin Company.

LEARNING ABOUT "REAL" CONTROL

Experiential Exercise

Purpose: The purpose of this exercise is to give you additional insights into how organizations deal with fundamental control issues.

Instructions:

Step One:
Working individually, interview a manager, owner, or employee of an organization. The individual can be a local entrepreneur, and manager in a larger company, or an administrator in your college or university, among other choices. If you currently work, interviewing your boss would be excellent.

Using your own words, ask these general questions:

1. In your organization, what are the most important resources to control?

2. Who is primarily responsible for control?

3. Which level of control is most important to your organization? (Briefly describe the three levels of operations control.)

4. Do you use budgets? If so, what kinds and in what ways?

5. Which of these types of control does your organization most typically use? (Briefly describe bureaucratic and clan control.)

6. Have you had any instances in which employees resisted control? Can you explain why and what you did about it?

Step Two:
Form small groups of four or five. Then do the following:

1. Have each member describe the organization and manager interviewed and the interview findings.

2. Identify as many commonalties across findings as possible.

3. Summarize the differences you found.

4. Select one group member to report your group's experiences to the rest of the class.

Ford Cuts Its Costs

As U.S. auto makers have gradually regained their competitive positions in the global marketplace, first one and then another has taken the occasional misstep and fallen back—like the old adage of two steps forward and one step back. The latest to drop behind by a step is Ford. While General Motors and Chrysler were charging ahead in the mid-1990s, Ford's costs had gotten out of line. Managers knew that significant steps were needed if the firm was to catch up again.

Jacques A. Nasser, a company executive from Australia, was installed as president of Ford in 1996 and given a mandate to cut costs. Nasser, in turn, readily accepted the challenge and quickly put into motion a variety of plans and ideas that he had already been formulating. His background is in engineering, and he is skilled in getting to the heart of an issue and taking quick and decisive action.

One of his immediate steps was to eliminate several unprofitable models from Ford's product line. Managers had been loathe to drop the slow-selling Thunderbird, for example, because the nameplate had long been part of the sporty image that Ford had tried to cultivate. But Nasser quickly—and with little sentiment—halted production and announced that the Thunderbird was dead. At the same time, he left the door open for a newly designed and reengineered Thunderbird at some point in the future. And indeed, Ford has announced its intentions to launch a new version of the Thunderbird in the spring of 2000.

As he was shutting down slow-selling products, he simultaneously boosted production on Ford's faster selling products. For example, the Ford Expedition—a full-size sport utility vehicle that got off to a quick start—was not being produced in sufficient numbers to meet demand. Nasser ordered an entire Michigan factory to be turned over to the production of the Expedition and its $10,000 per unit profit margin.

Nasser also implemented a broad-based plan of cost reductions throughout the firm. The Ford culture had long supported free spending, for example, with executives traveling first class and having virtually unlimited expense accounts. In addition, most top managers had discretionary spending accounts that they could use for virtually any purpose remotely related to work. For example, these funds could be used to support golf club memberships, to buy expensive gifts for associates, and so forth. Nasser moved quickly to cut travel budgets, however, and restricted access to first class travel privileges. He also froze all discretionary spending accounts until new policies could be developed to better regulate their use.

But Nasser's biggest undertaking was a makeover of Ford's entire organization design. Alexander Trotman, the firm's CEO, had previously launched an ambitious plan he called Ford 2000. This plan called for centralizing most international operations in Ford's Dearborn headquarters, with the goal of achieving worldwide efficiencies and coordination. But Nasser was already aware that Ford 2000 was not working out as well as expected. Thus, working behind the scenes to avoid embarrassing Trotman, Nasser quietly but firmly began to dismantle the Ford 2000 plan and to reverse its course by restoring control to regional operations in major marketplaces around the world.

So how have things worked out? So far, at least, Nasser's plans seem to be paying big dividends. For example, at the beginning of 1997 Ford announced a cost-reduction goal for the year of $1 billion. But as the year unfolded, Ford found its costs dropping even more significantly than expected and raised its goal to reductions in excess of $3 billion. Amazingly, this is the first time in Ford's history that its annual costs have ever dropped. One key part of Ford's success in this area was its European operations, which exceeded its own $500-million cost-reduction goal. Ford's executives were so happy with their results that they wanted to attempt to cut another $3 billion in 1998.

Case Questions

1. Identify as many forms of control as possible in this case.

2. Which forms of control seem to be working the best? Which are more and less likely to contribute to long-term success?

3. Use the Internet to research how well Ford is performing today.

Case References: Alex Taylor III, *Fortune*, June 22, 1998, pp. 71–75; "Ford Has a Tiger in Its Tank," *Business Week*, July 14, 1997, p. 30; and "Ford Triples Its Billion-Dollar Cost-Cutting Goal," *USA Today*, December 15, 1997, p. 1B.

CHAPTER NOTES

1. "No Detail Escapes the Attention of Abercrombie & Fitch's Chief," *Wall Street Journal*, October 7, 1997, pp. B1, B20 (quote on p. B1) and *Hoover's Handbook of American Business 1998* (Austin, Texas: Hoover's Business Press, 1998), pp. 876–877.

2. Thomas A. Stewart, "Welcome to the Revolution," *Fortune*, December 13, 1993, pp. 66–77.

3. William Taylor, "Control in an Age of Chaos," *Harvard Business Review*, November–December 1994, pp. 64–70.

4. "At Travelers, It's Trim, Trim, Trim," *Business Week*, February 10, 1997, p. 101.

5. Mark Kroll, Peter Wright, Leslie Toombs, and Hadley Leavell, "Form of Control: A Critical Determinant of Acquisition Performance and CEO Rewards," *Strategic Management Journal*, Vol. 18, No. 2, 1997, pp. 85–96.

6. Sim Sitkin, Kathleen Sutcliffe, and Roger Schroeder, "Distinguishing Control from Learning in Total Quality Management: A Contingency Perspective," *Academy of Management Review*, Vol. 19, No. 3, 1994, pp. 537–564.

7. Robert Lusch and Michael Harvey, "The Case for an Off-Balance-Sheet Controller," *Sloan Management Review*, Winter 1994, pp. 101–110.

8. Edward E. Lawler III and John G. Rhode, *Information and Control in Organizations* (Pacific Palisades, Calif.: Goodyear, 1976).

9. Charles W. L. Hill, "Establishing a Standard: Competitive Strategy and Technological Standards in Winner-Take-All Industries," *Academy of Management Executive*, Vol. 11, No. 2, 1997, pp. 7–16.

10. "Luxury's Mandarin," *Newsweek*, August 25, 1997, p. 43.

11. See Belverd E. Needles Jr., Henry R. Anderson, and James C. Caldwell, *Principles of Accounting*, 7th ed. (Boston: Houghton Mifflin, 1999.)

12. "The Tiger Is on the Prowl," *Forbes*, April 21, 1997, pp. 42–43.

13. Thomas A. Stewart, "Why Budgets Are Bad for Business," *Fortune*, June 4, 1990, pp. 179–190.

14. Needles, Anderson, and Caldwell, *Principles of Accounting*.

15. "Mickey Mouse, CPA," *Forbes*, March 10, 1997, pp. 42–43.

16. Needles, Anderson, and Caldwell, *Principles of Accounting*.

17. "Questions About U.S. Shoe Corp. Continue to Mount," *The Wall Street Street Journal*, April 5, 1990, p. A4.

18. "Auditors of Corporate Legal Bills Thrive," *Wall Street Journal*, February 13, 1991, p. B1.

19. William G. Ouchi, "The Transmission of Control Through Organizational Hierarchy," *Academy of Management Journal*, June 1978, pp. 173–192; Richard E. Walton, "From Control to Commitment in the Workplace," *Harvard Business Review*, March–April 1985, pp. 76–84.

20. See Diana Robertson and Erin Anderson, "Control System and Task Environment Effects on Ethical Judgment: An Exploratory Study of Industrial Salespeople," *Organization Science*, November 1993, pp. 617–629 for a recent study of effective control.

15

Managing for Total Quality

OBJECTIVES

After studying this chapter, you should be able to:

■ Explain the meaning and importance of managing quality and total quality management.
■ Explain the meaning and importance of managing productivity, discuss productivity trends, and describe ways to improve productivity.
■ Explain the nature of operations management and its role in managing quality.
■ Identify and discuss the components involved in using operations systems for quality.

Young Joseph Hartmann immigrated to the United States from Bavaria in 1877. Soon after arriving, he started a small trunk-making company, using the skills he had learned in his homeland. Today, Hartmann Luggage, based in Lebanon, Tennessee, is among the most respected names in the luggage industry.

The firm makes a full line of luggage products, ranging from business cases to suitcases to computer cases. Hartmann bags are also among the most expensive in the industry, with even a small bag costing hundreds of dollars. So why are consumers willing to pay such a premium price for a suitcase? One reason is the quality that characterizes Hartmann bags. Virtually all the work done on a Hartmann bag is performed by trained workers who excel at their craft. The company also uses only the highest quality materials, ranging from industrial-strength belting leather to the strongest metal hinges and cloth.

But it is in the testing lab that Hartmann truly excels. Every new case or bag Hartmann intends to make is first tested for a lifetime of use before being placed into production. And most of this testing is done with special machines that Hartmann managers have conceptualized and constructed.

One of its machines, for example, is called the "tumble tester." This large machine, which resembles a Ferris wheel, simulates the treatment that bags receive in an airport baggage-handling system. A bag inside the tester tumbles like a towel in a clothes dryer, crashing against sharp metal protrusions. Each test run is for seven thousand turns, simulating five years' worth of bouncing.

Another Hartmann testing machine moves a briefcase up and down every few seconds, as many as one hundred thousand times. This test measures the wear and tear that lifting creates on the briefcase handle. If the wear is excessive, the company will use stronger leather. Another machine tests the amount of energy or tension needed to pull apart the stitches that hold a bag together. Among the most interesting machines Hartmann uses is a treadmill-like device that simulates asphalt, tile, and carpet—testing how a bag holds up to being dragged or pulled from an airport to a parking lot. Other machines test wheel strength; the durability of shoulder straps; or how well a bag holds up to ultraviolet rays, rain, humidity, heat, and ice.

Given the extensive battery of tests that Hartmann bags must pass, it's little wonder that the firm backs them with such a praiseworthy guarantee. And there's little wonder that consumers who can afford to pay the price are eager to own the firm's products.[1]

"We have repaired or refurbished bags that are forty years old."

Gail Jamison, Hartmann repair section chief

Managers at Hartmann Luggage have made quality a hallmark of their company's operations. This quality, in turn, allows them to charge premium prices and earn superior profits. But to be successful with this strategy, the firm also must have the confidence that its products can withstand the demands of consumers and hold up to the rigors of daily and business use.

In this chapter we explore quality and its role in business today. We first discuss managing for total quality. We then discuss productivity, which is closely related to quality. Next we introduce operations management and its role in improving quality. The final section of the chapter discusses using operations systems for quality.

Managing Total Quality

Quality and productivity have become major determinants of business success or failure today and have become central issues in managing organizations.[2] But as we will see, achieving higher levels of quality is not an easy accomplishment. Simply ordering that quality be improved is about as effective as waving a magic wand.[3] The catalyst for its emergence as a mainstream management concern was foreign business, especially Japanese. And nowhere was it more visible than in the auto industry. During the energy crisis in the late 1970s, many people bought Toyotas, Hondas, and Nissans because they were more fuel efficient than U.S. cars. Consumers soon found, however, that not only were the Japanese cars more fuel efficient, they were also of higher quality than U.S. cars. Parts fit together better, the trim work was neater, and the cars were more reliable. Thus, after the energy crisis subsided, Japanese cars remained formidable competitors because of their reputations for quality.

■ The Meaning of Quality

quality The totality of features and characteristics of a product or service that bear on its ability to satisfy stated or implied needs

The American Society for Quality Control defines **quality** as the totality of features and characteristics of a product or service that bear on its ability to satisfy stated or implied needs.[4] Quality has several attributes. Table 15.1 lists eight basic dimensions that determine the quality of a particular product or service. For example, a product that has durability and is reliable is of higher quality than a product with less durability and reliability.

Quality is also relative. For example, a Lincoln Continental is a higher-grade car than a Ford Taurus, which, in turn, is a higher-grade car than a Ford Escort. The difference in quality stems from differences in design and other features. The Escort, however, is considered a high-quality car relative to its engineering specifications and price. Likewise, the Taurus and Continental may also be high-quality cars, given their standards and prices. Thus, quality is both an absolute and a relative concept.

Quality is relevant for both products and services. Although its importance for products like cars and computers was perhaps recognized first, service firms

1. **Performance.** A product's primary operating characteristic. Examples are automobile acceleration and a television set's picture clarity.
2. **Features.** Supplements to a product's basic functioning characteristics, such as power windows on a car.
3. **Reliability.** A probability of not malfunctioning during a specified period.
4. **Conformance.** The degree to which a product's design and operating characteristics meet established standards.
5. **Durability.** A measure of product life.
6. **Serviceability.** The speed and ease of repair.
7. **Aesthetics.** How a product looks, feels, tastes, and smells.
8. **Perceived quality.** As seen by a customer.

TABLE 15.1
Eight Dimensions of Quality

These eight dimensions generally capture the meaning of quality, which is a critically important ingredient to organizational success today. Understanding the basic meaning of quality is a good first step to more effectively managing it.

Source: Adapted and reprinted by permission of *Harvard Business Review,* from "Competing on the Eight Dimensions of Quality," by David A. Garvin, November–December 1987. Copyright © 1987 by the President and Fellows of Harvard College, all rights reserved.

ranging from airlines to restaurants have also come to see that quality is a vitally important determinant of their success or failure. Service quality, as we will discuss later in this chapter, has thus also become a major competitive issue in U.S. industry today.

■ The Importance of Quality

To help underscore the importance of quality, the U.S. government created the **Malcolm Baldrige Award**, named after the former Secretary of Commerce who championed quality in U.S. industry. The award, administered by an agency of the Commerce Department, is given annually to firms that achieve major improvements in the quality of their products or services. That is, the award is based on changes in quality, as opposed to absolute quality.

Recent winners of the Baldrige Award include Motorola, the Cadillac division of General Motors, and divisions of Texas Instruments, AT&T, Xerox, and Westinghouse. The 1998 winners were Boeing Airlift and Tanker (a division of Boeing), Texas Nameplate (maker of metal product-identification nameplates), and Solar Turbines (maker of gas turbine engines and compressors).[5] In addition, numerous other quality awards have also been created. For example, The Rochester Institute of Technology and *USA Today* award their Quality Cup award not to entire organizations but to individual teams of workers within organizations. Quality is also an important concern for individual managers and organizations for three very specific reasons: competition, productivity, and costs.[6]

Competition Quality has become one of the most competitive points in business today. For example, each major U.S. auto company—Ford, Chrysler, and General Motors—argues that its cars are higher in quality than the cars of the others. Similarly, each major airline, for example, American, United, and Delta, argues that it provides the best and most reliable service. Indeed, it seems that virtually every U.S. business has adopted quality as a major point of competition. Thus, a business that fails to keep pace may find itself falling behind not only foreign competition but also other U.S. firms.[7]

Productivity Managers have also come to recognize that quality and productivity are related. In the past many managers thought that they could increase

Malcolm Baldrige Award Named after a former Secretary of Commerce, this prestigious award is given to firms that achieve major quality improvements

output (productivity) only by decreasing quality. Managers today have learned the hard way that such an assumption is almost always wrong. If a firm installs a meaningful quality-enhancement program, three things are likely to result. First, the number of defects is likely to decrease, causing fewer returns from customers. Second, because the number of defects goes down, resources (materials and people) dedicated to reworking flawed output will be decreased. Third, because making employees responsible for quality reduces the need for quality inspectors, the organization is able to produce more units with fewer resources.

Costs   Improved quality also lowers costs. Poor quality results in higher returns from customers, high warranty costs, and lawsuits from customers injured by faulty products. Future sales are lost because of disgruntled customers. An organization with quality problems often has to increase inspection expenses just to catch defective products. We noted in Chapter 14, for example, how Whistler Corporation was using 100 of its 250 employees just to fix poorly assembled radar detectors.[8]

■ Total Quality Management

Once an organization makes a decision to enhance the quality of its products and services, it must then decide how to implement its decision. The most pervasive approach to managing quality has been called **total quality management**, or **TQM**—a real and meaningful effort by an organization to change its whole approach to business to make quality a guiding factor in everything the organization does.[9] Figure 15.1 highlights the major ingredients in TQM.

Strategic Commitment   The starting point for TQM is a strategic commitment by top management. Such commitment is important for several reasons. First, the organizational culture must change to recognize that quality is not just an ideal but is instead an objective goal that must be pursued.[10] Second, a decision to pursue the goal of quality carries with it some real costs—for expenditures such as new equipment and facilities. Thus, without a commitment from top management, quality improvement will prove to be just a slogan or gimmick, with little or no real change.

total quality management (TQM)
A strategic commitment by top management to change its whole approach to business to make quality a guiding factor in everything it does

FIGURE 15.1
Total Quality Management

Quality is one of the most important issues facing organizations today. Total quality management, or TQM, is a comprehensive effort to enhance an organization's product or service quality. TQM involves the five basic dimensions shown here. Each is important and must be effectively addressed if the organization truly expects to increase quality.

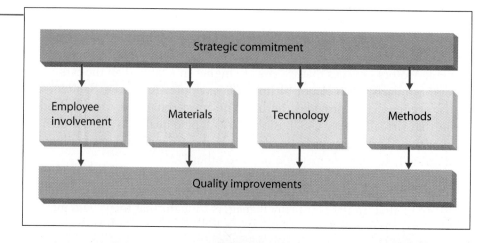

Employee Involvement   Employee involvement is another critical ingredient in TQM. Virtually all successful quality-enhancement programs involve making the person responsible for doing the job responsible for making sure it is done right.[11] By definition, then, employee involvement is a critical component in improving quality. Work teams, discussed in Chapter 13, are common vehicles for increasing employee involvement.

Technology   New forms of technology are also useful in TQM programs. Automation and robots, for example, can often make products with higher precision and better consistency than can people. Investing in higher-grade machines capable of doing jobs more precisely and reliably often improves quality. For example, AT&T has achieved notable improvements in product quality by replacing many of its machines with new equipment. Similarly, most U.S. auto and electronics firms have made significant investments in technology to help boost quality.

Materials   Another important part of TQM is improving the quality of the materials that organizations use. Suppose that a company that assembles stereos buys chips and circuits from another company. If the chips have a high failure rate, consumers will return defective stereos to the company whose nameplate appears on them, not to the company that made the chips. The stereo firm then loses in two ways: it must make refunds to customers, and it has a damaged reputation. As a result, many firms have increased the quality requirements they impose on their suppliers as a way of improving the quality of their own products. Recall from our opening incident that Hartmann uses only high-quality materials in its luggage.

Methods   Improved methods can improve product and service quality. Methods are operating systems used by the organization during the actual transformation process. American Express Company, for example, has found ways to cut its approval time for new credit cards from twenty-two days to only eleven. This change results in improved service quality.[12]

■ TQM Tools and Techniques

Beyond the strategic context of quality, managers can also rely on several specific tools and techniques for improving quality. Among the most popular today are benchmarking, outsourcing, speed, ISO 9000, and statistical quality control.

Benchmarking   **Benchmarking** is the process of learning how other firms do things in an exceptionally high-quality manner. Some approaches to benchmarking are simple and straightforward. For example, Xerox routinely buys copiers made by other firms and takes them apart to see how they work. This process enables the firm to stay abreast of its competitors' improvements and changes. When Ford was planning the Taurus, it identified the four hundred features that customers said were the most important to them. It then found the competing cars that did the best job on each feature. Ford's goal was to equal or surpass each of its competitors on those four hundred features. Other benchmarking strategies are more indirect. For example, many firms

benchmarking   The process of learning how other firms do things in an exceptionally high-quality manner

TABLE 15.2
Guidelines for Increasing the Speed of Operations

Many organizations today are using speed for competitive advantage. These are six common guidelines that organizations follow when they want to shorten the time they need to get things accomplished. Although not every manager can do each of these things, most managers can do at least some of them.

1. Start from scratch (it's usually easier than trying to do what the organization does now faster).
2. Minimize the number of approvals needed to do something (the fewer people who have to approve something, the faster it will get done).
3. Use work teams as a basis for organization (teamwork and cooperation work better than individual effort and conflict).
4. Develop and adhere to a schedule (a properly designed schedule can greatly increase speed).
5. Don't ignore distribution (making something faster is only part of the battle).
6. Integrate speed into the organization's culture (if everyone understands the importance of speed, things will naturally get done quicker).

study how L.L. Bean manages its mail-order business, how Disney recruits and trains employees, and how Federal Express tracks packages for applications they can employ in their own businesses.[13]

Outsourcing Another innovation for improving quality is outsourcing. **Outsourcing** is the process of subcontracting services and operations to other firms who can perform those functions less expensively and/or better. If a business performs each and every one of its own administrative and business services and operations, it is almost certain to be doing at least some of them in an inefficient and/or low-quality manner. If those areas can be identified and outsourced, the firm will save money and realize a higher-quality service or operation. For example, until recently Eastman Kodak handled all of its own computing operations. Now, however, those operations are subcontracted to IBM, which handles all of Kodak's computing. The result is higher-quality computing systems and operations at Kodak for less money than it was spending before.[14]

outsourcing Subcontracting services and operations to other firms that can perform them less expensively and/or better

Speed A third popular TQM technique is speed. **Speed** is the time needed by the organization to get something accomplished, and it can be emphasized in any area, including developing, making, and distributing products or services.[15] A good illustration of the power of speed comes from General Electric. At one point the firm needed six plants and three weeks to produce and deliver custom-made industrial circuit-breaker boxes. By emphasizing speed, the same product can now be delivered in three days, and only a single plant is involved. Table 15.2 identifies a number of basic suggestions that have helped companies increase the speed of their operations. For example, GE found it better to start from scratch with a remodeled plant. GE also wiped out the

speed The time needed by the organization to accomplish its activities, including developing, making, and distributing products or services

ISO 9000 is a relatively new technique for boosting quality. Managers should carefully assess its value and potential. When managers force it into situations where it's not needed, employees will be frustrated and the entire effort can degenerate into a bureaucratic nightmare of inefficiency.

need for approvals by eliminating most managerial positions and set up teams as a basis for organizing work. Stressing the importance of the schedule helped Motorola build a new plant and start production of a new product in only eighteen months.

ISO 9000 **ISO 9000** refers to a set of quality standards created by the International Organization for Standardization. There are five such standards, numbered 9000 to 9001. They cover areas such as product testing, employee training, record keeping, supplier relations, and repair policies and procedures. Firms that want to meet these standards apply for certification and are audited by a firm chosen by the organization's domestic affiliate (in the United States, this is the American National Standards Institute). These auditors review every aspect of the firm's business operations in relation to the standards. Many firms report that merely preparing for an ISO 9000 audit has been helpful. Many firms today, including General Electric, Du Pont, Eastman Kodak, British Telecom, and Philips Electronics are urging—or in some cases requiring—their suppliers to achieve ISO 9000 certification.[16]

ISO 9000 is an important TQM tool. These National Steel workers celebrate the announcement that their division, Pace, has met ISO 9000 standards and is now certified under all quality requirements imposed by the ISO. The firm believes that this designation will improve its competitiveness and generate new business.

Statistical Quality Control A final quality-control technique is **statistical quality control (SQC)**. SQC is primarily concerned with managing quality.[17] Moreover, it is a set of statistical techniques that can be used to monitor quality. *Acceptance sampling* involves sampling finished goods to ensure that quality standards have been met. Acceptance sampling is effective only when the correct percentage of products that should be tested (for example, 2, 5, or 25 percent) is determined. This decision is especially important when the test renders the product useless. Flash cubes, wine, and collapsible steering wheels, for example, are consumed or destroyed during testing. Another SQC method is *in-process sampling*. In-process sampling involves evaluating products during production so that needed changes can be made. The painting department of a furniture company might periodically check the tint of the paint it is using. The company can then adjust the color as necessary to conform to customer standards. The advantage of in-process sampling is that it detects problems before they accumulate.

ISO 9000 A set of quality standards created by the International Organization for Standardization

statistical quality control (**SQC**) A set of specific statistical techniques that can be used to monitor quality

Managing Productivity

While the current focus on quality by American companies is a relatively recent phenomenon, managers have been aware of the importance of productivity for several years. The stimulus for this attention was a recognition that the gap between productivity in the United States and productivity in other

productivity An economic measure of efficiency that summarizes what is produced relative to resources used to produce it

industrialized countries was narrowing. This section describes the meaning of productivity and underscores its importance. After summarizing recent productivity trends, we suggest ways that organizations can increase their productivity.

■ The Meaning of Productivity

In a general sense, **productivity** is an economic measure of efficiency that summarizes the value of outputs relative to the value of the inputs used to create them.[18] Productivity can be and often is assessed at different levels of analysis and in different forms.

Levels of Productivity   By level of productivity, we mean the units of analysis used to calculate or define productivity. For example, aggregate productivity is the total level of productivity achieved by a country. Industry productivity is the total productivity achieved by all the firms in a particular industry. Company productivity, just as the term suggests, is the level of productivity achieved by an individual company. Unit and individual productivity refer to the productivity achieved by a unit or department within an organization and the level of productivity attained by a single person.

Forms of Productivity   There are many different forms of productivity. Total factor productivity is defined by the following formula:

$$\text{Productivity} = \frac{\text{Outputs}}{\text{Inputs}}$$

Total factor productivity is an overall indicator of how well an organization uses all of its resources, such as labor, capital, materials, and energy to create all of its products and services. The biggest problem with total factor productivity is that all the ingredients must be expressed in the same terms—dollars (it is difficult to add hours of labor to number of units of a raw material in a meaningful way). Total factor productivity also gives little insight into how things can be changed to improve productivity. Consequently, most organizations find it more useful to calculate a partial productivity ratio. Such a ratio uses only one category of resource. For example, labor productivity could be calculated by this simple formula:

$$\text{Labor Productivity} = \frac{\text{Outputs}}{\text{Direct Labor}}$$

This method has two advantages. First, it is not necessary to transform the units of input into some other unit. Second, this method provides managers with specific insights into how changing different resource inputs affects productivity. Suppose that an organization can manufacture 100 units of a particular product with twenty hours of direct labor. The organization's labor productivity index is five (or five units per labor hour). Now suppose that worker efficiency is increased (through one of the ways to be discussed later in this chapter) so that the same twenty hours of labor results in the manufacture of 120 units of the product. The labor productivity index increases to six (six units per labor hour), and the firm can see the direct results of a specific managerial action.

■ The Importance of Productivity

Managers consider it important for their firms to maintain high levels of productivity for various reasons. Firm productivity is a primary determinant of an organization's level of profitability and, ultimately, its ability to survive. If one organization is more productive than another, it will have more products to sell at lower prices and have more profits to reinvest in other areas. Productivity also partially determines people's standards of living within a particular country. At an economic level, businesses consume resources and produce goods and services. The goods and services created within a country can be used by that country's citizens or exported for sale in other countries. The more goods and services the businesses within a country can produce, the more goods and services the country's citizens will have. Even goods that are exported result in financial resources flowing back into the home country. Thus, the citizens of a highly productive country are likely to have notably higher standards of living than are the citizens of a country with low productivity.

■ Productivity Trends

The United States has the highest level of productivity in the world. For example, Japanese workers produce only about 76 percent as much as U.S. workers, and German workers produce about 84 percent as much.[19] But in recent years, other countries have been closing the gap.[20] This trend was a primary factor in the decisions made by U.S. businesses to retrench, retool, and become more competitive in the world marketplace. For example, General Electric's dishwasher plant in Louisville has cut its inventory requirements by 50 percent, reduced labor costs from 15 percent to only 10 percent of total manufacturing costs, and cut product development time in half. As a result of these kinds of efforts, productivity trends have now leveled out and U.S. workers are generally maintaining their lead in most industries.

One important factor that has hurt U.S. productivity has been the tremendous growth of the service sector in the United States. While this sector grew, its productivity levels did not. One part of this problem relates to measurement. For example, it is fairly easy to calculate the number of tons of steel produced at a Bethlehem Steel mill and divide it by the number of labor hours used; it is more difficult to determine the output of an attorney or a certified public accountant. Still, virtually everyone agrees that improving service-sector productivity is the next major hurdle facing U.S. business.[21]

Figure 15.2 illustrates recent trends in productivity growth for the total U.S. economy, broken down into manufacturing and services (agricultural productivity is not included). As you can see, manufacturing productivity was stalled from the mid-1970s into the early 1980s but has been increasing since that time. Service sector productivity, meanwhile, has remained relatively stable. Total productivity, therefore, has been increasing but only at a modest pace.

■ Improving Productivity

How does a business or industry improve its productivity? Numerous specific suggestions made by experts generally fall into two broad categories: improving operations and increasing employee involvement.

Improving Operations   One way that firms can improve operations is by spending more on research and development (R&D). R&D spending helps identify new products, new uses for existing products, and new methods for making products. Each of these factors contributes to productivity. For example, Bausch & Lomb almost missed the boat on extended-wear contact lenses because the company had neglected R&D. When it became apparent that its major competitors were almost a year ahead of Bausch & Lomb in developing the new lenses, management made R&D a top priority. As a result, the company made several scientific breakthroughs, shortened the time needed to introduce new products, and greatly enhanced both total sales and profits—and all with a smaller workforce than the company used to employ. Even though other countries are greatly increasing their R&D spending, the United States continues to be the world leader in this area.

Another way firms can boost productivity through operations is by reassessing and revamping their transformation facilities. We noted earlier how one of GE's modernized plants does a better job than six antiquated facilities. Just building a new factory is no guarantee of success, but IBM, Ford, Allen-Bradley, Caterpillar, and many other businesses have achieved dramatic productivity gains by revamping their production facilities. Facilities refinements are not limited to manufacturers. Most McDonald's restaurants now have drive-through windows, and many are moving soft-drink dispensers out to the restaurant floor so that customers can get their own drinks. Each of these moves is an attempt to increase the speed with which customers can be served and thus to increase productivity.

Increasing Employee Involvement   The other major thrust in productivity enhancement has been toward employee involvement. We noted earlier that participation can enhance quality. Employee involvement can also boost productivity. Examples of this involvement are an individual worker being given a bigger voice in how she does her job, a formal agreement of cooperation between management and labor, and total involvement throughout the organization.[22] GE eliminated most of the supervisors at its new circuit-breaker plant and put control in the hands of workers.

Another method popular in the United States is increasing the flexibility of an organization's workforce by training employees to perform a

FIGURE 15.2
Manufacturing and Service Productivity Growth Trends (1970–1993)

Both manufacturing productivity and service productivity in the United States continue to grow, although manufacturing productivity is growing at a faster pace. Total productivity, therefore, also continues to grow.

Source: Graph "Productivity Growth" from Myron Magnet, "The Productivity Payoff Arrives," *Fortune,* June 27, 1994, p. 79. © 1994 Time Inc. All rights reserved. Reprinted by special permission.

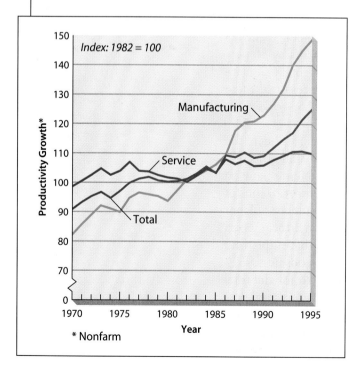

number of different jobs. Such cross training allows the firm to function with fewer workers because workers can be transferred easily to areas where they are most needed. For example, the Lechmere department store in Sarasota, Florida, encourages workers to learn numerous jobs within the store. One person in the store can operate a forklift in the stockroom, serve as a cashier, or provide customer service on the sales floor. At a Motorola plant, 397 of 400 employees have learned at least two skills under a similar program.

Rewards are essential to making employee involvement work. Firms must reward people for learning new skills and using them proficiently. At Motorola, for example, workers who master a new skill are assigned for five days to a job requiring them to use that skill. If they perform with no defects, they are moved to a higher pay grade, and then they move back and forth between jobs as they are needed. If there is a performance problem, they receive more training and practice. This approach is fairly new, but preliminary indicators suggest that it can increase productivity significantly. Many unions resist such programs because they threaten job security and reduce a person's identification with one skill or craft.

Managing Quality Through Operations Management

We noted earlier that both quality and productivity can be enhanced through various elements of operations. But what exactly are operations? And how are they managed? **Operations management** is the set of managerial activities used by an organization to transform resource inputs into products and services. When IBM buys electronic components, assembles them into computers, and then ships them to customers, it is relying on operations management. When a Pizza Hut employee orders food and paper products and then combines dough, cheese, and tomato paste to create a pizza, he or she is using operations management.

operations management The total set of managerial activities used by an organization to transform resource inputs into products, services, or both

■ The Importance of Operations

Operations is an important functional concern for organizations because efficient and effective operations management goes a long way toward ensuring quality and productivity. Inefficient or ineffective operations management, on the other hand, almost inevitably leads to lower levels of both quality and productivity. In an economic sense, operations management provides utility, or value, of one type or another, depending on the nature of the firm's products or services. If the product is a physical good, such as a Yamaha motorcycle, operations provides form utility by combining many dissimilar inputs (sheet metal, rubber, paint, combustion engines, and human craftsmanship) to produce the desired output. The inputs are converted from their incoming forms into a new physical form. This conversion is

manufacturing A form of business that combines and transforms resource inputs into tangible outcomes

typical of manufacturing operations and essentially reflects the organization's technology.

In contrast, the operations activities of American Airlines provide time and place utility through its services. The airline transports passengers and freight according to agreed-on departure and arrival places and times. Other service operations, such as a Coors Brothers Beer distributorship or the Gap retail chain, provide place and possession utility by bringing the customer and products made by others together. Although the organizations in these examples produce different kinds of products or services, their operations processes share many important features.[23]

Manufacturing and Production

Because manufacturing once dominated U.S. industry, the entire area of operations management used to be called production management. **Manufacturing** is a form of business that combines and transforms resources into tangible outcomes that are then sold to others. The Goodyear Tire and Rubber Company is a manufacturer because it combines rubber and chemical compounds and uses blending equipment and molding machines to ultimately create tires. Broyhill is a manufacturer because it buys wood and metal components, pads, and fabric and then combines them into furniture.

During the 1970s, manufacturing entered a long period of decline in the United States, primarily because of foreign competition. U.S. firms had grown lax and sluggish, and new foreign competitors came onto the scene with new equipment and much higher levels of efficiency. For example, steel companies in the Far East were able to produce high-quality steel for much lower prices than were U.S. companies like Bethlehem Steel and U.S. Steel (now USX Corporation). Faced with a battle for survival, many companies underwent a long and difficult period of change by eliminating waste and transforming themselves into leaner and more efficient and responsive entities. They reduced their workforces dramatically, closed antiquated or unnecessary plants, and modernized their remaining plants. In recent years, their efforts have started to pay dividends as U.S. business has regained its competitive position in many industries. Although manufacturers from other parts of the world are still formidable competitors and U.S. firms may never again be competitive in some markets, the overall picture is much better than it was just a few years ago. And prospects continue to look bright.

Properly designed operations systems can dictate the potential quality levels an organization can achieve. At Ipsilon Networks, for example, managers are hard at work creating new forms of network software that might one day challenge Cisco Systems for industry leadership. An open workplace where engineers work in cubicles is generally thought to be the most cost-effective way to facilitate interaction among engineers. As a prank, however, CEO Brian Nesmith and founder Tom Lyon recently built a temporary "office" for an engineer who complained about the lack of privacy in his cubicle.

Service Operations

During the decline of the manufacturing sector, a tremendous growth in the service sector kept the U.S. economy from declining at the same rate. A **service organization** is one that transforms resources into an intangible output and creates time or place utility for its customers. For example, Merrill Lynch Co. makes stock transactions for its customers, Avis leases cars to its customers, and your local hairdresser cuts your hair. In 1947 the service sector was responsible for less than half of the U.S. gross national product (GNP). By 1975, however, this figure reached 65 percent, and by 1995 it was over 75 percent. The service sector has been responsible for almost 90 percent of all new jobs created in the United States during the 1990s. Managers have come to see that many of the tools, techniques, and methods that are used in a factory are also useful to a service firm. For example, managers of automobile plants and hair salons have to decide how to design their facility, identify the best location for it, determine optimal capacity, make decisions about inventory storage, set procedures for purchasing raw materials, and set standards for productivity and quality.

service organization An organization that transforms resources into services

■ The Role of Operations in Organizational Strategy

It should be clear by this point that operations management is very important to organizations. Beyond its direct impact on quality and productivity, it also directly influences the organization's overall level of effectiveness. For example, the deceptively simple strategic decision whether to stress high quality regardless of cost, lowest possible cost regardless of quality, or some combination of the two, has numerous important implications. A highest-possible quality strategy will dictate state-of-the-art technology and rigorous control of product design and materials specifications. A combination strategy might call for lower-grade technology and less concern about product design and materials specifications. Just as strategy affects operations management, operations management affects strategy. Suppose that a firm decides to upgrade the quality of its products or services. The organization's ability to implement the decision partly depends on current production capabilities and other resources. If existing technology does not permit higher-quality work and if the organization lacks the resources to replace its technology, increasing quality to the desired new standards will be difficult.

Using Operations Systems for Quality

The basic functional purpose of operations systems is to control transformation processes to ensure that relevant goals are achieved in areas such as quality and costs. Operations has a number of special purposes within this control framework, including purchasing and inventory management.

■ Operations Management as Control

One way of using operations management as control is to coordinate it with other functions. Monsanto Company, for example, established a consumer products division that produces and distributes fertilizers and lawn chemicals. To facilitate control, the operations function was organized as an autonomous profit center. This approach is effective for Monsanto because its manufacturing division has the authority to determine not only the costs of creating the product but also the product price and the marketing programs.

In terms of overall organizational control, a division like the one used by Monsanto should be held accountable only for the activities over which it has decision-making authority. It would be inappropriate, of course, to make operations accountable for profitability in an organization that stresses sales and market share over quality and productivity. Misplaced accountability results in ineffective organizational control, to say nothing of hostility and conflict. Depending on the strategic role of operations, then, operations managers are accountable for different kinds of results. For example, in an organization using bureaucratic control, accountability will be spelled out in rules and regulations. In a clan system, on the other hand, accountability is likely to be understood and accepted by everyone.

Within operations, managerial control ensures that resources and activities achieve primary goals such as a high percentage of on-time deliveries, low unit-production cost, or high product reliability. Any control system should focus on the elements that are most crucial to goal attainment. For example, firms in which product quality is a major concern (as it is at Rolex) might adopt a screening control system to monitor the product as it is being created. If quantity is a pressing issue (as it is at Timex), a postaction system might be used to identify defects at the end of the system without disrupting the manufacturing process itself.

■ Purchasing Management

purchasing management Buying materials and resources needed to produce products and services

Purchasing management is concerned with buying the materials and resources needed to create products and services. Thus, the purchasing manager for a retailer like Sears, Roebuck is responsible for buying the merchandise the store will sell. The purchasing manager for a manufacturer buys raw materials, parts, and machines needed by the organization. Large companies like GE, IBM, and Westinghouse have large purchasing departments. The manager responsible for purchasing must balance a number of constraints. Buying too much ties up capital and increases storage costs. Buying too little might lead to shortages and high reordering costs. The manager must also make sure that the quality of what is purchased meets the organization's needs, that the supplier is reliable, and that the best financial terms are negotiated.

Many firms have recently changed their approach to purchasing as a means to lower costs and improve quality and productivity. In particular, rather than relying on hundreds or even thousands of suppliers, many companies are reducing their number of suppliers and negotiating special production-delivery arrangements. For example, the Honda plant in Marysville, Ohio, found a local business owner looking for a new opportunity. They negotiated an agreement whereby he would start a new company to mount car stereo speakers into plastic moldings. He delivers finished goods to the plant three times a day, and Honda buys all he can manufacture. Thus, he has a stable sales base, Honda has a local and reliable supplier, and both companies benefit.

■ Inventory Management

Inventory control, also called materials control, is essential for effective operations management. The four basic kinds of inventories are *raw materials*, *work-in-process*, *finished-goods*, and *in-transit* inventories. As shown in Table 15.3, the sources of control over these inventories are as different as their purposes. Work-in-process inventories, for example, are made up of partially completed products that need further processing; they are controlled by the shop-floor system. In contrast, the quantities and costs of finished-goods inventories are under the control of the overall production scheduling system, which is determined by high-level planning decisions. In-transit inventories are controlled by the transportation and distribution systems. Like most other areas of operations management, inventory management has changed notably in recent years. One particularly important breakthrough is the **just-in-time (JIT) method**. First popularized by the Japanese, the JIT system reduces the organization's investment in storage space for raw materials and in the materials themselves. Historically, manufacturers built large storage areas and filled them with materials, parts, and supplies that would be needed days, weeks, and even months in the future. In contrast, a manager using the JIT system orders materials and parts more often and in smaller quantities, thereby reducing investment in both storage space and actual inventory. The ideal arrangement is for materials to arrive just as they are needed—or just in time.

Recall our example about the small firm that assembles stereo speakers for Honda and delivers them three times a day, making it unnecessary for

inventory control Managing the organization's raw materials, work in process, finished goods, and products in transit

just-in-time (JIT) method An inventory system in which materials arrive as they are needed (just in time) so that the production process is not interrupted

Type	Purpose	Source of Control
Raw materials	Provide the materials needed to make the product	Purchasing models and systems
Work in process	Enables overall production to be divided into stages of the manageable size	Shop-floor control systems
Finished goods	Provide ready supply of products on customer demand and enable long, efficient production runs	High-level production scheduling systems in conjunction with marketing
In transit (pipeline)	Distributes products to customers	Transportation and distribution control systems

TABLE 15.3
Inventory Types, Purposes, and Sources of Control

JIT is a recent breakthrough in inventory management. With JIT inventory systems, materials arrive just as they are needed. JIT therefore helps an organization control its raw materials inventory by reducing the amount of space it must devote to storage.

Honda to carry large quantities of the speakers in inventory. In an even more striking example, Johnson Controls Inc. makes automobile seats for Chrysler and ships them by small truckloads to a Chrysler plant seventy-five miles away. Each shipment is scheduled to arrive two hours before it is needed. Clearly, the JIT approach requires high levels of coordination and cooperation between the company and its suppliers. If shipments arrive too early, Chrysler has no place to store them. If they arrive too late, the entire assembly line may have to be shut down, resulting in enormous expense. When properly designed and used, the JIT method controls inventory very effectively.

Summary of Key Points

Quality is a major consideration for all managers today. Quality is important because it affects competition, productivity, and costs. Total quality management is a comprehensive, organizationwide effort to enhance quality through a variety of avenues.

Productivity is also a major concern to managers. Productivity is a measure of how efficiently an organization is using its resources to create products or services. The United States still leads the world in individual productivity, but other industrialized nations are catching up.

Quality and productivity are often addressed via operations management, the set of managerial activities that organizations use in creating their products and services. Operations management is important to both manufacturing and service organizations. It plays an important role in an organization's strategy.

Operations systems serve an important role in quality control. Major areas of interest during the use of operations systems are purchasing and inventory management.

Discussion Questions

Questions for Review

1. What is quality? Why is it so important today?

2. How can an organization go about trying to increase the speed of its operations?

3. What are some of the basic TQM tools and techniques that managers can use to improve quality?

4. What is productivity? How can it be increased?

5. What is the relationship of operations management to overall organizational strategy? Where do productivity and quality fit into that relationship?

Questions for Analysis

1. How might the management functions of planning, organizing, and leading relate to the management of quality and productivity?

2. Some people argue that quality and productivity are inversely related; as one goes up, the other goes down. How can that argument be refuted?

3. Is operations management most closely linked to corporate-level, business-level, or functional strategies? Why or in what way?

4. Consider your college or university as an organization. How might it go about developing a TQM program?

5. Think of a product or service you purchased recently that subsequently failed to meet your expectations regarding quality. How could the product or service have been improved to make it of higher quality?

EXERCISE OVERVIEW

A manager's conceptual skills are her or his ability to think in the abstract. As this exercise demonstrates, there is often a relationship between the conceptual skills of key managers in an organization and that organization's ability to implement total quality initiatives.

EXERCISE BACKGROUND

Conceptual skills may help managers see opportunities for learning how to improve some aspect of their own operations from observations or experiences gleaned from dealings with other organizations.

To begin this exercise, carefully recall the last time you ate in a restaurant that involved some degree of self-service. Examples might include a fast-food restaurant like McDonald's, a cafeteria, or even a traditional restaurant with a salad bar. Recall as much about the experience as possible and develop some ideas as to why the restaurant is organized and laid out as it is.

Now carefully recall the last time you purchased something in a retail outlet. Possible examples might be an article of clothing from a specialty store, a book from a bookstore, or some software from a computer store. Again recall as much about the experience as possible and develop some ideas as to why the store is organized and laid out as it is.

EXERCISE TASK

Using the two examples you developed above, do the following:

1. Identify three or four elements of the service received at each location that you think most directly influenced—either positively or negatively—the quality and efficiency of your experience there.

2. Analyze the service elements from one organization and see whether they can somehow be used by the other.

3. Now repeat the process for the second organization.

EXERCISE OVERVIEW

As noted in this chapter, the quality of a product or service is relative to price and expectations. A manager's diagnostic skills—the ability to visualize responses to a situation—can be useful in helping to best position quality relative to price and expectations.

EXERCISE BACKGROUND

Think of a recent occasion in which you purchased a tangible product. For example, think about clothing, electronic equipment, luggage, or professional supplies that you subsequently came to feel to be of especially high quality. Now recall another product that you evaluated as having appropriate or adequate quality and a third that you felt had low or poor quality.

Next, recall parallel experiences involving purchases of services. Examples might include an airline, train, or bus trip; a meal in a restaurant; a haircut; or an oil change for your car.

Finally, recall three experiences in which both products and services were involved. Examples might include having questions answered by someone about a product you were buying, or returning a defective or broken product for a refund or warranty repair. Try to recall instances in which there was an apparent disparity between product and service quality (for example, a poor-quality product accompanied by outstanding service or a high-quality product with mediocre service).

EXERCISE TASK

Using the nine examples identified above, do the following:

1. Assess the extent to which the quality you associated with each was a function of price and your expectations.

2. Consider whether the quality of each item could be improved without greatly affecting its price. If so, how?

3. Consider whether high-quality service can offset only adequate or even poor product quality. Similarly, consider whether outstanding product quality can offset only adequate or even poor quality service.

Building Effective
Technical
Skills

EXERCISE OVERVIEW

Technical skills are the skills necessary to accomplish or understand the specific kind of work being done in an organization. This exercise helps you see how technical skills relate to quality, productivity, and operations management.

EXERCISE BACKGROUND

Select a product that you use on a regular basis. Examples might include computers, compact disks, books, or apparel. Next, do some research to learn as much as you can about how the product you chose is designed, produced, and distributed to consumers.

Assume that you have decided to go into business to make the product selected. Create two columns on a sheet of paper. In one column list all the relevant activities that you know how to do (for example, install software on a computer, sew two pieces of fabric together). In the second column, list the activities that you do not know how to do.

EXERCISE TASK

With the background information above as context, do the following:

1. Specify where people might learn the skills necessary to perform all the activities for the product you intend to make.

2. Rank-order the importance of the skills regarding the product.

3. Determine how many people you will likely need to employ to have a full skill set available.

Mark Spenser could hardly wait to get home. He had just attended a regional convention of nursery operators. During the convention he attended a workshop on total quality management and was excited about using some of the methods at Sunset Landscape Services.

For example, one thing he planned to start was a benchmarking program. He had not visited Lion Gardens, a competitor, in more than a year, and he had no idea how much the local Wal-Mart was charging for fertilizer or mulch. He had long ago decided to focus on service and quality rather than the competition; he realized, nonetheless, that he should know more about his competitors.

Mark also thought that perhaps he should outsource some of his operations. For example, he did his own payroll each week and managed his own employee benefits program. He was aware, however, that many other small businesses in town outsourced these human resource services to other firms. He decided to investigate this idea very soon.

Mark thought that applying what he had learned about speed might also help his operation. At present, for example, his customers were waiting at least a few days, and sometimes up to a week, for home delivery. He wondered if he could start promising same-day delivery and, if so, how this service might affect his business. He also wondered if he could get his suppliers to service his own purchases faster. It did seem to take longer than necessary to receive his orders. And although he was not a huge customer, he felt that he had sufficient clout to at least get them to try.

DISCUSSION QUESTIONS

1. How do you think Mark's efforts will affect his business?

2. Do you see any areas for concern in his plans?

3. Do you agree or disagree with his assumption that he should be more knowledgeable about his competitors even if he is not going to emulate them?

DEFINING QUALITY AND PRODUCTIVITY

Introduction: Quality is a complex term whose meaning has no doubt changed over time. The following assessment surveys your ideas about and approaches to quality.

Instructions: You will agree with some of the statements and disagree with others. In some cases making a decision may be difficult, but you should force a choice. Record your answers next to each statement according to the following scale:

Rating Scale

4 Strongly agree	2 Somewhat disagree
3 Somewhat agree	1 Strongly disagree

_____ 1. Quality refers to a product's or service's ability to fulfill its primary operating characteristics such as providing a sharp picture for a television set.

_____ 2. Quality is an absolute, measurable aspect of a product or service.

_____ 3. The concept of quality includes supplemental aspects of a product or service such as the remote control for a television set.

_____ 4. Productivity and quality are inversely related so that to get one you must sacrifice the other.

_____ 5. The concept of quality refers to the extent to which a product's design and operating characteristics conform to certain set standards.

_____ 6. Productivity refers to what is created relative to what it takes to create it.

_____ 7. Quality means that a product will not malfunction during a specified period of time.

_____ 8. Quality refers only to products; it is immeasurable for services.

_____ 9. The length of time that a product or service will function is what is known as quality.

_____ 10. Everyone uses exactly the same definition of quality.

_____ 11. Quality refers to the repair ease and speed of a product or service.

_____ 12. Being treated courteously has nothing to do with the quality of anything.

_____ 13. How a product looks, feels, tastes, or smells is what is meant by quality.

_____ 14. Price, not quality, is what determines the ultimate value of service.

_____ 15. Quality refers to what customers think of a product or service.

_____ 16. Productivity and quality cannot both increase at the same time.

For interpretation, turn to page 465.

Source: Adapted from Chapter 21, especially pp. 473–474, in David D. Van Fleet and Tim O. Peterson, _Contemporary Management_, Third Edition. Copyright © 1994 by Houghton Mifflin Company.

Experiential Exercise

PREPARING THE FISHBONE CHART

Purpose: The fishbone chart is an excellent procedure for identifying possible causes of a problem. It provides you with knowledge that you can use to improve the operations of any organization. This skill exercise focuses on the _administrative management model_. It helps you develop the _monitor role_ of the administrative management model. One of the skills of the monitor is the ability to analyze problems.

Introduction: Japanese quality circles often use the fishbone "cause and effect" graphic technique to initiate the resolution of a group work problem. Quite often the causes are clustered in categories such as materials, methods, people, and machines. The fishbone technique is usually accomplished in the following six steps.

1. Write the problem in the "head" of the fish (the large block).

2. Brainstorm the major causes of the problem and list them on the fish "bones."

3. Analyze each main cause and write in minor subcauses on bone subbranches.

4. Reach consensus on one or two of the major causes of the problem.

5. Explore ways to correct or remove the major cause(s).

6. Prepare a report or presentation explaining the proposed change.

Instructions: Your instructor will provide you with further instructions.

The fishbone will look something like this:

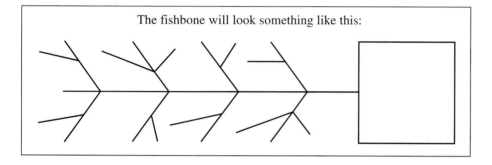

Source: Adapted from Burton, Gene E., *Exercises in Management,* 5th ed. Copyright © 1996 by Houghton Mifflin Company. Used with permission.

CASE STUDY

Honda Emphasizes Quality

Honda Motor Company, of course, is among the most successful and respected firms in the global automobile industry. Although Honda is only the ninth largest firm in its industry and just the third largest in Japan, the company enjoys a stellar reputation for producing high-quality cars in ways that are innovative and cost-efficient. Indeed, Honda is at the forefront of the industry in how it practices operations management.

The foundation of Honda's operations management strategy has long been the basic formula of well-engineered cars created to match consumer preferences and produced in an efficient manner. But like all companies, Honda has had to occasionally make adjustments in what it does. For example, its new products in the early 1990s were a bit off the mark with consumers, and sales dropped in both Japan and the United States. Its costs were also a bit higher than normal.

To get things back on track, Honda managers have begun to focus more of their attention on new product design and new methods for improving productivity. Among the newest wave of Honda products, for example, are the so-called recreational vehicles (RVs), smaller and more nimble than conventional sport utility vehicles but with the same characteristics and qualities as their larger brethren. The Odyssey, the CR-V, and the Orthia are three of Honda's very popular RVs.

Another interesting strategy at Honda is its plan to design and manufacture a so-called world car. Most cars today are made for specific countries or regions, with considerable differences across regions. These differences reflect variations in consumer tastes, environmental restrictions, preferred options, disposable income, and so forth. Honda's Accord, for example, is among the best-selling cars in the United States, but its styling does not have wide appeal in Japan.

But auto makers know that a car with global appeal would be enormously profitable because of the economies of scale they could gain. Ford has attempted to develop a world car twice, failing with the Escort but coming a bit closer with the Contour. Honda, meanwhile, is feverishly trying to make its Accord so universally appealing that it can be sold anywhere.

Honda's strategy hinges on the distinction between engineering and design. The firm plans to use the chassis, engine, and other "mechanics" everywhere. But is also intends to customize the exterior design to meet local tastes. Thus, Accords sold in the United States, Europe, and Japan will look very different on the outside, but will be essentially the same on the inside. By using the same platform in all markets, Honda will save millions of dollars.

Another key part of Honda's approach is based on speed. Honda can get new designs to market faster and adjust its production more quickly than any other car manufacturer in the world. For example, the firm recently made a changeover from producing 1997 Accords to 1998 Accords at its Maryville,

Ohio, factory in less than twelve hours. Rivals often spend weeks or even months in changing over between model years.

Such successes are necessary for Honda to keep its place in the industry. Because Honda has far fewer models than its bigger rivals have, it depends more on its core models like Accord and Civic than its competitors depend on a single model. Indeed, Accord accounts for half of Honda's sales in the United States and for more than a quarter of its worldwide production. But at least for now, Honda seems to be on the right track!

Case Questions

1. How does operations management contribute to Honda's success?

2. Describe Honda's apparent views on product quality.

3. Do you think a "world car" is really feasible? Why or why not?

Case References: "Can Honda Build a World Car?" *Business Week*, September 8, 1997, pp. 100–108; Alex Taylor III, "The Man Who Put Honda Back on Track," *Fortune*, September 9, 1996, pp. 92–100; and "Quick-Change Artists," *Newsweek*, September 1, 1997, p. 47.

CHAPTER NOTES

1. "The Quest for Quality Is in the Bag(gage)," *USA Today*, September 23, 1997, p. 12E (quote on p. 12E). Based on "The Quest for Quality is in the Bag(gage)," *USA Today*, September 23, 1997. Copyright 1997, *USA Today*. Reprinted with permission.

2. "Quality—How to Make It Pay," *Business Week*, August 8, 1994, pp. 54–59.

3. Rhonda Reger, Loren Gustafson, Samuel DeMarie, and John Mullane, "Reframing the Organization: Why Implementing Total Quality Is Easier Said Than Done," *Academy of Management Review*, Vol. 19, No. 3, 1994, pp. 565–584.

4. Ross Johnson and William O. Winchell, *Management and Quality* (Milwaukee: American Society for Quality Control, 1989). See also Carol Reeves and David Bednar, "Defining Quality: Alternatives and Implications," *Academy of Management Review*, Vol. 19, No. 3, 1994, pp. 419–445.

5. "Quality Sets These Three Companies Apart," *USA Today*, November 18, 1998, p. 5B.

6. W. Edwards Deming, *Out of the Crisis* (Cambridge, Mass.: MIT Press, 1986).

7. David Waldman, "The Contributions of Total Quality Management to a Theory of Work Performance," *Academy of Management Review*, Vol. 19, No. 3, 1994, pp. 510–536.

8. Joel Dreyfuss, "Victories in the Quality Crusade," *Fortune*, October 10, 1988, pp. 80–88.

9. Thomas Y. Choi and Orlando C. Behling, "Top Managers and TQM Success: One More Look After All These Years," *Academy of Management Executive*, Vol. 11, No. 1, 1997, pp. 37–48.

10. James Dean and David Bowen, "Management Theory and Total Quality: Improving Research and Practice Through Theory Development," *Academy of Management Review*, Vol. 19, No. 3, 1994, pp. 392–418.

11. Edward E. Lawler, "Total Quality Management and Employee Involvement: Are They Compatible?" *Academy of Management Executive*, Vol. 8, No. 1, 1994, pp. 68–79.

12. "Quality Is Becoming Job One in the Office, Too," *Business Week*, April 29, 1991, pp. 52–56.

13. Jeremy Main, "How to Steal the Best Ideas Around," *Fortune*, October 19, 1992, pp. 102–106.

14. James Brian Quinn and Frederick Hilmer, "Strategic Outsourcing," *Sloan Management Review*, Summer 1994, pp. 43–55.

15. Thomas Robertson, "How to Reduce Market Penetration Cycle Times," *Sloan Management Review*, Fall 1993, pp. 87–96.

16. Ronald Henkoff, "The Hot New Seal of Quality," *Fortune*, June 28, 1993, pp. 116–120. See also Mustafa V. Uzumeri, "ISO 9000 and Other Metastandards: Principles for Management Practice?" *Academy of Management Executive*, Vol. 11, No. 1, 1997, pp. 21–28.

17. Paula C. Morrow, "The Measurement of TQM Principles and Work-Related Outcomes," *Journal of Organizational Behavior*, July 1997, pp. 363–376.

18. John W. Kendrick, *Understanding Productivity: An Introduction to the Dynamics of Productivity Change* (Baltimore: Johns Hopkins, 1977).

19. "The Productivity Payoff Arrives," *Fortune*, June 27, 1994, pp. 79–84.

20. "Study: USA Losing Competitive Edge," *USA Today*, April 25, 1997, p. 9D.

21. Michael van Biema and Bruce Greenwald, "Managing Our Way to Higher Service-Sector Productivity," *Harvard Business Review*, July–August 1997, pp. 87–98.

22. David Wright and Paul Brauchle, "Teaming up for Quality," *Training & Development*, September 1994, pp. 67–75.

23. Paul M. Swamidass, "Empirical Science: New Frontier in Operations Management Research," *Academy of Management Review*, October 1991, pp. 793–814.

Appendix

Tools for Planning and Decision Making

This appendix discusses a number of the basic tools and techniques that managers can use to enhance the efficiency and effectiveness of planning and decision making. We first describe forecasting, an extremely important tool, and then discuss several other planning techniques. Next, we discuss several tools that relate more to decision making. We conclude by assessing the strengths and weaknesses of the various tools and techniques.

Forecasting

To plan, managers must make assumptions about future events. But unlike wizards of old, planners cannot simply look into a crystal ball. Instead, they must develop forecasts of probable future circumstances. **Forecasting** is the process of developing assumptions or premises about the future that managers can use in planning or decision making.

forecasting The process of developing assumptions or premises about the future that managers can use in planning or decision making

■ Sales and Revenue Forecasting

As the term implies, **sales forecasting** is concerned with predicting future sales. Because monetary resources (derived mainly from sales) are necessary to finance both current and future operations, knowledge of future sales is of vital importance. Sales forecasting is something that every business, from Exxon to a neighborhood pizza parlor, must do. Consider, for example, the following questions that a manager might need to answer:

sales forecasting The prediction of future sales

1. How much of each of our products should we produce next week? next month? next year?
2. How much money will we have available to spend on research and development and on new-product test marketing?
3. When and to what degree will we need to expand our existing production facilities?
4. How should we respond to union demands for a 15 percent pay increase?
5. If we borrow money for expansion, can we pay it back?

None of these questions can be adequately answered without some notion of what future revenues are likely to be. Thus, sales forecasting is generally one of the first steps in planning.

Unfortunately, the term *sales forecasting* suggests that this form of forecasting is appropriate only for organizations that have something to sell. But other kinds of organizations also depend on financial resources, and so they also must forecast. The University of South Carolina, for example, must forecast future state aid before planning course offerings, staff size, and so on. Hospitals must forecast their future income from patient fees, insurance payments, and other sources to assess their ability to expand. Although we will continue to use the conventional term, keep in mind that what is really at issue is **revenue forecasting**.

revenue forecasting The prediction of future revenues from all sources

Several sources of information are used to develop a sales forecast. Previous sales figures and any obvious trends, such as the company's growth or stability, usually serve as the base. General economic indicators, technological improvements, new marketing strategies, and the competition's behavior may be added together to ensure an accurate forecast. Once projected, the sales (or revenues) forecast becomes a guiding framework for a variety of other activities. Raw-material expenditures, advertising budgets, sales-commission structures, and similar operating costs are based on projected sales figures.

Organizations often forecast sales across several time horizons. The longer-run forecasts may then be updated and refined as various shorter-run cycles are completed. For obvious reasons, a forecast should be as accurate as possible, and the accuracy of sales forecasting tends to increase as organizations learn from their previous forecasting experience. But the more uncertain and complex future conditions are likely to be, the more difficult it is to develop accurate forecasts. To partially offset these problems, forecasts are more useful to managers if expressed as a range rather than as an absolute index or number. If projected sales increases are expected to be in the range of 10 to 12 percent, a manager can consider all the implications for the entire range. A 10 percent increase could dictate one set of activities; a 12 percent increase could call for a different set of activities.

■ Technological Forecasting

technological forecasting The prediction of what future technologies are likely to emerge and when they are likely to be economically feasible

Technological forecasting is another type of forecasting that many organizations use. It focuses on predicting what future technologies are likely to emerge and when they are likely to be economically feasible. In an era when technological breakthrough and innovation have become the rule rather than the exception, managers must be able to anticipate new developments. If a manager invests heavily in existing technology (such as production processes, equipment, and computer systems) and the technology becomes obsolete in the near future, the company has wasted its resources.

The most striking technological innovations in recent years have been in electronics, especially semiconductors. Home computers, electronic games, and sophisticated communications equipment are all evidence of the electronics explosion. Given the increasing importance of technology and the rapid pace of technological innovation, managers will grow increasingly concerned with technological forecasting in the years to come.

■ Other Types of Forecasting

Other types of forecasting are also important to many organizations. Resource forecasting projects the organization's future needs for and the availability of human resources, raw materials, and other resources. General economic conditions are the subject of economic forecasts. For example, some organizations undertake population or market-size forecasting. Some organizations also attempt to forecast future government fiscal policy and various government regulations that might be put into practice. Indeed, virtually any component in an organization's environment may be an appropriate area for forecasting.

■ Forecasting Techniques

To carry out the various kinds of forecasting we have identified, managers use several different techniques.[1] Time-series analysis and causal modeling are two common quantitative techniques.

Time-Series Analysis   The underlying assumption of **time-series analysis** is that the past is a good predictor of the future. This technique is most useful when the manager has a lot of historical data available and when stable trends and patterns are apparent. In a time-series analysis, the variable under consideration (such as sales or enrollment) is plotted across time, and a "best-fit" line is identified.[2] Figure A.1 shows how a time-series analysis might look. The dots represent the number of units sold for each year from 1993 through 2001. The best-fit line has also been drawn in. It is the line around which the dots cluster with the least variability. A manager who wants to know what sales to expect in 2002 simply extends the line. In this case the projection would be around eighty-two hundred units.

Real time-series analysis involves much more than simply plotting sales data and then using a ruler and a pencil to draw and extend the line. Sophisticated mathematical procedures, among other things, are necessary to account for seasonal and cyclical fluctuations and to identify the true best-fit line. In real situations data seldom follow the neat pattern found in Figure A.1. Indeed, the data points may be so widely dispersed that they mask meaningful trends from all but painstaking, computer-assisted inspection.

time-series analysis   A forecasting technique that extends past information into the future through the calculation of a best-fit line

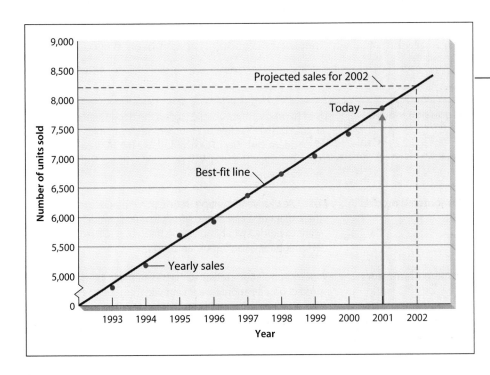

FIGURE A.1

An Example of Time-Series Analysis

Because time-series analysis assumes that the past is a good predictor of the future, it is most useful when historical data are available, trends are stable, and patterns are apparent. For example, it can be used for projecting estimated sales for products like shampoo, pens, and automobile tires.

causal modeling   A group of different techniques that determine causal relationships between different variables

regression model   An equation that uses one set of variables to predict another variable

econometric model   A causal model that predicts major economic shifts and their impact on the organization

Causal Modeling   Another useful forecasting technique is **causal modeling**. Actually, the term *causal modeling* represents a group of several techniques. Table A.1 summarizes three of the most useful approaches. **Regression models** are equations created to predict a variable (such as sales volume) that depends on a number of other variables (such as price and advertising). The variable being predicted is called the *dependent variable*; the variables used to make the prediction are called *independent variables*. A typical regression equation used by a small business might take this form:

$$y = ax_1 + bx_2 + cx_3 + d$$

where

y = the dependent variable (sales in this case)

x_1, x_2, and x_3 = independent variables (advertising budget, price, and commissions)

a, b, and c = weights for the independent variables calculated during development of the regression model

d = a constant

To use the model, a manager can insert various alternatives for advertising budget, price, and commissions into the equation and then compute y. The calculated value of y represents the forecasted level of sales, given various levels of advertising, price, and commissions.[3]

Econometric models employ regression techniques at a much more complex level. **Econometric models** attempt to predict major economic shifts and the potential impact of those shifts on the organization. Such models might be used to predict various age, ethnic, and economic groups that will characterize different regions of the United States in the year 2000 and to further predict the kinds of products and services these groups may want. A complete econometric model may consist of hundreds or even thousands of equations. Computers are almost always necessary to apply them. Given the complexities

TABLE A.1
Summary of Causal Modeling Forecasting Techniques

Managers use several types of causal models in planning and decision making. Three popular models are regression models, econometric models, and economic indicators.

Regression models	Used to predict one variable (called the dependent variable) on the basis of known or assumed other variables (called independent variables). For example, we might predict future sales based on the values of price, advertising, and economic levels.
Econometric models	Make use of several multiple-regression equations to consider the impact of major economic shifts. For example, we might want to predict what impact the migration toward the Sun Belt might have on our organization.
Economic indicators	Various population statistics, indexes, or parameters that predict organizationally relevant variables such as discretionary income. Examples include cost-of-living index, inflation rate, and level of unemployment.

involved in developing econometric models, many firms that decide to use them rely on outside consultants specializing in this approach.

Economic indicators, another form of causal model, are population statistics or indexes that reflect the economic well-being of a population. Examples of widely used economic indicators include the current rates of national productivity, inflation, and unemployment. In using such indicators, the manager draws on past experiences that have revealed a relationship between a certain indicator and some facet of the company's operations. Pitney Bowes Data Documents Division, for example, can predict future sales of its business forms largely on the basis of current GNP estimates and other economic growth indexes.

Qualitative Forecasting Techniques   Organizations also use several qualitative techniques to develop their forecasts. A **qualitative forecasting technique** relies more on individual or group judgment or opinion rather than on sophisticated mathematical analyses. The Delphi procedure, described in Chapter 4 as a mechanism for managing group decision-making activities, can also be used to develop forecasts. A variation of it—the *jury-of-expert-opinion* approach—involves using the basic Delphi process with members of top management. In this instance top management serves as a collection of experts asked to make a prediction about something—competitive behavior, trends in product demand, and so forth. Either a pure Delphi or a jury-of-expert-opinion approach might be useful in technological forecasting.

The *sales-force-composition* method of sales forecasting is a pooling of the predictions and opinions of experienced salespeople. Because of their experience, these individuals are often able to forecast quite accurately what various customers will do. Management combines these forecasts and interprets the data to create plans. Textbook publishers use this procedure to project how many copies of a new title they might sell.

The *customer evaluation* technique goes beyond an organization's sales force and collects data from customers of the organization. The customers provide estimates of their own future needs for the goods and services that the organization supplies. Managers must combine, interpret, and act on this information. This approach, however, has two major limitations. Customers may be less interested in taking time to develop accurate predictions than are members of the organization, and the method makes no provision for including any new customers that the organization may acquire. Wal-Mart helps its suppliers use this approach by providing them with detailed purchase projections several months in advance.

Selecting an appropriate forecasting technique can be as important as applying it correctly. Some techniques are appropriate only for specific circumstances. For example, the sales-force-composition technique is good only for sales forecasting. Other techniques, like the Delphi method, are useful in a variety of situations. Some techniques, such as the econometric models, require extensive use of computers, whereas others, such as customer evaluation models, can be used with little mathematical expertise. For the most part selection of a particular technique depends on the nature of the problem, the experience and preferences of the manager, and available resources.[4]

economic indicator   A key population statistic or index that reflects the economic well-being of a population

qualitative forecasting technique One of several techniques that rely on individual or group judgment rather than on mathematical analyses

Other Planning Techniques

Of course, planning involves more than just forecasting. Other tools and techniques that are useful for planning purposes include linear programming, breakeven analysis, simulations, and PERT.

■ Linear Programming

linear programming A planning technique that determines the optimal combination of resources and activities

Linear programming is one of the most widely used quantitative tools for planning. **Linear programming** is a procedure for calculating the optimal combination of resources and activities. It is appropriate when there is some objective to be met (such as a sales quota or a certain production level) within a set of constraints (such as a limited advertising budget or limited production capabilities).

To illustrate how linear programming can be used, assume that a small electronics company produces two basic products—a high-quality cable television tuner and a high-quality receiver for picking up television audio and playing it through a stereo amplifier. Both products go through the same two departments, first production and then inspection and testing. Each product has a known profit margin and a high level of demand. The production manager's job is to produce the optimal combination of tuners (T) and receivers (R) to maximize profits and use the time in production (PR) and in inspection and testing (IT) most efficiently. Table A.2 gives the information needed for the use of linear programming to solve this problem.

The *objective function* is an equation that represents what we want to achieve. In technical terms it is a mathematical representation of the desirability of the consequences of a particular decision. In our example the objective function can be represented as follows:

$$\text{Maximize profit} = \$30X_T + \$20X_R$$

where

R = the number of receivers to be produced

T = the number of tuners to be produced

TABLE A.2
Production Data for Tuners and Receivers

Linear programming can be used to determine the optimal number of tuners and receivers an organization might make. Essential information needed to perform this analysis includes the number of hours each product spends in each department, the production capacity for each department, and the profit margin for each product.

The $30 and $20 figures are the respective profit margins of the tuner and receiver, as noted in Table A.2. The objective, then, is to maximize profits.

However, this objective must be accomplished within a specific set of constraints. In our example the constraints are the time required to produce each product in each department and the total amount of time avail-

Department	Number of Hours Required per Unit		Production Capacity for Day (in Hours)
	Tuners (T)	Receivers (R)	
Production (PR)	10	6	150
Inspection and testing (IT)	4	4	80
Profit margin	$30	$20	

able. These data are also found in Table A.2 and can be used to construct the relevant constraint equations:

$$10T + 6R \leq 150$$

$$4T + 4R \leq 80$$

(that is, we cannot use more capacity than is available), and of course,

$$T \geq 0$$

$$R \geq 0$$

The set of equations consisting of the objective function and constraints can be solved graphically. To start, we assume that production of each product is maximized when production of the other is at zero. The resultant solutions are then plotted on a coordinate axis.

In the PR department, if $T = 0$, then:

$$10T + 6R \leq 150$$

$$10(0) + 6R \leq 150$$

$$R \leq 25$$

In the same department, if $R = 0$, then:

$$10T + 6(R) \leq 150$$

$$10T + 6(0) \leq 150$$

$$T \leq 15$$

Similarly, in the IT department, if no tuners are produced:

$$4T + 4R \leq 80$$

$$4(0) + 4R \leq 80$$

$$R \leq 20$$

And if no receivers are produced:

$$4T + 4R \leq 80$$

$$4T + 4(0) \leq 80$$

$$T \leq 20$$

The four resulting inequalities are graphed in Figure A.2. The shaded region represents the feasibility space, or production combinations that do not exceed the capacity of either department. The optimal number of products will be defined at one of the four corners of the shaded area— that is, the firm should produce twenty receivers only (point C), fifteen tuners only (point B), thirteen receivers and seven tuners (point E), or no products at all. With the constraint that production of both tuners and receivers must be greater than zero, it follows that point E is the optimal solution. That combination requires 148 hours in PR and 80 hours in IT and yields $470 in profit. (Note

**FIGURE A.2
The Graphical Solution of a Linear Programming Problem**

Finding the solution to a linear programming problem graphically is useful when only two alternatives are being considered. When problems are more complex, computers that can execute hundreds of equations and variables are necessary. Virtually all large firms, such as General Motors, Texaco, and Sears, use linear programming.

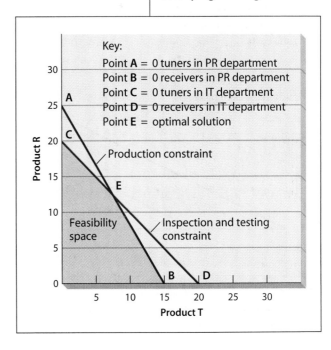

Key:
Point **A** = 0 tuners in PR department
Point **B** = 0 receivers in PR department
Point **C** = 0 tuners in IT department
Point **D** = 0 receivers in IT department
Point **E** = optimal solution

Production constraint

Feasibility space

Inspection and testing constraint

Product R

Product T

that if only receivers were produced, the profit would be $400; producing only tuners would mean $450 in profit.)

Unfortunately, only two alternatives can be handled by the graphical method, and our example was extremely simple. When other alternatives are possible, a complex algebraic method must be employed. Real-world problems may require several hundred equations and variables. Clearly, computers are necessary to execute such sophisticated analyses. Linear programming is a powerful technique, playing a key role in both planning and decision making. It can be used to schedule production, select an optimal portfolio of investments, allocate sales representatives to territories, or produce an item at some minimum cost.

■ Breakeven Analysis

Linear programming is called a *normative procedure* because it prescribes the optimal solution to a problem. Breakeven analysis is a *descriptive procedure* because it simply describes relationships among variables; then it is up to the manager to make decisions. We can define **breakeven analysis** as a procedure for identifying the point at which revenues start covering their associated costs. It might be used to analyze the effects on profits of different price and output combinations or various levels of output.

Figure A.3 represents the key cost variables in breakeven analysis. Creating most products or services includes three types of costs: fixed costs, variable costs, and total costs. *Fixed costs* are costs that are incurred regardless of what volume of output is being generated. They include rent or mortgage payments on the building, managerial salaries, and depreciation of plant and equipment. *Variable costs* vary with the number of units produced, such as the cost of raw materials and direct labor used to make each unit. *Total costs* are fixed costs plus variable costs. Note that because of fixed costs, the line for total costs never begins at zero.

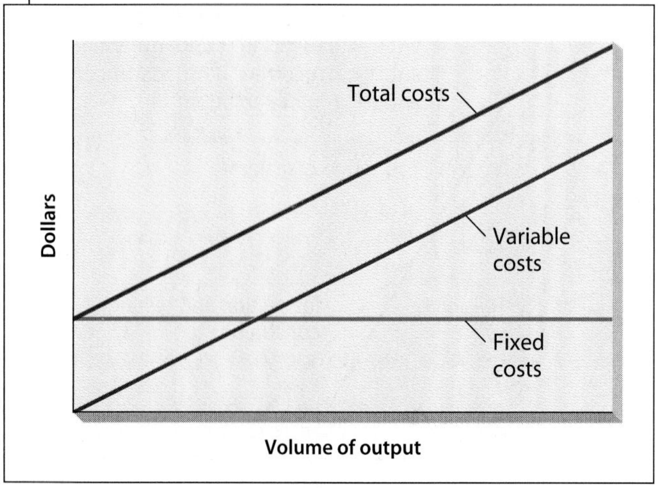

Other important factors in breakeven analysis are revenue and profit. *Revenue*, the total dollar amount of sales, is computed by multiplying the number of units sold by the sales price of each unit. *Profit* is then determined by subtracting total costs from total revenues. When revenues and total costs are plotted on the same set of axes, the breakeven graph shown in Figure A.4 emerges. The point at which the lines representing total costs and total revenues cross is the breakeven point. The company represented in Figure A.4 will realize a profit if it sells more units than are represented by point A; selling below that level will result in a loss.

Mathematically, the breakeven point (expressed as units of production or volume) is shown by the formula

$$BP = \frac{TFC}{P - VC}$$

breakeven analysis   A procedure for identifying the point at which revenues start covering costs

FIGURE A.3
An Example of Cost Factors for Breakeven Analysis

To determine the breakeven point for profit on sales for a product or service, the manager first must determine both fixed and variable costs. These costs are then combined to show total costs.

Total costs

Variable costs

Fixed costs

Dollars

Volume of output

where

    BP = breakeven point

    TFC = total fixed costs

    P = price per unit

    VC = variable cost per unit

Assume that you are considering the production of a new garden hoe with a curved handle. You have determined that an acceptable selling price will be $20. You have also determined that the variable costs per hoe will be $15, and you have total fixed costs of $400,000 per year. The question is, How many hoes must you sell each year to break even? Using the breakeven model, you find that

$$BP = \frac{TFC}{P - VC}$$

$$BP = \frac{400,000}{20 - 15}$$

$$BP = 80,000 \text{ units}$$

Thus, you must sell eighty thousand hoes to break even. Further analysis would also show that if you could raise your price to $25 per hoe, you would need to sell only forty thousand to break even, and so on.

The state of New York used a breakeven analysis to evaluate seven variations of prior approvals for its Medicaid service. Comparisons were conducted of the costs involved in each variation against savings gained from efficiency and improved quality of service. The state found that only three of the variations were cost-effective.[5]

Breakeven analysis is a popular and important planning technique, but it also has noteworthy weaknesses. It considers revenues only up to the breakeven point, and it makes no allowance for the time value of money. For example, because the funds used to cover fixed and variable costs could be used for other purposes (such as investment), the organization is losing interest income by tying up its money prior to reaching the breakeven point. Thus, managers often use breakeven analysis as the first step in planning. After the preliminary analysis has been completed, they use more-sophisticated techniques (such as rate-of-return analysis or

FIGURE A.4
Breakeven Analysis

After total costs are determined and graphed, the manager then graphs the total revenues that will be earned on different levels of sales. The regions defined by the intersection of the two graphs show loss and profit areas. The intersection itself shows the breakeven point—the level of sales at which all costs are covered but no profits are earned.

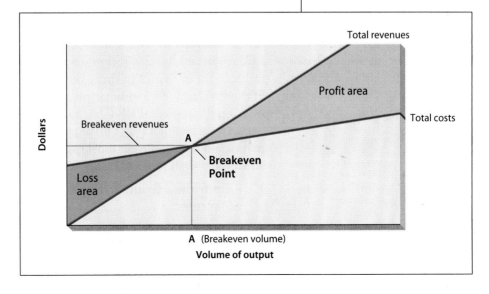

discounted-present-value analysis) to decide whether to proceed or to divert resources into other areas.

■ Simulations

Another useful planning device is simulation. The word *simulate* means to copy or to represent. An **organizational simulation** is a model of a real-world situation that can be manipulated to discover how it functions. Simulation is a descriptive, rather than a prescriptive, technique. Northern Research & Engineering Corporation is an engineering consulting firm that helps clients plan new factories. By using a sophisticated factory-simulation model, the firm recently helped a client cut several machines and operations from a new plant and to save more than $750,000.

To consider another example, suppose the city of Houston wants to build a new airport. Issues to be addressed might include the number of runways, the direction of those runways, the number of terminals and gates, the allocation of various carriers among the terminals and gates, and the technology and human resources needed to achieve a target frequency of takeoffs and landings. (Of course, actually planning such an airport would involve many more variables than these.) A model could be constructed to simulate these factors, as well as their interrelationships. The planner could then insert various values for each factor and observe the probable results.

Simulation problems are in some ways similar to those addressed by linear programming, but simulation is more useful in very complex situations characterized by diverse constraints and opportunities. The development of sophisticated simulation models may require the expertise of outside specialists or consultants, and the complexity of simulation almost always necessitates the use of a computer. For these reasons simulation is most likely to be used as a technique for planning in large organizations that have the required resources.

■ PERT

A final planning tool we will discuss is PERT. **PERT**, an acronym for Program Evaluation and Review Technique, was developed by the U.S. Navy to help coordinate the activities of three thousand contractors during the development of the Polaris nuclear submarine, and it was credited with saving two years of work on the project. PERT has subsequently been used by most large companies in a variety of ways. The purpose of PERT is to develop a network of activities and their interrelationships so as to highlight critical time intervals that affect the overall project. PERT follows six basic steps:

1. Identify the activities to be performed and the events that will mark their completion.
2. Develop a network showing the relationships among the activities and events.
3. Calculate the time needed for each event and the time necessary to get from one event to the next.

organizational simulation A model of a real-world situation that can be manipulated to discover how it functions

PERT A planning tool that uses a network to plan projects involving numerous activities and their interrelationships

4. Identify within the network the longest path that leads to completion of the project. This path is called the critical path.
5. Refine the network.
6. Use the network to control the project.

Suppose that a marketing manager wants to use PERT to plan the test marketing and nationwide introduction of a new product. Table A.3 identifies the basic steps involved in carrying out this project. The activities are then arranged in a network like the one shown in Figure A.5. In the figure each completed event is represented by a number in a circle. The activities are indicated by letters on the lines connecting the events. Notice that some activities are performed independently of one another and that others must be performed in sequence. For example, test production (activity a) and test site location (activity c) can be done at the same time, but test site location has to be done before actual testing (activities f and g) can be done.

The time needed to get from one activity to another is then determined. The normal way to calculate the time between each activity is to average the

TABLE A.3
Activities and Events for Introducing a New Product

PERT is used to plan schedules for projects and it is particularly useful when many activities with critical time intervals must be coordinated. Besides launching a new product, PERT is useful for projects like constructing a new factory or building, remodeling an office, or opening a new store.

Activities		Events	
a	Produce limited quantity for test marketing.	1	Origin of project.
		2	Completion of production for test marketing.
b	Design preliminary package.	3	Completion of design for preliminary package.
c	Locate test market.	4	Test market located.
d	Obtain local merchant cooperation.	5	Local merchant cooperation obtained.
e	Ship product to selected retail outlets.	6	Product for test marketing shipped to retail outlets.
f	Monitor sales and customer reactions.	7	Sales and customer reactions monitored.
g	Survey customers in test-market area.	8	Customers in test-market area surveyed.
h	Make needed product changes.	9	Product changes made.
I	Make needed package changes.	10	Package changes made.
j	Mass produce the product.	11	Product mass produced.
k	Begin national advertising.	12	National advertising carried out.
l	Begin national distribution.	13	National distribution completed.

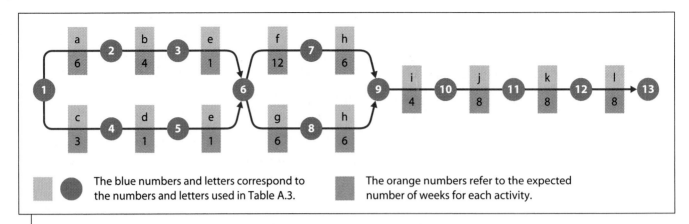

The blue numbers and letters correspond to the numbers and letters used in Table A.3.

The orange numbers refer to the expected number of weeks for each activity.

FIGURE A.5

A PERT Network for Introducing a New Product

critical path The longest path through a PERT network

most optimistic, most pessimistic, and most likely times, with the most likely time weighted by four. Time is usually calculated with the following formula:

$$\text{Expected time} = \frac{a + 4b + c}{6}$$

where

a = optimistic time

b = most likely time

c = pessimistic time

The expected number of weeks for each activity in our example is shown in parentheses along each path in Figure A.5. The **critical path**—or the longest path through the network—is then identified. This path is considered critical because it shows the shortest time in which the project can be completed. In our example the critical path is 1-2-3-6-7-9-10-11-12-13, totaling fifty-seven weeks. PERT thus tells the manager that the project will take fifty-seven weeks to complete.

The first network may be refined. If fifty-seven weeks to completion is too long a time, the manager might decide to begin preliminary package design before the test products are finished. Or the manager might decide that ten weeks rather than twelve is a sufficient time period to monitor sales. The idea is that if the critical path can be shortened, the overall duration of the project can also be shortened. The PERT network serves as an ongoing framework for both planning and control throughout the project. For example, the manager can use it to monitor where the project is relative to where it needs to be. Thus, if an activity on the critical path takes longer than planned, the manager needs to make up the time elsewhere or live with the fact that the entire project will be late.

Decision-Making Tools

Managers can also use a number of tools that relate more specifically to decision making than to planning. Two commonly used decision-making tools are payoff matrices and decision trees.

■ Payoff Matrices

A **payoff matrix** specifies the probable value of different alternatives, depending on different possible outcomes associated with each. The use of a payoff matrix requires that several alternatives be available, that several different events could occur, and that the consequences depend on which alternative is selected and on which event or set of events occurs. An important concept in understanding the payoff matrix, then, is probability. A **probability** is the likelihood, expressed as a percentage, that a particular event will or will not occur. If we believe that a particular event will occur seventy-five times out of one hundred, we can say that the probability of its occurring is 75 percent, or .75. Probabilities range in value from 0 (no chance of occurrence) to 1.00 (certain occurrence—also referred to as 100 percent). In the business world, there are few probabilities of either 0 or 1.00. Most probabilities that managers use are based on subjective judgment, intuition, and historical data.

The **expected value** of an alternative course of action is the sum of all possible values of outcomes due to that action multiplied by their respective probabilities. Suppose, for example, that a venture capitalist is considering investing in a new company. If he believes there is a .40 probability of making $100,000; a .30 probability of making $30,000; and a .30 probability of losing $20,000, the expected value (EV) of this alternative is

$$EV = .40(100,000) + .30(30,000) + .30(-20,000)$$

$$EV = 40,000 + 9,000 - 6,000$$

$$EV = \$43,000$$

The investor can then weigh the expected value of this investment against the expected values of other available alternatives. The highest EV signals the investment that should most likely be selected.

For example, suppose another venture capitalist wants to invest $20,000 in a new business. She has identified three possible alternatives: a leisure products company, an energy enhancement company, and a food-producing company. Because the expected value of each alternative depends on short-run changes in the economy, especially inflation, she decides to develop a payoff matrix. She estimates that the probability of high inflation is .30 and the probability of low inflation is .70. She then estimates the probable returns for each investment for both high and low inflation. Figure A.6 shows what the payoff matrix might look like (a minus sign indicates a loss). The expected value of investing in the leisure products company is

$$EV = .30(-10,000) + .70(50,000)$$

$$EV = -3,000 + 35,000$$

$$EV = \$32,000$$

Similarly, the expected value of investing in the energy enhancement company is

$$EV = .30(90,000) + .70(-15,000)$$

$$EV = 27,000 + (-10,500)$$

$$EV = \$16,500$$

payoff matrix A decision-making tool that specifies the probable value of different alternatives depending on different possible outcomes associated with each

probability The likelihood, expressed as a percentage, that a particular event will or will not occur

expected value When applied to alternative courses of action, the sum of all possible values of outcomes from that action multiplied by their respective probabilities

FIGURE A.6
An Example of a Payoff Matrix

A payoff matrix helps the manager determine the expected value of different alternatives. A payoff matrix is effective only if the manager ensures that probability estimates are as accurate as possible.

		High inflation (Probability of .30)	Low inflation (Probability of .70)
Investment alternative **1**	Leisure products company	−$10,000	+$50,000
Investment alternative **2**	Energy enhancement company	+$90,000	−$15,000
Investment alternative **3**	Food-processing company	+$30,000	+$25,000

And, finally, the expected value of investing in the food-processing company is

$$EV = .30(30,000) + .70(25,000)$$

$$EV = 9,000 + 17,500$$

$$EV = \$26,500$$

Investing in the leisure products company, then, has the highest expected value.

Other potential uses for payoff matrices include determining optimal order quantities, deciding whether to repair or replace broken machinery, and deciding which of several new products to introduce. Of course, the real key to using payoff matrices effectively is making accurate estimates of the relevant probabilities.

■ Decision Trees

decision tree A planning tool that extends the concept of a payoff matrix through a sequence of decisions

Decision trees are like payoff matrices in that they enhance a manager's ability to evaluate alternatives by making use of expected values. However, they are most appropriate when there are a number of decisions to be made in sequence.

Figure A.7 illustrates a hypothetical decision tree. The firm represented wants to begin exporting its products to a foreign market, but limited capacity restricts the firm to only one market at first. Managers feel that either France or China would be the best place to start. Whichever alternative is selected, sales for the product in that country may turn out to be high or low. In France there is a .80 chance of high sales and a .20 chance of low sales. The anticipated payoffs in these situations are predicted to be $20 million and $3 million, respectively. In China the probabilities of high versus low sales are .60 and .40, respectively, and the associated payoffs are presumed to be $25 million and $6 million. As shown in Figure A.7, the expected value of shipping to France is $16,600,000, whereas the expected value of shipping to China is $17,400,000.

The astute reader will note that this part of the decision could have been set up as a payoff matrix. However, the value of decision trees is that we can extend the model to include subsequent decisions. Assume, for example, that the company begins shipping to China. If high sales do in fact materialize, the

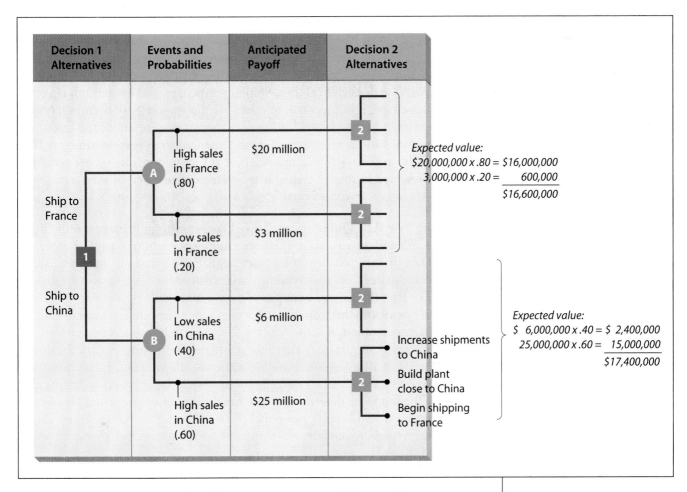

Decision 1 Alternatives	Events and Probabilities	Anticipated Payoff	Decision 2 Alternatives

Ship to France

Ship to China

A High sales in France (.80) — $20 million — 2

Low sales in France (.20) — $3 million — 2

Expected value:
$20,000,000 x .80 = $16,000,000
3,000,000 x .20 =   600,000
                    $16,600,000

B Low sales in China (.40) — $6 million — 2

High sales in China (.60) — $25 million — 2

Increase shipments to China

Build plant close to China

Begin shipping to France

Expected value:
$ 6,000,000 x .40 = $ 2,400,000
25,000,000 x .60 = 15,000,000
                    $17,400,000

FIGURE A.7
An Example of a Decision Tree

A decision tree extends the basic concepts of a payoff matrix through multiple decisions. This tree shows the possible outcomes of two levels of decisions. The first decision is whether to expand to China or France. The second decision, assuming that the company expands to China, is whether to increase shipments to China, build a plant close to China, or initiate shipping to France.

company will soon reach another decision situation. It might use the extra revenues to (1) increase shipments to China, (2) build a plant close to China to cut shipping costs, or (3) begin shipping to France. Various outcomes are possible for each decision, and each outcome will have both a probability and an anticipated payoff. It is therefore possible to compute expected values back through several tiers of decisions all the way to the initial one. As it is with payoff matrices, determining probabilities accurately is the crucial element in the process. Properly used, however, decision trees can provide managers with a useful road map through complex decision situations.

■ Other Techniques

In addition to payoff matrices and decision trees, a number of other quantitative methods are also available to facilitate decision making.

Inventory Models **Inventory models** are techniques that help the manager decide how much inventory to maintain. Target Stores uses inventory models to help determine how much merchandise to order, when to order it, and so forth. Inventory consists of both raw materials (inputs) and finished goods (outputs). Polaroid, for example, maintains a supply of the chemicals that it uses to make film, the cartons it packs film in, and packaged film ready to be shipped. For finished goods, both extremes are bad: excess inventory ties up

inventory model A technique that helps managers decide how much inventory to maintain

just-in-time (JIT) An inventory management technique in which materials are scheduled to arrive in small batches as they are needed, eliminating the need for resources such as big reserves and warehouse space

queuing model A model used to optimize waiting lines in organizations

capital, whereas a small inventory may result in shortages and customer dissatisfaction. The same holds for raw materials: too much inventory ties up capital, but if a company runs out of resources, work stoppages may occur. Finally, because the process of placing an order for raw materials and supplies has associated costs (such as clerical time, shipping expenses, and higher unit costs for small quantities), it is important to minimize the frequency of ordering. Inventory models help the manager make decisions so as to optimize the size of inventory. Innovations in inventory management such as **just-in-time**, or **JIT**, rely heavily on decision-making models. A JIT system involves scheduling materials to arrive in small batches as they are needed, thereby eliminating the need for a big reserve inventory, warehouse space, and so forth.[6]

Queuing Models   **Queuing models** help organizations manage waiting lines. We are all familiar with such situations: shoppers waiting to pay for groceries at Kroger, drivers waiting to buy gas at an Exxon station, travelers calling American Airlines for reservations, and customers waiting for a teller at Citibank. Take the Kroger example. If a store manager has only one check-out stand in operation, the store's cost for check-out personnel is very low; however, many customers are upset by the long line that frequently develops. To solve the problem, the store manager could decide to keep twenty check-out stands open at all times. Customers would like the short wait, but personnel costs would be very high. A queuing model would be appropriate in this case to help the manager determine the optimal number of check-out stands: the number that would balance personnel costs and customer waiting time. Target Stores uses queuing models to determine how many check-out lanes to put in its retail stores.

distribution model A model used to determine the optimal pattern of distribution across different carriers and routes

game theory A planning tool used to predict how competitors will respond to different actions the organization might take

Distribution Models   A decision facing many marketing managers relates to the distribution of the organization's products. Specifically, the manager must decide where the products should go and how to transport them. Railroads, trucking, and air freight have associated shipping costs, and each mode of transportation follows different schedules and routes. The problem is to identify the combination of routes that optimize distribution effectiveness and distribution costs. **Distribution models** help managers determine this optimal pattern of distribution.

Game Theory   **Game theory** was originally developed to predict the effect of one company's decisions on competitors. Models developed from game theory are intended to predict how a competitor will react to various activities that an organization might undertake, such as price changes, promotional changes, and the introduction of new products. If Bank of America were considering raising its prime lending rate by 1 percent, it might use a game theory model to predict whether Citicorp would follow suit. If the model revealed that Citicorp would do so, Bank of America would probably proceed; otherwise, it would probably maintain the current interest rates. Unfortunately, game theory is not yet as useful as it was originally expected to be. The complexities of the real world combined with the inherent limitations of the technique restrict its applicability. Game theory, however, does provide a useful conceptual framework for analyzing competitive behavior, and its usefulness may be improved in the future.

Artificial Intelligence   A fairly new addition to the manager's quantitative tool kit is **artificial intelligence (AI)**. The most useful form of AI is the expert system.[7] An expert system is essentially a computer program that tries to duplicate the thought processes of experienced decision makers. For example, Digital Equipment has developed an expert system that checks sales orders for new computer systems and then designs preliminary layouts for those new systems. Digital can now ship the computer to a customer in components for final assembly on site. This approach has enabled the company to cut back on its own final-assembly facilities.

artificial intelligence (AI)   A computer program that attempts to duplicate the thought processes of experienced decision makers

Strengths and Weaknesses of Planning Tools

Like all issues confronting management, planning tools of the type described here have a number of strengths and weaknesses.

■ Weaknesses and Problems

One weakness of the planning and decision-making tools discussed in this appendix is that they may not always adequately reflect reality. Even with the most sophisticated and powerful computer-assisted technique, reality must often be simplified. Many problems are also not amenable to quantitative analysis because important elements of them are intangible or nonquantifiable. Employee morale or satisfaction, for example, is often a major factor in managerial decisions.

The use of these tools and techniques may also be quite costly. For example, only larger companies can afford to develop their own econometric models. Even though the computer explosion has increased the availability of quantitative aids, some expense is still involved and it will take time for many of these techniques to become widely used. Resistance to change also limits the use of planning tools in some settings. If a manager for a retail chain has always based decisions for new locations on personal visits, observations, and intuition, she or he may be less than eager to begin using a computer-based model for evaluating and selecting sites. Finally, problems may arise when managers have to rely on technical specialists to use sophisticated models. Experts trained in the use of complex mathematical procedures may not understand or appreciate other aspects of management.

■ Strengths and Advantages

On the plus side, planning and decision-making tools offer many advantages. For situations that are amenable to quantification, these tools can bring sophisticated mathematical processes to bear on planning and decision making. Properly designed models and formulas also help decision makers "see reason." For example, a manager might not be inclined to introduce a new product line simply because she or he doesn't think it will be profitable. After seeing a forecast predicting first-year sales of one hundred thousand units coupled with a breakeven analysis showing profitability after only twenty thousand, however, the manager will probably change her or his mind. Thus, rational planning tools and techniques force the manager to look beyond personal prejudices and predispositions. Finally, the computer explosion is rapidly making sophisticated planning techniques available in a wider range of settings than ever before.

The crucial point to remember is that planning tools and techniques are a means to an end, not an end in themselves. Just as a carpenter uses a hand saw in some situations and an electric saw in others, a manager must recognize that a particular model may be useful in some situations but that others may call for a different approach. Knowing the difference is one mark of a good manager.

Summary of Key Points

Managers often use a variety of tools and techniques to develop plans and make decisions. Forecasting is one widely used method. Forecasting is the process of developing assumptions or premises about the future. Sales or revenue forecasting is especially important. Many organizations also rely heavily on technological forecasting. Time-series analysis and causal modeling are important forecasting techniques. Qualitative techniques are also widely used.

Managers also use other planning tools and techniques in different circumstances. Linear programming helps optimize resources and activities. Breakeven analysis helps identify how many products or services must be sold to cover costs. Simulations model reality. PERT helps plan how much time a project will require.

Other tools and techniques are useful for decision making. Constructing a payoff matrix, for example, helps a manager assess the expected value of different alternatives. Decision trees are used to extend expected values across multiple decisions. Other popular decision-making tools and techniques include inventory models, queuing models, distribution models, game theory, and artificial intelligence.

Various strengths and weaknesses are associated with each of these tools and techniques, as well as with their use by a manager. The key to success is knowing when each should and should not be used and knowing how to use and interpret the results that each provides.

APPENDIX NOTES

1. For a classic review, see John C. Chambers, S. K. Mullick, and D. Smith, "How to Choose the Right Forecasting Technique," *Harvard Business Review*, July–August 1971, pp. 45–74.
2. Charles Ostrom, *Time-Series Analysis: Regression Techniques* (Beverly Hills, Calif.: Sage Publications, 1980).
3. Fred Kerlinger and Elazar Pedhazur, *Multiple Regression in Behavioral Research* (New York: Holt, 1973).
4. Chambers, Mullick, and Smith, "How to Choose the Right Forecasting Technique"; see also J. Scott Armstrong, *Long-Range Forecasting: From Crystal Ball to Computers* (New York: Wiley, 1978).
5. Edward Hannan, Linda Ryan, and Richard Van Orden, "A Cost-Benefit Analysis of Prior Approvals for Medicaid Services in New York State," *Socio-Economic Planning Sciences*, Vol. 18, 1984, pp. 1–14.
6. Ramon L. Alonso and Cline W. Fraser, "JIT Hits Home: A Case Study in Reducing Management Delays," *Sloan Management Review*, Summer 1991, pp. 59–68.
7. Beau Sheil, "Thinking about Artificial Intelligence," *Harvard Business Review*, July–August 1987, pp. 91–97 and Dorothy Leonard-Barton and John J. Sviokla, "Putting Expert Systems to Work," *Harvard Business Review*, March–April 1988, pp. 91–98.

Interpretations of Skills Self-Assessment Instruments

CHAPTER 1:   SELF-AWARENESS

Total your scores for each skill area.

Skill Area	Items	Score
Self-disclosure and openness to feedback from others	1, 2, 3, 9, 11	_____
Awareness of own values, cognitive style, change orientation, and interpersonal orientation	4, 5, 6, 7, 8, 10	_____
Now total your score:		_____

To assess how well you scored on this instrument, compare your scores to three comparison standards. (1) Compare your scores with the maximum possible (66). (2) Compare your scores with the scores of other students in your class. (3) Compare your scores to a norm group consisting of five hundred business school students. In comparison to the norm group, if you scored

55 or above, you are in the top quartile.
52 to 54, you are in the second quartile.
48 to 51, you are in the third quartile.
47 or below, you are in the bottom quartile.

CHAPTER 2:   GLOBAL AWARENESS

All the statements are true. Thus, your score should be close to 40. The closer your score is to 40, the more you understand the global context of organizational environments. The closer your score is to 10, the less you understand the global context. For developmental purposes, you should note any particular items for which you had a low score and concentrate on improving your knowledge of those areas.

CHAPTER 3:   ARE YOU A GOOD PLANNER?

According to the author of this questionnaire, the "perfect" planner would have answered: (1) Yes, (2) No, (3) Yes, (4) Yes, (5) Yes, (6) Yes, (7) Yes, and (8) No.

CHAPTER 4:   DECISION-MAKING STYLES

Generally there are three decision-making styles: reflexive, consistent, and reflective. To determine your style, add up your score by totaling the numbers assigned to each response. The total will be between 10 and 30. A score of between 10 and 16 indicates a reflexive style, 17 to 23 indicates a consistent style, and 24 to 30 indicates a reflective style.

Reflexive Style: A reflexive decision maker likes to make quick decisions (to shoot from the hip) without taking the time to get all the information that may be needed and without considering all alternatives. On the positive side, reflexive decision makers are decisive; they do not procrastinate. On the negative side, making quick decisions can lead to waste and duplication when the best possible alternative is overlooked. Employees may see a decision maker as a poor supervisor if he or she consistently makes bad decisions. If you use a reflexive style, you may want to slow down and spend more time gathering information and analyzing alternatives.

Reflective Style: A reflective decision maker likes to take plenty of time to make decisions, gathering considerable information and analyzing several alternatives. On the positive side, the reflective type does not make hasty decisions. On the negative side, he or she may procrastinate and waste valuable time and other resources. The reflective decision maker may be viewed as wishy-washy and indecisive. If you use a reflective style, you may want to speed up your decision making. As Andrew Jackson once said, "Take time to deliberate; but when the time for action arrives, stop thinking and go on."

Consistent Style: Consistent decision makers tend to make decisions without rushing or wasting time. They know when they have enough information and alternatives to make a sound decision. Consistent decision makers tend to have the best record for making good decisions.

CHAPTER 5:   AN ENTREPRENEURIAL QUIZ

If most of your marks are in the first column, you probably have what it takes to run a business. If not, you are likely to have more trouble than you can handle by yourself. You should look for a partner who is strong on the points on which you are weak. If most marks are in the third column, not even a good partner will be able to shore you up. Now go back and answer the first question on the self-assessment.

CHAPTER 6:   HOW IS YOUR ORGANIZATION MANAGED?

0–9 10–19 20–29 30–39	Bureaucratic System 1
40–49 50–59 60–69 70–79	Mixed Systems 2 and 3
80–89 90–100	Organic System 4

High scores indicate a highly organic and participatively managed organization. Low scores are associated with a mechanistic or a bureaucratically managed organization.

CHAPTER 7: INNOVATIVE ATTITUDE SCALE

To determine your score, simply add the numbers associated with your responses to the twenty items. The higher your score, the more receptive to innovation you are. You can compare your score with that of others to see if you seem to be more or less receptive to innovation than a comparable group of business students.

Score	Percentile*
39	5
53	16
62	33
71	50
80	68
89	86
97	95

*Percentile indicates the percentage of the people who are expected to score below you.

CHAPTER 8: DIAGNOSING POOR PERFORMANCE AND ENHANCING MOTIVATION

Skill Area	Item	Rating
Diagnosing performance problems	1	_____
	11	_____
Establishing expectations and setting goals	2	_____
	12	_____
Facilitating performance (enhancing ability)	3	_____
	13	_____
	20	_____
Linking performance to rewards and discipline	5	_____
	14	_____
	6	_____
	15	_____
Using salient internal and external incentives	7	_____
	16	_____
	8	_____
	17	_____
Distributing rewards equitably	9	_____
	18	_____
Providing timely and straightforward performance feedback	4	_____
	10	_____
	19	_____
Total score:		_____

To assess how well you scored, compare your score to three comparison standards: (1) Compare your score with the maximum possible (120). (2) Compare your score with the scores of other students in your class. (3) Compare your score to a norm group consisting of five hundred business school students. In comparison to the norm group, if you scored

101 or above, you are in the top quartile.
94 to 100, you are in the second quartile.
85 to 93, you are in the third quartile.
84 or below, you are in the bottom quartile.

The higher your score, the better you are at identifying performance problems and the more skillful you are at taking steps to correct them. You can compare your score with that of others to see whether you seem to be more or less skillful than a comparable group of business students.

CHAPTER 9:   ASSESSING YOUR MENTAL ABILITIES

Research spanning fifty years has identified ten primary mental abilities. The higher your score on each statement, the more you see yourself as having the corresponding mental ability. The mental abilities associated with each statement are as follows:

1. Flexibility and speed of closure

2. Originality/fluency

3. Inductive reasoning

4. Associative memory

5. Span memory

6. Number facility

7. Perceptual speed

8. Deductive reasoning

9. Spatial orientation and visualization

10. Verbal comprehension

CHAPTER 10:   ASSESSING YOUR NEEDS

This set of needs was developed in 1938 by H. A. Murray, a psychologist, and operationalized by another psychologist, J. W. Atkinson. These needs correspond one-to-one to the items on the assessment questionnaire. Known as Murray's Manifest Needs because they are visible through behavior, they are:

1. Achievement

2. Affiliation

3. Aggression

4. Autonomy

5. Exhibition

6. Impulsivity

7. Nurturance

8. Order

9. Power

10. Understanding

Although little research has evaluated Murray's theory, the different needs have been researched. People seem to have a different profile of needs underlying their motivations at different ages. The more any one or more are descriptive of you, the more you see yourself as having that particular need active in your motivational makeup. For more information, see H. A. Murray, *Explorations in Personality* (New York: Oxford University Press, 1938) and J. W. Atkinson, *An Introduction to Motivation* (Princeton, N.J.: Van Nostrand, 1964).

CHAPTER 11:   MANAGERIAL LEADER BEHAVIOR QUESTIONNAIRE

These statements represent twenty-three behavior categories that are identified by research as descriptive of managerial leadership. Not all twenty-three are important in any given situation. Typically less than half of these behaviors are associated with effective performance in particular situations; thus, there is no "right" or "wrong" set of responses on this questionnaire. The behavior categories are

1. Emphasizing performance

2. Showing consideration

3. Career counseling

4. Inspiring subordinates

5. Providing praise and recognition

6. Structuring reward contingencies

7. Clarifying work roles

8. Goal setting

9. Training-coaching

10. Disseminating information

11. Encouraging decision participation

12. Delegating

13. Planning

14. Innovating

15. Problem solving

16. Facilitating the work

17. Monitoring operations

18. Monitoring the environment

19. Representing the unit

20. Facilitating cooperation and teamwork

21. Managing conflict

22. Criticism

23. Administering discipline

In military organizations at war, inspiring subordinates, emphasizing performance, clarifying work roles, problem solving, and planning seem most important. In military organizations during peacetime, inspiring subordinates, emphasizing performance, clarifying work roles, showing consideration, criticism, and administering discipline seem most important. In business organizations, emphasizing performance, monitoring the environment, clarifying work roles, goal setting, and sometimes innovating seem to be most important. In each of these instances, however, the level of organization, type of technology, environmental conditions, and objectives sought help determine the exact mix of behaviors that will lead to effectiveness. You should analyze your particular situation to determine which subset of these behavior categories is most likely to be important and then strive to develop that subset.

CHAPTER 12: SEX TALK QUIZ

1. **False**—According to studies there is no truth to the myth that women are more intuitive than men. However, research has shown that women pay greater attention to "detail." Linguist Robin Lakoff in her classic book, *Language and Woman's Place* (Harper Colophon, 1975), confirms this and states that women tend to use finer descriptions of colors.

2. **True**—Men are listened to more often than women. In "Sex Differences in Listening Comprehension," Kenneth Gruber and Jacqueline Gaehelein (*Sex Roles*, Vol. 5, 1979) found that both male and female audiences tended to listen more attentively to male speakers than to female speakers.

3. **False**—Contrary to popular stereotype it is men—not women—who talk more. Studies like the one done by linguist Lynnette Hirshman showed that men far outtalk women ("Analysis of Supportive and Assertive Behavior in Conversations." Paper presented at the Linguists Society of America, July 1974).

4. **False**—Although several studies show that women talk more rapidly than men, women don't necessarily talk extremely fast.

5. **False**—Numerous studies show that women, not men, tend to maintain more eye contact and facial pleasantries. Dr. Nancy Henley in her chapter "Power, Sex, and Non-Verbal Communication" in *Language and Sex: Dif-*

ference and Dominance (Newbury House Publishers, 1975), shows that women exhibit more friendly behavior such as smiles, facial pleasantries, and head nods than men.

6. **True**—Studies show that women are more open in their praise and give more "nods of approval" than men. They also use more complimentary terms throughout their speech according to Peter Falk in his book *Word-Play: What Happens When People Talk* (Knopf, 1973).

7. **True**—Donald Zimmerman and Candace West showed that 75 percent to 93 percent of the interruptions were made by men. ("Sex Roles, Interruptions and Silences in Conversation," in *Language and Sex: Difference and Dominance*, edited by B. Thorne and N. Henley, Newbury House Publishers, 1975.)

8. **False**—Men use more command terms or imperatives, which makes them sound more demanding. In essence, several researchers have concluded that women tend to be more polite in their speech.

9. **False**—Men and women definitely differ in their sense of humor. Women are more likely to tell jokes when there is a small, non-mixed sex group, and men were more likely to tell jokes in a larger, mixed sex group.

10. **False**—In a survey conducted for the Playboy Channel, people were asked what they wanted to hear when making love. In general, women wanted to be told they were beautiful and loved, and men wanted to hear how good they were in bed and how they pleased their women.

11. **True**—Deborah Tannen in her book, *You Just Don't Understand: Women and Men in Conversation* (William Morrow, 1990), found that men usually will not ask for help by asking for directions while women will.

12. **False**—Several surveys and numerous psychotherapists' observations have indicated that women tend to be more self-critical and more apt to blame themselves than men. Deborah Tannen's findings confirm this as she states that women also tend to use more "apologetic phrases" in their conversations such as, "I'm sorry," "I didn't mean to," or "Excuse me."

13. **True**—Naturalist Charles Darwin stated that making oneself appear smaller by bowing the head to take up less space can inhibit human aggression. Other researchers found that women tend to inhibit themselves by crossing their legs at the ankles or knees or keeping their elbows to their sides.

14. **False**—As mentioned earlier, women tend to be more detailed and more descriptive than men in what they say and in how they explain things. As Robin Lakoff's research shows (see Item 1), women tend to use more description in word choices.

15. **False**—Men tend to touch more than females. According to several researchers, women are more likely to be physically touched by men who guide them through the door, assist them with jackets and coats, and help them into cars.

16. **False**—Women, not men, appear to be more attentive when listening. Studies consistently show that women exhibit greater eye contact and express approval by smiling and head-nodding as a form of attentiveness and agreement.

17. **True**—Men and women are equally emotional when they speak. However, women appear to sound more emotional according to researchers such as Robin Lakoff (see item 1) because they use more psychological-state verbs: I *feel*, I *hope*, and I *wish*.

18. **False**—In general, men tend to bring up less personal topics than women. Women tend to discuss people, relationships, children, self-improvement, and how certain experiences have affected them. Men, on the other hand, tend to be more "outer directed" as they originate discussions about events, news, sports-related issues, and topics related to more concrete physical tasks.

19. **False**—Even though men do not bring up as many subjects of conversation as women, men interrupt more which ultimately gives them control of the topics that are raised by women.

20. **False**—Even though there are many progressive and socially enlightened parents in the modern world, parents still treat their male children differently than their female children. They tend to communicate differently to their children according to their sex, which in turn, induces sex-stereotyped behaviors.

21. **True**—Even though men make more direct statements, a recent survey indicated that women tend to confront and bring up a problem more often than men. Even though women bring up a problem more often, they tend to be more indirect and polite, as Deborah Tannen relates in her book.

22. **False**—In several studies, it was determined that women are more animated and livelier speakers than men. Studies also show that women make more eye contact, use more body movement, use more intonation, have a more varied pitch range, and use more emotionally laden words and phrases than men.

23. **False**—Just as women bring up more topics of conversation, they also ask more questions. According to researchers, this is usually done to facilitate the conversation.

24. **False**—Men and women usually talk about different things. Studies indicate that women enjoy talking about diet, personal relationships, personal appearance, clothes, self-improvement, children, marriages, personalities of others, actions of others, relationships at work, and emotionally charged issues that have a personal component. Men, on the other hand, enjoy discussing sports, what they did at work, where they went, news events, mechanical gadgets, latest technology, cars, vehicles, and music.

25. **True**—A recent Gallup poll survey commissioned for Lillian Glass, *He Says, She Says*, found that women rather than men were more likely to introduce the topics of AIDS testing and safe sex.

CHAPTER 13: USING TEAMS

Based on research conducted by J. Richard Hackman and others, all the statements are false.

1. An emphasis on individual accountability essentially undermines any effort to develop a team.

2. Complete authority is likely to lead to anarchy. Limits should be set.

3. Teams should be kept small, have clear boundaries, and have an enabling structure that ensures member motivation.

4. Teams need coaching, counseling, and support at certain intervals during their functioning.

5. The start-up period is critical, which is why managers must spend time and energy coaching and counseling the team during this period. Once the team gets going, the manager should pull back until it reaches a natural break or completes a performance cycle.

6. Training is absolutely critical and should be done before the team is assembled or shortly thereafter. If the needed skills and knowledge change, management should be ready to assist in training to help the team quickly learn the new skills and knowledge.

7. Providing support for teams is difficult. A reward system must recognize and reinforce team performance, an educational system must provide needed skills and knowledge, an information system must provide necessary information, and physical and fiscal resources must be available as needed.

8. Teams need some structure to work effectively.

9. The opposite is true. Managers should set the direction and establish wide limits on constraints with the means to the end determined by the team.

10. Teams cannot effectively be used in organizations that have strong individualistic cultures.

CHAPTER 14: UNDERSTANDING CONTROL

The odd-numbered items are all false, and the even-numbered ones are all true. Thus, you should have positive responses for the even-numbered items and negative responses for the odd-numbered ones. If you agreed strongly with all of the even ones and disagreed strongly with all of the odd ones, your total score would be zero.

Examine your responses to see which items you responded to incorrectly. Focus your attention on learning why the answers are what they are.

CHAPTER 15: DEFINING QUALITY AND PRODUCTIVITY

The odd-numbered items are all true; they refer to eight dimensions of quality (see Table 15.1). Those eight dimensions are performance, features, reliability, conformance, durability, serviceability, aesthetics, and perceived quality. The

even-numbered statements are all false. Thus, you should have positive responses for the odd-numbered items and negative responses for the even-numbered ones. If you agree strongly with all of the odd-numbered ones and disagree strongly with all of the even-numbered ones, your total score is zero.

Examine your responses to see which items you responded to incorrectly. Focus your attention on learning why the answers are what they are. Remember that the American Society for Quality Control defines quality as the *total* set of features and characteristics of a product or service that bears on its ability to satisfy stated or implied needs of customers.

Photo and Cartoon Credits (continued)

Name Index

Note: page numbers in italics refer to figures (*f*) or tables (*t*).

Organization and Product Index

Note: page numbers in italics refer to figures (*f*) or tables (*t*).

Subject Index